Crimes against humanity

AND INTERNATIONAL CRIMINAL LAW

Crimes against humanity

AND INTERNATIONAL CRIMINAL LAW

WILLEM-JAN VAN DER WOLF

INTERNATIONAL COURTS ASSOCIATION

INTERNATIONAL CRIMINAL LAW SERIES

Crimes against humanity, and international criminal law
International Courts Association Press
Editor: W van der Wolf

ISBN: 978-90-5887-081-0 (hardcover)
ISBN: 978-90-5887-082-7 (softcover)

This volume is published in the International Criminal Law series
Also available at this moment are:

- Genocide and international criminal law
- Aggression and international criminal law
- Crimes against Humanity and international criminal law
- The rights of parties and international criminal law
- The Ad Hoc tribunals and the International Criminal Court

Published by:
International Courts Association
P O Box 93567, 2509 AN The Hague, The Netherlands
tel: + 31 (0)13 5821366
info@ica-press com, http://www ica-press com

Contents

Appendix

Foreword

A crime against humanity is a crime against 'humaneness' that offends certain general principles of law and which becomes the concern of the international community. It has repercussions beyond international frontiers or exceeds in magnitude or savagery any limits tolerated by modern civilization.[1] Crimes against humanity differ from genocide in that no dolus specialis to destroy members of a particular group is required in case of crimes against humanity.[2]

The expressions 'humanity', 'laws of humanity', and 'dictates of humanity' were used in, for example, the Preamble to the 1907 Hague Convention IV Respecting the Laws and Customs of War on Land.[3] Paragraph 2 of the Preamble states that the contracting Parties desire to serve even in the case of war 'the interests of humanity and the ever-progressive needs of civilization'. Paragraph 8 of the Preamble (the so-called 'Martens Clause') provides that they declare, among other things, that 'the inhabitants and belligerents remain under the protection and governance of the principles of the law of nations, derived from the usages established among civilized peoples, from the laws of humanity, and from the dictates of the public conscience'. As pointed out by Egon Schwelb, the Preamble treats the 'interests of humanity' as the purpose which the laws and customs of war serve, and the 'laws of humanity' as one of the sources of the law of nations; there is no intention to indicate a set of norms different from war crimes.[4]

The terminology 'crimes against humanity' was used in a non-technical sense as far back as 1915, in the Declaration of 28 May 1915 of the Governments of France, Great Britain, and Russia denouncing the massacres of the Armenian population by Turkey as 'crimes against humanity and civilization for which all the members of the Turkish Government will be held responsible together with its agents implicated in the massacres'.[5] The terminology was also used in subsequent statements concerning World War I. The Commission of Fifteen Members was established by the Preliminary Peace Conference in January 1919 to inquire into the responsibilities relating to this war.

Chapter II of the Commission's report, dated 29 March 1919, stated, inter alia, that "all persons belonging to enemy countries (...) who have been guilty

1 E. Schwelb, 'Crimes Against Humanity' (1946) 23 BYBIL 178 at 195-7.
2 Prosecutor v. Jean-Paul Akayesu, Case No. ICTR-96-4-T, ICTR T. Ch. I, 2 Sept. 1998, pass. 565-8; Attorney-General of Israel v. Eichmann, District Ct, of Jerusalem (11 Dec. 1961) 36 ILR 5 at 41.
3 UK Treaties Series 9 (1910), Cd. 5030; 8 UNTS 279.
4 Schwelb, 180. For the use of 'dictates of humanity'.
5 The Armenian Memorandum presented by the Greek delegation to the Commission of Fifteen on 14 Mar. 1919. Quoted in ibid., at 181.

of offences against the laws and customs of war or the laws of humanity, are liable to criminal prosecution'. Annex I of the report listed, in addition to the charge of war crimes as they were generally understood at that time, the charges of murder and massacre, systematic terrorism, killing of hostages, torture of civilians, rape, abduction of female civilians for the purpose of enforced prostitution, deportation of civilians, and pillage, committed by Turkish and German authorities against Turkish subjects, as well as a charge of pillage by Austrian troops against the population of an Austrian town. The addition of the laws of humanity failed on an objection by the American members of the Commission essentially on the grounds that a judicial tribunal could only enforce existing law, not the vague notions of laws and principles of humanity that fall within the realm of moral law.[6]

Crimes against humanity were prosecuted at the Nuremberg and Tokyo trials after World War II. Article b(c) of the Nuremberg Charter[7] enumerated the following as crimes against humanity:

> '. . . murder, extermination, enslavement, deportation and other inhumane acts committed against any civilian populations, before or during the war; or persecutions on political, racial, or religious grounds in execution of or in connection with any crime within the jurisdiction of the Tribunal, whether or not in violation of the domestic law of the country where perpetrated.'

The semi-colon before 'or persecutions . . .' in the English and French texts was replaced subsequently by a comma by the Protocol signed at Berlin on 6 October 1945.[8] The change was made to harmonize these texts with the Russian text, all of which were equally authentic. As a result, the provisos 'in execution of or in connection with any crime within the jurisdiction of the Tribunal' and ', whether or not in violation of the domestic law of the country where perpetrated' applied to the whole text of Article 6(c).[9]

Although this was the first technical use of the terminology 'crimes against humanity', and the statesmen involved fully appreciated that crimes against humanity under the Nuremberg Charter were in a different category from war crimes[10], they were not treated by the Nuremberg Tribunal as a new concept.

6 Ibid., 180-3.
7 UK Treaty Series 27 (1946), Cd. 6903.
8 US Dept. of State Publication 2461, Executive Agreement Series 472 (US Govt. Printing Office, 1946), 45 ff.
9 Schwelb, 188, 192-5, 204-5.
10 Ibid., 186-7.

The Nuremberg Tribunal did not question the legality of the inclusion of crimes against humanity in the Nuremberg Charter, merely noting that 'from the beginning of the War in 1939 War Crimes were committed on a vast scale, which were also Crimes against Humanity'.[11] The Nuremberg Tribunal simply ruled that the Nuremberg Charter was decisive and binding on it, and that it was 'the expression of international law existing at the time of its creation; and to that extent [was] itself a contribution to international law'.[12] This was despite the fact that the Nuremberg Charter extended the jurisdiction of the Nuremberg Tribunal beyond war crimes in the traditional sense to encompass other serious crimes falling outside the purview of traditional war crimes, such as crimes where the victim was stateless, had the same nationality as the perpetrator, or had the nationality of a State allied with that of the perpetrator.[13] Indeed, crimes against humanity under the Nuremberg Charter corresponded roughly to violations of the 'laws of humanity' mentioned in the report of the 1919 Commission of Fifteen Members.[14]

The Nuremberg Tribunal, in practice, treated crimes against humanity and war crimes as overlapping and interchangeable, with the major discernible difference being that crimes against humanity were those committed in Germany or in Austria and Czechoslovakia annexed as part of Germany, whereas war crimes were committed in territories occupied by Germany.[15] As one commentator puts it, crimes against humanity under the Nuremberg Charter aimed to ensure that inhumane acts in violation of general principles of the laws of all civilized nations committed in connection with war should be punished; therefore, a crime against humanity was treated as an 'accompanying' or 'accessory' crime to either crimes against peace or war crimes.[16]

Crimes against humanity under the Nuremberg Charter fell into two main categories: (i) murder, extermination, enslavement, deportation, and other inhumane acts committed against any civilian populations, before or during the war; and (ii) persecutions on political, racial, or religious grounds. As mentioned, the commission of a crime against humanity under either of

11 Trial of the Major War Criminals, Proceedings of the International Military Tribunal, Nuremberg, pt. 22 (H.M. Stationery Office, 1950) (hereinafter 'Nuremberg Proceedings'), 468; (1947) 41 AJIL 249.

12 Nuremberg Proceedings, 443; (1947) 41 AJIL 216.

13 Prosecutor v. Dusko Tadic, Case No. IT-94-1-T, ICTY T. Ch. II, 7 May 1997 (hereinafter 'Tadic Judgment'), para. 619.

14 Schwelb, 181.

15 R. S. Clark, 'Nuremberg and Tokyo in Contemporary Perspective', in T. H. L. MacCormack and G. J. Simpson (eds.), The Law of War Crimes: National and International Approaches (Kluwer, 1997), 171 at 179.

16 Schwelb, 206.

these categories had to be in execution of or in connection with any crime within the jurisdiction of the Nuremberg Tribunal.

Control Council Law No. 10, dated 20 December 1945, enumerated the following as crimes against humanity:

> 'Atrocities and Offences, including but not limited to murder, extermination, enslavement, deportation, imprisonment, torture, rape, or other inhumane acts committed against any civilian population or persecution on political, racial or religious grounds, whether or not in violation of the domestic laws of the country where perpetrated.[17]

Control Council Law No. 10 added imprisonment, torture, and rape to the list of crimes against humanity under the Nuremberg Charter. Although the list of crimes against humanity under the Nuremberg Charter was exhaustive and that under Control Council Law No. 10 was illustrative, there was no practical difference between the two as the words 'other inhumane acts' in Article 6(c) of the Nuremberg Charter were sufficiently broad to cover other crimes of similar nature. Most changes in the wording adopted by Law No. 10 resulted in practically no difference between crimes against humanity under that Law and those under the Nuremberg Charter. However, the omission in Law No. 10 of the words 'in execution of or in connection with any crime within the jurisdiction of the Tribunal' had the effect of doing away with the requirement that a crime against humanity had to be committed in execution of, or in connection with, a crime against peace or a war crime.[18]

Article 5(c) of the Tokyo Charter[19] conferred jurisdiction on the Tokyo Tribunal to prosecute and punish crimes against humanity. The provision of the Nuremberg Charter on crimes against humanity, as amended by the Berlin Protocol, was followed in the Tokyo Charter, except that religious grounds of persecution were omitted, probably because persecutions on religious grounds had not been committed on a large scale in connection with the Japanese war effort. It has been noted that crimes against humanity prosecuted before the Tokyo Tribunal were in fact war crimes, being always committed against persons other than Japanese nationals and outside Japan.[20] This observation is correct, especially in light of the modification of the Tokyo Charter just before the commencement of the Tokyo proceedings by deleting from the definition of crimes against humanity the requirement that the crimes had to be directed against the civilian population. This modification was intended to make it possible to punish the wholesale killing

17 36 ILR 31.
18 Schwelb, 217-9.
19 4 Bevans 20.
20 Schwelb, 215-6.

of military personnel in an unlawful war. As a result, Counts 37 and 38 were the only counts dealing with the crimes not falling under the category of either crimes against peace or war crimes. Count 37 charged certain accused with 'conspiring to murder members of the armed forces and civilians of the United States, the Philippines, the British Commonwealth, the Netherlands, and Thailand by initiating unlawful hostilities against those countries in breach of the Hague Convention No. III of 18th October 1907'. Similarly, Count 38 charged these same accused with 'conspiring to murder the soldiers and civilians by initiating hostilities in violation of the [agreements]'.[21]
The prosecution of crimes against humanity was upheld subsequently by the UN General Assembly on 11 December 1946[22] and by the International Law Commission.[23] The concept of crimes against humanity continued to be refined in domestic courts of Israel and France, among others.[24]

As we will see in this book it is a settled rule of customary international law that crimes against humanity are international crimes and the perpetrators of these crimes incur individual criminal responsibility. Moreover, crimes against humanity under customary international law need not be linked to international armed conflict, as required in the Nuremberg and Tokyo Charters, or any conflict at all.[25]

Recent developments

Article 5 of the The International Criminal Tribunal for the former Yugoslavia (ICTY) Statute, under the heading 'Crimes against humanity', stipulates that the ICTY shall have the power to prosecute persons responsible for the following crimes 'when committed in armed conflict, whether international or internal in character, and directed against any civilian population: (a) murder; (b) extermination; (c) enslavement; (d) deportation; (e) imprisonment; (f) torture; (g) rape; (h) persecutions on political, racial and religious grounds; (i) other inhumane acts'.

While Article 3 of the International Criminal Tribunal for Rwanda (ICTR) Statute enumerates the same crimes against humanity as those in Article 5 of the ICTY Statute, it does away with the requirement in the ICTY Statute

21 B. V. A. Röling and C. F. Rüter (eds.), The Tokyo Judgment: The International Military Tribunal for the Far East (IMTFE) 29April 1946-12 November 1948, i (APA-University Press Amsterdam BV, 1977), xii, 21.

22 Resolution on the Affirmation of the Principles of International Law Recognized by the Charter of the Nuremberg Tribunal. UN GA Res. 95 (1) of 11 Dec. 1946.

23 Principle VI. c of the Principles of International Law Recognized in the Judgement of the Tribunal ('Nuremberg Principles') (1950) ii Yearbook of the ILC 374-8.

24 See Akayesu, pass. 567-77.

25 Prosecutor v. Dusko Tadic, Case No. IT-94-1, ICTY App. Ch., Decision on the Defence Motion for Interlocutory Appeal on Jurisdiction of 2 Oct. 1995 ('Tadic Jurisdiction Decision'), para. 141.

that such crimes be committed in armed conflict. However, Article 3 of the ICTR Statute confines the jurisdiction of the ICTR to the prosecution of persons responsible for these enumerated crimes 'when committed as part of a widespread or system attack against any civilian population on national, political, ethnic, racial or religious grounds'. Thus, the ICTR Statute contains a requirement of discriminatory intent in each of the enumerated crimes against humanity additional to the other requirements in the Nuremberg Charter, the Tokyo Charter, and the ICTY Statute.[26] Yet, the ICTR Statute is specifically tailor-made to punish the atrocities occurring in Rwanda in 1994, where Tutsis were singled out for attacks because of their ethnic origin. Tutsis and those Hutus who were believed to be political supporters of the Tutsi-dominated government were also singled out for attacks because of their political leaning.[27] Discrimination on the basis of a person's political ideology has been held to satisfy the requirement of 'political' grounds.[28] Inhumane acts committed against persons not falling within any one of the discriminatory categories could constitute crimes against humanity if the perpetrator intends to commit such acts to further his attacks on the group discriminated against on one of the discriminatory grounds.[29]

Article 7 of the International Criminal Courrt (ICC) Statute, under the heading 'Crimes against humanity', stipulates in paragraph 1 that these crimes mean any of the acts enumerated therein 'when committed as part of a widespread or systematic attack directed against any civilian population, with knowledge of the attack'. The enumerated acts are murder; extermination; enslavement; deportation or forcible transfer of population; imprisonment or other severe deprivation of physical liberty in violation of fundamental rules of international law; torture; rape, sexual slavery, enforced prostitution, forced pregnancy, enforced sterilization, or any other form of sexual violence of comparable gravity; persecution against any identifiable group or collectivity on political, racial, national, ethnic, cultural, religious, gender, or other grounds that are universally recognized as impermissible under international law, in connection with any act referred to in Article 7, paragraph 1, or any other crime within the ICUs jurisdiction; enforced disappearance of persons; the crime of apartheid; other inhumane acts of a similar character intentionally causing great suffering, or serious injury to the body or mental or physical health.[30]

26 The ICTR itself recognizes this fact. See Prosecutor v Kayishema and Obed Ruzindana, Case No. ICTR-95-1-T, ICTR T. Ch. II, 21 May 1999, para. 130.

27 Ibid.

28 Akayesu, para. 583.

29 Ibid., para. 584.

30 For a legislative history, see H. von Hebel and D. Robinson, 'Crimes within the Jurisdiction of the Court', in R. S. Lee (ed.), The International Criminal Court: The Making of the Rome Statute-Issues, Negotiations, Results (Kluwer, 1999), 79 at 90-103.

The definition of crimes against humanity under the ICC Statute is not an innovation; it reflects developments of international humanitarian law since Nuremberg.[31] The ICC Statute also adds 'forcible transfer of population' as an alternative offence to 'deportation'. Besides, it expands the offence of imprisonment to include 'other severe deprivation of physical liberty in violation of fundamental rules of international law'. In the case of sexual offences, the ICC Statute adds to the offence of rape those of 'sexual slavery, enforced prostitution, forced pregnancy, enforced sterilization, or any other form of sexual violence of comparable gravity'. With regard to the crime of persecution, the ICC Statute elaborates that it must be 'against any identifiable group or collectivity' on discriminatory grounds, with gender, national, ethnic, cultural, 'or other grounds that are universally recognized as impermissible under international law' added to the discriminatory grounds enumerated in the ICTY and the ICTR Statutes. The ICC Statute lists enforced disappearance of persons and the crime of apartheid as new grounds. As for 'other inhumane acts', the ICC Statute elucidates that they must be 'of a similar character intentionally causing great suffering, or serious injury to body or to mental, or physical health'.

In general, the essential elements shared among crimes against humanity are as follows: the act is inhumane in nature and character, causing great suffering, or serious injury to body or to mental or physical health; the act is committed as part of a widespread or systematic attack; and the act is committed against members of the civilian population.[32]

In this volume of the International Criminal Law Series we present background information on the issue of "Crimes against Humanity". First an in-depth account of the history and international legal implications is being presented. In the second part of the book the ICTY and ICTR jurisprudence is analysed in detail. Finally the most important texts and agreements relating to this subject can be found.

We hope that this book offers you useful tools in study or work.

The editors,

Reykjavik/Oisterwijk
April 2011

31 See D. Robinson, 'Defining "Crimes against Humanity" at the Rome Conference' (1999) 93 AJIL 43 at 43-4.

32 Cf. Akayesu, para. 578.

PART 1

DEFINITION OF CRIMES AGAINST HUMANITY

Introduction

Crimes against humanity are as old as humanity itself.[33] However, it is only in the last seven decades that the international legal prohibition on crimes against humanity has emerged, and it is only in the last fifteen years that the precise contours of the crime have been clarified.

Whereas genocide and war crimes have been codified in conventions with widely accepted definitions[34], crimes against humanity have appeared in a series of instruments with somewhat inconsistent definitions. The law of crimes against humanity was initially created to fill certain gaps in the law of war crimes, but many parameters were left undefined. The recent increase in the application of international criminal law has produced a fruitful interplay between international instruments, jurisprudence and commentaries, leading to a more coherent picture of the scope and definition of crimes against humanity today.

A crime against humanity involves the commission of certain inhumane acts, such as murder, torture, rape, sexual slavery, persecution and other inhumane acts, in a certain context: they must be part of a widespread or systematic attack directed against a civilian population. It is this context that elevates crimes that might otherwise fall exclusively under national jurisdiction to crimes of concern to the international community as a whole. An individual may be liable for crimes against humanity if he or she commits one or more inhumane acts within that broader context. It is not required that the individual be a ringleader or architect of the broader campaign.

1.1. Historical development

The most significant early reference to 'crimes against humanity' as a legal concept was a joint declaration by France, Great Britain and Russia in 1915. Responding to the massacre of Armenians by Turkey, the joint declaration denounced 'crimes against humanity and civilization' and warned of personal accountability.[35]

After the First World War, an international war crimes commission recommended the creation of an international tribunal to try not only war crimes but also 'violations of the laws of humanity'. However, the US

33 Jean Graven, 'Les Crimes Contre l'Humanité' (1950) 76 Hague Recueil 427 at 433.

34 See appendix and the other volumes in this series.

35 For more information on these historical developments, see United Nations War Crimes Commission, History of the United Nations War Crimes Commission and the Development of the Laws of War (London, 1948); Roger Clark, 'Crimes Against Humanity' in G. Ginsburgs and V. N. Kudriavstsev (eds.), The Nuremberg Trials and International Law (Dordrecht/Boston/London, 1990); Egon Schwelb, 'Crimes Against Humanity' (1946) 23 BYBIL 178.

representative objected to the references to the laws of humanity on the grounds that these were not yet precise enough for criminal law, and the concept was not pursued at that time.[36]

In the wake of the events of the Second World War, the drafters of the Nuremberg Charter[37] were confronted with the question of how to respond to the Holocaust and the massive crimes committed by the Nazi regime. The classic definition of war crimes did not include crimes committed by a government against its own citizens. The drafters therefore included 'crimes against humanity', defined in Article 6(c) as:

> murder, extermination, enslavement, deportation and other inhumane acts committed against any civilian population, before or during the war, or persecutions on political, racial or religious grounds in execution of or in connection with any crime within the jurisdiction of the Tribunal, whether or not in violation of the law of the country where perpetrated.

Three major features may be noted. First, the reference to 'any' civilian population meant that even crimes committed against a country's own population were included. This was a major advancement, given that at that time, prior to the advent of the human rights movement, international law generally regulated conduct between States and said little about a government's treatment of its own citizens. Second, the requirement of connection to war crimes or the crime of aggression meant in effect that crimes against humanity could occur only with some 'nexus' to armed conflict.[38] Third, the reference to 'population' was understood to create some requirement of scale, but the precise threshold was specified neither in the Charter nor in the Nuremberg Judgment.[39]

It remains controversial whether the Nuremberg Charter created new law, or whether it recognized an existing crime.[40] Among those concluding that it was a new crime, many argued that the principle of non-retroactivity had to give way to the overriding need for accountability for large-scale murder and atrocities recognized as criminal by all nations.[41] Perhaps because of

36 War Crimes Commission, History.

37 See appendix.

38 The text as originally adopted contained a semi-colon following the word 'war', which would give rise to the interpretation that the connection requirement applied only to persecution. This was promptly amended by the Berlin Protocol of 6 October 1945, which replaced the semi-colon with a comma, thereby supporting the interpretation that the connection requirement applied to all crimes against humanity. See Clark, 'Crimes',190–2.

39 War Crimes Commission, History, 192–3.

40 See, e.g. M. Cherif Bassiouni, Crimes Against Humanity in International Criminal Law, 2nd edn (The Hague, 1999) 123–76.

41 Hans Kelsen, 'Will the Judgment in the Nuremberg Trial Constitute a Precedent in Interna-

this uncertainty in the status of crimes against humanity, the Nuremberg Judgment tended to blur discussion of crimes against humanity and war crimes and provided very little guidance on the particular elements of the crime.[42]

The Tokyo Charter included a similar definition with some modifications[43]. The Allied Control Council, creating law for occupied Germany, adopted Law No. 10 with a similar definition, except that it added rape, imprisonment and torture to the list of inhumane acts, and did not require a connection to war crimes or aggression.

The concept of crimes against humanity was promptly endorsed by the UN General Assembly, [44] but in the decades that followed there was only a limited body of national cases[45] as well as a few treaties and instruments recognizing enforced disappearance and apartheid as crimes against humanity.[46] The International Law Commission also developed several drafts of an international code of crimes.

A major advance occurred when the Security Council created the ICTY and ICTR in response to mass crimes in the Former Yugoslavia and in Rwanda.[47] The Statute of each Tribunal contained a list of acts based on the Allied Control Council Law No. 10 list. The ICTY Statute (Article 5) defined the contextual threshold as 'when committed in armed conflict, whether international or internal in character, and directed against any civilian population'. The Tribunal itself, referring to the Report to the Secretary-

tional Law?' (1947) 1 International Law Quarterly 153 esp. at 165; see also E. Schwelb, 'Crimes' Against Humanity' (1946) 23 BYBIL 178; and see treatment of the question in R v. Finta [1994] 1 SCR 701; Polyukhovic [1991] HCA 32; (1991) 172 CLR 501 at 661–2, HCA; Eichmann 36 ILR 277 at 283, SC.

42 Nuremberg Judgment, reproduced (1947) 41 AJIL 172 esp. at 248–9.

43 Tokyo Charter, Art. 5(c), included the same definition with the omission of racial and religious persecution, on the grounds that such crimes had not occurred in that theatre of conflict. The term 'any civilian population' was also deleted, on which basis the prosecution argued that all killing during an aggressive war was murder. Such arguments were rejected at Nuremberg and Tokyo, as they would undermine the distinction between the law governing justification for armed conflict and the law governing conduct during armed conflict.

44 UNGA Res. 95(I), UN Doc A/64/Add.1 (1946).

45 Including cases in France, the Netherlands, Israel, Canada and Australia. See also Joseph Rikhof, 'Crimes Against Humanity, Customary International Law and the International Tribunals for Bosnia and Rwanda' (1995) 6 National Journal of Constitutional Law 231; Matthew Lippman, 'Crimes Against Humanity' (1997) 17 Boston College Third World Law Journal 171; Leila Sadat Wexler, 'The Interpretation of the Nuremberg Principles by the French Court of Cassation: From Touvier to Barbie and Back Again' (1994) 32 Columbia Journal of Transnational Law 289.

46 Examples include the Convention on the Non-Applicability of Statutory Limitations to War Crimes and Crimes Against Humanity 1968, the Apartheid Convention 1973, the Inter-American Convention on Enforced Disappearance 1994, and the UN Declaration on Enforced Disappearance 1992.

47 See also the special volume on this tribunal in this series.

General and other authorities, interpreted this threshold as requiring a 'widespread or systematic attack'.[48] The ICTR Statute (Article 3) defined the context as 'when committed as part of a widespread or systematic attack against any civilian population on national, political, ethnic, racial or religious grounds'. Thus, the definitions are similar, except that the ICTY Statute requires armed conflict and the ICTR Statute requires discriminatory grounds.

The ICC Statute contains the same list of acts but adds forced transfer of population, sexual slavery, enforced prostitution, forced pregnancy, enforced sterilization, sexual violence, enforced disappearance and the crime of apartheid. [49] The ICC Statute rejects both the armed conflict requirement and the requirement of discriminatory grounds. The contextual threshold in Article 7 of the ICC Statute is 'when committed as part of a widespread or systematic attack directed against any civilian population'. The ICC Statute includes supplementary definitions in Article 7(2), some of which have been generally welcomed as helpful clarifications, whereas others have been controversial, as will be discussed further in this chapter.

Additional sources on the definition of crimes against humanity may now be found in national and international jurisprudence, the ICC Elements of Crimes, and instruments of other tribunals (Sierra Leone, Iraq). Each of these includes a comparable list of acts as well as the now-standard requirement of widespread or systematic attack directed against any civilian population.

1.2. Relationship to other crimes

War crimes[50] and crimes against humanity can and do frequently overlap. For example, a mass killing of civilians during an armed conflict could constitute both types of crimes. There are, however, significant differences. First, unlike war crimes, crimes against humanity may occur even in the absence of armed conflict. Second, crimes against humanity require a context of widespread or systematic commission, whereas war crimes do not; a single isolated incident can constitute a war crime. Third, war crimes law was originally based on reciprocal promises between parties to conflict, and hence primarily focuses on protecting 'enemy' nationals or persons affiliated with the other party to the conflict. The law of crimes against humanity protects victims regardless of their nationality or affiliation. Fourth, war crimes law regulates conduct even on the battlefield and against

48 Tadic ICTY T. Ch. II 7.5.1997 para. 644; Tadic ICTY A. Ch. 15.7.1999 para. 248.
49 See Art. 7 ICC Statute.
50 See War Crimes and International Criminal Law, W.J. van der Wolf (ed.), ICA 2010.

military objectives, whereas the law of crimes against humanity concerns actions directed primarily against civilian populations.

Thus, the 'international dimension' of war crimes arises from the armed conflict, and the 'international dimension' of crimes against humanity arises from the attack on a civilian population. Cumulatively, the two bodies of law, working together, penalize atrocities committed during armed conflict or committed on a widespread or systematic basis.

Genocide was initially regarded as a particularly odious form of crime against humanity,[51] in that it was a crime against humanity committed with the intent to destroy, in whole or in part, a national, ethnical, racial or religious group as such. Over time, however, the definitions of the two crimes have evolved and pose differing requirements. Therefore it is no longer useful to describe genocide as a subset of crimes against humanity. Nonetheless, almost any conceivable example of genocide would also satisfy the requirements of crimes against humanity.

1.3. Common elements

As already noted, a crime against humanity entails the commission of a listed *inhumane act, in a certain context: a widespread or systematic attack directed against a civilian population.*

1.3.1 Aspects not required

No nexus to armed conflict

The Nuremberg and Tokyo Charters both required a connection to war crimes or to aggression, in effect requiring some nexus to armed conflict.[52] On the other hand, Allied Control Council Law No. 10 did not include such a requirement. Subsequent case law of military tribunals split over whether such a nexus must be read in to the definition, or was not required. For example, the Flick and Weizsäcker cases imported the requirement from the Nuremberg Charter, whereas the Ohlendorf and Altstötter decisions concluded that it was unnecessary. [53]

51 UN War Crimes Commission, History, 196–7. See also Genocide and International Criminal Law,
W.J. van der Wolf (ed.), ICA 2011.

52 See, e.g. Bassiouni, Crimes, 60–9.

53 United States v. Ohlendorf et al. 4 TWC 411; United States v. Altstötter et al. (the 'Justice Trial') VI LRTWC 1; United States v. Flick IX LRTWC 1; United States v. Weizsäcker, (the 'Ministries Trial') 14 TWC 1.

Subsequent international conventions[54] indicated that a nexus to armed conflict was not required. However, the ICTY Statute, adopted in 1993 by the Security Council, restricted crimes against humanity to those 'committed in armed conflict, whether international or internal in character' (Article 5). The Security Council promptly reversed this position in 1994, when it adopted the ICTR Statute without such a requirement (Article 3). Finally, after extensive debates at the 1998 Rome Conference, agreement was reached on a definition of crimes against humanity rejecting any such requirement (Article 7).[55]

Today, it seems well settled that a nexus to armed conflict is not required. The majority of instruments and precedents oppose such a requirement. The limitation in the Nuremberg Charter is generally seen as a jurisdictional limitation only,[56] and the ICTY Statute definition appears to be the anomaly. Indeed, the jurisprudence of the ICTY itself concludes that the requirement is a deviation from customary law.[57] This view is also supported by national case law, international bodies of experts, and the writings of commentators.[58] No requirement of armed conflict has appeared in subsequent definitions of crimes against humanity.

No requirement of discriminatory animus

The ICTR Statute, Article 3, requires that crimes against humanity be committed on 'national, ethnic, racial or religious grounds'. Such a requirement was supported by a few cases in France, but did not appear in most precedents.[59]

Although an early ICTY trial decision reluctantly adopted the 'discriminatory grounds' requirement for the purposes of consistency, it explicitly noted that it was not supported in previous authorities, and the ICTY Appeals Chamber subsequently ruled that discrimination is not a requirement.[60]

54 Including the Genocide Convention, the Convention on the Non-Applicability of Statutory Limitations to War Crimes and Crimes Against Humanity 1968, the Apartheid Convention 1973 and the Inter-American Convention on Enforced Disappearance 1994.

55 Darryl Robinson, 'Defining Crimes Against Humanity at the Rome Conference' (1999) 93 AJIL 43.

56 War Crimes Commission, History, 192–3; see also Clark, 'Crimes', 196; Diane Orentlicher, 'Settling Accounts: The Duty to Prosecute Human Rights Violations of a Prior Regime' (1991) 100 Yale Law Journal 2537 at 2588–90.

57 Tadic ICTY T. Ch. II 7.5.1997 para. 627; Tadic ICTY A. Ch. 15.7.1999 paras. 282–8.

58 Eichmann (1968) 36 ILR 5 at 49, DC; Barbie (1990) 78 ILR 124 at 136, Cour de Cassation; ILC Report 1996, UN Doc A/51/10 (1996) p. 96; Orentlicher, 'Settling Accounts' 2588–90; Theodor Meron, 'International Criminalization of Internal Atrocities' (1995) 89 AJIL 554; Beth van Schack, 'The Definition of Crimes Against Humanity: Resolving the Incoherence' (1999) 37 Columbia Journal of Transnational Law 787.

59 Some French cases, including Barbie (1990) 78 ILR 124, Cour de Cassation and Touvier 100 ILR 338, Cour d'Appel, suggested that a policy of discrimination is required.

60 Tadic ICTY T. Ch. II 7.5.1997 para. 652; Tadic ICTY A. Ch. 15.7.1999 paras. 282–305.

The ICC Statute, adopted in 1998, rejected a discrimination requirement. It appears reasonably well settled today that discriminatory animus is not a requirement, and it has not been included in subsequent instruments (Sierra Leone, Iraq). The ICTR Appeals Chamber has held that the restriction in the ICTR Statute relates only to the Tribunal, and also that the requirement relates to the attack as a whole; thus discriminatory intent of the perpetrator is not required.[61]

Thus, it would appear that discriminatory grounds are not required in customary law, except for the specific crime of persecution.

1.3.2 Widespread or systematic attack

Widespread or systematic

The concept of 'widespread or systematic attack directed against any civilian population' emerged in the 1990s as the accepted formulation for the contextual threshold, thus contributing to clarity and consistency in this area of law. Nonetheless, some aspects of the definition of these terms remain to be resolved.

The widespread or systematic test is disjunctive;[62] a prosecutor need only satisfy one or the other threshold. As discussed below, however, in addition to 'widespread or systematic', there must also be an 'attack', and some authorities indicate that an 'attack directed against a civilian population' necessarily entails at least some modest degree of scale and organization.[63] This would mean that, while the rigorous thresholds of 'widespread' or 'systematic' are disjunctive, the 'attack' requires at least some minimal aspect of each.

The term 'widespread' has been defined in various ways, and generally connotes the 'large-scale nature of the attack and the number of victims'.[64] No numerical limit has been set; the issue must be decided on the facts. While 'widespread' typically refers to the cumulative effect of numerous inhumane acts, it could also be satisfied by a singular massive act of extraordinary magnitude.[65]

61 Akayesu ICTR A. Ch. I 1.6.2001 paras. 461–9.

62 The French version of the ICTR Statute referred to the requirements conjunctively (généralisée et systématique), but this was held to be a simple error: Akayesu ICTR T. Ch. I 2.9.1998 para. 579.

63 See Art. 7(2)(a) ICC Statute, and see Haradinaj ICTY T. Ch. I 3.4.2008 para. 122.

64 Tadic ICTY T. Ch. II 7.5.1997 para. 206, Kunarac ICTY T. Ch. II 22.2.2001 para. 428; Nahimana, ICTR A. Ch. 28.11.2007 para. 920; Situation in Darfur (Al Bashir arrest warrant case) ICC PTC-I, 4.3.2009 para. 81.

65 Kordic ICTY T. Ch. 26.2.2001 para. 176; Blaškic ICTY T. Ch. I 3.3.2000 para. 206; ILC Draft Code, pp. 94–5.

The term 'systematic' has also been defined in various ways. Early decisions set high thresholds: in Akayesu, it was defined as (1) thoroughly organized, (2) following a regular pattern, (3) on the basis of a common policy and (4) involving substantial public or private resources.[66] In Blaškic, it was defined as requiring (1) a plan or objective, (2) large-scale or continuous commission of linked crimes, (3) significant resources, and (4) implication of high-level authorities.[67] It is understandable to pose a significant threshold, especially given that non-widespread crimes should not lightly be labelled as a crime against humanity, but these definitions may set the bar too high.[68] Other cases refer more simply to 'pattern or methodical plan', 'organized nature of the acts' or 'organized pattern of conduct'.[69] The most recent cases seem to be settling on 'the organized nature of the acts of violence and the improbability of their random occurrence'.[70] Consistent with the ordinary meaning of the term, it may be that the hallmark of 'systematic' is the high degree of organization, and that features such as patterns, continuous commission, use of resources, planning, and political objectives are important factors.

Attack

The term 'attack' is not used in the same sense as in the law of war crimes. An 'attack' need not involve the use of armed force, and can encompass mistreatment of the civilian population.[71] It refers to the broader course of conduct, involving prohibited acts, of which the acts of the accused form part.[72]

The ICC Statute and Tribunal jurisprudence indicate there must at least be multiple acts or multiple victims in order to warrant the label 'attack directed against a civilian population'.[73] These acts may be all of the same

66 Akayesu ICTR T. Ch. I 2.9.1998 para. 580.

67 Blaškic ICTY T. Ch. 3.3.2000 para. 203.

68 See also Kai Ambos and Steffen Wirth, 'The Current Law of Crimes Against Humanity: An Analysis of UNTAET Regulation 15/2000' (2002) 13 Criminal Law Forum 1at 18–20.

69 Tadic ICTY T Ch. II 7.5.1997 para. 648; Kunarac ICTY T. Ch. II 22.2.2001 para. 429; Ntakirutimana ICTR T. Ch. I 21.2.2003 para. 804.

70 See, e.g. Nahimana, ICTR A. Ch. 28.11.2007 para. 920; Al Bashir arrest warrant case ICC PTC-I, 4.4.2009 para. 81. As will be suggested below, improbability of random occurrence arguably should not only be an aspect of the disjunctive 'systematic' test, it should already be inherent in the concept of an 'attack'; otherwise widespread but random crime would constitute a crime against humanity.

71 ICC Elements, Crimes Against Humanity Introduction para. 3; Kunarac ICTY A. Ch. 12.6.2002 para. 86; Akayesu ICTR T. Ch. I 2.9.1998 para. 581.

72 Art. 7(2)(a) of the ICC Statute; Tadic ICTY T. Ch. 7.5.1997 para. 644; Akayesu ICTR T. Ch. I 2.9.1998 para. 205. See also the Jurisprudence part of this book.

73 Art. 7(2)(a) of the ICC Statute; Kunarac ICTY T Ch. II 22.2.2001 para. 415; Krnojelac ICTY T. Ch. II 15.3.2002 para. 54.

type or of different types, for example murder, rape and deportation.[74] This requirement of 'multiple acts' does not mean that 'widespread' is a requirement in all cases. Both terms measure scale, but 'multiple' is a low threshold and 'widespread' is a high threshold.

'Attack directed' and the controversy concerning the policy element

Crime, even on a 'widespread' basis – for example, a crime wave, or anarchy following a natural disaster – does not by itself constitute a crime against humanity. The random acts of individuals are not sufficient; some thread of connection between acts is needed so that they can accurately be described collectively as an attack directed against a civilian population. Some authorities seek to make this proposition explicit by indicating that there must be an underlying governmental or organizational policy that directs, instigates or encourages the crimes. Other authorities reject any requirement of plan or policy. It is therefore controversial whether the policy element is a necessary component of crimes against humanity.

The divide in the authorities

National jurisprudence on crimes against humanity following the Second World War frequently indicated that governmental policy is a requirement.[75] In the 1990s, the very same authorities that established the 'widespread or systematic' test also coupled this with a requirement of policy or of direction, instigation or encouragement by a State or organization.[76] Early Tribunal cases tended to follow this approach.[77]

At the Rome Conference, there was strong opposition to an unqualified disjunctive 'widespread or systematic' test, on the grounds that it would incorrectly include widespread but unconnected crimes, such as a crime wave. It was argued in response that the customary law concept of an 'attack' excluded random crimes. Agreement was reached on the disjunctive 'widespread or systematic' test, provided that the definition of 'attack'

74 Kayishema ICTR T. Ch. II 21.5.1999 para. 122.

75 Examples include: the Justice Trial VI LRTWC 1; Brandt (the 'Doctors' Trial') IV LRTWC 91 (US Military Tribunal); Barbie 78 ILR 124, Court of Cassation, 6 December 1983 (France); Menten 75 ILR 362–3 (Netherlands); R v. Finta [1994] 1 SCR 701 at 814 (Canada); Polyukhovic 172 CLR 501 (Australia); Pinochet (No. 3) [1999] 2 All ER 97 (United Kingdom) (Lord Hope, Lord Millet; but see contra Lord Browne-Wilkinson).

76 Commission of Experts (Former Yugoslavia), Final Report of the Commission of Experts Established Pursuant to Security Council Resolution 780 (1992), UN Doc. S/1994/674 at 23; Commission of Experts (Rwanda), Final Report of the Commission of Experts Established Pursuant to Security Council Resolution 935 (1994), UN Doc. G/SO 214 at para. 135; ILC, Report on the work of its forty-eighth session (ILC draft Code), UN Doc A/51/10 at 93 and 95–6; and see Final Report on Systematic Rape, Sexual Slavery and Slavery-like Practices During Armed Conflict, UN Doc. E/CN.4/Sub.2/1992/13 (1998).

77 Tadic ICTY T. Ch. II 7.5.1997 para. 644; Bagilishema ICTR T. Ch. I 7.6.2001 para. 78.

included this clarification. Article 7(2)(a) therefore defines 'attack' and includes the policy element, which was based on the authorities at the time. 'Policy' was understood as a low threshold which could be inferred from the manner in which the acts occur.[78] The definition followed more recent authorities indicating that the policy need not be that of a government, but could also be that of an organization.

Strong concerns were already growing about the policy element, both in Tribunal jurisprudence and the ICC negotiations. The major concerns were that it imposed a novel burden, that it would be difficult to prove, and that it contradicted the disjunctive test. [79] Tribunal cases began to split, with some supporting, then some declining to take a position, and then some expressing doubt.[80] Finally, in Kunarac, the ICTY Appeals Chamber held, rather succinctly, that 'nothing in the Statute or in customary international law ... required proof of the existence of a plan or policy to commit these crimes'.[81] Whereas decisions on other issues of customary law have tended to involve an extensive review of precedents, the Appeals Chamber resolved this major controversy with reasoning appearing only in a single footnote, and declining to address (or acknowledge) most of the contrary authorities.

Thus, the main indicators of customary law are now divided. On one hand, the ICC Statute indicates that policy is required. The Statute was adopted by a great number of States purporting to codify existing customary law, and hence it is a strong indicator of customary law. A similar requirement appears in much national jurisprudence, and in legislation based on the ICC Statute definitions, which will also shape State practice. On the other hand, Tribunal jurisprudence, which also purports to reflect customary law, and which is also a strong indicator, rejects the policy element. Moreover, Article 10 of the ICC Statute indicates that its definitions 'shall not be interpreted as limiting or prejudicing in any way existing or developing rules of international law for purposes other than this Statute'.

78 Tadic ICTY T. Ch. II 7.5.1997 paras. 653–5; Robinson, 'Defining Crimes Against Humanity',50–1; Timothy H. L. McCormack, 'Crimes Against Humanity' in Dominic McGoldrick, Peter Rowe and Eric Donnelly (eds.), The Permanent International Criminal Court: Legal and Policy Issues (Oxford, 2004) 186–9.

79 See Margaret McAuliffe de Guzman, 'The Road From Rome: The Developing Law of Crimes Against Humanity' (2000) 22 Human Rights Quarterly 335; Phyllis Hwang, 'Defining Crimes Against Humanity in the Rome Statute of the International Criminal Court' (1998) 22 Fordham International Law Journal 457. In relation to the latter concern, it may be noted that, in the same manner that 'multiple' was a lower threshold than 'widespread', 'policy' was understood as a lower threshold than 'systematic'. Thus the disjunctive test is not necessarily contradicted.

80 Kupreškic ICTY T. Ch. II 14.1.2000 paras. 554–5; Kunarac ICTY T. Ch. II 22.2.2001 para. 432; Kordic ICTY T. Ch. 26.2.2001 paras. 181–2; Krnojelac ICTY T. Ch. II 15.3.2002 para. 58.

81 Kunarac ICTY A. Ch. 12.6.2002 para. 98. The reasoning of the Chamber appears strikingly similar to that in Guénaël Mettraux, 'Crimes Against Humanity in the Jurisprudence of the International Criminal Tribunals for the Former Yugoslavia and Rwanda' (2002) 43 Harvard International Law Journal 237 at 270–82.

Interpretation of the authorities

In order for international criminal law to become a clear and credible edifice of law, it is desirable to resolve such issues in a consistent and coherent manner. It may be possible to read the authorities in light of the agreed properties of crimes against humanity, so as to reduce the apparent inconsistency of international criminal law. Much of the controversy over the policy element may result from differing understandings of what the element means.[82] Some commentators reject the policy element, but agree that random criminality of individuals does not amount to an 'attack'.[83] To other commentators, that is precisely what the policy element means:[84] indeed, the necessary logical corollary of excluding isolated individual acts is to require some instigation or encouragement by something other than individuals, namely a State or organization. Some scholars argue that the collective character reflected in the policy element is the fundamental essence of crimes against humanity; they are 'politics gone cancerous'.[85]

For those jurisdictions that apply a policy element, the policy element must be interpreted in accordance with the previous jurisprudence as a modest threshold that excludes random action.[86] First, as noted in jurisprudence, a 'policy' need not be formally adopted, nor expressly declared, nor even stated clearly and precisely.[87] Thus, it must be given an ordinary meaning such as 'a course of action adopted as advantageous or expedient',[88] rather than any connation of a formal and official strategy. Second, the element may be satisfied by inference from the manner in which the acts occur;[89] it is sufficient to show the improbability of random occurrence. Third, it is not required to show action by a State or organization; case law indicates that the requirement is satisfied by 'explicit or implicit approval or endorsement'

82 See, e.g. Mettraux, 'Crimes', 275, rejecting some authorities as precedent for a policy element because all they meant is to exclude isolated crimes. See also Hwang, 'Defining Crimes', 502–3, fearing that 'policy' might be misinterpreted as more stringent than 'systematic'.

83 Mettraux, 'Crimes', 254, 273 and 275.

84 See, e.g. Yoram Dinstein, 'Crimes Against Humanity After Tadic' (2000) 13 LJIL 273 at 389; Simon Chesterman, 'An Altogether Different Order: Defining the Elements of Crimes Against Humanity' (2000) Duke Journal of Comparative & International Law 283 at 316.

85 See, e.g. David Luban, 'A Theory of Crimes Against Humanity' (2004) 29 Yale Law Journal 85 at 90; see also Ambos and Wirth, 'The Current Law',26–34; William Schabas, 'State Policy as an Element of International Crimes' (2008) 98 Journal of Criminal Law & Criminology 953.

86 McAuliffe de Guzman, 'Road From Rome', 374.

87 Tadic ICTY T. Ch. II 7.5.1997 para. 653; Blaškic ICTY T. Ch. I 3.3.2000 paras. 204–5.

88 Oxford English Dictionary, 2nd edn (Oxford, 1989), vol. XII, 27 provides this as the 'chief living sense'.

89 Tadic ICTY T. Ch. II 7.5.1997 para. 653; Blaškic ICTY T. Ch. I 3.3.2000 para. 204.

or that the conduct is 'clearly encouraged' or 'clearly fits within' a general policy.[90] Thus, inaction designed to encourage the crimes would also suffice.[91]

For those jurisdictions that have rejected the term 'policy', it is essential not to lose sight of the principle that unconnected random acts cannot constitute an 'attack'.[92] Tribunal jurisprudence may partially achieve this result in its requirement to examine whether a 'population' was 'targeted' or was a 'primary object', all of which imply some direction from some source.[93] Recent Tribunal jurisprudence mentions the element of 'improbability of random occurrence', but only as part of the definition of 'systematic'. [94] The element of improbability of random occurrence must, however, be inherent in all 'attacks'; otherwise crime waves become included.[95] In the absence of such clarification, a literal and mechanistic application of Tribunal definitions would encompass widespread but random crimes of individuals, which reflects either a failure to describe the crime accurately, or else a loss of the basic conceptual foundation for crimes against humanity.[96]

1.3.3. 'Any civilian population'

The word 'any' highlights the central innovation and raison d'être of crimes against humanity. The law of crimes against humanity not only protects enemy nationals, it also covers, for example, crimes by a State against its own subjects.[97] The nationality or affiliation of the victim is irrelevant.

The term 'civilian' connotes crimes directed against non-combatants rather than combatants, while the term 'population' indicates that 'a larger body of victims is visualized', and that 'single or isolated acts against individuals' fall outside the scope of the concept.[98] The reference to population implies

90 Kupreškic ICTY T. Ch. II 14.1.2000 paras. 554–5.

91 Commission of Experts (former Yugoslavia), Final Report, 23. The ICC Elements, footnote 6, reach this result but in a particularly tortured manner, twice emphasizing a need for action, before acknowledging, in a restrictive manner, the possibility of passive encouragement. The ICC Elements also add that inaction alone is not enough to infer a policy; this cannot be interpreted as repudiating the preceding sentence. Rather, it acknowledges that there may be other reasons for inaction (lack of knowledge of crimes, lack of ability), and hence policy should not be inferred without considering alternative explanations.

92 Kunarac ICTY T. Ch. II 22.2.2001 para. 422.

93 See, e.g. Kunarac ICTY A. Ch. 12.6.2002 paras. 90–2. In Haradinaj ICTY T. Ch. I 3.4.2008, a Chamber found that a 'relative small number of incidents', lacking scale or frequency, and without significant evidence of structure, organization or targeting, did not amount to an attack directed against a civilian population.

94 Kunarac ICTY T. Ch. II 22.2.2001 para. 429; Krnojelac ICTY T. Ch. II 15.3.2002 para. 57.

95 Ambos and Wirth, 'The Current Law', 30–1.

96 See, e.g. David Luban, 'A Theory of Crimes Against Humanity' (2004) 29 Yale Law Journal 85; Ambos and Wirth, 'The Current Law',30–1; Bassiouni, Crimes, 245–7; Geoffrey Robertson, Crimes Against Humanity: The Struggle for Global Justice (London, 1999) 311 and 314.

97 War Crimes Commission, History, 193.

98 Ibid.

'crimes of a collective nature' but does not require that the entire population be targeted.[99]

Antonio Cassese has put forward a significant argument that in customary international law the crime is not restricted to 'civilian' populations, relying on certain Second World War cases that identify crimes against military personnel as crimes against humanity.[100] It is certainly important to scrutinize limitations to determine whether they are arbitrary or rational, and whether they are indeed supported by customary law. However, the major precedents – including the seminal Nuremberg Charter as well as the ICTY, ICTR, ICC and SCSL Statutes[101] and the great majority of case law – not only refer to 'civilian population' but regard it as a defining feature of crimes against humanity. Moreover, current international law clearly permits widespread and systematic attacks directed against military targets, in accordance with humanitarian law, even if it involves killing and injury.

There remains an open and important question as to the extent to which the law of crimes against humanity may protect military personnel outside combat situations. Is it possible to address persecution of military personnel without rejecting the 'time-honoured'[102] hallmark requirement of 'civilian population'? Many strands of the jurisprudence would suggest a positive answer. First, the population need only be 'predominantly civilian in nature'; the 'presence of certain non-civilians in their midst does not change the character of the population'.[103] Second, several early Trial Chamber decisions interpreted the term 'civilian' to include all those no longer taking part in hostilities at the time the crimes were committed.

This includes former combatants who had been decommissioned, as well as combatants placed hors de combat ('out of the fight') by being wounded or detained.[104]

Examining these cases, it is possible to form a hypothesis that the 'civilian' reference serves a rational purpose, which is simply to exclude military actions against legitimate military objectives in accordance with international humanitarian law. This would provide a coherent underlying rationale for the requirement: given that the laws of war are a special regime

99 Tadic ICTY T. Ch. II 7.5.1997 para. 644; Kunarac ICTY T. Ch. II 22.2.2001 para. 425.

100 A. Cassese, 'Crimes Against Humanity' in Cassese, Commentary, 375.

101 See appendix for these statutes.

102 Dinstein, 'Crimes Against Humanity After Tadic' (2000) 13 LJIL 273 at 381–2.

103 Tadic ICTY T. Ch. II 7.5.1997 para. 638; see also Kordic ICTY T. Ch. 26.2.2001 para. 180.

104 Akayesu ICTR T. Ch. 2.9.1998 para. 582; Tadic ICTY T. Ch. II 7.5.1997 para. 643; Kordic ICTY T. Ch. 26.2.2001 para. 180. Note that a current member of an armed force or organization remains a combatant even in moments when he or she is not armed or in combat, and thus may be lawfully attacked by an enemy party to the conflict. See, e.g. Blaškic ICTY A. Ch. 29.7.2004 para. 114.

in which killing, wounding and destruction can be allowed, attacks on military targets are more appropriately assessed under that law.[105]

Several doctrinal developments are consistent with this theory. In addition to the above mentioned developments to protect all non-combatants, the Tribunals' approach to determining an 'attack against a civilian population' distinguishes lawful attacks on military targets from other attacks. Tribunal jurisprudence requires that the civilian population be the 'primary object' of the attack,[106] thereby excluding attacks that appear to be directed primarily at military targets, with the result that such activities are assessed under the more appropriate lex specialis of the laws of war. Moreover, Tribunal jurisprudence expressly considers compliance with the laws of war as an indicator of whether there was an attack against a civilian population.[107] Thus, lawful military action would be excluded, whereas actions targeting civilians would be covered.[108] Patterns of indiscriminate or clearly excessive attacks would indicate that the attacks were in reality directed against a civilian population.

However, recent ICTY cases complicate this picture. In Martic , the Appeals Chamber clarified its interpretation that 'civilian' has the same meaning as in Article 50 of Additional Protocol I (AP I), and hence does not include persons hors de combat (such as prisoners of war).[109] The Chamber affirmed that persons hors de combat could be victims of crimes against humanity, but only where the broader attack was directed at civilians in the narrower sense.[110] The unfortunate effect of this interpretation is that large-scale extermination or torture directed entirely against prisoners of war would not constitute crimes against humanity.

Reliance on AP I was not the only available interpretation; 'civilian' could very plausibly have been interpreted as 'non-combatant', as was the prior trend in the authorities.[111] First, 'attack against a civilian population' is already given a different meaning in crimes against humanity than it receives in war crimes, since it does not require actual force but can refer to a series of non-violent

105 See, e.g. Ambos and Wirth, 'The Current Law',22–6, and on a related theme, see Akhavan, 'Reconciling'.

106 Kunarac ICTY A. Ch. 12.6.2002 para. 91.

107 Ibid. See also Mettraux, 'Crimes', 245–50.

108 See also Fofana, SCSL A. Ch. 28.5.2008 paras. 300–8; note that the emphasis is on the intentional targeting of civilians. This means that legitimate attacks on military targets are excluded, but intentionally indiscriminate or disproportionate attacks may be included: Chile Eboe-Osuji, 'Crimes Against Humanity: Directing Attacks Against a Civilian Population' (2008) 2 African Journal Legal Studies 118.

109 Martic , ICTY A. Ch. 8.10.2008 paras. 296–302.

110 Ibid., paras. 301–14. See also Mrkšic ICTY A. Ch. 5.5.2009 paras. 29–33.

111 Akayesu ICTR T. Ch. 2.9.1998 para. 582; Tadic ICTY T. Ch. II 7.5.1997 para. 643; Kordic ICTY T. Ch. 26.2.2001 para. 180. See also Ambos and Wirth, 'The Current Law', 22–6.

acts amounting to inhumane acts.[112] Second, the definition of 'civilian' in AP I arises in a detailed legislative regime that already grants protection to POWs, whereas the 'civilian' reference in crimes against humanity arose decades earlier, and likely harked to a simpler bifurcation between those taking part in hostilities and those who are not. Third, the Appeals Chamber relied on the principle of distinction,[113] but for the purposes of principle of distinction, a deliberate targeting of prisoners of war is also prohibited. As the language is open to more than one interpretation, it may be hoped that other jurisdictions will consider the function of the 'civilian' reference, the consequences of different interpretations, and consistency with past cases, before following the same path.[114]

1.3.4 The link between the accused and the attack

The rigorous requirements relating to the attack must be distinguished from the requirements relating to the accused. With respect to the individual accused, what is required is that the accused committed a prohibited act, that the act objectively falls within the broader attack, and that the accused was aware of this broader context.[115]

Only the attack, not the acts of the individual accused, must be widespread or systematic.[116] A single act by the accused may constitute a crime against humanity if it forms part of the attack.[117] The act of the accused may also in itself constitute the attack, if it is of great magnitude, for example, the use of a biological weapon against a civilian population.[118]

The accused need not be an architect of the attack, need not be involved in the formation of any policy, and need not be affiliated with any State or organization nor even share in the ideological goals of the attack.[119]

The acts of the accused need not be of the same type as other acts committed during the attack. For example, if a group launches a killing campaign,

112 See, e.g. Nahimana ICTR A. Ch. 28.11.2007 para. 918.

113 Martic ICTY A. Ch. 8.10.2008 note 806.

114 The position of the ICC is as yet unknown. In its decision on the Al Bashir arrest warrant case, a Pre-Trial chamber noted that killing of combatants is excluded from crimes against humanity: Al Bashir arrest warrant case ICC PTC-I, 4.3.2009. This proposition, which is clearly correct, is compatible with both the approach of the ICTY and the approach suggested above.

115 Tadic ICTY A. Ch. 15.7.1999 para. 271. To determine if an act is 'part of' an attack, one may consider its characterstics, aims, nature or consequence: Semanza ICTR T. Ch. 15.5.2003 para. 326. A crime may be committed several months after, or several kilometres away from, the main attack, and still, if sufficiently connected, be part of the attack: Krnojelac ICTY T. Ch. II 15.3.2002 para. 127.

116 Kunarac ICTY A. Ch. 12.6.2002 para. 96; Blaškic ICTY A. Ch. 29.7.2004 para. 101.

117 Kunarac ICTY A. Ch. 12.6.2002 para. 96; Blaškic ICTY A. Ch. 29.7.2004 para. 101.

118 Blaškic ICTY T. Ch. I 3.3.2000 para. 206.

119 Ibid.

and a person commits sexual violence in the execution of that campaign, the person is guilty of the crime against humanity of sexual violence. It is irrelevant whether the State or organization encouraged sexual violence, since the necessary contextual element is already satisfied because of the attack based on killing.[120]

1.3.5 Mental element

In addition to the requisite mental elements for the particular offences, the accused must also be aware of the 'broader context in which his actions occur', namely the attack directed against a civilian population.[121] It is the context of a widespread or systematic attack against a civilian population that makes an act a crime against humanity, and hence knowledge of this context is necessary in order to make one culpable for a crime against humanity as opposed to an ordinary crime or a war crime.[122]

Tribunal cases indicate that awareness, wilful blindness, or knowingly taking the risk that one's act is part of an attack, will suffice.[123] It is less clear if the ICC will take a similar approach, because of the different wording of Article 30 of the ICC Statute (mental element), but the ICC Elements of Crimes suggest that the mental element required for 'contextual elements' is lower.[124] It is not required that the perpetrator had detailed knowledge of the attack or its characteristics.[125] In most conceivable circumstances, the existence of a widespread or systematic attack would be notorious and knowledge could not credibly be denied. Thus, knowledge may be inferred from the relevant facts and circumstances.[126]

The perpetrator need not share in the purpose or goals of the overall attack.[127] The mental requirement relates to knowledge of the context, not motive.[128] After the Second World War, several cases dealt with instances

120 Art. 7(2)(a) of the ICC Statute.

121 Tadic ICTY A. Ch. 15.7.1999 para. 248; Kupreškic ICTY T. Ch. II 14.1.2000 para. 134.

122 Tadic ICTY T. Ch. II 7.5.1997 para. 656; Kupreškic ICTY T. Ch. II 14.1.2000 para. 138; Semanza ICTR T. Ch. 15.5.2003 para. 332; and see also R v. Finta [1994] 1 SCR 701 at 819: 'the mental element of a crime against humanity must involve an awareness of the facts or circumstances which would bring the acts within the definition of a crime against humanity'.

123 Tadic ICTY T. Ch. II 7.5.1997 para. 657; Kunarac ICTY A. Ch. 12.6.2002 para. 102; Blaškic ICTY T. Ch. I 3.3.2000 para. 251; Krnojelac ICTY T. Ch. II 15.3.2002 para. 59; see also R v. Finta [1994] 1 SCR 701 at 819.

124 See, e.g. Maria Kelt and Herman von Hebel, 'General Principles of Criminal Law and the Elements of Crimes' in Lee, Elements and Rules,34–5.

125 ICC Elements, Crimes Against Humanity Introduction, para. 2, states that it is not required that the perpetrator 'had knowledge of all characteristics of the attack or the precise details of the plan or policy of the State or organization'; see also Blaškic ICTY T. Ch. I 3.3.2000 para. 251; Kunarac ICTY A. Ch. 12.6.2002 para. 102.

126 ICC Elements, General Introduction, para. 3.

127 Kunarac ICTY A. Ch. II 22.2.2001 para. 103.

128 Tadic ICTY A. Ch. 15.7.1999 paras. 271–2, overturning a suggestion to the contrary by the Trial

where individuals had denounced others to the Nazi regime, for personal opportunistic reasons. Such persons were held liable for crimes against humanity, because even though they acted out of personal motives, their actions were objectively part of the persecutory system, and they acted with knowledge of the system and the likely consequences.[129]

Chamber.

129 See cases discussed in Tadic ICTY A. Ch. 15.7.1999 paras. 255–69.

PART 2

PROHIBITED ACTS WITHIN THE DEFINITION OF CRIMES AGAINST HUMANITY

2.1 Introduction

The definition of crime against humanity includes certain prohibited acts when committed in the necessary context (widespread or systematic attack). The list of prohibited acts has gradually evolved over the decades.

The first list, appearing in the Nuremberg Charter, comprised murder, extermination, enslavement, deportation, persecution and other inhumane acts. Shortly thereafter, Control Council Law No. 10 added rape, imprisonment and torture. The ICTY and ICTR Statutes follow the same expanded list.

In 1998, the ICC Statute added sexual slavery, enforced prostitution, forced pregnancy, other sexual violence, enforced disappearance and apartheid. At first glance, this may seem to be an expansion on existing customary law. However, the list of prohibited acts in the previous precedents ended with the residual clause 'or other inhumane acts'. If sexual slavery and these other acts are inhumane acts, the Article 7 simply codified explicitly what was already contained implicitly in the residual clause. The view that these acts were already inhumane acts is supported by the following considerations. First, each of these acts was already recognized as an inhumane act or crime against humanity in previous international instruments. Second, the agreed objective of States at the Rome Conference was to reflect, not to expand, existing customary law, and thus Article 7 reflects a simultaneous statement of opinio juris by 120 States. Third, their status has been supported in subsequent jurisprudence and instruments.[130]
For each of the following crimes, where no specific observations are made about the mental element, the normal mental element applies: the relevant conduct must be committed intentionally and with knowledge of the relevant circumstances.[131] With respect to legal requirements (for example 'unlawful') or other normative requirements (for example 'inhumane', 'severe'), it is not required that the perpetrator personally considered the conduct inhumane or severe; it is sufficient that the perpetrator was aware of the underlying facts.[132]

130 See, e.g. Kvočka ICTY T. Ch. I 2.11.2001 para. 208, and Kupreškic ICTY T. Ch. II 14.1.2000 para. 566, recognizing enforced disappearance, sexual violence, forced prostitution, and forced transfer of populations. Article 2 of the SCSL Statute recognizes the sexual violence offences, and the Iraq Special Tribunal Statute includes each of the ICC Statute crimes other than apartheid and enforced sterilization.

131 See, e.g. Art. 30 of the ICC Statute.

132 See, e.g. Art. 32(2) of the ICC Statute; ICC Elements, General Introduction, para. 4.

2.1.1 Murder

The crime of murder is well known to all legal systems and is an archetypal form of crime against humanity. There is general conformity between Tribunal jurisprudence and the ICC Elements that murder refers to unlawfully and intentionally causing the death of a human being.[133]

Tribunal jurisprudence, consistent with jurisprudence in many national systems, indicates that the mental element is satisfied if the perpetrator intends to kill, or intends to inflict grievous bodily harm likely to cause death and is reckless as to whether death ensues.[134] It is unclear whether the ICC will be able to adopt the same approach, in light of the different wording of Article 30 of the ICC Statute (mental element), although it may be possible to interpret the statute consistently with previous authorities.[135]

The conduct element of murder (crime against humanity) and wilful killing (war crime) is the same; the difference is the contextual element. The distinction between murder and extermination is discussed below.

2.1.2 Extermination

The issue of how to define extermination is inextricably linked to the question of how to distinguish it from the crime against humanity of murder. Both involve killing, but 'extermination' connotes killing on a large scale. Is extermination distinct from murder on the basis that the perpetrator must carry out killing on a large scale, or is there another way to distinguish between the two? Rather than requiring that the accused personally carried out or directed large-scale killing, both Tribunal jurisprudence and the ICC Elements indicate that extermination involves killing by the accused within a context of mass killing.[136]

Thus, the first and major difference between murder and extermination is that extermination requires a surrounding circumstance of mass killing.[137] The perpetrator need not carry out the mass killing personally; he only needs to know of the context of mass killing.

133 ICC Elements, Art. 7(1)(a); Akayesu ICTR T. Ch. I 2.9.1998 para. 589; Jelisic ICTY T. Ch. 14.12.1999 para. 35; Kupreškic ICTY T. Ch. II 14.1.2000 paras. 560–1.

134 See, e.g. Čelebic i ICTY T. Ch. II 16.11.1998 para. 439; Akayesu ICTR T. Ch. I 2.9.1998 para. 589; Kordic ICTY T. Ch. 26.2.2001 para. 236.

135 C. K. Hall, 'Article 7' in Triffterer, Observers' Notes, 188–9.

136 ICC Elements, Art. 7(1)(b); Kayishema ICTR T. Ch. 21.5.1999 para. 147.

137 Whereas a crime against humanity of murder can occur on the basis of a single killing, committed in the context of a widespread or systematic attack based on other crimes.

A second difference is that extermination expressly includes indirect means of causing death. This distinction was recognized as early as the 1948 UN War Crimes Commission, which included 'implication in the policy of extermination without any direct connection with actual acts of murder'.[138] Tribunal jurisprudence also includes indirect means of causing death,[139] as does the ICC Statute. Article 7(2)(b) of the ICC Statute expressly includes 'inflicting conditions of life ... calculated to bring about the destruction of part of a population', a phrase adapted from the Genocide Convention.[140]

A third issue is whether the crime of extermination requires that the accused personally be responsible for a substantial number of deaths. While some cases have held that 'responsibility for one or for a limited number of killings is insufficient',[141] the ICTY Appeals Chamber indicates that a single killing is sufficient provided that the accused is aware of the necessary context of mass killing.[142] The ICC Elements of Crimes also follow the latter interpretation.[143]

There are also significant overlaps between extermination and the crime of genocide. Indeed, the concepts of killing or inflicting conditions of life calculated to bring about the destruction of part of a population are common to both extermination and genocide. The major difference between the two crimes is the requisite special intent for the crime of genocide (the intent to destroy a group as such). Moreover, genocide can only be committed where there is an intent to target one of four types of groups (national, ethnical, racial or religious).[144]

2.1.3 Enslavement

The accepted definition of enslavement is 'exercising the powers attaching to the right of ownership' over one or more persons. This definition is drawn from the 1926 Slavery Convention and the 1956 Supplementary Slavery Convention, and has been adopted in the ICC Statute (Article 7(2)(c)) and in Tribunal jurisprudence.[145]

Enslavement may take various forms. It includes the traditional concept of 'chattel slavery', that is to say the treatment of persons as chattels, as in the

138 UN War Crimes Commission, History, 194.
139 Rutaganda ICTR T. Ch. 6.12.1999 para. 81; Kayishema ICTR T. Ch. 21.5.1999 para. 146.
140 Art. 2(c) of the Genocide Convention 1948.
141 Vasiljevic ICTY T. Ch. I 29.11.2002 para. 228.
142 Stakic ICTY A. Ch. 22.3.2006 paras. 260–1; see also Kayishema ICTR T. Ch. 21.5.1999 para. 147.
143 ICC Elements, Art. 7(1)(b), element 1.
144 Ibid.
145 1926 Slavery Convention, Art. 1; 1956 Supplementary Slavery Convention; Kunarac ICTY T. Ch. II 22.2.2001 para. 539; Krnojelac ICTY T. Ch. II 15.3.2002 para. 353.

slave trade. It also includes other practices, which are not limited to these 'transactional' or 'chattel slavery' examples, but which also involve exercising powers attaching to the right of ownership. [146]

First, with respect to 'chattel slavery', the Slavery Convention definition of 'slave trade' refers to the capture, acquisition, sale, exchange, transport or disposal of persons with intent to reduce them to slavery or to sell or exchange them. [147] The ICC Elements of Crimes also list, as examples, such transactions as 'purchasing, selling, lending or bartering'.

Second, the ICC Statute explicitly mentions the example of trafficking in persons, in particular, women and children (Article 7(2)(c)). [148]

Third, as noted in the ICC Elements of Crimes, enslavement also includes 'reducing a person to a servile status' as defined in the 1956 Supplementary Slavery Convention. This includes practices of debt bondage, serfdom, forced marriage and child exploitation, as defined in that Convention. [149]

Fourth, forced labour can also constitute enslavement.[150] In determining whether labour is 'forced' as prohibited under customary law, regard may be had to instruments such as the 1949 Geneva Convention III (Articles 49–57), the ICCPR (Article 8(3)(c)) and the 1930 Forced or Compulsory Labour Convention. In general, these instruments prohibit forced or compulsory labour, with various recognized exceptions, such as military and national service, normal civic obligations, hard labour as lawful punishment for crime, and certain forms of labour for prisoners of war. [151] In Krnojelac, the Appeals Chamber held that severely overcrowded conditions, deplorable sanitation, insufficient food, locked doors, frequent beatings, psychological abuse, and brutal living conditions rendered it impossible for detainees to consent to work and that their labour was indeed forced. [152]

Fifth, other activities may also amount to enslavement. The ICTY Appeals Chamber in the Kunarac decision indicated that relevant factors include 'control of someone's movement, control of physical environment, psychological control, measures taken to prevent or deter escape, force, threat of force or coercion, duration, assertion of exclusivity, subjection

146 Valerie Oosterveld, 'Sexual Slavery and the International Criminal Court: Advancing International Criminal Law' (2003) 25 Michigan Journal of International Law 605 at 643.

147 1926 Slavery Convention, Art. 1(2).

148 See also Tom Obokata, 'Trafficking of Human Beings as a Crime Against Humanity' (2005) 54 ICLQ 445.

149 ICC Elements, footnote 11; 1956 Supplementary Slavery Convention, Art. 1.

150 ICC Elements, footnote 11.

151 See, e.g. Geneva Convention III 1949, Arts. 49–57; Art. 8(3) of the ICCPR.

152 Krnojelac ICTY T. Ch. II 15.3.2002 paras. 193–5.

to cruel treatment and abuse, control of sexuality and forced labour'.[153] A specific form of enslavement, namely sexual slavery, is discussed below.

In Kunarac,[154] the victims were kept in an abandoned house for approximately six months, where they were raped and sexually assaulted whenever the soldiers returned to the house. The Chamber found that they were constantly and continuously raped, forced to do household chores and obey all demands. Although at some point they were given the keys to the house, they had nowhere to go or to hide and hence:

no realistic option whatsoever to flee the house ... or to escape their assailants. They were subjected to other mistreatments, such as Kunarac inviting a soldier into the house so that he could rape [the victim] for 100 Deutschmark if he so wished ... The two women were treated as ... personal property ...

The two men responsible were found guilty of enslavement.

2.1.4 Deportation or forcible transfer

Deportation and forcible transfer of population are frequently-seen examples of crimes against humanity, particularly in contexts of 'ethnic cleansing'. The terms refer to forced displacement of persons by expulsion or other coercive acts from the area in which they are lawfully present, without grounds permitted under international law.[155]

'Deportation' is generally regarded as referring to displacement across a border, whereas 'forcible transfer' is generally regarded as referring to internal displacement.[156]ICTY jurisprudence follows this distinction. In the Stakic case the Appeals Chamber confirmed that 'deportation' must be across a border, usually a de jure border, or in some circumstances a de facto border, but in any event crossing of 'constantly changing frontlines' would not suffice.[157]

Deportation or transfer must be forced in order to be a crime against humanity.[158]

153 Kunarac ICTY A. Ch. 12.6.2002 para. 119.
154 Kunarac ICTY T. Ch. II 22.2.2001 paras. 732–42.
155 Art. 7(2)(d) ICC Statute; Stakic ICTY A. Ch. 22.3.2006 para. 278.
156 ILC draft Code, 1996, p. 100.
157 Stakic ICTY A. Ch. 22.3.2006 para. 300. The Appeals Chamber therefore allowed the appeal from an anomalous Trial Chamber decision which had held that 'deportation' could be internal. The Appeals Chamber did not clarify the circumstances in which crossing a de facto border would suffice. For other cases see Krštic ICTY T. Ch. I 2.8.2001 para. 521; Krnojelac ICTY T. Ch. II 15.3.2002 para. 474; Kupreškic ICTY T. Ch. II 14.1.2000 para. 566.
158 ICC Statute, Art. 7(2)(d); Krštic ICTY T. Ch. I 2.8.2001 para. 528; Krnojelac ICTY T. Ch. II

This does not require actual physical force, but may also include the threat of force or coercion, psychological oppression, or other means of rendering displacement involuntary. [159] Thus, if a group flees of its own genuine volition, for example to escape a conflict zone, that would not be forced displacement.[160] On the other hand, if a group flees to escape deliberate violence and persecution, they would not be exercising a genuine choice.[161]

The forced displacement must also be unlawful under international law. Most or all States carry out legitimate acts of deportation on a frequent basis. Deportation of aliens not lawfully present in the territory is an established practice of States.[162] International humanitarian law, for example, allows transfers when the security of the population or imperative military reasons so demand; such transfers must meet certain stringent conditions and humanitarian safeguards.[163]

2.1.5 Torture

The crime of torture appeared in Allied Control Council Law No. 10 and subsequent definitions of crimes against humanity. The prohibition against torture is well established in numerous conventions and instruments, including the Universal Declaration of Human Rights, the International Covenant on Civil and Political Rights, the European Convention on Human Rights, the American Convention on Human Rights, the African Charter of Human and Peoples' Rights, the Convention Against Torture, the Inter-American Convention to Prevent and Punish Torture, and the Geneva Conventions and the Additional Protocols thereto. It is well recognized as a norm of customary law and amounts to jus cogens.[164]

Much of the definition in the 1984 Convention Against Torture (CAT) is also accepted as the core definition for torture as a crime against humanity or war crime: the intentional infliction of severe pain or suffering, whether physical or mental, upon a person.[165] There are, however, several open questions.

15.3.2002 para. 475.

159 ICC Elements, Art. 7(1)(d); Stakic ICTY A. Ch. 22.3.2006 para. 281; Krnojelac ICTY T. Ch. II 15.3.2002 para. 475; Kunarac ICTY T. Ch. II 22.2.2001 para. 129.

160 Jean Pictet, Commentary on Geneva Convention IV (ICRC, Geneva, 1960) 279; Akhavan, 'Reconciling', 34–5.

161 Krštic ICTY T. Ch. I 2.8.2001 para. 530.

162 The question whether an individual was 'lawfully' present would probably be assessed under international as well as national law. For example, a government could not circumvent the definition of this crime through an arbitrary legislative act declaring members of a group not lawfully present.

163 Art. 49 of the Geneva Convention IV 1949; Art. 87 of the AP I.

164 Čelebic i ICTY T. Ch. II 16.11.1998 para. 454. For discussion of the crime of torture under the Convention Against Torture.

165 Art. 1 of the CAT.

The first open question is that of official capacity. The CAT definition requires that the pain or suffering be 'inflicted by or at the instigation of or with the consent or acquiescence of a public official or other person acting in an official capacity'.[166] Early Tribunal cases adopted the requirement of official instigation or acquiescence.[167] However, in Kunarac, the Trial Chamber departed from this approach, noting structural differences between international criminal law and human rights law.[168] Human rights law focuses on the State because it regulates State treatment of human beings. International criminal law holds individuals accountable for crimes, and applies to everyone whether or not affiliated with a State. Similarly, the ICC Statute and the ICC Elements do not require a linkage between the act of torture and a public official.[169] Thus, torture by rebel groups, paramilitaries and others is included.
The second is the 'purpose' element. The CAT definition requires a specific purpose, such as 'obtaining from him or a third person information or a confession, punishing him for an act he or a third person has committed or is suspected of having committed, or intimidating or coercing him or a third person, or for any reason based on discrimination of any kind'.[170] It is not yet settled whether the customary law crime against humanity of torture requires the act to be committed with a specific purpose.

Many authorities, including the CAT and related international instruments, as well as Tribunal jurisprudence, regard the purpose element as a defining feature of torture.[171] On this approach, the presence of prohibited purpose distinguishes torture from inhuman treatment.[172] The purpose need not be the sole or predominant purpose, but must be part of the motivation.[173] The list is illustrative and some cases suggest the addition of 'humiliation' as a prohibited purpose.[174]

In other authorities, such as jurisprudence of the European Court of Human Rights, the difference between torture and lesser violations, such as inhuman treatment, is severity: the special stigma of torture requires infliction of

166 Ibid.

167 Akayesu ICTR T. Ch. I 2.9.1998 para. 594; Furundžija ICTY T. Ch. II 10.12.1998 para. 162.

168 Kunarac ICTY T. Ch. II 22.2.2001 paras. 387–91.

169 Art. 7(2)(e) of the ICC Statute; but see Art. 7(2)(a) which appears to require some sort of linkage between a State or organization and the attack as a whole, albeit not the particular crimes of the accused.

170 Art. 7(2)(e) of the ICC Statute.

171 Akayesu ICTR T. Ch. I 2.9.1998 paras. 593–5; Čelebic i ICTY T. Ch. II 16.11.1998 para. 459; Furundžija ICTY T. Ch. II 10.12.1998 para. 161; Krnojelac ICTY T. Ch. II 15.3.2002 para. 180.

172 Čelebic i ICTY T. Ch. II 16.11.1998 para. 469; Krštic ICTY T. Ch. I 2.8.2001 para. 516.

173 Kunarac ICTY A. Ch. 12.06.2002 para. 155; Kvočka ICTY T. Ch. I 2.11.2001 para. 153; Čelebic i ICTY T. Ch. II 16.11.1998 para. 470.

174 Furundžija ICTY T. Ch. II 10.12.1998 para. 162, but see Krnojelac ICTY T. Ch. II 15.3.2002 para. 186, doubting the customary law status of this extension.

'very serious and cruel suffering'.[175] Article 7 of the ICC Statute followed this approach, and did not include a purpose element.

Further adding to the uncertainty, the ICC Elements of Crimes adopted the 'purpose' requirement with respect to the war crime of torture but not with respect to the crime against humanity of torture.[176] Thus, it would seem that the divergent treatment in the Elements must either be given a principled explanation or else regarded as an anomaly.

Third, the ICC Statute, while dropping any requirements of purpose or link to an official, adds a requirement that the victim be in the 'custody or control' of the perpetrator. The requirement should not be onerous to prove since, as a practical matter, torture entails such custody or control. Various explanations have been offered for this addition, including establishing a link of power or control given the deletion of a link to a public official, or excluding the use of force against military objectives during armed conflict.[177]

It should also be noted that most definitions of torture, including the CAT and the ICC Statute, expressly exclude 'pain or suffering arising only from, inherent in or incidental to, lawful sanctions'. 'Lawful' in this context would appear to mean lawful in accordance with national law, provided, however, that the national law is not in violation of international law.[178]
Tribunal jurisprudence and regional human rights bodies have recognized that rape can constitute a form of torture.[179] Rape causes severe pain and suffering, both physical and psychological. In Furundžija, the accused was convicted of torture for acts during an interrogation, including sexual threats, rapes and forced nudity, inflicted on the victim for purposes of intimidation, humiliation and extracting confession.[180]

175 Ireland v. United Kingdom, 18 January 1978, Series A 25, (1978) ECHR 1 para. 167; Selmouni v. France, 28 July 1999, ECHR Appl. No. 25803/94 (1999) 29 EHRR 403 para. 105; Aydin v. Turkey (1998) 25 EHRR 251 para. 82.

176 Delegates followed Tribunal precedents with respect to war crimes, but they did not do so for crimes against humanity, out of fidelity to the decision taken at the Rome Conference not to require such an element for the crime against humanity of torture. Footnote 14 of the ICC Elements therefore specifies that no purpose element is required.

177 Darryl Robinson, 'Elements of Crimes Against Humanity' in Lee, Elements and Rules 90; Hall, 'Article 7', 253.

178 Report of the UN Special Rapporteur on Torture, UN Doc. E/CN.4/1988/17, para. 42.

179 Akayesu ICTR T. Ch. I 2.9.1998 para. 597; Kunarac ICTY A. Ch. 12.6.2002 para. 150; Semanza ICTR T. Ch. 15.5.2003 para. 482; Čelebici ICTY T. Ch. II 16.11.1998 para. 495; Fernando and Racquel Meiji v. Peru, Annual Report of the Inter-American Commission on Human Rights, Report No. 5/96, Case No. 10 970, 1 March 1996; Aydin v. Turkey (1998) 25 EHRR 251, para. 86.

180 Furundžija ICTY T. Ch. II 10.12.1998 para. 267.

2.1.6 Imprisonment

Although imprisonment did not appear in the Nuremberg or Tokyo Charters, it was listed in Allied Control Council Law No. 10 and subsequent definitions. The term 'imprisonment' is broadly construed, capturing not only detention in prison-like conditions but other serious forms of confinement and detention. Out of an abundance of caution, the ICC Statute added 'or other severe deprivation of physical liberty' to ensure that a narrow definition was not applied, and that situations such as house arrest were included.[181] It remains to be determined precisely how restrictive or how long a confinement must be in order to constitute imprisonment or severe deprivation of physical liberty.

Imprisonment must be arbitrary to constitute a crime against humanity. After all, there are many contexts in which persons may be lawfully detained, including following lawful arrest, conviction following trial, lawful deportation or extradition procedures, quarantine, and, during armed conflict, assigned residence, internment on security grounds and internment of prisoners of war.[182] Tribunal jurisprudence refers to imprisonment without due process of law.[183] Article 7(1)(e) of the ICC Statute refers to deprivation 'in violation of fundamental rules of international law'.

The requirement that the imprisonment be 'arbitrary' (and similarly, in violation of 'fundamental rules') does not mean that a minor procedural defect would expose the authorities involved to international prosecution; significant failings are required. For this reason, the ICC Elements refer to the 'gravity of the conduct' being such as to violate fundamental rules of international law.[184] Tribunal jurisprudence states that deprivation will be arbitrary and unlawful 'if no legal basis can be called upon to justify the initial deprivation of liberty'.[185] Even where the initial detention was justified, imprisonment will become arbitrary if the legal basis ceases to apply and the person remains imprisoned.[186]

While caution must always be used when relying on human rights standards in a criminal law context,[187] the three categories suggested by the UN Working Group on Arbitrary Detention seem to capture the forms of this

181 Hall, 'Article 7', 202.

182 Arts. 5, 42 and 43 of the Geneva Convention IV 1949; Arts. 21–32 of the Geneva Convention III 1949.

183 Kordic ICTY T. Ch. 26.2.2001 para. 302; Krnojelac ICTY T. Ch. II 15.3.2002 para. 113.

184 ICC Elements, Art. 7(1)(e), element 2.

185 Krnojelac ICTY T. Ch. II 15.3.2002 para. 114.

186 For example, if the procedural safeguards of Art. 43 of the Geneva Convention IV 1949 for internment of civilians are disregarded: Kordic ICTY T. Ch. 26.2.2001 para. 286; Čelebic i ICTY T. Ch. II 16.11.1998 para. 579.

187 See infra.

crime admirably: (1) absence of any legal basis for the deprivation of liberty, (2) deprivation of liberty resulting from exercise of specified rights and freedoms (that is to say political prisoners), and (3) 'when the total or partial nonobservance of the international human rights norms relating to the right to a fair trial ... is of such gravity as to give the deprivation of imprisonment an arbitrary character'.[188]

The material elements of arbitrary imprisonment are comparable to the material elements for unlawful confinement (war crime); the difference between the two is the contextual element (armed conflict or widespread or systematic attack).

2.1.7 Rape and other forms of sexual violence

The crime of rape appeared in Allied Control Council Law No. 10 and subsequent instruments, including the ICTY and ICTR Statutes. The 1996 draft Code of Crimes prepared by the International Law Commission proposed that the definition be updated by adding enforced prostitution and other forms of sexual abuse.[189] The ICC Statute took up the idea of modernizing the definition, by including 'rape, sexual slavery, forced pregnancy, enforced sterilization, or any other form of sexual violence of comparable gravity' (Article 7(1)(g)).[190] The inclusion was seen not as an expansion but rather as an acknowledgement that these acts, which have persisted in history, including during the violence in the Former Yugoslavia and Rwanda, are inhumane acts falling within the definition of crimes against humanity.[191]
The same definitions apply both in crimes against humanity and in war crimes, so the relevant issues for both war crimes and crimes against humanity will be discussed here.

Rape

The crime of rape has two components. The first is a physical invasion of a sexual nature. The second component is, according to some authorities, the presence of coercive circumstances, or according to other authorities, the absence of consent.

188 Report of the UN Working Group on Arbitrary Detention, UN Doc. E/CN.4/1998/44 para. 8.
189 Report of the International Law Commission on the work of its forty-eighth session, 1996, UN GAOR 51st Sess, Supp. No. 10 (A/51/10) at 102–3.
190 See, e.g. Vienna Declaration, World Conference on Human Rights, UN Doc. A/CONF.157/24 (1993) Part I, para. 28 and Part II, para. 38: Beijing Declaration and Platform for Action, Fourth World Conference on Women, 15 September 1995, A/CONF.177/20 (1995) and A/CONF.177/20/Add.1 (1995), Chapter II, paras. 114–15bis.
191 For a more detailed overview of the advances and difficulties, see Kelly Askin, 'Prosecuting Wartime Rape and Other Gender-Related Crimes under International Law: Extraordinary Advances, Enduring Obstacles' (2003) 21 Berkeley Journal International Law 288.

The first component, the conduct element, was described in Akayesu,the first case defining the crime against humanity of rape. The ICTR Trial Chamber held that rape 'is a form of aggression and ... cannot be captured in a mechanical description of objects and body parts', which led it to the definition 'a physical invasion of a sexual nature, committed on a person in circumstances which are coercive'.[192] A slight rift emerged in Tribunal jurisprudence, however, when a subsequent decision of an ICTY Trial Chamber (Furundžija) concluded that greater clarity was needed, and defined the physical element (rather mechanically) as: the sexual penetration, however slight, of (a) the vagina or anus of the victim by the penis of the perpetrator or any other object, or (b) the mouth of the victim by the penis of the perpetrator.[193] This definition was subsequently endorsed by the Appeals Chamber in Kunarac.[194]

The ICC Elements of Crimes falls in between the two definitions:

The perpetrator invaded the body of a person by conduct resulting in penetration, however slight, of any part of the body of the victim or of the perpetrator with a sexual organ, or of the anal or genital opening of the victim with any object or any other part of the body.[195]

This definition is closer to the later Tribunal jurisprudence, in that it is comparably specific, yet it is slightly broader and gender neutral.

The second component is less settled; some sources focus on coercive circumstances and some focus on absence of consent. Early Tribunal jurisprudence required coercive circumstances, that is to say coercion or force or threat of force against the victim or a third person.[196] This approach was followed in the ICC Elements of Crimes, albeit significantly expanded:

The invasion was committed by force, or by threat of force or coercion, such as that caused by fear of violence, duress, detention, psychological oppression or abuse of power, against such person or another person, or by taking advantage of a coercive environment, or the invasion was committed against a person incapable of giving genuine consent.[197]

192 Akayesu ICTR T. Ch. I 2.9.1998 paras. 597–8.
193 Furundžija ICTY T. Ch. II 10.12.1998 para. 185.
194 Kunarac ICTY T. Ch. II 22.2.2001 para. 127.
195 ICC Elements, Art. 7(1)(g)–1, element 1.
196 Akayesu ICTR T. Ch. I 2.9.1998 para. 598; Furundžija ICTY T. Ch. II 10.12.1998 para. 185.
197 ICC Elements, Art. 7(1)(g)–1, element 2.

This definition was an advance on previous definitions focused on coercive circumstances, as it more thoroughly encompasses the possible circumstances.

More recently, Tribunal jurisprudence has moved away from cataloguing coercive circumstances and has adopted a simpler element, known in most or all legal systems: the lack of consent of the victim. In Kunarac, the Trial Chamber analysed various legal systems and concluded that the correct element was lack of consent of the victim. This was the true common denominator and reflected the basic principle of penalizing violations of sexual autonomy.[198] The Appeals Chamber confirmed this approach, and held that force or threat of force may be relevant, in providing clear evidence of non-consent, but force is not an element per se of rape.[199]

Strong arguments can be made that the new line of cases better reflects national legal systems and indeed the underlying principle of sexual autonomy,[200] and that the newer interpretation is also more compatible with the ICC Rules of Procedure and Evidence.[201] If so, this may be an instance where, although the Elements should be given due weight as a consensus instrument, the ICC judges may find that the Elements do not reflect the correct reading of the Statute.

In a plausible counter-argument, Catharine MacKinnon argues that the 'coercion' approach is preferable to the 'nonconsent' approach.[202] She argues that in circumstances of 'mass sexual coercion', an inquiry into consent is decontextualized and unreal.[203] War crimes and crimes against humanity of sexual violence are almost invariably committed in coercive circumstances where consent or reasonable belief in consent is simply not a credible possibility. Where such circumstances are shown, inquiry into consent should not be necessary.[204]

198 Kunarac ICTY T. Ch. II 22.2.2001 paras. 440–60.

199 Kunarac ICTY A. Ch. 12.6.2002 para. 129.

200 Kristen Boon, 'Rape and Forced Pregnancy under the ICC Statute: Human Dignity, Autonomy and Consent' (2001) 32 Columbia Human Rights Law Review 625.

201 The ICC RPE contain rules on evidence of consent in cases of sexual violence, and yet the current elements do not refer to consent as a significant factor.

202 Catharine MacKinnon, 'Defining Rape Internationally: A Comment on Akayesu' (2005/6) 44 Columbia Journal International Law 940.

203 Ibid., at 950.

204 'In most cases relating to international crimes it is difficult to think of situations in which consent would be a genuine issue.' Suggestions have at times been made to go further, to legally exclude entirely the relevance of consent in any context of armed conflict. If such an approach were adopted, and consent were deemed irrelevant, then even consensual relations between longstanding sexual partners would become 'war crimes'. One might argue that 'prosecutorial discretion' is the solution to such problems, but the fact of liability in such circumstances indicates that the suggested rule is too broad. It therefore seems more appropriate to restrict consent defences to those circumstances where there is no air of reality to such a claim.

On either approach, it is desirable to adopt procedural and evidentiary rules to limit how the issue of consent may be raised, in order to prevent harassment of witnesses and spurious lines of questioning.

Sexual slavery

Sexual slavery is a particularly serious form of enslavement.[205] The first element of sexual slavery is therefore identical to enslavement.[206] The additional requirement is that the perpetrator caused the victim to engage in one or more acts of a sexual nature.[207] Particularly egregious examples include the 'comfort stations' maintained by the Japanese in the Second World War and the 'rape camps' in the Former Yugoslavia.[208] The examples of enslavement from the Tribunal cases discussed above,[209] would clearly qualify as sexual slavery.

Sexual slavery includes many acts that in the past would have been categorized as 'enforced prostitution'.[210] The latter concept is, however, problematic in that it obscures the violence involved, it is rooted in chastity and family honour, and it degrades the victim; thus 'sexual slavery' is generally preferred as properly reflecting the nature and seriousness of the crime.[211] Sexual slavery may also overlap with 'forced marriage'.

Enforced prostitution

Enforced prostitution is prohibited in the Geneva Convention IV 1949, but as an example of an attack upon a woman's honour; in Additional Protocol I it is prohibited as an outrage upon personal dignity.[212] The ICC Statute lists it as a crime against humanity and war crime in its own right, removing the outdated linkage to 'honour'.

The ICC Elements of Crimes refer to (1) causing one or more persons to engage in one or more acts of a sexual nature, (2) by force or by threat of force (or under the coercive circumstances as noted above in the discussion

205 Special Rapporteur, Final Report on Systematic Rape, Sexual Slavery and Slavery-Like Practices During Armed Conflict, UN Doc. E/CN.4/Sub.2/1998/13, 22 June 1998, para. 30.
206 ICC Elements, Art. 7(1)(g)–2, element 1.
207 ICC Elements, Art. 7(1)(g)–2, element 2.
208 Final Report on Systematic Rape, para. 30.
209 See infra.
210 Final Report on Systematic Rape, para. 31.
211 Oosterveld, 'Sexual Slavery'; Kelly D. Askin, 'Women and International Humanitarian Law' in Kelly D. Askin and Dorean M. Koening (eds.), Women and International Human Rights Law (1999), vol. I, 48; Rhonda Copelon, 'Surfacing Gender: Re-Engraving Crimes Against Women in Humanitarian Law' (1994) 5 Hastings Law Journal 243.
212 Art. 27 of GC IV 1949: 'Women shall be especially protected against any attack on their honour, in particular against rape, enforced prostitution, or any form of indecent assault.'

of rape).[213] In addition, pursuant to a US proposal, it is required that (3) 'the perpetrator or another person obtained or expected to obtain pecuniary or other advantage in exchange for or in connection with the acts of a sexual nature'.[214] There were considerable misgivings among some delegations concerning the paucity of precedent for this element. In the end, however, it was adopted, in order to create some distinction from sexual slavery and in light of the ordinary meaning of the term 'prostitution'. In the absence of such anticipated advantage, the relevant conduct could still be prosecuted as sexual slavery or sexual violence.

Forced pregnancy

The inclusion of 'forced pregnancy' was the subject of intense debate in the negotiation of the ICC Statute.[215] It had previously been recognized in instruments such as the Vienna Declaration and Programme of Action and the Beijing Declaration and Platform for Action.[216] The inclusion recognized a particular harm inflicted on women, including during the conflicts in the Former Yugoslavia, where captors indicated that they tried to impregnate women and hold them until it was too late to obtain an abortion.[217]

However, some delegations were concerned that the concept would be used to criminalize national systems that did not provide a right to abortion, which would conflict with their religious convictions and their constitutional provisions. It was agreed that discussion of the right to abortion will continue in a human rights context but was not part of the crimes against humanity debate. Agreement was reached on the following definition: (1) unlawful confinement (2) of a woman forcibly made pregnant (3) with the intent of affecting the ethnic composition of a population or carrying out other grave violations of international law.[218] The reference to grave violations of international law includes, for example, biological experiments. For greater clarity, Article 7(2)(f) states that '[t]his definition shall not in any way be interpreted as affecting national laws relating to pregnancy'.

213 ICC Elements, Art. 7(1)(g)–3, element 1.
214 ICC Elements, Art. 7(1)(g)–3, element 2.
215 Cate Steains, 'Gender Issues' in Lee, The Making of the Rome Statute, 363–9.
216 Vienna Declaration, World Conference on Human Rights, UN Doc. A/CONF.157/24 (1993) Part II, para. 38; Beijing Declaration and Platform for Action, Fourth World Conference on Women, 15 September 1995, A/ CONF.177/20 (1995) and A/CONF.177/20/Add.1 (1995) Chapter II, para. 115.
217 Commission of Experts (Former Yugoslavia), Report, paras. 248–50.
218 Art. 7(2)(f) of the ICC Statute.

Enforced sterilization

The ICC Statute is the first treaty expressly recognizing enforced sterilization as a crime against humanity and war crime. The conduct has, however, been prosecuted before, in the context of unlawful medical experiments such as were seen in the Second World War.[219] The ICC Elements of Crimes is the first instrument to define this particular crime. The elements are that (1) the perpetrator deprived one or more persons of biological reproductive capacity and (2) that the conduct was neither justified by the medical or hospital treatment of the persons concerned nor carried out with their genuine consent.[220] This definition is not restricted to medical operations, but could also include an intentional use of chemicals for this effect.[221] The concept of 'genuine consent' excludes consent obtained by deception.[222]

Enforced sterilization can also satisfy the conduct requirements of genocide (Article 6(e) of the ICC Statute) and can amount to genocide where genocidal intent is present.

Other sexual violence

The ICC Statute also includes 'other sexual violence of comparable gravity'. The ICC Elements document elaborates the following elements: (1) the perpetrator committed an act of a sexual nature against one or more persons or caused one or more persons to engage in an act of a sexual nature, (2) by force or threat of force or coercion[223] and (3) the gravity of the conduct was comparable to the other offences in Article 7(1)(g).[224]

The first element covers both acts against the victim as well as forcing the victim to perform sexual acts. It is not restricted to cases of assault, and therefore can include examples of forced nudity.[225] The second element, coercive circumstances, is discussed above in the context of rape. The third element creates a threshold of seriousness, so that the acts warrant being described as crimes against humanity.[226]

The UN Special Rapporteur on systematic rape, sexual slavery and slavery-like practices observed that sexual violence includes:

219 Brandt (The Doctors' Trial) IV LRTWC 91.
220 ICC Elements, Art. 7(1)(g)–5, elements 1 and 2.
221 Eve La Haye, 'Sexual Violence' in Lee, Elements and Rules, 195. The ICC Elements exclude 'birth control measures with a non-permanent effect'.
222 ICC Elements, footnote 55.
223 With the same list of coercive circumstances discussed above in the context of rape.
224 ICC Elements, Art. 7(1)(g)–6, elements 1 and 2.
225 Eve La Haye, 'Sexual Violence', 198; Final Report on Systematic Rape, paras. 21–2.
226 In the context of war crimes, the requirement refers to gravity comparable to a grave breach (or Common Article 3 in the case of internal armed conflicts) of the Geneva Conventions.

any violence, physical or psychological, carried out by sexual means or targeting sexuality. Sexual violence covers both physical and psychological attacks directed at a person's sexual characteristics, such as forcing a person to strip naked in public, mutilating a person's genitals or slicing off a woman's breasts. Sexual violence also characterizes situations in which two victims are forced to perform sexual acts on one another or to harm one another in a sexual manner.[227]

2.1.8 Persecution

Persecution involves the intentional and severe deprivation of fundamental rights, against an identifiable group or collectivity on prohibited discriminatory grounds. In addition, the ICC Statute requires that persecution be committed in connection with another crime or at least one inhumane act.

Severe deprivation of fundamental rights

Until recently, the crime of persecution was not well defined, and the need for adequate precision was highlighted both in Tribunal jurisprudence and in the drafting of the ICC Statute.[228] The test developed in Tribunal jurisprudence requires (1) a gross or blatant denial, (2) on discriminatory grounds, (3) of a fundamental right, laid down in international customary or treaty law, (4) reaching the same level of gravity as other crimes against humanity.[229] Although there is some different terminology, this is generally compatible with the ICC definition, which refers to intentional and severe deprivation of fundamental rights, on specified discriminatory grounds.
The emergent definition, with the notions of fundamental rights, severe deprivation, and discriminatory grounds, provides the needed precision for criminal law. Nonetheless, the test necessarily remains somewhat open with respect to the particular acts that may constitute persecution, as it is impossible to anticipate all future examples. Tribunal jurisprudence has noted that:

neither international treaty law nor case law provides a comprehensive list of illegal acts encompassed by the charge of persecution, and persecution as

227 Final Report on Systematic Rape, paras. 21–2.
228 Kupreškic ICTY T. Ch. II 14.1.2000 para. 618: 'However, this Trial Chamber holds the view that in order for persecution to amount to a crime against humanity it is not enough to define a core assortment of acts and to leave peripheral acts in a state of uncertainty. There must be clearly defined limits on the types of acts which qualify as persecution. Although the realm of human rights is dynamic and expansive, not every denial of a human right may constitute a crime against humanity.'
229 See, e.g. Kupreškic ICTY T. Ch. II 14.1.2000 para. 621.

such is not known in the world's major criminal justice systems. [Thus] the crime of persecution needs careful and sensitive development in light of the principle of nullum crimen sine lege.[230]

Gravity or severity

Tribunal jurisprudence indicates that persecution requires a gravity comparable to other crimes against humanity;[231] in the ICC definition this requirement may be subsumed in the requirements of 'severe' deprivation and the requirement of 'connection' to other acts.

Discriminatory grounds

The fundamental feature of persecution is that it be committed on discriminatory grounds. The ICTY and ICTR Statutes refer to persecution on political, racial or religious grounds.[232] The ICC Statute contains an updated and more inclusive list of prohibited grounds: political, racial, national, ethnic, cultural, religious, or gender.[233] In addition, the ICC list is cautiously openended in referring to 'other grounds that are universally recognized as impermissible under international law'.[234] The standard of 'universal' means that the threshold to read in additional grounds is a high one, but a high standard was considered necessary in order to satisfy the principle of legality.

Connection to other acts

The ICC Statute requires that persecution be committed in connection with (a) any crime within the jurisdiction of the Court or (b) any other act listed in Article 7(1). This requirement was included because of the concern of several States about the possible elasticity of the concept of persecution. The fear was that any practices of discrimination, more suitably addressed by human rights bodies, would be labelled as 'persecution', giving rise to international prosecutions. The connection requirement was inserted to ensure at least a context of more recognized forms of criminality. Although the original proposal was to require a link to another crime within the jurisdiction of the Court, this was widened to include a link to any other act referred to in Article 7(1).

230 Kordic ICTY T. Ch. 26.2.2001 para. 694.

231 See, e.g. Kupreškic ICTY T. Ch. II 14.1.2000 paras. 619 and 621; Kvočka ICTY T. Ch. I 2.11.2001 para. 185; Ruggiu ICTR T. Ch. 1.6.2000 para. 21.

232 Art. 5(h) of the ICTY Statute; Art. 3(h) of the ICTR Statute.

233 Art. 7(1)(h) of the ICC Statute.

234 Ibid.

The customary law status of this requirement is open to doubt. Such a requirement is not applied in Tribunal jurisprudence; in Kupreškic , an ICTY Trial Chamber found that 'although the Statute of the ICC may be indicative of the opinio juris of many States, Article 7(1)(h) is not consonant with customary international law'.[235] In any event, the requirement should not pose a significant obstacle for legitimate prosecutions of persecution, since it is satisfied by a linkage to even one other recognized act (a killing or other inhumane act), which one would expect to find in a situation warranting international prosecution. In so far as such an element exists, it is purely an objective element to ensure the seriousness of the situation, and does not require any mental element.[236]

Civilian population?

There is also a question whether persecution, unlike other crimes against humanity, need not be directed against a civilian population. On the one hand, the Nuremberg definition dealt separately with persecution, such that it was not linked to civilian population, and post-war cases have dealt with persecution of military personnel.[237] On the other hand, the Nuremberg approach may be overtaken by current practice, since all modern instruments unify the prohibited acts under a single chapeau, a move that was welcomed as rationalizing the structure and eliminating the 'awkward bifurcation'.[238] Concerns about protective coverage for military personnel may be addressed if a broad interpretation of 'civilian population' is adopted. [239]

Mental element

In addition to the normal mental element relating to the conduct and the broader context, persecution requires a particular intent to target a person or group on prohibited grounds of discrimination.[240] Tribunal jurisprudence indicates that a particular intent to discriminate is required, not simply a knowledge that one is acting in a discriminatory way.[241] With respect to the requirement in the ICC Statute of a 'connection' to other crimes or

235 Kupreškic T. Ch. II 14.1.2000 para. 580. Antonio Cassese argues persuasively that the requirement is inconsistent with the elimination of the general nexus requirement in the Nuremberg Charter and therefore is a restriction on customary law: Cassese, 'Crimes Against Humanity', 376.

236 ICC Elements, footnote 22.

237 Antonio Cassese, International Criminal Law, 2nd edn (Oxford, 2008) 117, 121.

238 Steven Ratner and Jason Abrams, Accountability for Human Rights Atrocities in International Law (Oxford, 2001) 59.

239 If the provision excludes only battlefield action against legitimate military objectives then there would be no gap in coverage. Protection would apply in all circumstances where military personnel could feasibly be victims of persecution – during peacetime, in their civilian lives, when captured or rendered hors de combat.

240 ICC Elements, Art. 7(1)(h), element 3; Kordic ICTY T. Ch. 26.2.2001 para. 212.

241 Krnojelac ICTY T. Ch. II 15.3.2002 para. 435; Kordic ICTY T. Ch. 26.2.2001 para. 212.

prohibited acts, this requirement is purely objective and no mental element is required. [242]

Relationship to other crimes

Persecution and genocide each require a particular discriminatory intent. In the case of genocide, however, the intent is more specific; it must be an intent to destroy a group as such, and the target must be a national, ethnical, racial or religious group. Genocide can only be based on the listed acts (see, for example Article 6 of the ICC Statute) whereas the conduct potentially amounting to persecution is broader. Acts amounting to other crimes against humanity can constitute persecution if the additional aggravating element of discriminatory intent is present.

Examples of persecutory acts

Persecutory acts include the prohibited acts already listed in the definition of crimes against humanity, when committed with discriminatory intent.[243] Examples that have been prosecuted include murder, extermination, imprisonment, deportation, transfer of populations, torture, enslavement and beatings (inhumane acts).[244] In addition, they can include other conduct that severely deprives political, civil, economic or social rights. Examples include the passing of discriminatory laws, restriction of movement and seclusion in ghettos, the exclusion of members of an ethnic or religious group from aspects of social, political and economic life, including exclusion from professions, business, educational institutions, public service and inter-marriage.[245] It also includes overt violence such as burning of homes and terrorization.[246] The ICTR Appeals Chamber has held that, while hate speech alone does not constitute persecution, hate speech and calls to violence, contributing to acts of violence, and in a broader context of persecution, can be of comparable gravity to other crimes and hence constitute acts of persecution. [247]

Attacks on property can constitute persecution. This includes 'systematic destruction of monuments or buildings representative of a particular social, religious, cultural or other group',[248] and destruction of homes and means of livelihood.[249] The Tadic decision noted doubts whether attacks on purely

242 ICC Elements, footnote 22.
243 Kupreškic ICTY T. Ch. II 14.1.2000 paras. 593–607.
244 Tadic ICTY T. Ch. II 7.5.1997 paras. 704–10; Kupreškic ICTY T. Ch. II 14.1.2000 para. 594.
245 Ibid., paras. 608–15.
246 Krštic ICTY T. Ch. I 2.8.2001 para. 537.
247 Nahimana ICTR A. Ch. 28.11.2007 paras. 986–8.
248 ILC Report, 1991, p. 268.
249 Kordic ICTY T. Ch. 26.2.2001 para. 205.

industrial property would suffice, but economic measures with personal effects, including deprivation of livelihood, would suffice.[250] The Blaškic decision affirmed that persecution includes 'targeting property, so long as the victimized persons were specially selected on grounds linked to their belonging to a particular community'.[251] This may be seen in destruction of private dwellings, businesses, symbolic buildings, looting and plunder of businesses and private property, boycott of businesses and shops, and forcing the group out of economic life.[252]

2.1.9 Enforced disappearance

The ICC Statute expressly includes enforced disappearance as a crime against humanity. Enforced disappearance was recognized previously as an international crime and indeed as a crime against humanity. It was exemplified in the 'Night and Fog Decree' issued by the Nazis, to execute people and to provide no information to the families as to their whereabouts or fate.[253] It was also a prevalent feature under military regimes in Latin America in the 1980s, and is still practised today in various regimes around the world. Enforced disappearance is expressly recognized as a crime against humanity in the 1992 UN Declaration on the Protection of All Persons from Enforced Disappearance, the 1994 Inter-American Convention on the Forced Disappearance of Persons and, more recently, in the 2005 International Convention on the Protection of All Persons from Enforced Disappearance.[254]

The definition in the ICC Statute is based on the UN Declaration and the Inter-American Convention,[255] and refers to the 'arrest, detention or abduction of persons by, or with the authorization, support or acquiescence of, a State or political organization, followed by a refusal to acknowledge that deprivation of freedom or to give information on the fate or whereabouts of those persons, with the intention of removing them from the protection of law for a prolonged period of time'.[256]

A welcome development in the negotiation of the ICC Elements was the realization that there are various ways in which an individual may be liable for this crime. Previous definitions described the whole system of enforced disappearance, but it is unlikely that a single individual would be involved in the arrest, detention or abduction phase, as well as the refusal to acknowledge

250 Tadic ICTY T. Ch. II 7.5.1997 para. 707.
251 Blaškic ICTY T. Ch. I 3.3.2000 para. 233.
252 Ibid., paras. 220–33.
253 Nuremberg Judgment, reproduced (1947) 41 AJIL 172 at 230.
254 Preamble paras. 4, 5 and 6 of the respective instruments.
255 Preamble para. 3 of the UN Declaration and Art. 2 of the Inter-American Convention.
256 Art. 7(2)(i) of the ICC Statute.

the deprivation or to provide information. Enforced disappearance typically involves many actors. Therefore, the ICC Elements recognize that the crime may be committed (a) by arresting, detaining or abducting a person, with knowledge that a refusal to acknowledge or give information would be likely to follow in the ordinary course of events, or (b) by refusing to acknowledge the deprivation of freedom or to provide information on the fate or whereabouts, with knowledge that such deprivation may well have occurred.[257]

Previous instruments required commission, authorization, support or acquiescence from the State. The ICC Statute expanded this to refer as well to 'political organizations', consistent with the fundamental proposition that crimes against humanity may be committed by non-State actors.

Those arresting, detaining or abducting a person must know that a refusal to acknowledge or give information would be likely to follow in the ordinary course of events. Those refusing to acknowledge the deprivation of freedom or to provide information on the fate or whereabouts must know that such deprivation may well have occurred. In addition, the crime of enforced disappearance requires a particular intention, to remove a person from the protection of the law.

Enforced disappearance may involve other crimes such as killing, torture or arbitrary imprisonment. The essence of the crime, however, is that the friends and families of the direct victims do not know whether the persons concerned are alive or dead. It is this uncertainty that is the hallmark of enforced disappearance, and indeed the friends and families of the direct victims are also the special victims of this crime.

2.1.10 Apartheid

The ICC Statute includes the crime of apartheid as a crime against humanity. Apartheid was recognized as a crime against humanity in instruments such as the 1968 Convention on the Non-Applicability of Statutory Limitations to War Crimes and Crimes Against Humanity and the 1973 Apartheid Convention.[258]

The definition was adjusted in order to refer not only to the situation which had prevailed in South Africa, but also any similar situations in the future. The ICC Statute, Article 7(2)(h), defines it as 'inhumane acts of a character

257 Georg Witschel and Wiebke Rückert, 'Crime Against Humanity of Enforced Disappearance of Persons' in Lee, Elements and Rules,98–103.

258 Art. 1(b) of the Convention on Statutory Limitations, quoted in Apartheid Convention, Preamble, para. 5.

similar to those referred to in paragraph 1, committed in the context of an institutionalized racial regime of systematic oppression and domination by one racial group over any other racial group and committed with the intention of maintaining that regime'.

The definition of crimes against humanity always included a residual clause encompassing other inhumane acts of a similar character. Thus, by requiring in the crime of apartheid definition that the inhumane acts be 'of a character similar to those referred to in paragraph 1', the drafters ensured that they did not exceed existing law. What the ICC Statute provides is simply an express recognition of the crime of apartheid where inhumane acts are committed in the context of an institutionalized racial regime of systematic oppression and domination.

Most or all of the acts listed in the Apartheid Convention are captured by the ICC definition. The requirement of 'similar character' naturally covers acts of identical character,[259] and hence the examples in the Apartheid Convention of murder, torture, arbitrary imprisonment and persecution are clearly included. In addition, inflicting conditions calculated to cause physical destruction of a group; legislative measures to prevent a racial group from participation in political, social, economic and cultural life; legislative measures to divide the population through ghettos, prohibiting mixed marriage, and expropriating property; and forced labour, appear to be of character similar to 'persecution' and 'other inhumane acts' and therefore would be covered. The significant difference between the two definitions is that the ICC Statute specifies that the crime must be committed 'in the context of an institutionalized regime of systematic oppression and domination by one racial group over any other racial group or groups'. To constitute the crime of apartheid, the conduct must be committed with the particular intent of maintaining the regime.

2.1.11 Other inhumane acts

All definitions of crimes against humanity close with the general residual clause 'or other inhumane acts'. A residual clause remains necessary because:

> [h]owever much care were taken in establishing all the various forms of infliction, one would never be able to catch up with the imagination of future torturers who wished to satisfy their bestial instincts; and the more specific and complete a list tries to be, the more restrictive it becomes.[260]

259 A point clarified in the ICC Elements, Art. 7(1)(j), element 2.

260 Blaškic ICTY T. Ch. I 3.3.2000 para. 237, referring to Jean Pictet, Commentary on Geneva Convention IV (Geneva, 1960) 54.

Jurists have, however, been aware that any such residual clause must be infused with adequate precision to satisfy the criminal law principle of legality. The ICC Statute provides the necessary threshold by requiring that the inhumane acts (1) be of a similar character to other prohibited acts and (2) that they cause great suffering or serious injury to body or to mental or physical health.[261] Tribunal jurisprudence provides the threshold by requiring 'similar gravity and seriousness' to other prohibited acts.[262]

The accused must carry out the conduct intentionally. It is not required that the accused considered his or her actions 'inhumane', it is sufficient that the accused was aware of the factual circumstances that established the character of the act.[263] The accused must intend to inflict serious bodily or mental harm.[264]

Tribunals have held the conduct element of 'inhumane acts' to be synonymous with the conduct element of the war crime of 'cruel treatment'. [265]

The Tribunal Statutes, unlike the ICC Statute, do not expressly include forced disappearance, sexual violence, forced prostitution, forced transfer of populations in their list of prohibited acts, and hence Tribunal jurisprudence has found that each of these are encompassed in the Tribunal Statutes under 'other inhumane acts'.[266] Other acts that have been characterized as inhumane acts include mutilation, severe bodily harm, beatings, serious physical and mental injury, inhumane or degrading treatment falling short of the definition of torture, imposing inhumane conditions in concentration camps, forced nudity and forced marriage.[267] More recently, Sierra Leone Special Court has recognized 'forced marriage' as an 'inhumane act', and defined it as 'forced conjugal association with another person resulting in great suffering, or serious physical or mental injury on the part of the victim'.[268]

261 Art. 7(1)(k) of the ICC Statute.

262 See, e.g. Kayishema ICTR A. Ch. 1.6.2001 para. 583.

263 ICC Elements, Art. 7(1)(k), element 3; Čelebic i ICTY T. Ch. II 16.11.1998 para. 543.

264 ICC Elements, Art. 7(1)(k); Blaškic ICTY T. Ch. I 3.3.2000 para. 243.

265 Jelisic ICTY T. Ch. 14.12.1999 para. 52. The ICC Elements use different terms for the two crimes, so it remains to be seen whether the ICC will adopt the same approach.

266 Kvočka ICTY T. Ch. I 2.11.2001 para. 208; Kupreškic ICTY T. Ch. II 14.1.2000 para. 566.

267 Akayesu ICTR T. Ch. I 2.9.1998 paras. 685–97; Tadic ICTY T. Ch. II 7.5.1997 para. 730; Blaškic ICTY T. Ch. I 3.3.2000 para. 239; Kvočka ICTY T. Ch. I 2.11.2001 para. 209; Čelebic i ICTY T. Ch. II 16.11.1998 paras. 554–8. 236 Brina SCSL A. Ch. 22.2.2008 para. 195. For discussion of this gender-based crime, see Valerie Oosterveld, 'International Decisions: Prosecutor v. Brima; Prosecutor v. Fofana' (2009) 103 AJIL 103.

268 Brina SCSL A. Ch. 22.2.2008 para. 195. For discussion of this gender-based crime, see Valerie Oosterveld, 'International Decisions: Prosecutor v. Brima; Prosecutor v. Fofana' (2009) 103 AJIL 103.

PART 3
JURISPRUDENCE OF THE ICTY

a) Statute

ICTY Statute, Article 5:

"The International Tribunal shall have the power to prosecute persons responsible for the following crimes when committed in armed conflict, whether international or internal in character, and directed against any civilian population:
(a) murder;
(b) extermination;
(c) enslavement;
(d) deportation;
(e) imprisonment;
(f) torture;
(g) rape;
(h) persecutions on political, racial and religious grounds;
(i) other inhumane acts."

b) General elements

Limaj et al., (Trial Chamber), November 30, 2005, para. 181: "To qualify as crimes against humanity the acts of an accused must be part of a widespread or systematic attack 'directed against any civilian population.'"

Limaj et al., (Trial Chamber), November 30, 2005, para. 181: "It is established in the jurisprudence of the Tribunal that the general elements required for the applicability of Article 5 of the Statute are that: (i) there must be an attack; (ii) the acts of the perpetrator must be part of the attack; (iii) the attack must be directed against any civilian population; (iv) the attack must be widespread or systematic; and (v) the perpetrator must know that his or her acts constitute part of a pattern of widespread or systematic crimes directed against a civilian population and know that his or her acts fit into such a pattern (*i.e.* knowledge of the wider context in which his or her acts occur and knowledge that his or her acts are part of the attack)." *See also Blagojevic and Jokic*, (Trial Chamber), January 17, 2005, para. 541 (same five elements); *Brdjanin*, (Trial Chamber), September 1, 2004, para. 130 (same five elements); *Galic*, (Trial Chamber), December 5, 2003, para. 140 (similar); *Simic, Tadic and Zaric*, (Trial Chamber), October 17, 2003, para. 37 (same five elements); *Stakic*, (Trial Chamber), July 31, 2003, para. 621 (same five elements); *Kunarac, Kovac, and Vukovic*, (Trial Chamber), February 22, 2001, para. 410 (same five elements).

Blagojevic and Jokic, (Trial Chamber), January 17, 2005, para. 541: "Additionally, the Statute of the Tribunal requires that the crimes be 'committed in armed conflict, whether international or internal in character.'

The Appeals Chamber has considered this requirement to be a jurisdictional requirement." *See also Brdjanin*, (Trial Chamber), September 1, 2004, para. 130 (the crime must be "committed in an armed conflict, whether international or internal in character. . ."); *Galic*, (Trial Chamber), December 5, 2003, para. 139 ("For a crime to be adjudicated under Article 5 of the Statute (crimes against humanity), there are two prerequisites: that there was an armed conflict, and that the alleged criminal acts occurred during that armed conflict."); *Stakic*, (Trial Chamber), July 31, 2003, para. 618 ("a jurisdictional requirement for the applicability of Article 5 is the existence of an armed conflict.").

i) jurisdictional prerequisites

(1) the Statute requires that there be an armed conflict

Kunarac, Kovac, and Vokovic, (Appeals Chamber), June 12, 2002, para. 83: "[T]he requirement [committed in armed conflict] contained in Article 5 of the Statute is a purely jurisdictional prerequisite which is satisfied by proof that there was an armed conflict (...)" *See also Stakic*, (Trial Chamber), July 31, 2003, para. 570 (quoting same).

Tadic, (Appeals Chamber), July 15, 1999, para. 251: "The armed conflict requirement is satisfied by proof that *there was* an armed conflict. . . ." (emphasis in original)

Limaj et al., (Trial Chamber), November 30, 2005, para. 180: "A crime listed in Article 5 of the Statute constitutes a crime against humanity only when 'committed in armed conflict.'" *See also Brdjanin*, (Trial Chamber), September 1, 2004, para. 133 (similar); *Simic, Tadic, and Zaric*, (Trial Chamber), October 17, 2003, para. 38 (similar); *Naletilic and Martinovic,* (Trial Chamber), March 31, 2003, para. 233 (similar).

(a) the armed conflict may be international or internal

Blagojevic and Jokic, (Trial Chamber), January 17, 2005, para. 541: "[T]he Statute of the Tribunal requires that the crimes be 'committed in armed conflict, whether international or internal in character.' The Appeals Chamber has considered this requirement to be a jurisdictional requirement."

Brdjanin, (Trial Chamber), September 1, 2004, para. 134: "The armed conflict can be international as well as internal in nature."

Kordic and Cerkez, (Trial Chamber), February 26, 2001, para. 23: "Article 5 vests the International Tribunal with the competence to prosecute crimes against humanity 'when committed in armed conflict, whether international or internal in character.'"

(b) armed conflict defined

Kunarac, Kovac, and Vokovic, (Appeals Chamber), June 12, 2002, para. 56: "An 'armed conflict' is said to exist 'whenever there is a resort to armed force between States or protracted armed violence between governmental authorities and organised armed groups or between such groups within a State.'" *See also Tadic,* (Appeals Chamber), Decision on the Defence Motion for Interlocutory Appeal on Jurisdiction, October 2, 1995, para. 70 (same).

Brdjanin, (Trial Chamber), September 1, 2004, para. 122: "It is settled in the jurisprudence of this Tribunal that an armed conflict exists 'whenever there is resort to armed forces between States or protracted armed violence between governmental authorities and organised armed groups or between such groups within a State.'" *See also Stakic,* (Trial Chambers), July 31, 2003, para. 568 (same).

(2) the acts of the accused and the armed conflict must be linked geographically as well as temporally

Kunarac, Kovac, and Vokovic, (Appeals Chamber), June 12, 2002, para. 83: "[T]he requirement [committed in armed conflict] contained in Article 5 of the Statute is a purely jurisdictional prerequisite which is satisfied by proof that there was an armed conflict and that objectively the acts of the accused are linked geographically as well as temporally with the armed conflict." *See also Simic, Tadic, and Zaric,* (Trial Chamber), October 17, 2003, para. 38 (quoting same); *Stakic,* (Trial Chamber), July 31, 2003, para. 570 (quoting same).

Tadic, (Appeals Chamber), July 15, 1999, para. 251: "A nexus between the accused's acts and the armed conflict is *not* required, as is (...) suggested by the [*Tadic* Trial] Judgment. The armed conflict requirement is satisfied by proof that *there was* an armed conflict; that is all that the Statute requires, and in so doing, it requires more than does customary international law." (emphasis in original) *See also Galic,* (Trial Chamber), December 5, 2003, para. 139 (there must exist "'. . . an armed conflict at the relevant time and place.'"); *Kordic and Cerkez,* (Trial Chamber), February 26, 2001, para. 23 (same as *Galic*).

Limaj et al., (Trial Chamber), November 30, 2005, para. 180: "A crime listed in Article 5 of the Statute constitutes a crime against humanity only when 'committed in armed conflict.' This requirement translates into a need for proof that there *was* an armed conflict at the relevant time and place, and that, objectively, the acts of the accused are linked geographically, as well as temporally, with the armed conflict. Proof of a nexus between the underlying crimes and the armed conflict is not required. Although the acts or omissions must be committed in the course of an armed conflict, the only nexus required is that between the acts of an accused and the attack on the civilian population(...)"

Brdjanin, (Trial Chamber), September 1, 2004, para. 133: "The Appeals Chamber in *Kunarac* held that this [requirement that crimes against humanity be committed in armed conflict] is not equivalent to the requirement contained in Article 3 of the Statute, where a 'close relationship' between the acts of the accused and the armed conflict is required. By contrast, according to the Appeals Chamber, the nexus with the armed conflict under Article 5 is (...) 'a purely jurisdictional prerequisite which is satisfied by proof that there was an armed conflict and that objectively the acts of the accused are linked geographically as well as temporally with the armed conflict.'"[14]

Stakic, (Trial Chambers), July 31, 2003, para. 567: "Article 5 of the Statute confers jurisdiction on the Tribunal to prosecute persons for crimes against humanity. While the Appeals Chamber has held that 'customary international law may not require a connection between crimes against humanity and any conflict at all,' Article 5 imposes a jurisdictional requirement limiting the Tribunal's jurisdiction to crimes against humanity 'when committed in armed conflict, whether international or internal in character.'"

Kordic and Cerkez, (Trial Chamber), February 26, 2001, para. 33: "The Appeal Chamber [in *Tadic*] (...) concluded in respect of Article 5 of the Statute that proof of a nexus between the conduct of the accused and the armed conflict is not required. . . ." "Although the acts or omissions must be committed in the course of an armed conflict, the nexus which is required is between the accused's acts and the attack on the civilian population." *See also Tadic,* (Appeals Chamber), July 15, 1999, para. 251: "A nexus with the accused's acts is required (...) only for the attack on 'any civilian population.'"

ii) there must be an "attack" (element 1)

Limaj et al., (Trial Chamber), November 30, 2005, para. 181: To show crimes against humanity, one element is "[t]here must be an attack." *See also Blagojevic and Jokic*, (Trial Chamber), January 17, 2005, para. 541 (same); *Brdjanin*, (Trial Chamber), September 1, 2004, para. 130 (same); *Simic, Tadic and Zaric*, (Trial Chamber), October 17, 2003, para. 37 (same);

Stakic, (Trial Chamber), July 31, 2003, para. 621 (same); *Kunarac, Kovac, and Vukovic,* (Trial Chamber), February 22, 2001, para. 410 (same).[269]

(1) defined

Blagojevic and Jokic, (Trial Chamber), January 17, 2005, para. 543: "'Attack' in the context of a crime against humanity can be defined as a course of conduct involving the commission of acts of violence." *See also Limaj et al.*, (Trial Chamber), November 30, 2005, para. 182 (similar); *Brdjanin,* (Trial Chamber), September 1, 2004, para. 131 (similar); *Galic,* (Trial Chamber), December 5, 2003, para. 141 (similar); *Naletilic and Martinovic,* (Trial Chamber), March 31, 2003, para. 233 (similar).

(2) "attack" and "armed conflict" are distinct

Tadic, (Appeals Chamber), July 15, 1999, para. 251: "[T]he two – the 'attack on the civilian population' and 'the armed conflict' – must be separate notions(...)"

Limaj et al., (Trial Chamber), November 30, 2005, para. 182: "The concepts of 'attack' and 'armed conflict' are distinct and separate notions(...)" *See also Brdjanin,* (Trial Chamber), September 1, 2004, para. 131 (similar); *Stakic,* (Trial Chamber), July 31, 2003, para. 623 (similar); *Vasiljevic,* (Trial Chamber), November 29, 2002, para. 30 (similar).

Simic, Tadic, and Zaric, (Trial Chamber), October 17, 2003, para. 39: "The concepts of 'attack' and 'armed conflict' are necessarily separate and distinct; the former being an element of a crime against humanity and the latter a jurisdictional requirement pursuant to the Statute."

Galic, (Trial Chamber), December 5, 2003, para. 141: "In comparing the content of customary international law concerning crimes against humanity to the Tribunal's Statute, the Appeals Chamber noted that 'the "attack on the civilian population" and the "armed conflict" must be separate notions(...)'"

(3) the "attack" may be, but need not be, part of the "armed conflict"

Kunarac, Kovac, and Vokovic, (Appeals Chamber), June 12, 2002, para. 86: "[T]he attack could precede, outlast, or continue during the armed conflict, but it need not be a part of it." *See also Limaj et al.*, (Trial Chamber), November

269 Most decisions use the word "nexus" to describe the relationship between the acts of the accused and the attack against the civilian population, not the armed conflict. See, e.g., Kordic and Cerkez, (Trial Chamber), February 26, 2001, para. 33 ("the nexus which is required is between the accused's acts and the attack on the civilian population.").

30, 2005, para. 182 (similar); *Blagojevic and Jokic*, (Trial Chamber), January 17, 2005, para. 543 (same); *Brdjanin*, (Trial Chamber), September 1, 2004, para. 131 (similar); *Stakic*, (Trial Chamber), July 31, 2003, para. 623 (similar).

Tadic, (Appeals Chamber), July 15, 1999, para. 251: "[U]nder Article 5 of the Statute the attack on 'any civilian population' may be part of an 'armed conflict.'" *See also Limaj et al.*, (Trial Chamber), November 30, 2005, para. 182 (same); *Galic*, (Trial Chamber), December 5, 2003, para. 141 (same); *Vasiljevic*, (Trial Chamber), November 29, 2002, para. 30 (same).

Galic, (Trial Chamber), December 5, 2003, para. 141: "In accordance with customary international law, the attack could precede, outlast, or continue during the armed conflict, but it need not be a part of it." *See also Simic, Tadic, and Zaric*, (Trial Chamber), October 17, 2003, para. 39 (similar); *Naletilic and Martinovic*, (Trial Chamber), March 31, 2003, para. 233 (similar).

Simic, Tadic, and Zaric, (Trial Chamber), October 17, 2003, para. 39: "The attack need not be part of the armed conflict because (i) the concept of 'attack' is not limited to the use of armed force, but has been held to encompass any mistreatment of the civilian population, and (ii) it is conceivable that where the existence of an armed conflict satisfies the jurisdictional requirement, an attack unconnected to the armed conflict, but nonetheless directed against a civilian population, could satisfy the customary international law requirements for a crime against humanity."

(4) "attack" not limited to use of armed force

Kunarac, Kovac, and Vokovic, (Appeals Chamber), June 12, 2002, para. 86: "[T]he attack in the context of a crime against humanity is not limited to the use of armed force; it encompasses any mistreatment of the civilian population." *See also Limaj et al.*, (Trial Chamber), November 30, 2005, para. 182 (similar); *Blagojevic and Jokic*, (Trial Chamber), January 17, 2005, para. 543 (same as *Limaj*); *Brdjanin*, (Trial Chamber), September 1, 2004, para. 131 (same as *Limaj*); *Stakic*, (Trial Chamber), July 31, 2003, para. 623 (same as *Kunarac*); *Vasiljevic*, (Trial Chamber), November 29, 2002, para. 29 (same as *Limaj*).

Limaj et al., (Trial Chamber), November 30, 2005, para. 194: "[T]o amount to an 'attack' the relevant conduct need not amount to a military assault or forceful takeover; the evidence need only demonstrate a 'course of conduct' directed against the civilian population that indicates a widespread or systematic reach."

Galic, (Trial Chamber), December 5, 2003, para. 141: "In the context of a crime against humanity, 'attack' is not limited to armed combat. It may also encompass situations of mistreatment of persons taking no active part in hostilities, such as of a person in detention."

(5) when establishing the attack, generally irrelevant that the other side committed atrocities or attack

Kunarac, Kovac, and Vukovic, (Appeals Chamber) June 12, 2002, paras. 97, 87-88: The Trial Chamber "correctly stated that the existence of an attack upon one side's civilian population would not disprove or cancel out that side's attack upon the other's civilian population."

"[W]hen establishing whether there was an attack upon a particular civilian population, it is not relevant that the other side also committed atrocities against its opponent's civilian population. The existence of an attack from one side against the other side's civilian population would neither justify the attack by that other side against the civilian population of its opponent nor displace the conclusion that the other side's forces were in fact targeting a civilian population as such. Each attack against the other's civilian population would be equally illegitimate and crimes committed as part of this attack could, all other conditions being met, amount to crimes against humanity."

"Evidence of an attack by the other party on the accused's civilian population may not be introduced unless it tends 'to prove or disprove any of the allegations made in the indictment,' notably to refute the Prosecutor's contention that there was a widespread or systematic attack against a civilian population. A submission that the other side is responsible for starting the hostilities would not, for instance, disprove that there was an attack against a particular civilian population."

Brdjanin, (Trial Chamber), September 1, 2004, para. 131: "To establish whether there was an attack, it is not relevant that the other side also committed atrocities against its opponent's civilian population. Each attack against the other side's civilian population would be equally illegitimate and crimes committed as part of such attack could, all other conditions being met, amount to crimes against humanity."

Galic, (Trial Chamber), December 5, 2003, para. 145: "Evidence of attack by opposing forces on the civilian population to which the accused belongs may not be introduced unless it tends to prove or disprove an allegation made in an indictment, such as the Prosecution's contention that there was a widespread or systematic attack against a civilian population. A submission that the opposing side is responsible for starting the hostilities is not relevant to disproving the allegation that there was an attack on the civilian population in question."

Simic, Tadic, and Zaric, (Trial Chamber), October 17, 2003, para. 40: "Once an 'attack' is established in the context of an armed conflict, it is irrelevant whether another side to the armed conflict is also involved in an attack upon a civilian population. Such other attacks would not amount to justification for the attack in question, and any crimes committed in the course of such an attack by another side to the armed conflict would themselves be subject to prosecution as crimes against humanity."

(6) application—there was an attack

For findings that there was an attack in the territory of Kosovo, see *Limaj et al.*, (Trial Chamber), November 30, 2005, paras. 195-204.

iii) the acts of the accused must form part of the attack (element 2)

(1) nexus

Prosecutor v. Deronjic, Case No. IT-02-61-A (Appeals Chamber), July 20, 2005, para. 109: "The acts of the accused need only be a part of the attack(...)"

Kunarac, Kovac, and Vokovic, (Appeals Chamber), June 12, 2002, para. 99: "The acts of the accused must constitute part of the attack. In effect, as properly identified by the Trial Chamber, the required nexus between the acts of the accused and the attack consists of two elements:
-the commission of an act which, by its nature or consequences, is objectively part of the attack; coupled with
-knowledge on the part of the accused that there is an attack on the civilian population and that his act is part thereof." *See also Limaj et al.*, (Trial Chamber), November 30, 2005, para. 188 (quoting same); *Blagojevic and Jokic*, (Trial Chamber), January 17, 2005, para. 547 (quoting same); *Simic, Tadic, and Zaric*, (Trial Chamber), October 17, 2003, para. 41 (similar first sentence).

Tadic, (Appeals Chamber), July 15, 1999, para. 251: "A nexus with the accused's acts is required (...) only for the attack on 'any civilian population.'"

Limaj et al., (Trial Chamber), November 30, 2005, para. 180: "[T]he only nexus required is that between the acts of an accused and the attack on the civilian population(...)" *See also Kordic and Cerkez*, (Trial Chamber), February 26, 2001, para. 33 (similar).

(2) crimes must be related to/part of the attack not isolated acts of the accused

Tadic, (Appeals Chamber), July 15, 1999, para. 271: "[T]o convict an accused of crimes against humanity, it must be proved that the crimes were *related* to the attack on a civilian population (occurring during an armed conflict). . . ." (emphasis in original) *See also Limaj et al.*, (Trial Chamber), November 30, 2005, para. 189 (same test).

Limaj et al., (Trial Chamber), November 30, 2005, para. 189: "[I]t must be established that the acts of the accused are not isolated, but rather, by their nature and consequence, are objectively part of the attack."
Limaj et al., (Trial Chamber), November 30, 2005, para. 194: "It has been emphasised, repeatedly, that the contextual element required for the application of Article 5 serves to exclude single, random or limited acts from the domain of crimes against humanity."

Blagojevic and Jokic, (Trial Chamber), January 17, 2005, para. 547: "The act or acts must not be isolated or random; they may not be so far removed from the attack that, having considered the context and circumstances in which it occurred, the act or acts cannot reasonably be said to have been part of the attack."

Brdjanin, (Trial Chamber), September 1, 2004, para. 132: "The acts of the accused need to objectively 'form part' of the attack by their nature or consequences, as distinct from being committed in isolation(...)" *See also Simic, Tadic, and Zaric*, (Trial Chamber), October 17, 2003, para. 41 (similar); *Naletilic and Martinovic,* (Trial Chamber), March 31, 2003, para. 234 (similar).

See also Simic, Tadic, and Zaric, (Trial Chamber), October 17, 2003, para. 41: "'Isolated acts' are defined as those acts 'so far removed from that attack that, having considered the context and circumstances in which it was committed, it cannot reasonably be said to have been part of the attack.' The acts of the accused are less likely to be considered random or isolated where they amount to a course of conduct against a civilian population."

(3) the acts need not be committed in the midst of, or at the height of, the attack

Limaj et al., (Trial Chamber), November 30, 2005, para. 189: "The acts [of the accused] need not be committed in the midst of that attack provided that they are sufficiently connected to that attack." *Brdjanin*, (Trial Chamber), September 1, 2004, para. 132: "The acts of the accused (...) do not need to be committed in the midst of the attack. For instance, the *Kunarac* Trial Chamber found that a crime committed several months after, or several kilometres away from the main attack could still, if sufficiently connected otherwise, be part of that attack."

Simic, Tadic, and Zaric, (Trial Chamber), October 17, 2003, para. 41: "The acts of the accused need not be committed in the midst, or at the height of the attack(...)"

iv) the attack must be "directed against any civilian population" (element 3)

Blaskic, (Appeals Chamber), July 29, 2004, para. 98: "It is well established in the jurisprudence of the International Tribunal that in order to constitute a crime against humanity, the acts of an accused must be part of a widespread or systematic attack directed against any civilian population."

Limaj et al., (Trial Chamber), November 30, 2005, para. 185: "The attack must be directed against a civilian population." *See also Galic,* (Trial Chamber), December 5, 2003, para. 143 (same).

Kunarac, Kovac, and Vukovic, (Trial Chamber), February 22, 2001, para. 410: To show crimes against humanity, one element is there must be an attack "directed against any civilian population."

(1) "directed against"

(a) an attack is "directed against" a civilian population if the civilian population is the primary object of the attack

Blaskic, (Appeals Chamber), July 29, 2004, para. 106: "The Appeals Chamber in *Kunarac* .
. . stated:
. . . the expression 'directed against' is an expression which 'specifies that in the
context of a crime against humanity the civilian population is the primary object of the attack.' . . ." *See also Kordic and Cerkez,* (Appeals Chamber), December 17, 2004, para. 96 (quoting same); *Kunarac, Kovac, and Vokovic,* (Appeals Chamber), June 12, 2002, para. 91 (same as *Blaskic*); *Limaj et al.*, (Trial Chamber), November 30, 2005, para. 185 (quoting same); *Brdjanin,* (Trial Chamber), September 1, 2004, para. 134 (similar); *Galic,* (Trial Chamber), December 5, 2003, para. 142 (quoting same); *Stakic,* (Trial Chamber), July 31, 2003, para. 624 (similar); *Naletilic and Martinovic,* (Trial Chamber), March 31, 2003, para. 235 (similar).

(b) not entire population, but a sufficient number must be subject to the attack, rather than a limited and randomly selected number of individuals

Kordic and Cerkez, (Appeals Chamber), December 17, 2004, para. 95: "In *Kunarac et al.*, the Appeals Chamber discussed the requirement that an attack is directed against a civilian population, stating that:
the use of the word 'population' does not mean that the entire population of the geographical entity in which the attack is taking place must have been subjected to that attack. It is sufficient to show that enough individuals were targeted in the course of the attack, or that they were targeted in such a way as to satisfy the Chamber that the attack was in fact directed against a civilian 'population,' rather than against a limited and randomly selected number of individuals."
Blaskic, (Appeals Chamber), July 29, 2004, para. 105 (same language as quoted); *Kunarac, Kovac, and Vokovic,* (Appeals Chamber), June 12, 2002, para. 90 (same); *Limaj et al.*, (Trial Chamber), November 30, 2005, para. 187 (same language as quoted); *Brdjanin,* (Trial Chamber), September 1, 2004, para. 134 (similar); *Galic,* (Trial Chamber), December 5, 2003, para. 143 (similar); *Simic, Tadic, and Zaric,* (Trial Chamber), October 17, 2003, para. 42 (similar); *Stakic,* (Trial Chamber), July 31, 2003, para. 624 (similar); *Naletilic and Martinovic,* (Trial Chamber), March 31, 2003, para. 235 (same).

(c) factors for assessing whether the attack was directed against the civilian population

Blaskic, (Appeals Chamber), July 29, 2004, para. 106: "The Appeals Chamber in *Kunarac* .
. . stated: (...) In order to determine whether the attack may be said to have been so directed [against the civilian population], the Trial Chamber will consider, *inter alia*, the means and method used in the course of the attack, the status of the victims, their number, the discriminatory nature of the attack, the nature of the crimes committed in its course, the resistance to the assailants at the time and the extent to which the attacking force may be said to have complied or attempted to comply with the precautionary requirements of the laws of war. . . ."

See also Kordic and Cerkez, (Appeals Chamber), December 17, 2004, para. 96 (quoting same); *Limaj et al.*, (Trial Chamber), November 30, 2005, para. 185 (quoting same); *Brdjanin,* (Trial Chamber), September 1, 2004, para. 134 (similar); *Galic,* (Trial Chamber), December 5, 2003, para. 142 (similar); *Simic, Tadic, and Zaric,* (Trial Chamber), October 17, 2003, para. 42 (similar); *Kunarac, Kovac, and Vokovic,* (Appeals Chamber), June 12, 2002, para. 90 (source of quoted language).

(d) attack directed against a civilian population will most often occur at the behest of a state

Limaj et al., (Trial Chamber), November 30, 2005, para. 191: "Due to structural factors and organisational and military capabilities, an 'attack directed against a civilian population' will most often be found to have occurred at the behest of a State. Being the locus of organised authority within a given territory, able to mobilise and direct military and civilian power, a sovereign State by its very nature possesses the attributes that permit it to organise and deliver an attack against a civilian population; it is States which can most easily and efficiently marshal the resources to launch an attack against a civilian population on a 'widespread' scale, or upon a 'systematic' basis. In contrast, the factual situation before the Chamber involves the allegation of an attack against a civilian population perpetrated by a non-state actor with extremely limited resources, personnel and organisation."

Limaj et al., (Trial Chamber), November 30, 2005, para. 194: "[T]he existence of an attack is most clearly evident when a course of conduct is launched on the basis of massive state action. This can be seen from a number of examples. In *Prosecutor v. Nikolic* the Trial Chamber looked to the existence of discriminatory measures and an 'authoritarian take-over' that installed a new 'authoritarian power structure' as evidence of an attack in the relevant geographical region. In *Prosecutor v. Mrksic et al.,* the Trial Chamber looked to, as relevant factors in discerning the existence of an attack, a number of factors that included: the 'massive land, naval and air offensive by the forces of the JNA [Army of the Socialist Federal Republic of Yugoslavia]; intensive shelling of the city of Vukovar for a period of three months; and the deportation of women and children *en masse*."

(e) targeting a number of political opponents insufficient

Limaj et al., (Trial Chamber), November 30, 2005, para. 187: "It is established that the targeting of a select group of civilians—for example, the targeted killing of a number of political opponents—cannot satisfy the requirements of Article 5."

(f) the laws of war provide a benchmark to assess the nature of the attack and legality of acts committed

Blaskic, (Appeals Chamber), July 29, 2004, para. 106: "The Appeals Chamber in *Kunarac* .
. . stated:

. . . To the extent that the alleged crimes against humanity were committed in the course of an armed conflict, the laws of war provide a benchmark against which the Chamber may assess the nature of the attack and the legality of the acts committed in its midst." *See also Kordic and Cerkez,* (Appeals Chamber), December 17, 2004, para. 96 (same); *Limaj et al.*, (Trial Chamber), November 30, 2005, para. 185 (same).

Galic, (Trial Chamber), December 5, 2003, para. 144: "The Trial Chamber accepts that when considering the general requirements of Article 5, the body of [the] laws of war plays an important part in the assessment of the legality of the acts committed in the course of an armed conflict and whether the population may be said to have been targeted as such."

(2) civilian population

Kordic and Cerkez, (Appeals Chamber), December 17, 2004, para. 97: "In determining the scope of the term 'civilian population,' the Appeals Chamber recalls its obligation to ascertain the state of customary law in force at the time the crimes were committed. The Appeals Chamber considers that Article 50 of Additional Protocol I [to the Geneva Conventions] contains a definition of civilians and civilian populations, and the provisions in this article may largely be viewed as reflecting customary law. As a result, they are relevant to the consideration at issue under Article 5 of the Statute, concerning crimes against humanity." *See also Blaskic,* (Appeals Chamber), July 29, 2004, para. 110 (similar).

See also Limaj et al., (Trial Chamber), November 30, 2005, para. 223: "The provisions of Article 50 [of Additional Protocol I to the Geneva Conventions] have been considered by the Appeals Chamber to reflect customary international law. The Chamber acknowledges, however, that the definition of 'civilian' employed in the laws of war cannot be imported wholesale into discussion of crimes against humanity. In this regard the Chamber notes that the Trial Chamber in *Prosecutor v Tadic* determined that:

[The] definition of civilians contained in Common Article 3 is not immediately applicable to crimes against humanity because it is a part of the laws or customs or war and can only be applied by analogy. The same applies to the definition contained in Protocol I and the Commentary, Geneva Convention IV, on the treatment of civilians, both of which advocate a broad interpretation of the term 'civilian.'"

(a) defined

Blagojevic and Jokic, (Trial Chamber), January 17, 2005, para. 544: "The term 'civilian' refers to persons not taking part in hostilities, including members of armed forces who have laid down their arms and those placed *hors de combat* by sickness, wounds detention or any other cause. It is a principle of customary international law that these persons are protected in armed conflicts."

(b) population must be "predominantly" civilian

Limaj et al., (Trial Chamber), November 30, 2005, para. 186: "The Chamber recalls that there is an absolute prohibition against targeting civilians in customary international law. The terms 'civilian population' must be interpreted broadly and refers to a population that is predominantly civilian in nature. A population may qualify as 'civilian' even if non-civilians are among it, as long as it is predominantly civilian."
Brdjanin, (Trial Chamber), September 1, 2004, para. 134: "It is not required that every single member of that population be a civilian – it is enough if it is predominantly civilian in nature, and may include, *e.g.*, individuals *hors de combat*."

Galic, (Trial Chamber), December 5, 2003, para. 143: "A population may qualify as 'civilian' even if non-civilians are among it, as long as the population is predominantly civilian." *See also Blagojevic and Jokic*, (Trial Chamber), January 17, 2005, para. 544 (similar); *Naletilic and Martinovic*, (Trial Chamber), March 31, 2003, para. 235 (similar); *Kordic and Cerkez*, (Trial Chamber), February 26, 2001, para. 180 (similar).

Simic, Tadic, and Zaric, (Trial Chamber), October 17, 2003, para. 42: "Both the primary object of the attack and its victims must be 'any civilian population,' a phrase that pertains to any predominantly civilian population, notwithstanding the presence of noncivilians."

(c) construe civilian population liberally/ cases of doubt

Blaskic, (Appeals Chamber), July 29, 2004, para. 111: "Article 50, paragraph 1, of Additional Protocol I states (...) 'In case of doubt whether a person is a civilian, that person shall be considered to be a civilian.' The Appeals Chamber notes that the imperative 'in case of doubt' is limited to the expected conduct of a member of the military. However, when the latter's criminal responsibility is at issue, the burden of proof as to whether a person is a civilian rests on the Prosecution."

Limaj et al., (Trial Chamber), November 30, 2005, para. 186: "The terms 'civilian population' must be interpreted broadly(...)"

Limaj et al., (Trial Chamber), November 30, 2005, para. 223: "The Chamber recalls that Article 50, paragraph 1 of Additional Protocol I to the Geneva Conventions (which the Defence invite the Chamber to apply in the present situation) states that '[i]n case of doubt whether a person is a civilian, that person shall be considered a civilian.'"

Prosecutor v. Kupreskic et al., Case No. IT-95-16 (Trial Chamber), January 14, 2000, para. 547: "It would seem that a wide definition of 'civilian' and 'population' is intended. This is warranted first of all by the object and purpose of the general principles and rules of humanitarian law, in particular by the rules prohibiting crimes against humanity. The latter are intended to safeguard basic human values by banning atrocities directed against human dignity. [A] broad interpretation should (...) be placed on the word 'civilians,' the more so because the limitation [safeguarding civilians and not combatants] in Article 5 constitutes a departure from customary international law."

Jelisic, (Trial Chamber), December 14, 1999, para. 54: "It follows from the letter and the spirit of Article 5 that the term 'civilian population' must be interpreted broadly."

(d) those excluded from civilian status

Blaskic, (Appeals Chamber), July 29, 2004, para. 111: "Article 50, paragraph 1, of Additional Protocol I states that a civilian is 'any person who does not belong to one of the categories of persons referred to in Article 4A(1), (2), (3) and (6) of the Third Convention and in Article 43 of this Protocol. . . ."

Blaskic, (Appeals Chamber), July 29, 2004, para. 112: "As the ICRC [International Committee of the Red Cross] Commentary to the Additional Protocol explains, the following categories of persons, derived from Article 4A of the Third Geneva Convention, are excluded from civilian status:
(1) Members of the armed forces of a Party to the conflict, as well as members of militias or volunteer corps forming part of such armed forces.
(2) Members of other militias and members of other volunteer corps, including those of organized resistance movements, belonging to a Party to the conflict and operating in or outside their own territory, even if this territory is occupied, provided that such militias or volunteer corps, including such organized resistance movements, fulfil the following conditions:
(a) that of being commanded by a person responsible for his subordinates;
(b) that of having a fixed distinctive sign recognizable at a distance;

(c) that of carrying arms openly;
(d) that of conducting their operations in accordance with the laws and customs of war.
(3) Members of regular armed forces who profess allegiance to a government or an authority not recognized by the Detaining Power. [(...)]
(6) Inhabitants of a non-occupied territory, who on the approach of the enemy spontaneously take up arms to resist the invading forces, without having had time to form themselves into regular armed units, provided they carry arms openly and respect the laws and customs of war."

Blaskic, (Appeals Chamber), July 29, 2004, para. 113: "Read together, Article 50 of Additional Protocol I and Article 4A of the Third Geneva Convention establish that members of the armed forces, and members of militias or volunteer corps forming part of such armed forces, cannot claim civilian status. Neither can members of organized resistance groups, provided that they are commanded by a person responsible for his subordinates, that they have a fixed distinctive sign recognizable at a distance, that they carry arms openly, and that they conduct their operations in accordance with the laws and customs of war."

(i) member of armed group, even if not armed or in combat, not a civilian

Blaskic, (Appeals Chamber), July 29, 2004, para. 114: "[T]he Trial Chamber's view [in *Blaskic*] that the specific situation of the victim at the time the crimes were committed must be taken into account in determining his standing as a civilian may be misleading. The ICRC [International Committee of the Red Cross] Commentary is instructive on this point and states:

All members of the armed forces are combatants, and only members of the armed forces are combatants. This should therefore dispense with the concept of quasi-combatants, which has sometimes been used on the basis of activities related more or less directly with the war effort. Similarly, any concept of a parttime status, a semi-civilian, semi-military status, soldier by night and peaceful citizen by day, also disappears. A civilian who is incorporated in an armed organization such as that mentioned in paragraph 1, becomes a member of the military and a combatant throughout the duration of the hostilities (or in any case, until he is permanently demobilized by the responsible command referred to in paragraph 1), whether or not he is in combat, or for the time being armed. If he is wounded, sick or shipwrecked, he is entitled to the protection of the First and Second Conventions (Article 44, paragraph 8), and, if he is captured, he is entitled to the protection of the Third Convention (Article 44, paragraph 1).

As a result, the specific situation of the victim at the time the crimes are committed may not be determinative of his civilian or non-civilian status. If he is indeed a member of an armed organization, the fact that he is not armed or in combat at the time of the commission of crimes, does not accord him civilian status."

(e) civilian includes those who were members of a resistance movement, former combatants, and others hors de combat

Limaj et al., (Trial Chamber), November 30, 2005, para. 186: "[T]he definition of a 'civilian' is expansive and includes individuals who at one time performed acts of resistance, as well as persons who were *hors de combat* when the crime was committed." *See also Galic*, (Trial Chamber), December 5, 2003, para. 143 (similar).

Naletilic and Martinovic, (Trial Chamber), March 31, 2003, para. 235: "[T]he definition of civilian population includes individuals who may at one time have performed acts of resistance and persons *hors de combat. . . .*"
Kordic and Cerkez, (Trial Chamber), February 26, 2001, para. 180: "[I]ndividuals who at one time performed acts of resistance may in certain circumstances be victims of a crime against humanity."

Blaskic, (Trial Chamber), March 3, 2000, para. 214: "Crimes against humanity (...) do not mean only acts committed against civilians in the strict sense of the term but include also crimes against two categories of people: those who were members of a resistance movement and former combatants - regardless of whether they wore wear uniform or not – but who were no longer taking part in hostilities when the crimes were perpetrated because they had either left the army or were no longer bearing arms or, ultimately, had been placed *hors de combat*, in particular, due to their wounds or their being detained."

Jelisic, (Trial Chamber), December 14, 1999, para. 54: "[T]he notion of civilian population as used in Article 5 of the Statute includes, in addition to civilians in the strict sense, all persons placed *hors de combat* when the crime is perpetrated."

See also Blaskic, (Appeals Chamber), July 29, 2004, para. 113: "[T]he Appeals Chamber considers that the presence within a population of members of resistance groups, or former combatants, who have laid down their arms, does not alter its civilian characteristic." *See also Limaj et al.*, (Trial Chamber), November 30, 2005, para. 186 (similar); *Blagojevic and Jokic*, (Trial Chamber), January 17, 2005, para. 544 (similar).

(f) to determine whether presence of soldiers deprives population of its civilian nature, examine number of soldiers and whether they are on leave

Blaskic, (Appeals Chamber), July 29, 2004, para. 115: "The Trial Chamber (...) stated that the 'presence of soldiers within an intentionally targeted civilian population does not alter the civilian nature of that population.' The ICRC [International Committee of the Red Cross] Commentary on this point states: (...) in wartime conditions it is inevitable that individuals belonging to the category of combatants become intermingled with the civilian population, for example, soldiers on leave visiting their families. However, provided that these are not regular units with fairly large numbers, this does not in any way change the civilian character of a population. Thus, in order to determine whether the presence of soldiers within a civilian population deprives the population of its civilian character, the number of soldiers, as well as whether they are on leave, must be examined."

Limaj et al., (Trial Chamber), November 30, 2005, para. 186: "Relevant to the determination whether the presence of soldiers within a civilian population deprives the population of its civilian character are the number of soldiers as well as whether they are on leave."
Brdjanin, (Trial Chamber), September 1, 2004, para. 134: "[T]he presence of soldiers, provided that they are on leave and do not amount to 'fairly large numbers,' within an intentionally targeted civilian population does not alter the civilian nature of that population."

Naletilic and Martinovic, (Trial Chamber), March 31, 2003, para. 235: "[T]he presence of a number of non-civilians cannot refute the predominantly civilian character of a population." *See also Blaskic,* (Trial Chamber), March 3, 2000, para. 214 (similar); *Jelisic,* (Trial Chamber), December 14, 1999, para. 54 (similar).

Kupreskic et al., (Trial Chamber), January 14, 2000, para. 549: "[T]he presence of those actively involved in the conflict should not prevent the characterization of a population as civilian and those actively involved in a resistance movement can qualify as victims of crimes against humanity."

(g) protects "any" civilian population

Limaj et al., (Trial Chamber), November 30, 2005, para. 186: "There is no requirement that the victims are linked to any particular side of the conflict."[270]

270 The Limaj Trial Chamber is looking at the existence of a "policy" as an indicia of a systematic attack against a civilian population, not as a legal element for crimes against humanity. See Limaj

Blagojevic and Jokic, (Trial Chamber), January 17, 2005, para. 544: "It is not necessary to demonstrate that the victims are linked to any particular side of the armed conflict. The Appeals Chamber has recently emphasised that 'there is an absolute prohibition on the targeting of civilians in customary international law.'"

Vasiljevic, (Trial Chamber), November 29, 2002, para. 33: "The protection of Article 5 extends to 'any' civilian population including, if a state takes part in the attack, that state's own population. It is therefore unnecessary to demonstrate that the victims were linked to any particular side of the conflict."

(3) application—attack directed against a civilian population

(a) abduction, detention or mistreatment of Serbian civilians by the Kosovo Liberation Army

(i) perceived collaborators generally entitled to civilian status

Limaj et al., (Trial Chamber), November 30, 2005, paras. 223, 224: "The Chamber is satisfied that the KLA [Kosovo Liberation Army] definition of 'collaborators' encompassed civilians as well as perceived combatants." "Taking account of [*inter alia*, the provisions of Article 50 of Additional Protocol I to the Geneva Conventions], and in light of the evidence before the Chamber concerning those apprehended and detained because of their alleged or suspected acts of collaboration, the Chamber concludes that, at least as a general rule, perceived collaborators abducted by the KLA were entitled to civilian status."

(ii) abductions, detentions or mistreatment not on a scale or frequency to be considered an attack directed against a civilian population

Limaj et al., (Trial Chamber), November 30, 2005, paras. 225, 228: "To acknowledge the abduction of specific civilians, whether Serbian or Kosovo Albanian, (...) does not demonstrate, however, at least in the established circumstances of this case, that the KLA [Kosovo Liberation Army] had a policy[[15]] to target a 'civilian population.' The evidence does indicate that some abducted Serbs suspected of being military or police were subjected to considerable violence and otherwise mistreated as an interrogation technique

et al., (Trial Chamber), November 30, 2005, paras. 212, 184 ("The existence of a plan or policy can be indicative of the systematic character of offences charged as crimes against humanity." However, "[t]he existence of a policy or plan (...) is not a legal requirement, to establish the widespread or systematic nature of the attack and that it was directed against a civilian population.").

as the KLA sought to verify suspicions. A number of abducted Serbs, apparently civilian, were later murdered by the KLA. Others have not been heard from since their abduction or since they were seen in KLA custody. However, some were released. The evidence does not allow a determination in most cases as to why some were released, but others not. Clearly, in many cases there was a process of decision by the KLA. On what basis that process of decision turned is not, however, established by the evidence. In many, but not all, cases, connection with the Serbian police or military or involvement in armed civilian or paramilitary forces engaged against the KLA may be a, or the, determinative factor. Whatever was the basis, the existence of a process of decision which affected the consequences of KLA abduction tells with some force against the existence and perpetration of a general KLA strategy of abduction of the Serbian civilian population of Kosovo. The evidence does not establish that the abduction, detention or mistreatment of Serbian civilians was on a scale or frequency such that the attack could be considered to have been directed against a civilian population."

"Upon consideration of the evidence before it, the Chamber finds that at the time relevant to the Indictment there was no attack by the KLA directed against a 'civilian population,' whether Kosovo Albanian or Serbian in ethnicity, and no attack that could be said to indicate a 'widespread' scale; however, as indicated earlier there is evidence of a level of systematic or coordinated organisation to the abduction and detention of certain individuals. While the KLA evinced a policy to target those Kosovo Albanians suspected of collaboration with the Serbian authorities, the Chamber finds that there was no attack directed against a civilian population, whether of Serbian or Albanian ethnicity (...) It has not been established that Article 5 applies in the present case."

(b) events in Prijedor constituted an attack directed against a civilian population

Stakic, (Trial Chamber), July 31, 2003, para. 627: "The Trial Chamber is satisfied that the events which took place in [the] Prijedor municipality between 30 April and 30 September 1992 constitute an attack directed against a civilian population. The scale of the attack was such that it cannot be characterised as having been directed against only a limited and randomly selected group of individuals. Rather, most of the non-Serb population in the Municipality of Prijedor was directly affected. Moreover, it is clear from the combat reports that the Serb military forces had the overwhelming power as compared to the modest resistance forces of the non-Serbs. General Wilmot, who testified as the military expert in the Defence case, acknowledged that the scale of the attack on Hambarine was disproportionate to the threat posed by the resistance forces active in those areas. Those attacks, and the ones that followed in the broader Brdo region, coupled with the arrests, detention and deportation of citizens that came next, were primarily directed against the non-Serb civilian population in the Municipality of Prijedor."

v) the attack must be "widespread or systematic" (element 4)

(1) widespread or systematic

Deronjic, (Appeals Chamber), July 20, 2005, para. 109: "[I]n order to constitute a crime against humanity, the acts of an accused must be part of a widespread or systematic attack directed against any civilian population(...)" *See also Kordic and Cerkez,* (Appeals Chamber), December 17, 2004, para. 93 (similar).

Blaskic, (Appeals Chamber), July 29, 2004, para. 102: "[T]he Appeals Chamber concludes that the Trial Chamber [in *Blaskic*] was correct in stating that acts constituting crimes against humanity must be part of a widespread or systematic attack against civilians."

Kunarac, Kovac, and Vukovic, (Appeals Chamber) June 12, 2002, para. 97: "The Trial Chamber thus correctly found that the attack must be either 'widespread' or 'systematic', that is, that the requirement is disjunctive rather than cumulative." *See also Limaj et al.*, (Trial Chamber), November 30, 2005, para. 183 (similar); *Brdjanin,* (Trial Chamber), September 1, 2004, para. 135 (same as *Limaj*).

Galic, (Trial Chamber), December 5, 2003, para. 146: "The attack must be widespread or systematic." *See also Simic, Tadic, and Zaric,* (Trial Chamber), October 17, 2003, para. 43 (similar); *Naletilic and Martinovic,* (Trial Chamber), March 31, 2003, para. 236 (similar).

(2) only the attack, not the accused's acts, must be widespread or systematic

Deronjic, (Appeals Chamber), July 20, 2005, para. 109: "[T]his requirement [of a widespread or systematic attack] only applies to the attack and not to the individual acts of the accused."

Kordic and Cerkez, (Appeals Chamber), December 17, 2004, para. 94: "Only the attack, not the individual acts of the accused, must be widespread or systematic." *See also Blaskic,* (Appeals Chamber), July 29, 2004, para. 101 (same); *Kunarac, Kovac, and Vukovic,* (Appeals Chamber) June 12, 2002, para. 96 (same); *Limaj et al.*, (Trial Chamber), November 30, 2005, para.

189 (same); *Brdjanin*, (Trial Chamber), September 1, 2004, para. 135 (similar); *Simic, Tadic, and Zaric*, (Trial Chamber), October 17, 2003, para. 43; *Kunarac, Kovac and Vukovic*, (Trial Chamber), February 22, 2001, para. 431 (same).

(3) widespread

Kordic and Cerkez, (Appeals Chamber), December 17, 2004, para. 94: "In relation to the widespread or systematic nature of the attack, the Appeals Chamber notes the jurisprudence of the International Tribunal according to which the phrase 'widespread' refers to the large-scale nature of the attack and the number of targeted persons(...)" *See also Blaskic*, (Appeals Chamber), July 29, 2004, para. 101 (same).

Limaj et al., (Trial Chamber), November 30, 2005, para. 183: "The term 'widespread' refers to the large scale nature of the attack and the number of victims(...)" *See also Blagojevic and Jokic*, (Trial Chamber), January 17, 2005, para. 545 (same); *Brdjanin*, (Trial Chamber), September 1, 2004, para. 135 (similar); *Galic*, (Trial Chamber), December 5, 2003, para. 146 (similar); *Simic, Tadic, and Zaric*, (Trial Chamber), October 17, 2003, para. 43 (similar); *Stakic*, (Trial Chamber), July 31, 2003, para. 625 (same).

Blagojevic and Jokic, (Trial Chamber), January 17, 2005, para. 545: A crime may be widespread by the 'cumulative effect of a series of inhumane acts or the singular effect of an inhumane act of extraordinary magnitude.'" *See also Naletilic and Martinovic*, (Trial Chamber), March 31, 2003, para. 236 (same as *Kordic*); *Kordic and Cerkez*, (Trial Chamber), February 26, 2001, para. 179 (similar).

(4) systematic

Kordic and Cerkez, (Appeals Chamber), December 17, 2004, para. 94: "[T] he phrase 'systematic' refers to the organised nature of the acts of violence and the improbability of their random occurrence." *See also Blaskic*, (Appeals Chamber), July 29, 2004, para. 101 (same); *Limaj et al.*, (Trial Chamber), November 30, 2005, para. 183 (same); *Simic, Tadic, and Zaric*, (Trial Chamber), October 17, 2003, para. 43 (same); *Stakic*, (Trial Chamber), July 31, 2003, para. 625 (same); *Naletilic and Martinovic*, (Trial Chamber), March 31, 2003, para. 236 (similar).

Kordic and Cerkez, (Appeals Chamber), December 17, 2004, para. 94: "Patterns of crimes, in the sense of the non-accidental repetition of similar criminal conduct on a regular basis, are a common expression of such systematic occurrence." *See also Blaskic*, (Appeals Chamber), July 29, 2004, para. 101 (same); *Kunarac, Kovac, and Vokovic,* (Appeals Chamber), June 12, 2002 (similar); *Limaj et al.*, (Trial Chamber), November 30, 2005, para. 183 (same).

Blagojevic and Jokic, (Trial Chamber), January 17, 2005, para. 545: "The term 'systematic' refers to an 'organised nature of the acts of violence and the improbability of their random occurrence,' and is often expressed through patterns of crimes, in the sense of non-accidental repetition of similar criminal conduct on a regular basis."

Brdjanin, (Trial Chamber), September 1, 2004, para. 135: "[T]he term 'systematic' refers to the organised nature of the acts of violence and the non-accidental recurrence of similar criminal conduct on a regular basis."

Galic, (Trial Chamber), December 5, 2003, para. 146: "'[S]ystematic' refers to the organized nature of the attack."

Blaskic, (Trial Chamber), March 3, 2000, para. 203: "The systematic character refers to four elements which (...) may be expressed as follows: [1] the existence of a political objective, a plan pursuant to which the attack is perpetrated or an ideology, in the broad sense of the word, that is, to destroy, persecute or weaken a community; [2] the perpetration of a criminal act on a very large scale against a group of civilians or the repeated and continuous commission of inhumane acts linked to one another; [3] the preparation and use of significant public or private resources, whether military or other; [4] the implication of high-level political and/or military authorities in the definition and establishment of the methodical plan."[16]

(5) assessing widespread or systematic

Kunarac, Kovac, and Vukovic, (Appeals Chamber) June 12, 2002, para. 95: "A Trial Chamber must (...) 'first identify the population which is the object of the attack and, in light of the means, methods, resources and result of the attack upon the population, ascertain whether the attack was indeed widespread or systematic.'" *See also Limaj et al.*, (Trial Chamber), November 30, 2005, para. 183 (similar); *Galic,* (Trial Chamber), December 5, 2003, para. 146 (similar); *Simic, Tadic, and Zaric,* (Trial Chamber), October 17, 2003, para. 43 (similar).

(a) factors to consider

Kunarac, Kovac, and Vukovic, (Appeals Chamber) June 12, 2002, para. 95: "The consequences of the attack upon the targeted population, the number of victims, the nature of the acts, the possible participation of officials or authorities or any identifiable patterns of crimes, could be taken into account to determine whether the attack satisfies either or both requirements of a 'widespread' or 'systematic' attack vis-à-vis this civilian population." *See also Limaj et al.*, (Trial Chamber), November 30, 2005, para. 183 (same);

Simic, Tadic, and Zaric, (Trial Chamber), October 17, 2003, para. 43 (similar); *Stakic*, (Trial Chamber), July 31, 2003, para. 625 (similar).

Blagojevic and Jokic, (Trial Chamber), January 17, 2005, para. 546: "The Appeals Chamber (...) provided a non-exhaustive list of factors that could be taken into account in determining whether an attack meets the requirements of 'widespread' or 'systematic.' These factors are: the consequences of the attack upon the targeted population, the number of victims, the nature of the acts, the possible participation of officials or authorities or any identifiable patterns of crimes." *See also Brdjanin*, (Trial Chamber), September 1, 2004, para. 136 (similar).

Jelisic, (Trial Chamber), December 14, 1999, para. 53: "The existence of an acknowledged policy targeting a particular community, the establishment of parallel institutions meant to implement this policy, the involvement of high-level political or military authorities, the employment of considerable financial, military or other resources and the scale or the repeated, unchanging and continuous nature of the violence committed against a particular civilian population are among the factors which may demonstrate the widespread or systematic nature of an attack."[17]

(6) single act, if linked to a widespread or systematic attack, may qualify as a crime against humanity

Deronjic, (Appeals Chamber), July 20, 2005, para. 109: "[A]ll other conditions being met, a single or limited number of acts on [the accused's] part would qualify as a crime against humanity, unless those acts may be said to be isolated or random." *See also Kordic and Cerkez,* (Appeals Chamber), December 17, 2004, para. 94 (similar); *Blaskic,* (Appeals Chamber), July 29, 2004, para. 101 (same as *Kordic*); *Kunarac, Kovac, and Vukovic,* (Appeals Chamber) June 12, 2002, para. 96 (same as *Kordic*); *Brdjanin*, (Trial Chamber), September 1, 2004, para. 135 (similar).

Simic, Tadic, and Zaric, (Trial Chamber), October 17, 2003, para. 43: "Provided that the acts of the individual are sufficiently linked to the widespread or systematic attack, and are not found to be random or isolated, it is possible that a single act could be found to be a crime against humanity." *Kordic and Cerkez,* (Trial Chamber), February 26, 2001, para. 178: "[A] single isolated act by a perpetrator, if linked to a widespread or systematic attack, could constitute a crime against humanity."

Kupreskic et al., (Trial Chamber), January 14, 2000, para. 550: "[I]n certain circumstances, a single act has comprised a crime against humanity when it occurred within the necessary context. An *isolated* act, however – i.e. an atrocity which did not occur within such a context – cannot."

(7) no plan or policy required, although may be useful to show the attack was widespread or systematic

Kordic and Cerkez, (Appeals Chamber), December 17, 2004, para. 98: "The Appeals Chamber notes that the Prosecution has withdrawn its first ground of appeal [regarding whether the acts of the accused and the attack must have been committed in pursuance to a pre-existing criminal policy or plan]. [S]ince the *Kunarac et al.* Appeal Judgement, the jurisprudence on this point is settled."

Blaskic, (Appeals Chamber), July 29, 2004, para. 120: "In relation to this issue [whether the existence of a plan is a legal element of a crime against humanity], the Appeals Chamber has stated, on a previous occasion:

. . . neither the attack nor the acts of the accused needs to be supported by any form of 'policy' or 'plan.' There was nothing in the Statute or in customary international law at the time of the alleged acts which required proof of the existence of a plan or policy to commit these crimes. As indicated above, proof that the attack was directed against a civilian population and that it was widespread or systematic, are legal elements of the crime. But to prove these elements, it is not necessary to show that they were the result of the existence of a policy or plan. It may be useful in establishing that the attack was directed against a civilian population and that it was widespread or systematic (especially the latter) to show that there was in fact a policy or plan, but it may be possible to prove these things by reference to other matters. Thus, the existence of a policy or plan may be evidentially relevant, but it is not a legal element of the crime.

The Appeals Chamber agrees that a plan or policy is not a legal element of a crime against humanity, though it may be evidentially relevant in proving that an attack was directed against a civilian population and that it was widespread or systematic." *See also Limaj et al.*, (Trial Chamber), November 30, 2005, para. 184 (similar to last sentence).

Blaskic, (Appeals Chamber), July 29, 2004, paras. 100, 126: "In the view of the Appeals Chamber, the existence of a plan or policy may be evidentially relevant, but is not a legal element of the crime." "There is no legal requirement of a plan or policy, and the Trial Chamber's statement is misleading in this regard(...)" *Reversing on this point Blaskic*, (Trial Chamber), March 3, 2000, para. 204. *See also Krstic*, (Appeals Chamber), April 19, 2004, para. 225 (similar to *Blaskic*); *Kunarac, Kovac, and Vokovic*, (Appeals Chamber), June 12, 2002, para. 98 (similar to *Blaskic*).

Limaj et al., (Trial Chamber), November 30, 2005, para. 212: "The existence of a plan or policy can be indicative of the systematic character of offences charged as crimes against humanity. The existence of a 'policy' to conduct an attack against a civilian population is most easily determined or inferred when a State's conduct is in question; but absence of a policy does not mean that a widespread or systematic attack against a civilian population has not occurred. Although not a legal element of Article 5, evidence of a policy or plan is an important indication that the acts in question are not merely the workings of individuals acting pursuant to haphazard or individual design, but instead have a level of organisational coherence and support of a magnitude sufficient to elevate them into the realm of crimes against humanity. It stands to reason that an attack against a civilian population will most often evince the presence of policy when the acts in question are performed against the backdrop of significant State action and where formal channels of command can be discerned."

Blagojevic and Jokic, (Trial Chamber), January 17, 2005, para. 546: "Neither the attack nor the acts of the accused need to be supported by a 'policy' or 'plan.'"

Brdjanin, (Trial Chamber), September 1, 2004, para. 137: "There is no requirement under customary international law that the acts of the accused need to be supported by any form of policy or plan. The existence of a policy or plan may evidentially be relevant to the requirements of a widespread or systematic attack and the accused's participation in the attack, but it is not a legal element of the crime." *See also Galic*, (Trial Chamber), December 5, 2003, para. 147 (similar); *Simic, Tadic, and Zaric*, (Trial Chamber), October 17, 2003, para. 44 (similar).

(a) a level of de facto control over territory necessary to demonstrate that a sub-state unit or armed opposition group has a policy to direct an attack

Limaj et al., (Trial Chamber), November 30, 2005, para. 213: "Special issues arise (...) in considering whether a sub-state unit or armed opposition group, whether insurrectionist or trans-boundary in nature, evinces a policy to direct an attack. One requirement such an organisational unit must demonstrate in order to have sufficient competence to formulate a policy is a level of *de facto* control over territory. As was said by the Trial Chamber in *Prosecutor v Tadic*: 'the law in relation to crimes against humanity has developed to take into account forces which, although not those of the legitimate government, have de facto control over, or are able to move freely within, defined territory.'"[18]

(8) both civilian status of the victims and scale or level of organization characterize a crime against humanity

Blaskic, (Appeals Chamber), July 29, 2004, para. 107: "In this case, the Trial Chamber correctly recognized that a crime against humanity applies to acts directed against any civilian population. However, it stated that 'the specificity of a crime against humanity results not from the status of the victim but the scale and organisation in which it must be committed.' The Appeals Chamber considers that *both* the status of the victim as a civilian and the scale on which it is committed or the level of organization involved characterize a crime against humanity." (emphasis added)

(9) application—widespread or systematic attack

(a) attacks carried out by Croats against the Bosnian Muslim civilian population in Central Bosnia widespread, systematic and directed against a civilian population

Kordic and Cerkez, (Appeals Chamber), December 17, 2004, paras. 666-669: "[F]or determining when the common elements of crimes against humanity have been established,' [t]he first issue is whether a reasonable trier of fact could have concluded beyond reasonable doubt that there was a widespread or systematic attack directed against any civilian population(...)"
"In January 1993 in the town of Busovaca, numerous civilians were targeted and killed, and the following crimes were committed:
-murder, a crime against humanity;
-unlawful attacks on civilians and civilian objects;
-wanton destruction not justified by military necessity;
-and plunder of public or private property."
"The following crimes were committed in Central Bosnia, in April and/or June 1993, *inter alia*, in:
-Ahmici: the massacre, which was directed against the civilian population;
-Santici: unlawful attack on civilians and civilian objects; murder, a crime against humanity; and wanton destruction not justified by military necessity;
-Nadioci, Pirici: unlawful attack on civilians; murder, a crime against humanity;
-Gacice: wanton destruction not justified by military necessity;

-Veceriska/Donja Veceriska: unlawful attack on civilian objects and wanton destruction not justified by military necessity;
-Ocehnici: wanton destruction not justified by military necessity;
-Kiseljak municipality: unlawful attack on civilians, murder, a crime against humanity, inhumane acts, a crime against humanity, and plunder of public or private property in Rotilj in April 1993; wanton destruction not justified by military necessity in Svinjarevo, Gomionica, Visnjica, Polje Visnjica, Behrici, and Gromiljak in April 1993; plunder of public or private property in Gomionica; murder and inhumane acts, crimes against humanity, and plunder of public or private property in Tulica in June 1993; and murder, a crime against humanity, and destruction or wilful damage to institutions dedicated to religion or education in Han-Ploca in June 1993; and wanton destruction not justified by military necessity and plunder of public or private property in Han-Ploca-Grahovci in June 1993;
-Kaonik, the Dubravica Elementary School, the SDK building, the Vitez Cinema, the village of Rotilj, the Kiseljak barracks; and the Kiseljak municipal building: unlawful confinement of civilians." "These findings, upheld above by the Appeals Chamber and underpinned by evidence discussed at length in this Judgement, demonstrate that there were attacks carried out by Croats against the Bosnian Muslim civilian population in Central Bosnia from January to June 1993. They have to be characterised as widespread, systematic and directed against a civilian population."

(b) there was a widespread or systematic attack against the Bosnian Muslim and Bosnian Croat civilian population in the Bosnian Krajina

Brdjanin, (Trial Chamber), September 1, 2004, paras. 157-158: "The Trial Chamber is satisfied beyond reasonable doubt that there was a widespread or systematic attack against the Bosnian Muslim and Bosnian Croat civilian population in the Bosnian Krajina during the period relevant to the Indictment [April 1, 1992 through December 31, 1992]. The attack took many forms. By the end of 1992, nearly all Bosnian Muslims and Bosnian Croats had been dismissed from their jobs in, amongst others, the media, the army, the police, the judiciary and public companies. Numerous crimes were committed against Bosnian Muslims and Bosnian Croats, including murder, torture, beatings, rape, plunder and the destruction of property. Villages were shelled, houses were torched and looted. In the spring of 1992, a number of detention camps where Bosnian Muslim and Bosnian Croat civilians were arrested and detained *en masse* were established throughout the [Autonomous Region of Krajina ("ARK")]. In several instances, mass killings of civilians took place. Moreover, a policy of 'ethnically cleansing' the ARK of its non-Serb population was systematically implemented by the Bosnian Serbs. Indeed, tens of thousands of Bosnian Muslims and Bosnian Croats were forcibly expelled from the ARK by the Bosnian Serbs and taken in convoys of buses and trains to Bosnian Muslim held territory in [Bosnia-Herzegovina] or to Croatia. On the basis of the pattern of conduct by which these crimes were committed throughout the Bosnian Krajina, the Trial Chamber is satisfied that they were mostly perpetrated with a view to implement the Strategic Plan." *See Brdjanin,* (Trial Chamber), September 1, 2004, para. 65 (the "Strategic Plan" consisted of "the Bosnian Serb leadership, including the members of the Main Board of the [Serbian Democratic Party] and other members of the [Serbian Democratic Party], as well as Bosnian Serb representatives of the armed forces, form[ing] a plan to link Serb-populated areas in [Bosnia and Herzegovina] together, to gain control over these areas and to create a separate Bosnian Serb state, from which most non-Serbs would be permanently removed(...)").

(c) plan to rid Prijedor municipality of non-Serbs was a widespread and systematic attack against the civilian population

Stakic, (Trial Chamber), July 31, 2003, paras. 629-630: The Trial Chamber stated as to the "systematic" nature of the attack: "The Chamber is satisfied that the attack directed against the civilian population was prepared as of 7 January 1992 when the Assembly of the Serbian People in Prijedor was first established. The plan to rid the Prijedor municipality of non-Serbs and others not loyal to the Serb authorities was activated through the takeover of power by Serbs on 30 April 1992. Thereafter the attack directed against the civilian population intensified, according to the plan, culminating with the attacks on Hambarine and Kozarac in late May 1992. Attacks on predominantly non-Serb areas including the Brdo region ensued, with hundreds of non-Serbs killed and many more arrested and detained by the Serb authorities, *inter alia* in detention facilities."

"Having established that the attack was systematic, it is not strictly necessary to consider the requirement that the attack be widespread. Nonetheless, the Chamber finds that the attack on the non-Serb population of Prijedor was also widespread. The attacks, as such, occurred throughout the municipality of Prijedor, initially in Hambarine and Kozarac, and then spreading to the whole of the Brdo region. Moreover, thousands of citizens of Prijedor municipality passed through one or more of the three main detention camps, Omarska, Keraterm and Trnopolje, established in the towns of Omarska, Prijedor and Trnopolje respectively."

vi) mens rea (element 5)

Kordic and Cerkez, (Appeals Chamber), December 17, 2004, para. 99: "The Appeals Chamber considers that the *mens rea* of crimes against humanity is satisfied when the accused has the requisite intent to commit the underlying offence(s) with which he is charged, and when he knows that there is an attack on the civilian population and also knows that his acts comprise part of that attack." *See also Blaskic,* (Appeals Chamber), July 29, 2004, para. 124 (same).

Blagojevic and Jokic, (Trial Chamber), January 17, 2005, para. 548: "The accused must possess the necessary *mens rea,* which includes:
(i) the intent to commit the underlying offence or offences with which he is charged;
(ii) the knowledge that there is an attack against the civilian population; and
(iii) the knowledge that his acts comprise part of that attack."

See also Brdjanin, (Trial Chamber), September 1, 2004, para. 138 (similar); *Galic,* (Trial Chamber), December 5, 2003, para. 148 (similar).

Kupreskic et al., (Trial Chamber), January 14, 2000, para. 556: "[T]he requisite *mens rea* for crimes against humanity appears to be comprised by (1) the *intent* to commit the underlying offence, combined with (2) *knowledge* of the broader context in which that offence occurs."

(1) intent

(a) the perpetrator must have intent to commit the underlying offense(s)

Kordic and Cerkez, (Appeals Chamber), December 17, 2004, para. 99: "[T] he accused [must have had] the requisite intent to commit the underlying offence(s) with which he is charged(...)" *Blaskic,* (Appeals Chamber), July 29, 2004, para. 124 (same); *Vasiljevic,* (Trial Chamber), November 29, 2002, para. 37 (similar).

(b) discriminatory intent only required for persecution

Tadic, (Appeals Chamber), July 15, 1999, paras. 283, 292, 305: "The ordinary meaning of Article 5 makes it clear that this provision does not require all crimes against humanity to have been perpetrated with a discriminatory intent. Such intent is only made necessary for one sub-category of those crimes, namely 'persecutions provided for in Article 5 (h).'" "[C]ustomary international law, as it results from the gradual development of international instruments and national case-law into general rules, does not presuppose a discriminatory or persecutory intent for all crimes against humanity." "[T] he Trial Chamber erred in finding that all crimes against humanity require a discriminatory intent. Such an intent is an indispensable legal ingredient of the offence only with regard to those crimes for which this is expressly required, that is, for Article 5 (h), concerning various types of persecution."

Kordic and Cerkez, (Trial Chamber), February 26, 2001, para. 186: "The Appeals Chamber in *Tadic* clarified another issue in relation to the requisite *mens rea* for crimes against humanity. It rejected the view that to constitute a crime against humanity all relevant acts or omissions must be undertaken by the perpetrator on discriminatory grounds. [D]iscriminatory intent 'is an indispensable legal ingredient of the offence only with regard to those crimes for which this is expressly required, that is, for Article 5(h), concerning various types of persecution.'"

Blaskic, (Trial Chamber), March 3, 2000, paras. 244, 260: "[T]o be judged guilty of crimes against humanity, except in the case of persecution, [the perpetrator] [need] not have had the intent of targeting civilians because of their race or their religious or political beliefs."
"[F]or a widespread or systematic attack and the resultant crimes – murder, extermination, enslavement, deportation, imprisonment, torture, rape or other inhumane acts with the exception of persecution – to be characterised as crimes against humanity they need not have been perpetrated with the deliberate intent to cause injury to a civilian population on the basis of specific characteristics. [T]o be found guilty of such an offence, those responsible for the attack need not necessarily have acted with a particular racial, national, religious or political intent in mind."

Todorovic, Case No. IT-95-9/1 (Trial Chamber), July 31, 2001, para. 113: The crime of persecution "is the only crime against humanity which requires that the perpetrator act with a discriminatory intent and, by its nature, it incorporates other crimes."

(2) knowledge

(a) the perpetrator must knowingly participate in a widespread or systematic attack, i.e., have knowledge of the attack and that his act is part of the attack

Kordic and Cerkez, (Appeals Chamber), December 17, 2004, para. 100: "The Appeals Chamber reiterates its case law pursuant to which knowledge on the part of the accused that there is an attack on the civilian population, as well as knowledge that his act is part thereof, is required." *See also Blaskic,* (Appeals Chamber), July 29, 2004, para. 126 (same).

Kunarac, Kovac, and Vokovic, (Appeals Chamber), June 12, 2002, para. 99: There must be "knowledge on the part of the accused that there is an attack on the civilian population and that his act is part thereof." *See also Limaj et al.*, (Trial Chamber), November 30, 2005, para. 188 (same); *Blagojevic and Jokic,* (Trial Chamber), January 17, 2005, para. 547 (same).

Tadic, (Appeals Chamber), July 15, 1999, para. 271: "The Trial Chamber correctly recognised that crimes which are unrelated to widespread or systematic attacks on a civilian population should not be prosecuted as crimes against humanity. Thus to convict an accused of crimes against humanity, it must be proved that the crimes were *related* to the attack on a civilian population (occurring during an armed conflict) and that the accused *knew* that his crimes were so related."

Limaj et al., (Trial Chamber), November 30, 2005, para. 190: "The second requirement to be established as part of the 'nexus' requirement is the knowledge of the accused that there is an attack on a civilian population and that his or her acts are part thereof."

Simic, Tadic and Zaric, (Trial Chamber), October 17, 2003, para. 45: "To satisfy the subjective or *mens rea* element of the nexus between the acts of the accused and the attack, the perpetrator must know of the wider context in which his acts occur, and know that his acts are part of the attack."

Kordic and Cerkez, (Trial Chamber), February 26, 2001, para. 185: "'[T] he perpetrator must knowingly commit crimes against humanity in the sense that he must understand the overall context of his act. [. . .] Part of what transforms an individual's act(s) into a crime against humanity is the inclusion of the act within a greater dimension of criminal conduct; therefore an accused should be aware of this greater dimension in order to be culpable thereof. Accordingly, actual or constructive knowledge of the broader context of the attack, meaning that the accused must know that his act(s) is part of a widespread or systematic attack on a civilian population and pursuant to some sort of policy or plan, is necessary to satisfy the requisite *mens rea* element of the accused.'"[19]
Kunarac, Kovac, and Vukovic, (Trial Chamber), February 22, 2001, para. 410: In addition to the statutory requirement of an armed conflict, the following sub-elements are necessary: " (...) v) The perpetrator must know of the wider context in which his acts occur and know that his acts are part of the attack."

Blaskic, (Trial Chamber), March 3, 2000, para. 244: "The perpetrator must knowingly participate in a widespread or systematic attack against a civilian population."

Blaskic, (Trial Chamber), March 3, 2000, para. 247: "The accused must first have knowledge of the general context in which his acts occur and then of the nexus between his action and that context."

Jelisic, (Trial Chamber), December 14, 1999, para. 56: "The accused must (...) be aware that the underlying crime which he is committing forms part of the widespread and systematic attack."

(b) it does not suffice that the perpetrator knew of the attack and took the risk his acts were part of it

Blaskic, (Appeals Chamber), July 29, 2004, para. 126: "In relation to the *mens rea* applicable to crimes against humanity, the Appeals Chamber reiterates its case law pursuant to which knowledge on the part of the accused that there is an attack on the civilian population, as well as knowledge that his act is part thereof, is required. The Trial Chamber, in stating that it 'suffices that he knowingly took the risk of participating in the implementation of the ideology, policy or plan,' did not correctly articulate the *mens rea* applicable to crimes against humanity. Moreover, as stated above, there is no legal requirement of a plan or policy, and the Trial Chamber's statement is misleading in this regard."

See also Limaj et al., (Trial Chamber), November 30, 2005, para. 190: "It does not suffice that an accused knowingly took the risk of participating in the implementation of a policy."

But see Kunarac, Kovac, and Vokovic, (Appeals Chamber), June 12, 2002, para. 102: "[T]he accused must have had the intent to commit the underlying offence or offences with which he is charged, and that he must have known 'that there is an attack on the civilian population and that his acts comprise part of that attack, or at least that he took the risk that his acts were part of the attack.'" *See also Simic, Tadic, and Zaric,* (Trial Chamber), October 17, 2003, para. 46 (similar); *Stakic*, (Trial Chamber), July 31, 2003, para. 626 (similar); *Vasiljevic,* (Trial Chamber), November 29, 2002, para. 37 (the perpetrator "must know 'that there is an attack on the civilian population and that his acts comprise part of that attack, or at least [that he took] the risk that his acts were part of the attack.'"); *Krnojelac,* (Trial Chamber), March 15, 2002, para. 59 (similar to *Kunarac*); *Krnojelac,* (Trial Chamber), March 15, 2002, para. 59 (similar to *Vasiljevic*).

(c) knowledge of the details of the attack not required

Kunarac, Kovac, and Vokovic, (Appeals Chamber), June 12, 2002, para. 102: "This requirement [that the accused have knowledge of the attack] does not entail knowledge of the details of the attack." *See also Blagojevic and Jokic,* (Trial Chamber), January 17, 2005, para. 548: "The *mens rea* requirement (...) does not entail knowledge of the details of the attack." *See also Brdjanin*, (Trial Chamber), September 1, 2004, para. 138 (similar); *Galic*,

(Trial Chamber), December 5, 2003, para. 148 (similar); *Krnojelac,* (Trial Chamber), March 15, 2002, para. 59 (similar).

Limaj et al., (Trial Chamber), November 30, 2005, para. 190: "[T]he accused need not know the details of the attack (...) The accused merely needs to understand the overall context in which his or her acts took place."

Simic, Tadic and Zaric, (Trial Chamber), October 17, 2003, para. 45: "It is well established that the accused need not know the details of the attack, (...) :
It is the attack, not the acts of the accused, which must be directed against the target population, and the accused need only know that his acts are part thereof."

(d) no requirement that the perpetrator approve of the context or share the purpose or goal behind the attack

Kordic and Cerkez, (Appeals Chamber), December 17, 2004, para. 99: "'[T] he accused need not share the purpose or goal behind the attack.'" *See also Blaskic,* (Appeals Chamber), July 29, 2004, para. 124 (same); *Kunarac, Kovac, and Vokovic,* (Appeals Chamber), June 12, 2002, para. 103 (same); *Blagojevic and Jokic,* (Trial Chamber), January 17, 2005, para. 548 (same); *Brdjanin,* (Trial Chamber), September 1, 2004, para. 138 (same); *Galic,* (Trial Chamber), December 5, 2003, para. 148 (similar).

Limaj et al., (Trial Chamber), November 30, 2005, para. 190: "[T]he accused need not (...) approve of the context in which his or her acts occur." *See also Kordic and Cerkez,* (Trial Chamber), February 26, 2001, para. 185 (similar).

Simic, Tadic and Zaric, (Trial Chamber), October 17, 2003, para. 45: The accused need not "share the motive, intent, or purpose of those involved in the attack."

(e) motive generally irrelevant

Kordic and Cerkez, (Appeals Chamber), December 17, 2004, para. 99: "[T] he Appeals Chamber considers that: "[f]or criminal liability pursuant to Article 5 of the Statute [to attach], 'the motives of the accused for taking part in the attack are irrelevant and a crime against humanity may be committed for purely personal reasons(...) At most, evidence that [the perpetrator] committed the acts for purely personal reasons could be indicative of a rebuttable assumption that he was not aware that his acts were part of that attack.'" *See also Blaskic,* (Appeals Chamber), July 29, 2004, para. 124 (same language as quoted); *Kunarac, Kovac, and Vokovic,* (Appeals Chamber), June 12, 2002, para. 103 (quoting some of the same language).

Krnojelac, (Appeals Chamber), September 17, 2003, para. 102: "The Appeals Chamber (...) recalls its case-law in the *Jelisic* case which, with regard to the specific intent required for the crime of genocide, sets out 'the necessity to distinguish specific intent from motive. The personal motive of the perpetrator of the crime of genocide may be, for example, to obtain personal economic benefits, or political advantage or some form of power. The existence of a personal motive does not preclude the perpetrator from also having the specific intent to commit genocide.' It is the Appeals Chamber's belief that *this distinction between intent and motive must also be applied to the other crimes laid down in the Statute.*" (emphasis added) *See also Jelisic,* (Appeals Chamber), July 5, 2001, para. 49 (same quoted language).

Tadic, (Appeals Chamber), July 15, 1999, paras. 270, 272: "[U]nder customary law, 'purely personal motives' do not acquire any relevance for establishing whether or not a crime against humanity has been perpetrated." "[I]n the opinion of the Appeals Chamber, the requirement that an act must not have been carried out for the purely personal motives of the perpetrator does not form part of the prerequisites necessary for conduct to fall within the definition of a crime against humanity under Article 5 of the Tribunal's Statute."

Limaj et al., (Trial Chamber), November 30, 2005, para. 190: "The motives for the accused's participation in the attack are irrelevant. . . ." *See also Brdjanin,* (Trial Chamber), September 1, 2004, para. 138 (similar); *Kordic and Cerkez,* (Trial Chamber), February 26, 2001, para. 187 (similar).

(f) it is irrelevant whether the accused intended his acts to be directed against the targeted population or merely against the victim

Kordic and Cerkez, (Appeals Chamber), December 17, 2004, para. 99: "'It is (...) irrelevant whether the accused intended his acts to be directed against the targeted population or merely against his victim. It is the attack, not the acts of the accused, which must be directed against the target population and the accused need only know that his acts are part thereof.'" *See also Blaskic,* (Appeals Chamber), July 29, 2004, para. 124 (same); *Kunarac, Kovac, and Vokovic,* (Appeals Chamber), June 12, 2002, para. 103 (same); *Limaj et al.*, (Trial Chamber), November 30, 2005, para. 190 (similar).

(g) evidence of knowledge will vary from case to case

Blaskic, (Appeals Chamber), July 29, 2004, para. 126: "[T]he Appeals Chamber considers that evidence of knowledge on the part of the accused depends on the facts of a particular case; as a result, the manner in which this legal element may be proved may vary from case to case. Therefore, the Appeals Chamber declines to set out a list of evidentiary elements which, if proved, would establish the requisite knowledge on the part of the accused."

Limaj et al., (Trial Chamber), November 30, 2005, para. 190: "Evidence of knowledge depends on the facts of a particular case; as a result, the manner in which this legal element may be proved may vary from case to case."

(h) whether there are factors from which to infer knowledge of context

Blaskic, (Appeals Chamber), July 29, 2004, paras. 125, 127-128: "[The Trial Chamber stated:]
it must, for example, be proved that:
– the accused willingly agreed to carry out the functions he was performing;
– that these functions resulted in his collaboration with the political, military or civilian authorities defining the ideology, policy or plan at the root of the crimes;
– that he received orders relating to the ideology, policy or plan; and lastly
– that he contributed to its commission through intentional acts or by simply refusing of his own accord to take the measures necessary to prevent their perpetration."
"The Appeals Chamber (...) observes that the Trial Chamber's list of four points which may serve as proof of the *mens rea* suffers from a number of defects. The first point, that the accused 'willingly agreed to carry out the functions he was performing,' is vague and does not necessarily relate to the *mens rea* applicable to crimes against humanity. The second and third points, as well as the first part of the fourth point, may be misleading because they could be interpreted as suggesting that an ideology, policy, or plan is required. Further, they too do not relate with sufficient precision to the requirement that the accused must know that his acts form part of the criminal attack. Finally, the second part of the fourth point seems to relate to command responsibility under Article 7(3), rather than Article 7(1) responsibility for crimes against humanity."
"For the foregoing reasons, the Appeals Chamber finds that the Trial Chamber erred in part in its articulation of the *mens rea* applicable to crimes against humanity."

Compare Blaskic, (Trial Chamber), March 3, 2000, paras. 258-259: "[K]nowledge of the political context in which the offence fits may be surmised from the concurrence of a number of concrete facts" and "these are: [a] the historical and political circumstances in which the acts of violence occurred; [b] the functions of the accused when the crimes were committed; [c] his responsibilities within the political or military hierarchy; [d] the direct and indirect relationship between the political and military hierarchy; [e] the scope and gravity of the acts perpetrated; [f] the nature of the crimes committed and the degree to which they are common knowledge."

(i) application—mens rea: whether the acts of the accused formed part of a widespread and systematic attack and the accused knew of the attack

Vasiljevic, (Appeals Chamber), February 25, 2004, paras. 28, 30: "The Appellant argues that the Trial Chamber erroneously concluded that the acts of the Appellant formed part of a widespread and systematic attack and that he knew of the attack." "It must be stressed that the Trial Chamber's finding relevant to the present ground relates to the Appellant's knowledge of on-going attacks against the Muslim civilian population in the region of Visegrad. The Appeals Chamber finds that (...) it is obvious from the various findings of the Trial Chamber (...) that the Appellant participated with Milan Lukic and others in the searching of the house of [a witness'] father in Musici, and that he was present at the Vilina Vlas Hotel on 7 June 1992 when the seven Muslim men [who were later shot, five of whom died] arrived escorted by Milan Lukic and his men. Further, the Trial Chamber found that 'in view of the sheer scale and systematic nature of the attack, the Accused must have noticed the consequences of this campaign upon the non-Serb civilian population of the Visegrad municipality.' The Appeals Chamber is of the view that a reasonable Trial Chamber could conclude from the above that the Appellant knew about the on-going attack against the Muslim civilian population in Visegrad."

c) Application—general elements for Article 5

i) Srebrenica

(1) armed conflict

Blagojevic and Jokic, (Trial Chamber), January 17, 2005, para. 549: "It has not been disputed that an armed conflict existed between the Republic of Bosnia and Herzegovina and its forces, and the Republika Srpska and its forces during the period relevant for the Indictment. Nor has it been disputed that this armed conflict existed in eastern Bosnia. Based on the evidence set out above in the Factual Background relevant to this case, the Trial Chamber finds that there is sufficient evidence to establish that there was an armed conflict in eastern Bosnia between 11 July and 1 November 1995."

(2) widespread or systematic attack

Blagojevic and Jokic, (Trial Chamber), January 17, 2005, para. 551: "The Trial Chamber further finds that the attack was widespread or systematic. The attack, carried out by the [Army of the Republika Srpska] and [the Ministry of the Interior in Republika Srpska] was planned and defined in the 'Krivaja 95' order. The attack continued after the fall of Srebrenica and affected the approximately 40,000 people who lived within the Srebrenica enclave at the time of the attack."

(3) directed against a civilian population

Blagojevic and Jokic, (Trial Chamber), January 17, 2005, para. 552: "The attack was clearly directed against the Bosnian Muslim civilian population in the Srebrenica enclave. The Trial Chamber has heard evidence that the 28th Division of the [Army of Bosnia-Herzegovina] was located in the Srebrenica enclave and that members of that division were among the men that formed the column. However, The Trial Chamber finds that the estimated number of members of the [Army of Bosnia-Herzegovina] present in the enclave and among the column, ranging from about 1,000 soldiers to 4,000 soldiers do not amount to such numbers that the civilian character of the population would be affected, as the vast majority of the people present in the enclave itself and in the column were civilians."

(4) acts of the accused were part of the attack and the accused knew their acts were part of the attack

Blagojevic and Jokic, (Trial Chamber), January 17, 2005, paras. 553-554: "Both Accused were high-ranking officers in brigades which took part in the attack on the Srebrenica enclave and as such had knowledge of the wider context in which their own acts occurred. The Trial Chamber finds that it has been established beyond reasonable doubt that the acts of both Accused were part of the attack and that both Accused knew that their acts were part of the attack." "Therefore, the Trial Chamber finds that the general requirements of Article (...) 5 have been met."

ii) Sarajevo

Galic, (Trial Chamber), December 5, 2003, para. 598: "[T]he Trial Chamber finds that the required elements under Article 5 of the Statute that there must be an attack, that the attack must be directed against any civilian population, and that the attack be widespread or systematic have been satisfied. The Trial Chamber also finds that the crimes committed in Sarajevo during the Indictment Period [from around 10 September 1992 to 10 August 1994,] formed part of an attack directed against the civilian population and this would have had been known to all who were positioned in and around Sarajevo at that time." *See also Galic*, (Trial Chamber), December 5, 2003, para. 3 (discussing that there was 3 and ½ years of armed conflict in and around Sarajevo).

iii) Bosanski Samac and Odzak

(1) attack on the civilian population and existence of armed conflict

Simic, Tadic, and Zaric, (Trial Chamber), October 17, 2003, para. 978: "The Trial Chamber finds that the events, which took place in Bosanski Samac and Odzak between 17 April 1992 and 31 December 1993, constituted an attack on the civilian population. This attack included the forcible takeover of power in Bosanski Samac, and the subsequent acts of persecution and deportation against non-Serb civilians. The Trial Chamber is satisfied that a state of armed conflict existed in the Republic of Bosnia and Herzegovina during the above mentioned period and that there was a nexus between the armed conflict and the acts of the Accused."

(2) the attack was widespread and systematic

Simic, Tadic, and Zaric, (Trial Chamber), October 17, 2003, paras. 979-980: "While Article 5 of the Statute requires that the attack must be either widespread or systematic, the Trial Chamber finds that the attack against non-Serb civilians in the Bosanski Samac and Odzak Municipalities was both systematic and widespread. The attack was preceded by a series of acts, which indicate that it was planned and carried out in an organized fashion. These acts include military training of Serb men from Bosanksi Samac at a camp near Ilok in mid March 1992, securing the presence of Serb paramilitary forces who arrived in Batkusa on 11 April 1992, and the establishment of the Crisis Staff on 15 April 1992. The forcible takeover on 17 April 1992 was followed by acts of systematic persecution against non-Serb civilians which included the arbitrary arrests of Bosnian Muslim and Bosnian Croat civilians and their unlawful detention in various facilities in Bosanski Samac, and in camps in Zasavica and Crkvina. Many were subjected to repeated beatings and other cruel and inhumane acts, in addition to deportation and forcible transfer."

"The Trial Chamber finds that the attack in Bosanski Samac and Odzak was also widespread. It affected the vast majority of the residents of the Municipality. Approximately 250 non-Serb civilians were detained at the

Territorial Defence Building in Bosanski Samac, the number of people detained at the secondary schools in Bosanski Samac was between 300 and 500. In May 1992 almost 1000 people were detained at the Omladinski Dom in Crkvina. A large number of them were subjected to torture or to cruel and inhumane treatment. Hundreds of non-Serbs were deported or focrcibly transferred."

(3) the accuseds' knowledge of the attack and that their acts were part of the attack

Simic, Tadic, and Zaric, (Trial Chamber), October 17, 2003, paras. 981-982: "The Trial Chamber is satisfied that the three Accused knew of the attack against the non-Serb civilians in Bosanski Samac and that their acts were part of this attack. Blagoje Simic telephoned Lt. Col. Stevan Nikolic on 17 April 1992 to inform him that the Crisis Staff of the Serbian Municipality of Bosanski Samac has been established and that with the assistance from members of the Serb police and the paramilitaries had taken over the vital facilities in town. As the head of the *de facto* government, in the following months, Blagoje Simic was informed of the persecutory acts against non-Serb civilians, often organized or greatly facilitated by members of the Crisis Staff."

"The Trial Chamber also accepts that, as a member of the Crisis Staff and as the member of the Exchange Commission, Miroslav Tadic became aware of the forcible takeover and of the following events. Simo Zaric was a member of the 4th Detachment since its establishment and served as the Assistant Commander for Intelligence, Reconnaissance, Morale and Information. In this capacity he was aware of the acts of mistreatment of non-Serb civilians. In view of the above, the Trial Chamber is satisfied that the general requirements of Article 5 are met with respect to each of the Accused."

d) Underlying offenses

i) murder (Article 5(a))

(1) elements

Blagojevic and Jokic, (Trial Chamber), January 17, 2005, para. 556: "In the jurisprudence of both the Tribunal and the ICTR, murder has consistently been defined as the death of the victim which results from an act or omission by the accused, committed with the intent either to kill or to cause serious bodily harm with the reasonable knowledge that it would likely lead to death." *See also Krstic*, (Trial Chamber), August 2, 2001, para. 485 (similar);

Blaskic, (Trial Chamber), March 3, 2000, para. 217 (similar); *Kordic and Cerkez,* (Trial Chamber), February 26, 2001, para. 236 (similar).

Brdjanin, (Trial Chamber), September 1, 2004, para. 381: "Save for some insignificant variations in expressing the constituent elements of the crime of murder and wilful killing, which are irrelevant for this case, the jurisprudence of this Tribunal has consistently defined the essential elements of these offences as follows:
1. The victim is dead;
2. The death was caused by an act or omission of the accused, or of a person or persons for whose acts or omissions the accused bears criminal responsibility; and
3. The act was done, or the omission was made, by the accused, or a person or persons for whose acts or omissions he bears criminal responsibility, with an intention:
- to kill, or
- to inflict grievous bodily harm or serious injury, in the reasonable knowledge that such act or omission was likely to cause death."

Brdjanin, (Trial Chamber), September 1, 2004, para. 382: "The *actus reus* consists in the action or omission of the accused resulting in the death of the victim. The Prosecution need only prove beyond reasonable doubt that the accused's conduct contributed substantially to the death of the victim."

Galic, (Trial Chamber), December 5, 2003, para. 150: "The basic requirements for murder as a crime against humanity are that:
(a) the victim died;
(b) the victim's death was caused by an act or omission of the accused, or of a person or persons for whose acts or omissions the accused bears criminal responsibility; and
(c) the act was done, or the omission was made, by the accused, or by a person or persons for whose acts or omissions the accused bears criminal responsibility, with an intention:
(i) to kill, or
(ii) to inflict serious injury, in reckless disregard of human life."

Kupreskic et al., (Trial Chamber), January 14, 2000, para. 560: "The constituent elements of murder under Article 5(a) of the Statute (...) comprise the death of the victim as a result of the acts or omissions of the accused, where the conduct of the accused was a substantial cause of the death of the victim. It can be said that the accused is guilty of murder if he or she engaging in conduct which is unlawful, intended to kill another person or to cause this person grievous bodily harm, and has caused the death of that person."

Jelisic, (Trial Chamber), December 14, 1999, para. 35: "Murder is defined as homicide committed with the intention to cause death. The legal ingredients of the offence as generally recognised in national law may be characterised as follows: [a] the victim is dead, [b] as a result of an act of the accused, [c] committed with the intention to cause death."

See also Kordic and Cerkez, (Appeals Chamber), December 17, 2004, para. 114: "The elements of murder as a crime against humanity are undisputed."

(2) "murder" under Article 5 of the Statute, compared to Article 2 ("wilful killing") and Article 3 ("murder")

Blagojevic and Jokic, (Trial Chamber), January 17, 2005, para. 556: "The elements of the offence of murder as a crime against humanity and as a violation of the laws or customs of war are the same." *See also Stakic*, (Trial Chamber), July 31, 2003, para. 631 (similar); *Krnojelac*, (Trial Chamber), March 15, 2002, paras. 323-324 (similar).

Brdjanin, (Trial Chamber), September 1, 2004, para. 380: "It is clear from the Tribunal's jurisprudence that the elements of the underlying crime of wilful killing under Article 2 of the Statute are identical to those required for murder under Article 3 and Article 5 of the Statute."

Kordic and Cerkez, (Trial Chamber), February 26, 2001, para. 236: "[The] elements [of murder under Article 5] are similar to those required in connection to wilful killing under Article 2 and murder under Article 3 of the Statute, with the exception that in order to be characterised as a crime against humanity a 'murder' must have been committed as part of a widespread or systematic attack against a civilian population."

(3) proof of dead body not required

Brdjanin, (Trial Chamber), September 1, 2004, para. 383: "The Trial Chamber concurs with the *Tadic* Trial Chamber that: 'Since these were not times of normalcy, it is inappropriate to apply rules of some national systems that require the production of a body as proof to death. However, there must be evidence to link injuries received to a resulting death.'"

Brdjanin, (Trial Chamber), September 1, 2004, para. 385: "In *Krnojelac*, the Trial Chamber held that: 'Proof beyond reasonable doubt that a person was murdered does not necessarily require proof that the dead body of that person has been recovered. [T]he fact of a victim's death can be inferred circumstantially from all of the evidence presented to the Trial Chamber.'" "The Trial Chamber added that a victim's death may be established by circumstantial evidence provided that the *only* reasonable inference is that the victim is dead as a result of the acts or omissions of the accused." (emphasis in original) *See also Krnojelac,* (Trial Chamber), March 15, 2002, para. 326 (same language as quoted).

(4) suicide as murder

Krnojelac, (Trial Chamber), March 15, 2002, para. 329: "The crucial issues [for determining whether suicide can constitute murder] are causation and intent. The relevant act or omission by the Accused or by those for whose acts or omissions the Accused bears criminal responsibility must have caused the suicide of the victim and the Accused, or those for whom he bears criminal responsibility, must have intended by that act or omission to cause the suicide of the victim, or have known that the suicide of the victim was a likely and foreseeable result of the act or omission. The Accused cannot be held criminally liable unless the acts or omissions for which he bears criminal responsibility induced the victim to take action which resulted in his death, and that his suicide was either intended, or was an action of a type which a reasonable person could have foreseen as a consequence of the conduct of the Accused, or of those for whom he bears criminal responsibility."

(5) mens rea

Blagojevic and Jokic, (Trial Chamber), January 17, 2005, para. 556: Murder must be "committed with the intent either to kill or to cause serious bodily harm with the reasonable knowledge that it would likely lead to death." *See also Krstic,* (Trial Chamber), August 2, 2001, para. 485 (similar); *Blaskic,* (Trial Chamber), March 3, 2000, para. 217 (similar); *Kordic and Cerkez,* (Trial Chamber), February 26, 2001, para. 236 (similar).

Brdjanin, (Trial Chamber), September 1, 2004, para. 381: "[The required mental state is:]

The act was done, or the omission was made, by the accused, or a person or persons for whose acts or omissions he bears criminal responsibility, with an intention: - to kill, or -to inflict grievous bodily harm or serious injury, in the reasonable knowledge that such act or omission was likely to cause death."

Kupreskic et al., (Trial Chamber), January 14, 2000, para. 560: The *mens rea* for murder is that the accused "engaging in conduct which is unlawful, intended to kill another person or to cause this person grievous bodily harm, and has caused the death of that person."

Jelisic, (Trial Chamber), December 14, 1999, para. 35: "Murder [is] (...) committed with the intention to cause death."
Compare Galic, (Trial Chamber), December 5, 2003, para. 150: "The *[mens rea]* requirements for murder as a crime against humanity are that:
the act was done, or the omission was made, by the accused, or by a person or persons for whose acts or omissions the accused bears criminal responsibility, with an intention:
(i) to kill, or
(ii) to inflict serious injury, in reckless disregard of human life."

(a) "murder" not "premeditated murder" is the underlying offense

Kordic and Cerkez, (Trial Chamber), February 26, 2001, para. 235: "[T]he *Blaskic* Trial Chamber held that 'it is murder ("meurtre") and not premeditated murder ("assassinat") which must be the underlying offence of a crime against humanity.'" *See also Blaskic*, (Trial Chamber), March 3, 2000, para. 216 (same).

Jelisic, (Trial Chamber), December 14, 1999, para. 51: "The Trial Chamber notes (...) that the English text of the Statute uses the term 'murder'" and "observes" that "it is appropriate to adopt this as the accepted term in international custom."

But see Kupreskic et al., (Trial Chamber), January 14, 2000, para. 561: "The requisite *mens rea* of murder under Article 5(a) is the intent to kill or the intent to inflict serious injury in reckless disregard of human life. [T]he standard of *mens rea* required is intentional and premeditated killing. The result is premeditated when the actor formulated his intent to kill after a cool moment of reflection. The result is intended when it is the actor's purpose, or the actor is aware that it will occur in the ordinary course of events."

(6) application—murder

(a) Srebrenica

Blagojevic and Jokic, (Trial Chamber), January 17, 2005, para. 569: "[T]he Trial Chamber finds that it has been established beyond reasonable doubt that more than 7,000 Bosnian men any [*sic*] boys were killed [subsequent to the takeover of Srebrenica] by the members of the [Army of the Republika Srpska] and/or [Ministry of the Interior in Republika Srpska]. It is further proven that the direct perpetrators had the intention to kill or inflict serious injury in the reasonable knowledge that their acts or omissions were likely to cause the death of the victim."

(b) Sarajevo

Galic, (Trial Chamber), December 5, 2003, para. 599: "The Trial Chamber is (...) satisfied that (...) murder (...) falling within the meaning of Article 5 of the Statute [was] committed in Sarajevo during the Indictment Period [from around 10 September 1992 to 10 August 1994]." For detailed factual findings, see *Galic*, (Trial Chamber), December 5, 2003, paras. 192-594.

(c) Prijedor

Stakic, (Trial Chamber), July 31, 2003, para. 632: "The Trial Chamber is satisfied that, in relation to those killings for which the Trial Chamber has held Dr. Stakic criminally responsible under Article 3 [the deaths of over 1500 Bosnian Muslim and Bosnian Croat non-combatants killed in camps and other detention facilities, during organized convoys by police and/or military units, and committed as a result of armed military and/or police action, in the Municipality of Prijedor in 1992], he is also criminally responsible under Article 5, since it finds that those killings were committed in the context of a widespread and systematic attack directed against the civilian population of the Municipality of Prijedor and that Dr. Stakic was aware that his acts formed part of that attack."

ii) extermination (Article 5(b))

(1) relationship to crimes of murder (Articles 3 and 5) and willful killing (Article 2)

Blagojevic and Jokic, (Trial Chamber), January 17, 2005, para. 571: "The jurisprudence of this Tribunal and the ICTR has on several occasions held that the core elements of extermination are essentially similar to those required for wilful killing under Article 2 and murder under Articles 3 and 5 of the Statute. The scale of the crimes is, however, distinct: extermination is 'to be interpreted as murder on a larger scale - mass murder.' The International Law Commission has found that 'the act used to carry out the offence of extermination involves an element of mass destruction which is not required for murder.'"

Brdjanin, (Trial Chamber), September 1, 2004, para. 388: "The jurisprudence of this Tribunal and the ICTR has consistently held that, apart from the question of scale, the core elements of wilful killing (Article 2) and murder (Article 3 and Article 5) on the one hand and extermination (Article 5) on the other are the same."

(2) elements

Blagojevic and Jokic, (Trial Chamber), January 17, 2005, para. 572: "The Trial Chamber finds that the elements for the crime extermination are as follows: a) act or omission that results in the death of persons on a massive scale (*actus reus*), and b) the intent to kill persons on a massive scale, or to inflict serious bodily injury or create conditions of life that lead to the death in the reasonable knowledge that such act or omission is likely to cause the death of a large number of persons (*mens rea*)."

Brdjanin, (Trial Chamber), September 1, 2004, para. 388: "In addition to the preconditions which must be established for a finding of a crime against humanity under Article 5 of the Statute, the elements of the crime of extermination under Article 5(b) are the following:

1. the killing of persons on a massive scale (*actus reus*), and
2. the accused's intention to kill persons on a massive scale or to create conditions of life that lead to the death of a large number of people (*mens rea*)."

Vasiljevic, (Trial Chamber), November 29, 2002, para. 229: "[T]he elements of the crime of 'extermination' are as follows: 1. The material element of extermination consists of any one act or combination of acts which contributes to the killing of a large number of individuals (*actus reus*). 2. The offender must intend to kill, to inflict grievous bodily harm, or to inflict serious injury, in the reasonable knowledge that such act or omission is likely to cause death, or otherwise intends to participate in the elimination of a number of individuals, in the knowledge that his action is part of a vast murderous enterprise in which a large number of individuals are systematically marked for killing or killed (*mens rea*)."[22]

(3) actus reus

Blagojevic and Jokic, (Trial Chamber), January 17, 2005, para. 573: "The *actus reus* of extermination consists of acts or omissions, which directly or indirectly lead to the death of a large number of persons."

Brdjanin, (Trial Chamber), September 1, 2004, para. 389: "The *actus reus* of the crime of extermination consists of any act, omission or combination thereof which contributes directly or indirectly to the killing of a large number of individuals."

Stakic, (Trial Chamber), July 31, 2003, para. 638: "This Trial Chamber agrees with the parties that the core element of extermination is the killing of persons on a massive scale."

(a) may include acts such as the deprivation of food and medicine, calculated to cause the destruction of part of the population

Brdjanin, (Trial Chamber), September 1, 2004, para. 389: "An act amounting to extermination may include the killing of a victim as such as well as conduct which creates conditions provoking the victim's death and ultimately mass killings, such as the deprivation of food and medicine, calculated to cause the destruction of part of the population."

Krstic, (Trial Chamber), August 2, 2001, para. 503: "[F]or the crime of extermination to be established, in addition to the general requirements for a crime against humanity, there must be evidence that a particular population was targeted and that its members were killed *or otherwise subjected to conditions of life calculated to bring about the destruction* of a numerically significant part of the population." (emphasis added)

(b) number of individuals involved

Blagojevic and Jokic, (Trial Chamber), January 17, 2005, para. 573: "While some Trial Chamber's have discussed whether the element of mass destruction includes a minimum number of victims, the Trial Chamber finds that there is no such requirement. In the Trial Chamber's opinion, any such attempt to set a minimum number of victims in the abstract will ultimately prove unhelpful; the element of massive scale must be assessed on a case-by-case basis in light of the proven criminal conduct and all relevant factors."

Brdjanin, (Trial Chamber), September 1, 2004, para. 391: "The question has often arisen whether the element of killings on a massive scale implies a numerical requirement. The Trial Chamber agrees with the approach adopted by the *Krstic* Trial Chamber that: 'The very term "extermination" strongly suggests the commission of a massive crime, which in turn assumes a substantial degree of preparation and organisation(...)[W]hile extermination generally involves a large number of victims, it may be constituted even where the number of victims is limited.' Furthermore, the Trial Chamber recalls that the element of massiveness of the crime allows for the possibility to establish the evidence of the *actus reus* of extermination on an accumulation of separate and unrelated incidents, meaning on an aggregated basis. The Trial Chamber in that respect agrees with the finding of the *Stakic* Trial Chamber, which clarified that the requirement of massiveness as a constitutive element of the *actus reus* of extermination has to be determined on a case-by-case analysis of all relevant factors."

Stakic, (Trial Chamber), July 31, 2003, para. 640: "This Trial Chamber does not find that the case-law provides support for the Defence submission that the killings must occur on a vast scale in a concentrated place over a short period. Such a claim does not follow from the requirement that the killings must be massive. Nor does the Trial Chamber believe that a specific minimum number of victims is required. As the Trial Chamber in *Prosecutor v. Vasiljevic* held, the lowest figure from the Second World War cases to which the crime of extermination was applied was a total of 733 killings. The Chamber added in a however that it does not suggest 'that a lower number of victims would disqualify that act as "extermination" as a crime against humanity, nor does it suggest that such a threshold must necessarily be met.' In the opinion of this Trial Chamber, an assessment of whether the element of massiveness has been reached depends on a case-by-case analysis of all relevant factors. As the Trial Chamber in *Krstic* held, the massiveness of the crime automatically assumes a substantial degree of preparation and organisation which may serve as indicia for the existence of a murderous 'scheme' or 'plan,' but not, as proposed by the Defence, of a 'vast scheme of collective murder' as a separate element of crime."[23]

Vasiljevic, (Trial Chamber), November 29, 2002, para. 227: The "Trial Chamber concludes (...) that criminal responsibility for 'extermination' only attaches to those individuals responsible for a large number of deaths, even if their part therein was remote or indirect. Responsibility for one or for a limited number of such killings is insufficient."

Krstic, (Trial Chamber), August 2, 2001, para. 503: "[F]or the crime of extermination to be established, in addition to the general requirements for a crime against humanity, there must be evidence that a particular population was targeted and that its members were killed or otherwise subjected to conditions of life calculated to bring about the destruction of *a numerically significant part of the population*." (emphasis added)

Krstic, (Trial Chamber), August 2, 2001, para. 502: "[T]he definition should be read as meaning the destruction of a numerically significant part of the population concerned."

Compare Krstic, (Trial Chamber), August 2, 2001, para. 501: "[W]hile extermination generally involves a large number of victims, it may be constituted even where the number of victims is limited."

(i) application—number of victims: at least 1669 Bosnian Muslims and Bosnian Croats killed by Bosnian Serb forces in the Autonomous Region of Krajina

Brdjanin, (Trial Chamber), September 1, 2004, para. 465: Where "at least 1669 Bosnian Muslims and Bosnian Croats were killed by Bosnian Serb forces [in the Autonomous Region of Krjina], all of whom were non-combatants," the Trial Chamber was "satisfied that these killings fulfil the element of massiveness for the crime of extermination."

(c) extermination must be collective, not directed toward singled out individuals

Brdjanin, (Trial Chamber), September 1, 2004, para. 390: "[E]xtermination 'must be collective in nature rather than directed towards singled out individuals. However, in contrast to genocide, the offender need not have intended to destroy the *group* or part of the group to which the victims belong.'" (emphasis in original)

Stakic, (Trial Chamber), July 31, 2003, para. 639: "An act amounting to extermination, as explained by the Trial Chamber in *Prosecutor v. Vasiljevic*, 'must be collective in nature rather than directed towards singled out individuals.'" *See also Vasiljevic,* (Trial Chamber), November 29, 2002, para. 227 (source of quoted language).

(d) responsibility may be remote or indirect/ not required to prove the accused had de facto control over a large number of individuals

Brdjanin, (Trial Chamber), September 1, 2004, para. 390: "Criminal responsibility for extermination can also be established in situations where the accused's participation in mass killings is remote or indirect. This Trial Chamber also recalls that, although 'the charge of extermination seems to have been restricted to individuals who, by reason of either their position or authority, could decide upon the fate or had control over a large number of individuals,' the Prosecution is not required to prove that the accused had *de facto* control over a large number of individuals because of his position or authority."

(4) mens rea

Blagojevic and Jokic, (Trial Chamber), January 17, 2005, para. 574: "[T]he *mens rea* required for the crime of extermination consists of the intent to kill persons on a massive scale or to inflict serious bodily injury or create conditions of life that lead to the death of a large number of individuals."

Brdjanin, (Trial Chamber), September 1, 2004, paras. 392-393, 395: "The *mens rea* of the crime of extermination has not been defined consistently in the jurisprudence of this Tribunal and of the ICTR. In general, three approaches can be differentiated. The first approach was articulated by the *Kayishema and Ruzindana* Trial Chamber (...) The second approach was formulated by the *Krstic* Trial Judgement (...) The *Stakic* Trial Chamber has refined this second approach(...)" "The third approach was adopted by the *Vasiljevic* Trial Chamber(...)" "The Trial Chamber (...) endorses the *mens rea* formulation as identified in the *Krstic* and *Stakic* Trial Judgements as the correct legal one for the final determination of the factual findings in this case. The *mens rea* standard for extermination is the same as the *mens rea* required for murder as a crime against humanity with the difference that 'extermination can be said to be murder on a massive scale.' The Prosecution is thus required to prove beyond reasonable doubt that the accused had the intention to kill persons on a massive scale or to create conditions of life that led to the death of a large number of people. The *mens rea* standard required for extermination does not include a threshold of negligence or gross negligence: the accused's act or omission must be done with intention or recklessness (*dolus eventualis*)."

Stakic, (Trial Chamber), July 31, 2003, paras. 641-642: "[T]his Trial Chamber finds that the *mens rea* required for extermination is that the perpetrator intends to kill persons on a massive scale or to create conditions of life that lead to the death of large numbers of individuals. This includes the requirement that the perpetrator's mental state encompasses all objective elements of the crime: the annihilation of a mass of people."

"Relying on the Judgement of the Trial Chamber in *Prosecutor v. Kayishema,* the Prosecution argues that an accused can be held liable for his acts or omissions if they have been committed 'with intention, recklessness, or gross negligence.' This Trial Chamber does not agree and finds that it would be incompatible with the character of the crime of extermination and with the system and construction of Article 5 if recklessness or gross negligence sufficed to hold an accused criminally responsible for such a crime. It therefore considers that the threshold for the *mens rea* cannot be lower than the intent required for murder as a crime against humanity (i.e. *dolus directus* or *dolus eventualis*)."

Krstic, (Trial Chamber), August 2, 2001, para. 495: "The offences of murder and extermination have a similar element in that they both intend the death of the victims. They have the same *mens rea*, which consists of the intention to kill or the intention to cause serious bodily injury to the victim which the perpetrator must have reasonably foreseen was likely to result in death."

(a) discriminatory intent not required

Krstic, (Trial Chamber), August 2, 2001, para. 500: "[E]xtermination may be retained when the crime is directed against an entire group of individuals even though no discriminatory intent nor intention to destroy the group as such on national, ethnical, racial or religious grounds has been demonstrated; or where the targeted population does not share any common national, ethnical, racial or religious characteristics."

(5) no plan or policy requirement/ "vast scheme of collective murder" or "vast murderous enterprise" not an element

Krstic, (Appeals Chamber), April 19, 2004: "The Trial Chamber also concluded that the definitions of intent for extermination and genocide 'both require that the killings be part of an extensive plan to kill a substantial part of a civilian population.' The Appeals Chamber has explained, however, that 'the existence of a plan or policy is not a legal ingredient of the crime' of genocide. While the existence of such a plan may help to establish that the accused possessed the requisite genocidal intent, it remains only evidence supporting the inference of intent, and does not become a legal ingredient of the offence. Similarly, the Appeals Chamber has rejected the argument that the legal elements of crimes against humanity (which include extermination) require a proof of the existence of a plan or policy to commit these crimes. The presence of such a plan or policy may be important evidence that the attack against a civilian population was widespread or systematic, but it is not a legal element of a crime against humanity. As neither extermination nor genocide requires the proof of a plan or policy to carry out the underlying act, this factor cannot support the Trial Chamber's conclusion that the offence of extermination is subsumed in genocide."

Blagojevic and Jokic, (Trial Chamber), January 17, 2005, para. 576: "The Appeals Chamber held in the *Krstic* case that extermination does not require the proof of a plan or policy to carry out the underlying act, adding that the presence of such a plan or policy may be important evidence of the widespread or systematic nature of the attack. In view of this holding, the *Brdjanin* Trial Chamber recently found that 'the *Vasiljevic* "knowledge that [the offender's] action is part of a vast murderous enterprise in which a larger number of individuals are systematically marked for killing or killed," if proven, will be considered as evidence tending to prove the accused's knowledge that his act was part of a widespread or systematic attack against a civilian population, and not beyond that.' This Trial Chamber endorses this view and does not consider the existence of a 'vast scheme of collective murder' or 'vast murderous enterprise' as a separate element of the crime nor as an additional layer of the *mens rea* required for the commission of the crime."

Brdjanin, (Trial Chamber), September 1, 2004, para. 394: "*Krstic* Appeal Judgement has crystallised the legal position on the matter in stating that for the purpose of extermination, no proof is required of the existence of a plan or policy to commit that crime. In its decision, the Appeals Chamber added that the presence of such a plan or policy may be important evidence that the attack against a civilian population was widespread or systematic. In view of this pronouncement, the Trial Chamber makes it clear that the *Vasiljevic* 'knowledge that his action is part of a vast murderous enterprise in which a larger number of individuals are systematically marked for killing or killed,' if proven, will be considered as evidence tending to prove the accused's knowledge that his act was part of a widespread or systematic attack against a civilian population, and not beyond that."

Stakic, (Trial Chamber), July 31, 2003, para. 640: "As the Trial Chamber in *Krstic* held, the massiveness of the crime automatically assumes a substantial degree of preparation and organisation which may serve as indicia for the existence of a murderous 'scheme' or 'plan,' but not, as proposed by the Defence, of a 'vast scheme of collective murder' as a separate element of crime."

But see Vasiljevic, (Trial Chamber), November 29, 2002, paras. 228, 229: "[I] t is not sufficient to establish extermination for the offender to have intended to kill a large number of individuals, or to inflict grievous bodily harm, or to inflict serious injury, in the reasonable knowledge that such act or omission was likely to cause death as in the case of murder. He must also have known of the vast scheme of collective murder and have been willing to take part therein."

"The offender must intend to kill, to inflict grievous bodily harm, or to inflict serious injury, in the reasonable knowledge that such act or omission is likely to cause death, or otherwise intends to participate in the elimination of a number of individuals, in the knowledge that his action is part of a vast murderous enterprise in which a large number of individuals are systematically marked for killing or killed (*mens rea*)."

(6) application—extermination

(a) Srebrenica—killing more than 7,000 thousand Bosnian Muslim men and boys was extermination

Blagojevic and Jokic, (Trial Chamber), January 17, 2005, para. 577: "The Trial Chamber finds that the killings [subsequent to the fall of Srebrenica] were part of one murder operation, which led to the death of more than 7,000 thousands [*sic*] Bosnian Muslim men and boys. The crime of extermination in the present case is clearly indicated by the massive scale of the number of victims and by the intent of the perpetrators to kill on massive scale. The Trial Chamber inferred this intent from the nature of the murder operation, which (...) was carried out in a short time period, with similar pattern of killings, in locations near to each other and by perpetrators who in some cases were active in more than one of these locations."

(b) Prijedor—killing more than 1,500, including at the Keraterm camp, at Koricanske Stijene on Mount Vlasic, and the village of Brisevo was extermination

Stakic, (Trial Chamber), July 31, 2003, para. 651-655: "The Indictment (...) charges the Accused with a number of killings committed in Prijedor municipality between 30 April and 30 September 1992."

"[T]he proven large-scale killings were of three kinds: 1) killings committed in camps and other detention facilities, 2) killings committed during organised convoys by police and/or military units, and 3) killings committed as a result of armed military and/or police action in non-Serb or predominantly non-Serb areas of the municipality."

"The evidence shows that the proven killings, many of which independently would reach the requisite level of massiveness for the purposes of an evaluation under Article 5(b) of the Statute, were aimed at the collective group of targeted individuals and not at the victims in their individual capacity. This holds true *inter alia* for:
a) the massacre in Room 3 of the Keraterm camp;
b) the killings of around 120 men who were called out in an organised fashion on 5
August in the Keraterm camp;
c) the closely controlled and cold-blooded executions at Koricanske Stijene on
Mount Vlasic on 21 August 1992;
d) the Serb armed attack on the mainly Croat village of Brisevo, which started on 27 May 1992."

"Although the total number of victims of the killings (...) for which Dr. Stakic incurs criminal liability, can never be accurately calculated, the Trial Chamber finds that based on a conservative estimate, more than 1,500 persons were killed. Considering the scale of the killings and in an effort not to lose sight of the fact that these crimes were committed against individual victims, the Trial Chamber has included a List of Victims known by name, in which are enumerated the names of those persons identified as killed in Prijedor municipality in 1992, in total 486 human beings."

"The Trial Chamber therefore considers that the killings committed in the Municipality of Prijedor during the relevant period of 1992 were part of a campaign of annihilation of non-Serbs carried out by Serb police and military forces, and that the killings thus perpetrated fulfil the requisite element of massiveness for the purposes of Article 5(b) of the Statute. It is proven that acts of extermination were committed by the Accused."

(i) application—mens rea—extermination: Prijedor

Stakic, (Trial Chamber), July 31, 2003, para. 661: "Killings were perpetrated on a massive scale against the non-Serb population of Prijedor municipality. The lives of the non-Serb population were of very little, if any, value to the Serb perpetrators. The Trial Chamber has found that the Accused, because of his political position and role in the implementation of the plan to create a purely Serb municipality, was familiar with the details and the progress of the campaign of annihilation directed against the non-Serb population. Dr. Stakic was aware of the killings of non-Serbs and of their occurrence on a massive scale. The Trial Chamber is therefore convinced that the Accused acted with the requisite intent, at least *dolus eventualis*, to exterminate the non-Serb population of Prijedor municipality in 1992 and finds the Accused guilty of this crime, punishable under Article 5(b) of the Statute."

(7) extermination distinguished from genocide

Stakic, (Trial Chamber), July 31, 2003, para. 639: "Extermination must form part of a widespread or systematic attack against a civilian population. An act amounting to extermination, as explained by the Trial Chamber in *Prosecutor v. Vasiljevic*, 'must be collective in nature rather than directed towards singled out individuals. However, in contrast to genocide, the offender need not have intended to destroy the *group* or part of the group to which the victims belong,' and it is not required that the victims share national, ethnical, racial or religious characteristics. In this context it should be emphasised that the crime of extermination may apply to situations where some members of a group are killed but others spared. It suffices that the victims be defined by political affiliation, physical attributes or simply the fact that they happened to be in a certain geographical area. Moreover, the victims may be defined in the negative, *i.e.* as not belonging to, not being affiliated with or not loyal to the perpetrator or the group to which the perpetrator belongs." (emphasis in original)

iii) enslavement (Article 5(c))

(1) actus reus and mens rea

Kunarac, Kovac, and Vokovic, (Appeals Chamber), June 12, 2002, para. 116: "'[T]he *actus reus* of the violation [of enslavement] is the exercise of any or all of the powers attaching to the right of ownership over a person,' and the '*mens rea* of the violation consists in the intentional exercise of such powers.'"

Krnojelac, (Trial Chamber), March 15, 2002, para. 350: "Enslavement under Article 5 (...) has been defined by the Tribunal as the exercise of any or all of the powers attaching to the right of ownership over a person. The *actus reus* of enslavement is the exercise of those powers, and the *mens rea* is the intentional exercise of such powers."

(2) same as "slavery" under Article 3

Simic, Tadic, and Zaric, (Trial Chamber), October 17, 2003, para. 85: "Trial Chambers of the Tribunal have held that the charge of 'forced labour assignments' may constitute the basis of the crime of enslavement as a crime against humanity under Article 5(c), and the offence of slavery as a violation of the laws or customs of war under Article 3 of the Statute(...)"

Krnojelac, (Trial Chamber), March 15, 2002, para. 356: "The Trial Chamber is satisfied that the offence of slavery under Article 3 (...) is the same as the offence of enslavement under Article 5. As such, slavery under Article 3 requires proof of the same elements as constitute enslavement under Article 5."

(3) indicia of enslavement

Kunarac, Kovac, and Vokovic, (Appeals Chamber), June 12, 2002, para. 119: In determining whether enslavement has been established, the indicia of enslavement identified by the Trial Chamber include: "control of someone's movement, control of physical environment, psychological control, measures taken to prevent or deter escape, force, threat of force or coercion, duration, assertion of exclusivity, subjection to cruel treatment and abuse, control of sexuality and forced labour."

Krnojelac, (Trial Chamber), March 15, 2002, para. 359: "'[T]he exaction of forced or compulsory labour or service' is an 'indication of enslavement,' and a 'factor to be taken into consideration in determining whether enslavement was committed.'"

(a) keeping someone in captivity usually not enough

Kunarac, Kovac, and Vukovic, (Trial Chamber), February 22, 2001, para. 542: "Detaining or keeping someone in captivity, without more, [existence of other indications of enslavement] would, depending on the circumstances of a case, usually not constitute enslavement." "Further indications of enslavement include exploitation; the exaction of forced or compulsory labour or service, often without remuneration and often, though not necessarily, involving physical hardship; sex; prostitution; and human trafficking."

(b) duration of enslavement is a factor, but not a required element

Kunarac, Kovac, and Vokovic, (Appeals Chamber), June 12, 2002, paras. 121, 356: "The duration of the enslavement is not an element of the crime. The question turns on the quality of the relationship between the accused and the victim. A number of factors determine that quality. One of them is the duration of the relationship." "[D]uration may be a factor 'when considering whether someone was enslaved.' This means that duration is not an element of the crime, but a factor in the proof of the elements of the crime. The longer the period of enslavement, the more serious the offence."

(4) lack of resistance is not a sign of consent; lack of consent is not an element

Kunarac, Kovac, and Vokovic, (Appeals Chamber), June 12, 2002, para. 120: The "lack of resistance or the absence of a clear and constant lack of consent during the entire time of the detention" cannot be interpreted as a sign of consent. Lack of consent is not an element of the crime of enslavement.

(5) forced labor assignments may constitute slavery

Simic, Tadic, and Zaric, (Trial Chamber), October 17, 2003, paras. 85-87: "Trial Chambers of the Tribunal have held that the charge of 'forced labour assignments' may constitute the basis of the crime of enslavement as a crime against humanity under Article 5(c), and the offence of slavery as a violation of the laws or customs of war under Article 3 of the Statute, and as such this offence is of sufficient gravity to support a charge of persecution." "The underlying acts of the charge of 'forced labour assignments' infringe upon certain provisions of Geneva Conventions III and IV, and as such may constitute a violation of the laws or customs of war other than grave breaches of the Geneva Conventions, falling within the scope of Article 3 of the Statute. It is settled case-law of the Tribunal that the law of the Geneva Conventions is part of customary international law." "International humanitarian law generally prohibits forced or involuntary labour in international, as well as internal armed conflicts."

Krnojelac, (Trial Chamber), March 15, 2002, para. 359: "'[T]he exaction of forced or compulsory labour or service' is an 'indication of enslavement,' and a 'factor to be taken into consideration in determining whether enslavement was committed.'"

iv) deportation (Article 5(d))

(1) defined

Brdjanin, (Trial Chamber), September 1, 2004, para. 544: "The Trial Chamber by a majority vote is satisfied that the *actus reus* of 'deportation' under Article 5(d) of the Statute consists of the forcible displacement of individuals across a State border from the area in which they are lawfully present without grounds permitted under international law(...)"

Simic, Tadic, and Zaric, (Trial Chamber), October 17, 2003, para. 122: "Trial Chambers of the Tribunal have held in several judgements that deportation is defined as the forced displacement of persons by expulsion or other coercive acts from the area in which they are lawfully present, across a national border, without lawful grounds(...) The Trial Chamber agrees with these findings."

Stakic, (Trial Chamber), July 31, 2003, para. 672: "The Trial Chamber in the *Krnojelac* case noted that deportation is clearly and specifically prohibited under the law as a crime against humanity and has long been so and that deportation was defined as 'the forced displacement of persons by expulsion or other coercive acts from the area in which they are lawfully present, without grounds permitted under international law.' It added the requirement that the persons deported be displaced across a national border(...)"

See also Simic, Tadic, and Zaric, (Trial Chamber), October 17, 2003, para. 121: "Both deportation and unlawful or forcible transfer relate to the involuntary and unlawful displacement, or movement, or relocation, or removal of persons from the territory in which they reside."

See also Stakic, (Trial Chamber), July 31, 2003, para. 681: "Any forced displacement of population involves 'abandoning one's home, losing property and being displaced under duress to another location.'"

(2) distinction between deportation and forcible transfer

Brdjanin, (Trial Chamber), September 1, 2004, para. 544: "[D]isplacement within the boundaries of a State constitutes 'forcible transfer,' punishable as 'other inhumane acts' pursuant to Article 5(i) of the Statute."

Simic, Tadic, and Zaric, (Trial Chamber), October 17, 2003, para. 122: "Forcible transfer has been defined as a forced removal or displacement of people from one area to another which may take place within the same national borders."

Stakic, (Trial Chamber), July 31, 2003, para. 671: "The jurisprudence of this Tribunal has drawn a distinction between deportation under Article 5(d) of the Statute and other inhumane acts (forcible transfer) under Article 5(i) of the Statute. This distinction was set out in *Krstic*, where the Trial Chamber ruled that '[b]oth deportation and forcible transfer relate to the involuntary and unlawful evacuation of individuals from the territory in which they reside. Yet, the two are not synonymous in customary international law. Deportation presumes transfer beyond State borders, whereas forcible transfer relates to displacements within a State.'"

Stakic, (Trial Chamber), July 31, 2003, para. 672: "[The Trial Chamber in the *Krnojelac* case] added the requirement that [for the crime of deportation] the persons deported be displaced across a national border in order 'to be distinguished from forcible transfer which may take place within national boundaries.'"

See also Simic, Tadic, and Zaric, (Trial Chamber), October 17, 2003, para. 122: "In *Krnojelac* the Trial Chamber found that the concept of expulsion formed part of the definition of deportation, and may be treated in the same way as deportation."

(3) transfer over de facto boundaries that are not internationally recognized, such as constantly changing frontlines

Brdjanin, (Trial Chamber), September 1, 2004, para. 542: "The Trial Chamber by a majority vote is unable to agree with the *Stakic* approach. Significant evidence has been advanced in previous judgements of this Tribunal to the effect that, under customary international law, 'deportation' requires that an internationally recognised border be crossed. While the

Stakic Trial Judgement (and the Prosecution's Final Brief in the instant case) may advance excellent policy arguments in favour of dispensing with a cross-border element for the crime of deportation, the Trial Chamber is not convinced that this reflects customary international law as it stood at the relevant time. It is customary international law, and not policy, which the Trial Chamber is bound to apply. The Trial Chamber therefore maintains the cross-border element as a criterion in order to distinguish between 'deportation' and 'forcible transfer.'"

But see Stakic, (Trial Chamber), July 31, 2003, paras. 677-679, 684: "The Trial Chamber is (...) of the view that it is the *actus reus* of forcibly removing, essentially uprooting, individuals from the territory and the environment in which they have been lawfully present, in many cases for decades and generations, which is the rationale for imposing criminal responsibility and not the destination resulting from such a removal. The Trial Chamber believes that, should a definite destination requirement be specified, it would often be difficult to determine whether and when the crime occurred because the victims may have been transferred in several stages and therefore through several territories and across borders that may have changed every day. A fixed destination requirement might consequently strip the prohibition against deportation of its force."

"[I]t would make little or no sense to prohibit acts of deportation, in the words of the Security Council, 'regardless of whether they are committed in an armed conflict, international or internal in character' and at the same time to limit the possibility of punishment to cases involving transfers across internationally recognised borders only."

"For the purposes of the present case, the Trial Chamber finds that Article 5(d) of the Statute must be read to encompass forced population displacements both across internationally recognised borders and *de facto* boundaries, such as constantly changing frontlines, which are not internationally recognised. The crime of deportation in this context is therefore to be defined as the forced displacement of persons by expulsion or other coercive acts for reasons not permitted under international law from an area in which they are lawfully present to an area under the control of another party."

"[I]n the context of the Statute the question of whether a border was internationally recognised or merely *de facto* is immaterial. To hold otherwise would not sufficiently take into account the broader meaning of the word, the initial concept, the legislator's purpose and the sense and spirit of the norm. The Trial Chamber emphasizes that the underlying act – i.e. irrespective of whether the displacement occurred across an internationally recognized border or not – was already punishable under public international law by the time relevant to the present case. The Trial Chamber points to the fact that the International Military Tribunal at Nuremberg, on the basis of Article 6(c) of the Nuremberg Charter referring to 'deportations' as a crime against humanity, applied this provision *de facto* in cases where victims were displaced within internationally recognised borders."

See also Krnojelac, (Appeals Chamber), Separate Opinion of Judge Schomburg, September 17, 2003, para. 15: "The question of whether a border is internationally recognised or merely de facto is immaterial. This was also the approach taken by the International Military Tribunal at Nuremberg and the District Court of Jerusalem in the case of *Attorney General v. Adolf Eichmann*."

(4) unlawful character of the displacement—when displacement is involuntary

Simic, Tadic, and Zaric, (Trial Chamber), October 17, 2003, para. 125: "The displacement of persons is only illegal where it is forced, i.e. not voluntary, and 'when it occurs without grounds permitted under international law.' In other words, displacement motivated by an individual's own genuine wish to leave an area is lawful. The requirement that the displacement be forced or forcible has been interpreted broadly by Trial Chambers. The term 'forced' is not limited to physical force; it may also include the 'threat of force or coercion, such as that caused by fear of violence, duress, detention, psychological oppression or abuse of power against such person or persons or another person, or by taking advantage of a coercive environment.' The essential element is that the displacement be *involuntary* in nature, that 'the relevant persons had *no real choice*.' In other words, a civilian is involuntarily displaced if he is 'not faced with a genuine choice as to whether to leave or to remain in the area.' As noted by the *Krnojelac* Trial Chamber, an apparent consent induced by force or threat of force should not be considered to be real consent." (emphasis in original)

Stakic, (Trial Chamber), July 31, 2003, para. 682: "The definition of deportation requires 'forced' or 'forcible' displacement. Thus, transfers based on an individual's free will to leave are lawful. In the jurisprudence, the requirement of 'forced displacement' has been interpreted to refer not only to acts of physical violence but also to other forms of coercion. The Trial Chamber in *Krstic* made reference to the Elements of Crimes for the International Criminal Court which provides that the term 'forcibly:'

- is not restricted to physical force, but may include threat of force or coercion,
- such as that caused by fear of violence, duress, detention, psychological

- oppression or abuse of power against such person or persons or another person,
- or by taking advantage of a coercive environment." *See Krstic*, (Trial Chamber), August 2, 2001, para. 529 (source of quoted language).

(5) assistance by humanitarian agencies does not render displacement lawful

Stakic, (Trial Chamber), July 31, 2003, para. 683: "The Trial Chamber emphasises that, with regard to a subsequent legal evaluation of the behaviour of a warring party, assistance by humanitarian agencies is not a factor rendering a displacement lawful."

(6) need not involve a minimum number of individuals

Stakic, (Trial Chamber), July 31, 2003, para. 685: "[A] minimum number of individuals [need not] have been forcibly transferred for the perpetrator to incur criminal responsibility. [Such a] submission finds no support in the case-law of this Tribunal and is tantamount to negating the protective effect of the prohibition against deportation."

(7) return of victim has no impact on criminal responsibility

Stakic, (Trial Chamber), July 31, 2003, para. 687: "If a victim were to return, this would consequently not have an impact on the criminal responsibility of the perpetrator who removed the victim."

(8) mens rea

Stakic, (Trial Chamber), July 31, 2003, paras. 686-687: "For this Trial Chamber, all the objective elements (...) must be covered by the intent of the perpetrator. This approach is fully consonant with the aim of prohibiting the practice of ethnic cleansing." "The Trial Chamber agrees with the Trial Chamber in the *Prosecutor v. Mladen Naletilic and Vinko Martinovic* that the intent of the perpetrator must be that the victim is 'removed, which implies the aim that the person is not returning.'"

(9) application—deportation

(a) deportation of the non-Serb population from the Municipality of Prijedor

Stakic, (Trial Chamber), July 31, 2003, paras. 814, 712: "'Deportation' under Article 5(d) of the Statute has already been established beyond reasonable doubt. The Trial Chamber is convinced that the deportations of non-Serb population from Prijedor municipality took place throughout the period relevant to the Indictment."

"[T]he Trial Chamber is convinced that the Accused intended to deport the non-Serb population from Prijedor municipality and that, based on this intent, he not only committed the crime of deportation as a co-perpetrator, but also planned and ordered this crime. The Trial Chamber consequently finds the Accused guilty of the crime of deportation, a crime against humanity under Article 5(d) of the Statute." *See also Stakic*, (Trial Chamber), July 31, 2003, paras. 314-334, for detailed facts as to the deportation and forcible transfer of the non-Serb population.

(b) deportation of non-Serb civilians from the Municipality of Bosanski Samac to Croatia

Simic, Tadic, and Zaric, (Trial Chamber), October 17, 2003, paras. 1051-1053: "[T]he Trial Chamber is satisfied beyond reasonable doubt that Blagoje Simic is criminally responsible as a perpetrator of the deportation of [16 individuals]."

"The Trial Chamber is also satisfied that it has been proven beyond reasonable doubt that Miroslav Tadic is criminally responsible as a perpetrator for the deportation of [16 individuals from their homes in the Municipality of Bosanski Samac]. The Trial Chamber finds that sufficient evidence has been adduced to prove that Miroslav Tadic had the *actus reus* of deportation of the above-mentioned non-Serb civilians."

"With regard to his *mens rea*, the Trial Chamber does not accept Miroslav Tadic's statements that he never wished that some of his fellow citizens would leave forever, and that there was always a possibility to return. The Trial Chamber is satisfied beyond reasonable doubt that the Prosecution has adduced sufficient evidence to prove that Miroslav Tadic had the intent to permanently displace non-Serb civilians from their he only inference from his substantial and continuing activity in the exchange of non-Serb civilians is that Miroslav Tadic had the intent that these non-Serb civilians are not returning, or that he at least knew that his actions were likely to permanently displace these non-Serb civilians and was reckless thereto."

But see Simic, Tadic, and Zaric, (Trial Chamber), Separate and Partly Dissenting Opinion of Judge Per-Johan Lindholm, October 17, 2003, para. 27: "I am convinced that Miroslav Tadic sincerely believed that the exchanges [from Bosanski Samac] were the only means to get the non-Serb civilians out of their miserable and – in many cases – terrifying living conditions, and that he helped them to a better life. As Miroslav Tadic stated at the closure of the case: 'I thought I was doing something humane, helping people in distress.' His participation in their deportation helped them to exercise their right to freedom to a greater degree than during their detention and avoided the constant danger to the life and limb of the non-Serb prisoners in the detention facilities in Bosanski Samac. Furthermore, it has not been made out on the evidence that any other adequate means was available to Miroslav Tadic to free the non-Serb civilians from the situation they were in."

(i) involuntary character of the exchanges/ lack of genuine consent

Simic, Tadic, and Zaric, (Trial Chamber), October 17, 2003, paras. 967, 968: "The Trial Chamber accepts the evidence that some of the non-Serb civilians who were to be exchanged were asked whether they wanted to cross over to the other side. This, however, does not necessarily indicate that these persons voluntarily agreed to be exchanged, as they could have been left without a genuine choice as to whether to leave or to remain in the area when they made their statement. In this context, the Trial Chamber notes the atmosphere of terror and fear created for the non-Serbs who were taken from their homes and held in various detention centres in the municipality of Bosanski Samac and in other locations. When these detainees had to state whether or not they wanted to be exchanged, they were not given guarantees that they would not be mistreated again. The Trial Chamber also accepts the evidence that some of the non-Serb civilians who were exchanged were not asked whether they wanted to be exchanged. In the view of the Trial Chamber, this is a strong indicator that these civilians were not voluntarily exchanged."

"The Trial Chamber accepts the evidence on the seven exchanges from Bosanski Samac and Batkovic to Croatia (...) The Trial Chamber finds that the displacement of the witnesses involved in these exchanges constitutes unlawful deportation, as the witnesses were forcibly relocated. In this respect, the Trial Chamber reiterates that the term 'force' is not limited to physical force. Instead, the essential requirement is that the relocation is involuntary in nature, i.e., that the victim does not have a real choice(...) The detention conditions constituted a coercive environment that left the detainees without a real choice as to whether or not they wanted to be exchanged(...) The Trial Chamber is satisfied that there was no justification for the deportation of the above-mentioned witnesses."

Compare Simic, Tadic, and Zaric, (Trial Chamber), October 17, 2003, para. 1033: "The Trial Chamber finds that none of the Accused is criminally responsible for forcibly transferring non-Serb prisoners from one detention facility to another, as the Trial Chamber is not satisfied that the Accused had the intent to permanently displace these prisoners."

For findings as to transfers of non-Serb prisoners between detention centers within Serb-held territory in Bosnia and Herzegovina, see *Simic, Tadic, and Zaric*, (Trial Chamber), October 17, 2003, paras. 973-977.

v) imprisonment (Article 5(e))

(1) elements

Kordic and Cerkez, (Appeals Chamber), December 17, 2004, paras. 114-115: "The Appeals Chamber notes the finding of the Trial Chamber that imprisonment of civilians is unlawful where

- civilians have been detained in contravention of Article 42 of Geneva Convention IV, *i.e.* that they are detained without reasonable grounds to believe that the security of the Detaining Power makes it absolutely necessary;

1. the procedural safeguards required by Article 43 of Geneva Convention IV are not complied with in respect of detained civilians, even where initial detention may have been justified; and
2. the imprisonment occurs as part of a widespread or systematic attack directed against a civilian population." "[T]he existence of an international armed conflict, an element of Articles 42 and 43 of Geneva Convention IV, is not required for imprisonment as a crime against humanity."

Simic, Tadic, and Zaric, (Trial Chamber), October 17, 2003, para. 64: "The Trial Chamber considered that deprivation of an individual's liberty is arbitrary if imposed without due process of law. The Trial Chamber outlined the following elements to establish a crime of imprisonment (or unlawful confinement) as a crime against humanity under Article 5 (e) of the Statute:

1. An individual is deprived of his or her liberty.
2. The deprivation of liberty is imposed arbitrarily, that is, no legal basis can be invoked to justify the deprivation of liberty.
3. The act or omission by which the individual is deprived of his or her physical liberty is performed by the accused or a person or persons for whom the accused bears criminal responsibility with the intent to deprive the individual arbitrarily of his or her physical liberty or in the reasonable knowledge that his act or omission is likely to cause arbitrary deprivation of physical liberty."

See also Krnojelac, (Trial Chamber), March 15, 2002, para. 115 (same elements).

(2) requires "arbitrary" imprisonment

Kordic and Cerkez, (Appeals Chamber), December 17, 2004, para. 116: "The Appeals Chamber agrees with the Trial Chamber's finding 'that the term imprisonment in Article 5(e) of the Statute should be understood as arbitrary imprisonment, that is to say, the deprivation of liberty of the individual without due process of law, as part of a widespread or systematic attack directed against a civilian population.'"

Simic, Tadic, and Zaric, (Trial Chamber), October 17, 2003, para. 64: "The Trial Chamber in *Kordic* concluded that imprisonment in Article 5(e) of the Statute should be understood as arbitrary imprisonment, defined as 'deprivation of liberty of the individual without due process of law, as part of a widespread or systematic attack directed against the civilian population.' The Trial Chamber in *Krnojelac* held that 'any form of arbitrary physical deprivation of liberty of an individual may constitute imprisonment under Article 5 (e) as long as the other requirements of the crime are fulfilled.'"
Kordic and Cerkez, (Trial Chamber), February 26, 2001, para. 302: "[T]he term imprisonment in Article 5(e) of the Statute should be understood as arbitrary imprisonment, that is to say, the deprivation of liberty of the individual without due process of law, as part of a widespread or systematic attack directed against a civilian population. In that respect, the Trial Chamber will have to determine the legality of imprisonment as well as the procedural safeguards pertaining to the subsequent imprisonment of the person or group of persons in question, before determining whether or not they occurred as part of a widespread or systematic attack directed against a civilian population."

(3) same elements as "unlawful confinement" under Article 2

Simic, Tadic, and Zaric, (Trial Chamber), October 17, 2003, para. 6 3: "The Trial Chamber in *Kordic* held that the elements of the crime of unlawful confinement under Article 2 of the Statute, and the elements of the crime of imprisonment under Article 5 of the Statute are identical. The Trial Chamber in the *Krnojelac* Judgement shared this view, but also considered that as a crime against humanity, the definition of imprisonment was not restricted by the grave breaches provisions of the Geneva Conventions."

vi) torture (Article 5(f))

(1) same regardless of Article

Brdjanin, (Trial Chamber), September 1, 2004, para. 482: "The definition of 'torture' remains the same regardless of the Article of the Statute under which the Accused has been charged." *See also Simic, Tadic, and Zaric,* (Trial Chamber), October 17, 2003, para. 79 (similar).

(2) elements

Kunarac, Kovac, and Vokovic, (Appeals Chamber), June 12, 2002, para. 142: The definition [of torture] is based on the following constitutive elements: "(i) The infliction, by act or omission, of severe pain or suffering, whether physical or mental. (ii) The act or omission must be intentional. (iii) The act or omission must aim at obtaining information or a confession, or at punishing, intimidating or coercing the victim or a third person, or at discriminating, on any ground, against the victim or a third person." *See also Brdjanin,* (Trial Chamber), September 1, 2004, para. 481 (similar); *Simic, Tadic, and Zaric,* (Trial Chamber), October 17, 2003, para. 79 (similar); *Krnojelac,* (Trial Chamber), March 15, 2002, para. 179 (same); *Stakic,* (Trial Chamber), July 31, 2003, para. 750 (same elements).

(3) requirement of severe pain and suffering

Kunarac, Kovac, and Vokovic, (Appeals Chamber), June 12, 2002, para. 142: The first element for the crime of torture is "[t]he infliction, by act or omission, of severe pain or suffering, whether physical or mental."

Brdjanin, (Trial Chamber), September 1, 2004, para. 483: "The seriousness of the pain or suffering sets torture apart from other forms of mistreatment. The jurisprudence of this Tribunal and of the ICTR has not specifically set the threshold level of suffering or pain required for the crime of torture, and it consequently depends on the individual circumstances of each case."

Brdjanin, (Trial Chamber), September 1, 2004, para. 484: "In assessing the seriousness of any mistreatment, the objective severity of the harm inflicted must be considered, including the nature, purpose and consistency of the acts committed. Subjective criteria, such as the physical or mental condition of the victim, the effect of the treatment and, in some cases, factors such as the victim's age, sex, state of health and position of inferiority will also be relevant in assessing the gravity of the harm. Permanent injury is not a requirement for torture; evidence of the suffering need not even be visible after the commission of the crime."

Simic, Tadic, and Zaric, (Trial Chamber), October 17, 2003, para. 80: "The expression 'severe pain or suffering' requires that 'only acts of substantial gravity may be considered to be torture;' therefore, '[n]either interrogation by itself, nor minor contempt for the physical integrity of the victim, satisfies this requirement.' As stated in the *Krnojelac* Trial Judgement, when assessing the seriousness of the acts charged as torture, a Trial Chamber must consider:

[a]ll the circumstances of the case, including the nature and context of the infliction of pain, the premeditation and institutionalization of the ill-treatment, the physical condition of the victim, the manner and method used, and the position of inferiority of the victim. In particular, to the extent that an individual has been mistreated over a prolonged period of time, or that he or she has been subjected to repeated or various forms of mistreatment, the severity of the acts should be assessed as a whole to the extent that it can be shown that this lasting period or the repetition of acts are inter-related, follow a pattern or are directed towards the same prohibited goal."

(a) rape necessarily implies severe pain or suffering

Kunarac, Kovac, and Vokovic, (Appeals Chamber), June 12, 2002, paras. 149, 150: "[S]ome acts establish *per se* the suffering of those upon whom they were inflicted. Rape is (...) such an act(...) Sexual violence necessarily gives rise to severe pain or suffering, whether physical or mental, and in this way justifies its characterisation as an act of torture." "Severe pain or suffering, as required by the definition of the crime of torture, can thus be said to be established once rape has been proved, since the act of rape necessarily implies such pain or suffering."

Brdjanin, (Trial Chamber), September 1, 2004, para. 485: "Some acts, like rape, appear by definition to meet the severity threshold. Like torture, rape is a violation of personal dignity and is used for such purposes as intimidation, degradation, humiliation and discrimination, punishment, control or destruction of a person. Severe pain or suffering, as required by the definition of the crime of torture, can be said to be established once rape has been proved, since the act of rape necessarily implies such pain or suffering."

Kvocka et al., (Trial Chamber), November 2, 2001, para. 145: "[R]ape may constitute severe pain and suffering amounting to torture, provided that the other elements of torture, such as a prohibited purpose, are met."

(4) requirement of a prohibited purpose

Kunarac, Kovac, and Vokovic, (Appeals Chamber), June 12, 2002, para. 142: "The act or omission must aim at obtaining information or a confession, or at punishing, intimidating or coercing the victim or a third person, or at discriminating, on any ground, against the victim or a third person." *See also Krnojelac,* (Trial Chamber), March 15, 2002, para. 179 (same).

Brdjanin, (Trial Chamber), September 1, 2004, para. 486: "Acts of torture aim, through the infliction of severe mental or physical pain, to attain a certain result or purpose. Thus, in the absence of such purpose or goal, even a very severe infliction of pain would not qualify as torture for the purposes of Article 2 and Article 5 of the Statute."

Simic, Tadic, and Zaric, (Trial Chamber), October 17, 2003, para. 81: "The act of torture must have been committed deliberately and for one of the prohibited purposes outlined in the definition(...)"

Delalic et al., (Trial Chamber), November 16, 1998, para. 470: The prohibited purposes listed in the Torture Convention "do not constitute an exhaustive list, and should be regarded as merely representative."

(a) prohibited purpose need not be the predominating or sole purpose

Kunarac, Kovac, and Vokovic, (Appeals Chamber), June 12, 2002, para. 155: "[A]cts need not have been perpetrated solely for one of the purposes prohibited by international law. If one prohibited purpose is fulfilled by the conduct, the fact that such conduct was also intended to achieve a non-listed purpose (even one of a sexual nature) is immaterial."

Brdjanin, (Trial Chamber), September 1, 2004, para. 487: "The prohibited purposes [of aiming at obtaing information or a confession, or to punish, intimidate or coerce the victim or a third person, or to discriminate, on any ground, against the victim or a third person] do not constitute an exhaustive list, and there is no requirement that the conduct must *solely* serve a prohibited purpose. If one prohibited purpose is fulfilled by the conduct, the fact that such conduct was also intended to achieve a non-listed purpose is immaterial." (emphasis in original)

Simic, Tadic, and Zaric, (Trial Chamber), October 17, 2003, para. 81: "It is sufficient that one of the prohibited purposes forms part of the motivation behind the conduct, and it need not be the 'predominant or sole purpose.'"

Kvocka et al., (Trial Chamber), November 2, 2001, para. 153: "[T]he prohibited purpose need be neither the sole nor the main purpose of inflicting the severe pain or suffering."

Delalic et al., (Trial Chamber), November 16, 1998, para. 470: "[T]here is no requirement that the conduct must be solely perpetrated for a prohibited purpose. Thus, in order for this requirement to be met, the prohibited purpose must simply be part of the motivation behind the conduct and need not be the predominating or sole purpose."

(5) role of a state official not necessary

Kunarac, Kovac, and Vokovic, (Appeals Chamber), June 12, 2002, para. 148: "[T]he public official requirement is not a requirement under customary international law in relation to the criminal responsibility of an individual for torture outside of the framework of the Torture Convention."

Brdjanin, (Trial Chamber), September 1, 2004, paras. 488, 489: "Even though the [Convention Against Torture] envisages that torture be committed 'with the consent or acquiescence of a public official or other person acting in an official capacity,' the jurisprudence of this Tribunal does not require that the perpetrator of the crime of torture be a public official, nor does the torture need to have been committed in the presence of such an official."

"[T]he Trial Chamber notes that the definition of the [Convention Against Torture] relies on the notion of human rights, which is largely built on the premises that human rights are violated by States or Governments. For the purposes of international criminal law, which deals with the criminal responsibility of an individual, this Trial Chamber agrees with and follows the approach of the *Kunarac* Trial Chamber that 'the characteristic trait of the offence [under the Tribunal's jurisdiction] is to be found in the nature of the act committed rather than in the status of the person who committed it.'"

Simic, Tadic, and Zaric, (Trial Chamber), October 17, 2003, para. 82: "The presence or involvement of a state official or any other authority-wielding person in the process of torture is not necessary for the offence to be regarded as 'torture.'"

Kvocka et al., (Trial Chamber), November 2, 2001, para. 139: "[T]he state actor requirement imposed by international human rights law is inconsistent with the application of individual criminal responsibility for international crimes found in international humanitarian law and international criminal law."

(6) mens rea

Kunarac, Kovac, and Vokovic, (Appeals Chamber), June 12, 2002, para. 142: "The act or omission must be intentional." *See also Brdjanin*, (Trial Chamber), September 1, 2004, para. 481 (same); *Simic, Tadic, and Zaric*, (Trial Chamber), October 17, 2003, para. 79 (similar); *Krnojelac,* (Trial

Chamber), March 15, 2002, para. 179 (same); *Stakic*, (Trial Chamber), July 31, 2003, para. 750 (same).

Kunarac, Kovac, and Vokovic, (Appeals Chamber), June 12, 2002, para. 153: "[E]ven if the perpetrator's motivation is entirely sexual, it does not follow that the perpetrator does not have the intent to commit an act of torture or that his conduct does not cause severe pain or suffering, whether physical or mental, since such pain or suffering is a likely and logical consequence of his conduct. In view of the definition, it is important to establish whether a perpetrator intended to act in a way which, in the normal course of events, would cause severe pain or suffering, whether physical or mental, to his victims."

(7) distinction between cruel and inhumane treatment as an underlying act of persecution, and torture

Simic, Tadic and Zaric, (Trial Chamber), October 17, 2003, para. 83: "The Trial Chamber notes that beatings committed on discriminatory grounds and causing severe pain or suffering, physical or mental, constitute cruel and inhumane treatment as an underlying act of persecution. The deliberate infliction of severe physical or mental pain or suffering through beatings in order to discriminate [*sic*] a victim constitutes torture."

vii) rape (Article 5(g))

Kunarac, Kovac, and Vokovic, (Appeals Chamber), June 12, 2002, paras. 127-129: After an extensive review of the Tribunal's jurisprudence and domestic laws from multiple jurisdictions, the Trial Chamber concluded: "'[T]he *actus reus* of the crime of rape in international law is constituted by: the sexual penetration, however slight: (a) of the vagina or anus of the victim by the penis of the perpetrator or any other object used by the perpetrator; or (b) the mouth of the victim by the penis of the perpetrator; where such sexual penetration occurs without the consent of the victim. Consent for this purpose must be consent given voluntarily, as a result of the victim's free will, assessed in the context of the surrounding circumstances. The *mens rea* is the intention to effect this sexual penetration, and the knowledge that it occurs without the consent of the victim.'" "Resistance" is not a requirement. "Force or threat of force provides clear evidence of non-consent, but force is not an element *per se* of rape." "[T]here are 'factors [other than force] which would render an act of sexual penetration nonconsensual or non-voluntary on the part of the victim.' A narrow focus on force or threat of force could permit perpetrators to evade liability for sexual activity to which the other party had not consented by taking advantage of coercive circumstances without relying on physical force."

Kvocka et al., (Trial Chamber), November 2, 2001, paras. 175, 180: "Rape was succinctly defined in the *Akayesu* Trial Chamber Judgement as 'a physical invasion of a sexual nature, committed on a person under circumstances which are coercive.'" "[S]exual violence is broader than rape and includes such crimes as sexual slavery or molestation. Moreover, the *Akayesu* Trial Chamber emphasized that sexual violence need not necessarily involve physical contact and cited forced public nudity as an example."

viii) persecution (Article 5(h))

(1) elements

Deronjic, (Appeals Chamber), July 20, 2005, para. 109: "With regard to the crime of persecutions, the Appeals Chamber (...) recalls that this crime is defined as 'an act or omission which: 1. discriminates in fact and which denies or infringes upon a fundamental right laid down in international customary or treaty law (the *actus reus*); and 2. was carried out deliberately with the intention to discriminate on one of the listed grounds, specifically race, religion or politics (the *mens rea*).'" *See also Kvocka et al.*, (Appeals Chamber), February 28, 2005, paras. 320, 454; *Kordic and Cerkez,* (Appeals Chamber), December 17, 2004, paras. 101, 671; *Blaskic* (Appeals Chamber), July 29, 2004, para. 131; *Vasiljevic* (Appeals Chamber) February 25, 2004, para. 113; *Krnojelac* (Appeals Chamber), September 17, 2003, para. 185; *Blagojevic and Jokic*, (Trial Chamber), January 17, 2005, para. 579; *Brdjanin*, (Trial Chamber), September 1, 2004, para. 992; *Simic, Tadic, and Zaric*, (Trial Chamber), October 17, 2003, para. 47; *Stakic*, (Trial Chamber), July 31, 2003, para. 732 (same elements for all).

Kvocka et al., (Appeals Chamber), February 28, 2005, paras. 319-320: "Referring to the case-law of the Tribunal, the Trial Chamber defined the constitutive elements of the crime of persecution as follows: '(1) the occurrence of a discriminatory act or omission;
(2) a basis for that act or omission founded on race, religion, or politics; and (3) the intent to infringe an individual's enjoyment of a basic or fundamental right' and, in more general terms, defined persecutions as 'the gross or blatant denial, on discriminatory grounds, of a fundamental right, laid down in international customary or treaty law, reaching the same level of gravity as the other acts prohibited in Article 5.'" "The Appeals Chamber finds no error in the constitutive elements identified by the Trial Chamber but prefers to adopt the wording of the *Krnojelac* Appeal Judgement(...)"

Prosecutor v. Momir Nikolic, Case No. IT-02-60/1-S (Trial Chamber), December 2, 2003, para. 16: The elements of Article 5(h) are: "(a) the existence of an armed conflict during the time alleged in the Indictment; (b) a widespread or systematic attack directed against a civilian population and, in a manner related to that attack, (...) [acts] committed (...) against the civilian population that violated fundamental human rights; (c) (...) conduct (...) committed on political, racial or religious grounds and (...) committed with discriminatory intent; and (d) (...) aware[ness] of the wider context in which [the perpetrator's] conduct occurred."

Simic, Tadic, and Zaric, (Trial Chamber), October 17, 2003, para. 47: "The *Kupreskic* Trial Chamber defines persecution as 'the gross or blatant denial, on discriminatory grounds, of a fundamental right, laid down in international customary or treaty law, reaching the same level of gravity as the other acts prohibited in Article 5.'"

Naletilic and Martinovic, (Trial Chamber), March 31, 2003, para. 634: "The following elements must be proven to establish that persecution as a crime against humanity has been committed: i) the perpetrator commits a discriminatory act or omission; ii) the act or omission denies or infringes upon a fundamental right laid down in international customary or treaty law; iii) the perpetrator carries out the act or omission with the intent to discriminate on racial, religious or political grounds; iv) the general requirements for a crime against humanity pursuant to Article 5 of the Statute are met." *See also Nikolic - Momir*, (Trial Chamber), December 2, 2003, para. 104 (similar); *Prosecutor v. Obrenovic*, Case No. IT-02-60/2-S (Trial Chamber), December 10, 2003, para. 64 (same).

(2) actus reus

(a) persecutory acts include those listed in Article 5, acts found elsewhere in the Statute and acts not expressly prohibited under the Statute

Krnojelac, (Appeals Chamber), September 17, 2003, para. 219: "The Appeals Chamber holds that the crime of persecution may take different forms. It may be one of the other acts constituting a crime under Article 5 of the Statute or one of the acts constituting a crime under other articles of the Statute."

Brdjanin, (Trial Chamber), September 1, 2004, para. 994: "While a comprehensive list of such acts has never been established, it is clear that persecution may encompass acts which are listed in the Statute, as well as acts which are not listed in the Statute." *See also Prosecutor v. Deronjic*, Case No. IT-02-61-S (Trial Chamber), March 30, 2004, para. 118; *Stakic*, (Trial Chamber), July 31, 2003, para. 735 (similar); *Stakic*, (Trial Chamber), July 31, 2003, para. 735 (same as *Stakic*); *Vasiljevic*, (Trial Chamber), November

29, 2002, para. 246 (similar); *Krnojelac*, (Trial Chamber), March 15, 2002, para. 433 (similar).

Simic, Tadic, and Zaric, (Trial Chamber), October 17, 2003, para. 48: "Not every denial of a fundamental human right is serious enough to constitute a crime against humanity. It is clear that, for the purposes of this Tribunal, persecution may encompass acts which are listed in the Statute, as well as acts which are not listed in the Statute."

Kvocka et al., (Trial Chamber), November 2, 2001, para. 185: "The Tribunal's caselaw has specified that persecutory acts include those crimes enumerated in other sub-clauses of Article 5, crimes found elsewhere in the Statute, and acts not enumerated in the Statute but which may entail the denial of other fundamental human rights. . . ."

Kupreskic et al., (Trial Chamber), January 14, 2000, paras. 581, 614-615: "[T]he Trial Chamber rejects the notion that persecution must be linked to crimes found elsewhere in the Statute of the International Tribunal. [N] o such requirement is imposed on it by the Statute of the International Tribunal." "A narrow definition of persecution is not supported in customary international law." "[P]ersecution can consist of the deprivation of a wide variety of rights. A persecutory act need not be prohibited explicitly either in Article 5 or elsewhere in the Statute." *See also Kvocka et al.*, (Trial Chamber), November 2, 2001, para. 185 (persecution includes "acts not enumerated in the Statute").

Kupreskic et al., (Trial Chamber), January 14, 2000, paras. 605-606: "[A]cts enumerated in other sub-clauses of Article 5 can (...) constitute persecution. (...) A narrow interpretation of persecution, excluding other sub-headings of Article 5, is (...) not an accurate reflection of the notion of persecution which has emerged from customary international law." "[I]f persecution was given a narrow interpretation, so as not to include the crimes found in the remaining sub-headings of Article 5, a *lacuna* would exist in the Statute of the Tribunal. There would be no means of conceptualising those crimes against humanity which are committed on discriminatory grounds, but which, for example, fall short of genocide, which requires a specific intent 'to destroy, in whole or in part, a national, ethnical, racial, or religious group.'"

(b) acts or omissions not enumerated in Article 5 must be of equal gravity to those listed

Kordic and Cerkez, (Appeals Chamber), December 17, 2004, para. 102: "[T]he acts underlying persecutions as a crime against humanity, whether considered in isolation or in conjunction with other acts, must constitute a crime of persecutions of gravity equal to the crimes listed in Article 5 of the Statute." *See also Kvocka et al.*, (Appeals Chamber), February 28, 2005, para. 321 (similar); *Kordic and Cerkez,* (Appeals Chamber), December 17, 2004, para. 671 (same); *Blaskic,* (Appeals Chamber), July 29, 2004, para. 135 (same) and para. 138 (similar) (criticizing Blaskic Trial Chamber); *Krnojelac,* (Appeals Chamber), September 17, 2003, para. 199 (same); *Vasiljevic,* (Trial Chamber), November 29, 2002, para. 247 (similar); *Kvocka et al.*, (Trial Chamber), November 2, 2001, para. 185 (similar).

Blagojevic and Jokic, (Trial Chamber), January 17, 2005, para. 580: "It is settled in the jurisprudence of the Tribunal that the acts or omissions that can amount to persecutions not only include acts or omissions enumerated in other sub-clauses of Article 5, but also acts or omissions of equal gravity to the acts listed in Article 5 of the Statute. The requirement of 'equal gravity' defines the limits on the types of acts which qualify as persecutions."

Brdjanin, (Trial Chamber), September 1, 2004, para. 995: "Not every act or omission denying a fundamental right is serious enough to constitute a crime against humanity. While acts or omissions listed under other sub-paragraphs of Article 5 of the Statute are by definition serious enough, others (either listed under other Articles of the Statute or not listed in the Statute at all) must meet an additional test. Such acts or omissions must reach the same level of gravity as the other crimes against humanity enumerated in Article 5 of the Statute. This test will only be met by gross or blatant denials of fundamental rights." *See also Simic, Tadic, and Zaric*, (Trial Chamber), October 17, 2003, para. 48 (similar).

Deronjic, (Trial Chamber), March 30, 2004, para. 118: "[T]he common denominator of all persecutory acts must be that the acts are committed on the basis of one of the listed discriminatory grounds and must be of an equal gravity as other acts enumerated under Article 5 of the Statute."

Stakic, (Trial Chamber), July 31, 2003, para. 736: "In order to comply with the principle of *nullum crimen sine lege certa*, there must be 'clearly defined limits on the types of acts which qualify as persecution.' The acts of persecution not enumerated in Article 5 or elsewhere in the Statute must be of an equal gravity or severity as the other acts enumerated under Article 5."

Kupreskic et al., (Trial Chamber), January 14, 2000, paras. 618-619: "[I] in order for persecution to amount to a crime against humanity it is not enough to define a core assortment of acts and to leave peripheral acts in a state of uncertainty. There must be clearly defined limits on the types of acts which qualify as persecution." "[A]t a minimum, acts of persecution must be of an equal gravity or severity to the other acts enumerated under Article 5." (underlining removed)

Kupreskic et al., (Trial Chamber), January 14, 2000, para. 621: "The Trial Chamber (...) defines persecution as the gross or blatant denial, on discriminatory grounds, of a fundamental right, laid down in international customary or treaty law, reaching the same level of gravity as the other acts prohibited in Article 5." (underlining removed)

(c) separately or combined, the acts must amount to persecution

Kordic and Cerkez, (Appeals Chamber), December 17, 2004, para. 102: "[T]he acts underlying persecutions as a crime against humanity, *whether considered in isolation or in conjunction with other acts*, must constitute a crime of persecutions of gravity equal to the crimes listed in Article 5 of the Statute." (emphasis added) *See also Kvocka et al.*, (Appeals Chamber), February 28, 2005, para. 321 (similar); *Kordic and Cerkez,* (Appeals Chamber), December 17, 2004, para. 671 (same); *Blaskic,* (Appeals Chamber), July 29, 2004, para. 135 (same) and para. 138 (similar); *Krnojelac,* (Appeals Chamber), September 17, 2003, para. 199 (same).

Krnojelac, (Appeals Chamber), Separate Opinion of Judge Shahabuddeen, September 17, 2003, paras. 6-7: "Under paragraph (h) of the provision, the relevant supporting crime is 'persecution,' the underlying act or acts being only evidence of the persecution. It is the 'persecution' which must have the same gravity as that of enumerated crimes. The underlying act does not have to be a crime listed in article 5 of the Statute. It does not have to be a crime specified elsewhere in the Statute. Indeed, by itself it does not have to be a crime specified anywhere in international criminal law: it may be a non-crime.

As was recalled in the *Ministries Case*: The persecution of Jews went on steadily from step to step and finally to death in foul form. The Jews of Germany were first deprived of the rights of citizenship. They were then deprived of the right to teach, to practice professions, to obtain education, to engage in business enterprises, they were forbidden to marry except among themselves and those of their own religion; they were subject to arrest and confinement in concentration camps, to beatings, mutilation, and torture; their property was confiscated; they were herded into ghettos; they were forced to emigrate and to buy leave to do so; they were deported to the East, where they were worked to exhaustion and death; they became slave laborers; and finally over six million were murdered.

Citing that case, the *Kvocka* Trial Chamber later said: [J]urisprudence from World War II trials found acts or omissions such as denying bank accounts, educational or employment opportunities, or choice of spouse to Jews on the basis of their religion, constitute persecution. Thus, acts that are not inherently criminal may nonetheless become criminal and persecutorial if committed with discriminatory intent."

"It follows that an underlying act may not by itself constitute a crime; therefore, there can be no question of its having the same gravity as an enumerated crime. But the act, taken separately or cumulatively with other acts, can give rise to the crime of persecution. The question which then arises is what is the level of persecution that the Statute is concerned with. It is possible that there can be persecution at different levels. It is here, I think, that it would be reasonable to say that the Statute is concerned only with cases in which the level of the gravity of the proven persecution matches the level of the gravity of an enumerated crime."

Blagojevic and Jokic, (Trial Chamber), January 17, 2005, para. 582: "The acts or omissions may be evaluated separately or together in their context considering their cumulative effect." *See also Kupreskic et al.*, (Trial Chamber), January 14, 2000, para. 622 (similar).

Brdjanin, (Trial Chamber), September 1, 2004, para. 995: "[A]cts should not be considered in isolation but rather should be examined in their context and with consideration of their cumulative effect. Separately or combined, the acts must amount to persecution, though it is not required that each alleged underlying act be regarded as a violation of international law." *See also Vasiljevic,* (Trial Chamber), November 29, 2002, para. 247 (similar).

Prosecutor v. Dragan Nikolic, Case No. IT-94-2-S (Trial Chamber), December 18, 2003, para. 110: "The Trial Chamber reiterates what it stated in *Stakic:* The acts of persecution not enumerated in Article 5 or elsewhere in the Statute must be of an equal gravity or severity as the other acts enumerated under Article 5. When considering whether acts or omissions satisfy this threshold, they should not be considered in isolation but in their context and with consideration to their cumulative effect. An act which may not appear comparable to the other acts enumerated in Article 5 might reach the required level of gravity if it had, or was likely to have, an effect similar to that of the other acts because of the context in which it was undertaken." *Stakic*, (Trial Chamber), July 31, 2003, para. 736 (same).

Simic, Tadic, and Zaric, (Trial Chamber), October 17, 2003, para. 48: "When invoking this test [of when acts not listed in the Statute reach the same level of gravity as the other crimes against humanity enumerated in

Article 5], acts or omissions should not be considered in isolation but rather, in their context by looking at their cumulative effect. The *Krnojelac* Trial Chamber went on to state that, jointly or severally, 'the acts must amount to persecution, though it is not required that each alleged underlying act be regarded as a violation of international law.'"

(d) the acts underlying persecution, separately or combined, must constitute a denial of, or infringement upon, a fundamental right under international customary law

Kvocka et al., (Appeals Chamber), February 28, 2005, paras. 323, 325: "The Appeals Chamber recalls incidentally that acts underlying persecution under Article 5(h) of the Statute need not be considered a crime in international law. (...) The Appeals Chamber has no doubt that, in the context in which they were commited and taking into account their cumulative effect, the acts of harassment, humiliation and psychological abuse ascertained by the Trial Chamber are acts which by their gravity constitute material elements of the crime of persecution."

Kordic and Cerkez, (Appeals Chamber), December 17, 2004, para. 103: "[I] t must be demonstrated that the acts underlying the crime of persecutions constituted a crime against humanity in customary international law or in international treaty law at the time the accused is alleged to have committed the offence. As stated above, these acts must constitute a denial of or infringement upon a fundamental right laid down in international customary or treaty law; not every act, if committed with the requisite discriminatory intent, amounts to persecutions as a crime against humanity." *See also Blaskic,* (Appeals Chamber), July 29, 2004, para. 139 (same).

Brdjanin, (Trial Chamber), September 1, 2004, para. 995: "Separately or combined, the acts must amount to persecution, though it is not required that each alleged underlying act be regarded as a violation of international law." *See also Simic, Tadic, and Zaric,* (Trial Chamber), October 17, 2003, para. 48 (similar).

Blaskic, (Appeals Chamber), July 29, 2004, para. 160: "The Appeals Chamber considers that a Trial Chamber, when making a determination on a charge of persecutions, is obliged to assess whether the underlying acts amount to persecutions as a crime against humanity in international customary law."

Simic, Tadic, and Zaric, (Trial Chamber), October 17, 2003, para. 48: "'This test [of when acts not listed in the Statute reach the same level of gravity as the other crimes against humanity enumerated in Article 5] will only be met by gross or blatant denials of fundamental human rights.'"

Kupreskic et al., (Trial Chamber), January 14, 2000, para. 621: "The Trial Chamber (...) defines persecution as the gross or blatant denial, on discriminatory grounds, of a fundamental right, laid down in international customary or treaty law, reaching the same level of gravity as the other acts prohibited in Article 5." (underlining omitted)

But see Stakic, (Trial Chamber), July 31, 2003, para. 773: "This Trial Chamber opines that it is immaterial to identify which rights may amount to fundamental rights for the purpose of persecution. Persecution can consist of the deprivation of a wide variety of rights, whether fundamental or not, derogable or not."

(e) acts may encompass physical or mental harm or infringements upon individual freedom, as well as acts which appear less serious

Brdjanin, (Trial Chamber), September 1, 2004, para. 994: "The persecutory act or omission may encompass physical and mental harm, as well as infringements upon fundamental rights and freedoms of individuals." *See also Vasiljevic,* (Trial Chamber), November 29, 2002, para. 246 (similar); *Krnojelac*, (Trial Chamber), March 15, 2002, para. 433 (similar).

Simic, Tadic, and Zaric, (Trial Chamber), October 17, 2003, para. 50: "The persecutory act(s) or omission(s) may encompass physical and mental harm, infringements upon individual freedom, as well as acts which appear less serious, such as those targeting property, provided that the victimised persons were specially selected or discriminated on political, racial, or religious grounds."

(f) act is discriminatory where victim targeted because of group membership

Blagojevic and Jokic, (Trial Chamber), January 17, 2005, para. 583: "An act is discriminatory when a victim is targeted because of his or her membership in a group defined by the perpetrator on a political, racial or religious basis."

(g) targeted individuals may include those defined by the perpetrator as belonging to the victim group due to their close affiliations to, or sympathies for, the victim group

Simic, Tadic, and Zaric, (Trial Chamber), October 17, 2003, para. 49: "In relation to the targeted group's possession of the religious, racial or political characteristics required for the crime of persecution, the Trial Chamber refers to the *Naletilic* Trial Judgement:

. . . the targeted group does not only comprise persons who *personally* carry the (religious, racial, or political) criteria of the group. The targeted group must be interpreted broadly, and may, in particular include such persons who are *defined by the perpetrator as belonging to the victim group due to their close affiliations or sympathies for the victim group*." (emphasis in original)

Stakic, (Trial Chamber), July 31, 2003, para. 734: "The targeted individuals may include persons 'who are *defined by the perpetrator as belonging to the victim group due to their close affiliations or sympathies for the victim group*,' 'as it is the perpetrator who defines the victim group while the targeted victims have no influence on the definition of their status.'" (emphasis in original)

(h) each of the three grounds listed in Article 5(h) sufficient

Stakic, (Trial Chamber), July 31, 2003, para. 732: "Each of the three grounds listed in Article 5(h) of the Statute is in itself sufficient to qualify conduct as persecutions, notwithstanding the conjunctive 'and' in the text of Article 5(h)."

(i) actual discrimination must result

Vasiljevic (Appeals Chamber), February 25, 2004, para. 113: "Although persecution often refers to a series of acts, a single act may be sufficient, as long as this act or omission discriminates *in fact* and is carried out deliberately with the intention to discriminate on one of the listed grounds." (emphasis added) *See also Krnojelac*, (Appeals Chamber), September 17, 2003, para. 185 (discussing "the requirement for discrimination in fact (or a discriminatory act) established by the case-law"); *Brdjanin*, (Trial Chamber), September 1, 2004, para. 993 (requiring "discrimination in fact").

Blagojevic and Jokic, (Trial Chamber), January 17, 2005, para. 583: "The act or omission needs to discriminate in fact, *i.e.*, a discriminatory intent is not sufficient, but the act or omission must have discriminatory consequences."

Stakic, (Trial Chamber), July 31, 2003, para. 733: "The Trial Chamber recognises that 'the persecutory act must be *intended* to cause, *and result in*, an infringement on an individual's enjoyment of a basic or fundamental right.' Although the Statute does not explicitly require that the discrimination take place against a member of a targeted group, the act or omission must in fact have discriminatory consequences rather than have been committed only with discriminatory intent."

Compare Kordic and Cerkez, (Appeals Chamber), December 17, 2004, para. 105: "With respect to the question as to whether a particular result of [an attack launched deliberately against civilians or civilian objects] is required, the Appeals Chamber recalls that acts may constitute a crime of persecutions if they are of gravity equal to the other crimes listed in Article 5 of the Statute, whether considered in isolation or in conjunction with other acts. Therefore, the Appeals Chamber finds that [an] unlawful attack launched deliberately against civilians or civilian objects may constitute a crime of persecutions without the requirement of a particular result caused by the attack(s)."

(i) application—actual discrimination against the detainees in the Omarska camp and the non-Serb population of Prijedor

Kvocka et al., (Appeals Chamber), February 28, 2005, paras. 362, 363: "Radic submits that the Trial Chamber erred in concluding that a criminal act can be discriminatory if the perpetrator acts with discriminatory intent only. In his view, there must be discriminatory consequences to hold an act discriminatory." "The Trial Chamber found that all the detainees in the Omarska camp were non-Serbs or persons suspected of sympathizing with non-Serbs. Virtually all offences were committed against non-Serbs. The establishment of the camp formed only one element of a common plan to drive the non-Serb population of Prijedor out of the territory. Radic does not challenge these findings, nor does he dispute that the crimes committed in the Omarska camp, for which he was convicted under this count, deny or infringe fundamental rights of the victims. In the present case, the Appeals Chamber found that the Trial Chamber correctly defined the crime of persecution. Under the given circumstances, there is no doubt that the underlying crimes were committed upon discriminatory grounds, and had discriminatory effects."

(j) mistaken target of persecution is still persecution

Krnojelac, (Appeals Chamber), September 17, 2003, para. 185: "[T]he Appeals Chamber does not agree with the interpretation given to this definition [of persecution] in (...) the [*Krnojelac* Trial] Judgment (...) which reads as follows:

The crime of persecution, the only crime in the Statute which must be committed on discriminatory grounds (see *Tadic* Appeal Judgment, par 305), has as its object the protection of members of political, racial and religious groups from discrimination on the basis of belonging to one of these groups. If a Serb deliberately murders someone on the basis that he is Muslim, it is clear that the object of the crime of persecution in that instance is to provide protection from such discriminatory acts to members of the Muslim religious group. If it turns out that the victim is not Muslim, to argue that this act amounts nonetheless to persecution if done with a discriminatory intent needlessly extends the protection afforded by that crime to a person who is not a member of the listed group requiring protection in that instance (Muslims).

The Appeals Chamber finds this assertion to be incorrect. It is an erroneous interpretation of the requirement for discrimination in fact (or a discriminatory act) established by the case-law. To use the example provided in the footnote, the Appeals Chamber considers that a Serb mistaken for a Muslim may still be the victim of the crime of persecution. The Appeals Chamber considers that the act committed against him institutes discrimination in fact, *vis-à-vis* the other Serbs who were not subject to such acts, effected with the will to discriminate against a group on grounds of ethnicity."

Brdjanin, (Trial Chamber), September 1, 2004, para. 993: "With respect to the discriminatory element of the *actus reus*, although Tribunal jurisprudence is clear that the act must have discriminatory consequences, the Appeals Chamber has stated that it is not necessary that the victim of the crime of persecution be a member of the group against whom the perpetrator of the crime intended to discriminate. In the event that the victim does not belong to the targeted ethnic group, 'the act committed against him institutes discrimination in fact, *vis-à-vis* other [members of that different group] who were not subject to such acts, effected with the will to discriminate against a group on grounds of ethnicity.'"

(k) single act may constitute persecution if discriminatory intent proven

Kordic and Cerkez, (Appeals Chamber), December 17, 2004, para. 102: "The Appeals Chamber considers that:

although persecution often refers to a series of acts, a single act may be sufficient, as long as this act or omission discriminates in fact and was carried out deliberately with the intention to discriminate on one of the listed grounds." *See also Blaskic,* (Appeals Chamber), July 29, 2004, para. 135 (same); *Vasiljevic,* (Appeals Chamber), February 25, 2004, para. 113 (same); *Blagojevic and Jokic,* (Trial Chamber), January 17, 2005, para. 582 (quoting same).

Brdjanin, (Trial Chamber), September 1, 2004, para. 994: "Although persecution usually refers to a series of acts, a single act may be sufficient."

See also Simic, Tadic, and Zaric, (Trial Chamber), October 17, 2003, para. 50 (same); *Krnojelac*, (Trial Chamber), March 15, 2002, para. 433 (same).

Kupreskic et al., (Trial Chamber), January 14, 2000, para. 624: "[P]ersecution was often used to describe a series of acts. However, the Trial Chamber does not exclude the possibility that a single act may constitute persecution. In such a case, there must be clear evidence of the discriminatory intent."

(i) application—single act may constitute persecution: murder at the Drina River, in the municipality of Visegrad in south-eastern Bosnia-Herzegovina

Vasiljevic, (Appeals Chamber), February 25, 2004, paras. 112-113: "[T]he Appellant submits that the Trial Chamber made an error of law 'by convicting the accused for persecution solely on the basis of one incident which occurred on June 7, 1992 at the Drina River.'" "The Appeals Chamber does not subscribe to the views of the Appellant that the Trial Chamber erred in finding him guilty of persecution 'solely on the basis of one incident[.]' First, the Drina River incident consists of the murder of five people and the inhumane acts inflicted on two others. This incident cannot be described as a single act but rather as a series of acts. Second, as held by the Appeals Chamber in the *Krnojelac* Appeals Judgement, persecution is 'an act or omission which discriminates in fact and which: denies or infringes upon a fundamental right laid down in international customary or treaty law (the *actus reus*); and was carried out deliberately with the intention to discriminate on one of the listed grounds, specifically race, religion or politics (the *mens rea*).' Although persecution often refers to a series of acts, a single act may be sufficient, as long as this act or omission discriminates in fact and is carried out deliberately with the intention to discriminate on one of the listed grounds."

(l) prosecution must charge particular acts or omissions amounting to persecution

Blaskic, (Appeals Chamber), July 29, 2004, para. 139: "The Appeals Chamber notes that the Prosecution is required to charge particular acts as persecutions."

Prosecutor v. Kupreskic et al., Case No. IT-95-16-A (Appeals Chamber), October 23, 2001, para. 98: "[T]he fact that the offence of persecution is a so-called 'umbrella' crime does not mean that an indictment need not specifically plead the material aspects of the Prosecution case with the same detail as other crimes. Persecution cannot, because of its nebulous character, be used as a catch-all charge. Pursuant to elementary principles of criminal pleading, it is not sufficient for an indictment to charge a crime in generic terms. An indictment must delve into particulars. This does not mean, however, as correctly noted in the jurisprudence of this Tribunal, that the Prosecution is required to lay a separate charge in respect of each basic crime that makes up the general charge of persecution. What the Prosecution must do, as with any other offence under the Statue, is to particularize the material facts of the alleged criminal conduct of the accused that, in its view, goes to the accused's role in the alleged crime. Failure to do so results in the indictment being unacceptably vague since such an omission would impact negatively on the ability of the accused to prepare his defence." *See also Stakic*, (Trial Chamber), July 31, 2003, paras. 771-772 (quoting same).

Blagojevic and Jokic, (Trial Chamber), January 17, 2005, para. 581: "While the crime of persecutions is considered to be an 'umbrella' crime, the Appeals Chamber has warned that '[p]ersecution cannot, because of its nebulous character, be used as a catch-all charge.' The Prosecution must plead particular acts or omissions which it alleges amount to persecutions in the Indictment."

Brdjanin, (Trial Chamber), September 1, 2004, para. 994: "The act or omission constituting the crime of persecution may assume different forms. However, the principle of legality requires that the Prosecution must charge particular acts amounting to persecution rather than persecution in general." *See also Simic, Tadic, and Zaric*, (Trial Chamber), October 17, 2003, para. 50 (similar); *Krnojelac*, (Trial Chamber), March 15, 2002, para. 433 (same as *Brdjanin*).

Stakic, (Trial Chamber), July 31, 2003, para. 735: "In charging persecutions, the Prosecutor must plead with precision the particular acts amounting to persecutions."

(3) examples of persecution

(a) destruction of property or means of subsistence

(i) prohibition of pillage is customary international law

Blaskic, (Appeals Chamber), July 29, 2004, paras. 147, 148: "Acts of plunder, which have been deemed by the International Tribunal to include pillage, infringe various norms of international humanitarian law. Pillage is explicitly prohibited in Article 33 of Geneva Convention IV, and Article 4, para. 2(g), of Additional Protocol II. In addition, Articles 28 and 47 of the Hague Regulations of 1907 expressly forbid pillage."

"The prohibition against pillage may therefore be considered to be part of customary international law. In addition, it may be noted that the Nuremberg Charter and Control Council Law No. 10 prohibited the war crime of 'plunder of public and private property,' and the crime of pillage was the subject of criminal proceedings before the International Military Tribunal at Nuremberg and other trials following the Second World War, where in certain cases, it was charged both as a war crime and a crime against humanity. There may be some doubt, however, as to whether acts of plunder, in and of themselves, may rise to the level of gravity required for crimes against humanity."

(ii) destruction of property, depending on the nature and extent of the destruction, may be of equal gravity to other crimes listed in Article 5

Kordic and Cerkez, (Appeals Chamber), December 17, 2004, paras. 108, 109: "The Appeals Chamber finds that the destruction of property, depending on the nature and extent of the destruction, may constitute a crime of persecutions of equal gravity to other crimes listed in Article 5 of the Statute." "It has to be noted that the crime of pillage was the subject of criminal proceedings before the International Military Tribunal at Nuremberg and other trials following the Second World War, where in certain cases, it was charged both as a war crime and a crime against humanity. The Appeals Chamber has to consider whether an act of plunder, committed separately or cumulatively, with discriminatory intent *in concreto* amounts to persecutions being of an equal gravity as the other crimes against humanity listed in Article 5 of the Statute."

Blaskic, (Appeals Chamber), July 29, 2004, para. 149: "The Appeals Chamber finds that the destruction of property, depending on the nature and extent of the destruction, may constitute a crime of persecutions of equal gravity to other crimes listed in Article 5 of the Statute." *See also Blagojevic and Jokic,* (Trial Chamber), January 17, 2005, para. 594 (similar).

iii)examine severity of impact

Blaskic, (Appeals Chamber), July 29, 2004, para. 146: "The destruction of property has been considered by various Trial Chambers of the International Tribunal to constitute persecutions as a crime against humanity. The Trial Chamber in *Kupreskic* considered that whether such attacks on property constitute persecutions may depend on the type of property involved, and that 'certain types of property whose destruction may not have a severe enough impact on the victim as to constitute a crime against humanity, even if such a destruction is perpetrated on discriminatory grounds: an example is the burning of someone's car (unless the car constitutes an indispensable and vital asset to the owner).' The *Kupreskic* Trial Chamber held, however, that in the circumstances of that case, which concerned the comprehensive destruction of homes and property, this constituted 'a destruction of the livelihood of a certain population,' and may have the 'same inhumane consequences as a forced transfer or deportation.' The Trial Chamber concluded that the act 'may constitute a gross or blatant denial of fundamental human rights, and, if committed on discriminatory grounds, it may constitute persecution.' The Appeals Chamber agrees with this assessment." *See also Blagojevic and Jokic*, (Trial Chamber), January 17, 2005, para. 594 (similar); *Kupreskic*, (Trial Chamber), January 14, 2000, para. 631 (same language as quoted).

(iv) various acts covered, including plunder and looting that render a people homeless and with no means of economic support

Simic, Tadic, and Zaric, (Trial Chamber), October 17, 2003, paras. 102-103: "The jurisprudence of the Tribunal, as well as previous war crimes jurisprudence has established that the acts of plundering if carried out with the requisite discriminatory intent may form the basis of the crime of persecution. As held in *Blaskic* Trial Judgement, in the context of persecution, plunder will involve unlawful, extensive and wanton appropriation of private or 'quasi-state' public property belonging to a particular population. The *Kordic* Trial Chamber held:

[i]n the context of an overall campaign of persecution, rendering a people homeless and with no means of economic support may be the method used to coerce, intimidate, terrorise and forcibly transfer civilians from their homes and villages. Thus when the cumulative effect of (...) [these acts] is the removal of civilians from their homes on discriminatory grounds, the 'wanton and extensive destruction or plundering of Bosnian Muslim civilian dwellings, buildings, businesses, and civilian personal property and livestock' may constitute the crime of persecution." "The Trial Chamber finds no reason to disagree with the above jurisprudence and accepts that the acts of plundering and looting, as defined above, may constitute persecution."

Stakic, (Trial Chamber), July 31, 2003, paras. 763-764: "The Trial Chamber notes that prior jurisprudence has held that '[i]n the context of an overall campaign of persecution, rendering a people homeless and with no means of economic support may be the method used to "coerce, intimidate, terrorise [...] civilians [...]."' When the cumulative effect of such property destruction is the removal of civilians from their homes on discriminatory grounds, the 'wanton and extensive destruction and /or plundering of Bosnian Muslim civilian dwellings, buildings, business, and civilian personal property and livestock' may constitute the crime of persecution."

"This Trial Chamber therefore concludes that acts of 'destruction, wilful damage and looting of residential and commercial properties,' even if not listed in Article 5 of the Statute, may amount to persecution."

Kordic and Cerkez, (Trial Chamber), February 26, 2001, para. 205: "Prior jurisprudence of the International Tribunal has made clear that the destruction of property with the requisite discriminatory intent may constitute persecution." "[W]hen the cumulative effect of such property destruction is the removal of civilians from their homes on discriminatory grounds, the 'wanton and extensive destruction and/or plundering of Bosnian Muslim civilian dwellings, buildings, businesses, and civilian personal property and livestock' may constitute the crime of persecution."

Blaskic, (Trial Chamber), March 3, 2000, paras. 227, 233, 234: "[P]ersecution may take forms other than injury to the human person, in particular those acts rendered serious not by their apparent cruelty but by the discrimination they seek to instil within humankind. [P]ersecution may (...) take the form of confiscation or destruction of private dwellings or businesses, symbolic buildings or means of subsistence belonging to the Muslim population of Bosnia-Herzegovina."

"[T]he crime of 'persecution' encompasses not only bodily and mental harm and infringements upon individual freedom but also acts which appear less serious, such as those targeting property, so long as the victimised persons were specially selected on grounds linked to their belonging to a particular community."

"In the context of the crime of persecution, the destruction of property must be construed to mean the destruction of towns, villages and other public or private property belonging to a given civilian population or extensive devastation not justified by military necessity and carried out unlawfully, wantonly and discriminatorily. In the same context the plunder of property is defined as the unlawful, extensive and wanton appropriation of property belonging to a particular population, whether it be the property of private individuals or of state or 'quasi-state' public collectives(...)"

(v) institutions dedicated to religion, charity and education, the arts and sciences, historic monuments and works of art and science

Deronjic, (Trial Chamber), March 30, 2004, para. 122: "The destruction of an institution dedicated to religion is not listed under Article 5 of the Statute, but it was held in *Stakic* that 'the seizure of, destruction or wilful damage done to institutions dedicated to religion, charity and education, the arts and sciences, historic monuments and works of art and science,' a crime punishable under Article 3 (d) of the Statute, when perpetrated with the requisite discriminatory intent, amounts to Persecutions."

Stakic, (Trial Chamber), July 31, 2003, paras. 765-768: "Article 3(d) of the Statute penalises 'the seizure of, destruction or wilful damage done to institutions dedicated to religion, charity and education, the arts and sciences, historic monuments and works of art and science' as violations of the laws or customs of war." "The International Military Tribunal, and the 1991 ILC Report, *inter alia*, have singled out the destruction of religious buildings as a clear case of persecution as a crime against humanity." "This Trial Chamber shares the view that '[t]his act, when perpetrated with the requisite discriminatory intent, amounts to an attack on the very religious identity of a people.'" "The Trial Chamber therefore concludes that acts of 'destruction of, or wilful damage to, religious and cultural buildings,' even if not listed in Article 5 of the Statute, may amount to persecutions."

Kordic and Cerkez, (Trial Chamber), February 26, 2001, paras. 206-207: The following "acts may constitute the crime of persecution provided they are performed with the requisite discriminatory intent:" destruction and damage of religious or educational institutions. "The Trial Chamber (...) finds that the destruction and wilful damage of institutions dedicated to Muslim religion or education, coupled with the requisite discriminatory intent, may amount to an act of persecution."

(vi) application—equal gravity

Brdjanin, (Trial Chamber), September 1, 2004, para. 1023: "The Trial Chamber is satisfied that the destruction, wilful damage and looting of residential and commercial properties in the parts of towns, villages and other areas [in Bosnia and Herzegovina] inhabited predominantly by a Bosnian Muslim and Bosnian Croat population and destruction of, or wilful damage to, Bosnian Muslim and Bosnian Croat religious and cultural buildings in the instant case occupy the same level of gravity as the other crimes enumerated in Article 5 of the Statute."

Deronjic, (Trial Chamber), March 30, 2004, paras. 123-124: "Although the wanton destruction of property is not a crime listed under Article 5 of the Statute, it was held in *Stakic* that '[w]hen the cumulative effect of such property destruction is removal of civilians from their homes on discriminatory grounds, the "wanton and extensive destruction […] of Bosnian Muslim civilian dwellings, buildings, business, and civilian personal property and livestock" may constitute the crime of persecution.'" "The Trial Chamber finds (...) that the aforementioned acts [including killing, forcible displacement, attacks on a village and destruction of an institution dedicated to religion [committed in Glogova, in eastern Bosnia] fulfil the legal requirements of Article 5 (h) of the Statute, i.e. are of an equal gravity as the other crimes listed under Article 5 of the Statute."

(vii) application—destruction of property generally

(a) Autonomous Region of Krajina

Brdjanin, (Trial Chamber), September 1, 2004, paras. 1022, 1024: "Earlier in this judgement, the Trial Chamber established the extensive destruction and appropriation of non-Serb property [in the Autonomous Region of Krajina] located in areas predominantly inhabited by Bosnian Muslims and Bosnian Croats during the period relevant to the Indictment. The Trial Chamber also found that Muslim and Roman Catholic institutions dedicated to religion were targeted and suffered severe damage during the summer months of 1992. Unlike non-Serb property, Bosnian Serb property was systematically left intact and only sporadically damaged. The Trial Chamber, therefore, finds that the destruction and appropriation of non-Serb property and religious buildings was discriminatory in fact."

"With regard to the requisite *mens rea*, the Trial Chamber finds that the circumstances surrounding the commission of the acts of destruction and appropriation of property and the destruction or damage to religious buildings, such as the marking of Bosnian Muslim and Bosnian Croat houses to be destroyed and the destruction and subsequent flattening of non-Serb religious sites and their subsequent use as parking lots, are indicative that the acts were carried out with the intent to discriminate on racial, religious or political grounds."[25]

(b) Srebrenica

Obrenovic, (Trial Chamber), December 10, 2003, para. 37: Where the accused pled guilty to persecution as a crime against humanity, the Trial Court recognized: "Beginning around 12 July 1995 and continuing throughout the period of the executions, the personal property of the Bosnian Muslim prisoners [from Srebrenica], including their identification documents, was confiscated and destroyed by members of the VRS [Army of the Serbian Republic of Bosnia and Herzegovina/Republika Srpska] and the MUP [Ministry of the Interior] in the Zvornik area."

Nikolic – Momir, (Trial Chamber), December 2, 2003, para. 39: "Beginning around 12 July 1995 and continuing throughout the period of executions [subsequent to the fall of Srebrenica], the personal property of Bosnian Muslim men was confiscated and destroyed by members of the VRS [Army of the Serbian Republic of Bosnia and Herzegovina/Republika Srpska] and MUP [Ministry of the Interior]. This included identification documents and valuables. As the Bosnian Muslim refugees travelled along the Bratunac-Milici road, personal property was taken and destroyed. Additionally, at various execution sites, Bosnian Muslim men had any property still in their possession confiscated, and subsequently destroyed." *See also Nikolic – Momir*, (Trial Chamber), December 2, 2003, paras. 21, 31 (the destruction of personal property and effects belonging to the Bosnian Muslims was part of the crime of persecution to which Nikolic pled guilty).

Compare Blagojevic and Jokic, (Trial Chamber), January 17, 2005, paras. 615, 620: "It has been established that the Bosnian Muslim men who were taken to the 'White House' [in Potocari] had to leave their personal belongings including their wallets and identification papers outside the building and that all those belongings were subsequently burned. The Trial Chamber further recalls evidence as to a pile of burning personal belongings on the football field near Nova Kasaba where hundreds of Bosnian Muslim men had been detained. The Trial Chamber finds that the destruction of those personal belongings was not justified by military necessity."[26] "However, in relation to the destruction of the personal belongings such as clothes and wallets, the Trial Chamber does not find that those personal belongings constituted indispensable assets to their owners. The Trial Chamber therefore does not find that the burning of those personal belongings had a severe enough impact on the victims to reach the threshold of equal gravity as the acts listed in Article 5 of the Statute."

(c) Bosanski Samac

Simic, Tadic, and Zaric, (Trial Chamber), October 17, 2003, paras. 873-874, 1027: "The Trial Chamber accepts that immediately after the forcible takeover of Bosanski Samac individual looting on a large scale occurred. Cars, money, and jewellery were plundered from civilians. Furniture, kitchen appliances, and personal belongings were removed from private houses and apartments. Commercial property and farm equipment belonging to civilians in Bosanski Samac and the neighbouring villages was looted. Sometimes property was taken by force or by threat of use of force. Property exclusively belonging to non-Serbs was targeted. It has been established that paramilitaries, individual members of the 4th Detachment, policemen, and ordinary Serb civilians, were involved in acts of plundering of non-Serb property."

"While there is extensive evidence of the occurrence of unlawful appropriation of property, the Trial Chamber is not satisfied that the role of the Crisis Staff in these acts has been proved beyond reasonable doubt."

"The Trial Chamber is not satisfied that the widespread plundering and looting of the property of Bosnian Muslims and Croats was part of the common plan to persecute non-Serb civilians. While the Accuseds' knowledge of the occurrence of acts of looting is not contested in this case, the Trial Chamber is not satisfied that the Accused's intentional participation in any form has been proved beyond reasonable doubt."

(d) Prijedor municipality

Stakic, (Trial Chamber), July 31, 2003, paras. 809-810: "The Trial Chamber has already found that many residential and commercial properties were looted and destroyed in the parts of towns, villages and other areas in Prijedor municipality inhabited predominantly by Bosnian Muslims and Bosnian Croats." "The Trial Chamber is convinced that these acts amount to crimes against humanity [as persecution]."

Stakic, (Trial Chamber), July 31, 2003, paras. 811-813: "The Trial Chamber has already found that Bosnian Muslim and Bosnian Croat religious buildings were destroyed or wilfully damaged in a number of villages whereas Serb Orthodox churches remained intact." "The Catholic Church in Prijedor, for example, was blown up on 28 August 1992 by a group of soldiers and police." "The Trial Chamber is satisfied that these acts amount to crimes against humanity, committed by the direct perpetrators with the discriminatory purpose to destroy such non-Serb religious buildings."

(b) unlawful arrest

Simic, Tadic, and Zaric, (Trial Chamber), October 17, 2003, paras. 60, 62: "Unlawful arrest has not been defined in the jurisprudence of the Tribunal. The Body of Principles for the Protection of All Persons under Any Form of Detention or Imprisonment ('Body of Principles'), defines an arrest as 'the act of apprehending a person for the alleged commission of an offence or by the action of an authority.' International Conventions enshrine the right to be free from arbitrary arrest and imprisonment. Article 5 of the European Convention of Human Rights provides for the right to liberty and security and that no one shall be deprived thereof except in particular cases detailed in that Convention and in accordance with a procedure prescribed by law. Article 9 of the International Covenant on Civil and Political Rights provides that everyone has the right to liberty and security of the person and no one shall be subjected to arbitrary arrest or detention, except in accordance with procedures established by law. The Trial Chamber considers, therefore, that the act of unlawful arrest means to apprehend a person, without due process of law."

"The Trial Chamber is of the opinion that while unlawful arrest may in itself not constitute a gross or blatant denial of a fundamental right reaching the same level of gravity as the other acts prohibited under Article 5, when considered in context, together with unlawful detention or confinement, such acts may constitute the crime of persecution as a crime against humanity."

(i) application—unlawful arrest: Bosanski Samac

Simic, Tadic, and Zaric, (Trial Chamber), October 17, 2003, paras. 654, 656, 657: "The Trial Chamber is satisfied that following the takeover in Bosanski Samac Municipality on 17 April 1992, and continuing throughout 1992, large-scale arrests of Bosnian Muslims and Bosnian Croats were carried out in the Municipality." "The majority of persons arrested were non-Serb civilians in Bosanski Samac, namely Bosnian Muslims and Bosnian Croats. One category of persons arrested, who were civilians, were the women, children, and elderly who were taken from their homes and brought to Zasavica." "The Trial Chamber concludes that the arrests of groups of women, children and elderly, who were subsequently detained in Zasavica and Crkvina were arbitrary, with no lawful basis. They were arrested because they were non-Serbs, not because there was a reasonable suspicion that they had committed any offences, or for reasons of their safety."

(c) unlawful detention

Simic, Tadic, and Zaric, (Trial Chamber), October 17, 2003, para. 59: "[T]he *Blaskic* Trial Chamber has considered unlawful detention as a form of the crime of persecution, defining unlawful detention as 'unlawfully depriving a group of discriminated civilians of their freedom.' The *Kupreskic* Trial Chamber also held that the organised detention of civilians may constitute persecution. Unlawful confinement of civilians is a grave breach of the Geneva Conventions of 1949 found in Article 2(g) of the Statute, and the crime of imprisonment is listed as a crime against humanity in Article 5(e) of the Statute."

Simic, Tadic, and Zaric, (Trial Chamber), October 17, 2003, para. 61: "[U]nlawful detention, confinement and imprisonment have each been considered acts of persecution and constituting crimes against humanity(...)"

Simic, Tadic, and Zaric, (Trial Chamber), October 17, 2003, para. 66: "The Trial Chamber considers that the elements of the offence of unlawful detention are the same as those for unlawful confinement and imprisonment as set out in the *Krnojelac* Judgement (...)It has noted that the Body of Principles refers to the terms detention and imprisonment interchangeably, and defines detention and imprisonment as the condition of detained or imprisoned persons, which is further described as 'any person deprived of personal liberty except as a result of conviction for an offence.'" *See Krnojelac,* (Trial Chamber), March 15, 2002, para. 115.

Blaskic, (Trial Chamber), March 3, 2000, para. 234: "The unlawful detention of civilians, as a form of the crime of persecution, means unlawfully depriving a group of discriminated civilians of their freedom."

(i) application—unlawful detention

(a) Lasva River Valley region in central Bosnia

Blaskic, (Appeals Chamber), July 29, 2004, para. 155: "The Appeals Chamber considers that the acts charged in the Indictment which encompass *the detention of Bosnian Muslim civilians* who were killed, used as human shields, beaten, subjected to physical or psychological abuse and intimidation, inhumane treatment, and deprived of adequate food and water [in the Lasva River Valley region in central Bosnia], all rise to the level of gravity of the other crimes enumerated in Article 5." (emphasis added).

(b) Bosanski Samac, north-eastern Bosnia and Herzegovina

Simic, Tadic, and Zaric, (Trial Chamber), October 17, 2003, paras. 684-685: "The Trial Chamber finds that the Bosnian Croat, Bosnian Muslims and other non-Serbs detained in the detention facilities above, namely at the [Secretariat of the Interior], [Territorial Defence], primary and secondary schools, Brcko, and Bijeljina [in Bosanski Samac, in north-eastern Bosnia and Herzegovina], were deprived of their liberty arbitrarily. The evidence has clearly established that there was no legal basis which could be relied upon to justify their deprivation of liberty under national or international law. The small group of members of the SDA [Party of Democratic Action] paramilitary unit, which the Trial Chamber accepted may have been arrested upon a reasonable suspicion of committing a crime, were not subject to fair or lawful criminal proceedings to justify their detention. Others who were detained were not under suspicion of having ever committed a crime, and again, were not subjected to fair and lawful proceedings to justify their continued detention."

"The Trial Chamber is satisfied that non-Serb persons were arrested and detained because of their non-Serb ethnicity and political affiliations. The overwhelming majority of those detained were Bosnian Croats and Bosnian Muslims civilians. The Trial Chamber finds that the arrest and detention of the non-Serb civilian population in Bosanski Samac was carried out on a discriminatory basis, as the Bosnian Muslim and Bosnian Croat population was targeted specifically, while their Serb neighbours were on the whole left unharmed. In addition, members of the SDA and [Croatian Democratic Union], Bosnian Muslim and Croat political parties were arrested and detained, while again, members of the Serb parties were not."

(c) Ahmici, located in the municipality of Vitez in the Lasva River Valley in central Bosnia and Herzegovina

Kupreskic, (Trial Chamber), January 14, 2000, para. 629: "[T]he Trial Chamber finds that the 'deliberate and systematic killing of Bosnian Muslim civilians' [in Ahmici] as well as their 'organised detention and expulsion from Ahmici' can constitute persecution. This is because these acts qualify as murder, imprisonment, and deportation, which are explicitly mentioned in the Statute under Article 5."

(d) unlawful confinement

Simic, Tadic, and Zaric, (Trial Chamber), October 17, 2003, para. 63: "Unlawful confinement has been considered by the Tribunal to constitute persecution and a crime against humanity. The Trial Chamber in *Kordic* held that the elements of the crime of unlawful confinement under Article 2 of the Statute, and the elements of the crime of imprisonment under Article 5 of the Statute are identical. The Trial Chamber in the *Krnojelac* Judgement shared this view, but also considered that as a crime against humanity, the definition of imprisonment was not restricted by the grave breaches provisions of the Geneva Conventions."

Simic, Tadic, and Zaric, (Trial Chamber), October 17, 2003, para. 65: "[T]he Trial Chamber adopts the elements of the crime of imprisonment under Article 5(e) of the Statute, as set out in the *Krnojelac* Trial Judgement, and applies this test to the charge of unlawful detention and confinement in the Amended Indictment."

See Krnojelac, (Trial Chamber), March 15, 2002, para. 115: "To establish the crime of imprisonment as a crime against humanity under Article 5(e) of the Tribunal's Statute, the Trial Chamber accordingly finds that the following elements must be established in the circumstances of the present case:

1 An individual is deprived of his or her liberty.

2 The deprivation of liberty is imposed arbitrarily, that is, no legal basis can be invoked to justify the deprivation of liberty.

3 The act or omission by which the individual is deprived of his or her physical liberty is performed by the accused or a person or persons for whom the accused bears criminal responsibility with the intent to deprive the individual arbitrarily of his or her physical liberty or in the reasonable

knowledge that his act or omission is likely to cause arbitrary deprivation of physical liberty."

(i) application—unlawful confinement: Municipalities of Bosanski Samac and Odzak

See Simic, Tadic, and Zaric, (Trial Chamber), October 17, 2003, paras. 684-685 (finding that Bosnian Croats, Bosnian Muslims, and other non-Serbs detained at the SUP (Secretariat of the Interior), TO (Territorial Defense), primary and secondary schools, Brcko, and Bijeljina detention facilities [in the Municipalities of Bosanski Samac and Odzak] were arbitrarily deprived of their liberty).

(e) deportation, forcible transfer and forcible displacement

(i) are crimes of equal gravity to other crimes listed in Article 5

Blaskic, (Appeals Chamber), July 29, 2004, paras. 152-153: "The Appeals Chamber in the *Krnojelac* case held that:

Forcible displacements, taken separately or cumulatively, can constitute a crime of persecution of equal gravity to other crimes listed in Article 5 of the Statute. [...] The Appeals Chamber concludes that displacements within a state or across a national border, for reasons not permitted under international law, are crimes punishable under customary international law, and these acts, if committed with the requisite discriminatory intent, constitute the crime of persecution under

Article 5(h) of the Statute." "In light of the foregoing analysis and jurisprudence, the Appeals Chamber considers that at the time relevant to the Indictment in this case, deportation, forcible transfer, and forcible displacement constituted crimes of equal gravity to other crimes listed in Article 5 of the Statute and therefore could amount to persecutions as a crime against humanity." *See also Blaskic*, (Appeals Chamber), July 29, 2004, para. 151 (discussing deportation and forcible transfer under the Geneva Conventions).

Blagojevic and Jokic, (Trial Chamber), January 17, 2005, para. 602: "The Trial Chamber finds that forcible transfer, taken separately or cumulatively, and when committed on discriminatory grounds it is of equal gravity to other crimes listed in Article 5 of the Statute and therefore it may constitute persecutions."

Brdjanin, (Trial Chamber), September 1, 2004, para. 1025: "The Prosecution charges 'the deportation or transfer of Bosnian Muslims and Bosnian Croats [...] from areas within the [Autonomous Region of Krajina] municipalities

[...] to areas under the control of the legitimate government of Bosnia and Herzegovina (Travnik) and Croatia (Karlovac)' as persecutions. These acts are separately charged as deportation (a crime against humanity under Article 5(d) of the Statute) and as inhumane acts (forcible transfer) (a crime against humanity under Article 5(i) of the Statute) and as such are by definition of sufficient gravity to constitute persecution."

See also Simic, Tadic and Zaric, (Trial Chamber), October 17, 2003, para. 121: "While Article 5(d) of the Statute prohibits 'deportation,' forcible transfer is not explicitly mentioned in Article 5(d) and (h) of the Statute. Thus, forcible transfer can only constitute a persecutory act if it amounts to a 'gross and blatant denial, on discriminatory grounds, of a fundamental right, laid down in international customary or treaty law, reaching the same level of gravity as the other acts prohibited in Article 5' of the Statute."

(ii) displacements punishable under customary international law

Krnojelac, (Appeals Chamber), September 17, 2003, para. 223: "[T]he Appeals Chamber holds that at the time of the conflict in the former Yugoslavia, displacements both within a state and across a national border were crimes under customary international law."

Blagojevic and Jokic, (Trial Chamber), January 17, 2005, para. 595: "It is well established that displacements within a state or across national borders, for reasons not permitted under international law, are crimes punishable under customary international law."

(iii)deportation, forcible transfer and forcible displacement defined

Blagojevic and Jokic, (Trial Chamber), January 17, 2005, para. 595: "The crime of forcible transfer has been defined in the jurisprudence of this Tribunal as the forced displacement of individuals from the area in which they are lawfully present without grounds permitted under international law. Traditionally, the distinction between forcible transfer and deportation is that the first one consists of forced displacements of individuals within state borders, while the second one consists of forced displacement beyond internationally recognised state borders."

Brdjanin, (Trial Chamber), September 1, 2004, para. 540: "Traditionally, the distinction between the *actus reus* of 'deportation' and 'forcible transfer' is identified with the destination to which individuals are displaced. The Trial Chamber notes that the majority of trial judgements from this Tribunal that have addressed the issue have held that under customary international law, 'deportation' consists of the forced displacement of individuals *beyond* internationally recognised state borders. In contrast, 'forcible transfer' may consist of forced displacement *within* state borders." (emphasis in original)

Blaskic, (Trial Chamber), March 3, 2000, para. 234: "The deportation or forcible transfer of civilians [as a form of the crime of persecution] means 'forced displacement of the persons concerned by expulsion or other coercive acts from the area in which they are lawfully present, without grounds permitted under international law.'"

For the holding that the failure to distinguish persecution by way of deportation and expulsion from expulsion or forcible transfer was not reversible error where there was no ambiguity that the indictment covered displacements both within and outside the borders of Bosnia and Herzegovina, see *Krnojelac*, (Appeals Chamber), September 17, 2003, paras. 214-215.

For discussion of when deportation and imprisonment should be classified as crimes under Article 5 (d) and (e) of the Statute, respectively, or as persecution under Article 5(h), see *Krnojelac*, (Appeals Chamber), Separate Opinion of Judge Schomburg, September 17, 2003, paras. 4, 11.

(a) forcible displacement not limited to displacements across a national border

Krnojelac, (Appeals Chamber), September 17, 2003, para. 218: "The Appeals Chamber holds that acts of forcible displacement underlying the crime of persecution punishable under Article 5(h) of the Statute are not limited to displacements across a national border. The prohibition against forcible displacements aims at safeguarding the right and aspiration of individuals to live in their communities and homes without outside interference. The forced character of displacement and the forced uprooting of the inhabitants of a territory entail the criminal responsibility of the perpetrator, not the destination to which these inhabitants are sent."

Krnojelac, (Appeals Chamber), September 17, 2003, paras. 221-222: "On several occasions, the Tribunal's Trial Chambers have found that the forced displacement of the population within a state or across its borders constituted persecution."

"The Appeals Chamber concludes that displacements within a state or across a national border, for reasons not permitted under international law, are crimes punishable under customary international law, and these acts, if committed with the requisite discriminatory intent, constitute the crime of persecution under Article 5(h) of the Statute."

(b) error of law not to examine whether forcible displacement constituted a crime under customary international law at the time committed

Krnojelac, (Appeals Chamber), September 17, 2003, paras. 223-224: "[T]he Appeals Chamber holds that at the time of the conflict in the former Yugoslavia, displacements both within a state and across a national border were crimes under customary international law. Consequently, the principle *nullum crimen sine lege* has been respected." "The Appeals Chamber finds that by failing to establish whether the alleged acts of forcible displacement constituted persecution, the Trial Chamber committed an error of law which invalidates its decision."

(vi) elements

Simic, Tadic and Zaric, (Trial Chamber), October 17, 2003, para. 124: "[T]he following common elements need to be ascertained for a finding that an act of deportation or forcible transfer has occurred: (i) the unlawful character of the displacement; (ii) the area where the person displaced lawfully resided and the destination to which the person was displaced; and [(iii)] the intent of the perpetrator to deport or forcibly transfer the victim."

Simic, Tadic and Zaric, (Trial Chamber), October 17, 2003, para. 123: "From the jurisprudence of the Tribunal it is clear that the elements of the offences of deportation and forcible transfer are substantially similar. As noted by the Trial Chamber in *Krstic*, 'any forced displacement is by definition a traumatic experience which involves abandoning one's home, losing property and being displaced under duress to another location.' Accordingly, the Trial Chamber is satisfied that deportation and forcible transfer share the same substantial elements, apart from deportation requiring that a national border must be crossed."

(vii) assessing voluntariness of displacement

Blagojevic and Jokic, (Trial Chamber), January 17, 2005, para. 596: "It is the 'forced character of displacement and the forced uprooting of the inhabitants of a territory' that give rise to criminal responsibility. The requirement of 'forcible' describes a situation where individuals do not have a free or 'genuine' choice to remain in the territory where they were present. The element of 'forcible' has been interpreted to include threats or the use of force, fear of violence, and illegal detention. It is essential therefore that the displacement takes place under coercion. Even in cases where those displaced may have wished – and in fact may have even requested – to be removed, this does not necessarily mean that they had or exercised a genuine choice. The trier of fact must consequently consider the prevailing situation and atmosphere, as well as all relevant circumstances, including in particular the victims' vulnerability, when assessing whether the displaced victims had a genuine choice to remain or leave and thus whether the resultant displacement was unlawful."

Simic, Tadic, and Zaric, (Trial Chamber), October 17, 2003, paras. 126, 128: "The Trial Chamber is of the view that in assessing whether the displacement of a person was voluntary or not, it should look beyond formalities to all the circumstances surrounding the person's displacement, to ascertain that person's genuine intention. For instance, in situations where persons are relocated following detention in one or several places, coupled with various forms of mistreatment, an expression of consent does not necessarily reflect a person's genuine desire to leave, as the person may not be faced with a real choice. Whether a person would have wished to leave the area absent circumstances of discrimination or persecution may also be considered as indicative of a person's wish. A lack of genuine choice may be inferred from, *inter alia*, threatening and intimidating acts that are calculated to deprive the civilian population of exercising its free will, such as the shelling of civilian objects, the burning of civilian property, and the commission of – or the threat to commit – other crimes 'calculated to terrify the population and make them flee the area with no hope of return.'" "[W]hat matters is the *personal* consent or wish of an individual, as opposed to collective consent as a group, or a consent expressed by official authorities, in relation to an individual person, or a group of persons." (emphasis in original)

(viii) application—lack of possibility of genuine consent

(a) KP Dom Prison Complex in Foca, located in Bosnia and Herzegovina

Krnojelac, (Appeals Chamber), September 17, 2003, para. 233: "The Trial Chamber finds that living conditions in the KP Dom [prison complex in Foca] made the non-Serb detainees subject to a coercive prison regime which was such that they were not in a position to exercise genuine choice. This leads the Appeals Chamber to conclude that the 35 detainees were under duress and that the Trial Chamber erred in finding that they had freely chosen to be exchanged."

Krnojelac, (Appeals Chamber), Separate Opinion of Judge Shahabuddeen, September 17, 2003, paras. 9-10: "The circumstances of this case have been recalled in (...) the judgment of the Appeals Chamber (...) There were many vacant cells in KP Dom [prison complex]; yet the non-Serb detainees were heaped into crowded cells, each of which was designed to accommodate one prisoner in solitary confinement but which now held up to 18 detainees, without the possibility of lying down and with little hygiene. There was no provision for warmth even during a severe winter, and detainees were forbidden to make any necessary extra clothing. They were given bare survival food; they lost weight, between 20 and 40 kilos per detainee. They were generally required to stay in their cells, sometimes placed in isolation for small infractions. There were frequent beatings; the cries and moans of those being beaten could be heard. There was torture. Fresh bloodstains were visible. Detainees knew that colleagues were taken out never to return – that they were made to 'disappear.' There was evidence that detainees had been killed on the premises; surviving detainees knew this. The atmosphere was one of violence and fear; the climate was oppressive; detainees were vulnerable; the situation was inhuman."

"In such circumstances, it is difficult to appreciate what more the prosecution could be asked to show in discharge of its burden to prove that there was no possibility of genuine consent to work or to be relocated. The fact that some detainees were eager for the opportunity to go out of KP Dom to work or to be relocated has been dealt with in the judgment. That does not show that there was a possibility of genuine consent; on the contrary, it is only evidence of the consequence of the absence of any possibility of genuine consent."

(b) Srebrenica

See Blagojevic and Jokic, (Trial Chamber), January 17, 2005, paras. 617-618 (discussing lack of ability to genuinely consent whether to remain in or leave Srebrenica).

(ix) location to which victim is displaced must be sufficiently distant

Simic, Tadic and Zaric, (Trial Chamber), October 17, 2003, para. 130: "[T]he Trial Chamber notes that among the legal values protected by deportation and forcible transfer are the right of the victim to stay in his or her home and community and the right not to be deprived of his or her property by being forcibly displaced to another location. Therefore, the Trial Chamber finds that the location to which the victim is forcibly displaced is sufficiently distant if the victim is prevented from effectively exercising these rights."

(x) evacuation is permissible to ensure the security of the population or for imperative military reasons

Blagojevic and Jokic, (Trial Chamber), January 17, 2005, paras. 597, 598: "[F]orced displacement of individuals is a crime when it is not carried out for one of the grounds recognised under international law. Both Article 49(2) of the Fourth Geneva Convention and Article 17(1) of Additional Protocol II, which have been cited above, contain provisions providing for exceptions, namely, when 'the security of the civilians involved or imperative military reasons so demand.' The term used to describe the displacement in such exceptional situations is 'evacuation.' Evacuation is by definition a temporary and provisional measure and the law requires that individuals who have been evacuated shall be transferred back to their homes as soon as hostilities in the area in question have ceased. From this it may be concluded that it is unlawful to use evacuation measures as a pretext to remove the population and effectuate control over a desired territory. It should be recalled here that, while evacuation is undertaken in the interests of the civilian population, it is by definition an extreme measure for those displaced."

"The exceptions when evacuations may be carried out are somewhat overlapping. Evacuation to ensure the security of the population is authorised when the area in which the population is located is in danger as a result of 'military operations' or 'intense bombing.' In such situations, in the interest of the protection of the civilian population a military commander may, and is in fact duty bound to, evacuate the population. This situation is similar to that when evacuations for 'imperative military reasons' may be carried out, *i.e.* when the presence of the population hampers military operations. There is an important distinction, however, in that evacuations in this latter situation may only be carried out when necessitated by overriding, *i.e.* imperative, military reasons. In considering whether these exceptions justify proven acts of forcible population displacements, the trier of fact will consider whether there was in actual fact a military or other significant threat to the physical security of the population, and whether the military operation in question was 'imperative.'"

(xi) evacuation is permissible for humanitarian reasons

Blagojevic and Jokic, (Trial Chamber), January 17, 2005, para. 600: "In light of the particular factual situation in the present case, the Trial Chamber has considered whether the law also provides for an exception to the general prohibition against forcible displacements that would permit evacuations for humanitarian reasons. It finds that it does. The Trial Chamber reiterates the general obligation of all parties to a conflict to protect and respect the civilian population as well as other protected persons. The Trial Chamber has already found that Article 17 of Additional Protocol II is applicable in this case. Article 17 provides in part that '[t]he displacement of the civilian population shall not be ordered for reasons related to the conflict.' The Commentary to this provision indicates that for other reasons – such as the outbreak or risk of outbreak of epidemics, natural disasters, or the existence of a generally untenable and life-threatening living situation – forcible displacement of the civilian population may be lawfully carried out by parties to the conflict. Such displacement must, however, comply with the requirements of evacuation, including among others, that they be of a temporary character."

(xii) obligations incumbent upon the evacuating party

Blagojevic and Jokic, (Trial Chamber), January 17, 2005, para. 599: "If an evacuation is carried out, it is incumbent upon the evacuating party to ensure that the civilian population, to the extent possible and practicable, is properly provided for in terms of accommodation, hygiene, health, safety and nutrition. With regard to international armed conflicts, the Fourth Geneva Convention provides that the evacuating party shall ensure that members of the same family are not separated to the greatest practicable extent. While Article 17 of Additional Protocol II does not contain the same provision, this Trial Chamber does not find any reason why this general principle should not be applicable also to non-international armed conflicts."

(xiii) mens rea

Krnojelac, (Appeals Chamber), Separate Opinion of Judge Schomburg, September 17, 2003, para. 16: "The *mens rea* for deportation is the intent to remove the victim, which implies the intention that the victim can or will not return."

Blagojevic and Jokic, (Trial Chamber), January 17, 2005, para. 601: "As for the *mens rea*, the perpetrator must intent [*sic*] to remove the victims, which implies the intention that they should not return. By definition, therefore, lawful evacuations, under any of the three recognised exceptions, cannot form part of this crime. The fact that no step is taken by the perpetrator to secure the return of those displaced, when the circumstances that necessitated the evacuation have ceased, is among the factors that may prove an intent to permanently displace the victims rather than the intent to secure the population through a lawful – and therefore temporary – evacuation."

Simic, Tadic and Zaric, (Trial Chamber), October 17, 2003, paras. 134, 974: "[T]he Trial Chamber accepts that a finding of forced displacement, either as deportation or forcible transfer, requires an element of permanency in relation to the intention of the accused. An important consideration in this context will be the intended goal of the relocation." "[T]he Trial Chamber finds that relocations of non-Serb prisoners from one detention centre to another within Serb-held territory in Bosnia and Herzegovina do not constitute forcible transfer unless the Accused had the intent that the victims did not return."

(xiv) subsequent voluntary return does not impact on criminal responsibility

Blagojevic and Jokic, (Trial Chamber), January 17, 2005, para. 601: "The Trial Chamber finds that the fact that victims subsequently return to the area by their own volition does not have an impact on the criminal responsibility."

Simic, Tadic and Zaric, (Trial Chamber), October 17, 2003, para. 134: "[T] he Trial Chamber finds that whether persons forcibly displaced were able to return to their former place of residence at a later time has no bearing on the assessment of the legality of the original displacement; thus, the duration of the displacement has no impact on its illegality. Otherwise, the perpetrator who had the intent to permanently displace the victim would unjustifiably benefit from such return."

(xv) application—deportation, forcible transfer and forcible displacement

(a) from Foca municipality

Krnojelac, (Appeals Chamber), September 17, 2003, paras. 236-238: "The Trial Chamber reached the following conclusion: The expulsion, exchange or deportation of non-Serbs, both detainees at the KP Dom [prison complex in Foca] and those who had not been detained, was the final stage of the Serb attack upon the non-Serb civilian population in Foca municipality. Initially there was a military order preventing citizens from leaving Foca. However, most of the non-Serb civilian population was eventually forced to leave Foca. In May 1992, buses were organized to take civilians out of town, and around 13 August 1992 the remaining Muslims in Foca, mostly women and children, were taken away to Rozaje, Montenegro. On 23 October 1992, a group of women and children from the municipality, having been detained for a month at Partizan Sports Hall, were deported by bus to Gorazde. [...] In late 1994, the last remaining Muslim detainees at the KP Dom were exchanged, marking the end of the attack upon those civilians and the achievement of a Serbian region ethically cleansed of Muslims. By the end of the war in 1995, Foca had become an almost purely Serb town."

"Given these conclusions, as well as the discriminatory character of unlawful detention and the imposition of the living conditions described above on non-Serb KP Dom [prison complex] detainees, the Appeals Chamber considers that it was not reasonable for the Trial Chamber to conclude that there was no evidence that the 35 detainees had been transferred to Montenegro on the requisite discriminatory grounds."

"The Appeals Chamber holds that the reasoning with regard to the forcible displacement of the 35 non-Serb detainees to Montenegro is applicable *mutatis mutandis* to other displacements recognised by the Trial Chamber. The same holds for Krnojelac's discriminatory intent." *See also Krnojelac*, (Appeals Chamber), September 17, 2003, para. 233 (discussing lack of genuine consent regarding exchanges).

(b) from Srebrenica

Blagojevic and Jokic, (Trial Chamber), January 17, 2005, paras. 616-618: "It is established that the Bosnian Muslim population was forcibly displaced from the Srebrenica enclave through Potocari, including the women, children and elderly who were transported to Kladanj, and the Bosnian Muslim men who were bussed out of Potocari to temporary detention facilities in Bratunac."

"The evidence establishes that the Bosnian Muslim refugees in Potocari did not have a genuine choice of whether to remain in or leave the Srebrenica enclave. This lack of a genuine choice was a result of the actions and behaviour of the officers and soldiers of the [Army of the Republika Srpska] towards the refugees. In particular the Trial Chamber observes the following evidence testimony:

– the widespread knowledge among the Bosnian Muslim refugees of serious crimes committed by members of the Bosnian Serb forces in Potocari,
– the organised, inhumane and frequently aggressive process of separating out and removing the male members of the population,
– the evidence regarding the conditions in Potocari during the nights of 11 and, in particular, 12 July,
– that many [Army of the Republika Srpska] soldiers were cursing at the Bosnian Muslim refugees, saying that they would be slaughtered, and
– the demonstrative attack by the [Army of the Republika Srpska] on Potocari in the morning of 12 July."

"All these actions by members of the Bosnian Serb forces served to show the Bosnian Muslim refugees that they did not have a genuine choice to remain in the enclave. The transport of the Bosnian Muslim refugees out of the enclave was consequently forcible in character. Although documentary evidence indicates that the [Army of the Republika Srpska] used the term 'evacuation' to describe the forcible transfer, the Trial Chamber is unable to find that any of the exceptions to the general prohibition of forcible population displacements apply to the actions of the [Army of the Republika Srpska]. Moreover, the evidence is clear that the perpetrators did not intend that those displaced would be able to return once the situation had normalised in the area. The Trial Chamber therefore concludes that the elements of the crime of forcible transfer, as a component crime of persecution, have been met and that this crime was committed."

Nikolic - Momir, (Trial Chamber), December 2, 2003, paras. 40-42: "On the evening of 11 July 1995, Ratko Mladic and other VRS [Army of the Serbian Republic of Bosnia and Herzegovina/Republika Srpska] officers held two meetings at the Hotel Fontana with members of the Dutch Battalion and, in the case of the second meeting, a representative of the Bosnian Muslim refugees who had fled from Srebrenica. Momir Nikolic was present at the Hotel Fontana during both meetings. During the second meeting, Mladic told the Bosnian Muslim representative that his people could either 'survive or disappear.' At a third meeting held at the Hotel Fontana on 12 July 1995 attended by members of the VRS, Bosnian Serb representatives, Dutch Battalion officers and representatives of the Bosnian Muslim refugees, Ratko Mladic 'explained that he would supervise the "evacuation" of refugees from Potocari and that he wanted to see all military-aged Bosnian Muslim men so that they could be screened as possible war criminals.' It was during these meetings that 'the plan to transport the civilian refugee population from Potocari was developed.'"

"Buses began arriving on 12 July 1995 in Potocari; Momir Nikolic was present at that time. The forcible transfer process of Bosnian Muslim women and children began. Bosnian Muslim men, however, were not permitted to board the buses; they were separated and transported to detention sites in Bratunac."

"In his Statement of Facts, Momir Nikolic states that '[d]uring the attack and takeover of the Srebrenica enclave by the VRS forces in July 1995 it was the intention of the VRS forces to cause the forcible removal of the entire Muslim population from Srebrenica to Muslim-held territory.' The statement continues: 'On 11 July 1995, VRS forces captured and occupied the town of Srebrenica causing the Muslim population to move to the Dutch UN base in Potocari.'"

(c) from Banja Luka, Prijedor, Sanski Most and Bosanski Novi in the Autonomous Region of Krajina

Brdjanin, (Trial Chamber), September 1, 2004, paras. 1027-1028: "On the basis of the evidence adduced by the parties, the Trial Chamber earlier established that numerous acts of deportation and forcible transfer did take place in the period relevant to the Indictment, notably in the municipalities of Banja Luka, Prijedor, Sanski Most and Bosanski Novi. The individuals displaced as a result of these acts were almost exclusively Bosnian Muslims and Bosnian Croats. This policy was implemented through armed force, expulsion, intimidation, the imposition of intolerable living conditions, and the establishment of punitive departure conditions, all of which were targeted specifically at the Bosnian Muslim and Bosnian Croat communities.

The Trial Chamber therefore finds that these acts of deportation and forcible transfer were discriminatory in fact."

"With respect to the requisite *mens rea*, the Trial Chamber finds that the circumstances surrounding the commission of the acts of deportation and forcible transfer are indicative that the acts were carried out by the direct perpetrators with the intent to discriminate. The displacements which occurred were the result of a systematic policy on the part of the Bosnian Serb authorities to cleanse the municipalities [in the Autonomous Region of Krajina] of non-Serbs."

(d) from the Serbian Autonomous Region of Krajina

Prosecutor v. Babic, Case No. IT-03-72-S (Trial Chamber), June 29, 2004, paras. 14-16: "In the period of the Indictment, from about 1 August 1991 to 15 February 1992, Serb forces comprised of JNA [Yugoslav People's Army] units, local Serb TO [Territorial Defence] units, TO units from Serbia and Montenegro, local MUP [Serbian Ministry of Internal Affairs] police units, MUP police units from Serbia, and paramilitary units attacked and took control of towns, villages, and settlements in the [Serbian Autonomous District of] Krajina."

"After the take-over, in cooperation with the local Serb authorities, the Serb forces established a regime of persecutions designed to drive the Croat and other non-Serb civilian populations from these territories. The regime, which was based on political, racial, or religious grounds, included the extermination or murder of hundreds of Croat and other non-Serb civilians in Dubica, Cerovljanji, Bacin, Saborsko, Poljanak, Lipovaca, and the neighbouring hamlets of Skabrnja, Nadin, and Bruska in Croatia; the prolonged and routine imprisonment and confinement of several hundred Croat and other non-Serb civilians in inhumane living conditions in the old hospital and the JNA barracks in Knin, which were used as detention facilities; the deportation or forcible transfer of thousands of Croat and other non-Serb civilians from the [Serbian Autonomous District of] Krajina; and the deliberate destruction of homes and other public and private property, cultural institutions, historic monuments, and sacred sites of the Croat and other non-Serb populations in Dubica, Cerovljani, Bacin, Saborsko, Poljanak, Lipovaca, and the neighbouring hamlets of Vaganac, Skabrnja, Nadin, and Bruska."

"These acts were intended to permanently and forcibly remove the majority of the Croat and other non-Serb populations from approximately one-third of Croatia in order to transform that territory into a Serb-dominated state. The acts started on or about 1 August 1991 and continued until June 1992, at least, that is until after the indictment period, which runs only until 15

February 1992." As to Babic's participation in the campaign of persecutions and his *mens rea*, as part of evaluating his guilty plea, see *Babic*, (Trial Chamber), June 29, 2004, paras. 24-28.

(f) harassment, humiliation, degradation, and psychological abuse

Kvocka et al., (Appeals Chamber), February 28, 2005, para. 323: "Harassment, humiliation and psychological abuse are not listed as such under Article 5 of the Statute nor do they constitute specific offences under other articles of the Statute. The Appeals Chamber notes however that Common Article 3(1)(c) of the Geneva Conventions prohibits 'outrages upon personal dignity, in particular humiliating and degrading treatment.' The specific offence of outrages upon personal dignity also appears in Article 75(2)(b) of Additional Protocol I. The Appeals Chamber also considers that acts of harassment and other psychological abuse, depending on the circumstances, can clearly be assimilated to violations of the 'mental well-being of persons' prohibited under Article 75(2)(a) of Additional Protocol I. The Appeals Chamber recalls incidentally that acts underlying persecution under Article 5(h) of the Statute need not be considered a crime in international law."

Brdjanin, (Trial Chamber), September 1, 2004, para. 1014: "Humiliating and degrading treatment is prohibited under common Article 3 of the Geneva Conventions, although such acts are not explicitly listed under Article 5 or elsewhere in the Statute. In order to rise to the level of crimes against humanity, they must meet the test of gravity which satisfies the criteria for persecution."

Simic, Tadic, and Zaric, (Trial Chamber), October 17, 2003, para. 95: "The Trial Chamber [in *Kvocka*] went on to examine harassment, humiliation and psychological abuse stating that 'these acts are not explicitly listed under Article 5 nor do they appear as specific offences under other Articles of the Statute,' and concluded that: the horrendous conditions of detention and the demoralizing treatment of detainees in Omarska camp were sufficiently degrading and traumatizing to constitute per se an outrage upon personal dignity, which qualifies as persecution since it was clearly committed on discriminatory grounds. In addition to the harassment, humiliation, and psychological trauma endured by the detainees as part of their daily life in the camp, psychological abuse was also inflicted upon them through having to see and hear torturous interrogations and random brutality perpetrated on fellow inmates. The Trial Chamber is satisfied that the harassment, humiliation, and psychological abuses fall under the *actus reus* of persecution."

Stakic, (Trial Chamber), July 31, 2003, paras. 759-760: "When examining the allegations of 'harassment, humiliation and psychological abuse' and describing the conditions of detention prevailing in a camp, the Trial Chamber in the *Kvocka et. al.* case found that 'humiliating treatment that forms part of a discriminatory attack against a civilian population may, in combination with other crimes or, in extreme cases alone, similarly constitute persecution.'" "This Trial Chamber holds that the alleged acts of constant humiliation and/or degradation may amount to persecutions."

Kvocka et al., (Trial Chamber), November 2, 2001, para. 190: "In order to constitute persecution, harassment, humiliation, and psychological abuse must occupy the same level of seriousness as other listed or recognized crimes against humanity, or together with other crimes cognizable under Article 5, they must form part of a course of conduct which satisfies the criteria for persecution." "[H]umiliating treatment that forms part of a discriminatory attack against a civilian population may, in combination with other crimes or, in extreme cases alone, similarly constitute persecution."

(i) application—harassment, humiliation, degradation and psychological abuse

(a) the Omarska Camp

Kvocka et al., (Appeals Chamber), February 28, 2005, paras. 324-325: "Contrary to Kvocka's claim, the Trial Chamber endeavoured to show in what respect the acts of harassment, humiliation and psychological abuse committed in the [Omarska] camp reached the degree of gravity of the crimes against humanity explicitly listed in the Statute. The Trial Chamber argued as follows: (…) The conditions of detention prevailing in the camp – gross overcrowding in small rooms without ventilation, requiring the detainees to beg for water, and forcing them to relieve bodily functions in their clothes – were themselves a form of abuse, and were intended to harass, humiliate, and inflict mental harm on the detainees. The constant berating, demoralizing, and threatening of detainees, including the guards' coercive demands for money from detainees, and the housing of detainees in lice-infected and cramped facilities were calculated by participants in the operation of the camp to inflict psychological harm upon detainees. Just as rape and forced nudity are recognized as crimes against humanity or genocide if they form part of an attack directed against a civilian population or if used as an instrument of the genocide, humiliating treatment that forms part of a discriminatory attack against a civilian population may, in combination with other crimes or, in extreme cases alone, similarly constitute persecution. The Trial Chamber is also satisfied that the horrendous conditions of detention and the demoralizing treatment of detainees in Omarska camp were sufficiently degrading and traumatizing to constitute *per se* an outrage upon personal dignity, which qualifies as persecution since it was clearly committed on discriminatory grounds."

"The Appeals Chamber has no doubt that, in the context in which they were commited [*sic*] and taking into account their cumulative effect, the acts of harassment, humiliation and psychological abuse ascertained by the Trial Chamber are acts which by their gravity constitute material elements of the crime of persecution. The Appeals Chamber finds the conclusion reached by the Trial Chamber reasonable."

(b) camps and detention facilities in the Autonomous Region of the Krajina

Brdjanin, (Trial Chamber), September 1, 2004, paras. 1015-1020: "There are no specific incidents expressly charged as constant humiliation and degradation of Bosnian Muslims and Bosnian Croats in the Indictment. The Trial Chamber has already established the horrific conditions in which Bosnian Muslims and Bosnian Croats were forced to live in camps and other detention facilities [in the Autonomous Region of the Krajina], which were themselves humiliating and degrading. As part of the attack on human dignity, Bosnian Muslims and Bosnian Croats were constantly called by pejorative names while being forced to sing 'Cetnik' songs, show the three-fingered Serbian greeting and show devotion for Serbian national symbols. Such treatment was humiliating and degrading to all non-Serbs. Beatings inside and outside camps were ubiquitous and merciless."

"There are many more examples of incidents in which the human dignity of Bosnian Muslims and Bosnian Croats was treated with outright contempt. The conditions in which people were transported to and from camps bear a resemblance to the transportation of livestock. In the camps and other places of detention, it was commonplace that detainees had no choice but to relieve themselves in the room in which they were detained."

"During interrogations, detainees were made to adopt uncomfortable postures while being held at gunpoint. Once, a Bosnian Muslim was forced to drink whisky. A Bosnian Croat was made to eat the piece of paper on which he had written a statement because he had used Latin, not Cyrillic script."

"As part of the ill-treatment by camp guards, Bosnian Muslims and Bosnian Croats were also forced to beat and perform sexual acts on each other. It was announced that their mothers and sisters would be raped in front of them. Bosnian Muslims and Bosnian Croats were forced to watch other members of their group being killed, raped, and beaten. Detainees were provided with totally inadequate food over long periods. On one occasion, when some bread was thrown into their room, they started to fight over it like animals. People licked walls in order to get water from condensation.

Some detainees started to hallucinate or became mentally disturbed as a result of the conditions."

"As a final humiliating gesture, the bodies of killed Bosnian Muslims and Bosnian Croats were often treated with disrespect or even mutilated, buried in mass graves and sometimes re-buried in order to cover up the crimes committed. Some of these gravesites have not been discovered to date. There can be no doubt that these acts were discriminatory in fact. The Trial Chamber also finds that in the given situation, these acts amount to the level of gravity of crimes against humanity."

"With regard to the requisite *mens rea*, taking into account the circumstances surrounding the commission of these acts of humiliation and degradation, the Trial Chamber has no doubt at all that the direct perpetrators possessed the requisite discriminatory intent based on racial, religious and political grounds."[27]

(c) the Omarska, Keraterm and Trnopolje camps

Stakic, (Trial Chamber), July 31, 2003, paras. 807-808: "The Trial Chamber is satisfied beyond reasonable doubt that thousands of non-Serbs detained in the Omarska, Keraterm and Trnopolje camps were constantly subjected to acts of humiliation and degradation. Apart from the already established terrible conditions in which the detainees were forced to live in the camps, which were themselves humiliating and degrading, several Muslim and Croat witnesses testified that, during their detention, on different occasions, they were forced to show Serbian signs (three fingers) and sing 'Chetnik' songs. These songs were abusing and humiliating to all non-Serb people. In addition, they were cursed, insulted and called 'ustasa,' 'balija' or 'Green Berets.' A witness testified that in the Prijedor SUP [Secretariat of the Interior] Building prisoners were regularly threatened and insulted."

"The Trial Chamber is satisfied that these acts were committed by the direct perpetrators with the intent to inflict humiliating and degrading treatment upon the victims. The Trial Chamber is also convinced that these acts amount to crimes against humanity [as a form of persecution]."

(g) murder

Kordic and Cerkez, (Appeals Chamber), December 17, 2004, para. 106: "With respect to the charges of wilful killing, murder, causing serious injury, and inhuman treatment, the Appeals Chamber considers that the inherent right to life and to be free from cruel, inhuman or degrading treatment or punishment is recognised in customary international law and is embodied in Articles 6 and 7 of the ICCPR [International Covenant on Civil and

Political Rights], and Articles 2 and 3 of the ECHR [European Convention for the Protection of Human Rights and Fundamental Freedoms]. It is clear in the jurisprudence of the International Tribunal that acts of wilful killing, murder, and of serious bodily and mental harm are of sufficient gravity as compared to the other crimes enumerated in Article 5 of the Statute and therefore may constitute persecutions. As concluded by *inter alia* the *Kupreskic et al.* Trial Chamber, the crime of persecutions has developed in customary international law to encompass acts that include 'murder, extermination, torture, and other serious acts on the person such as those presently enumerated in Article 5.'" *See also Blaskic,* (Appeals Chamber), July 29, 2004, para. 143 (same).

Blaskic, (Appeals Chamber), July 29, 2004, para. 143: "With respect to the charges of killing and causing serious injury, the Trial Chamber stated that 'there is no doubt that serious bodily and mental harm [...] may be characterised as persecution when [...] they target the members of a group because they belong to a specific community.'"

Blagojevic and Jokic, (Trial Chamber), January 17, 2005, para. 585: "Murder is set out as a crime against humanity pursuant to Article 5(a) of the Statute and, as such, can therefore amount to persecutions."

Brdjanin, (Trial Chamber), September 1, 2004, para. 999: "Because the elements of acts of wilful killings are identical to those required for murder under Article 5 of the Statute, they are as such of sufficient gravity to constitute persecution."

Deronjic, (Trial Chamber), March 30, 2004, para. 119: "Although the term 'killing' as such is not mentioned in the list of crimes punishable under Article 5 of the Statute, it is used interchangeably with the term 'murder,' which is a crime punishable pursuant to Article 5 (a) of the Statute."

Kupreskic et al, (Trial Chamber), January 14, 2000, para. 615: "In their interpretation of persecution courts have included acts such as murder, extermination, torture, and other serious acts on the person such as those presently enumerated in Article 5."

(i) application—murder

(a) Srebrenica

Blagojevic and Jokic, (Trial Chamber), January 17, 2005, para. 604: "[T]he Trial Chamber finds that during the days following the fall of Srebrenica thousands of Bosnian Muslim men were murdered. The Trial Chamber further finds that amongst the killed there were also elderly and children.

It also recalls the stabbing to death of a baby by [Army of the Republika Srpska] soldiers when they were told that it was a boy. The Trial Chamber also finds that babies were killed intentionally by not satisfying their essential needs. The Trial Chamber further finds that women were killed and recalls evidence as to dead female bodies that were found in a stream near the UN compound in Potocari." *See also Blagojevic and Jokic*, (Trial Chamber), January 17, 2005, para. 620 (finding that murder, *inter alia*, amounted to the crime of persecution).

Obrenovic, (Trial Chamber), December 10, 2003, para. 30: Where the accused pled guilty to persecution as a crime against humanity, the Trial Court recognized: "Within approximately one week in mid-July 1995, approximately 6,000 Bosnian men who had escaped in 'the column' from Srebrenica were captured, detained and executed in various locations in the Bratunac and Zvronik municipalities. Along the route between Bratunac and Zvornik, the names previously used to mark settlements and communities or places of learning, culture and work or for geographic features are now used to identify mass execution sites: Jadar River, Cerska Valley, Petkovci School, Pilica Cultural Centre, and the villages of Tisca and Orahovac. At one location, Branjevo Military Farm, approximately 1,200 Bosnian Muslim men who had been captured from the column were executed by automatic weapon fire. Over 1,000 prisoners were executed at the Kravica warehouse on 13 July 1995. . . ."

(b) Autonomous Region of Krajina

Brdjanin, (Trial Chamber), September 1, 2004, paras. 1000-1001: "Earlier in this Judgement, the Trial Chamber defined the legal requirements for the crime of killings and established that at least 1669 Bosnian Muslims and Bosnian Croats were killed in the [Autonomous Region of Krajina] at the time relevant to the Indictment. The Trial Chamber finds that these killings were discriminatory in fact."

"With respect to the requisite *mens rea*, the Trial Chamber observes that the use of pejorative names such as 'Balijas' for Muslims, 'Ustasas' for Croats and other verbal abuse often accompanied the killings. The Bosnian Serb direct perpetrators frequently celebrated their deeds by singing 'Cetnik' songs. On occasion, Bosnian Muslims were deprived of their lives because they were believed to be members or supporters of the SDA [Party for Democratic Action]. Before they were killed, Bosnian Muslims and Bosnian Croats were hit with or forced to kiss Serbian religious and national symbols, and made to sing Serbian songs. In contrast, a detainee who claimed to have a Serbian mother was spared execution. The Trial Chamber concludes that the circumstances surrounding the killings of Bosnian Muslims and Bosnian

Croats substantiate the finding of discriminatory intent on racial, religious or political grounds on the part of the direct perpetrators."[28]

(c) Municipality of Prijedor

For findings that killings of the non-Serb population in the Municipality of Prijedor constitute murder underlying the charge of persecution, see *Stakic*, (Trial Chamber), July 31, 2003, paras. 775-779.

(h) torture

Kordic and Cerkez, (Appeals Chamber), December 17, 2004, para. 106: "As concluded by *inter alia* the *Kupreskic et al.* Trial Chamber, the crime of persecutions has developed in customary international law to encompass acts that include 'murder, extermination, torture, and other serious acts on the person such as those presently enumerated in Article 5.'"

Brdjanin, (Trial Chamber), September 1, 2004, para. 1002: "Torture (...) [under] Article 5(f) of the Statute (...) is of sufficient gravity to constitute persecution."

Simic, Tadic, and Zaric, (Trial Chamber), October 17, 2003, para. 79: "Torture is contained in Article 5(f) of the Statute, and as such, is of sufficient gravity to constitute an underlying offence of persecution."

Kupreskic et al, (Trial Chamber), January 14, 2000, para. 600: "It is clear that the courts understood persecution to include severe attacks on the person such as murder, extermination and torture; acts which potentially constitute crimes against humanity under the other subheadings of Article 5."

(i) application—torture

(a) camps and detention facilities in the Autonomous Region of Krajina

Brdjanin, (Trial Chamber), September 1, 2004, paras. 1003-1004: "The Trial Chamber has (...) found that in many instances, Bosnian Muslims and Bosnian Croats were subjected to severe ill-treatment and abuse amounting to torture. The Trial Chamber finds that these acts of torture were discriminatory in fact."

"With regard to the requisite *mens rea*, the Trial Chamber recalls that in camps and detention facilities, Bosnian Muslims and Bosnian Croats were commonly beaten up severely by their Bosnian Serb guards, as well as by Bosnian Serbs admitted from outside into the places of detention. Before and during these acts, detainees were frequently cursed, insulted, and called by derogatory names referring to their ethnicity. When Bosnian

Muslims refused to kiss the Serbian flag or the four Serbian S's, they were stabbed or beaten until they fell unconscious. In many instances, severe pain or suffering was inflicted on Bosnian Muslims because they were allegedly supporting an independent Bosnian state or the SDA [Party for Democratic Action]. Serbian songs were chanted very frequently during this ill-treatment and at times the victims themselves were forced to sing them. The Trial Chamber concludes that the circumstances surrounding the commission of acts of torture leave no doubt that they were carried out with the intention to discriminate against the victims on racial, religious or political grounds."[29]

(b) detention facilities in Bosanski Samac, Crkvina, Brcko, Bijeljina

Simic, Tadic, and Zaric, (Trial Chamber), October 17, 2003, para. 772: "The Trial Chamber is further satisfied that the other heinous acts that witnesses testified about, including sexual assaults, the extraction of teeth, and the threat of execution, constitute torture. These acts caused severe physical and mental pain and suffering and occurred in order to discriminate on ethnic grounds against the victims."

(c) the Omarska, Keraterm and Trnopolje camps and elsewhere

Stakic, (Trial Chamber), July 31, 2003, paras. 780-785: "The Trial Chamber has already found that many of the detainees at the Omarska, Keraterm and Trnopolje camps were subjected to serious mistreatment and abuse amounting to torture. Detainees were severely beaten, often with weapons such as cables, batons and chains. In Omarska and Keraterm, this occurred on a daily basis. As a result of these brutal beatings detainees were seriously injured. The Trial Chamber is convinced that severe beatings were also committed in the Miska Glava community centre, the Ljubija football stadium, the SUP [Secretariat of the Interior] building, and outside the camps."

"These examples of serious mistreatment lead the Trial Chamber to the following conclusions. First, all the mistreatment was of such a serious nature that it amounted to the infliction of severe pain or suffering. Second, the examples provided show that the direct perpetrators had the intent to inflict such pain or suffering for one of the purposes set out in the definition of torture. Some examples demonstrate that the direct perpetrator intended to obtain information from the victim. Other examples indicate that the direct perpetrator inflicted the pain or suffering with a discriminatory intent towards the victim."

(i) cruel and inhumane treatment

(i) defined

Blagojevic and Jokic, (Trial Chamber), January 17, 2005, para. 586: "Cruel and inhumane treatment is defined as an intentional act or omission, which causes serious mental harm, physical suffering or injury, or which constitutes a serious attack on human dignity."

(ii) elements

Simic, Tadic, and Zaric, (Trial Chamber), October 17, 2003, para. 74: "In assessing the content of cruel and inhumane treatment [as a form of persecution], the Trial Chamber finds that it is assisted by the Tribunal's jurisprudence regarding other inhumane acts under Article 5 (i) of the Statute, inhuman treatment under Article 2 (b) of the Statute, and cruel treatment under Article 3 of the Statute. The elements of these offences are the same, namely:

(a) an intentional act or omission of similar gravity to the other enumerated acts under the Article concerned;
(b) the act or omission caused serious mental or physical suffering or injury or constituted a serious attack on human dignity; and
(c) the act or omission was performed deliberately by the accused or a person or persons for whose acts and omissions he bears criminal responsibility."

(iii)customary international law

Blagojevic and Jokic, (Trial Chamber), January 17, 2005, para. 587: "The Appeals Chamber has found that, *inter alia*, the right to be free from cruel, inhuman or degrading treatment is recognised in customary international law and is enshrined in international human rights instruments."

(iv) acts of serious bodily and mental harm are of sufficient gravity compared to the other crimes enumerated in Article 5

Blagojevic and Jokic, (Trial Chamber), January 17, 2005, para. 587: "The Appeals Chamber has further found that '[i]t is clear in the jurisprudence of the International Tribunal that acts of serious bodily and mental harm are of sufficient gravity as compared to the other crimes enumerated in Article 5 of the Statute and therefore may constitute persecutions.'"

(a) application—gravity

Blaskic, (Appeals Chamber), July 29, 2004, para. 155: "The Appeals Chamber considers that the acts charged in the Indictment which encompass the detention of Bosnian Muslim civilians who were killed, used as human shields, beaten, subjected to physical or psychological abuse and intimidation, inhumane treatment, and deprived of adequate food and water, all rise to the level of gravity of the other crimes enumerated in Article 5."

(v) determining seriousness/severity of the harm suffered

Blagojevic and Jokic, (Trial Chamber), January 17, 2005, para. 586: "The seriousness of the harm or injury must be assessed on a case by case basis, taking into consideration various factors including the nature of the act or omission, the context in which it occurs, its duration and/or repetition, its physical and mental effects on the victim and, in some instances, the personal circumstances of the victim, including age, gender and health. The harm inflicted does not need to be permanent and irremediable; it must, however, have more than a short-term or temporary effect on the victim."

Simic, Tadic, and Zaric, (Trial Chamber), October 17, 2003, para. 75: "Consideration must be given to all the factual circumstances in the determination of the seriousness of the act, including the nature of the act or omission, the context in which it occurred, the personal circumstances of the victim, including age, sex and health, as well as the physical, mental and moral effects of the act upon the victim. While there is no requirement that the suffering imposed by the act has long term effects on the victim, the fact that an act has had long term effects may be relevant to the determination of the seriousness of the act."

(vi) cruel and inhumane treatment is a lesser included offense of torture

Simic, Tadic and Zaric, (Trial Chamber), October 17, 2003, para. 71: "The Trial Chamber notes that the words 'cruel and inhumane treatment' appear to be superfluous with regard to torture, as it is well-established that torture may in itself constitute a persecutory act pursuant to Article 5 (h) of the Statute. It is also generally accepted that cruel and inhumane treatment is a lesser included offence of torture, and that the latter is considered *lex specialis* in relation to cruel and inhumane treatment."

(vii) beatings as a form of cruel and inhumane treatment

Simic, Tadic, and Zaric, (Trial Chamber), October 17, 2003, paras. 77-78, 83: "The Trial Chamber emphasises that the mere description of bodily assaults as 'beatings' does not by itself establish that these beatings constitute the *actus reus* of cruel and inhumane treatment as persecutory acts. Instead, the beatings have to amount to a 'gross or blatant denial, on discriminatory grounds, of a fundamental right, laid down in international customary or treaty law, reaching the same level of gravity as the other acts prohibited in Article 5.'"

"Taking into consideration the requirements of Article 5(i) of the Statute as set out above, the Trial Chamber finds that beatings constitute cruel and inhumane treatment if the following elements can be proved:

(a) the beatings caused serious mental or physical suffering or injury or constituted a serious attack on human dignity, and

(b) the beatings were performed deliberately."

"The Trial Chamber notes that beatings committed on discriminatory grounds and causing severe pain or suffering, physical or mental, constitute cruel and inhumane treatment as an underlying act of persecution. The deliberate infliction of severe physical or mental pain or suffering through beatings in order to discriminate [*sic*] a victim constitutes torture [but was not pled as such]."

(viii) forced labor as a form of cruel and inhumane treatment

Simic, Tadic, and Zaric, (Trial Chamber), October 17, 2003, paras. 91-92: "The Trial Chamber notes that certain types of forced labour may amount to cruel and inhumane treatment if the conditions under which the labour is rendered are such as to create danger for the life or health of the civilians, or may arouse in them feelings of fear, and humiliation. It should be noted here that the principle of humane treatment enshrined in the Geneva Conventions implies an obligation for the occupying powers to protect civilians against inhumane acts. Forcing protected persons to work in life-threatening circumstances fails to meet the obligation for protection against acts of violence and may result in inflicting upon these persons physical and mental suffering. It has been held that placing detainees in life-threatening situations constitutes cruel and inhuman treatment."

"It is important to emphasize that inhumane treatment encompasses not only acts or omissions that cause serious mental or physical suffering, but also acts or omissions that constitute a serious attack on human dignity. Among the provisions prohibiting humiliating and degrading treatment, Article 52, paragraph 2 of Geneva Convention III explicitly proscribes compelling prisoners of war to do humiliating labour. The Commentary to Geneva Convention III notes that the prohibition is against making the prisoner 'the laughing stock of those around him.' An inquiry into the specific circumstances in each case will be necessary in order to determine whether the conditions under which civilians were forced to work constituted a serious attack on human dignity."

(ix)confinement under inhumane conditions as a form of cruel and inhumane treatment

Simic, Tadic, and Zaric, (Trial Chamber), October 17, 2003, paras. 94, 96, 97: "When discussing 'confinement under inhumane conditions,' the *Kvocka* Trial Chamber found that:

Confinement in camps under inhumane conditions can be included under sub-clauses (e) and (i) prohibiting 'imprisonment' and 'other inhumane acts' and also meets the definition of a persecutory act." "The *Krnojelac* Trial Chamber further observed:

The establishment and perpetuation of inhumane conditions is separately charged as inhumane acts, a crime against humanity pursuant to Article 5(i) of the Statute, and as cruel treatment, a violation of the law or customs of war pursuant to Article 3 of the Statute, and as such is of sufficient gravity to constitute persecution." "The Trial Chamber finds that harassment, humiliation, the creation of an atmosphere of fear through torture and other forms of physical and psychological abuse, an insufficient supply of food and water, lack of space, unhygienic detention conditions, and an insufficient access to medical care are circumstances that may constitute confinement under inhumane conditions and meet the *actus reus* of cruel and inhumane treatment as a persecutory act."

(x) mens rea

Simic, Tadic, and Zaric, (Trial Chamber), October 17, 2003, para. 74: The *mens rea* of cruel and inhumane treatment is: "the act or omission was performed deliberately by the accused or a person or persons for whose acts and omissions he bears criminal responsibility."

Simic, Tadic, and Zaric, (Trial Chamber), October 17, 2003, para. 76: "The *Vasiljevic* Trial Chamber held that the *mens rea* for inhumane acts is met 'where the offender, at the time of the act or omission, had the intention to inflict serious physical or mental suffering or to commit a serious attack on the human dignity of the victim, or where he knew that his act or omission was likely to cause serious physical or mental suffering or a serious attack upon human dignity and was reckless thereto.' The Trial Chamber accepts this definition."

(xi)application—cruel and inhumane treatment

(a) following the fall of Srebrenica

Blagojevic and Jokic, (Trial Chamber), January 17, 2005, paras. 605-610: "The Prosecution has charged 'the cruel and inhumane treatment of Bosnian Muslim civilians, including severe beatings at Potocari and in detention facilities in Bratunac and Zvornik' as a persecutory act."

"It has been established that the Bosnian Muslim refugees who were forced to flee to Potocari were exposed to horrific and inhumane conditions and found themselves, as described by a [Dutch Battalion of UNPROFOR] member, in a 'hopeless [...] and extremely uncertain and unsecure' situation. The 20,000 to 30,000 people, who were very exhausted, had very limited access to water despite the heat, almost no food and were exposed to a lack of basic medical treatment and toilet facilities. In addition, the refugees were exposed to insults and physical abuse aimed at creating an atmosphere of intimidation and panic that increased during the night of 12 July –'the night of horror'

– when the refugees suffered from extreme fear as the soldiers moved among the refugees, shouting and firing their weapons, and taking people away. The Trial Chamber finds that the continued exposure to such intimidating and life threatening conditions caused serious mental and physical suffering among the refugees."

"The Trial Chamber also finds that there is sufficient evidence to establish beyond reasonable doubt that the brutal separation of the men from the women and children throughout the Potocari area on 12 and 13 July amounts to cruel and inhumane treatment. The Trial Chamber finds that the refugees who experienced the pulling apart of their families – who were aggressively separated and taken away from their beloved ones without knowing if they would ever see them again – suffered serious mental harm. As one example of an extremely aggressive separation that also caused serious bodily harm, the Trial Chamber recalls the evidence that a young boy was grabbed by the throat and 'more or less strangled' when a [Army of the Republika Srpska] soldier tried to pull him away from his family."

"The Trial Chamber also finds that there is sufficient evidence to establish beyond reasonable doubt that the Bosnian Muslim men who were taken by [Army of the Republika Srpska] soldiers from the UN compound to the 'White House' suffered serious mental and bodily harm. . . ."

"The Trial Chamber further finds that there is sufficient evidence to establish beyond reasonable doubt that the Bosnian Muslim men who were detained on buses in Bratunac or in other detention facilities in Bratunac and Zvornik were subjected to horrific conditions and mistreatment. The Trial Chamber recalls that the buses and detention centres were packed with men who were suffering from the heat and were not provided with sufficient, if any, water or food. The prisoners were prevented from relieving themselves; they were badly beaten; and repeatedly men were singled out for further abuse and often were finally killed while the remaining men had to witness their moaning in pain and the shots. The Trial Chamber finds that the Bosnian Muslim men who experienced these atrocities and the uncertainty of their fate, were suffering serious mental and bodily harm."

"The Trial Chamber conclusively finds that there is sufficient evidence to establish beyond reasonable doubt that the terrible mistreatment as summarily described above caused serious mental harm and physical suffering and was a continuous attack on the human dignity of the Bosnian Muslims subjected to the mistreatment."

Obrenovic, (Trial Chamber), December 10, 2003, para. 35: Where the accused pled guilty to persecution as a crime against humanity, the Trial Court recognized the following as to cruel and inhuman treatment of Bosnian Muslim civilians: "The Bosnian Muslim civilians were subjected to acts of violence, including beatings at schools and other detention centres in the Zvornik area. In Luke, near Tisca, some of the women who had been separated from their male relatives in Potocari were 'selected' by VRS [Army of the Serbian Republic of Bosnia and Herzegovina/Republika Srpska] soldiers to go to a school, on 13 July 1995 where they were abused and assaulted; men and boys were also selected and abused before being taken for execution."

Nikolic – Momir, (Trial Chamber), December 2, 2003, paras. 36-37: Under the heading "Cruel and Inhumane Treatment of Bosnian Muslim Civilians," the Trial Chamber stated: "Following the fall of the Srebrenica enclave, Bosnian Muslim civilians were subjected to acts of violence, including severe beatings at Potocari. In Potocari, men were separated from women and children and detained. Furthermore, Bosnian Muslim men who were detained in Bratunac and Zvornik were subjected to cruel and inhumane treatment." "In his Statement of Facts, Momir Nikolic confirms that during the time that Bosnian Muslims were detained in Potocari and around Bratunac, they were not given any food or medical aid, and were only given enough water to sustain them until they were transported to Zvornik."

(b) beatings at detention facilities in Bosanski Samac and in Crkvina, Brcko, and Bijeljina

Simic, Tadic, and Zaric, (Trial Chamber), October 17, 2003, paras. 770-771: "The Trial Chamber is convinced that on 17 April 1992 and in the following months, a large number of non-Serb civilians were repeatedly beaten in the detention facilities in Bosanski Samac and in Crkvina, Brcko, and Bijeljina. Some of the victims had already been beaten upon their arrest. During their imprisonment in the detention facilities, detainees were severely beaten with various objects, such as rifles, metal bars, baseball bats, metal chains, police batons, and chair legs. The detainees were beaten on all parts of their bodies, and many of them suffered serious injuries. Some prisoners were beaten while undergoing interrogation. The beatings were applied by paramilitary forces from Serbia, local policemen, and a few members of the [Yugoslavia Peoples' Army]. The beatings took place on a daily basis, day and night. The Defence for all three accused did not contest that such beatings occurred as described by the witnesses."

"The Trial Chamber is satisfied that these beatings caused severe pain and suffering, both physically and mentally, to the detainees. The Trial Chamber is also satisfied that the beatings were committed on discriminatory grounds. The evidence shows that practically all detainees who were beaten were non-Serbs. On one occasion, a victim was beaten in the crotch, and his assailants told him that Muslims should not propagate. Prisoners were regularly insulted on the basis of their ethnicity. For these reasons, the Trial Chamber finds that the beatings that were committed on discriminatory grounds constitute cruel and inhumane treatment as an underlying act of persecution."

(c) confinement under inhumane conditions at detention centers in Bosanski Samac, Crkvina and Bijeljina

Simic, Tadic, and Zaric, (Trial Chamber), October 17, 2003, paras. 773, 775: "The Trial Chamber is (...) satisfied that the detainees who were imprisoned in the detention centres in Bosanski Samac were confined under inhumane conditions. The prisoners were subjected to humiliation and degradation. The forced singing of 'Chetnik' songs and the verbal abuse of being called 'ustasha' or 'balija' were forms of such abuse and humiliation of the detainees. They did not have sufficient space, food or water. They suffered from unhygienic conditions, and they did not have appropriate access to medical care. These appalling detention conditions, the cruel and inhumane treatment through beatings and the acts of torture caused severe physical suffering, thus attacking the very fundamentals of human dignity. The Trial Chamber finds that this confinement under inhumane conditions constitutes cruel and inhumane treatment [as a form of persecution]. This was done because of the non-Serb ethnicity of the detainees."

"The Trial Chamber is satisfied that during detention in the detention centres in Crkvina and Bijeljina, the prisoners did not have sufficient space and sufficient food and water supply. They were kept in unhygienic conditions and did not have access to sufficient medical care. Furthermore, detainees were subjected to beatings that constituted cruel and inhumane treatment and torture. For these reasons, the Trial Chamber finds that these prisoners were also confined under inhumane conditions that constituted cruel and inhumane treatment [as a form of persecution]."

(d) forced labor—digging trenches, building bunkers, carry sandbags or railway sleepers for the construction of trenches, and building other fortifications on the frontline

Simic, Tadic, and Zaric, (Trial Chamber), paras. 834-835: "The Trial Chamber is satisfied that civilians who had to report every day in front of the Pensioner's Home as well as civilians who were detained were forced to dig trenches, build bunkers, carry sandbags or railway sleepers for the construction of trenches, and build other fortifications on the frontline. It has been established that this work was not rendered voluntarily. Civilians were compelled to work under the supervision of armed guards, who beat, or fired at those who tried to escape. The Trial Chamber also accepts that the civilians who were forced to dig trenches, and to work on the frontline were not paid for their work.

The Trial Chamber is satisfied that civilians working on military assignments on the frontline were exposed to dangerous conditions and were under a high risk of being injured or killed. The Trial Chamber accepts that the acts of forcing civilians to work in life-threatening circumstances where they could be exposed to physical and mental suffering fail to meet the obligation for humane treatment of civilians enshrined in the Geneva Conventions and amount to cruel and inhumane treatment. The Trial Chamber is satisfied that these assignments were made on a discriminatory basis and that they reach the level of seriousness required for persecution."

(e) confinement under inhumane conditions at the Omarska camp

For findings of confinement in inhumane conditions at the Omarska camp in Prijedor as a form of persecution, see *Kvocka et al.*, (Appeals Chamber), February 28, 2005, paras. 335-338.

(j) extermination

Kordic and Cerkez, (Appeals Chamber), December 17, 2004, para. 106: "As concluded by *inter alia* the *Kupreskic et al.* Trial Chamber, the crime of persecutions has developed in customary international law to encompass acts that include 'murder, extermination, torture, and other serious acts on the person such as those presently enumerated in Article 5.'"

Kupreskic et al, (Trial Chamber), January 14, 2000, para. 615: "In their interpretation of persecution courts have included acts such as murder, extermination, torture, and other serious acts on the person such as those presently enumerated in Article 5."

(k) serious bodily and mental harm/ physical violence

Kordic and Cerkez, (Appeals Chamber), December 17, 2004, para. 106: "With respect to the charges of wilful killing, murder, causing serious injury, and inhuman treatment, the Appeals Chamber considers that the inherent right to life and to be free from cruel, inhuman or degrading treatment or punishment is recognised in customary international law and is embodied in Articles 6 and 7 of the ICCPR [International Covenant on Civil and Political Rights], and Articles 2 and 3 of the ECHR [European Convention for the Protection of Human Rights and Fundamental Freedoms]. It is clear in the jurisprudence of the International Tribunal that acts of wilful killing, murder, and of serious bodily and mental harm are of sufficient gravity as compared to the other crimes enumerated in Article 5 of the Statute and therefore may constitute persecutions."

Brdjanin, (Trial Chamber), September 1, 2004, para. 1005: "The term 'physical violence' does not appear anywhere in the Statute. The Trial Chamber finds that 'physical violence' may comprise treatment that does not amount to torture as defined above, such as 'conditions in which detainees (are) forced to live, such as overcrowded conditions, deprivation of food, water and sufficient air, exposure to extreme heat or cold, random beatings of detainees as a general measure to instill terror amongst them and similar forms of physical assaults not amounting to torture(...)' Such treatment may fall under the crime of persecution if it reaches the same level of gravity as the other crimes against humanity enumerated in Article 5 of the Statute."

Stakic, (Trial Chamber), July 31, 2003, paras. 752-753: "In the Trial Chamber's view, 'physical violence' is a broad term which focuses *inter alia* on the conditions in which detainees were forced to live, such as overcrowded conditions, deprivation of food, water and sufficient air, exposure to extreme heat or cold, random beating of detainees as a general measure to instil terror amongst them and similar forms of physical assaults not amounting to torture as defined above." "The Trial Chamber therefore holds that even if physical violence is not listed under Article 5 of the Statute and the alleged acts do not qualify as torture, they may nonetheless fall under the crime of persecution."

(i) application—serious bodily and mental harm/ physical violence

(a) detention camps and facilities: the Manjaca Camp; the Mlavke football stadium and Bosanski Novi fire station in Bosanski Novi; the Kotor Varos Prison in Kotor Varos; the Omarska, Keraterm and Trnopolje camps in Prijedor; the Sloga shoe factory in Prnjavor; Betonirka in Sanski Most; and Pribinic and Territorial Defense buildings in Teslic

Brdjanin, (Trial Chamber), September 1, 2004, paras. 1006-1007: "The Trial Chamber recalls that conditions in the majority of camps and facilities in which Bosnian Muslims and Bosnian Croats were detained [including the Manjaca Camp set up on a mountain outside the city of Banja Luka; the Mlavke football stadium and Bosanski Novi fire station in Bosanski Novi; the Kotor Varos Prison in Kotor Varos; the Omarska, Keraterm and Trnopolje camps in Prijedor; the Sloga shoe factory in Prnjavor; Betonirka in Sanski Most; Pribinic and Territorial Defense buildings in Teslic] can only be characterised as absolutely appalling. Constant and random beatings were the order of the day. Detainees were beaten on the way to and during their daily meal, as well as when they asked to use toilet facilities. Sanitation and hygienic conditions were hideous. Detention facilities were intensely crowded. The Trial Chamber is thus satisfied that these incidents of physical violence were discriminatory in fact, and, placed in context, occupy the same level of gravity as the other crimes against humanity enumerated in Article 5 of the Statute."

"With respect to the requisite *mens rea*, the Trial Chamber observes that the circumstances surrounding the commission of acts of physical violence were the same as those in which torture was inflicted on detainees as described above. Consequently, the Trial Chamber concludes that the circumstances clearly show that they were carried out with the intention to discriminate against the Bosnian Muslims and Bosnian Croats concerned on racial, religious or political grounds."[30]

(b) the Omarska, Keraterm and Trnopolje camps

Stakic, (Trial Chamber), July 31, 2003, para. 790: "The Trial Chamber concludes that the perpetuation of the inhumane conditions [at the Omarska, Keraterm and Trnopolje camps] constituting cruel and inhuman treatment of the non-Serb detainees was carried out by the direct perpetrators with the intent to cause serious physical suffering to the victims and to attack their human dignity. The direct perpetrators caused such physical suffering because the victims were non-Serbs. The Trial Chamber is satisfied that these acts of physical violence amount to crimes against humanity."

(l) rape

Brdjanin, (Trial Chamber), September 1, 2004, paras. 1008-1009: "Rape is set out as a crime against humanity under Article 5(g) of the Statute and as such is of sufficient gravity to constitute persecution. Under the jurisprudence of the Tribunal, it is defined as follows:

the *actus reus* of the crime of rape in international law is constituted by: the sexual penetration, however slight: (a) of the vagina or anus of the victim by the penis of the perpetrator or any other object used by the perpetrator; or (b) the mouth of the victim by the penis of the perpetrator; where such sexual penetration occurs without the consent of the victim. Consent for this purpose must be consent given voluntarily, as a result of the victim's free will, assessed in the context of the surrounding circumstances. The *mens rea* is the intention to effect this sexual penetration, and the knowledge that it occurs without the consent of the victim."

Citing Kunarac Trial Judgement, para. 460; *Kunarac* Appeal Judgement, paras. 127-128. "It should be noted that the Appeals Chamber has held that force or threat of force provides clear evidence of non-consent, but is not an element *per se* of rape, since 'a narrow focus on force or threat of force could permit perpetrators to evade liability for sexual activity to which the other party had not consented by taking advantage of coercive circumstances without relying on physical force.' The Trial Chamber agrees that 'for a woman, rape is by far the ultimate offence.'"

Stakic, (Trial Chamber), July 31, 2003, paras. 755-756: "The Trial Chamber concurs with the definition of the crime of rape adopted by the *Kunarac et al.* Appeals Chamber." "In this context, '[f]orce or threat of force provide clear evidence of non- consent, but force is not an element *per se* of rape. [...] A narrow focus on force or threat of force could permit perpetrators to evade liability for sexual activity to which the other party had not consented by taking advantage of coercive circumstances without relying on physical force.'"

(i) application—rape

(a) municipalities of Prijedor, Teslic, Banja Luka, Bosanska Krupa, Donji Vakuf, and in Kotor Varos

Brdjanin, (Trial Chamber), September 1, 2004, paras. 1010, 1011: "Earlier in this judgement, the Trial Chamber established that a number of Bosnian Muslim women were raped in Prijedor and in Teslic municipalities. The Trial Chamber finds that, apart from these municipalities, rapes of Bosnian Muslim and Bosnian Croat women occurred in the municipalities of Banja Luka, Bosanska Krupa, Donji Vakuf, and in Kotor Varos. In each incident, armed Bosnian Serb soldiers or policemen were the perpetrators. There can be no doubt that these rapes were discriminatory in fact."

"With regard to the requisite *mens rea*, the Trial Chamber notes that the direct perpetrators made abundant use of pejorative language. One of them made no secret that he wanted a Bosnian Muslim woman to 'give birth to a little Serb.' The Trial Chamber is satisfied beyond reasonable doubt that, in the circumstances surrounding the commission of these rapes, these acts were carried out with the intent to discriminate against the Bosnian Muslim and Bosnian Croat women on racial, religious or political grounds."[31]

(b) the Trnopolje, Keraterm and Omarska camps

Stakic, (Trial Chamber), July 31, 2003, para. 806: "The Trial Chamber is (...) convinced that rape based on discriminatory intent was committed also in the Trnopolje camp.

The Trial Chamber has already established the commission of other cases of rape and sexual assaults in the Keraterm and Omarska camps. (...) [T]hese crimes were committed with a discriminatory intent."

(m) sexual assault

Brdjanin, (Trial Chamber), September 1, 2004, para. 1012: "Any sexual assault falling short of rape may be punishable as persecution under international criminal law, provided that it reaches the same level of gravity as the other crimes against humanity enumerated in Article 5 of the Statute. This offence embraces all serious abuses of a sexual nature inflicted upon the integrity of a person by means of coercion, threat of force or intimidation in a way that is humiliating and degrading to the victim's dignity."

Stakic, (Trial Chamber), July 31, 2003, para. 757: "This Trial Chamber holds that, under international criminal law, not only rape but also any other sexual assault falling short of actual penetration is punishable. This offence embraces all serious abuses of a sexual nature inflicted upon the integrity of a person by means of coercion, threat of force or intimidation in a way that is humiliating and degrading to the victim's dignity."

(i) application—sexual assault in various prison camps and complexes including the Omarska and Keraterm camps and other detention facilities in the Prijedor area

Brdjanin, (Trial Chamber), September 1, 2004, para. 1013: "The Trial Chamber finds that many incidents of sexual assault occurred [in various prison camps and complexes including the Omarska Camp and other camps in the Prijedor area], including the case of a Bosnian Croat woman who was forced to undress herself in front of cheering Bosnian Serb policemen and soldiers. In another incident, a knife was run along the breast of a Bosnian Muslim woman. Frequently, it was demanded that detainees perform sex with each other. In each incident, armed Bosnian Serb soldiers or policemen were the perpetrators. The Trial Chamber is satisfied that, evaluated in their context, these acts are serious enough to rise to the level of crimes against humanity. Moreover, the Trial Chamber is satisfied that the circumstances surrounding the commission of sexual assaults leave no doubt at all that there was discrimination in fact and discriminatory intent on the part of the direct perpetrators, based on racial, religious or political grounds."

Stakic, (Trial Chamber), July 31, 2003, para. 806: "The Trial Chamber has already established the commission of (...) cases of (...) sexual assaults in the Keraterm and Omarska camps. As discussed above, these crimes were committed with a discriminatory intent."

(n) terrorizing the civilian population

(i) elements

Blagojevic and Jokic, (Trial Chamber), January 17, 2005, para. 589: "While the act of 'terrorising the civilian population' is not found in the Statute, the Trial Chamber finds that it is similar to '[a]cts or threats of violence the primary purpose of which is to spread terror among the civilian population' prohibited under Article 51(2) of Additional Protocol I and Article 13(2) of Additional Protocol II to the Geneva Conventions. Based on the prohibitions enshrined in these two Articles and taking into consideration the *Galic* Trial Judgement, the Trial Chamber defines the elements of 'terrorising the civilian population' as follows:

1 Acts or threats of violence;
2 The offender wilfully made the civilian population or individual civilians not taking part in hostilities the object of those acts or threats of violence; and

3 The acts or threats of violence were carried out with the primary purpose of spreading terror among the civilian population."

(ii) actual infliction of terror unnecessary

Blagojevic and Jokic, (Trial Chamber), January 17, 2005, para. 590: "The Trial Chamber concurs with the *Galic* Trial Chamber finding that 'terror' means 'extreme fear.' The plain wording of Article 51(2) of Additional Protocol I does not suggest that the 'terrorising of the civilian population' requires an actual infliction of terror. The Trial Chamber therefore finds that the Prosecution only needs to prove that acts or threats of violence were carried out to create an atmosphere of extreme fear or uncertainty of being subjected to violence among the civilian population."

(iii)primary purpose must be spreading terror

Blagojevic and Jokic, (Trial Chamber), January 17, 2005, para. 591: "As one element of the offence is the primary purpose of spreading terror, the offender must have intended to terrorise the civilian population. The Trial Chamber finds that 'primary' does not mean that the infliction of terror needed to be the only objective of the acts or threats of violence, but that it was the principal aim."

(iv) terrorization violates a fundamental right laid down in international customary and treaty law

Blagojevic and Jokic, (Trial Chamber), January 17, 2005, para. 592: "In addition to the prohibition against acts or threats of violence enshrined in the Geneva Conventions, the Trial Chamber observes that the exposure to terror is a denial of the fundamental right to security of person which is recognised in all national systems and is contained in Article 9 of the ICCPR [International Covenant on Civil and Political Rights] and Article 5 of the ECHR [European Convention for the Protection of Human Rights and Fundamental Freedoms]. Accordingly, the Trial Chamber finds that terrorisation violates a fundamental right laid down in international customary and treaty law."

(v) application—terrorizing the civilian population

(a) Srebrenica and Potocari

Blagojevic and Jokic, (Trial Chamber), January 17, 2005, paras. 611-614, 620: "It has been established that the UN compound in Srebrenica town was shelled while thousands of Bosnian Muslim refugees were seeking protection there. It has further been established that while the refugees were fleeing from Srebrenica to Potocari, elements of the Bratunac Brigade [a unit of the Army of Republika Srpska], among others, fired at them. The Trial Chamber finds that the aim of the shellings was to cause fear and panic among the civilian population and force the people to flee the Srebrenica enclave."

"The Trial Chamber further finds that the Bosnian Muslims who sought shelter in Potocari were continuously subjected to terrifying threats and physical attacks. It has been established that during the meetings in the Hotel Fontana, the Bosnian Muslim representatives were threatened repeatedly and told that they 'could either survive or disappear.' Many [Army of the Republika Srpska] soldiers cursed at the Bosnian Muslims, calling them names and saying that they would be 'slaughtered.' Especially during the night of 12 July, 'the night of horror,' the refugees suffered from extreme fear."

"It has also been proven that the Bosnian Muslim men who were taken to the 'White House' were forced to leave their personal belongings and identity cards outside the building. The Trial Chamber finds the message sent to the men when their identity cards were taken – that they would no longer need this most basic document – was intended to terrify the men as it suggested that their fate – death – had been sealed. It has been further established that Bosnian Muslim men were told to take off their clothes and shoes before they were transported from the detention to the execution sites. The Trial Chamber finds this to be another tool used to instil fear and suggest to the men that they were marked for death."

"The Trial Chamber finds that there is sufficient evidence to establish that the described unlawful acts and threats of violence against the Bosnian Muslim civilians, including individual civilians not taking part in hostilities, were carried out with the primary purpose to create an atmosphere of extreme fear among the population."

"The Trial Chamber finds that there is sufficient evidence to establish beyond reasonable doubt that the murder, the cruel and inhumane treatment and the terrorising of the civilian population as described above constitute blatant denials of fundamental rights that had a severe impact on the victims and therefore amount to persecutions."

Obrenovic, (Trial Chamber), December 10, 2003, para. 36: Where the accused pled guilty to persecution as a crime against humanity, the Trial Court recognized: "The Bosnian Muslim civilians who had been transferred from Srebrenica and Potocari to Zvornik during the dates of 13 to 16 July

1995 were subjected to terrorisation. At detention centres and execution sites, the civilians were mistreated and abused."

Nikolic – Momir, (Trial Chamber), December 2, 2003, para. 38: "During the time-period that the Bosnian Muslim refugee population from Srebrenica was in and around Potocari, members of the VRS [Army of the Serbian Republic of Bosnia and Herzegovina/Republika Srpska] terrorised the population (...) [T]his took the form of intimidation and abuse, with the purpose of compelling the Muslim population to get on the buses and trucks to Kladanj."

(o) attacks launched deliberately against civilians or civilian objects/ attacks on civilians, cities, towns and villages

Kordic and Cerkez, (Appeals Chamber), December 17, 2004, paras. 104, 105: "[T]he Appeals Chamber holds that attacks launched deliberately against civilians or civilian objects may constitute persecutions as a crime against humanity." An "unlawful attack launched deliberately against civilians or civilian objects may constitute a crime of persecutions without the requirement of a particular result caused by the attack(s)."

Blaskic, (Appeals Chamber), July 29, 2004, para. 159: "In light of the customary rules on the issue [specifically, Articles 51(2) – 51(4) of Additional Protocol I, Article 13(2) of Additional Protocol II, and Article 25 of the Fourth Hague Convention of 1907], the Appeals Chamber holds that attacks in which civilians are targeted, as well as indiscriminate attacks on cities, towns, and villages, may constitute persecutions as a crime against humanity." *See also Blaskic,* (Appeals Chamber), July 29, 2004, paras. 157, 158.

Deronjic, (Trial Chamber), March 30, 2004, para. 121: "An attack on a village is not listed under Article 5 of the Statute. The Trial Chamber in *Kordic and Cerkez,* when assessing the level of gravity of this crime, held that the unlawful attack on cities, towns and villages, 'is akin to an "attack, or bombardment, by whatever means, of undefended towns, villages, dwellings, or buildings," a violation of the laws or customs of war enumerated under Article 3 (c) of the Statute' and therefore when committed on discriminatory grounds constitutes the act of Persecutions."

Kordic and Cerkez, (Trial Chamber), February 26, 2001, para. 203: The following "acts may constitute the crime of persecution provided they are performed with the requisite discriminatory intent:" attacking cities, towns and villages.

(p) forced labor

Krnojelac, (Appeals Chamber), September 17, 2003, para. 199: "[F]orced labour must be considered as part of a series of acts comprising unlawful detention and beatings whose cumulative effect is of sufficient gravity to amount to a crime of persecution, given that the unlawful detention and beatings were based on one or more of the discriminatory grounds listed under Article 5 of the Statute. Accordingly, the degree of gravity of persecution based on those acts is the same as that of the crimes expressly laid down under Article 5 of the Statute."

Simic, Tadic, and Zaric, (Trial Chamber), October 17, 2003, paras. 85, 93: "Trial Chambers of the Tribunal have held that the charge of 'forced labour assignments' may constitute the basis of the crime of enslavement as a crime against humanity under Article 5(c), and the offence of slavery as a violation of the laws or customs of war under Article 3 of the Statute, and as such this offence is of sufficient gravity to support a charge of persecution."

"The Trial Chamber finds that forced labour assignments which require civilians to take part in military operations violate the fundamental norms of international humanitarian law (...)The Trial Chamber is also satisfied that forced labour assignments which result in exposing civilians to dangerous or humiliating conditions amount to cruel and inhumane treatment. These acts reach the same level of gravity as the other crimes against humanity and if performed with the requisite discriminatory intent may constitute persecution."

(i) permissible work distinguished

Krnojelac, (Appeals Chamber), September 17, 2003, para. 200: "There is a principle which states that the work required of a person in the ordinary course of lawful detention is not regarded as forced or compulsory labour. This principle is enshrined in, *inter alia*, Article 4(3) of the [European] Convention for the Protection of Human Rights and Fundamental Freedoms ('ECHR'). It sets out that '"forced or compulsory labour" shall not include: a) any work required to be done in the ordinary course of detention imposed according to the provisions of Article 5 of this Convention [governing notably the lawfulness of an arrest or detention] or during conditional release from such detention.'"

Simic, Tadic, and Zaric, (Trial Chamber), October 17, 2003, para. 836: "The Trial Chamber accepts the argument of the Defence that certain types of work even if compulsory were permissible under international humanitarian law and consequently do not amount to persecution."

(ii) application—forced labor

(a) KP Dom prison complex in Foca

Krnojelac, (Appeals Chamber), September 17, 2003, paras. 194-195, 201: "The Appeals Chamber notes that the living conditions at the KP Dom [prison complex in Foca] were clearly appalling. Of the facts set out above, some are particularly significant and should be emphasised. The Trial Chamber concluded that, at the KP Dom, there was a deliberate policy to feed the non-Serb detainees barely enough for their survival. All non-Serb detainees suffered considerable weight loss ranging from 20 to 40 kilograms during their detention at the KP Dom. Moreover, non-Serb detainees were locked up in their rooms for most of the day, being allowed out only to go to the canteen and back. Some, however, were taken out to work knowing that they would receive additional and much needed food if they did. Finally, the non-Serb detainees were subjected to harrowing psychological abuse during their period of detention at the KP Dom. The detainees were exposed to the sounds of people being beaten and tortured over a period of months, in particular in June and July 1992, and they constantly feared that they would be the next to be selected. The Appeals Chamber holds that, given the specific detention conditions of the non-Serb detainees at the KP Dom, a reasonable trier of fact should have arrived at the conclusion that the detainees' general situation negated any possibility of free consent. The Appeals Chamber is satisfied that the detainees worked to avoid being beaten or in the hope of obtaining additional food. Those who refused to work did so out of fear on account of the disappearances of detainees who had gone outside of the KP Dom. The climate of fear made the expression of free consent impossible and it may neither be expected of a detainee that he voice an objection nor held that a person in a position of authority need threaten him with punishment if he refuses to work in order for forced labour to be established. In such circumstances, the fact that a detainee raised an objection is immaterial in ascertaining whether it was truly impossible to object."

"The Appeals Chamber holds that the specific circumstances of the KP Dom detainees' prison life were therefore such as to make free consent impossible."

"In the Appeals Chamber's opinion, there can be no doubt that the non-Serb prisoners were detained and forced to work on account of their ethnicity. The Trial Chamber emphasised that '[t]he few Serb convicts who were detained at the KP Dom [prison complex] were kept in a different part of the building from the non-Serbs. They were not mistreated like the non-Serb detainees. The quality and quantity of their food was somewhat better, sometimes including additional servings. They were not beaten or otherwise abused, they were not locked up in their rooms, they were released once they had served their time, they had access to hygienic facilities and enjoyed other benefits which were denied to non-Serb detainees.' It is clear, however, that the non-Serb detainees were subjected to a wholly different regime. The overcrowding of the solitary confinement cells in which the detainees were so packed that they were unable to move around or lie down, the starvation and its principal effects in terms of weight loss, the widespread nature of the beatings and mistreatment and the psychological abuse linked to the detention conditions and mistreatment constitute circumstances particularly indicative of the discriminatory character of the acts of forced labour imposed upon the non-Serb detainees."

(b) Bosanski Samac, Brijeljina, Grebnice, Zasavia, Pisaria, Lijekovica, Brvnik, Prud, Teocak

Simic, Tadic, and Zaric, (Trial Chamber), October 17, 2003, paras. 834, 835, 837, 841: "The Trial Chamber is satisfied that civilians who had to report every day in front of the Pensioner's Home [in Bosanski Samac] as well as civilians who were detained were forced to dig trenches, build bunkers, carry sandbags or railway sleepers for the construction of trenches, and build other fortifications on the frontline. It has been established that this work was not rendered voluntarily. Civilians were compelled to work under the supervision of armed guards, who beat, or fired at those who tried to escape. The Trial Chamber also accepts that the civilians who were forced to dig trenches, and to work on the frontline were not paid for their work."

"The Trial Chamber is satisfied that civilians working on military assignments on the frontline were exposed to dangerous conditions and were under a high risk of being injured or killed. The Trial Chamber accepts that the acts of forcing civilians to work in life-threatening circumstances where they could be exposed to physical and mental suffering fail to meet the obligation for humane treatment of civilians enshrined in the Geneva Conventions and amount to cruel and inhumane treatment. The Trial Chamber is satisfied that these assignments were made on a discriminatory basis and that they reach the level of seriousness required for persecution."

"The Trial Chamber is satisfied that non-Serb civilians were subjected to humiliating forced labour. Sulejman Tihic was forced to sweep the street outside the municipality building and the [Secretariat of the Interior] building, while people walked by. Dragan Lukac had to clean a room in front of two Bosnian women and felt humiliated. Ahmet Hadzialijagic had to sweep the streets in front of the bank, which he used to manage. The director of a textile company had to sweep the compounds of the Samac textile industry. The Trial Chamber is satisfied that these assignments were such as to arouse feelings of fear and subordination, capable of causing the said persons psychological suffering, and of debasing them and the group to which they belonged, and as such constitute cruel and inhumane treatment. While single incidences of humiliating assignments may not reach the level of gravity required for persecution, the Trial Chamber accepts that these assignments were part of a pattern targeting the Bosnian Muslim and Bosnian Croat political and economic leadership. The Trial Chamber is satisfied that the humiliating assignments reach the level of gravity to amount to persecution." "The Trial Chamber finds that through the Secretariat for National Defence the Crisis Staff was ultimately responsible for managing the forced labour program and sending civilians to work in dangerous or humiliating conditions."

(c) Bosanski Samac, Zasavica, Novi Grad, Pisari and other neighboring villages, and Odzak—not forced labor

Simic, Tadic, and Zaric, (Trial Chamber), October 17, 2003, para. 836: "Civilians were forced to do agricultural work in Bosanski Samac, Zasavica, Novi Grad, Pisari and other neighbouring villages, to chop wood, to prepare food for the army or for the civilians, to work on the water supply system, to clean and rebuild Odzak, or to work for state owned companies. While the civilians had no real choice as to whether to work or not, these types of labour are lawful *per se* under international humanitarian law, and in the absence of other aggravating circumstances do not amount to persecution. It has not been established beyond reasonable doubt that the conditions under which this labour was rendered were such as to amount to cruel and inhumane treatment, or that the assignments are of sufficient gravity to constitute persecution."

(q) forcible transfer, sexual violence, subjection to inhumane conditions and atmosphere of terror

(i) application—the Susica camp

Nikolic - Dragan, (Trial Chamber), December 18, 2003, para. 111: "The Trial Chamber finds that the situation in [the] Susica camp, as previously described, was that serious that the acts of forcible transfer, sexual violence, subjection to inhumane conditions and atmosphere of terror rise without further explanation to a level of gravity that falls within the ambit of Article 5 of the Statute."

See *Nikolic - Dragan,* (Trial Chamber), December 18, 2003, paras. 57-61 for a discussion of conditions at the Susica detention camp, where, in a warehouse or hangar approximately 50 by 30 meters, as many as 8,000 Muslim civilians and other non-Serbs from Vlasenica and the surrounding villages were successively detained, with the number of detainees at any one time usually between 300 and 500.

(r) killings, beatings, unlawful attacks on civilians and civilian objects, the unlawful imprisonment of civilians, destruction of civilian objects, and looting

Kordic and Cerkez, (Appeals Chamber), December 17, 2004, paras. 672, 673: "The underlying acts include killings, beatings, unlawful attacks on civilians and civilian objects, the unlawful imprisonment of civilians, destruction of civilian objects, and looting. All of them, considered in conjunction, amount to a criminal conduct of gravity equal to crimes listed in Article 5 of the Statute." "In accordance with settled jurisprudence, the Appeals Chamber holds that these acts constitute criminal conduct of a gravity equal to the crimes listed in Article 5 of the Statute."

(s) political, social, economic rights violations, including the right to employment, right to freedom of movement, right to proper judicial process, and right to proper medical care

Kupreskic et al, (Trial Chamber), January 14, 2000, para. 615: "Persecution can also involve a variety of other discriminatory acts, involving attacks on political, social, and economic rights."

Blaskic, (Trial Chamber), March 3, 2000, para. 220: "[I]nfringements of the elementary and inalienable rights of man, which are 'the right to life, liberty and the security of person,' the right not to be 'held in slavery or servitude,' the right not to 'be subjected to torture or to cruel, inhuman or degrading treatment or punishment' and the right not to be 'subjected to arbitrary arrest, detention or exile' as affirmed in Articles 3, 4, 5 and 9 of the Universal Declaration of Human Rights, by their very essence may constitute persecution when committed on discriminatory grounds."

(i) rights violations need not be set out in the ICTY Statute

Brdjanin, (Trial Chamber), September 1, 2004, paras. 1029, 1030: "The Prosecution charges the Accused with 'the denial of fundamental rights to Bosnian Muslims and Bosnian Croats, including the right to employment, freedom of movement, right to proper judicial process, or right to proper medical care' as persecutions." "As a preliminary matter, the Trial Chamber notes the argument raised by the Accused that 'no conviction may be based on the denial of any of these [four] rights since they are not specifically set out in the Statute. Any conviction for a violation of these rights violates the principle of legality.' The Trial Chamber finds that this argument is misconceived as the Accused is obviously confusing the underlying acts or violations with the actual crime charged, namely that of persecution. The underlying acts (and corresponding violations) alleged are encompassed by the crime of persecution, set out in the Statute and charged under Count 3 of the Indictment. Any possible conviction would be for this crime and not for the underlying acts or violations. It is well established in the jurisprudence of this Tribunal that a conviction for the crime of persecution does not violate the principle of legality. This argument is therefore rejected."

(ii) evaluate rights violations on a case by case basis to determine gravity, considering the cumulative effect of the violations

Brdjanin, (Trial Chamber), September 1, 2004, para. 1031: "The jurisprudence of this Tribunal has specified that acts which deny fundamental rights may amount to persecution provided they are of sufficient gravity or severity. The Trial Chamber reiterates its view that there is no list of established fundamental rights and that such decisions are best taken on a case by case basis. In order to establish the crime of persecution, underlying acts should not be considered in isolation, but in context, looking at their cumulative effect. The Trial Chamber considers that it is not necessary to examine the fundamental nature of each right individually, but rather to examine them as a whole. It is appropriate, therefore, to look at the cumulative denial of the rights to employment, freedom of movement, proper judicial process and proper medical care in order to determine whether these are fundamental rights for the purposes of establishing persecutions."

(iii)application—violations of the right to employment, the right to freedom of movement, the right to proper judicial process and the right to proper medical care

Brdjanin, (Trial Chamber), September 1, 2004, paras. 1032-49: The court determined that the following rights violations "taking into account the cumulative effect of their denial" were committed on discriminatory grounds: right to employment; right to freedom of movement; right to proper judicial process; right to proper medical care. These rights violations were "fundamental rights for the purposes of establishing persecution." "The Trial Chamber is also satisfied that the denial of these rights to Bosnian Muslims and Bosnian Croats was of equal gravity to other crimes listed in Article 5 of the Statute as well as discriminatory in fact and was carried out with the requisite discriminatory intent by the direct perpetrators on racial, religious and political grounds."

(t) issuance of discriminatory orders, policies, decisions or other regulations

Simic, Tadic and Zaric, (Trial Chamber), October 17, 2003, para. 58: "[I] ssuance of discriminatory orders, policies, decisions or other regulations may constitute the *actus reus* of persecution, provided that these orders infringe upon a person's basic rights and that the violation reaches the level of gravity of the other crimes against humanity listed in Article 5 of the Statute. Such a determination has to be made on a case by case basis, taking account of the specific factual circumstances, and of the cumulative effect of such decisions or regulations."

(u) use of civilians as hostages and human shields

Kordic and Cerkez, (Appeals Chamber), December 17, 2004, para. 107: "The Appeals Chamber considers that the acts charged in the Indictment which encompass the use of detained Bosnian Muslim civilians as hostages and human shields, their use to dig trenches in hostile, hazardous and combat conditions, and their subjection to physical and psychological abuse all rise to the level of gravity of the other crimes enumerated in Article 5 of the Statute."

Blaskic, (Appeals Chamber), July 29, 2004, para. 155: "The Appeals Chamber considers that the acts charged in the Indictment which encompass the detention of Bosnian Muslim civilians who were (...) [among other things] used as human shields (...) all rise to the level of gravity of the other crimes enumerated in Article 5."

Kordic and Cerkez, (Trial Chamber), February 26, 2001, para. 204: The following "acts may constitute the crime of persecution provided they are performed with the requisite discriminatory intent:" trench-digging and use of hostages and human shields.

(v) summary of acts covered

Kvocka et al., (Trial Chamber), November 2, 2001, para. 186: "[T]he ICTY have found that the following acts may constitute persecution when committed with the requisite discriminatory intent: imprisonment, unlawful detention of civilians or infringement upon individual freedom, murder, deportation or forcible transfer, 'seizure, collection, segregation and forced transfer of civilians to camps,' comprehensive destruction of homes and property, the destruction of towns, villages and other public or private property and the plunder of property, attacks upon cities, towns and villages, trenchdigging and the use of hostages and human shields, the destruction and damage of religious or educational institutions, and sexual violence."

(w) acts that alone did not rise to the level of persecution: encouraging and promoting hatred on political grounds; dismissing and removing individuals from government; forcible takeover; and interrogations

Simic, Tadic, and Zaric, (Trial Chamber), October 17, 2003, paras. 55-56 "The Trial Chamber notes that a forcible takeover, as an illegal *coup d'état*, is a political move to overthrow an existing government by force, and does not necessarily encompass all the elements and the gravity associated with an attack on cities, towns or villages. The Trial Chamber notes the *Kordic* Trial Judgement finding that the exclusion of Bosnian Muslims from the government does not rise to the level of gravity as the other crimes against humanity and consequently does not constitute persecution. The *Kordic* Trial Chamber held further that the criminal prohibition of removal of members of government on discriminatory grounds has not reached the level of customary international law."

"[A] forcible takeover, *per se*, does not reach the level of gravity as the other crimes against humanity and on its own does not amount to persecution. The Trial Chamber notes however that a forcible takeover may serve as the basis for perpetration of other persecutory acts as it provides the conditions necessary for adoption and enforcement of policies infringing upon basic rights of citizens on the basis of their political, ethnic, or religious background."

Simic, Tadic and Zaric, (Trial Chamber), October 17, 2003, paras. 67, 69: "[I]nterrogations alone have not been considered by the Tribunal to be of sufficient gravity to constitute offences charged in the Statute, such as persecution or torture, as crimes against humanity." "The Trial Chamber concludes that the interrogation of Bosnian Croats, Bosnian Muslims and other non-Serb civilians who had been arrested and detained, and forcing them to sign false and coerced statements, *as alleged in themselves*, do not meet the seriousness requirement to constitute persecution and a crime against humanity. They may, however, form part of a series of acts which comprise an underlying persecutory act, for example, when considered with the charge of persecution on political, racial or religious grounds for the acts of unlawful arrest or confinement of Bosnian Croats, Bosnian Muslims and other non-Serb civilians (...) ; and specifically, when considering the legality of the alleged unlawful arrest or confinement. Such acts are also related to the charge of persecution for acts of cruel and inhumane treatment, that include beatings and torture (...) ; and may be considered cumulatively."

Kordic and Cerkez, (Trial Chamber), February 26, 2001, paras. 208-210: The following acts do not constitute persecution as a crime against humanity because they do not rise to the same level of gravity as the other crimes against humanity enumerated in Article 5:

- encouraging and promoting hatred on political grounds;
- dismissing and removing Bosnian Muslims from government.

(4) mens rea for persecution

(a) discriminatory intent required for persecution

Kvocka et al., (Appeals Chamber), February 28, 2005, para. 460: "With regard to the required *mens rea* [for persecution], the Appeals Chamber reiterates that persecution as a crime against humanity requires evidence of a specific intent to discriminate on political, racial or religious grounds." *See also Kordic and Cerkez,* (Appeals Chamber), December 17, 2004, paras. 110, 674 (same); *Blaskic,* (Appeals Chamber), July 29, 2004, para. 164 (same).

Kordic and Cerkez, (Appeals Chamber), December 17, 2004, para. 711: "The (...) *mens rea* for all crimes against humanity [requires the following showing]: namely, the accused must know that there is a widespread or systematic attack on the civilian population and that his acts comprise part of that attack. In addition, for persecutions, a crime against humanity, the specific intent to discriminate on political, racial, or religious grounds must be proved."

Vasiljevic, (Appeals Chamber), February 25, 2004, para. 113: "[A]s held by the Appeals Chamber in the *Krnojelac* Appeals Judgement, [the *mens rea* of the crime of persecution requires proof that the act or omission] 'was carried out deliberately with the intention to discriminate on one of the listed grounds, specifically race, religion or politics(...)'"

Krnojelac, (Appeals Chamber), September 17, 2003, para. 184: "The Appeals Chamber reiterates that, in law, persecution as a crime against humanity requires evidence of a specific intent to discriminate on political, racial or religious grounds and that it falls to the Prosecution to prove that the relevant acts were committed with the requisite discriminatory intent."

Brdjanin, (Trial Chamber), September 1, 2004, para. 996: "The crime of persecution also derives its unique character from the requirement of a specific discriminatory intent. It is not sufficient for the accused to be aware that he is in fact acting in a way that is discriminatory; he must consciously intend to discriminate."

Simic, Tadic, and Zaric, (Trial Chamber), October 17, 2003, para. 51: "The crime of persecution is uniquely distinguishable from the other Article 5 crimes by the requirement of an intent to discriminate on racial, religious or political grounds. It is not sufficient for the accused to be aware that he is in fact acting in a way that is discriminatory; he must consciously intend to discriminate."

Stakic, (Trial Chamber), July 31, 2003, para. 738: "The Trial Chamber recalls that the *mens rea* of the crime of persecutions, apart from the knowledge required for all crimes against humanity listed in Article 5 of the Statute, consists of:

- the intent to commit the underlying act, and
- the intent to discriminate on political, racial or religious grounds.

Kordic and Cerkez, (Trial Chamber), February 26, 2001, para. 212: "[A] particular intent is required, in addition to the specific intent (to commit the act and produce its consequences) and the general intent (objective knowledge of the context in which the accused acted). This intent – the discriminatory intent – is what sets the crime of persecution apart from other Article 5 crimes against humanity. This discriminatory intent requirement for the crime of persecution is thus different from the more general level of intent required for the other crimes against humanity under Article 5, when mere 'knowledge of the context' of a widespread or systematic attack against a civilian population is sufficient." (underlining removed)

See also Stakic, (Trial Chamber), July 31, 2003, para. 737: "The Trial Chamber opines that the terms 'discriminatory intent' amounts to the requirement of a '*dolus specialis*.'"

(b) mens rea requirement for persecution higher than for other crimes against humanity, but lower than for genocide

Kupreskic et al., (Trial Chamber), January 14, 2000, para. 636: "[T]he *mens rea* requirement for persecution is higher than for ordinary crimes against humanity, although lower than for genocide. [P]ersecution as a crime against humanity is an offence belonging to the same *genus* as genocide. Both persecution and genocide are crimes perpetrated against persons that belong to a particular group and who are targeted because of such belonging. In both categories what matters is the intent to discriminate: to attack persons on account of their ethnic, racial, or religious characteristics (as well as, in the case of persecution, on account of their political affiliation). While in the case of persecution the discriminatory intent can take multifarious inhumane forms and manifest itself in a plurality of actions including murder, in the case of genocide that intent must be accompanied by the intention to destroy, in whole or in part, the group to which the victims of the genocide belong. [F]rom the viewpoint of *mens rea*, genocide is an extreme and most inhuman form of persecution. To put it differently, when persecution escalates to the extreme form of wilful and deliberate acts designed to destroy a group or part of a group, it can be held that such persecution amounts to genocide."

(c) intent to target group, not individuals

Blaskic, (Appeals Chamber), July 29, 2004, para. 165: "The Trial Chamber was correct when it held (...) that the *mens rea* for persecutions 'is the specific intent to cause injury to a human being because he belongs to a particular community or group.'"

Naletilic and Martinovic, (Trial Chamber), March 31, 2003, para. 636: "A discriminatory basis exists where a person is targeted on the basis of religious, political or racial considerations, i.e. for his or her membership in a certain victim group that is targeted by the perpetrator group(...)[T]he targeted group does not only comprise persons who *personally* carry the (religious, racial or political) criteria of the group. The targeted group must be interpreted broadly, and may, in particular, include such persons who are *defined by the perpetrator as belonging to the victim group due to their close affiliations or sympathies for the victim group*(...) [T]his interpretation is consistent with the underlying *ratio* of the provision prohibiting persecution, as it is the perpetrator who defines the victim group while the targeted victims have no influence on the definition of their status. The Chamber finds that in such cases, a factual discrimination is given as the victims are *discriminated in fact* for who or what they are on the basis of the perception of the perpetrator."

Blaskic, (Trial Chamber), March 3, 2000, para. 235: The "perpetrator of the acts of persecution does not initially target the individual but rather membership in a specific racial, religious or political group."

(d) discriminatory intent may be shown by political, racial or religious discrimination

Simic, Tadic, and Zaric, (Trial Chamber), October 17, 2003, para. 52: "Although the Statute refers to the listed grounds in the conjunctive ["persecution on political, racial and religious grounds"], it is settled in the jurisprudence of the Tribunal that the presence of discriminatory intent on any one of these grounds is sufficient to fulfil the *mens rea* requirement for persecution."

(e) discriminatory intent may be shown by positive or negative criteria

Kvocka et al., (Trial Chamber), November 2, 2001, para. 195: "[T]he discriminatory act could result from the application of positive or negative criteria." For example, "an attack 'conducted against only the non-Serb portion of the population because they were non-Serbs' was indicative of the necessary discriminatory intent."

(f) inferring discriminatory intent

(i) discriminatory intent may not be inferred directly from the general discriminatory nature of an attack

Kvocka et al., (Appeals Chamber), February 28, 2005, para. 460: "This intent [for persecution as a crime against humanity] may not be inferred directly from the general discriminatory nature of an attack characterized as a crime against humanity; such a context may not in and of itself amount to evidence of discriminatory intent." *See also Kvocka et al.*, (Appeals Chamber), February 28, 2005, para. 366; *Kordic and Cerkez,* (Appeals Chamber), December 17, 2004, paras. 110, 674; *Blaskic,* (Appeals Chamber), July 29, 2004, para. 164; *Krnojelac,* (Appeals Chamber), September 17, 2003, para. 184; *Blagojevic and Jokic,* (Trial Chamber), January 17, 2005, para. 584; *Brdjanin,* (Trial Chamber), September 1, 2004, para. 997.

But see Blagojevic and Jokic, (Trial Chamber), January 17, 2005, para. 584: "When those acts [charged as persecution] formed part of an attack of a discriminatory nature, this context can be a sufficient basis to infer the discriminatory intent in relation to each particular act."

For discussion that discriminatory intent may be inferred directly from the general discriminatory nature of an attack where there is an indirect perpetrator, see "where indirect perpetrator, proof is required only of general discriminatory intent in relation to the attack,"

(ii) discriminatory intent may be inferred from the context of the attack if it is substantiated by surrounding circumstances

Kvocka et al., (Appeals Chamber), February 28, 2005, para. 366: "[D] iscriminatory intent may be inferred from the context of the attack, provided it is substantiated by the surrounding circumstances of the crime." *See also Kvocka et al.*, (Appeals Chamber), February 28, 2005, para. 460 (similar); *Kordic and Cerkez,* (Appeals Chamber), December 17, 2004, paras. 110, 674; *Blaskic,* (Appeals Chamber), July 29, 2004, para. 164; *Krnojelac,* (Appeals Chamber), September 17, 2003, para. 184; *Blagojevic and Jokic,* (Trial Chamber), January 17, 2005, para. 584; *Brdjanin,* (Trial Chamber), September 1, 2004, para. 997.

See also Krnojelac, (Appeals Chamber), September 17, 2003, para. 185: "[T] he Appeals Chamber considers that the fact that [circumstances surrounding the commission of the alleged acts] may allow the *actus reus* of persecution (i.e. the discriminatory nature of an act) to be established does not preclude a Trial Chamber from giving consideration to those circumstances, as well as other factors, to establish the *mens rea* of the offence, that is the discriminatory intent on the basis of which the discriminatory act was committed."

(iii)factors to consider

Kvocka et al., (Appeals Chamber), February 28, 2005, para. 460: "Circumstances which may be taken into consideration [when inferring discriminatory intent regarding persecution] include the systematic nature of the crimes committed against a racial or religious group and the general attitude of the alleged perpetrator as demonstrated by his behaviour."

Kordic and Cerkez, (Appeals Chamber), December 17, 2004, para. 715: "The Appeals Chamber now turns to the specific intent to discriminate on political, racial, or religious grounds and wants to stress first that such a specific intent in general can only be inferred from objective facts and the general conduct of an accused seen in its entirety. Only on rare occasions it will be possible to establish such an intent on documents laying down a perpetrator's own *mens rea*."

Krnojelac, (Appeals Chamber), September 17, 2003, para. 184: "Circumstances which may be taken into consideration [in inferring discriminatory intent] include the operation of the prison (in particular, the systematic nature of the crimes committed against a racial or religious group) and the general attitude of the offence's alleged perpetrator as seen through his behaviour."

(iv) intent may be inferred from a perpetrator's knowing participation in a system

Simic, Tadic, and Zaric, (Trial Chamber), October 17, 2003, para. 51: "Trial Chambers have inferred discriminatory intent through a perpetrator's knowing participation in a system or enterprise that discriminates on political, racial or religious grounds."

Kvocka et al., (Trial Chamber), November 2, 2001, para. 201: "[D] iscriminatory intent of a perpetrator [where there exists a joint criminal enterprise] can be inferred from knowingly participating in a system or enterprise that discriminates on political, racial or religious grounds."

(v) application—inferring discriminatory intent from the fact that beatings were inflicted only on non-Serb prison detainees

Kvocka et al., (Appeals Chamber), February 28, 2005, para. 366: "[T] he Appeals Chamber found in the case *Prosecutor v. Krnojelac* that, when beatings were inflicted only on the non-Serb detainees in a prison, it was reasonable to conclude that these beatings were committed because of the political or religious affiliation of the victims, and that these acts were committed with the requisite discriminatory intent. In the present case, it appears that almost all the detainees in the camp belonged to the non-Serb group. It was reasonable to conclude that the reason for their detention was their membership in this group and therefore of a discriminatory nature."

(g) no requirement of discriminatory policy

Kvocka et al., (Appeals Chamber), February 28, 2005, para. 341: "In his Reply Brief, Kvocka accepts that there is no requirement that a discriminatory policy existed or that the accused took part in the formulation of such a policy and submits that this subsection of his ground of appeal does not need to be considered."

Blagojevic and Jokic, (Trial Chamber), January 17, 2005, para. 582: "While persecutory acts might often be part of a discriminatory policy, the existence of a discriminatory policy is not a necessary requirement for persecutions." *See also Kupreskic et al.*, (Trial Chamber), January 14, 2000, para. 625 (similar).

Brdjanin, (Trial Chamber), September 1, 2004, para. 997: "'There is no requirement under persecution that a discriminatory policy exist or that, in the event that such a policy is shown to have existed, the accused need to have taken part in the formulation of such discriminatory policy or practice by a governmental authority.'" *See also Simic, Tadic, and Zaric*, (Trial Chamber), October 17, 2003, para. 51 (same); *Vasiljevic*, (Trial Chamber), November 29, 2002, para. 248 (similar); *Krnojelac*, (Trial Chamber), March 15, 2002, para. 435 (same).

Stakic, (Trial Chamber), July 31, 2003, para. 739: "The requirement that an accused intend to discriminate does not require the existence of a discriminatory policy."

(h) persecutory intent—the removal of targeted persons from society or humanity—not required

Kordic and Cerkez, (Appeals Chamber), December 17, 2004, para. 111: "Pursuant to the jurisprudence of the International Tribunal, the Appeals Chamber holds that a showing of a specific persecutory intent behind an alleged persecutory plan or policy, that is, the removal of targeted persons from society or humanity, is not required to establish the *mens rea* of the perpetrator carrying out the underlying physical acts of persecutions. The Appeals Chamber holds that the *mens rea* for persecutions 'is the specific intent to cause injury to a human being because he belongs to a particular community or group.' The Appeals Chamber stresses that there is no requirement in law that the actor possess a 'persecutory intent' over and above a discriminatory intent."

Blaskic, (Appeals Chamber), July 29, 2004, para. 165: "Pursuant to the jurisprudence of the International Tribunal, the Appeals Chamber holds that a showing of a specific persecutory intent behind an alleged persecutory plan or policy, that is, the removal of targeted persons from society or humanity, is not required to establish the *mens rea* of the perpetrator carrying out the underlying physical acts of persecutions. The Appeals Chamber further dismisses the Appellant's allegation that a discriminatory purpose alone is insufficient to establish the *mens rea* for the crime of persecutions. The Trial Chamber was correct when it held at paragraph 235 of the Trial Judgement that the *mens rea* for persecutions 'is the specific intent to cause injury to a human being because he belongs to a particular community or group.' The Appeals Chamber stresses that there is no requirement in law that the actor possess a 'persecutory intent' over and above a discriminatory intent."

(i) knowledge that one is acting in a way that is discriminatory is insufficient; must intend to discriminate

Vasiljevic, (Trial Chamber), November 29, 2002, para. 248: "The accused must consciously intend to discriminate for persecution to be established. It is not sufficient that the accused was merely aware that he is in fact acting in a discriminatory way."

Krnojelac, (Trial Chamber), March 15, 2002, para. 435: "The crime of persecution also derives its unique character from the requirement of a specific discriminatory intent. It is not sufficient for the accused to be aware that he is in fact acting in a way that is discriminatory; he must consciously intend to discriminate."

(j) intent to discriminate need not be the primary intent, but must be a significant one

Krnojelac, (Trial Chamber), March 15, 2002, para. 435: "While the intent to discriminate need not be the primary intent with respect to the act, it must be a significant one."

(k) personal motives irrelevant to finding of intent

Kvocka et al., (Appeals Chamber), February 28, 2005, para. 463: "The Trial Chamber explicitly noted that crimes against humanity can be committed for purely personal reasons. The Appeals Chamber confirms that the relevant case-law and the spirit of international rules concerning crimes against humanity make it clear that under customary law, 'purely personal motives' do not acquire any relevance for establishing whether or not a crime against humanity has been perpetrated. Motive and intent must be distinguished. Personal motives, such as settling old scores, or seeking personal gain, do not exclude discriminatory intent. They may become relevant at the sentencing stage in mitigation or aggravation of the sentence, but they do not form part of the prerequisites necessary for conduct to fall within the definition of a crime against humanity."

(i) application—personal motives: the Omarska camp

Kvocka et al., (Appeals Chamber), February 28, 2005, paras. 367, 369-370: "Radic argues that he did not share the goal of the discriminatory policy, but that he reluctantly served in the [Omarska] camp only because of the explicit orders of his superior. The Appeals Chamber recalls that discriminatory intent must be distinguished from the motive for doing so. The Trial Chamber inferred Radic's discriminatory intent from his knowledge of the persecutory nature of the crimes, and his knowing participation in the system of persecution pervading Omarska camp. The Appeals Chamber finds that it was reasonable to reach the conclusion that Radic acted with discriminatory intent from the facts of the case, regardless of his personal motives for doing so. His personal motives may become relevant at the sentencing stage, but not as to the finding of his criminal intent."

"Radic also asserts that the acts of rape and sexual violence charged do not involve discrimination based on religion, ethnicity, or political belief. He submits that the Trial Chamber found personal motives in the acts of rape as persecution, but failed to establish what constituted his discriminatory intent." "The Appeals Chamber finds that Radic, again, does not distinguish between intent and motive. The Trial Chamber found that the sexual violence was directed only against women of non-Serb origin, and Radic does not contest this finding. It was, for the reasons set out in the preceding section, reasonable to conclude that Radic acted with the required discriminatory intent, notwithstanding his personal motives for committing these acts."

(l) generally, discriminatory intent must relate to the act charged as persecution, not the attack

Blagojevic and Jokic, (Trial Chamber), January 17, 2005, para. 584: "The intent to discriminate must be related to the particular act(s) charged as persecutions."

Simic, Tadic, and Zaric, (Trial Chamber), October 17, 2003, para. 51: "The discriminatory intent must relate to the specific act or omission underlying the charge of persecution as opposed to the attack in general, notwithstanding the fact that the attack may also in practice have a discriminatory aspect."

Stakic, (Trial Chamber), July 31, 2003, para. 740: "In the *Vasiljevic* case, the Trial

Chamber held that [...] the discriminatory intent must relate to the specific act charged as persecution. It is not sufficient that the act merely occurs within an attack which has a discriminatory aspect. In this context, the Trial Chamber in that case criticised the fact that, in other cases before the Tribunal, it was held that 'a discriminatory attack is a sufficient basis from which to infer the discriminatory intent of acts carried out within that attack.' It continued by stating that [t]his approach may lead to the correct conclusion with respect to most of the acts carried out within the context of a discriminatory attack, but there may be acts committed within the context that were committed either on discriminatory grounds not listed in the Statute, or for purely personal reasons. Accordingly, this approach does not necessarily allow for an accurate inference regarding intent to be drawn with respect to all acts that occur within that context."

Krnojelac, (Trial Chamber), March 15, 2002, para. 436: "The discriminatory intent must relate to the specific act charged as persecution rather than the attack in general, even though the latter may also in practice have a discriminatory aspect. This is clear from the definition of persecution which requires an act or omission that is in fact persecutory. There is no requirement, either under the crime of persecution or under the general requirements for crimes against humanity, that the attack in general be discriminatory. [T]he law has (...) been applied by this Tribunal on the basis that an attack on discriminatory grounds is a sufficient basis from which to infer the necessary discriminatory intent for persecution. While such an approach would probably reach the correct conclusion for most acts occurring within the context of a discriminatory attack, there may be certain acts committed within the context of the attack either on discriminatory grounds not listed in the Statute, or for purely personal reasons. Therefore, this approach does not necessarily allow for an accurate inference regarding intent to be drawn with respect to all acts." *See also Vasiljevic,* (Trial Chamber), November 29, 2002, para. 249 (similar).

(i) where indirect perpetrator, proof is required only of general discriminatory intent in relation to the attack

Stakic, (Trial Chamber), July 31, 2003, paras. 741-743, 746, 774: "This Trial Chamber (...) is of the view that the role of the particular accused has a significant impact on the question whether proof is required of a discriminatory intent in relation to each specific act charged, or whether it would suffice that proof of a discriminatory attack is a sufficient basis from which to infer the discriminatory intent in relation to acts forming part of that attack. In both the *Vasiljevic* and *Krnojelac* cases, the accused were closely related to the actual commission of crimes. In such cases, this Trial Chamber might agree that proof is required of the fact that the direct perpetrator acted with discriminatory intent in relation to the specific act. In the present case, however, the Accused is not alleged to be the direct perpetrator of the crimes. Rather, as the leading political figure in Prijedor municipality, he is charged as the perpetrator behind the direct perpetrator/actor and is considered the co-perpetrator of those crimes together with other persons with whom he co-operated in many leading bodies of the Municipality. The Trial Chamber deliberately uses both terms 'perpetrator' and 'actor' because it is immaterial for the assessment of the intent of the indirect perpretator whether or not the actor had such a discriminatory intent; the actor may be used as an innocent instrument or tool only."

"In such a context, to require proof of the discriminatory intent of both the Accused and the acting individuals in relation to all the single acts committed would lead to an unjustifiable protection of superiors and would run counter to the meaning, spirit and purpose of the Statute of this International Tribunal. This Trial Chamber, therefore, holds that proof of a discriminatory attack against a civilian population is a sufficient basis to infer the discriminatory intent of an accused for the acts carried out as part of the attack in which he participated as a (co-) perpetrator."

"In cases of indirect perpetratorship, proof is required only of the general discriminatory intent of the indirect perpetrator in relation to the attack committed by the direct perpetrators/actors. Even if the direct perpetrator/actor did not act with a discriminatory intent, this, as such, does not exclude the fact that the same act may be considered part of a discriminatory attack if only the indirect perpetrator had the discriminatory intent." "[I]t is immaterial whether or not the direct perpetrator had, or even shared, the intent of the indirect perpetrator who acts on a higher level. What counts is the discriminatory intent of the indirect perpetrator."

"[T]he Trial Chamber has determined that for a persecutorial act, a different discriminatory intent must be proved depending on the position of the perpetrator. In case of a persecutorial attack, it must be proved on the level of the indirect (co-) perpretator behind the perpetrator/actor. However, proof of individual crimes committed by the direct perpetrators with discriminatory intent may be of assistance."

(m)mens rea for ordering, planning or instigating crime of persecution

Kordic and Cerkez, (Appeals Chamber), December 17, 2004, para. 112: "[T]he Appeals Chamber considers that a person who orders, plans or instigates an act or omission with the awareness of the substantial likelihood that a crime will be committed in the execution of that order, plan or instigation, has the requisite *mens rea* for establishing liability under Article 7(1) of the Statute pursuant to ordering, planning or instigating. Ordering, planning or instigating with such awareness has to be regarded as accepting that crime. Thus, an individual who orders, plans or instigates an act with the awareness of a substantial likelihood that persecutions as a crime against humanity will be committed in the execution of the order, plan or instigation, may be liable under Article 7(1) of the Statute for the crime of persecutions."

Blaskic, (Appeals Chamber), July 29, 2004, para. 166: "[T]he correct legal standard (...) is that a person who orders an act or omission with the awareness of the substantial likelihood that a crime will be committed in the execution of that order, has the requisite *mens rea* for establishing liability under Article 7(1) pursuant to ordering. Ordering with such awareness has to be regarded as accepting that crime. Thus, an individual who orders an act with the awareness of a substantial likelihood that persecutions as a crime against humanity will be committed in the order's execution, may be liable under Article 7(1) for the crime of persecutions."

(n) mens rea for crime of persecution where joint criminal enterprise/ mens rea for aider and abettor of persecution

Kvocka et al., (Appeals Chamber), February 28, 2005, para. 110: "[F]or crimes of persecution, the Prosecution must demonstrate that the accused shared the common discriminatory intent of the joint criminal enterprise. If the accused does not share the discriminatory intent, then he may still be liable as an aider and abettor if he knowingly makes a substantial contribution to the crime."

Compare Vasiljevic, (Appeals Chamber), February 25, 2004, para. 142: "In order to convict [Vasiljevic] for aiding and abetting the crime of persecution, the Appeals Chamber must establish that the Appellant had knowledge that the principal perpetrators of the joint criminal enterprise intended to commit the underlying crimes, and by their acts they intended to discriminate against the Muslim population, and that, with that knowledge, the Appellant made a substantial contribution to the commission of the discriminatory acts by the principal perpetrators."

(o) application—persecution—mens rea

(i) the Omarska, Keraterm and Trnopolje camps

Kvocka et al., (Appeals Chamber), February 28, 2005, paras. 461, 345-347, 455: "Considering that all the crimes Zigic was convicted of were committed in the framework of the Omarska, Keraterm and Trnopolje camps, that these camps were part of a widespread and systematic attack on the non-Serb civilian population, and that the overwhelming majority of detainees in these camps belonged to this group, the Trial Chamber correctly found that the discriminatory intent of Zigic against the detainees could be inferred from his activities within these camps."

"Kvocka submits that his association with the Muslim community, his political affiliation and his duty as a professional policeman are facts that disprove the existence of a discriminatory intent." "The Appeals Chamber concurs with the Trial Chamber's reasonable and cogent finding that the crimes committed in the camp were committed with the intent to discriminate against and subjugate the non-Serb detainees, the ultimate aim of the joint criminal enterprise. Regarding Kvocka, the Trial Chamber found that he had the intent to discriminate against the non-Serbs detained in the camp. In this respect, the Appeals Chamber recalls that, on the question of Kvocka's *mens rea*, it concluded that the Trial Chamber did not err when it found, based on the evidence before it, that Kvocka had the intent to contribute to the joint criminal enterprise of the Omarska camp. The Appeals Chamber is of the opinion that, in the context of the case, the intent to contribute to the joint criminal enterprise and discriminatory intent is one and the same thing."

"[T]he Trial Chamber considered that when all the detainees were non-Serbs or those suspected of sympathizing with non-Serbs, it would be disingenuous to contend that religion, politics, and ethnicity did not define the group targeted for attack. In relation to the facts of the present case, the Trial Chamber noted: [V]irtually all the offences alleged were committed against non-Serb detainees of the camps. The victims were targeted for attack on discriminatory grounds. While discriminatory grounds form the requisite criteria, not membership in a particular group, the discriminatory grounds in this case are founded upon exclusion from membership in a particular group, the Serb group. [...] There is no doubt that the attacks specifically targeted the non-Serb population of Prijedor and purported to drive this population out of the territory or to subjugate those remaining. The Trnopolje and Keraterm camps appear to have been each established as part of a common plan to effectuate this goal, and the Omarska camp was clearly established to effectuate this goal. Although the Trial Chamber made these observations in the context of the discussion of the *mens rea* for persecution, they also support the conclusion that the crimes committed in the camps discriminated in fact. In the Omarska camp, a few Bosnian Serbs were also detained, reportedly because they were suspected of having collaborated with the Muslims. Although the Trial Chamber's arguments mainly relate to the Omarska camp, it did not leave any doubt that the same conditions prevailed in the Keraterm and Trnopolje camps."

(ii) Prijedor municipality

Stakic, (Trial Chamber), July 31, 2003, paras. 818, 826: "The (...) findings lead the Trial Chamber to the conclusion that various crimes such as murder, torture, physical violence, rapes and sexual assaults were committed by the direct perpetrators with a discriminatory intent. What is crucial is that these crimes formed part of a persecutorial campaign headed *inter alia* by Dr. Stakic as (co-)perpetrator behind the direct perpetrators. He is criminally responsible for all the crimes and had a discriminatory intent in relation to all of them, whether committed by the direct perpetrator/actor with a discriminatory intent or not." "The Trial Chamber is satisfied beyond reasonable doubt that the Accused had the intent to discriminate against non-Serbs or those affiliated or sympathising with them because of their political or religious affiliations in the Prijedor municipality during the relevant time in 1992. The Trial Chamber therefore finds the Accused guilty as a co-perpetrator of the proven acts alleged under persecution, a crime against humanity under Article 5(h) of the Statute."

(iii)the Drina River incident in the municipality of Visegrad in south-eastern Bosnia-Herzegovina

Vasiljevic, (Appeals Chamber), February 25, 2004, paras. 1, 143: The Trial Chamber found that on June 7, 1992, the Appellant, together with Milan Lukic and two unidentified men, forcibly transported seven Muslim men to the eastern bank of the Drina River, where they were shot. Five of the seven men died as a result of the shooting and two survived by falling into the river, pretending to be dead. This incident is referred to as the Drina River incident.

"In the Appeals Chamber's view, it is beyond doubt that the acts committed by Milan Lukic and the two other men amount to the crime of persecution: They killed the five Muslim men and committed inhumane acts against the two survivors with the deliberate intent to discriminate on religious or political grounds. Furthermore, the Appeals Chamber concurs with the findings of the Trial Chamber that the Appellant participated in the Drina River incident 'with full awareness that the intent of the Milan Lukic's group was to persecute the local Muslim population of Visegrad through the commission of the underlying crimes.' The only reason why the seven

Muslim men were arrested and killed was because of their belonging to the Muslim population of Visegrad. The Appellant was aware of these facts and he willingly participated in the Drina River incident by pointing his gun at the victims and preventing them from fleeing. Even if it has not been established beyond reasonable doubt that he personally killed the five Muslim men, his support had a substantial effect upon the perpetration of the crimes on the bank of the Drina River. He was at that time fully aware that his participation assisted the commission of the crime of persecution by the principal perpetrators. The Appellant is therefore responsible for having aided and abetted the crime of persecution by way of murder of the five Muslim men and of inhumane acts against the two other Muslim men (Count 3)."

(iv) detention of non-Serbs in the KP Dom prison complex in Foca, Bosnia-Herzegovina

Krnojelac, (Appeals Chamber), September 17, 2003, para. 186: "In this case, the Trial Chamber indicated that the 'detention of non-Serbs in the KP Dom [prison complex], and the acts or omissions which took place therein, were clearly related to the widespread and systematic attack against the non-Serb civilian population in the Foca municipality.' The Appeals Chamber holds that it may be inferred from this finding that the treatment meted out to the non-Serb detainees was the consequence of the aforementioned discriminatory policy[[32]] at the root of their detention. Furthermore, the Appeals Chamber recalls the Trial Chamber's findings in paragraph 47 of the Judgment:

The few Serb convicts who were detained at the KP Dom were kept in a different part of the building from the non-Serbs. They *were not mistreated like the non-Serb detainees*. The quality and quantity of their food was somewhat better, sometimes including additional servings. *They were not beaten or otherwise abused*, they were not locked up in their rooms, they were released once they had served their time, they had access to hygienic facilities and enjoyed other benefits which were denied to non-Serb detainees. The Appeals Chamber observes that this finding shows that only the non-Serb detainees were, in actual fact, subject to beatings. It holds that the differences in the way that the Serb and non-Serb detainees were treated cannot reasonably be attributed to the random posting of the guards. This finding therefore confirms the above presumption. Accordingly, the Appeals Chamber considers that the only reasonable finding that could be reached on the basis of the Trial Chamber's relevant findings of fact was that the beatings were inflicted upon the non-Serb detainees because of their political or religious affiliation and that, consequently, these unlawful acts were committed with the requisite discriminatory intent. The Appeals Chamber considers that, even if it were to be assumed that the blows inflicted upon the non-Serb detainees were meted out in order to punish them for violating the regulations, the decision to inflict such punishment arose out of a will to discriminate against them on religious or political grounds since punishment was only inflicted upon non-Serb detainees."

(5) application—persecution as a crime against humanity

(a) Srebrenica massacre and related crimes

Blagojevic and Jokic, (Trial Chamber), January 17, 2005, paras. 619-621: "The Trial Chamber has found that the widespread and systematic attack against the Bosnian Muslim population in Srebrenica was carried out on the basis of the ethnic, national and religious affiliation of the population. The Trial Chamber recalls in this respect the announcement of General Mladic that 'the time has come for us to take revenge upon the Turks in this region.' It further notes that many [Army of the Republika Srpska] soldiers were cursing at the Bosnian Muslims and calling them names. [Army of the Republika Srpska] soldiers told refugees to leave the area calling it 'Serb country' and part of 'Greater Serbia.' When Bosnian Muslim prisoners arrived at detention centres they were forced to repeat pro-Serb texts including that 'this [area] is Serbia.' The Trial Chamber therefore finds that the circumstances accompanying the terrorising and the cruel and inhumane treatment of the Bosnian Muslim civilians, the subsequent forcible transfer of the women and children and the organised executions of the men substantiate the existence of a discriminatory intent on racial, religious or political grounds of the perpetrators."

"The Trial Chamber finds that there is sufficient evidence to establish beyond reasonable doubt that the murder, the cruel and inhumane treatment and the terrorising of the civilian population as described above constitute blatant denials of fundamental rights that had a severe impact on the victims and therefore amount to persecutions. However, in relation to the destruction of the personal belongings such as clothes and wallets, the Trial Chamber does not find that those personal belongings constituted indispensable assets to their owners. The Trial Chamber therefore does not find that the burning of those personal belongings had a severe enough impact on the victims to reach the threshold of equal gravity as the acts listed in Article 5 of the Statute."

"In summary the Trial Chamber finds that the murder, cruel and inhumane treatment, terrorising and forcible transfer of the Bosnian Muslim civilians constituted a persecutorial campaign against the Bosnian Muslim population."

Nikolic – Momir, (Trial Chamber), December 2, 2003, paras. 30-33: "'[I]n the several days following this attack on Srebrenica, VRS [Army of the Serbian Republic of Bosnia and Herzegovina/Republika Srpska] forces captured, detained, summarily executed, and buried over 7000 Bosnian Muslim men and boys from the Srebrenica enclave, and forcibly transferred the Bosnian Muslim women and children of Srebrenica out of the enclave.' These acts form the basis of the crime of persecutions to which Momir Nikolic has pled guilty."

"The crime of persecutions (...) was carried out by the following means: (a) the murder of thousands of Bosnian Muslim civilians, including men, women, children and elderly persons; (b) the cruel and inhumane treatment of Bosnian Muslim civilians, including severe beatings at Potocari and in detention facilities in Bratunac and Zvornik;

(c) the terrorising of Bosnian Muslim civilians in Srebrenica and Potocari; (d) the destruction of personal property and effects belonging to the Bosnian Muslims; and (e) the forcible transfer of Bosnian Muslims from the Srebrenica enclave."

"Beginning on 12 and 13 July 1995 in Potocari, a number of Bosnian Muslim men and women were shot and killed in and around the area of the United Nations compound, where they had gathered after fleeing Srebrenica; one group of approximately 80 -100 men were summarily executed by decapitation. Within a five-day period, approximately 6,000 Bosnian Muslim men who were escaping in 'the column' from Srebrenica were captured, detained and executed in various locations in the Bratunac and Zvornik municipalities. In the town of Bratunac on 13 July 1995, some of the Bosnian Muslim men who were detained there were taken from their places of detention, including schools, hangars and buses, and summarily executed. Along the route between Bratunac and Zvornik, the names previously used to mark settlements and communities or places of learning, culture and work or geographic features are now used to identify mass execution sites: Jadar River, Cerska Valley, Kravica Warehouse, Petkovci School, Pilica Cultural Centre, and the villages of Tisca and Orahovac. At one location, Branjevo Military Farm, approximately 1,200 Bosnian Muslim men who had been captured from the column were executed by automatic weapon fire."

"In his Statement of Facts, Momir Nikolic describes his role in the initial stages of planning the murder operation, including the detention of able-bodied men and the selection of execution sites:

In the morning of 12 July, prior to the above-mentioned meeting, I met with Lt. Colonel Vujadin Popovic, Chief of Security, Drina Corps, and Lt. Colonel

Kosoric, Chief of Intelligence, Drina Corps, outside the Hotel Fontana. At that time Lt. Colonel Popovic told me that the thousands of Muslim women and children in Potocari would be transported out of Potocari toward Muslim-held territory near Kladanj and that the able-bodied Muslim men within the crowd of Muslim civilians would be separated from the crowd, detained temporarily in Bratunac, and killed shortly thereafter. I was told that it was my responsibility to help coordinate and organise this operation. Lt. Colonel Kosoric reiterated this information and we discussed the appropriate locations to detain the Muslim men prior to their execution. I identified several specific areas: the Old Elementary School 'Vuk Karadzic' (including the gym), the old building of the secondary School 'Duro Pucar Stari,' and the Hangar (which is 50 meters away from the old secondary School). Lt. Colonel Popovic and Kosoric talked with me about sites of executions of temporarily detained Muslim men in Bratunac and we discussed two locations which were outside Bratunac town. These were: State company 'Ciglane' and a mine called 'Sase' in Sase."

(b) attack on Muslim residents of Glogova in the Municipality of Bratunac with the goal of taking over territory in Bosnia-Herzegovina

(i) underlying acts

Deronjic, (Trial Chamber), March 30, 2004, para. 128: "From the end of April to 9 May 1992, Miroslav Deronjic, individually as President of the Crisis Staff of the Municipality of Bratunac and in concert with other members of the joint criminal enterprise, committed Persecutions of Bosnian Muslims on political, racial or religious grounds, in the village of Glogova in the Municipality of Bratunac. These Persecutions resulted in the killings of 64 Bosnian Muslims, the forcible displacement of the Bosnian Muslim population from Glogova and the destruction of the village of Glogova."

(ii) intent

Deronjic, (Trial Chamber), March 30, 2004, paras. 129, 132: "Miroslav Deronjic committed the aforementioned acts with the specific intent to discriminate against the Bosnian Muslim residents of Glogova and the Municipality of Bratunac on political and religious grounds." "The decision to attack Glogova and to displace permanently its Muslim residents was taken in order to further the plan to create Serb ethnic territories within Bosnia and Herzegovina."

(iii)existence of a widespread or systematic attack against a civilian population and knowledge that the acts form part of that attack

Deronjic, (Trial Chamber), March 30, 2004, para. 130: "Miroslav Deronjic knew that the attack on Glogova and the forcible displacement of the Bosnian Muslim population formed part of a widespread and systematic attack directed against the Bosnian Muslim civilian population within parts of Bosnia and Herzegovina designated as the Republika Srpska."

(iv) armed conflict

Deronjic, (Trial Chamber), March 30, 2004, para. 131: "The attack on Glogova occurred within the context of an armed conflict between Serb and Muslim forces within Bosnia and Herzegovina."

ix) other inhumane acts (Article 5(i))

(1) generally

Kordic and Cerkez, (Appeals Chamber), December 17, 2004, para. 117: "The Appeals Chamber notes that inhumane acts as crimes against humanity were deliberately designed as a residual category, as it was felt undesirable for this category to be exhaustively enumerated. An exhaustive categorization would merely create opportunities for evasion of the letter of the prohibition." *See also Kupreskic et al.*, (Trial Chamber), January 14, 2000, para. 563 (same language as quoted).

Galic, (Trial Chamber), December 5, 2003, para. 152: "The crime of inhumane acts is a residual clause for serious acts which are not otherwise enumerated in Article 5 but which require proof of the same chapeau elements."

Naletilic and Martinovic, (Trial Chamber), March 31, 2003, para. 247: "Article 5(i) of the Statute (other inhumane acts) is a residual clause, which applies to acts that do not fall within any of other sub-clause [*sic*] of Article 5 of the Statute but are sufficiently similar in gravity to the other enumerated crimes. Inhumane acts are '[…] acts or omissions intended to cause deliberate mental or physical suffering to the individual.' As constituting crimes against humanity, these acts must also be widespread or systematic."

(2) part of international customary law

Blagojevic and Jokic, (Trial Chamber), January 17, 2005, para. 624: "Mindful of the principle *nullum crimen sine lege*, the Trial Chamber finds that the category of Other Inhumane Acts, as a residual category of crimes against humanity, forms part of customary international law. It should be stressed that other inhumane acts is in itself a crime under international criminal law. The Trial Chamber observes that convictions have been entered on this ground by the International Military Tribunal at Nuremberg, this Tribunal and the Rwanda Tribunal."

(3) potential nullum crimen sine lege issue

Kordic and Cerkez, (Appeals Chamber), December 17, 2004, para. 117: "The Appeals Chamber considers that the potentially broad range of the crime of inhumane acts may raise concerns as to a possible violation of the *nullum crimen* principle. In the present case, however, 'other inhumane acts' are charged exclusively as injuries."

Blagojevic and Jokic, (Trial Chamber), January 17, 2005, para. 625: "The crime of Other Inhumane Acts exists in order not to unduly restrict the Statute's application with regard to crimes against humanity. It must be stressed, however, that the principle of legality requires that a trier of fact exercise great caution in finding that an alleged act, not regulated elsewhere in Article 5 of the Statute, forms part of this crime: norms of criminal law must always provide individuals with sufficient notice of what is criminal behaviour and what is not."

Stakic, (Trial Chamber), July 31, 2003, paras. 719-721: "The Trial Chamber recalls that '[t]he use of "other inhumane acts" as a crime against humanity under Article 5(i) of the Statute to attach criminal liability to forcible transfers, which are not otherwise punishable as deportations, raises serious concerns.' While noting that '[n]ot every law can be defined with ultimate precision and that it is for the jurisprudence to interpret and apply legal provisions which need, in part, to be formulated in the abstract,' the Trial Chamber declared that the description of a criminal offence extends beyond the permissible when the specific form of conduct prohibited can not be identified.' The Trial Chamber therefore held that as '[t]he crime of "other inhumane acts" subsumes a potentially broad range of criminal behaviour and may well be considered to lack sufficient clarity, precision and definiteness' it might violate the fundamental criminal law principle *nullum crimen sine lege certa*."

"This legal issue was addressed in *Kupreskic*, where the Trial Chamber held that the category 'other inhumane acts' was: deliberately designed as a residual category, as it was felt undesirable for this category to be exhaustively enumerated. An exhaustive categorization would merely create opportunities for evasion of the letter of the prohibition. After referring to several international human rights instruments such as the Universal Declaration of Human Rights of 1948 and the two United Nations

Covenants of 1966, the *Kupreskic* Trial Chamber concluded that by referring to such instruments one would be able to identify 'less broad parameters for the interpretation of "other inhumane acts"' and 'identify a set of basic rights appertaining to human beings, the infringement of which may amount, depending on the accompanying circumstances, to a crime against humanity.'"

"This Trial Chamber disagrees with that approach and notes that the international human rights instruments referred to by the *Kupreskic* Trial Chamber provide somewhat different formulations and definitions of human rights. However, regardless of the status of the enumerated instruments under customary international law, the rights contained therein do not necessarily amount to norms recognised by international criminal law. The Trial Chamber recalls the report of the Secretary-General according to which 'the application of the principle *nullum crime sine lege* requires that the international tribunal should apply rules of international humanitarian law which are beyond doubt part of customary law.' Accordingly, this Trial Chamber hesitates to use such *human rights* instruments automatically as a basis for a norm of *criminal law*, such as the one set out in Article 5(i) of the Statute. Its hesitation is even more pronounced when, as in the present case, there is no need to undertake such an exercise. A norm of criminal law must always provide a Trial Chamber with an appropriate yardstick to gauge alleged criminal conduct for the purposes of Article 5(i) so that individuals will know what is permissible behaviour and what is not."

(4) elements

Kordic and Cerkez, (Appeals Chamber), December 17, 2004, para. 117: "Inhumane acts as a crime against humanity is comprised of acts which fulfill the following conditions:

- the victim must have suffered serious bodily or mental harm; the degree of severity must be assessed on a case-by-case basis with due regard for the individual circumstances;

- the suffering must be the result of an act or omission of the accused or his subordinate; and

-when the offence was committed, the accused or his subordinate must have been motivated by the intent to inflict serious bodily or mental harm upon the victim."

See also Kordic and Cerkez, (Trial Chamber), February 26, 2001, para. 271 (same elements); *Blaskic*, (Trial Chamber), March 3, 2000, para. 243 (similar).

Vasiljevic, (Appeals Chamber), February 25, 2004, para. 165: "In the present case, when recalling the applicable law (...) on inhumane acts, the Trial Chamber held that:

The elements to be proved [for an act to constitute an inhumane act as a crime against humanity] are:

(i) the occurrence of an act or omission of similar seriousness to the other enumerated acts under the Article;

(ii) the act or omission caused serious mental or physical suffering or injury or constituted a serious attack of [*sic*] human dignity;

(iii) the act or omission was performed deliberately by the accused or a person or persons for whose acts and omissions he bears criminal responsibility."

See also Blagojevic and Jokic, (Trial Chamber), January 17, 2005, para. 626 (same elements but using "intentionally" instead of "deliberately" in last prong of test); *Galic*, (Trial Chamber), December 5, 2003, para. 152 (same elements but using "intentionally" instead of "deliberately" in last prong of test); *Vasiljevic,* (Trial Chamber), November 29, 2002, para. 234 (same elements).

Kordic and Cerkez, (Trial Chamber), February 26, 2001, para. 271: "In addition [to the elements of the crime], as discussed in relation to the requirements for the application of Article 5 of the Statute, the acts must have been committed as part of a widespread or systematic attack against a civilian population."

(a) factors for assessing seriousness of the act

Vasiljevic, (Appeals Chamber), February 25, 2004, para. 165: "To assess the seriousness of an act, consideration must be given to all the factual circumstances. These circumstances may include the nature of the act or omission, the context in which it occurred, the personal circumstances of the victim including age, sex and health, as well as the physical, mental and moral effects of the act upon the victim." *See also Galic*, (Trial Chamber), December 5, 2003, para. 153 (similar); *Vasiljevic,* (Trial Chamber), November 29, 2002, para. 235 (same).

Blagojevic and Jokic, (Trial Chamber), January 17, 2005, para. 627: "The element of 'similar seriousness' is to be evaluated in light of all factual circumstances, such as the nature of the act or omission, the context within which it occurred, the individual circumstances of the victim(s) as well as the physical, mental and moral effects on the victim(s)."

(b) no requirement that the suffering have long term effects

Vasiljevic, (Appeals Chamber), February 25, 2004, para. 165: "While there is no requirement that the suffering imposed by the act have long term effects on the victim, the fact that an act has had long term effects may be relevant to the determination of the seriousness of the act."

Blagojevic and Jokic, (Trial Chamber), January 17, 2005, para. 627: "There is no requirement that the effects on the victim(s) be long-lasting, however the fact that such were the effects will impact the determination of the seriousness of the act or omission."

Vasiljevic, (Trial Chamber), November 29, 2002, para. 235: "[T]he fact that an act has had long term effects may be relevant to the determination of the seriousness of the act."

Krnojelac, (Trial Chamber), March 15, 2002, para. 131: "The suffering inflicted by the act upon the victim does not need to be lasting so long as it real and serious."

(c) mens rea

Blagojevic and Jokic, (Trial Chamber), January 17, 2005, para. 628: "It is required that the perpetrator, at the time of the act or omission, had the intention to inflict serious physical or mental suffering or to commit a serious attack on the human dignity of the victim(s), or that the perpetrator knew that his act or omission was likely to cause such suffering to, or amount to a serious attack on, the human dignity of the victim(s) and, with that knowledge, acted or failed to act."

Galic, (Trial Chamber), December 5, 2003, para. 154: "The intention to inflict inhumane acts is satisfied where the offender, at the time of the act or omission, had the intention to inflict serious physical or mental suffering or to commit a serious attack upon the human dignity of the victim, or where he knew that his or her act or omission was likely to cause serious physical or mental suffering or a serious attack upon human dignity."

Krnojelac, (Trial Chamber), March 15, 2002, para. 132: "The required *mens rea* is met where the principal offender, at the time of the act or omission, had the intention to inflict serious physical or mental suffering or to commit a serious attack on the human dignity of the victim, or where he knew that his act or omission was likely to cause serious physical or mental suffering or a serious attack upon human dignity and was reckless as to whether such suffering or attack would result from his act or omission." *See also Vasiljevic,* (Trial Chamber), November 29, 2002, para. 236 (similar).

(5) equivalent to "cruel treatment" under Article 3 and "inhumane treatment" under Article 5

Jelisic, (Trial Chamber), December 14, 1999, para. 52: "The sub-characterisation 'other inhumane acts' specified under Article 5(i) of the Statute is an generic charge which encompasses a series of crimes. [T]he notion of cruel treatment set out in Article 3 of the Statute 'carries an equivalent meaning [(...)] as inhuman treatment does in relation to grave breaches of the Geneva Conventions.' Likewise (...) the notions of cruel treatment within the meaning of Article 3 and of inhumane treatment set out in Article 5 of the Statute have the same legal meaning."

(6) acts covered

(a) forcible displacement and forcible transfer

Blagojevic and Jokic, (Trial Chamber), January 17, 2005, paras. 629-630: "[T]he Trial Chamber is of the opinion that the prohibition against forcible population displacements, whether in international or non-international armed conflicts, forms part of customary international law. The Trial Chamber finds that the crime of forcible transfer as defined satisfies the three requirements above. This crime, therefore, clearly forms part of the category of Other Inhumane Acts under Article 5(i) of the Statute." "Consequently, it is a crime against humanity to forcibly displace members of the civilian population unless any of the law's exceptions applies justifying the displacement."

Brdjanin, (Trial Chamber), September 1, 2004, para. 544: "[D]isplacement within the boundaries of a State constitutes 'forcible transfer,' punishable as 'other inhumane acts' pursuant to Article 5(i) of the Statute."

Krstic, (Trial Chamber), August 2, 2001, para. 523: "[F]orcible displacement within or between national borders is included as an inhumane act under Article 5(i) defining crimes against humanity."

See also Stakic, (Trial Chamber), July 31, 2003, para. 723: "This Trial Chamber has used a definition of deportation that covers different forms of forcible transfers. The Prosecution has proposed that various forms of forcible transfer should be covered by Article 5(i) of the Statute. The Trial Chamber has concluded that the vast majority of these forms fall under the definition of deportation as laid down in Article 5(d)."

(i) distinction between deportation, forcible transfer and forced displacement

For discussion of the distinctions between deportation, forcible transfer and forcible displacement, see (IV)(d)(viii)(3)(e)(iii).

(ii) coercion required for both deportation and forcible transfer

Brdjanin, (Trial Chamber), September 1, 2004, para. 543: "It is essential for both 'deportation' [under Article 5(d)] and 'forcible transfer' [under Article 5(i)] that the displacement takes place under coercion. The essential element in establishing coercion is that the displacement be involuntary in nature, where the persons concerned had no real choice."

(iii)displacement must be unlawful

Brdjanin, (Trial Chamber), September 1, 2004, para. 543: "In addition, the displacement must be unlawful."

(iv)mens rea

Brdjanin, (Trial Chamber), September 1, 2004, para. 545: "With regard both to deportation and forcible transfer as crimes against humanity, the Prosecution needs to prove beyond reasonable doubt that the Accused acted with the intent that the removal of the person or persons be permanent."

(b) mutilation and other types of severe bodily harm, beatings and other acts of violence, serious physical and mental injury, forcible transfer, inhumane and degrading treatment, forced prostitution, and forced disappearance

Kvocka et al., (Trial Chamber), November 2, 2001, para. 208: "Mutilation and other types of severe bodily harm, beatings and other acts of violence, serious physical and mental injury, forcible transfer, inhumane and degrading treatment, forced prostitution, and forced disappearance are listed in the jurisprudence of the Tribunal as falling under this category [other inhumane acts]."

(c) serious physical and mental injury

Blaskic, (Trial Chamber), March 3, 2000, para. 239: "[S]erious physical and mental injury – excluding murder – is without doubt an 'inhumane act' within the meaning of Article 5 of the Statute."

(d) removal of individuals to detention facilities excluded

Stakic, (Trial Chamber), July 31, 2003, para. 723: "In relation to other examples provided by the Prosecution (such as removal of individuals to detention facilities), the Trial Chamber is not convinced that they a) reached the same level as other listed crimes under Article 5 of the Statute, b) suffice to base a conviction cumulatively on Article 5(i), and c) in this case might amount to an infringement of the principle *nullum crime sine lege certa*."

(e) application—other inhumane acts

(i) forcible transfer of women and children from Srebrenica to Kladanj

Blagojevic and Jokic, (Trial Chamber), January 17, 2005, paras. 631, 707: "[T]he Trial Chamber has found that the crime of forcible transfer, as a component crime of persecution, was committed." "It has been proved beyond reasonable doubt that the women and children from the Srebrenica enclave were forcibly transferred to Kladanj on 12 and 13 July 1995."

(ii) campaign of sniping, artillery fire and mortar attacks on civilians in Sarajevo

Galic, (Trial Chamber), December 5, 2003, para. 599: "The Trial Chamber is further satisfied that, as examined in this Part of the Judgement, (...) inhumane acts falling within the meaning of Article 5 of the Statute were committed in Sarajevo during the Indictment Period [from around 10 September 1992 to 10 August 1994]." For detailed factual findings, see *Galic*, (Trial Chamber), December 5, 2003, paras. 192-594.

PART 4
JURISPRUDENCE OF THE ICTR

II) CRIMES AGAINST HUMANITY (ARTICLE 3)

a) Statute

ICTR Statute, Article 3:

"The International Tribunal for Rwanda shall have the power to prosecute persons responsible for the following crimes when committed as part of a widespread or systematic attack against any civilian population on national, political, ethnic, racial or religious grounds:

a) Murder;

b) Extermination;

c) Enslavement;

d) Deportation;

e) Imprisonment;

f) Torture;

g) Rape;

h) Persecutions on political, racial and religious grounds;

i) Other inhumane acts."

b) Overall requirements/chapeau

Bagosora, Kabiligi, Ntabakuze and Nsengiyumva, (Trial Chamber), December 18, 2008, para. 2165: "For an enumerated crime under Article 3 to qualify as a crime against humanity, the Prosecution must prove that there was a widespread or systematic attack against the civilian population on national, political, ethnic, racial or religious grounds." *See also Zigiranyirazo,* (Trial Chamber), December 18, 2008, para. 430 (similar); *Bikindi*, (Trial Chamber), December 2, 2008, paras. 428 (similar); *Nzabirinda,* (Trial Chamber), February 23, 2007, para. 20 (similar); *Rwamakuba*, (Trial Chamber), September 20, 2006, para. 1 (similar); *Bisengimana,* (Trial Chamber), April 13, 2006, para. 41 (similar); *Simba,* (Trial Chamber), December 13, 2005, para. 421 (similar).

Seromba, (Trial Chamber), December 13, 2006, para. 354: "Article 3 of the Statute, which deals with crimes against humanity, contains a general element that is applicable to all the acts listed therein: perpetration of any of those acts by an accused will constitute a crime against humanity only if it was committed as part of a widespread or systematic attack against any civilian population on national, political, ethnic, racial or religious grounds." *See also Nchamihigo,* (Trial Chamber), November 12, 2008, para. 340 (similar); *Muhimana,* (Trial Chamber), April 28, 2005, para. 525 (similar); *Rutaganira,* (Trial Chamber), March 14, 2005, para. 48 (similar); *Gacumbitsi*, (Trial Chamber), June 17, 2004, para. 297 (similar).

Muvunyi, (Trial Chamber), September 12, 2006, para. 511: "[U]nder Article 3 of the Statute, the definition of 'Crimes Against Humanity' consists of two layers. The first layer, ('General Elements') is to the effect that a crime against humanity must be committed as part of a 'widespread or systematic attack against any civilian population on national, ethnic, racial or religious grounds.' The second layer lists six specific ('underlying') crimes, plus one residual category of 'other inhumane acts' which qualify as crimes against humanity when committed in the context of a widespread or systematic attack on a civilian population on any of the enumerated discriminatory grounds."

Mpambara, (Trial Chamber), September 11, 2006, para. 11: "[T]he chapeau requirements for a crime against humanity must (...) be satisfied. First, the crime must have been committed as part of a widespread or systematic attack (...) Second, the attack must be carried out against a civilian population on 'national, political, ethnic, racial or religious grounds.'" *See also Kamuhanda,* (Trial Chamber), January 22, 2004, para. 657 (similar); *Kajelijeli,* (Trial Chamber), December 1, 2003, para. 864 (same as *Kamuhanda*).

Ntagerura, Bagambiki, and Imanishimwe, (Trial Chamber), February 25, 2004, para. 698: "The Chamber explained in the *Semanza* Judgement that in connection with crimes against humanity, the Prosecutor must prove: (1) that there was an attack; (2) that the attack was widespread or systematic; (3) that the attack was directed against any civilian population; (4) that the attack was committed on national, political, ethnical, racial or religious grounds; and (5) that the accused acted with knowledge of the broader context of the attack and with knowledge that his act(s) formed part of the attack."

But see Akayesu, (Trial Chamber), September 2, 1998, para. 578: Crimes against humanity can be broken down into four essential elements, namely: "(i) *the act must be inhumane in nature and character, causing great suffering, or serious injury to body or to mental or physical health;*

(ii) the act must be committed as part of a wide spread [*sic*] or systematic attack; (iii) the *act* must be committed against members of the civilian population; (iv) the *act* must be committed on one or more discriminatory grounds, namely, national, political, ethnic, racial or religious grounds." (emphasis added.) *See also Semanza*, (Appeals Chamber), May 20, 2005, para. 268 (quoting *Akayesu* approvingly).[15]

i) the act must be committed as part of a "widespread or systematic attack" (element 1)

Semanza, (Trial Chamber), May 15, 2003, para. 326: "A crime against humanity must have been committed as part of a widespread or systematic attack against any civilian population on discriminatory grounds."

1) attack

(a) defined

Nahimana, Barayagwiza and Ngeze, (Appeals Chamber), November 28, 2007, para. 918: "[F]or purposes of Article 3 of the Statute, an attack against a civilian population means the perpetration against a civilian population of a series of acts of violence, or of the kind of mistreatment referred to in sub-paragraphs (a) to (i) of the Article." *See also Bagosora, Kabiligi, Ntabakuze and Nsengiyumva,* (Trial Chamber), December 18, 2008, para. 2165 (similar).

Nahimana, Barayagwiza and Ngeze, (Appeals Chamber), November 28, 2007, para. 917:

"According to the *Kayishema and Ruzindana* Trial Judgement:

The attack is the event of which the enumerated crimes must form part. Indeed, within a single attack, there may exist a combination of the enumerated crimes, for example murder, rape and deportation." *See also Kayishema and Ruzindana,* (Trial Chamber), May 21, 1999, para. 122 (source).

Nahimana, Barayagwiza and Ngeze, (Appeals Chamber), November 28, 2007, para. 916: "According to the [ICTY's] *Kunarac et al.* Trial Judgement, an attack 'can be described as a course of conduct involving the commission of acts of violence.'"

Nzabirinda, (Trial Chamber), February 23, 2007, para. 21: "'[A]ttack' has been defined as 'an unlawful act, event, or series of events of the kind listed in Article 3 (a) through (i) of the Statute.'" *See also Seromba,* (Trial Chamber), December 13, 2006, para. 355 (similar);

The *Akayesu* Trial Chamber, in the quotation in text, also uses the word "act" in places where other cases use the word "attack." Indeed, the *Akayesu* Trial Chamber later contradicts itself by using the (more accurate) formulation with the word "attack." *See Akayesu,* (Trial Chamber), September 2, 1998, para. 595 ("a) [the underlying act] must be perpetrated as part of a widespread or systematic attack; b) the *attack* must be against the civilian population; c) the *attack* must be launched on discriminatory grounds, namely: national, ethnic, racial, religious and political grounds") (emphasis added).

Muvunyi, (Trial Chamber), September 12, 2006, para. 512 (similar); *Bisengimana,* (Trial Chamber), April 13, 2006, para. 42 (same); *Muhimana,* (Trial Chamber), April 28, 2005, para. 526 (similar); *Gacumbitsi,* (Trial Chamber), June 17, 2004, para. 298 (similar); *Kamuhanda,* (Trial Chamber), January 22, 2004, para. 660 (similar); *Kajelijeli,* (Trial Chamber), December 1, 2003, para. 867 (same as *Kamuhanda*); *Akayesu,* (Trial Chamber), September 2, 1998, para. 581 (similar).

(b) not same as armed conflict/ need not require use of armed force

Nahimana, Barayagwiza and Ngeze, (Appeals Chamber), November 28, 2007, paras. 916-17:

"[T]he Appeals Chamber of [the] ICTY [in *Kunarac*], (...) added the following: The concepts of 'attack' and 'armed conflict' are not identical. Under customary international law, the attack could precede, outlast, or continue during the armed conflict, but it need not be a part of it. Also, the attack in the context of a crime against humanity is not limited to the use of armed force; it encompasses any mistreatment of the civilian population." "This position is reiterated in the [ICTY's] *Kordić and Čerkez* Appeal Judgement and was adopted in a number of ICTY Trial judgements."

Kamuhanda, (Trial Chamber), January 22, 2004, para. 661: "[A]n attack committed on specific discriminatory grounds need not necessarily require the use of armed force; it could also involve other forms of inhumane treatment of the civilian population." *See also Kajelijeli,* (Trial Chamber), December 1, 2003, para. 868 (same).

Akayesu, (Trial Chamber), September 2, 1998, para. 581: An attack may (...) be non violent in nature, like imposing a system of apartheid (...) or exerting pressure on the population to act in a particular manner." *See also Semanza,* (Trial Chamber), May 15, 2003, para. 327 (similar); *Musema,* (Trial Chamber), January 27, 2000, para. 205 (similar); *Rutaganda,* (Trial Chamber), December 6, 1999, para. 70 (similar).

(c) attack distinct from underlying acts

Muvunyi, (Trial Chamber), September 12, 2006, para. 516: "The 'attack' is an element distinct from the acts enumerated in Article 3 of the Statute. There must exist an attack on a civilian population which is discriminatory and widespread or systematic before the perpetrator can be found to have committed a crime against humanity."

(d) random acts or acts committed for personal reasons excluded

Kayishema and Ruzindana, (Trial Chamber), May 21, 1999, paras. 122-23, n.28: "The elements of the attack effectively exclude (...) acts carried out for purely personal motives and those outside of a broader policy or plan." "Either of these conditions [widespread or systematic] will serve to exclude isolated or random inhumane acts committed for purely personal reasons."

Akayesu, (Trial Chamber), September 2, 1998, paras. 578-79: The act must be committed as "part of a wide spread [*sic*] or systematic attack and not just a random act of violence." *See also Rutaganda* (Trial Chamber), December 6, 1999, para. 67 ("the *actus reus* cannot be a random inhumane act, but rather an act committed as part of an attack").

2) either "widespread or systematic"

Nahimana, Barayagwiza and Ngeze, (Appeals Chamber), November 28, 2007, para. 920: "It is well established that the attack must be widespread *or* systematic. In particular, the Appeals Chamber has held that the conjunction '*et*' in the French version of Article 3 of the Statute is a translation error." (emphasis in original) *See also Kamuhanda,* (Trial Chamber), January 22, 2004, paras. 662-63 (similar); *Kajelijeli,* (Trial Chamber), December 1, 2003, paras. 869-70 (same as *Kamuhanda*).

Karera, (Trial Chamber), December 7, 2007, para. 551: "The general requirements for a crime against humanity are intended to be read as disjunctive elements." *See also Bagosora, Kabiligi, Ntabakuze and Nsengiyumva,* (Trial Chamber), December 18, 2008, para. 2165 (similar); *Simba,* (Trial Chamber), December 13, 2005, para. 421 (similar).

Muvunyi, (Trial Chamber), September 12, 2006, para. 512: "In accordance with customary international law, the twin elements 'widespread' or 'systematic' should be read disjunctively and not as cumulative requirements."

Bisengimana, (Trial Chamber), April 13, 2006, para. 43: "The Chamber notes that, based on the practice of this Tribunal and the ICTY, the applicable standard is 'widespread or systematic' and not 'widespread and systematic.'"

Ndindabahizi, (Trial Chamber), July 15, 2004, para. 477: "The enumerated offence must be part of an attack which has two characteristics before qualifying as a crime against humanity. First, the attack must be either widespread or systematic (...)Second, the attack must be 'against any civilian population on national, political, ethnic racial or religious grounds.' In other words, the attack as a whole, but not the individual offence, must be committed on these particular grounds."

Gacumbitsi, (Trial Chamber), June 17, 2004, para. 299: "The attack must be widespread or systematic." *See Gacumbitsi,* (Appeals Chamber), July 7, 2006, para. 101 (approving of same).

Akayesu, (Trial Chamber), September 2, 1998, para. 579, n. 144: The attack must contain one of the alternate conditions of being widespread or systematic, not both, as in the French text of the Statute. "Customary international law requires only that the attack be either widespread or systematic." *See also Niyitegeka,* (Trial Chamber), May 16, 2003, para. 439; *Semanza,* (Trial Chamber), May 15, 2003, para. 328; *Ntakirutimana and Ntakirutimana,* (Trial Chamber), February 21, 2003, para. 804; *Bagilishema,* (Trial Chamber), June 7, 2001, para. 77; *Musema,* (Trial Chamber), January 27, 2000, para. 203; *Rutaganda,* (Trial Chamber), December 6, 1999, para. 68; *Kayishema and Ruzindana,* (Trial Chamber), May 21, 1999, para. 123 & n. 26.

See also Seromba, (Trial Chamber), December 13, 2006, para. 356: "This attack must be widespread or systematic. In practice, these two criteria tend to overlap."

3) widespread

Nahimana, Barayagwiza and Ngeze, (Appeals Chamber), November 28, 2007, para. 920: "The Appeals Chamber (...) recalls that: 'widespread' refers to the large-scale nature of the attack and the number of victims(...)" *See also Bagosora, Kabiligi, Ntabakuze and Nsengiyumva,* (Trial Chamber), December 18, 2008, para. 2165 (similar).

Nchamihigo, (Trial Chamber), November 12, 2008, para. 340: "'[W] idespread' refers to the scale of the attack(...)" *See also Simba,* (Trial Chamber), December 13, 2005, para. 421 (similar).

Karera, (Trial Chamber), December 7, 2007, para. 551: "'[W]idespread' refers to the large scale of an attack, involving many victims(...)" *See also Gacumbitsi,* (Appeals Chamber), July 7, 2006, para. 101 (similar); *Nzabirinda,* (Trial Chamber), February 23, 2007, para. 21 (similar); *Muvunyi,* (Trial Chamber), September 12, 2006, para. 512 (similar); *Mpambara,* (Trial Chamber),

September 11, 2006, para. 11 (similar); *Muhimana,* (Trial Chamber), April 28, 2005, para. 527 (similar); *Ndindabahizi,* (Trial Chamber), July 15, 2004, para. 477 (same); *Gacumbitsi,* (Trial Chamber), June 17, 2004, para. 299 (similar); *Ntakirutimana and Ntakirutimana,* (Trial Chamber), February 21, 2003, para. 804 (similar); *Bagilishema* (Trial Chamber), June 7, 2001, para. 77 (similar); *Kayishema and Ruzindana,* (Trial Chamber), May 21, 1999, para. 123 (similar).

Seromba, (Trial Chamber), December 13, 2006, para. 356: "'Widespread' may be defined as massive, frequent, large scale action, carried out collectively with considerable seriousness and directed against a multiplicity of victims." *See also Musema,* (Trial Chamber), January 27, 2000, para. 204 (same); *Rutaganda,* (Trial Chamber), December 6, 1999, para. 69 (same); *Akayesu,* (Trial Chamber), September 2, 1998, para. 580 (source).

Bisengimana, (Trial Chamber), April 13, 2006, para. 44: "The 'widespread' element of the attack has been given slightly different meanings in the Tribunal's judgements. The Chamber notes, however, that this element is always taken to refer to the scale of the attack, and sometimes to the number of victims. The Chamber adopts the *Kajelijeli* Judgement definition, which is 'large scale, involving many victims.'" *See also Kamuhanda,* (Trial Chamber), January 22, 2004, para. 664 (similar); *Kajelijeli,* (Trial Chamber), December 1, 2003, para. 871 (similar).

4) systematic

Nahimana, Barayagwiza and Ngeze, (Appeals Chamber), November 28, 2007, para. 920:

"The Appeals Chamber (...) recalls that: (...) 'systematic' refers to 'the organised nature of the acts of violence and the improbability of their random occurrence.' Patterns of crimes – that is the nonaccidental repetition of similar criminal conduct on a regular basis – are a common expression of such systematic occurrence."

See also Bagosora, Kabiligi, Ntabakuze and Nsengiyumva, (Trial Chamber), December 18, 2008, para. 2165 (similar to first sentence of quote).

Nchamihigo, (Trial Chamber), November 12, 2008, para. 340: "'[S]ystematic' describes [an attack's] organised nature, as distinguished from random and unrelated acts." *See also Karera,* (Trial Chamber), December 7, 2007, para. 551 (same); *Muvunyi,* (Trial Chamber), September 12, 2006, para. 512 (similar); *Mpambara,* (Trial Chamber), September 11, 2006, para. 11 (similar).

Nzabirinda, (Trial Chamber), February 23, 2007, para. 21: "The Chamber adopts the *Kajelijeli* Judgement's definition of (...) 'systematic' which describes the organised nature of the attack." *See also Bisengimana,* (Trial Chamber), April 13, 2006, para. 45 (similar); *Simba,* (Trial Chamber), December 13, 2005, para. 421 (similar).

Seromba, (Trial Chamber), December 13, 2006, para. 356: "'Systematic' may be defined as thoroughly organised and following a regular pattern on the basis of a common policy involving substantial public or private resources."[17]

Ndindabahizi, (Trial Chamber), July 15, 2004, para. 477: "'[S]ystematic' refers to an organized pattern of conduct, as distinguished from random or unconnected acts committed by independent actors." *See also Kamuhanda,* (Trial Chamber), January 22, 2004, para. 666 (similar); *Kajelijeli,* (Trial Chamber), December 1, 2003, para. 872 (same as *Kamuhanda*).

(a) plan or policy relevant but not required

Seromba, (Appeals Chamber), March 12, 2008, para. 149: "[W]hile the existence of a plan can be evidentially relevant, it is not a separate legal element of a crime against humanity(...)" *See also Nahimana, Barayagwiza and Ngeze,* (Appeals Chamber), November 28, 2007, para. 922 (similar); *Gacumbitsi,* (Appeals Chamber), July 7, 2006, para. 84 (similar); *Seromba,* (Trial Chamber), December 13, 2006, para. 356 (similar); *Muhimana,* (Trial Chamber), April 28, 2005, para. 527 (similar); *Semanza,* (Trial Chamber), May 15, 2003, para. 329 (similar).

Semanza, (Appeals Chamber), May 20, 2005, para. 269: "[T]he Prosecution did not have to prove the existence of a high-level policy against the Tutsi: although the existence of a policy or plan may be useful to establish that the attack was directed against a civilian population and that it was widespread and systematic, it is not an independent legal element." *See also Muvunyi,* (Trial Chamber), September 12, 2006, para. 512 (similar); *Gacumbitsi,* (Trial Chamber), June 17, 2004, para. 299 (similar); *Gacumbitsi,* (Appeals Chamber), July 7, 2006, para. 101 (approving of *Gacumbitsi* Trial Chamber formulation).

Muhimana, (Trial Chamber), April 28, 2005, para. 527: "The concept of a 'systematic' attack, within the meaning of Article 3 of the Statute, refers to a deliberate pattern of conduct but does not necessarily require the proof of a plan." *See also Gacumbitsi,* (Trial Chamber), June 17, 2004, para. 299 (similar); *Gacumbitsi,* (Appeals Chamber), July 7, 2006, para. 101 (approving of *Gacumbitsi* Trial Chamber formulation).

Kamuhanda, (Trial Chamber), January 22, 2004, para. 665: "There has been some debate in the jurisprudence of this Tribunal about whether or not the term 'systematic' necessarily contains a notion of a policy or a plan. The Chamber agrees with the reasoning followed in Semanza [*sic*] and finds that the existence of a plan is not [*sic*] independent legal element of Crimes against Humanity. In Semanza [*sic*], ICTR Trial Chamber II endorsed the jurisprudence of the Appeals Chamber of the ICTY in Kunarac [*sic*], that whilst 'the existence of a policy or plan may be evidentially relevant, in that it may be useful in establishing that the attack was directed against a civilian population and that it was widespread or systematic, [...] the existence of such a plan is not a separate legal element of the crime.'" *See also Kajelijeli,* (Trial Chamber), December 1, 2003, para. 872 (same with italics).

But see Akayesu, (Trial Chamber), September 2, 1998, para. 580: "There must however be some kind of preconceived plan or policy." *See also Bagilishema,* (Trial Chamber), June 7, 2001, para. 77; *Musema,* (Trial Chamber), January 27, 2000, para. 204; *Rutaganda,* (Trial Chamber), December 6, 1999, para. 69; *Kayishema and Ruzindana,* (Trial Chamber), May 21, 1999, paras. 123-24, 581.

(b) use of substantial resources not an element

Nahimana, Barayagwiza and Ngeze, (Appeals Chamber), November 28, 2007, para. 922: "Contrary to what certain early Tribunal judgements might be taken to imply, 'substantial resources' do not constitute a legal element of crimes against humanity."

5) crime must form part of the widespread or systematic attack

Nahimana, Barayagwiza and Ngeze, (Appeals Chamber), November 28, 2007, para. 934: "Whereas the crime *per se* must be committed as part of a widespread and systematic attack, preparatory acts, instigation or aiding and abetting can be accomplished before the commission of the crime and the occurrence of the widespread and systematic attack."

Seromba, (Trial Chamber), December 13, 2006, para. 360: "There must be a nexus between the criminal act and the attack."

See also Nahimana, Barayagwiza and Ngeze, (Appeals Chamber), Partly Dissenting Opinion of Judge Meron, November 28, 2007, paras. 17-21 (there was a lack of nexus between Nahimana and the widespread and systematic attack).

Compare Semanza, (Appeals Chamber), May 20, 2005, para. 269: "[T]he Prosecution did not have to prove the existence of an armed conflict: contrary to Article 5 of the ICTY Statute, Article 3 of the ICTR Statute does not require that the crimes be committed in the context of an armed conflict."

(a) need not share all the same features

Bisengimana, (Trial Chamber), April 13, 2006, para. 50: "The victim(s) of the enumerated act need not necessarily share geographic or other defining features with the civilian population that forms the primary target of the underlying attack, but such characteristics may be used to demonstrate that the enumerated act forms part of the attack." *See also Kamuhanda*, (Trial Chamber), January 22, 2004, para. 669 (same); *Kajelijeli,* (Trial Chamber), December 1, 2003, paras. 875-76 (same); *Semanza,* (Trial Chamber), May 15, 2003, para. 330 (source).

Kajelijeli, (Trial Chamber), December 1, 2003, para. 866: "An act may form part of the widespread or systematic attack without necessarily sharing all the same features, such as the time and place of commission of the other acts constituting the attack. In determining whether an act forms part of a widespread or systematic attack, the Chamber will consider its characteristics, aims, nature, and consequence." *See also Kamuhanda*, (Trial Chamber), January 22, 2004, para. 659 (same as first sentence).

Semanza, (Trial Chamber), May 15, 2003, para. 326: "Although the act need not be committed at the same time and place as the attack or share all of the features of the attack, it must, by its characteristics, aims, nature, or consequence objectively form part of the discriminatory attack."

(b) underlying crime need not be widespread or systematic

Gacumbitsi, (Appeals Chamber), July 7, 2006, para. 102: "[I]t is not rape *per se* that must be shown to be widespread or systematic, but rather the attack itself (of which the rapes formed part)."

Seromba, (Trial Chamber), December 13, 2006, para. 357: "It is in not a requirement that the criminal act must, in and of itself, be widespread or systematic."

(c) a single murder may constitute a crime against humanity/ multiplicity of victims of act not required except for extermination

Nahimana, Barayagwiza and Ngeze, (Appeals Chamber), November 28, 2007, para. 924: "The Appeals Chamber considers that, except for extermination, a crime need not be carried out against a multiplicity of victims in order to constitute a crime against humanity. Thus an act directed against a limited number of victims, or even against a single victim, can constitute a crime against humanity, provided it forms part of a widespread or systematic attack against a civilian population.".

Seromba, (Trial Chamber), December 13, 2006, para. 357: "A single murder may constitute a crime against humanity if it is perpetrated within the context of a widespread or systematic attack."

Compare case law discussing "widespread," Section (II)(b)(i)(3), where it is relevant that the "attack" be against a multiplicity of victims.

6) application—widespread or systematic attack

Bikindi, (Trial Chamber), December 2, 2008, para. 430: "It is not disputed in this case that a genocide characterised by widespread killings of Tutsi civilians occurred from April to July 1994 in Rwanda."

Bisengimana, (Trial Chamber), April 13, 2006, paras. 46-47: "In the Plea agreement, the Accused admits that from 7 April 1994, massacres of the Tutsi population and the murder of numerous political opponents were perpetrated throughout the territory of Rwanda, including Gikoro *commune*. These crimes were carried out by militiamen, military personnel, and *gendarmes*." "Based on the facts contained in the Plea Agreement, the Chamber is convinced that widespread attacks were committed in Gikoro *commune* in April 1994 because the attacks resulted in a lager number of victims."

Ntagerura, Bagambiki, and Imanishimwe, (Trial Chamber), February 25, 2004, paras. 707-08: "Prosecution Expert Witness Guichaoua testified that, subsequent to 6 April 1994, there were widespread attacks against the Tutsi population across Rwanda. This opinion was amply supported by the evidence presented in this case, particularly with respect to the various massacre sites. Imanishimwe acknowledged that there was 'inter-ethnic killing' throughout Rwanda in April and May 1994. Moreover, Bagambiki does not dispute that there were widespread attacks against the civilian population in Cyangugu during the events referred to in the indictment. Having considered the totality of the evidence, and in particular the evidence concerning the ethnic composition of the individuals who sought refuge at the various sites in Cyangugu, the Chamber finds that from April to June 1994 there was a widespread attack against the civilian Tutsi population of Cyangugu."

"The Chamber further finds that the evidence reflects that there was a related systematic attack on political grounds against civilians with suspected ties to the RPF [Rwandan Patriotic Front]. For example, the Chamber recalls that assailants demanded the removal of seventeen people from Kamarampaka

Stadium and Cyangugu Cathedral because they were suspected of financially contributing to or communicating with the RPF. Sixteen of these refugees were later killed. The Chamber further notes that the assailants threatening to attack Shangi parish demanded the removal of a number of refugees whom the assailants thought to be armed and connected with the RPF. Furthermore, the Chamber's findings concerning the events at the Karambo military camp indicate that a number of civilians were arrested, detained, mistreated, and executed because of suspected ties to the RPF."

Kajelijeli, (Trial Chamber), December 1, 2003, para. 686: "[B]etween 7 and 14 April 1994, killings of members of the Tutsi group occurred on a mass scale in Mukingo *commune*, Nkuli *commune* and at the Ruhengeri Court of Appeal in Kigombe *commune*. These attacks were carried out by groups of attackers and were directed against a large number of victims on the basis of their Tutsi ethnicity. The targets were whole populations of people of Tutsi ethnicity such as neighbourhoods, or places of shelter and refuge. Entire families and neighbourhoods were eliminated. Thus, the Chamber finds that during April 1994 in Mukingo *commune* and neighbouring *communes* within Ruhengeri *prefecture*, there was a widespread attack upon a civilian Tutsi group, carried out on the basis of ethnicity."

Akayesu, (Trial Chamber), September 2, 1998, para. 173: The "widespread" requirement was met, in part, because of the scale of the events that took place. "Around the country, a massive number of killings took place within a very short time frame. Tutsi were clearly the target of the attack." The systematic nature of the attack was evidenced by the "unusually large shipments of machetes into the country shortly before it occurred," "the structured manner in which the attack took place," the fact that "[t]eachers and intellectuals were targeted first," and the fact that through the "media and other propaganda, Hutu were encouraged systematically to attack Tutsi."

ii) the attack must be directed against a civilian population (element 2)

Nzabirinda, (Trial Chamber), February 23, 2007, para. 22: "[T]he attack must be directed against a civilian population." *See also Seromba,* (Trial Chamber), December 13, 2006, para. 358 (same); *Muhimana,* (Trial Chamber), April 28, 2005, para. 528 (same); *Gacumbitsi*, (Trial Chamber), June 17, 2004, para. 300 (same).

Semanza, (Trial Chamber), May 15, 2003, para. 326: "A crime against humanity must have been committed as part of a widespread or systematic attack against any civilian population on discriminatory grounds."

But see Akayesu, (Trial Chamber), September 2, 1998, para. 578: "[T]he *act* must be committed against members of the civilian population." (emphasis added). *See also Akayesu*, (Trial Chamber), September 2, 1998, para. 582 (similar); *Bagilishema*, (Trial Chamber), June 7, 2001, para. 80 (similar).[18]

1) civilian defined

Bisengimana, (Trial Chamber), April 13, 2006, para. 48: "The *Akayesu* Judgement definition of 'civilian population' has been consistently followed in the jurisprudence of the Tribunal:

[…] people who are not taking any active part in the hostilities, including members of the armed forces who laid down their arms and those persons placed *hors de combat* by sickness, wounds, detention or any other cause." *See also Seromba,* (Trial Chamber), December 13, 2006, para. 358 (quoting same language from *Akayesu*); *Muvunyi,* (Trial Chamber), September 12, 2006, para. 513 (relying on same language from *Akayesu*); *Kamuhanda,* (Trial Chamber), January 22, 2004, para. 667 (quoting same language from *Akayesu*); *Kajelijeli,* (Trial Chamber), December 1, 2003, paras. 873-74 (quoting same language from *Akayesu*); *Musema,* (Trial Chamber), January 27, 2000, para. 207 ("'civilian population,' (...) was defined as people who were not taking any active part in the hostilities"); *Rutaganda,* (Trial Chamber), December 6, 1999, para. 72 (same as *Musema*); *Akayesu,* (Trial Chamber), September 2, 1998, para. 582 (source of quote in *Bisengimana*).

See also Kayishema and Ruzindana, (Trial Chamber), May 21, 1999, paras. 127-29: Because crimes against humanity may be committed "inside or outside the context of an armed conflict," "the term civilian must be understood within the context of war as well as relative peace." Thus, "a wide definition of civilian is applicable and, in the context of the situation of Kibuye *Prefecture* where there was no armed conflict, includes all persons *except* those who have the duty to maintain public order and have the legitimate means to exercise force."

2) presence of non-civilians does not change civilian character of population/ civilians must be the primary object of the attack

Nzabirinda, (Trial Chamber), February 23, 2007, para. 22: "As stated in the *Semanza* Judgement, 'a civilian population remains civilian in nature even if there are individuals within it who are not civilians.'" *See Semanza,* (Trial Chamber), May 15, 2003, para. 330 (source of quote).

Seromba, (Trial Chamber), December 13, 2006, para. 358: "The presence of certain noncivilians in this group does not change its civilian character." *See also Muhimana,* (Trial Chamber), April 28, 2005, para. 528 (similar); *Bagilishema,* (Trial Chamber), June 7, 2001, para. 79 (similar); *Musema,* (Trial Chamber), January 27, 2000, para. 207 (similar); *Rutaganda,*

(Trial Chamber), December 6, 1999, para. 72 (similar); *Kayishema and Ruzindana,* (Trial Chamber), May 21, 1999, para. 128 (similar); *Akayesu,* (Trial Chamber), September 2, 1998, para. 582 (similar).

Bisengimana, (Trial Chamber), April 13, 2006, para. 48: According to the *Akayesu* Judgement: "Where there are certain individuals within the civilian population who do not come within the definition of civilians, this does not deprive the population of its civilian character." *See also Muvunyi,* (Trial Chamber), September 12, 2006, para. 513 (relying on same language from *Akayesu*); *Gacumbitsi,* (Trial Chamber), June 17, 2004, para. 300 (similar); *Kamuhanda,* (Trial Chamber), January 22, 2004, para. 667 (quoting same language from *Akayesu*); *Kajelijeli,* (Trial Chamber), December 1, 2003, paras. 87374 (quoting same language from *Akayesu*).

Semanza, (Trial Chamber), May 15, 2003, para. 330: "A civilian population must be the primary object of the attack."

3) consider situation of victim when crimes committed, not status

Bisengimana, (Trial Chamber), April 13, 2006, para. 49: "As noted in [the] *Blaškic* Judgement, 'the specific situation of the victim at the moment the crimes were committed, rather than his status, must be taken into account in determining his standing as a civilian.'" *See also Kamuhanda,* (Trial Chamber), January 22, 2004, para. 668 (similar).

4) population—does not require that crimes against humanity be directed against the entire population

Bisengimana, (Trial Chamber), April 13, 2006, para. 50: "[T]he term 'population' does not require that crimes against humanity be directed against the entire population of a geographical territory or area." *See also Kamuhanda,* (Trial Chamber), January 22, 2004, para. 669 (same); *Kajelijeli,* (Trial Chamber), December 1, 2003, paras. 875-76 (same); *Bagilishema,* (Trial Chamber), June 7, 2001, para. 80 (source).

Bagilishema, (Trial Chamber), June 7, 2001, para. 80: "The requirement that the prohibited acts must be directed against a civilian 'population' does not mean that the entire population of a given State or territory must be victimised by these acts in order for the acts to constitute a crime against humanity." "Instead the 'population' element is intended to imply crimes of a collective nature and thus excludes single or isolated acts which, although possibly constituting crimes under national penal legislation, do not rise to the level of crimes against humanity."

5) application—civilian population

Bisengimana, (Trial Chamber), April 13, 2006, paras. 52-53: "In the Plea Agreement, the Accused admits that massacres of the Tutsi population and the murder of numerous political opponents were perpetrated. He further admits that the attacks against Tutsi civilians gathered at Musha Church and at Ruhanga Protestant Church and School in Gikoro *commune* were part of the ongoing attacks against Tutsi civilians occurring in most parts of Rwanda during April 1994." "Based on the facts contained in the Plea Agreement, the Chamber is convinced that the widespread attacks in Gikoro *commune* were committed against a civilian population."

iii) the attack must be committed on national, political, ethnic, racial or religious grounds (discriminatory grounds) (element 3)

1) the attack must be on discriminatory grounds

Nzabirinda, (Trial Chamber), February 23, 2007, para. 23: "[T]he attack must be committed on discriminatory grounds. The Chamber recalls the *Akayesu* Judgement, where the 'discriminatory grounds' element was considered to be jurisdictional in nature, limiting the jurisdiction of the Tribunal to crimes committed on 'national, political, ethnic, racial or religious grounds.'" *See also Bisengimana,* (Trial Chamber), April 13, 2006, para. 54 (same as second sentence); *Gacumbitsi,* (Trial Chamber), June 17, 2004, para. 301 (similar to *Nzabirinda*).

Seromba, (Trial Chamber), December 13, 2006, para. 359: "The attack against a civilian population must have been committed with discriminatory intent. That is, it must have been committed against a population 'on national, political, ethnic, racial or religious grounds.'"

Muhimana, (Trial Chamber), April 28, 2005, para. 529: "The attack against the civilian population must have been carried out on a discriminatory basis, that is, on national, political, ethnic, racial or religious grounds."

Kamuhanda, (Trial Chamber), January 22, 2004, para. 671: "Article 3 of the Statute provides that the attack against the civilian population be committed on 'national, political, ethnical, racial or religious grounds.' This provision is jurisdictional in nature, limiting the jurisdiction of the Tribunal to a narrow category of Crimes, and not intended to alter the definition of Crimes against Humanity in international law." *See also Muvunyi,* (Trial Chamber), September 12, 2006, para. 514 (similar); *Kamuhanda,* (Trial Chamber), January 22, 2004, para. 672; *Kajelijeli,* (Trial Chamber), December 1, 2003, para. 877 (same).

Semanza, (Trial Chamber), May 15, 2003, para. 331: "Article 3 of the Statute requires that the attack against the civilian population be committed 'on national, political, ethnical, racial or religious grounds.'" *See also Akayesu,* (Trial Chamber), September 2, 1998, para. 595 (similar).[19]

2) describes nature of the attack, not mens rea of the accused/perpetrator

Bagosora, Kabiligi, Ntabakuze and Nsengiyumva, (Trial Chamber), December 18, 2008, para. 2166: "The (...) requirement that crimes against humanity have to be committed 'on national, political, ethnic, racial or religious grounds' does not mean that a discriminatory *mens rea* must be established." *See also Seromba,* (Trial Chamber), December 13, 2006, para. 359 (similar).

Bagilishema, (Trial Chamber), June 7, 2001, para. 81: "[T]he qualifier 'on national, political, ethnic, racial or religious grounds,' which is peculiar to the ICTR Statute should, as a matter of construction, be read as a characterisation of the nature of the 'attack' rather than of the *mens rea* of the perpetrator. The perpetrator may well have committed an underlying offence on discriminatory grounds identical to those of the broader attack; but neither this, nor for that matter any discriminatory intent whatsoever, are prerequisites of the crime, so long as it was committed as part of the broader attack."

See also Semanza, (Appeals Chamber), May 20, 2005, paras. 268-69: "The *Akayesu* (...)

Appeals Chamber (...) explained: The meaning to be collected from Article 3 of the Statute is that even if the accused did not have a discriminatory intent when he committed the act charged against a particular victim, he nevertheless knew that his act could further a discriminatory attack against a civilian population; the attack could even be perpetrated by other persons and the accused could even object to it. As a result, where it is shown that the accused had knowledge of such objective nexus, the Prosecutor is under no obligation to go forward with a showing that the crime charged was committed against a particular victim with a discriminatory intent. In this connection, the only known exception in customary international law relates to cases of persecutions."

"The Appeals Chamber considers that the above is a correct statement of the law." *See Akayesu,* (Appeals Chamber), June 1, 2001, para. 467 (source of quote).

See also "discriminatory intent not required for acts other than persecution," Section (II)(b)(iv)(2).

3) acts committed against persons outside discriminatory categories may be covered

Nzabirinda, (Trial Chamber), February 23, 2007, para. 23: "[I]n the *Kajelijeli* Judgement the Chamber noted that: such acts committed against persons outside the discriminatory categories need not necessarily fall out with the jurisdiction of the Tribunal, if the perpetrator's intention in committing these acts is to support or further the attack on the group discriminated against on one of the enumerated grounds." *See also Bisengimana,* (Trial Chamber), April 13, 2006, para. 54 (same); *Gacumbitsi,* (Trial Chamber), June 17, 2004, para. 301 (similar); *Kamuhanda,* (Trial Chamber), January 22, 2004, paras. 672-73 (same language as quoted); *Kajelijeli,* (Trial Chamber), December 1, 2003, para. 878 (source of quoted language).

Muhimana, (Trial Chamber), April 28, 2005, para. 529: "[T]he victim's membership in a national, political, ethnic, racial or religious group is irrelevant, provided that the perpetrator's intention is to support or further an attack against a civilian population on one of the enumerated discriminatory grounds." *See also Muvunyi,* (Trial Chamber), September 12, 2006, para. 514 (similar).

Semanza, (Trial Chamber), May 15, 2003, para. 331: "Acts committed against persons outside the discriminatory categories may nevertheless form part of the attack where the act against the outsider supports or furthers or is intended to support or further the attack on the group discriminated against on one of the enumerated grounds."

See, e.g., Muhimana, (Trial Chamber), April 28, 2005, para. 561: "The Chamber finds that the Accused chose his rape victims because he believed that they were *Tutsi*. Whether the victims were in fact *Tutsi* [one, in fact, was Hutu] is irrelevant in the determination of the Accused's criminal responsibility. The Chamber concludes, on the basis of the Accused's conduct, that he raped his victims with the knowledge that the rapes formed part of a widespread and systematic attack on the *Tutsi* civilian population."

4) political grounds

Kayishema and Ruzindana, (Trial Chamber), May 21, 1999, para. 130: "Political grounds include party political beliefs and political ideology."

5) national, ethnical, racial, or religious grounds

See Sections (I)(c)(iv)(4)–(7).

6) application—discriminatory grounds

Bisengimana, (Trial Chamber), April 13, 2006, paras. 55-56: "In the Plea Agreement, Paul Bisengimana acknowledges that massacres of the Tutsi population and the murder of numerous political opponents were perpetrated. He acknowledges that from 7 April 1994, in all regions of the country, Tutsis fleeing from massacres sought refuge in locations that they considered to be safe. In many of these places, the refugees were attacked, abducted, and massacred, often with the complicity of some of the authorities." "Based on the Plea Agreement, the Chamber finds that the widespread attacks against the civilian population were committed on discriminatory grounds because most of the victims were Tutsis."

iv) mens rea (element 4)

1) knowledge of the broader context of the attack and that acts form part of the attack

Gacumbitsi, (Appeals Chamber), July 7, 2006, para. 86: "[F]or crimes against humanity 'the accused must have acted with knowledge of the broader context of the attack, and with knowledge that his act formed part of the widespread and systematic attack against the civilian population.'" *See also Nzabirinda,* (Trial Chamber), February 23, 2007, para. 24 (same language as quoted); *Seromba,* (Trial Chamber), December 13, 2006, para. 360 (similar); *Bisengimana,* (Trial Chamber), April 13, 2006, para. 57 (similar); *Gacumbitsi,* (Trial Chamber), June 17, 2004, para. 302 (similar); *Kamuhanda,* (Trial Chamber), January 22, 2004, paras. 675-76 (same language as quoted); *Kajelijeli,* (Trial Chamber), December 1, 2003, paras. 880-81 (similar).

Bagosora, Kabiligi, Ntabakuze and Nsengiyumva, (Trial Chamber), December 18, 2008, para. 2166: "As concerns the *mens rea* [for crimes against humanity], the perpetrator must have acted with knowledge of the broader context and knowledge that his acts formed part of the attack, but need not share the purpose or goals of the broader attack." *See also Zigiranyirazo,* (Trial Chamber), December 18, 2008, para. 430 (similar); *Karera,* (Trial Chamber), December 7, 2007, para. 551 (similar); *Muvunyi,* (Trial Chamber), September 12, 2006, para. 516 (similar); *Simba,* (Trial Chamber), December 13, 2005, para. 421 (similar).

Mpambara, (Trial Chamber), September 11, 2006, para. 11: "The perpetrator must know that his acts form part of this discriminatory attack but need not possess the discriminatory intent."[20]

Muhimana, (Trial Chamber), April 28, 2005, para. 530: "[T]he perpetrator must have acted knowing that the act formed part of a widespread or systematic attack against a civilian population."

Ndindabahizi, (Trial Chamber), July 15, 2004, para. 478: "The requirement that the commission of the enumerated offence be 'part of' the attack supplies the *mens rea* unique to crimes against humanity. The perpetrator need not intend to discriminate on one of the enumerated grounds, but must, at a minimum, know that his action is part of a widespread or systematic attack against civilians on discriminatory grounds."

Niyitegeka, (Trial Chamber), May 16, 2003, para. 442: "[T]he crime must be committed as part of a widespread or systematic attack against a civilian population on national, political, ethnic, racial or religious grounds. The Accused need not act with discriminatory intent, but he must know that his act is part of this widespread or systematic attack."[21]

Kayishema and Ruzindana, (Trial Chamber), May 21, 1999, paras. 133-34: "The perpetrator must knowingly commit crimes against humanity in the sense that he must understand the overall context of his act(...)" "[T]he accused must have acted with knowledge of the broader context of the attack (...) Part of what transforms an individual's act(s) into a crime against humanity is the inclusion of the act within a greater dimension of criminal conduct; therefore an accused should be aware of this greater dimension in order to be culpable. Accordingly, actual or constructive knowledge of the broader context of the attack, meaning that the accused must know that his act(s) is part of a widespread or systematic attack on a civilian population and pursuant to some kind of policy or plan, is necessary to satisfy the requisite *mens rea* element of the accused." *See also Bagilishema,* (Trial Chamber), June 7, 2001, para. 94 (similar); *Ruggiu,* (Trial Chamber), June 1, 2000, para. 20 (same as *Kayishema*).

Kayishema and Ruzindana, (Trial Chamber), May 21, 1999, paras. 133-34: To be held responsible, the perpetrator must have "actual or constructive knowledge of the broader context of the attack, meaning that the accused must know that his act(s) is part of a widespread or systematic attack on a civilian population and pursuant to some kind of policy or plan." *See also Rutaganda,* (Trial Chamber), December 6, 1999, para. 71; *Musema,* (Trial Chamber), January 27, 2000, para. 206.

But see "plan or policy relevant but not required," Section (II)(b)(i)(4)(a).

2) discriminatory intent not required for acts other than persecution

Akayesu, (Appeals Chamber), June 1, 2001, paras. 447-69: The Appeals Chamber ruled that the Trial Chamber had committed an error of law in finding that intent to discriminate on national, political, ethnic, racial or religious grounds was an essential element for crimes against humanity. "Article 3 (...) does not require that all crimes against humanity (...) be committed with a discriminatory intent." The Appeals Chamber held that "Article 3 restricts the jurisdiction of the Tribunal to crimes against humanity committed in a specific situation, that is, 'as part of a widespread or systematic attack against any civilian population' on discriminatory grounds."

Muvunyi, (Trial Chamber), September 12, 2006, para. 514: "In *Akayesu,* the Appeals Chamber stated that except for the offence of persecution, international humanitarian law does not require proof of a discriminatory intent for all crimes against humanity."

Zigiranyirazo, (Trial Chamber), December 18, 2008, para. 430: The perpetrator need not posess discriminatory intent.

Semanza, (Trial Chamber), May 15, 2003, para. 332: "There is no requirement that the enumerated acts other than persecution be committed with discriminatory intent."

See also "discriminatory grounds" "describes nature of the attack, not *mens rea* of the accused/perpetrator," Section (II)(b)(iii)(2).

For the *mens rea* requirements as to the underlying crimes, see Section (II)(c).

3) application

Bisengimana, (Trial Chamber), April 13, 2006, paras. 58-60: "In the Plea Agreement, the Accused admits that from 7 April 1994, massacres of the Tutsi population and the murder of numerous political opponents were perpetrated in Gikoro *commune.* He acknowledges that the attacks against the Tutsi civilians gathered at Musha Church and at Ruhanga Protestant Church and School were part of the ongoing attacks against Tutsi civilians which were occurring in most parts of Rwanda." "Based on the Plea Agreement, the Chamber is convinced that the Accused knew the broader context of the attacks occurring in Rwanda in April 1994 and knew that his acts formed part of widespread attacks committed against Tutsi civilians." "The Chamber finds that the attacks at Musha Church and at Ruhanga Protestant Church and School in Gikoro *commune* in April 1994 were launched against Tutsi civilians on discriminatory grounds and were of a widespread nature because they resulted in a large number of victims."

Muhimana, (Trial Chamber), April 28, 2005, paras. 559-60: "The Chamber recalls its finding that the Accused participated in attacks against *Tutsi* during April, May, and June 1994 and that in doing so, he intended to destroy the *Tutsi* ethnic group." "Consequently, the Chamber finds that the Accused knew that all of these rapes were part of a discriminatory, widespread, and systematic attack against *Tutsi* civilians." *See also id.*, paras. 579-80 (similar findings regarding the underlying crime of killing).

Ntagerura, Bagambiki, and Imanishimwe, (Trial Chamber), February 25, 2004, paras. 709, 742: "Given the respective positions of authority of Bagambiki and Imanishimwe during the relevant period, and considering, in particular, the evidence concerning the various prefectural security council meetings in which they discussed the ongoing events, it is inconceivable that Bagambiki or Imanishimwe could have been unaware of these attacks at the time of the events." "From the totality of the evidence of what occurred at the [Cyangugu] military camp and in the region, the only reasonable inference that may be drawn is that Imanishimwe acted intentionally in ordering civilians to be killed and with an awareness that he was ordering the principal perpetrators to commit murder as part of the widespread attack against the civilian population against the civilian population in Cyangugu."

v) both state and non-state actors covered

Kayishema and Ruzindana, (Trial Chamber), May 21, 1999, paras. 125-26: Stating that "crimes against humanity are (...) 'instigated or directed by a Government or by any organization or group,'" the Chamber held that the "Tribunal's jurisdiction covers both State and non-State actors."

vi) application—chapeau

Zigiranyirazo, (Trial Chamber), December 18, 2008, para. 433: "The Chamber recalls it took judicial notice that between 6 April and 17 July 1994, there were, throughout Rwanda, widespread and systematic attacks against the civilian population based on Tutsi ethnic identification. The Chamber considers that someone in the Accused's position of authority, particularly after seeing corprses [*sic*] at the Kiyovu roadblock [in Kiyovu cellule, Kigali-*ville* prefecture], would have been aware of the aforementioned context of widespread and systematic attacks against Tutsi in Rwanda. Accordingly, the Chamber finds beyond reasonable doubt that when the Accused participated in the Kesho Hill massacre [in Rwili secteur, Gaseke commune, in Gisenyi prefecture], and issued instructions at the Kiyovu roadblock, as found above, he did so with knowledge of the broader context and knowledge that his acts formed part of the discriminatory attacks occurring throughout Rwanda in 1994. The Chamber therefore finds that the *chapeau* requirements for crimes against humanity are met."

Bagosora, Kabiligi, Ntabakuze and Nsengiyumva, (Trial Chamber), December

18, 2008, para. 2167: "The Chamber has considered the totality of the evidence, in particular concerning the ethnic composition of the individuals who sought refuge at various sites as well as the actual or perceived political leanings of many of those killed or singled out at roadblocks in the days after President Habyarimana's death. It finds that there were widespread and systematic attacks against the civilian population on ethnic and political grounds between April and July 1994. It is inconceivable that the principal perpetrators of these attacks as well as the Accused did not know that their actions formed part of this attack. As high-ranking military officers, the Accused would have been familiar with the situation unfolding both nationally and in areas under their control. Many of the attacks or massacres where open and notorious. The Chamber has also concluded that Bagosora, Ntabakuze and Nsengiyumva ordered *or* authorised many of these attacks." (emphasis added.)[22]

Nchamihigo, (Trial Chamber), November 12, 2008, paras. 341-42: "The Chamber has found that there were attacks against the civilian population of Cyangugu prefecture. Thousands of civilians were killed. These civilians were Tutsi or Hutu political opponents, and they were killed at places where they had sought refuge (Gihundwe sector, Hanika parish, Mibilizi parish and hospital, Nyakanyinya school, Nyamasheke parish, and Shangi parish). Civilians were killed after being removed from Kamarampaka Stadium. Civilians were killed at their homes and in the street. There was evidence that at the roadblocks those trying to flee were stopped, their identities controlled, and their fate decided accordingly. The Chamber believed that the killings were planned at PSC [Cyangugu Prefecture Security Council] meetings and has found that Nchamihigo participated in two of those meetings. The Chamber is satisfied that the attack against the civilian population was both widespread and systematic. The Chamber believed the evidence that these attacks were aimed at destroying the Tutsi and RPF [Rwandan Patriotic Front] supporters or those who were opposed to the incumbent authorities. They were therefore committed on ethnic or racial, and political grounds." "On the basis of all the evidence, the Chamber has found that there was a widespread and systematic attack against [*sic*] civilian population of Cyangugu prefecture on racial or ethnic and political grounds. Considering Nchamihigo's position as Deputy Prosecutor in Cyangugu and his role in the events as established in the factual findings, the Chamber has no doubt that he knew that his acts were part of such widespread and systematic attack."

Karera, (Trial Chamber), December 7, 2007, para. 553: "[I]t is clear that a widespread or systematic attack against Tutsi civilians took place in the prefectures of Kigali-Ville and Kigali-Rural, between 6 April and June 1994. Considering Karera's participation in attacks in Kigali-Ville and Kigali-Rural prefectures (...) , as well as his high official position in the Rwandan administration, the Chamber finds that Karera was aware that such an attack took place." *See also id.*, paras. 554-56.

Seromba, (Trial Chamber), December 13, 2006, paras. 369-70: "The Chamber finds that the conditions required for the commission of crime against humanity have been satisfied in this case. Indeed, the Chamber is satisfied that there were attacks against the Tutsi in Kivumu *commune* in April 1994. The attack which culminated in the destruction of Nyange church on 16 April 1994 was 'widespread' in the sense that it was massive, carried out collectively and directed against a multiplicity of victims. The attack was also 'systematic' inasmuch as the factual findings tend to show that it was thoroughly organized and followed a regular pattern, starting with the surrounding of the church on 12 April 1994 up to its destruction on 16 April 1994, coupled with the intensification of the attacks against the refugees on 14 and 15 April 1994. Lastly, the Chamber finds that the attack was directed against the Tutsi civilian population that had sought refuge in Nyange church on discriminatory grounds (...)Furthermore, the Chamber finds that Accused Athanase Seromba had knowledge of the widespread and systematic nature of the attack and the underlying discriminatory grounds. The Chamber is satisfied that Seromba also knew that the crime of extermination committed against the Tutsi refugees was part of that attack."

Simba, (Trial Chamber), December 13, 2005, paras. 423-24: "The evidence in this case amply supports the conclusion that there were widespread attacks against the Tutsi population in Gikongoro prefecture in April 1994. Witnesses recounted Hutu militiamen burning and looting Tutsi homes in the days immediately following the death of President Habyarimana on 6 April. Thousands of Tutsi then congregated at parishes and schools. The evidence of the killings at the five massacre sites as well as their massive scale can lead to no other conclusion. Having considered the totality of the evidence, and in particular the evidence concerning the ethnic composition of the individuals who sought refuge at the various sites, the Chamber finds that in April 1994 there was a widespread attack against the civilian Tutsi population of Gikongoro on ethnic grounds."

"The Chamber finds it inconceivable that Simba, and the other participants in the joint criminal enterprise, did not know during the massacres of 21 April that their actions formed part of a widespread attack against the Tutsi civilian population. Simba was familiar with the situation in Rwanda nationally from his time in Kigali and Gitarama town. Those who sought refuge at his home in Kigali recounted soldiers looking for Tutsi. He passed roadblocks from Kigali to Gitarama town where militiamen threatened his Tutsi passengers. He was warned by Witness MIB that the road to Gikongoro was not safe because assailants were killing Tutsi. The Chamber found that on 21 April, Simba was present at two massacre sites distributing weapons and speaking with assailants. In addition, other prominent participants in the joint criminal enterprise, such as Prefect Bucyibartua, Captain Sebuhura, and Bourgmestre Semakwavu, attended various meetings with local authorities to discuss the lack of security in the region. They were present during the massacres and directed attackers from Murambi Technical School to Cyanika Parish [in Gikongoro prefecture]. The assailants who physically perpetrated the massacres also must have been aware of the broader context, particularly given the scale of the atrocities."

Muhimana, (Trial Chamber), April 28, 2005, paras. 531-33: "In the instant case, the Chamber has found that several attacks were carried out against *Tutsi* refugees between April and May 1994 in Gishyita *Commune*: on 9 and 11 April 1994, *Tutsi* residents were attacked at Nyarutovu; on 15 April 1994, numerous *Tutsi* refugees were attacked at Mubuga Church; the next day, 16 April 1994, refugees, mainly *Tutsi*, were attacked at Mugonero Complex; in May 1994, *Tutsi* were attacked on Kanyinya Hill; on 13 and 14 May 1994, *Tutsi* were attacked on Muyira Hill. At Mubuga Church and Mugonero Complex, the assailants instructed *Hutu* refugees to separate from the crowd. During these attacks, many *Tutsi* were killed or seriously injured." "Considering the circumstances and nature of the attacks, as well as evidence that, in some instances, assailants instructed *Hutu* refugees to separate from the *Tutsi*, the Chamber finds that the *Tutsi* civilians were targeted on the basis of their ethnicity, within the meaning of Article 3 of the Statute and that many died or were seriously injured." "The Chamber, therefore, finds that discriminatory, widespread, and systematic attacks were directed against groups of *Tutsi* civilians in Gishyita *Commune* and in the Bisesero area, between April and June 1994."

Gacumbitsi, (Trial Chamber), June 17, 2004, paras. 303-04, 306: "The Chamber has already found that there were attacks against Tutsi refugees in Nyarubuye Parish during three consecutive days, from 15 to 17 April 1994. Hutu refugees at the parish had been asked to separate themselves from the crowd, thus an indeterminate number of them were saved from the attack. Many Tutsi were killed there. After the first attack on the parish on 15 April 1994, the attackers returned there the following day, and the day after, to finish off survivors. Between 7 April and 18 April 1994, other Tutsi were killed or subjected to attacks and acts of discrimination. Tutsi refugees and Tutsi inhabitants of Rusumo *commune* were attacked and their property looted. On 13 April 1994, the Accused expelled his tenants, Tutsi women, knowing that by so doing he was exposing them to the imminent risk of being targeted by Hutu attackers. The utterances and actions of the Accused at the meeting of 9 April 1994, and during the public meetings he held on the days preceding the attack on the parish, demonstrate the systematic nature of the attack. Weapons were assembled in preparation for the attacks. The Accused conferred daily with military officials to coordinate actions to be undertaken. He travelled to various locations in Rusumo *commune* disseminating his instructions. Once the population was mobilized, it started attacking Tutsi in different locations, but the most serious attack – the attack on the parish – occurred after reinforcements had come from a group of *Interahamwe*." "The Chamber finds that the Accused's instructions to the attackers contained a discriminatory element, which prevailed during the attacks and in the selection of victims." "The said attacks, which were carried out by groups of attackers, were directed against numerous victims, on the ground that they belonged to the Tutsi ethnic group. The victims were attacked particularly in their areas of residence or in places where they had sought refuge. Tutsi families were decimated. The Chamber therefore finds that a discriminatory, widespread and systematic attack was carried against a group of Tutsi civilians during the month of April 1994 in Rusumo *commune*."

Kamuhanda, (Trial Chamber), January 22, 2004, paras. 677-83: "[T]he Accused admitted that between 1 January 1994 and 17 July 1994 there were throughout Rwanda widespread or systematic attacks against a civilian population with the specific objective of extermination of the Tutsi." "The Chamber has accepted that by 12 April 1994, several thousand men, women and children, mainly of Tutsi origin, along with their cattle, had taken refuge at the Parish." "The Chamber has found that a large number of Tutsi were killed on 12 April 1994 at the Gikomero Parish Compound, Gikomero commune." "The Chamber has also found that a large number of Tutsi were killed on or about the 13 April 1994 in Gishaka, Gikomero commune." "The evidence of both Parties shows that these Tutsi victims had taken refuge in Gikomero Parish Compound and Gishaka fleeing prior attacks against them that occurred in other areas of Kigali-Rural, such as Rubungo." "Thus, the Chamber finds that killings of members of the Tutsi ethnic group occurred on a mass scale in Gikomero commune during April 1994. The targets were whole populations of Tutsi ethnicity, attacked at places such as where they took shelter and refuge. The Chamber further finds that this constitutes a widespread attack upon a civilian Tutsi ethnic group." "The Chamber finds that the attack of Gikomero Parish Compound on 12 April 1994 was part of a widespread attack against the Tutsi civilian population in Rwanda and particularly in Kigali-Rural."

c) Underlying offenses

i) the individual acts contain their own elements and need not contain the elements of crimes against humanity

Kayishema and Ruzindana, (Trial Chamber), May 21, 1999, para. 135: "The crimes themselves need not contain the three elements of the attack (i.e. widespread or systematic, against any civilian population, on discriminatory grounds), but must form *part of* such an attack. Indeed, the individual crimes contain their own specific elements."

ii) murder

1) defined/ actus reus

Zigiranyirazo, (Trial Chamber), December 18, 2008, para. 442: "Murder requires proof of the following three elements: (1) the death of a victim; (2) that the death was the result of an act or an omission of the perpetrator; and (3) that the perpetrator, at the time of the act or omission, intended to kill the victim or, in the absence of such a specific intent, knew that death was a probable consequence of the act or omission." *See also Bikindi*, (Trial Chamber), December 2, 2008, para. 429 (same).

Bagosora, Kabiligi, Ntabakuze and Nsengiyumva, (Trial Chamber), December 18, 2008, para. 2169: "Murder is the intentional killing of a person without any lawful justification or excuse or the intentional infliction of grievous bodily harm leading to death with knowledge that such harm will likely cause the victim's death." *See also Karera*, (Trial Chamber), December 7, 2007, para. 558 (same); *Muhimana,* (Trial Chamber), April 28, 2005, para. 568 (similar).

Nzabirinda, (Trial Chamber), February 23, 2007, para. 25: "Murder is the intentional killing of a person by an act or an omission, or the intentional infliction of grievous bodily harm, committed by the offender with knowledge that such harm is likely to cause the victim's death or with reckless disregard as to whether or not death will result, with no lawful justification or excuse." *See also Bisengimana,* (Trial Chamber), April 13, 2006, para. 87 (similar); *Ndindabahizi,* (Trial Chamber), July 15, 2004, para. 487 (similar).

Kayishema and Ruzindana, (Trial Chamber), May 21, 1999, para. 140: "The accused is guilty of murder if the accused, engaging in conduct which is unlawful:

1. causes the death of another;

2. by a premeditated act or omission;

3. intending to kill any person or, [*sic*]

4. intending to cause grievous bodily harm to any person." *See also Bagilishema,* (Trial Chamber), June 7, 2001, para. 84 (same elements).

Akayesu, (Trial Chamber), September 2, 1998, para. 589: "The Chamber defines murder as the unlawful, intentional killing of a human being. The requisite elements of murder are:

1. the victim is dead;

2. the death resulted from an unlawful act or omission of the accused or a subordinate;

3. at the time of the killing the accused or a subordinate had the intention to kill or inflict grievous bodily harm on the deceased having known that such bodily harm is likely to cause the victim's death, and is reckless whether death ensures [*sic*] or not."

See also Musema, (Trial Chamber), January 27, 2000, para. 215 (similar, including crimes against humanity *chapeau*); *Rutaganda,* (Trial Chamber), December 6, 1999, paras. 80-81 (same).

(a) omissions covered

See Nzabirinda, (Trial Chamber), February 23, 2007, para. 25 (omissions covered); *Kayishema and Ruzindana,* (Trial Chamber), May 21, 1999, para. 140 (same).

(b) when punishable as a crime against humanity

Nzabirinda, (Trial Chamber), February 23, 2007, para. 25: "Murder is punishable as a crime against humanity when it has been committed as part of a widespread or systematic attack against a civilian population on discriminatory grounds." *See also Bisengimana,* (Trial Chamber), April 13, 2006, para. 87 (similar); *Muhimana,* (Trial Chamber), April 28, 2005, para. 568 (similar); *Ndindabahizi,* (Trial Chamber), July 15, 2004, para. 487 (similar).

(c) no requirement that the accused personally commit the killing

Ntakirutimana and Ntakirutimana, (Appeals Chamber), December 13, 2004, para. 546: "Murder as a crime against humanity under Article 3(a) does not require the Prosecution to establish that the accused personally committed the killing. Personal commission is only one of the modes of [responsibility] identified under Article 6(1) of the ICTR Statute. All modes of [responsibility] under that Article are applicable to the crimes defined in Articles 2 to 4 of the Statute. Similarly, an accused can also be convicted of a crime defined in Articles 2 to 4 of the Statute on the basis of his responsibility as a superior according to Article 6(3) of the ICTR Statute."

See also Akayesu, (Trial Chamber), September 2, 1998, para. 589 (death may result from the act or omission of the accused "or a subordinate," and the intent may be that of the accused "or a subordinate").

(d) murder and extermination same except for scale

Bisengimana, (Trial Chamber), April 13, 2006, para. 87: "The Chamber recalls that it is the scale of the killings that distinguishes extermination from murder as a crime against humanity."

Kamuhanda, (Trial Chamber), January 22, 2004, para. 686: "The Chamber notes that apart from the question of scale, the essence of the crimes of murder as a Crime against Humanity and extermination as a Crime against Humanity is the same." *See also Kajelijeli,* (Trial Chamber), December 1, 2003, para. 886 (same).

For discussion of extermination, see Section (II)(c)(iii), *see also* "difference from crime of murder," under "extermination," Section (II)(c)(iii)(1)(c).

2) mens rea

Nzabirinda, (Trial Chamber), February 23, 2007, para. 25: "The *mens rea* as to murder includes "the intentional infliction of grievous bodily harm, committed by the offender with knowledge that such harm is likely to cause the victim's death or with reckless disregard as to whether or not death will result(...)" *See also Bisengimana,* (Trial Chamber), April 13, 2006, para. 87 (similar); *Akayesu,* (Trial Chamber), September 2, 1998, para. 589 (similar).

Muhimana, (Trial Chamber), April 28, 2005, para. 569: "The Chamber agrees with the Trial Chamber in *Semanza* that: (...) it is premeditated murder (assassinat) that constitutes a crime against humanity in Article 3(a) of the Statute. Premeditation requires that, at a minimum, the accused held a deliberate plan to kill prior to the act causing death, rather than forming the intention simultaneously with the act. The prior intention need not be held for very long; a cool moment of reflection is sufficient. The Chamber observes that the requirement that the accused must have known that his acts formed part of a wider attack on the civilian population generally suggests that the murder was pre-planned. The Chamber emphasises that the accused need not have premeditated the murder of a particular individual; for crimes against humanity it is sufficient that the accused had a premeditated intention to murder civilians as part of the widespread or systematic attack on discriminatory grounds." *See also Semanza,* (Trial Chamber), May 15, 2003, para. 339 (source of quoted language).

Ntagerura, Bagambiki, and Imanishimwe, (Trial Chamber), February 25, 2004, para. 700: "In the *Semanza* Judgement, the Chamber found that premeditated murder constitutes a crime against humanity under Article

3(a) of the Statute. The Chamber explained that premeditation requires that the accused held the intention to murder prior to committing the act causing death. The Chamber emphasises that the accused need not have premeditated the murder of a particular individual; it is sufficient that the accused had a premeditated intention to murder civilians as part of the widespread or systematic attack on discriminatory grounds."

Kayishema and Ruzindana, (Trial Chamber), May 21, 1999, paras. 137-40: The Chamber disagreed with the Trial Chamber's holding in *Akayesu,* and stated that "*assassinat*" in the French version of the Statute, and not "murder," (in the English version of the Statute) was the correct term. The Chamber noted that "premeditation is always required for *assassinat*" whereas it is not with "murder." "If in doubt, a matter of interpretation should be decided in favour of the accused; in this case, the inclusion of premeditation is favourable to the accused." The Chamber thus held that "murder and *assassinat* should be considered together in order to ascertain the standard of *mens rea*." "When murder is considered along with *assassinat* the Chamber finds that the standard of *mens rea* required is intentional and premeditated killing." The Chamber held that "[t]he result is premeditated when the actor formulated his intent to kill after a cool moment of reflection," and that "[t]he result is intended when it is the actor's purpose, or the actor is aware that it will occur in the ordinary course of events." *See also Bagilishema,* (Trial Chamber), June 7, 2001, para. 84 (relying on *Kayishema and Ruzindana*).

But see Akayesu, (Trial Chamber), September 2, 1998, para. 588: "Customary International Law dictates that it is the act of 'Murder' that constitutes a crime against humanity and not 'Assassinat.' There are therefore sufficient reasons to assume that the French version of the Statute suffers from an error in translation." *See also Rutaganda,* (Trial Chamber), December 6, 1999, para. 79; *Musema,* (Trial Chamber), January 27, 2000, para. 214.

See also discussion of murder under Article 4 (war crimes), Section (III)(d)(i)(1).

(a) mens rea of an aider or abettor of murder

Bisengimana, (Trial Chamber), April 13, 2006, para. 88: "With respect to the Accused's *mens rea* as an aider or abettor of murder as a crime against humanity, the Chamber should consider whether the Accused knew of the criminal intent of the principal perpetrator and knew that his actions assisted in the commission of the crime."

For discussion of the *mens rea* for aiding and abetting generally, see Section (IV)(g)(iii).

3) application

(a) killings of Tutsis and Hutus believed to be RPF accomplices were murder

Bagosora, Kabiligi, Ntabakuze and Nsengiyumva, (Trial Chamber), December 18, 2008, paras. 2170-72: "The Chamber has already determined that the killing of Tutsis at roadblocks in Kigali between 7 and 9 April 1994, as well as during the attacks in Kabeza, Kibagabaga Mosque, the Saint Josephite Centre, Karama hill, Kibagabaga Catholic Church, Nyanza hill, IAMSEA [*L'Institut Africain et Mauricien de Statistiques et d'Economie*], Gisenyi town on 7 April, Mudende University, Nyundo Parish and Bisesero constituted genocide. On the same basis, the Chamber is satisfied that these intentional murders were conducted on ethnic grounds."

"Some Hutus were likely killed during these attacks, even though they were principally directed at Tutsis. As they formed part of the attack on ethnic grounds they constitute murder as a crime against humanity. At roadblocks, in Kabeza, and during the targeted killings in Gisenyi town on 7 April, there is evidence that the killings were also conducted on political grounds. In particular, roadblocks were equally established to identify members of the political opposition and those suspected of being RPF [Rwandan Patriotic Front] accomplices. Kabeza was viewed as a neighbourhood populated by Tutsis and individuals sympathetic to the RPF. The killings in Gisenyi town also mirror targeted assassinations on political grounds conducted at the same time in Gisenyi and in Kigali. These crimes therefore formed part of the attack on political grounds." (Concluding that "Bagosora bears responsibility for the crimes committed at Kigali area roadblocks, Kabeza, Kibagabaga Mosque, the Saint Josephite Centre, Karama hill, Kibagabaga Catholic Church, Gisenyi town on 7 April, Mudende University and Nyundo Parish as a superior under Article 6(3)"; "Ntabakuze is responsible as a superior for crimes committed in Kabeza, Nyanza hill and IAMSEA"; "Nsengiyumva is responsible for ordering or aiding and abetting the killings in Gisenyi town on 7 April, Mudende Universiy, Nyundo Parish and Bisesero"; and that "the assailants and the Accused were aware that these events formed part of widespread and systematic attacks against the civilian population on ethnic and political grounds.")

(b) killing of Belgian Peacekeepers was murder

Bagosora, Kabiligi, Ntabakuze and Nsengiyumva, (Trial Chamber), December 18, 2008, paras. 2174-77: "On the morning of 7 April 1994, 10 Belgian peacekeepers dispatched to escort Prime Minister Agathe Uwilingiyimana to Radio Rwanda were arrested and disarmed during an attack by Rwandan soldiers on her residence. The peacekeepers were taken to Camp Kigali where four were beaten to death by a mob of soldiers. The beatings did not stop even though some officers at the camp tried to verbally intervene. Six peacekeepers were able to seek refuge in the UNAMIR [United Nations Assistance Mission for Rwanda] office there and fend off the assailants for several hours after disarming a Rwandan soldier. They were later killed by high powered weapons. In view of the circumstances surrounding these attacks, the Chamber finds that these murders were premeditated."

"Considering their status as United Nations peacekeepers and that they were disarmed, the Chamber is satisfied that the victims could not be considered as combatants. The fact that the peacekeepers were able to obtain a weapon during the course of the attack in order to defend themselves against a mob of soldiers intending to kill them can in no way alter this conclusion."

"The peacekeepers were arrested and disarmed during the course of an attack on the Prime Minister, which the Chamber concluded above was part of the attack against the civilian population on political grounds. UNAMIR and the Belgian contingent in particular were also seen as sympathetic to the RPF [Rwandan Patriotic Front] and Tutsis in general (...) Immediately after the death of the President, the Belgian contingent was blamed for downing his plane by RTLM [*Radio Télévision Libre des Mille Collines*] as well as by some of the assailants at the camp. Therefore, it is clear that the killing of the peacekeepers formed part of the widespread and systematic attack on political and ethnic grounds." (Concluding that "Bagosora bears superior responsibility for the crimes committed against these individuals" and that "[t]he assailants and Bagosora were aware that these attacks formed part of widespread and systematic attacks against the civilian population on ethnic and political grounds(...)")

(c) killing of prominent personalities or opposition political officials was murder

See Bagosora, Kabiligi, Ntabakuze and Nsengiyumva, (Trial Chamber), December 18, 2008, paras. 2178-79 (concluding that Bagosora bore superior responsibility for the murders on April 7, 1994, by "members of elite army units, including the Presidential Guard, Para Commando Battalion and Reconnaissance Battalion," of Prime Minister "Agathe Uwilingiyimana, Joseph Kavaruganda, Frédéric Nzamurambaho, Landoald Ndasingwa and Faustin Rucogoza, who were all prominent personalities or opposition political officials").

(d) additional murders

See Bagosora, Kabiligi, Ntabakuze and Nsengiyumva, (Trial Chamber), December 18, 2008, paras. 2180-85 (concluding that Bagosora bore superior responsibility for 17 murders at *Centre Christus* in the Remera area of Kigali; individual responsibility (ordering) for the murder of Augustin Muharangari, Director of the Rwandan Bank of Development on April 8, 1994; and superior responsibility for the murder of Alphonse Kabiligi on April 7, 1994; also concluding that Nsengiyumva bore individual responsibility (ordering) for the murder of Alphonse Kabiligi).

Bisengimana, (Trial Chamber), April 13, 2006, paras. 92-95: "It is not disputed that a Tutsi man named Rusanganwa was murdered with premeditation. On the basis of the facts admitted by the Accused, the Chamber finds that the Accused was present when Rusanganwa was murdered during the attack at Musha Church [in Gikoro commune]."

"The Chamber is convinced that Paul Bisengimana knew that the murder of Rusanganwa was part of a widespread attack against Tutsis [*sic*] civilians on ethnic grounds. The Chamber is also convinced, based on the factual circumstances of the case that Paul Bisengimana knew the criminal intent of the perpetrator of the murder of Rusanganwa(...)"

"The Chamber finds that the Accused participated in Rusanganwa's murder by being present when the crime was committed. The Accused was aware that his presence would encourage the criminal conduct of the principal perpetrator and give the impression that he endorsed the murder. Moreover, the Chamber recalls that the Accused acknowledges that he had the means to oppose the killings of Tutsi civilians but that he remained indifferent to the attacks."

"The Chamber is satisfied that the Accused is individually criminally responsible pursuant to Article 6(1) of the Statute for aiding and abetting the murder of a Tutsi civilian named Rusanganwa at Musha Church in Gikoro *commune* in April 1994." (Due to cumulative conviction concerns, however, the conviction was entered for aiding and abetting extermination, *see id.*, paras. 102-03.)[23]

Ntagerura, Bagambiki, and Imanishimwe, (Trial Chamber), February 25, 2004, para. 689: "[T]he Chamber has found beyond a reasonable doubt that soldiers participated in the massacre of mainly Tutsi civilian refugees at the Gashirabwoba football field on 12 April 1994. The Chamber has found that at least fifteen soldiers arrived at the field, surrounded the mainly Tutsi refugees, opened fire with their guns, and threw grenades at them for thirty minutes after the refugees asked for peace. The scale of these killings of the Tutsi refugees and the length of time required to kill such a large number of victims prove that these killings were intentional." (However, Imanishimwe's conviction as to crimes at the Gashirabwoba football field was overturned on appeal due to indictment defects, *Ntagerura, Bagambiki and Imanishimwe,* (Appeals Chamber), July 7, 2006, at para. 150; Ntagerura and Bagambiki were acquitted as to all crimes.)

See also Karera, (Trial Chamber), December 7, 2007, paras. 559-61 (finding Karera guilty of murder as a crime against humanity); *Muhimana,* (Trial Chamber), April 28, 2005, para. 570 (findings as to murder).

iii) extermination

1) defined/actus reus

Seromba, (Appeals Chamber), March 12, 2008, para. 189: "The Appeals Chamber recalls that extermination as a crime against humanity under Article 3(b) of the Statute is the act of killing on a large scale. The Appeals Chamber stresses that in the jurisprudence of both *ad hoc* Tribunals, the necessary *actus reus* underlying the crime of extermination consists of any act, omission, or combination thereof which contributes directly or indirectly to the killing of a large number of individuals." *See also Bagosora, Kabiligi, Ntabakuze and Nsengiyumva,* (Trial Chamber), December 18, 2008, para. 2191 (similar).

Ntakirutimana and Ntakirutimana, (Appeals Chamber), December 13, 2004, para. 522: "[T]he crime of extermination requires proof that the accused participated in a widespread or systematic killing or in subjecting a widespread number of people or systematically subjecting a number of people to conditions of living that would inevitably lead to death, and that the accused intended by his acts or omissions this result." *See also Zigiranyirazo,* (Trial Chamber), December 18, 2008, para. 431 (similar); *Karera*, (Trial Chamber), December 7, 2007, para. 552 (similar); *Seromba,* (Trial Chamber), December 13, 2006, para. 361 (similar); *Mpambara*, (Trial Chamber), September 11, 2006, para. 9 (similar); *Simba,* (Trial Chamber), December 13, 2005, para. 422 (similar).[24]

Mpambara, (Trial Chamber), September 11, 2006, para. 9: "The *actus reus* of the offence is that the perpetrator participates with others in a collective or ongoing mass killing event."

Bisengimana, (Trial Chamber), April 13, 2006, para. 70: "[E]xtermination consists of an act or a combination of acts, which contributes to the killing of a large number of individuals." *See also Niyitegeka,* (Trial Chamber), May 16, 2003, para. 450 (same).

Ndindabahizi, (Trial Chamber), July 15, 2004, para. 479: "[E]xtermination requires that the perpetrator intend to commit acts directed at a group of individuals collectively, and whose effect is to bring about a mass killing."

Kamuhanda, (Trial Chamber), January 22, 2004, para. 698: "The material element of extermination is the large-scale killing of a substantial number of civilians."

Kayishema and Ruzindana, (Trial Chamber), May 21, 1999, para. 144: The Chamber defined the requisite elements of extermination: (1) "[t]he actor participates in the mass killing of others or in the creation of conditions of life that lead to the mass killing of others, through his act(s) or omission(s);" (2) "having intended the killing, or being reckless, or grossly negligent as to whether the killing would result and;" (3) "being aware that his act(s) or omission(s) forms part of a mass killing event;" (4) "where, his act(s) or omission(s) forms part of a widespread or systematic attack against any civilian population on national, political, ethnic, racial or religious grounds."[25] *See also Bagilishema,* (Trial Chamber), June 7, 2001, para. 89 (similar).

Akayesu, (Trial Chamber), September 2, 1998, para. 592: The Chamber defined the following as essential elements of extermination:

(1) "the accused or his subordinate participated in the killing of certain named or described persons; (2) the act or omission was unlawful and intentional; (3) the unlawful act or omission must be part of a widespread or systematic attack; (4) the attack must be against the civilian population; (5) the attack must be on discriminatory grounds, namely: national, political, ethnic, racial, or religious grounds."

See also Musema, (Trial Chamber), January 27, 2000, para. 218 (same elements); *Rutaganda,* (Trial Chamber), December 6, 1999, paras. 83-84 (same elements).

(a) how large in scale: no numerical minimum/determine case-by-case

Ntakirutimana and Ntakirutimana, (Appeals Chamber), December 13, 2004, para. 516: "The expressions 'on a large scale' or 'large number' do not (...) suggest a numerical minimum." *See also Bagosora, Kabiligi, Ntabakuze and Nsengiyumva,* (Trial Chamber), December 18, 2008, para. 2191 (similar); *Karera,* (Trial Chamber), December 7, 2007, para. 552 (similar); *Rugambarara,* (Trial Chamber), November 16, 2007, para. 23 (similar); *Simba,* (Trial Chamber), December 13, 2005, para. 422 (similar); *Bagilishema,* (Trial Chamber), June 7, 2001, para. 87 (similar).

Gacumbitsi, (Trial Chamber), June 17, 2004, para. 309: "'Large scale' does not suggest a numerical minimum; it must be determined on case-by-case basis using a common sense approach."

Kamuhanda, (Trial Chamber), January 22, 2004, para. 692: "[T]he killings must have been committed on a large scale for the Chamber to find the Accused guilty of extermination. There is no conclusive authority on how many murders constitute extermination. The first judgments concerning extermination as a Crime against Humanity considered that 'large scale' does not suggest a numeric minimum. It must be determined on a case-by-case basis, using a common-sense approach."

(b) perpetrator's contribution/indirect contributions

Seromba, (Appeals Chamber), March 12, 2008, para. 189: "[A]s the Appeals Chamber has previously considered in the *Ndindabahizi* Appeal Judgement, for the *actus reus* of extermination to be fulfilled, it is sufficient that the accused participated in measures *indirectly* causing death." *See Ndindabahizi,* (Appeals Chamber), January 16, 2007, para. 123 & n. 268.

Mpambara, (Trial Chamber), September 11, 2006, para. 9: "The [perpetrator's] act need not directly cause any single victim's death, but must contribute to a mass killing event. As to the nature of the contribution required, a standard of 'sufficient contribution' has been adopted in some cases, assessed according to 'the actions of the perpetrator, their impact on a defined [victim] group, and awareness [by the accused] of the impact on the defined group.'"

Bisengimana, (Trial Chamber), April 13, 2006, para. 70: "It is irrelevant that the accused's participation in the act is remote or indirect."

Ndindabahizi, (Trial Chamber), July 15, 2004, para. 479: "Extermination may be committed less directly than murder, as by participation in measures intended to bring about the deaths of a large number of individuals, but without actually committing a killing of any person. Causation must nevertheless be established by naming or describing the victims, and by establishing the manner in which the accused contributed to, or participated in, their deaths. Whether an accused has contributed sufficiently to the mass killing depends on a concrete assessment of the facts."

Rutaganda, (Trial Chamber), December 6, 1999, para. 84: "[T]his act or omission [for the crime of extermination] includes, but is not limited to the direct act of killing. It can be any act or omission, or cumulative acts or omissions, that cause the death of the targeted group of individuals."

See also Semanza, (Appeals Chamber), May 20, 2005, para. 271: "The Appellant (...) argues that the Trial Chamber erred in convicting him of extermination because there was no proof of preparation and organization of the murders (...) However, an accused need not have planned, ordered or executed the massacres to be convicted of extermination. Indeed, Article 6(1) refers also to other modes of participation."

See also "*actus reus*/ participation (element 1): contribution must have substantially contributed to, or had a substantial effect on, the completion of the crime," Section (IV)(b)(iv)(1).

(c) difference from crime of murder

Ntakirutimana and Ntakirutimana, (Appeals Chamber), December 13, 2004, para. 516: "[T]he Trial Chamber followed the *Akayesu* Trial Judgement in defining extermination as 'a crime which by its very nature is directed against a group of individuals. Extermination differs from murder in that it requires an element of mass destruction, which is not required for murder.'" *See Ntakirutimana and Ntakirutimana*, (Trial Chamber), February 21, 2003, para. 813 (similar); *Akayesu*, (Trial Chamber), September 2, 1998, paras. 591, 813.

Zigiranyirazo, (Trial Chamber), December 18, 2008, para. 431: "Extermination as a crime against humanity is (...) distinguishable from murder as it requires that the killings occur on a mass scale." *See also Seromba*, (Trial Chamber), December 13, 2006, para. 361 (similar); *Bisengimana*, (Trial Chamber), April 13, 2006, para. 70 (similar); *Simba*, (Trial Chamber), December 13, 2005, para. 422 (similar).

Rutaganira, (Trial Chamber), March 14, 2005, para. 49: "[T]he Tribunal has consistently held that, by its very nature, extermination is a crime which is directed against a group of individuals as distinct from murder in that it must be perpetrated on a 'large scale.'" *See Nahimana*, (Trial Chamber), December 3, 2003, para. 1061; *Akayesu*, (Trial Chamber), September 2, 1998, para. 591.

Ndindabahizi, (Trial Chamber), July 15, 2004, para. 479: "This [mass killing requirement] distinguishes the offence [of extermination] from murder, whose material element may be satisfied by the killing of a single person, and proof that the perpetrator intended the death of that single person alone, albeit as part of a widespread or systematic attack."

Gacumbitsi, (Trial Chamber), June 17, 2004, para. 309: "It is the settled jurisprudence of this Tribunal that extermination, by its very nature, is a crime that is directed against a group of individuals, but different from murder in that it requires an element of mass destruction that is not required for murder." *See also Kamuhanda*, (Trial Chamber), January 22, 2004, para. 691 (similar).

Ntagerura, Bagambiki, and Imanishimwe, (Trial Chamber), February 25, 2004, para. 701: "Extermination is mass or large scale killing; it may be differentiated from murder in that it is directed against a population rather than against individuals."

Kamuhanda, (Trial Chamber), January 22, 2004, para. 694: "In order to give practical meaning to the charge of extermination, as distinct from murder, there must in fact be a large number of killings, and the attack must be directed against a group, such as a neighbourhood, as opposed to any specific individuals within it."

Nahimana, Barayagwiza and Ngeze, (Trial Chamber), December 3, 2003, para. 1061: "The Chamber agrees that in order to be guilty of the crime of extermination, the Accused must have been involved in killings of civilians on a large scale but considers that the distinction is not entirely related to numbers. The distinction between extermination and murder is a conceptual one that relates to the victims of the crime and the manner in which they were targeted."

See also "murder and extermination same except for scale" under the crime of murder, Section (II)(c)(ii)(1)(d).

(d) extermination as a crime against humanity

Ntakirutimana and Ntakirutimana, (Appeals Chamber), December 13, 2004, para. 516: "As a crime against humanity, for the purposes of the ICTR Statute, the act of killing must occur within the context of a widespread or systematic attack against the civilian population for national, political, ethnic, racial or religious grounds."

(e) single or limited number of killings not extermination/ killing or aiding single or limited number of killings in context of mass killing

Gacumbitsi, (Trial Chamber), June 17, 2004, para. 309: "Responsibility for a single or a number of killings is insufficient for a finding of extermination." *See also Ntagerura, Bagambiki, and Imanishimwe*, (Trial Chamber), February 25, 2004, para. 701 (similar).

Kamuhanda, (Trial Chamber), January 22, 2004, paras. 692-94: "Trial Chamber I in

Bagilishema [*sic*] held that:

A perpetrator may nonetheless be guilty of extermination if he kills, or creates conditions of life that kill, a single person, providing that the perpetrator is aware his or her acts or omissions form part of a mass killing event, namely mass killings that are proximate in time and place and thereby are best understood as a single or sustained attack."

"In contrast, more recent judgments have held that 'responsibility for a single or a limited number of killings is insufficient.' This most recent approach appears to be more in conformity with established jurisprudence that an element of mass destruction is required for extermination."

"The Chamber is satisfied that a single killing or a small number of killings do not constitute extermination. In order to give practical meaning to the charge of extermination, as distinct from murder, there must in fact be a large number of killings, and the attack must be directed against a group, such as a neighbourhood, as opposed to any specific individuals within it. However, the Chamber may consider evidence under this charge relating to the murder of specific individuals as an illustration of the extermination of the targeted group." *See also Kajelijeli,* (Trial Chamber), December 1, 2003, paras. 890-93 (same with italics).

Compare Ntakirutimana and Ntakirutimana, (Appeals Chamber), December 13, 2004, paras. 529, 530: If the Trial Chamber "meant that aiding and abetting the crime of extermination requires that the acts of assistance provided by the Accused to the main perpetrators effectively resulted in the killing of a large number of people. This interpretation of aiding and abetting would (...) constitute a legal error." "[I]f the mass killing in question occurs, the fact that the weapon procured by the accused 'only' killed a limited number of persons is irrelevant to determining the accused's responsibility as an aider and abettor of the crime of extermination."

Compare Bagosora, Kabiligi, Ntabakuze and Nsengiyumva, (Trial Chamber), December 18, 2008, paras. 2192-93: "Several of the events charged as extermination when viewed separately do not satisfy the threshold of killing on a large-scale, in particular the targeted political assassinations. However, the Chamber has considered the events for which the Accused have been held responsible together since they are essentially part of the same widespread and systematic attacks against the civilian population on political and ethnic grounds."

Compare Bagilishema, (Trial Chamber), June 7, 2001, para. 88: "A perpetrator may nonetheless be guilty of extermination if he kills, or creates the conditions of life that kill, a single person, providing that the perpetrator is aware that his or her acts or omissions form part of a mass killing event, namely mass killings that are proximate in time and place and thereby are best understood as a single or sustained attack."

Compare Kayishema and Ruzindana, (Trial Chamber), May 21, 1999, n. 8. to para. 645: "It is important to note that an accused may be guilty of extermination (...) when sufficient evidence is produced that he or she killed a single person as long as this killing was a part of a mass killing event."

See also Mpambara, (Trial Chamber), September 11, 2006, para. 9: "The [perpetrator's] act need not directly cause any single victim's death, but must contribute to a mass killing event."

(f) no plan or policy required

Gacumbitsi, (Appeals Chamber), July 7, 2006, para. 84: "[T]he ICTY Appeals Chamber has emphasized that proof of a plan or policy is not a prerequisite to a conviction for extermination."

(g) responsibility not limited to persons exercising power and authority or who had the capacity to be instrumental in large scale killings

Ntakirutimana and Ntakirutimana, (Appeals Chamber), December 13, 2004, paras. 538-39: "Elizaphan and Gérard Ntakirutimana argued that extermination charges are reserved for persons exercising power and authority or who otherwise had the capacity to be instrumental in the large scale killings." "The argument (...) stems from an erroneous interpretation of the *Vasiljević* Trial Judgement."

(h) precise description or designation by name of victims not required

Ntakirutimana and Ntakirutimana, (Appeals Chamber), December 13, 2004, paras. 517, 518, 521: "In finding that an element of the crime of extermination was the 'killing of certain named or described persons' the Trial Chamber purported to be following the *Akayesu* Trial Judgement, which it found had since been followed in *Rutaganda* and *Musema*(...)" "The Appeals Chamber agrees with the Prosecution that customary international law does not consider a precise description or designation by name of victims to be an element of the crime of extermination(...)" "It is sufficient that the Prosecution satisfy the Trial Chamber that mass killings occurred. In this case that element was satisfied by the Trial Chamber's findings that hundreds of people were killed at the Mugonero Complex and that thousands of people were killed in Bisesero. To require greater identification of those victims would, as the Prosecution argued, increase the burden of proof to such an extent that it hinders a large number of prosecutions for extermination." *See Akayesu,* (Trial Chamber), September 2, 1998, para. 592.

Karera, (Trial Chamber), December 7, 2007, para. 552: "[F]or the crime of extermination,] [t]he Prosecution need not name the victims."

See also "pleading mass crimes: scale of crimes may make it impracticable to require a high degree of specificity," Section (VIII)(c)(xix)(6)(l).

(i) particularly large number of victims may be an aggravating factor

Ndindabahizi, (Appeals Chamber), January 16, 2007, para. 135: "As for extermination, the *actus reus* requires 'killing on a large scale.' While this does not 'suggest a numerical minimum,' a particularly large number of victims can be an aggravating circumstance in relation to the sentence for this crime if the extent of the killings exceeds that required for extermination."

See "large number of victims/deaths of women, children and orphans" as an aggravating factor, Section (VII)(b)(iii)(6)(b)(*iii*).

(j) aiding and abetting extermination—elements

Ntakirutimana and Ntakirutimana, (Appeals Chamber), December 13, 2004, para. 530: "The *actus reus* for aiding and abetting the crime of extermination is that the accused carries out acts specifically directed to assist, encourage or lend moral support to the perpetration of that crime. This support must have a substantial effect upon the perpetration of the crime. The requisite *mens rea* is knowledge that the acts performed by the aider and abettor assist the commission of the crime of extermination committed by the principal. If it is established that the accused provided a weapon to one principal, knowing that the principal will use that weapon to take part with others in a mass killing, as part of a widespread and systematic attack against the civilian population, and if the mass killing in question occurs, the fact that the weapon procured by the accused 'only' killed a limited number of persons is irrelevant to determining the accused's responsibility as an aider and abettor of the crime of extermination."

See also "aiding and abetting," Section (IV)(g).

See "*actus reus*/participation (element 1): contribution must have substantially contributed to, or had a substantial effect on, the completion of the crime," Section (IV)(b)(iv)(1).

See "single or limited number of killings not extermination/killing or aiding single or limited number of killings in context of mass killing," Section (II) (c)(iii)(1)(e).

2) mens rea

Gacumbitsi, (Appeals Chamber), July 7, 2006, para. 86: "The Trial Chamber (...) implicitly applied the correct requirement [for the crime of extermination] by finding that the actions of the Appellant revealed his 'intention to participate in a large scale massacre in Nyarubuye.' As the Appeals Chamber recently explained: the crime of extermination requires proof that the accused participated in a widespread or systematic killing or in subjecting a widespread number of people or systematically subjecting a number of people to conditions of living that would inevitably lead to death, *and that the accused intended by his acts or omissions this result.*"[26]

Zigiranyirazo, (Trial Chamber), December 18, 2008, para. 431: "The *mens rea* for extermination is the intent to perpetrate or to participate in a mass killing." *See also Seromba,* (Trial Chamber), December 13, 2006, para. 361 (similar).

Bagosora, Kabiligi, Ntabakuze and Nsengiyumva, (Trial Chamber), December 18, 2008, para. 2191: "The *mens rea* of extermination requires that the accused intend to kill persons on a massive scale or to subject a large number of people to conditions of living that would lead to their deaths in a widespread or systematic manner."[27]

Mpambara, (Trial Chamber), September 11, 2006, para. 10: "The *mens rea* of extermination is that the accused must intend by his actions to bring about the deaths on a large-scale."

Ndindabahizi, (Trial Chamber), July 15, 2004, para. 480: "The *mens rea* for the offence of extermination is that the Accused participated in the imposition of measures against many individuals intending that their deaths should be brought about on a large-scale."

Semanza, (Trial Chamber), May 15, 2003, para. 341: "[I]n the absence of express authority in the Statute or in customary international law, international criminal [responsibility] should be ascribed only on the basis of intentional conduct. [T]he mental element for extermination is the intent to perpetrate or participate in a mass killing." *See also Simba,* (Trial Chamber), December 13, 2005, para. 422 (same as second sentence); *Ntagerura, Bagambiki, and Imanishimwe,* (Trial Chamber), February 25, 2004, para. 701 (similar to second sentence).

See, e.g., Gacumbitsi, (Appeals Chamber), July 7, 2006, paras. 86, 88: "While the Trial Chamber did not expressly outline the *mens rea* requirement specific to the crime of extermination, it implicitly applied the correct requirement by finding that the actions of the Appellant revealed his 'intention to participate in a large scale massacre in Nyarubuye.'" "The actions of the Appellant in planning the extermination of Tutsis from 8 through 15 April 1994, as well as his subsequent actions from 15 through 17 April 1994, show that the Appellant had the intent to massacre a large number of individuals, and that he knew that his acts furthered a widespread and systematic attack against the Tutsis (...) [T]he Trial Chamber did not err in assessing the Appellant's *mens rea*."

(a) whether recklessness suffices *Kamuhanda*, (Trial Chamber), January 22, 2004, paras. 695-96: "In Bagilishema [*sic*] and Kayishema and Ruzindana [*sic*] it was held that extermination is not limited to intentional acts or omissions but also covers reckless or grossly negligent conduct of the accused. The Chamber notes that more recent judgments have taken a slightly different approach, with Semanza [*sic*] holding that:

[...] in the absence of express authority in the Statute or in customary international law, international criminal [responsibility] should be ascribed only on the basis of intentional conduct."

"We do not interpret Bagilishema [*sic*] and Kayishema and Ruzindana [*sic*] to suggest that a person may be found guilty of a Crime against Humanity if he or she did not possess the requisite *mens rea* [*sic*] for such a crime, but rather to suggest that reckless or grossly negligent conduct are indicative of the offender's *mens rea* [*sic*]. Understood in that way, the Semanza [*sic*] position is not at odds with the Bagilishema [*sic*] and Kayishema and Ruzindana [*sic*] judgments." *See also Kajelijeli,* (Trial Chamber), December 1, 2003, paras. 894-95 (same with italics).

See Ndindabahizi, (Trial Chamber), July 15, 2004, para. 480: "Given the facts of the present case, there is no need to consider whether recklessness would also satisfy the *mens rea* of extermination."

But see Bisengimana, (Trial Chamber), April 13, 2006, paras. 71-72: "To establish the *mens rea* of extermination, the Prosecution must prove that the accused intended the killings, or *was reckless or grossly negligent* as to whether the killings would result and was aware that his acts or omissions formed part of a mass killing event. The accused must also be shown to have known of the vast scheme of collective murders directed against a civilian population on discriminatory grounds and to have been willing to take part in that scheme. As an aider or abettor of extermination as a crime against humanity, the Chamber should consider whether the Accused knew of the criminal intent of the principal perpetrator and knew that his actions assisted in the commission of the crime."

"Therefore, in order to be convicted of extermination as a crime against humanity, an accused must have (i) participated in the mass killing of others, or in the creation of conditions of life leading to the mass killing of others; (ii) intended the killings, or been *reckless or grossly negligent* as to whether the killings would result; and (iii) been aware that his acts or omissions formed part of a mass killing event." (emphasis added.)

But see Kayishema and Ruzindana, (Trial Chamber), May 21, 1999, para. 144: The mental state for extermination is that the accused "intended the killing" or was "reckless *or grossly negligent* as to whether the killing would result," and was "aware that his act(s) or omission(s) form[] part of a mass killing event." (emphasis added.) *See also Bagilishema,* (Trial Chamber), June 7, 2001, para. 89 (quoting same).

3) application

Nahimana, Barayagwiza and Ngeze, (Appeals Chamber), November 28, 2007, para. 941: "Regarding RTLM [*Radio Télévision Libre des Mille Collines*] broadcasts after 6 April 1994, the Appeals Chamber has already found that these broadcasts substantially contributed to the killing of large numbers of Tutsi. It accordingly follows that they substantially contributed to the extermination of Tutsi."

Ntakirutimana and Ntakirutimana, (Appeals Chamber), December 13, 2004, paras. 532,

534: "With respect to Elizaphan Ntakirutimana, the remaining findings [after various factual findings were quashed due to lack of notice] are: one day in May or June 1994, he transported armed attackers who were chasing Tutsi survivors at Murambi Hill [Bisesero region, Kibuye prefecture]; one day in the middle of May 1994, he brought armed attackers in the rear hold of his vehicle to Nyarutovu Hill, and the group was searching for Tutsi refugees and chasing them; on this occasion, Elizaphan Ntakirutimana pointed out the fleeing refugees to the attackers, who then chased these refugees singing, 'Exterminate them; look for them everywhere; kill them; and get it over with, in all the forests'; one day on May or June 1994 Elizaphan Ntakirutimana was seen arriving at Ku Cyapa in a vehicle followed by two buses of attackers, and he was part of a convoy which included attackers; and sometime between 17 April and early May 1994, Elizaphan Ntakirutimana was in Murambi within the area of Bisesero, and he went to a church in Murambi where many Tutsi were seeking refuge and ordered attackers to destroy the roof of the church."

"The Appeals Chamber finds that in carrying out these acts of participation Elizaphan Ntakirutimana knew that the intent of the actual perpetrators was the extermination of the Tutsi refugees and that he was making a substantial contribution to the acts of mass killing of the Tutsi victims that occurred at Murambi. Accordingly, the Appeals Chamber holds that these factual findings support the mass killing element of the crime of extermination, that Elizaphan Ntakirutimana had the required *mens rea* for aiding and abetting extermination and accordingly finds that Elizaphan Ntakirutimana incurred individual criminal responsibility for aiding and abetting the extermination of the Tutsi as a crime against humanity."

Bagosora, Kabiligi, Ntabakuze and Nsengiyumva, (Trial Chamber), December 18, 2008, paras. 2192-93: "Several of the events charged as extermination when viewed separately do not satisfy the threshold of killing on a large-scale, in particular the targeted political assassinations. However, the Chamber has considered the events for which the Accused have been held responsible together since they are essentially part of the same widespread and systematic attacks against the civilian population on political and ethnic grounds. In this respect, the Chamber emphasises the relatively brief time period in which these crimes were committed and that each of them were [*sic*] based on the same set of orders or authorisation from the Accused."

"It is clear therefore that the following killings satisfy either in themselves or collectively the requirement of killings on a large-scale: Agathe Uwilingiyimana, Joseph Kavaruganda, Frédéric Nzamurambaho, Landoald Ndasingwa, Faustin Rucogoza. . . , Alphonse Kabiligi (...) and Augustin Maharangari (...) as well as civilians at roadblocks in the Kigali area between 7 and 9 April (...) , at *Centre Christus* (...) , the Kibagabaga Mosque (...) , Kabeza (...) , the Saint Josephite Centre (...) , Karama hill and Kibagabaga Catholic Church (...) , Gikondo Parish (...) , Nyanza hill (...) , IAMSEA [*L'Institut Africain et Mauricien de Statistiques et d'Economie*] (...) , Gisenyi town (...) , Nyundo Parish (...) , Mudende University (...) and Bisesero (...) Each of these killings were [*sic*] conducted on the basis of ethnic and political grounds (...) As also noted above, the assailants and the Accused were aware that these attacks formed part of widespread and systematic attacks against the civilian population on ethnic and political grounds(...)" *See id.,* paras. 2194, 2196-97 (finding Bagosora, Ntabakuze and Nsengiyumva responsible for extermination as a crime against humanity).

Zigiranyirazo, (Trial Chamber), December 18, 2008, paras. 434-36: "The Chamber recalls that hundreds and possibly over a thousand Tutsi were killed on Kesho Hill [in Rwili secteur, Gaseke commune, in Gisenyi prefecture] on 8 April 1994. The Chamber therefore finds beyond reasonable doubt that the *actus reus* requirement of large scale killings, for the crime of extermination as a crime against humanity, is met." "With regard to the Accused's criminal responsibility, (...) the Chamber found that he participated in a JCE [joint criminal enterprise] to kill Tutsi on Kesho Hill. In view of the large scale killings which occurred, as well as the large number of assailants who were armed with a variety of weapons, the Chamber finds that the only reasonable inference is that all those who participated in the JCE intended to kill Tutsi on a mass scale. Accordingly, the Chamber finds beyond reasonable doubt that the Accused and the assailants intentionally participated in a JCE at Kesho Hill to kill members of the Tutsi ethnic group on a mass scale." "The Chamber therefore finds that the Accused committed extermination as a crime against humanity through his participation in the JCE to kill Tutsi at Kesho Hill."[28]

Seromba, (Trial Chamber), December 13, 2006, para. 365: The Chamber is of the view that the destruction of the [Nyange] church [Nyange parish, Kibuye prefecture], which resulted in the death of 1,500 Tutsi refugees, constitutes the crime of extermination within the meaning of Article 3 of the Statute." *See also Seromba,* (Appeals Chamber), March 12, 2008, para. 190: "With respect to Athanase Seromba's *mens rea*, the Appeals Chamber is satisfied that the role he played in the events that led to the destruction of the church, his knowledge that such destruction would inevitably result in the death of a large number of Tutsi civilians, as well as his awareness of the widespread and systematic attack against the Tutsi population occurring at the time, all demonstrate that he possessed the required intent to commit extermination."

Bisengimana, (Trial Chamber), April 13, 2006, paras. 65-66, 73-76: "The Accused acknowledges that: a) On or about 12 April 1994, weapons such as guns and grenades were distributed to *Interahamwe* militiamen and other armed civilians at Musha Church [in Gikoro commune] by members of the Rwandan Army. b) He was aware of this and the fact that these weapons would be used to attack Tutsi civilians seeking refuge at Musha Church. c) On or about 13 April 1994, an attack was launched against the Tutsi civilians seeking refuge at Musha Church. The attackers used guns, grenades, machetes, pangas and other traditional weapons. d) This attack resulted in the killing of more than a thousand Tutsi civilians. e) During the attack, a civilian militiaman named Manda set fire to the Church, causing the death of many refugees. f) The Accused was present during the attack, along with Laurent Semanza, soldiers from the Rwandan Army, *Interahamwe* militiamen, armed civilians and communal policemen. g) His presence at Musha Church during the attack would have had an encouraging effect on the perpetrators and given them the impression that he endorsed the killing of Tutsi civilians gathered there."

"Paul Bisengimana acknowledges that he had the means to oppose the killings of Tutsi civilians in Gikoro *commune*, but that he remained indifferent to the attack." "Based on the facts admitted by the Accused and recalling the Chamber's findings that the attack on Musha Church in Gikoro *commune* was launched against Tutsi civilians on discriminatory grounds, was widespread and resulted in a large number of victims, the Chamber finds that this attack amounts to extermination." "The Chamber finds that the Accused participated in the attack against Musha Church by being present and that he was aware that his presence would have encouraged the criminal conduct of the perpetrators of the attack." "The Chamber is convinced that the Accused knew of the criminal intent of the principal perpetrators because of his admission that he was aware that arms had been distributed to *Interahamwe* militiamen and other armed civilians at Musha Church and that these weapons would be used to attack the Tutsi population who had sought refuge there." "Accordingly, the Chamber is satisfied that Paul Bisengimana's presence at Musha Church on or about 13 April 1994 aided and abetted the extermination of Tutsi civilians there." *See id.*, paras. 67-69, 77-80 (similar findings as to extermination at Ruhanga Protestant Church and School).

Simba, (Trial Chamber), December 13, 2005, paras. 425, 426: "The assailants at Murambi Technical School and Kaduha Parish [in Gikongoro prefecture in southern Rwanda] killed thousands of Tutsi civilians in what can only be said to be a large-scale killing, which was part of the widespread attack on ethnic grounds. Simba participated in this large-scale killing as a participant in the joint criminal enterprise to kill Tutsi at these two sites by distributing weapons and lending approval and encouragement to the physical perpetrators. In its findings on criminal responsibility, the Chamber described this assistance as having a substantial effect on the killings that followed. Given the manner in which the attacks were conducted, the nature of the weapons used, and the number of victims, the Chamber finds beyond reasonable doubt that Simba and the assailants intentionally participated in a mass killing of members of the Tutsi ethnic group." "The Chamber finds beyond reasonable doubt that Simba is criminally responsible under Article 6(1) of the Statute based on his participation in a joint criminal enterprise to kill Tutsi civilians at Murambi Technical School and Kaduha Parish. Therefore, the Chamber finds Simba guilty on Count 3 of the Indictment for extermination as a crime against humanity."[29]

Rutaganira, (Trial Chamber), March 14, 2005, para. 53: "[T]he Chamber finds that the massacres committed at Mubuga church [Gishyita commune, Kibuye prefecture] between 14 and 17 April 1994 [in which thousands of Tutsi refugees were killed or wounded] had been perpetrated on a large scale and had caused thousands of casualties" and qualified as the crime of extermination.

Ndindabahizi, (Trial Chamber), July 15, 2004, paras. 482-84: "The Chamber has found that the Accused visited Gitwa Hill [in the Bisesero Hills, Kibuye prefecture] on two occasions, urging the attackers to kill the Tutsi refugees, and distributing machetes and other weapons. On one occasion, he also transported attackers who were identified as *Interahamwe* to Gitwa Hill. He was known to be a Government Minister and people gathered around him during these visits attentively and respectfully. His words and deeds would undoubtedly have had a substantial motivating impact on the attackers. As little as two days after the Accused's final visit, there was a massive attack on the Hill, resulting in the deaths of thousands of Tutsi. This final attack had been preceded by smaller-scale attacks, including one which occurred in his presence and which he appears to have initiated."

"[T]he specific requirements for the offence of extermination are satisfied. The Accused intended to bring about the deaths of the Tutsi besieged on Gitwa Hill on a massive scale. He manifested this intent directly, by urging that the Tutsi be killed. The material element of the crime is satisfied by his distribution of weapons, transportation of attackers, and verbal encouragement of the attack. As a Government Minister, these words and deeds contributed substantial moral support and official approval for the devastating attack which occurred shortly thereafter. Accordingly, the Accused contributed substantially to the mass killing of Tutsi which ensued."

"The general requirements for a crime against humanity are also satisfied. The evidence is overwhelming that there were widespread attacks against Tutsi in Rwanda, and in Kibuye Prefecture, during this period. The Accused overtly manifested his intent to kill the civilian refugees at Gitwa Hill because they were Tutsi, knowing that ethnic massacres were occurring throughout Rwanda. At the least, he had knowledge of the widespread nature of the attacks and their discriminatory nature, and knew that an attack on Gitwa Hill would be part of those widespread attacks."

Gacumbitsi, (Trial Chamber), June 17, 2004, paras. 310-12: "[T]he Chamber is of the view that the high numerical strength of the victims of the Nyarubuye Parish massacres [in Rusumo commune] supports a finding of widespread killing. It is established that many persons of Tutsi and Hutu origin had taken refuge in the parish on the days preceding the attack. Some witnesses testified that there were several thousand refugees there. It is also established that Hutu were asked to separate themselves from Tutsi during the massacre. The massacre lasted several hours and the attackers returned to finish off survivors during the following two days. Witness accounts show sufficiently that it was a large-scale massacre that resulted in numerous deaths. The fact is corroborated by Prosecution Witness Patrick Fergal Keane who, weeks later, saw many corpses." "Considering the leading role of the Accused in preparing and launching the attack, as well as his subsequent visits to the parish to instigate attackers to kill survivors, and the fact that he supervised their actions, the Chamber does not doubt the Accused's intention to participate in a large scale massacre in Nyarubuye."

"The Chamber finds that the Accused had knowledge of such a widespread and systematic attack against a civilian population in Rusumo in April 1994 because, at the local level, he planned and led certain operations."

Kamuhanda, (Trial Chamber), January 22, 2004, paras. 697-99: "The Chamber recalls its findings (...) that Tutsis were killed at Gikomero Parish Compound [in Gikomero commune, Kigali-Rural prefecture] and that the Accused participated in this killing by ordering, instigating and aiding and abetting the commission of the crime." "The material element of extermination is the large-scale killing of a substantial number of civilians. Although the evidence does not indicate the specific number of victims to enable a specific finding of the number of deaths at the Gikomero Parish Compound, the evidence clearly shows that large numbers of Tutsi civilians were killed there during the attack, in which the Accused participated. On the basis of reliable and credible evidence, the Chamber finds that the scale of killings at the Gikomero Parish Compound is sufficient to be termed extermination, and that the principal perpetrators of the killings committed extermination as a Crime against Humanity." "The Chamber finds that the Accused participated in the attack at Gikomero Parish Compound, and that the Accused was fully aware that his actions formed part of a widespread attack. On the basis of the evidence and in view of the scale of this event, the Chamber is convinced that the Accused ordered, instigated, and aided and abetted the principal perpetrators of the attack at the Gikomero Parish Compound against the Tutsi civilians, who had gathered there in large numbers to seek shelter and refuge."

Kajelijeli, (Trial Chamber), December 1, 2003, para. 904: "The Chamber finds that within the context of th[e] attack, and in full knowledge that his actions formed a part of that attack, the Accused directed attacks against neighbourhoods and places of shelter and refuge where Tutsis were grouped in large numbers. Hundreds of Tutsis within Mukingo, Nkuli and Kigombe *communes* in Ruhengeri prefecture were exterminated as a direct result of the Accused's participation by ordering and supervising, or, in the case of the attack upon the Ruhengeri Court of Appeal, by aiding, these attacks. *See id.*, paras. 896-903 (additional details as to extermination).

Niyitegeka, (Trial Chamber), May 16, 2003, para. 454: "[B]y his participation in attacks against Tutsi, and his acts of shooting at Tutsi refugees, which contributed to the killing of a large number of individuals, and his killing of the three persons, the Accused is (...) responsible (...) for extermination committed as part of a widespread and systematic attack on the civilian Tutsi population on ethnic grounds(...)"

Compare Zigiranyirazo, (Trial Chamber), December 18, 2008, para. 438: "In view of the Chamber's finding that at least 10 to 20 people were killed at the Kiyovu roadblock [in Kiyovu cellule, Kigali-*ville* prefecture], it does not find beyond reasonable doubt that the requirement of large scale killings, as required for the crime of extermination, has been met."

iv) enslavement

(no law presently)

v) deportation

(no law presently)

vi) imprisonment

1) defined

Ntagerura, Bagambiki, and Imanishimwe, (Trial Chamber), February 25, 2004, para. 702: "Imprisonment as a crime against humanity refers to arbitrary or otherwise unlawful detention or deprivation of liberty. It is not every minor infringement of liberty that forms the material element of imprisonment as a crime against humanity; the deprivation of liberty must be of similar gravity and seriousness as the other crimes enumerated as crimes against humanity enumerated in Article 3 (a) to (i). In assessing whether the imprisonment constitutes a crime against humanity, the Chamber may take into account whether the initial arrest was lawful, by considering, for example, whether it was based on a valid warrant of arrest, whether the detainees were informed of the reasons for their detention, whether the detainees were ever formally charged, and whether they were informed of any procedural rights. The Chamber may also consider whether the continued detention was lawful. When a national law is relied upon to justify a deprivation of liberty, this national law must not violate international law."

2) application

Ntagerura, Bagambiki, and Imanishimwe, (Trial Chamber), February 25, 2004, paras. 754-56: "[T]he Chamber has found that an unknown number of Tutsi and Hutu civilians were arrested under suspicion of being RPF [Rwandan Patriotic Front] accomplices and were taken to Karambo military camp [in Cyangugu] where soldiers mistreated them. The Chamber has found that the only reasonable inference to be drawn from the totality of the evidence is that Imanishimwe issued orders authorizing the arrest and detention of civilians with suspected ties to the RPF (...)These arrests were not based on valid warrants, nor were these civilians ever formally charged and informed of their procedural rights. The Chamber finds that the soldiers acted intentionally in the execution of Imanishimwe's orders to incarcerate civilians at Karambo military camp. The Chamber finds that the principal perpetrators, soldiers who were also involved in the mistreatment and questioning of these detainees about suspected ties to the RPF, were aware that their acts formed part of a systematic attack on political grounds against the civilian population in Cyangugu." "The Chamber finds that by issuing orders authorizing the arrest and detention of civilians with suspected ties to the RPF and by having knowledge that these acts were carried out, Imanishimwe acted intentionally and with awareness that he was encouraging his subordinates to commit crimes against humanity. These orders substantially contributed to the imprisonment of civilians at the Karambo military camp, given Imanishimwe's authority as the camp commander." "Consequently, the Chamber finds beyond a reasonable doubt that Imanishimwe is criminally responsible under Article 6(1) of the Statute for imprisonment as a crime against humanity(...)" (The conviction was affirmed on appeal.)

vii) torture

1) defined/ actus reus

Ntagerura, Bagambiki, and Imanishimwe, (Trial Chamber), February 25, 2004, para. 703: "Torture as a crime against humanity is the intentional infliction of severe physical or mental pain or suffering for prohibited purposes including: obtaining information or a confession; punishing, intimidating, or coercing the victim or a third person; or discriminating against the victim or a third person."

Akayesu, (Trial Chamber), September 2, 1998, paras. 593-95: "The Tribunal interprets the word 'torture'. . . in accordance with the definition of torture set forth in the United Nations Convention Against Torture and Other Cruel, Inhuman or Degrading Treatment or Punishment." "The Chamber defines the essential elements of torture as:

(i) The perpetrator must intentionally inflict severe physical or mental pain or suffering upon the victim for one or more of the following purposes:

(a) to obtain information or a confession from the victim or a third person;

(b) to punish the victim or a third person for an act committed or suspected of having been committed by either of them;

(c) for the purpose of intimidating or coercing the victim or the third person;

(d) for any reason based on discrimination of any kind.

(ii) The perpetrator was himself an official, or acted at the instigation of, or with the consent or acquiescence of, an official or person acting in an official capacity."

But see "no 'public official requirement,'" Section (II)(c)(vii)(4).

2) torture as a crime against humanity

Akayesu, (Trial Chamber), September 2, 1998, para. 595: "The Chamber finds that torture is a crime against humanity if the following further elements are satisfied: a) Torture must be perpetrated as part of a widespread or systematic attack; b) the attack must be against the civilian population; c) the attack must be launched on discriminatory grounds, namely: national, ethnic, racial, religious and political grounds."

3) rape constitutes torture

Akayesu, (Trial Chamber), September 2, 1998, paras. 597, 687: "Like torture, rape is used for such purposes as intimidation, degradation, humiliation, discrimination, punishment, control or destruction of a person. Like torture, rape is a violation of personal dignity, and rape in fact constitutes torture when inflicted by or at the instigation of or with the consent of acquiescence of a public official or other person acting in an official capacity."

But see "no 'public official requirement,'" directly below.

4) no "public official requirement"

Semanza, (Appeals Chamber), May 20, 2005, para. 248: "In the *Kunarac et al.* Appeal Judgement, the ICTY Appeals Chamber explained that the public official requirement is not a requirement outside the framework of the Torture Convention:

Furthermore, in the [ICTY's] *Furundžija* Trial Judgement, the Trial Chamber noted that the definition provided in the Torture Convention related to 'the purposes of [the] Convention.' The accused in that case had not acted in a private capacity, but as a member of armed forces during an armed conflict, and he did not question that the definition of torture in the Torture Convention reflected customary international law. In this context, and with the objectives of the Torture Convention in mind, the Appeals Chamber in the *Furundžija* case was in a legitimate position to assert that 'at least one of the persons involved in the torture process must be a public official or must at any rate act in a nonprivate capacity, *e.g.*, as a de facto organ of a State or any other authoritywielding entity.' This assertion, which is tantamount to a statement that the definition of torture in the Torture Convention reflects customary international law as far as the obligation of States is concerned, must be distinguished from an assertion that this definition wholly reflects customary international law regarding the meaning of the crime of torture generally. The Trial Chamber in the present case was therefore right in taking the position that the public official requirement is not a requirement under customary international law in relation to the criminal responsibility of an individual for torture outside of the framework of the Torture Convention.

This was recently reaffirmed in the [ICTY's] *Kvočka et al.* Appeal Judgement."

Semanza, (Trial Chamber), May 15, 2003, paras. 342-43: "In *Akayesu*, the Trial Chamber relied on the definition of torture found in the (...) Convention Against Torture (...)The ICTY Appeals Chamber has since explained that while the definition contained in the Convention Against Torture is reflective of customary international law (...) , it is not identical to the definition of torture as a crime against humanity. [T]he ICTY Appeals Chamber has confirmed that, outside the framework of the Convention Against Torture, the 'public official' requirement is not a requirement under customary international law in relation to individual criminal responsibility for torture as a crime against humanity." Thus, the Chamber rejected the "public official" requirement.

5) application

Ntagerura, Bagambiki, and Imanishimwe, (Trial Chamber), February 25, 2004, paras. 759-60: "The Chamber has (...) found that soldiers [in the Karambo military camp in Cyangugu] under Imanishimwe's effective control and in his presence severely beat Witness MG and another detainee and hammered a long nail into the foot of one of the other detainees, removed the nail, and then hammered it into the foot of another detainee while questioning them about their suspected affiliation with the RPF [Rwandan Patriotic Front] and accusing them of collaborating with the enemy. As a result of this treatment, Witness MG could not stand up for several days. In addition, the two detainees who were injured with the nail screamed in pain in their cell. Soldiers later removed the two detainees who were never seen or heard from again."

"[T]he Chamber finds that, in mistreating Witness MG and the other three detainees at the Karambo camp, the soldiers were acting intentionally and with the prohibited purpose of obtaining information or confessions from the detainees or of punishing them. Additionally, the Chamber finds that the severe beating as well as the mistreatment with the long nail amounted to infliction of severe physical pain. The Chamber has found that the soldiers at the camp had knowledge that their actions formed part of a systematic attack on political grounds. Thus, the Chamber finds that the soldiers committed torture as a crime against humanity." *See also id.*, paras. 761-62 (finding Imanishimwe responsible for ordering and aiding and abetting the torture). (The convictions were affirmed on appeal.)

Compare Ntagerura, Bagambiki, and Imanishimwe, (Trial Chamber), February 25, 2004, para. 758: Where "two of the [other] victims were in a position to forcibly escape from detention, the Chamber conclude[d] that the mistreatment was not such as to cause severe suffering or pain sufficient for a finding of torture." *See also id.*, paras. 799-800 (finding mistreatment that was not "torture" to be the war crime of cruel treatment).

See also discussions of torture and cruel treatment under Article 4 (war crimes), Sections (III)(d)(i)(2)-(3).

viii) rape

1) defined/ actus reus

(a) the original "Akayesu" approach

Akayesu, (Trial Chamber), September 2, 1998, paras. 597-98, 688: "[R]ape is a form of aggression and (...) the central elements of the crime of rape cannot be captured in a mechanical description of object and body parts (...) Like torture, rape is used for such purposes as intimidation, degradation, humiliation, discrimination, punishment, control or destruction of a person. Like torture, rape is a violation of personal dignity. . . ." "The Chamber defines rape as a physical invasion of a sexual nature, committed on a person under circumstances which are coercive. Sexual violence which includes rape, is considered to be any act of a sexual nature which is committed on a person under circumstances which are coercive."

Musema, (Trial Chamber), January 27, 2000, paras. 220-21, 226-29: The Chamber adopted the definition of rape and sexual violence set forth in *Akayesu*, and further stated that "variations on the acts of rape may include acts which involve the insertions of objects and/or the use of bodily orifices not considered to be intrinsically sexual." Concurring with the approach set forth in *Akayesu*, the Chamber stated that the "essence of rape is not the particular details of the body parts and objects involved, but rather the aggression that is expressed in a sexual manner under conditions of coercion." Since "there is a trend in national legislation to broaden the definition of rape" and an ongoing evolution and incorporation of the understanding of rape into principles of international law, "a conceptual definition is preferable to a mechanical definition of rape" because it will "better accommodate evolving norms of criminal justice."

Muhimana, (Trial Chamber), April 28, 2005, paras. 537-40: "The first judgement in which an international criminal tribunal defined rape as a crime against humanity and an instrument of genocide was issued on 2 September 1998 in the case *Prosecutor v. Akayesu*, by Trial Chamber I of the ICTR (...) Emphasizing that 'the central elements of the crime of rape cannot be captured in a mechanical description of objects and body parts,' the *Akayesu* Judgement defined rape and sexual violence as: a physical invasion of a sexual nature, committed on a person under circumstances which are coercive. Sexual violence, which includes rape, is considered to be any act of a sexual nature which is committed on a person under circumstances which are coercive."

"Recognizing that rape has been historically defined in national jurisdictions as 'non-consensual sexual intercourse,' the *Akayesu* Trial Chamber found this description too mechanical, insofar as 'variations on the form of rape may include acts which involve the insertion of objects and/or the use of bodily orifices not considered to be intrinsically sexual.' As an example, the *Akayesu* Trial Chamber referred to its factual finding that a piece of wood was thrust into the sexual organs of a woman as she lay dying - a physically invasive act of the victim's body, which it found to constitute rape."

"Consonant with the definition of rape in *Akayesu*, this Chamber notes with approval the *Furundžija* Trial Chamber's conclusion that: The general principle of respect for human dignity is the basic underpinning and indeed the very *raison d'être* of international humanitarian law and human rights law; indeed in modern times it has become of such paramount importance as to permeate the whole body of international law. This principle is intended to shield human beings from outrages upon their personal dignity, whether such outrages are carried out by unlawfully attacking the body or by humiliating and debasing the honour, the self-respect or the mental well being of a person. It is consonant with this principle that such an extremely serious sexual outrage as forced oral penetration should be classified as rape."

"The Chamber observes that the *Akayesu* definition of rape was endorsed by Trial Chamber I of this Tribunal in *Musema* and *Niyitegeka*, and by Trial Chamber II of the ICTY in *Delalic*. No appeal was taken as to this issue in any of these cases." *See Akayesu,* (Trial Chamber), September 2, 1998, paras. 598, 688; *Musema,* (Trial Chamber), January 27, 2000, paras. 229, 907, 933, 936; *Niyitegeka,* (Trial Chamber), May 16, 2003, para. 456 ("rape being 'a physical invasion of a sexual nature, committed on a person under circumstances which are coercive.'").

(b) the "Kunarac" approach—retreat from "Akayesu"?

Gacumbitsi, (Appeals Chamber), July 7, 2006, para. 151: "In the *Kunarac* case, the ICTY

Appeals Chamber defined rape as follows: the *actus reus* of the crime of rape in international law is constituted by: the sexual penetration, however slight: (a) of the vagina or anus of the victim by the penis of the perpetrator or any other object used by the perpetrator; or (b) the mouth of the victim by the penis of the perpetrator; where such sexual penetration occurs without the consent of the victim. Consent for this purpose must be consent given voluntarily, as a result of the victim's free will, assessed in the context of the surrounding circumstances. The *mens rea* is the intention to effect this sexual penetration, and the knowledge that it occurs without the consent of the victim."

See also Bagosora, Kabiligi, Ntabakuze and Nsengiyumva, (Trial Chamber), December 18, 2008, para. 2199 (similar).

Gacumbitsi, (Trial Chamber), June 17, 2004, para. 321: "The Chamber is of the opinion that any penetration of the victim's vagina by the rapist with his genitals or with any object constitutes rape, although the definition of rape under Article 3(g) of the Statute is not limited to such acts alone."

Kamuhanda, (Trial Chamber), January 22, 2004, paras. 705-07, 709: "In Akayesu [*sic*] the Trial Chamber considered that the traditional mechanical definition of rape did not adequately capture its true nature and instead offered a definition of rape as:

A physical invasion of a sexual nature, committed on a person under circumstances which are coercive. Sexual violence which includes rape is considered to be any act of a sexual nature which is committed on a person under circumstances which are coercive." "This conceptual definition of rape was approved in Musema [*sic*], where the Chamber highlighted the difference between 'a physical invasion of a sexual nature', and 'any act of a sexual nature' as being the difference between rape and sexual assault. Meanwhile, a Trial Chamber of the ICTY handed down the Furundžija [*sic*] Judgment, in which that Chamber preferred the following more detailed definition related to objects and body parts:

Most legal systems in the common and civil law world consider rape to be the forcible sexual penetration of the human body by the penis or the forcible insertion of any other object into either the vagina or the anus.'" "This definition substantially modified and completed by Trial Chamber II in the Kunarac [*sic*] Judgment has been endorsed by the Appeals Chamber. It reads as follow: The *actus reus* [*sic*] of the crime of rape in international law is constituted by: the sexual penetration, however slight:

(a) of the vagina or anus of the victim by the penis of the perpetrator or any other object used by the perpetrator; or

(b) of the mouth of the victim by the penis of the perpetrator; where such sexual penetration occurs without the consent of the victim. Consent for this purpose must be consent given voluntarily, as a result of the victim's free will, assessed in the context of the surrounding circumstances."

"Given the evolution of the law in this area, endorsed in the Furundžija/Kunarac [*sic*] approach by the ICTY Appeals Chamber, the Chamber finds the latter approach of persuasive authority and hereby adopts the definition as given in Kunarac [*sic*] and quoted above." *See also Kajelijeli,* (Trial Chamber), December 1, 2003, paras. 910-15 (same with italics).

Semanza, (Trial Chamber), May 15, 2003, paras. 344-45: "The *Akayesu* Judgement enunciated a broad definition of rape (...) The Appeals Chamber of the ICTY [in *Kunarac*] (...) affirmed a narrower interpretation defining the material element of rape (...) as the non-consensual penetration, however slight, of the vagina or anus of the victim by the penis of the perpetrator or by any other object used by the perpetrator, or of the mouth of the victim by the penis of the perpetrator." "While this mechanical style of defining rape was originally rejected by this Tribunal, the Chamber finds the comparative analysis in *Kunarac* to be persuasive and thus will adopt the definition of rape approved by the ICTY Appeals Chamber."

(c) interpreting the "Kunarac" and "Akayesu" approaches as consonant

Muvunyi, (Trial Chamber), September 12, 2006, paras. 517-18, 520-22: "The jurisprudence of the *ad hoc* Tribunals reveals a rather chequered history of the definition of rape. Initially, in the *Akayesu* Judgement, this Tribunal proposed that a conceptual approach to defining rape would be more useful to international law and opined that a mechanical approach with its focus on objects and body parts, was unsuitable. The *Akayesu* Trial Chamber therefore proceeded to define rape as 'a physical invasion of a sexual nature, committed on a person under circumstances which are coercive.' The broader concept of 'sexual violence,' according to Akayesu, 'includes rape [and] is considered to be any act of a sexual nature which is committed on a person under circumstances which are coercive.' The Chamber notes that this definition was endorsed in the *Musema*, *Niyitegeka*, and *Muhimana* Judgements."

"However, in both *Furundžija* and *Kunarac,* ICTY Trial Chambers reverted to defining rape in terms of sexual penetration through the use of body parts or other objects under forceful or otherwise coercive circumstances. The definition of rape as sexual penetration of the vagina, anus, or mouth of the victim by the penis of the perpetrator or some other object used by him under coercive or forceful circumstances was partially approved by the Appeals Chamber in *Kunarac.* However, the Appeals Chamber expressed the view that *Furundžija* and earlier decisions defined rape more narrowly than was required under international law and reasoned that the emphasis on coercion, force, or threat of force did not recognise other factors that could render an act of sexual penetration non-consensual or non-voluntary. Consequently, the Appeals Chamber approved the definition of rape as:

[t]he sexual penetration, however slight: (a) of the vagina or anus of the victim by the penis of the perpetrator or any other object used by the perpetrator; or

(b) of the mouth of the victim by the penis of the perpetrator; where such sexual penetration occurs without the consent of the victim. Consent for this purpose must be consent given voluntarily, as a result of the victim's free will, assessed in the context of the surrounding circumstances."

"In *Muhimana* this Tribunal expressed the view that the *Akayesu* and *Kunarac* definitions of rape are not incompatible and noted that '[w]hereas *Akayesu* referred broadly to a "physical invasion of a sexual nature," *Kunarac* went on to articulate the parameters of what would constitute a physical invasion of a sexual nature amounting to rape.'"

"The Chamber agrees with the above analysis and considers that the underlying objective of the prohibition of rape at international law is to penalise serious violations of sexual autonomy. A violation of sexual autonomy ensues whenever a person is subjected to sexual acts of the genre listed in *Kunarac* to which he/she has not consented, or to which he/she is not a voluntary participant. Lack of consent therefore continues to be an important ingredient of rape as a crime against humanity. The fact that unwanted sexual activity takes place under coercive or forceful circumstances may provide evidence of lack of consent on the part of the victim."

"The Chamber considers that in their result, both the *Akayesu* and *Kunarac* definitions of rape reflect this objective of protecting individual sexual autonomy and therefore are not incompatible. The broad language in *Akayesu* that rape constitutes 'physical invasion of a sexual nature,' when properly interpreted, could include 'sexual penetration' as stipulated in *Kunarac.* The Chamber therefore concludes that the offence of rape exists whenever there is sexual penetration of the vagina, anus or mouth of the victim, by the penis of the perpetrator or some other object under, circumstances where the victim did not agree to the sexual act or was otherwise not a willing participant to it."

Muhimana, (Trial Chamber), April 28, 2005, paras. 542-43, 547, 549-51: "The [ICTY's *Kunarac*] Trial Chamber's articulation of the elements of the crime of rape was as follows:

The *actus reus* of the crime of rape in international law is constituted by: the sexual penetration, however slight:

(a) of the vagina or anus of the victim by the penis of the perpetrator or any other object used by the perpetrator; or

(b) of the mouth of the victim by the penis of the perpetrator; where such sexual penetration occurs without the consent of the victim. Consent for this purpose must be consent given voluntarily, as a result of the victim's free will, assessed in the context of the surrounding circumstances. The *mens rea* is the intention to effect this sexual penetration, and the knowledge that it occurs without the consent of the victim."

"When the *Kunarac* Appeals Chamber concurred with the Trial Chamber's 'definition,' it is clear that it was approving the elements set out by the Trial Chamber(...)"

"The Chamber notes that the definition of rape, as enunciated in *Akayesu*, has not been adopted *per se* in all subsequent jurisprudence of the *ad hoc* Tribunals. The ICTR Trial Chambers in *Semanza*, *Kajelijeli* and *Kamuhanda*, for example, described only the physical elements of the act of rape, as set out in *Kunarac*, and thus seemingly shifted their analyses away from the conceptual definition established in *Akayesu*."

"This Chamber considers that *Furundžija* and *Kunarac*, which sometimes have been construed as departing from the *Akayesu* definition of rape – as was done in *Semanza* -actually are substantially aligned to this definition and provide additional details on the constituent elements of acts considered to be rape." "The Chamber takes the view that the *Akayesu* definition and the *Kunarac* elements are not incompatible or substantially different in their application. Whereas *Akayesu* referred broadly to a 'physical invasion of a sexual nature,' *Kunarac* went on to articulate the parameters of what would constitute a physical invasion of a sexual nature amounting to rape." "On the basis of the foregoing analysis, the Chamber endorses the conceptual definition of rape established in *Akayesu*, which encompasses the elements set out in *Kunarac*."

(d) that rapist knew victim and may have had personal motivation, does not preclude finding rape

Gacumbitsi, (Appeals Chamber), July 7, 2006, paras. 103, 107: "The Appellant specifically contends that the rape of Witness TAQ was isolated because she had known her attacker previously. But this fact does not mean that her rape was isolated from the widespread and systematic attack. Indeed, the genocide and extermination campaign in Rwanda was characterized in significant part by neighbours killing and raping neighbours. Moreover, as the ICTY Appeals Chamber has recognized, even in the event that 'personal motivations can be identified in the defendant's carrying out of an act, it does not necessarily follow that the required nexus with the attack on a civilian population must also inevitably be lacking.' Whether or not the perpetrator and victim are acquainted, the question is simply whether the totality of the evidence proves a nexus between the act and the widespread or systematic attack." "[T]he acquaintance between Witness TAQ and her assailant does not mean that her rape cannot constitute a crime against humanity."

(e) non-consent and knowledge thereof are elements of rape *Gacumbitsi*, (Appeals Chamber), July 7, 2006, para. 153: "*Kunarac* establishes that non-consent and knowledge thereof are elements of rape as a crime against humanity."

Muvunyi, (Trial Chamber), September 12, 2006, para. 521: "Lack of consent (...) continues to be an important ingredient of rape as a crime against humanity."

(i) force or threat of force provides evidence of nonconsent, but force is not an element of rape

Bagosora, Kabiligi, Ntabakuze and Nsengiyumva, (Trial Chamber), December 18, 2008, para. 2199: "Force or threat of force provides clear evidence of non-consent, but force is not an element *per se* of rape."

Muhimana, (Trial Chamber), April 28, 2005, paras. 544-46: "In analyzing the relationship between consent and coercion, the Appeals Chamber acknowledged that coercion provides clear evidence of non-consent. The Appeals Chamber in *Kunarac* opined as follows:

. . . with regard to the role of force in the definition of rape, the Appeals

Chamber notes that the Trial Chamber appeared to depart from the Tribunal's prior definitions of rape. However, in explaining its focus on the absence of consent as the condition sine qua non of rape, the Trial Chamber did not disavow the Tribunal's earlier jurisprudence, but instead sought to explain the relationship between force and consent. Force or threat of force provides clear evidence of non-consent, but force is not an element per se of rape. In particular, the Trial Chamber wished to explain that there are 'factors [other than force] which would render an act of sexual penetration non-consensual or nonvoluntary on the part of the victim.' A narrow focus on force or threat of force could permit perpetrators to evade [responsibility] for sexual activity to which the other party had not consented by taking advantage of coercive circumstances without relying on physical force. The Appeals Chamber notes, for example, that in some domestic jurisdictions, neither the use of a weapon nor the physical overpowering of a victim is necessary to demonstrate force. A threat to retaliate 'in the future against the victim or any other person' is a sufficient indicium of force so long as 'there is a reasonable possibility that the perpetrator will execute the threat.' While it is true that a focus on one aspect gives different shading to the offence, it is worth observing that the circumstances giving rise to the instant appeal and that prevail in most cases charged as either war crimes or crimes against humanity will be almost universally coercive. That is to say, true consent will not be possible."

"Similarly, the Chamber also recalls that the *Furundžija* Trial Chamber acknowledged that 'any form of captivity vitiates consent.'"

"Accordingly, the Chamber is persuaded by the Appellate Chamber's analysis that coercion is an element that may obviate the relevance of consent as an evidentiary factor in the crime of rape."

See also Akayesu, (Trial Chamber), September 2, 1998, para. 688: "[C]oercive circumstances need not be evidenced by a show of physical force. Threats, intimidation, extortion and other forms of duress which prey on fear or desperation may constitute coercion, and coercion may be inherent in certain circumstances (...)"

(ii) circumstances prevailing in most genocide, war crimes and crimes against humanity cases will be almost universally coercive/true consent not possible

Gacumbitsi, (Appeals Chamber), July 7, 2006, para. 151: "The ICTY Appeals Chamber in *Kunarac* 'immediately emphasized that "the circumstances giving rise to the instant appeal and that prevail in most cases charged as either war crimes or crimes against humanity will be almost universally coercive. That is to say, true consent [or a rape victim] will not be possible."'"

Muhimana, (Trial Chamber), April 28, 2005, para. 546: "[T]his Chamber concurs with the opinion that circumstances prevailing in most cases charged under international criminal law, as either genocide, crimes against humanity, or war crimes, will be almost universally coercive, thus vitiating true consent."

(iii) not necessary to introduce evidence of victim's words, conduct or relationship to the perpetrator

Gacumbitsi, (Appeals Chamber), July 7, 2006, paras. 155, 157: "The Prosecution can prove non-consent beyond reasonable doubt by proving the existence of coercive circumstances under which meaningful consent is not possible. As with every element of any offence, the Trial Chamber will consider all of the relevant and admissible evidence in determining whether, under the circumstances of the case, it is appropriate to conclude that non-consent is proven beyond reasonable doubt. But it is not necessary, as a legal matter, for the Prosecution to introduce evidence concerning the words or conduct of the victim or the victim's relationship to the perpetrator. Nor need it introduce evidence of force. Rather, the Trial Chamber is free to infer non-consent from the background circumstances, such as an ongoing genocide campaign or the detention of the victim. Indeed, the Trial Chamber did so in this case." "Knowledge of non[-]consent may be proven, for instance, if the Prosecution establishes beyond reasonable doubt that the accused was aware, or had reason to be aware, of the coercive circumstances that undermined the possibility of genuine consent."

(iv) accused may seek to prove consent, subject to caveats

Gacumbitsi, (Appeals Chamber), July 7, 2006, para. 156: "Under certain circumstances, the accused might raise reasonable doubt by introducing evidence that the victim specifically consented. However, pursuant to Rule 96(ii) of the Rules, such evidence is inadmissible if the victim:

(a) Has been subjected to or threatened with or has had reason to fear violence, duress, detention or psychological oppression; or

(b) Reasonably believed that if the victim did not submit, another might be so subjected, threatened or put in fear. Additionally, even if it admits such evidence, a Trial Chamber is free to disregard it if it concludes that under the circumstances the consent given was not genuinely voluntary."

Gacumbitsi, (Appeals Chamber), July 7, 2006, para. 151: ""Consent for this purpose must be consent given voluntarily, as a result of the victim's free will, assessed in the context of the surrounding circumstances."' *See also Bagosora, Kabiligi, Ntabakuze and Nsengiyumva,* (Trial Chamber), December 18, 2008, para. 2199 (same); *Semanza,* (Trial Chamber), May 15, 2003, para. 344 (same).

(f) acts of sexual violence short of rape may be prosecuted as other inhumane acts, torture, persecution or enslavement

Kamuhanda, (Trial Chamber), January 22, 2004, para. 710: "Other acts of sexual violence which may fall outside of this specific definition may of course be prosecuted, and would be considered by the Chamber under other categories of crimes for which the Tribunal has jurisdiction, such as other inhumane acts." *See also Kajelijeli,* (Trial Chamber), December 1, 2003, para. 916 (same).

Semanza, (Trial Chamber), May 15, 2003, para. 45: "[T]he Chamber recognises that other acts of sexual violence that do not satisfy this narrow definition [of rape] may be prosecuted as other crimes against humanity (...) such as torture, persecution, enslavement, or other inhumane acts."

See "other inhumane acts," "torture" and "persecution" as crimes against humanity, Sections (II)(c)(x), (II)(c)(vii), (II)(c)(ix).

2) mens rea

Gacumbitsi, (Appeals Chamber), July 7, 2006, para. 151: "In the *Kunarac* case, the ICTY

Appeals Chamber (...) [stated]: (...) The *mens rea* [for rape] is the intention to effect this sexual penetration, and the knowledge that it occurs without the consent of the victim."

Bagosora, Kabiligi, Ntabakuze and Nsengiyumva, (Trial Chamber), December 18, 2008, para. 2200: "The *mens rea* for rape as a crime against humanity is the intention to effect the prohibited sexual penetration with the knowledge that it occurs without the consent of the victim." *See also Muvunyi,* (Trial Chamber), September 12, 2006, para. 519 (similar); *Kamuhanda*, (Trial Chamber), January 22, 2004, para. 710 (similar); *Kajelijeli,* (Trial Chamber), December 1, 2003, para. 915 (similar); *Semanza,* (Trial Chamber), May 15, 2003, para. 346 (similar).

3) application

Gacumbitsi, (Appeals Chamber), July 7, 2006, paras. 107, 102: "[T]he Trial Chamber found: on 16 April 1994, around 9 a.m., the Accused, who was driving around in Rubare *cellule*, Nyarubuye *secteur*, using a megaphone, asked that Hutu young men whom (...) girls had refused to marry should be looked for so that they should have sex with the young girls, adding that 'in the event that they—the young girls—resisted, they had to be killed in an atrocious manner.' Placed in context, and considering the attendant audience, such an utterance from the Accused constituted an incitement, directed at this group of attackers on which the *bourgmestre* had influence, to rape Tutsi women. That is why, immediately after the utterance, a group of attackers attacked Witness TAQ and seven other Tutsi women and girls with whom she was hiding, and raped them.

Given these factual findings, which have not been shown to be unreasonable, it was reasonable for the Trial Chamber to conclude that the Appellant's words substantially contributed to the rapes of Witness TAQ, as well as that of the seven other Tutsis."

"In the case at hand, the Trial Chamber reasonably concluded that there was a widespread and systematic attack against Tutsis in Rusumo Commune. Its further conclusion that the rapes formed part of this attack was also reasonable in light of the finding that 'the victims of rape were chosen because of their Tutsi ethnic origin, or because of their relationship with a person of the Tutsi ethnic group.'" *See also Gacumbitsi*, (Trial Chamber), June 17, 2004, paras. 321, 323-25, 328, 330.

Bagosora, Kabiligi, Ntabakuze and Nsengiyumva, (Trial Chamber), December 18, 2008, para. 2201-03: "The Chamber has found that acts of rape occurred during attacks on civilians at Kigali area roadblocks (...) , the Saint Josephite Centre (...) and Gikondo Parish (...)It is clear that, given the circumstances surrounding these attacks, there could have been no consent for these acts of sexual violence and that the perpetrators would have known this fact. The Chamber has determined that the crimes at these locations were committed as part of a wide-spread and systematic attack on ethnic and political grounds(...)" (Concluding Bagosora bore superior responsible for those rapes as a crime against humanity.)

Muvunyi, (Trial Chamber), September 12, 2006, para. 524: "The evidence provided in this case shows that Tutsi women as young as 17 years old were raped by soldiers during the months of April and May 1994 in the Butare and Gikongoro *préfectures*. The evidence before the Chamber establishes that Witnesses TM, QY and AFV were raped at various locations in Butare between April and May 1994. In each case, the evidence points to sexual penetration of the victim's vagina under circumstances in which they did not consent to such penetration. Moreover, each of these events took place in the context of widespread attacks against civilians in Butare in 1994. The legal requirements for the offence of rape as a crime against humanity have therefore been satisfied." *But see id.*, para. 526 (finding the Accused not guilty of rape because the Indictment alleged soldiers from the Ngoma Camp committed the rapes, and the evidence at trial was that soldiers from the ESO Camp committed the rapes); *see also Muvunyi,* (Appeals Chamber), August 29, 2008, paras. 160-65 (affirming same).

See also Muhimana, (Trial Chamber), April 28, 2005, paras. 552-54 (rape convictions); *but see Muhimana,* (Appeals Chamber), May 21, 2007, paras. 50-52 (reversing two of the rape convictions); *see also Muhimana,* (Appeals Chamber), Joint Partly Dissenting Opinion of Judge Shahabuddeen and Judge Schomburg, May 21, 2007 (disagreeing with reversals).

See also Kajelijeli, (Trial Chamber), December 1, 2003, paras. 917-25 (detailing how rape as a crime against humanity occurred, but concluding that Article 6(1) and Article 6(3) responsibility were not found regarding the Accused).

But see Kajelijeli, (Trial Chamber), December 1, 2003, Dissenting Opinion Of Judge Arlette Ramaroson, paras. 61, 69, 72, 97-100: Detailing testimony as to rape and showing the Accused's link to various rapes and maintaining he should have been found guilty for instigating, ordering and aiding and abetting rape as a crime against humanity:

"Kajelijeli not only instigated the *Interahamwe*, but he also, by the same token, gave orders to forcefully rape and kill Tutsi women. Following this instigation, Tutsi women were raped at different locations where Kajelijeli was with his *lnterahamwe*, either when he dropped them off at the location or when he sent them there. There is no doubt that in the cases listed earlier, the *lnterahamwe* acted on the orders of Kajelijeli, the more so as he appeared in the immediate vicinity of the sites of the rapes, at the very locations where the rapes took place, or had just left the location."

"The presence of Kajelijeli at the scene of the crime and the fact that he witnessed the rape prove that he abetted and supported the perpetrators of the crime and that he knew that his presence was interpreted by his *Interahamwe* as an encouragement. . . ."

"With regard to *mens rea*, Kajelijeli had the intent and willingness to participate in the commission of rape, and he was quite aware that by his acts (in this case, the act of ordering, instigating the commission of a crime, aiding and abetting the *Interahamwe*), he knowingly contributed to the criminal conduct of his *lnterahamwe*, and he was aware that his participation had a significant effect on the commission of the rape."

"I am convinced that the acts of rape and sexual violence were exclusively perpetrated against Tutsi women (of which only some cases were reported to us) and were committed grounds of their ethnicity. The women were raped on orders from Kajelijeli because they were Tutsi, that is, members of the group that was targeted by the attacks. The reactions of some *Interahamwe* during the rapes prove that too. According to Witness GDF, for example, three *lnterahamwe* who raped her spoke in shocking and contemptuous terms such as: 'Allow me to taste the vagina of a Tutsi woman.' the fourth said 'I cannot fall on a Tutsi [woman]' and jabbed a cigarette stub into her sexual organ and kicked her."

"Rape is a component of the process to destroy the Tutsi ethnic group, especially its mind and its very existence. The intent to destroy the minds and lives of Tutsi women can be inferred from the utterances made by Kajelijeli when he arrived at the location where [Witness] GDO's daughter was raped. GDO was traumatized by the rape of her disabled daughter and still suffers the consequences (...) GDF was also traumatized by the rape that she suffered, and her sister lost her mind due to her own experience. Joyce was raped and killed in an atrocious manner."

"*Rapes were part of a widespread attack.* They were committed throughout Ruhengeri *préfecture* where the *Interahamwe* gang-raped. The victims were found in different locations. These rapes took place at the same time as the genocide."

"I am satisfied beyond a reasonable doubt that (...) Kajelijeli is, pursuant to Article 6(1) of the Statute, criminally responsible for the crime of rape(...)"

ix) persecution on political, racial and religious grounds

1) defined/ actus reus

Nahimana, Barayagwiza and Ngeze, (Appeals Chamber), November 28, 2007, para. 985: "The Appeals Chamber reiterates that 'the crime of persecution consists of an act or omission which discriminates in fact and which: denies or infringes upon a fundamental right laid down in international customary or treaty law (the *actus reus*); and was carried out deliberately with the intention to discriminate on one of the listed grounds, specifically race, religion or politics (the *mens rea*).'" *See also Bagosora, Kabiligi, Ntabakuze and Nsengiyumva,* (Trial Chamber), December 18, 2008, para. 2208 (similar); *Bikindi,* (Trial Chamber), December 2, 2008, para. 435 (similar).

Serugendo, (Trial Chamber), June 12, 2006, para. 10: "The elements of the crime against humanity of persecution under Article 3 (h) of the Statute are described in both the Plea Agreement and the Tribunal jurisprudence as:

- the accused committed specific violations of basic or fundamental rights;
- the specific crimes were committed due to political or racial discrimination;

- the accused had real or constructive knowledge of the general context in which the offences were committed;

- the crimes were committed as part of widespread or systematic attacks against a civilian population; and

- the attacks were carried out on political, ethnic, racial or religious grounds."

Semanza, (Trial Chamber), May 15, 2003, paras. 348-49: "Persecution may take diverse forms and does not necessarily require a physical act." "[P] ersecution may include acts enumerated under other sub-headings of crimes against humanity, such as murder or deportation, when they are committed on discriminatory grounds. Persecution may also involve a variety of other discriminatory acts, not enumerated elsewhere in the Statute, involving serious deprivations of human rights."

Ruggiu, (Trial Chamber), June 1, 2000, para. 21: Quoting the ICTY [in *Kupreskic*], the Trial Chamber "summarized the elements that comprise the crime of persecution as follows: a) those elements required for all crimes against humanity under the Statute, b) a gross or blatant denial of a fundamental right reaching the same level of gravity as the other acts prohibited under Article 5, c) discriminatory grounds."

(a) whether discrimination on ethnic grounds is covered

Bagosora, Kabiligi, Ntabakuze and Nsengiyumva, (Trial Chamber), December 18, 2008, para. 2209: "The enumerated grounds of discrimination for persecution in Article 3 (h) of the Statute do not expressly include ethnic grounds, which is included in the list of discriminatory grounds for the attack contained in the *chapeau* of Article 3. Notwithstanding, the Appeals Chamber in the *Nahimana et al.* case held that discrimination on ethnic grounds could constitute persecution if the accompanying violation of rights was sufficiently serious, such as killings, torture and rape. It affirmed a conviction for persecution based on the supervision of roadblocks where Tutsis were killed." *See Nahimana, Barayagwiza and Ngeze,* (Appeals Chamber), November 28, 2007, paras. 986-88, 1002.

See also Semanza, (Trial Chamber), May 15, 2003, para. 350 ("[T]he enumerated grounds of discrimination for persecution in Article 3(h) (...) do not include national or ethnic grounds, which are included in the list of discriminatory grounds for the attack contained in the chapeau of Article 3.").

(b) persecution also defined in terms of impact

Nahimana, Barayagwiza and Ngeze, (Trial Chamber), December 3, 2003, para. 1073: "[T]he crime of persecution is defined also in terms of impact. It is not a provocation to cause harm. It is itself the harm. Accordingly, there need not be a call to action in communications that constitute persecution. For the same reason, there need be no link between persecution and acts of violence."

(c) persecution is broader than incitement

Nahimana, Barayagwiza and Ngeze, (Trial Chamber), December 3, 2003, para. 1078: "[P]ersecution is broader than direct and public incitement, including advocacy of ethnic hatred in other forms."

(d) not necessary that every act of persecution be of same gravity as other crimes against humanity, but must be cumulatively

Nahimana, Barayagwiza and Ngeze, (Appeals Chamber), November 28, 2007, paras. 987, 985: "[I]t is not necessary that every individual act underlying the crime of persecution should be of a gravity corresponding to other crimes against humanity: underlying acts of persecution can be considered together. It is the cumulative effect of all the underlying acts of the crime of persecution which must reach a level of gravity equivalent to that for other crimes against humanity. Furthermore, the context in which these underlying acts take place is particularly important for the purpose of assessing their gravity." "Furthermore, it is not necessary that these underlying acts of persecution amount to crimes in international law."

Compare Bikindi, (Trial Chamber), December 2, 2008, para. 435: "The underlying acts of persecution, whether considered in isolation or in conjunction with other acts, must be of equal gravity to the crimes listed under Article 3 of the Statute."

2) mens rea: discriminatory intent required

Nahimana, Barayagwiza and Ngeze, (Appeals Chamber), November 28, 2007, para. 985: The *mens rea* for persecution is that the acts are "carried out deliberately with the intention to discriminate on one of the listed grounds, specifically race, religion or politics (the *mens rea*)." *See also Bikindi*, (Trial Chamber), December 2, 2008, para. 435 (same).

Kamuhanda, (Trial Chamber), January 22, 2004, para. 674: "The Chamber notes that a specific discriminatory intent is required for the charge of persecution as Crime against Humanity." *See also Kajelijeli,* (Trial Chamber), December 1, 2003, para. 879 (same).

Nahimana, Barayagwiza and Ngeze, (Trial Chamber), December 3, 2003, para. 1071: "[T]he crime of persecution specifically requires a finding of discriminatory intent on racial, religious or political grounds. The Chamber notes that this requirement has been broadly interpreted by the International Criminal Tribunal for the Former Yugoslavia (ICTY) to include discriminatory acts against all those who do not belong to a particular group."

See also "discriminatory intent not required for acts other than persecution," Section (II)(b)(iv)(2).

(a) discriminatory intent may be inferred

Bagosora, Kabiligi, Ntabakuze and Nsengiyumva, (Trial Chamber), December 18, 2008, para. 2208: "The required discriminatory intent can be inferred from circumstantial evidence, such as the nature of the attack and the circumstances surrounding it."

3) hate speech as persecution

Nahimana, Barayagwiza and Ngeze, (Appeals Chamber), November 28, 2007, para. 986: "The Appeals Chamber considers that hate speech targeting a population on the basis of ethnicity, or any other discriminatory ground, violates the right to respect for the dignity of the members of the targeted group as human beings, and therefore constitutes 'actual discrimination.' In addition, the Appeals Chamber is of the view that speech inciting to violence against a population on the basis of ethnicity, or any other discriminatory ground, violates the right to security of the members of the targeted group and therefore constitutes 'actual discrimination.' However, the Appeals Chamber is not satisfied that hate speech alone can amount to a violation of the rights to life, freedom and physical integrity of the human being. Thus other persons need to intervene before such violations can occur; a speech cannot, in itself, directly kill members of a group, imprison or physically injure them." *See also Nahimana, Barayagwiza and Ngeze,* (Trial Chamber), December 3, 2003, para. 1072.

Nahimana, Barayagwiza and Ngeze, (Appeals Chamber), Partly Dissenting Opinion of Judge Fausto Pocar, November 28, 2007, para. 3: "[T]he Appeal Judgement does not appear to rule definitively on the question whether a hate speech can *per se* constitute an underlying act of persecution. In my opinion, the circumstances of the instant case are, however, a perfect example where a hate speech fulfils the conditions necessary for it to be considered as an underlying act of persecution. Indeed, the hate speeches broadcast on RTLM [*Radio Télévision Libre des Mille Collines*] by Appellant Nahimana's subordinates were clearly aimed at discriminating against the Tutsi and led the population to discriminate against them, thus violating their basic rights. Taken together and in their context, these speeches amounted to a violation of equivalent gravity as other crimes against humanity. Consequently, the hate speeches against the Tutsi that were broadcast after 6 April 1994 – that is, after the beginning of the systematic and widespread attack against this ethnic group – were *per se* underlying acts of persecution." *See also Nahimana, Barayagwiza and Ngeze*, (Appeals Chamber), Partly Dissenting Opinion of Judge Shahabuddeen, November 28, 2007, para. 20 ("where statements are relied upon, the gravity of persecution as a crime against humanity can be established without need for proof that the accused advocated the perpetration of genocide or extermination.").

Bikindi, (Trial Chamber), December 2, 2008, paras. 390-95, 397: "In contrast to the crime of direct and public incitement to commit genocide (...) , hate speech that does not directly call for genocide may, in certain contexts, constitute persecution as a crime against humanity."

"The crime of persecution consists of an act or omission that discriminates in fact and that denies or infringes upon a fundamental right laid down in international customary or treaty law, and was carried out deliberately with the intention to discriminate on one of the listed grounds, specifically race, religion or politics."

"Underlying acts of persecution need not be considered crimes in international law. For example, harassment, humiliation, psychological abuse, as well as denial of the rights of employment, freedom of movement, proper judicial process, and proper medical care have been recognised as underlying acts of persecution. It follows that it is not necessary to find that certain hate speech was in and of itself a crime under international law in order to regard such a speech as an underlying act of persecution. The Chamber is satisfied that hate speech may in certain circumstances constitute a violation of fundamental rights, namely a violation of the right to respect for dignity when that speech incites to hate and discrimination, or a violation of the right to security when it incites to violence."

"The Appeals Chamber [in *Nahimana*] recently recalled that the underlying acts of persecution, whether considered in isolation or in conjunction with other acts, must be of equal gravity to the crimes listed under Article 3 of the Statute. It also held that hate speeches may be considered of equal gravity to the crimes listed under Article 3 of the Statute if they occur as part of a larger campaign of persecution. In its determination, the Appeals

Chamber considered the cumulative effect of all the underlying acts of the crime of persecution, namely the cumulative effect of the hate speeches and the direct calls to commit genocide broadcast in the context of a campaign of anti-Tutsi violence."

"The question remains as to whether hate speech occurring in isolation could be considered to be of equal gravity to the other crimes listed under Article 3. In such a scenario, the hate speech would occur without any other underlying acts of persecution, and as such, would be the only act discriminating against the group. However, given that a widespread or systematic attack against a civilian population on national, political, ethnic, racial or religious grounds would have to be established in order to support a conviction for persecution under the Tribunal's Statute, the Chamber considers that the same facts that would lead it to find the existence of such an attack could also support a finding of many other underlying acts of persecution, as both must be committed on discriminatory grounds."

"Finally, depending on the message conveyed and the context, the Chamber does not exclude the possibility that songs may constitute persecution as a crime against humanity."

"While there is murky ground between some forms of expression, at some point, in the words of Judge Shahabuddeen, '[n]o margin of delicate appreciation is involved.' There are cases that are made up of simple criminality, in which the perpetrators know what they are doing and why they are doing it. These are the cases that will be punished under the Statute, no less."

(a) application—hate speech as persecution

Nahimana, Barayagwiza and Ngeze, (Appeals Chamber), November 28, 2007, paras. 988, 995: "In the present case, the hate speeches made after 6 April 1994 were accompanied by calls for genocide against the Tutsi group and all these speeches took place in the context of a massive campaign of persecution directed at the Tutsi population of Rwanda, this campaign being also characterized by acts of violence (killings, torture and ill-treatment, rapes . . .) and of destruction of property. In particular, the speeches broadcast by RTLM [*Radio Télévision Libre des Mille Collines*] – all of them by subordinates of Appellant Nahimana – , considered as a whole and in their context, were, in the view of the Appeals Chamber, of a gravity equivalent to other crimes against humanity. The Appeals Chamber accordingly finds that the hate speeches and calls for violence against the Tutsi made after 6 April 1994 (thus after the beginning of a systematic and widespread attack against the Tutsi) themselves constituted underlying acts of persecution. In addition, as explained below, some speeches made after

6 April 1994 did in practice substantially contribute to the commission of other acts of persecution against the Tutsi; these speeches thus also instigated the commission of acts of persecution against the Tutsi."

"The acts characterized as acts of genocide committed against the Tutsi also constituted acts of persecution, and hence these broadcasts also instigated the commission of acts of persecution. Furthermore, the Appeals Chamber is of the view that hate speeches and direct calls for genocide broadcast by RTLM after 6 April 1994, while a massive campaign of violence against the Tutsi population was being conducted, also constituted acts of persecution." *But see Nahimana, Barayagwiza and Ngeze*, (Appeals Chamber), Partly Dissenting Opinion of Judge Meron, November 28, 2007, paras. 3-16, 21, 22 ("hate speech" cannot be the basis of a crimes against humanity conviction for persecution; Nahimana's crimes against humanity conviction should be reversed and his sentence reduced).

Compare Bikindi, (Trial Chamber), December 2, 2008, paras. 436-40 (finding that Bikindi's composition of songs to encourage ethnic hatred was not persecution where there was no evidence of him performing or disseminating the songs in 1994).

4) application—persecution

Nahimana, Barayagwiza and Ngeze, (Appeals Chamber), November 28, 2007, paras. 1002, 1010: "The Appeals Chamber considers that murders of Tutsi at the roadblocks after 6 April 1994 (...) constituted acts of persecution. In consequence, it finds that the supervision of roadblocks by the Appellant [Barayagwiza] substantially contributed to the commission of acts of persecution, and it finds the Appellant guilty pursuant to Article 6(1) of the Statute for having instigated persecution." "As the Trial Chamber found, a person who possesses genocidal intent necessarily possesses the intent required for persecution. The Appeals Chamber finds that the Appellant [Ngeze] had the required *mens rea* for persecution. It also finds that, on the basis of the acts committed by the Appellant, he also possessed the intent to instigate others to commit persecution against Tutsi."

Bagosora, Kabiligi, Ntabakuze and Nsengiyumva, (Trial Chamber), December 18, 2008, paras. 2210-16: "The Chamber has found Bagosora, Ntabakuze and Nsengiyumva responsible variously for the killings of Agathe Uwilingiyimana, Joseph Kavaruganda, Frédéric Nzamurambaho, Landoald Ndasingwa, Faustin Rucogoza, Alphonse Kabiligi and Augustin Maharangari as well as of civilians at Kigali area roadblocks between 7 and 9 April, *Centre Christus*, Kabeza, the Kibagabaga Mosque, the Saint Josephite Centre, Karama hill, Kibagabaga Catholic Church, Gikondo Parish, Nyanza hill, IAMSEA [*L'Institut Africain et Mauricien de Statistiques et d'Economie*],

Gisenyi town on 7 April, Mudende University, Nyundo Parish and Bisesero (...)It has also held Bagosora responsible for the rapes committed at Kigali area roadblocks, the Saint Josephite Centre and Gikondo Parish."

"The Chamber has already determined that these crimes formed part of the widespread and systematic attack against civilians on ethnic and political grounds (...)These crimes are also charged in their respective Indictments as persecution."

"In the Chamber's view, these acts of killing and rape equally establish the *actus reus* of persecution. Furthermore, the circumstances surrounding the attacks clearly evince that the perpetrators had the requisite discriminatory intent on ethnic or political grounds. In particular, for many of these crimes, the Chamber has already found that the assailants possessed genocidal intent (...) The assailants and the Accused were aware that these attacks formed part of widespread and systematic attacks against the civilian population on ethnic and political grounds(...)" (Finding Bagosora, Ntabakuze and Nsengiyumva responsible for persecution as a crime against humanity.)

Ruggiu, (Trial Chamber), June 1, 2000, para. 22: In the case at hand, the Trial Chamber discerned "a common element" when examining the acts of persecution admitted to by the accused. "Those acts were direct and public radio broadcasts all aimed at singling out and attacking the Tutsi ethnic group and Belgians on discriminatory grounds, by depriving them of the fundamental rights to life, liberty and basic humanity enjoyed by members of wider society. The deprivation of these rights can be said to have as its aim the death and removal of those persons from the society in which they live alongside the perpetrators, or eventually from humanity itself." (Ruggiu pled guilty to persecution as a crime against humanity.)

See also "application—hate speech as persecution," immediately prior section.

x) other inhumane acts

1) residual category recognized by customary international law/does not violate nullum crimen sine lege

Muvunyi, (Trial Chamber), September 12, 2006, para. 527: "The crime of 'other inhumane acts' encompasses acts not specifically listed as crimes against humanity, but which are nevertheless of comparable nature, character, gravity and seriousness to the enumerated acts in sub-articles (a) to (h) of Article 3. The inclusion of a residual category of crimes in Article 3 recognizes the difficulty in creating an exhaustive list of criminal conduct and the need for flexibility in the law's response. The ICTY Appeals

Chamber recently noted that the crime of 'other inhumane acts' cannot in itself violate the principle of *nullum crimen sine lege certa* as it proscribes conduct which is forbidden under customary international law."[30]

See also Kamuhanda, (Trial Chamber), January 22, 2004, para. 716: "In Kayishema and Ruzindana [*sic*] the Trial Chamber noted that since the Nuremberg Charter, the category 'other inhumane acts' has been maintained as a useful category for acts not specifically stated but which are of comparable gravity."[31] *See also Kajelijeli,* (Trial Chamber), December 1, 2003, para. 931 (same with italics).

2) defined/ actus reus

Bagosora, Kabiligi, Ntabakuze and Nsengiyumva, (Trial Chamber), December 18, 2008, para. 2218: "The crime of inhumane acts is a residual clause for serious acts which are not otherwise enumerated in Article 3. They must be similar in gravity to the acts envisaged in Article 3 and must cause mental or physical suffering or injury or constitute a serious attack on human dignity." *See also Niyitegeka,* (Trial Chamber), May 16, 2003, para. 460 (similar).

Muvunyi, (Trial Chamber), September 12, 2006, para. 527: "The crime of 'other inhumane acts' encompasses acts not specifically listed as crimes against humanity, but which are nevertheless of comparable nature, character, gravity and seriousness to the enumerated acts in sub-articles (a) to (h) of Article 3."

Kamuhanda, (Trial Chamber), January 22, 2004, para. 718: "In Kayishema and Ruzindana [*sic*] the position was summarised that:

[…] for an accused to be has [*sic*] found guilty of Crimes against Humanity for other inhumane acts, he must commit an act of similar gravity and seriousness to the other enumerated crimes(...)" *See also Kajelijeli,* (Trial Chamber), December 1, 2003, para. 933 (same with italics).

Musema, (Trial Chamber), January 27, 2000, para. 232: "[T]he inhumane act or omission must: (a) [b]e directed against member(s) of the civilian population; (b)[t]he perpetrator must have discriminated against the victim(s), on one or more of the enumerated discriminatory grounds; (c) [t]he perpetrator's act or omission must form part of a widespread or systematic attack and the perpetrator must have knowledge of this attack."

Akayesu, (Trial Chamber), September 2, 1998, para. 585: The list of acts enumerated in Article 3(a)-(h) of the Statute is not exhaustive. "Any act which is inhumane in nature and character may constitute a crime against humanity, provided the other elements are met. This is evident in (i) which caters for all other inhumane acts not stipulated in (a) to (h) of Article 3." *See also Rutaganda,* (Trial Chamber), December 6, 1999, para. 77 (similar).

(a) gravity determined on a case-by-case basis

Muvunyi, (Trial Chamber), September 12, 2006, para. 527: The crime of other inhumane acts encompasses crimes "of comparable nature, character, gravity and seriousness to the enumerated acts in sub-articles (a) to (h) of Article 3 (...) Whether an act falls within the ambit of Article 3(i) has to be determined on a case-by-case basis." *See also Kamuhanda,* (Trial Chamber), January 22, 2004, para. 717 (similar); *Kajelijeli,* (Trial Chamber), December 1, 2003, para. 932 (similar); *Niyitegeka,* (Trial Chamber), May 16, 2003, para. 460; *Bagilishema,* (Trial Chamber), June 7, 2001, para. 92 (similar); *Kayishema and Ruzindana,* (Trial Chamber), May 21, 1999, paras. 150-51 (similar).

(b) nexus required

Kamuhanda, (Trial Chamber), January 22, 2004, para. 717: "[T]he Prosecution must prove a nexus between the inhumane act and the great suffering or serious injury to the mental or physical health of the victim." *See also Kajelijeli,* (Trial Chamber), December 1, 2003, para. 932 (same); *Kayishema and Ruzindana,* (Trial Chamber), May 21, 1999, para. 151 (similar).

(c) types of crimes covered

Muvunyi, (Trial Chamber), September 12, 2006, para. 528: "With respect to the *actus reus* of the offence, inhumane acts have been found to include sexual violence, forcible transfer of civilians, mutilation, beatings and other types of severe bodily harm."

Akayesu, (Trial Chamber), September 2, 1998, para. 688: "Sexual violence falls within the scope of 'other inhumane acts,' set forth [in] Article 3(i) of the Tribunal's Statute."

See also discussion of rape and sexual violence as causing serious bodily or mental harm to members of the group under Article 2 (genocide), Section (I)(d)(ii)(3); rape under Article 3 (crimes against humanity), Section (II)(c)(viii); sexual violence as an outrage upon personal dignity under Article 4 (war crimes), Section (III)(d)(v)(1).

(d) third party mental suffering covered

Kayishema and Ruzindana, (Trial Chamber), May 21, 1999, para. 153: "The

Chamber is in no doubt that a third party could suffer serious mental harm by witnessing acts committed against others, particularly against family or friends."

See., e.g., Kamuhanda, (Trial Chamber), January 22, 2004, para. 718: Kayishema and Ruzindana [*sic*] states:

In the Niyitegeka [*sic*] Judgment, Trial Chamber I has found that by perpetrating gross acts of sexual violence upon a dead woman's body, the Accused caused mental suffering to civilians, his actions constituted a serious attack on the human dignity of the Tutsi community as a whole, and that these acts were part of a widespread and systematic attack against the civilian Tutsi population on ethnic grounds." *See also Kajelijeli,* (Trial Chamber), December 1, 2003, para. 933 (same with italics); *see Niyitegeka*, Trial Chamber, May 16, 2003, paras. 316, 465-67 (crime constituted "other inhumane acts").

3) mens rea

(a) generally

Bagosora, Kabiligi, Ntabakuze and Nsengiyumva, (Trial Chamber), December 18, 2008, para. 2218: "The *mens rea* required [for other inhumane acts] is the intent to inflict serious bodily or mental harm upon the victim and the knowledge that the act or omission is part of a widespread and systematic attack."

Muvunyi, (Trial Chamber), September 12, 2006, para. 529: "The act or omission must *deliberately* cause serious mental or physical suffering or injury or constitute a serious attack on human dignity." *See also Bagilishema,* (Trial Chamber), June 7, 2001, para. 92 (similar); *Kayishema and Ruzindana,* (Trial Chamber), May 21, 1999, para. 151 (similar).

Kamuhanda, (Trial Chamber), January 22, 2004, para. 718: Quoting *Kayishema* and *Ruzindana*, [for the crime against humanity of other inhumane acts, the *mens rea* is] "the intention to cause the other inhumane act, (...) with knowledge that the act is perpetrated within the overall context of the attack(...)" *See also Kajelijeli,* (Trial Chamber), December 1, 2003, para. 933 (same); *Kayishema and Ruzindana,* (Trial Chamber), May 21, 1999, paras. 154, 583 (source).

(b) mental state where act causes third party suffering

Muvunyi, (Trial Chamber), September 12, 2006, para. 529: "If the inhumane act is witnessed by a third party, 'an accused may be held [responsible] under these circumstances only where, at the time of the act, the accused had the intention to inflict serious mental suffering on the third party, or where the accused knew that his act was likely to cause serious mental suffering and was reckless as to whether such suffering would result. Accordingly, if at the time of the act, the accused was unaware of the third party bearing witness to his act, then he cannot be held responsible for the mental suffering of the third party.'" *See also Kayishema and Ruzindana,* (Trial Chamber), May 21, 1999, para. 153 (similar).

Compare Kamuhanda, (Trial Chamber), January 22, 2004, para. 717: "Inhumane Acts are only those which deliberately cause suffering. Therefore, where third parties observe acts committed against others, in circumstances in which the Accused may not have had an intention to injure those third parties by their observation of these acts, the Accused may still be held accountable for their mental suffering." *See also Kajelijeli,* (Trial Chamber), December 1, 2003, para. 923 (same).

4) application

Bagosora, Kabiligi, Ntabakuze and Nsengiyumva, (Trial Chamber), December 18, 2008, paras. 2219, 2221-23: "The sole reference in the Indictments to inhumane treatment is the sexual assault of Prime Minister Uwilingiyimana. The Chamber found that a bottle was inserted into her vagina after her death(...)" "However, (...) notice was provided in the Prosecution's Pre-Trial Brief for the prevention of refugees killed at Nyanza hill from seeking sanctuary, the sheparding of Tutsis to Gikondo Parish to be killed in a house of worship, the stripping of women at the Saint Josephite centre and the torture and murder of Alphonse Kabiligi in front of his family."[32]

"The Chamber is satisfied that each of these acts conducted in the course of the attacks against the Prime Minister, Alphonse Kabiligi as well as the civilians at Gikondo Parish, Nyanza hill and the Saint Josephite Centre constitutes a serious attack on human dignity. In the circumstances of the attacks, it is clear that they were perpetrated with the intent to cause serious bodily or mental harm to the victims. The Chamber has already determined that the assailants would have been aware that they formed part of the widespread and systematic attack against the civilian population on ethnic and political grounds(...)" (Concluding Bagosora bore superior responsibility for the crimes against the Prime Minister, Alphonse Kabiligi and the civilians at the Saint Josephite Centre and Gikondo Parish; Ntabakuze bore superior responsibility for the crimes committed during the Nyanza hill massacre; Nsengiyumva bore individual responsibility as to Alphonse Kabiligi.)

Muvunyi, (Trial Chamber), September 12, 2006, para. 530: "The Chamber recalls its factual findings relating to the treatment of [certain witnesses] at the *Économat General*, the Butare Cathedral and at [the] ESO [*École des sous-Officiers* Camp in Butare prefecture], the open humiliation of the two Tutsi women (...) at various roadblocks in Butare, the beatings and injuries caused to Tutsi civilians by ESO soldiers at Beneberika Covent and *Groupe scolaire*, and is satisfied that the treatment meted out to these people by ESO soldiers constitute inhumane treatment within the meaning of Article 3(i) of the Statute. *See also id.*, paras. 426, 436-37, 456 (detailing mistreatement at Butare Cathedral, Beneberika Convent, the *Groupe scolaire*—where orphan children were beaten—and at various roadblocks in Butare and Gikongoro).

Kajelijeli, (Trial Chamber), December 1, 2003, paras. 934-36: "The Chamber found that, at Rwankeri cellule [Mukingo commune, Ruhengeri prefecture] on 7 April 1994, the *Interahamwe* raped and killed a Tutsi woman called Joyce. Furthermore, the Chamber found that they pierced her side and her sexual organs with a spear, and then covered her dead body with her skirt." "The Chamber found that, at Rwankeri cellule on 7 April 1994, a Tutsi girl named Nyiramburanga was mutilated by an *Interahamwe* who cut off her breast and then licked it." "The Chamber finds that these acts constitute a serious attack on the human dignity of the Tutsi community as a whole. Cutting a woman's breast off and licking it, and piercing a woman's sexual organs with a spear are nefarious acts of a comparable gravity to the other acts listed as crimes against humanity, which would clearly cause great mental suffering to any members of the Tutsi community who observed them. Furthermore, given the circumstances under which these acts were committed, the Chamber finds that they were committed in the course of a widespread attack upon the Tutsi civilian population." *But see id.,* paras. 937-39 (Kajelijeli's responsibility for other inhumane acts not proven).

Niyitegeka, (Trial Chamber), May 16, 2003, paras. 465, 467: "[T]he acts committed with respect to Kabanda [decapitation, castration and piercing his skull with a spike] and the sexual violence to the dead woman's body [insertion of a sharpened piece of wood into her genitalia] are acts of seriousness comparable to other acts enumerated in the Article, and would cause mental suffering to civilians, in particular, Tutsi civilians, and constitute a serious attack on the human dignity of the Tutsi community as a whole." "[B]y his act of encouragement during the killing, decapitation and castration of Kabanda, and the piercing of his skull, and his association with the attackers who carried out these acts, and his ordering of Interahamwe to perpetrate the sexual violence on the body of the dead woman, the Accused is (...) responsible for inhumane acts committed as part of a widespread and systematic attack on the civilian Tutsi population on ethnic grounds." (The convictions were affirmed on appeal.)

Akayesu, (Trial Chamber), September 2, 1998, para. 697: Akayesu was "judged criminally responsible under Article 3(i) for the following other inhumane acts: (i) the forced undressing of [a woman] outside the bureau communal, after making her sit in the mud (...) ; (ii) the forced undressing and public marching of [a woman] naked at the bureau communal; (iii) the forced undressing of [three women] and the forcing of the women to perform exercises naked in public near the bureau communal."

Appendix

Convention on the Prevention and Suppression of the Crime of Genocide

Paris, 9 December 1948

Article 1.

The Contracting Parties confirm that genocide, whether committed in time of peace or in time of war, is a crime under international law which they undertake to prevent and to punish.

Article 2.

In the present Convention, genocide means any of the following acts committed with intent to destroy, in whole or in part, a national, ethnical, racial or religious group, as such:
(a) Killing members of the group;
(b)Causing serious bodily or mental harm to members of the group;
(c) Deliberately inflicting on the group conditions of life calculated to bring about its physical destruction in whole or in part;
(d)Imposing measures intended to prevent births within the group;
(e)Forcibly transferring children of the group to another group.

Article 3.

The following acts shall be punishable:
(a)Genocide;
(b)Conspiracy to commit genocide;
(c) Direct and public incitement to commit genocide;
(d)Attempt to commit genocide;
(e)Complicity in genocide.

Article 4.

Persons committing genocide or any of the other acts enumerated in Article III shall be punished, whether they are constitutionally responsible rulers, public officials or private individuals.

Article 5.

The Contracting Parties undertake to enact, in accordance with their respective Constitutions, the necessary legislation to give effect to the provisions of the present Convention, and, in particular, to provide effective penalties for persons guilty of genocide or any of the other acts enumerated in Article III.

Article 6.

Persons charged with genocide or any of the other acts enumerated in Article III shall be tried by a competent tribunal of the State in the territory of which the act was committed, or by such international penal tribunal as may have jurisdiction with respect to those Contracting Parties which shall have accepted its jurisdiction.
Article 7.

Genocide and the other acts enumerated in Article III shall not be considered as political crimes for the purpose of extradition. The Contracting Parties pledge themselves in such cases to grant extradition in accordance with their laws and treaties in force.

Article 8.

Any Contracting Party may call upon the competent organs of the United Nations to take such action under the Charter of the United Nations as they consider appropriate for the prevention and suppression of acts of genocide or any of the other acts enumerated in Article III.

Article 9.

Disputes between the Contracting Parties relating to the interpretation, application or fulfilment of the present Convention, including those relating to the responsibility of a State for genocide or for any of the other acts enumerated in Article III, shall be submitted to the International Court of Justice at the request of any of the parties to the dispute.

Convention on the Non-Applicability of Statutory Limitations to War Crimes and Crimes Against Humanity

Adopted and opened for signature, ratification and accession by General Assembly resolution 2391 (XXIII) of 26 November 1968

Entry into force: 11 November 1970, in accordance with Article VIII

Preamble

The States Parties to the present Convention ,

Recalling resolutions of the General Assembly of the United Nations 3 (I) of 13 February 1946 and 170 (II) of 31 October 1947 on the extradition and punishment of war criminals, resolution 95 (I) of 11 December 1946 affirming the principles of international law recognized by the Charter of the International Military Tribunal, Nürnberg, and the judgement of the Tribunal, and resolutions 2184 (XXI) of 12 December 1966 and 2202 (XXI) of 16 December 1966 which expressly condemned as crimes against humanity the violation of the economic and political rights of the indigenous population on the one hand and the policies of apartheid on the other,

Recalling resolutions of the Economic and Social Council of the United Nations 1074 D (XXXIX) of 28 July 1965 and 1158 (XLI) of 5 August 1966 on the punishment of war criminals and of persons who have committed crimes against humanity,

Noting that none of the solemn declarations, instruments or conventions relating to the prosecution and punishment of war crimes and crimes against humanity made provision for a period of limitation,

Considering that war crimes and crimes against humanity are among the gravest crimes in international law,

Convinced that the effective punishment of war crimes and crimes against humanity is an important element in the prevention of such crimes, the protection of human rights and fundamental freedoms, the encouragement of confidence, the furtherance of co-operation among peoples and the promotion of international peace and security,

Noting that the application to war crimes and crimes against humanity of the rules of municipal law relating to the period of limitation for ordinary crimes is a matter of serious concern to world public opinion, since it prevents the prosecution and punishment of persons responsible for those crimes,

Recognizing that it is necessary and timely to affirm in international law, through this Convention, the principle that there is no period of limitation for war crimes and crimes against humanity, and to secure its universal application,

Have agreed as follows:

Article I

No statutory limitation shall apply to the following crimes, irrespective of the date of their commission:
(a) War crimes as they are defined in the Charter of the International Military Tribunal, Nürnberg, of 8 August 1945 and confirmed by resolutions 3 (I) of 13 February 1946 and 95 (I) of 11 December 1946 of the General Assembly of the United Nations, particularly the "grave breaches" enumerated in the Geneva Conventions of 12 August 1949 for the protection of war victims;
(b) Crimes against humanity whether committed in time of war or in time of peace as they are defined in the Charter of the International Military Tribunal, Nürnberg, of 8 August 1945 and confirmed by resolutions 3 (I) of 13 February 1946 and 95 (I) of 11 December 1946 of the General Assembly of the United Nations, eviction by armed attack or occupation and inhuman acts resulting from the policy of apartheid , and the crime of genocide as defined in the 1948 Convention on the Prevention and Punishment of the Crime of Genocide, even if such acts do not constitute a violation of the domestic law of the country in which they were committed.

Article II

If any of the crimes mentioned in Article I is committed, the provisions of this Convention shall apply to representatives of the State authority and private individuals who, as principals or accomplices, participate in or who directly incite others to the commission of any of those crimes, or who conspire to commit them, irrespective of the degree of completion, and to representatives of the State authority who tolerate their commission.

Article III

The States Parties to the present Convention undertake to adopt all necessary domestic measures, legislative or otherwise, with a view to making possible the extradition, in accordance with international law, of the persons referred to in Article II of this Convention.

Article IV

The States Parties to the present Convention undertake to adopt, in accordance with their respective constitutional processes, any legislative or other measures necessary to ensure that statutory or other limitations shall not apply to the prosecution and punishment of the crimes referred to in Articles I and II of this Convention and that, where they exist, such limitations shall be abolished.

Article V

This Convention shall, until 31 December 1969, be open for signature by any State Member of the United Nations or member of any of its specialized agencies or of the International Atomic Energy Agency, by any State Party to the Statute of the International Court of Justice, and by any other State which has been invited by the General Assembly of the United Nations to become a Party to this Convention.

Article VI

This Convention is subject to ratification. Instruments of ratification shall be deposited with the Secretary-General of the United Nations.

Article VII

This Convention shall be open to accession by any State referred to in Article V. Instruments of accession shall be deposited with the Secretary-General of the United Nations.

Article VIII

1. This Convention shall enter into force on the ninetieth day after the date of the deposit with the Secretary-General of the United Nations of the tenth instrument of ratification or accession.
2. For each State ratifying this Convention or acceding to it after the deposit of the tenth instrument of ratification or accession, the Convention shall enter into force on the ninetieth day after the date of the deposit of its own instrument of ratification or accession.

Article IX

1. After the expiry of a period of ten years from the date on which this Convention enters into force, a request for the revision of the Convention may be made at any time by any Contracting Party by means of a notification in writing addressed to the Secretary-General of the United Nations.
2. The General Assembly of the United Nations shall decide upon the steps, if any, to be taken in respect of such a request.

Article X

This Convention shall be deposited with the Secretary-General of the United Nations.
1. The Secretary-General of the United Nations shall transmit certified copies of this Convention to all States referred to in Article V.
2. The Secretary-General of the United Nations shall inform all States referred to in Article V of the following particulars:
(a) Signatures of this Convention, and instruments of ratification and accession deposited under Articles V, VI and VII;
(b) The date of entry into force of this Convention in accordance with Article VIII;
(c) Communications received under Article IX.

Article XI

This Convention, of which the Chinese, English, French, Russian and Spanish texts are equally authentic, shall bear the date of 26 November 1968.
In witness whereof the undersigned, being duly authorized for that purpose, have signed this Convention.

International Convention on the Suppression and Punishment of the Crime of Apartheid (ICSPCA)

The States Parties to the present Convention,

Recalling the provisions of the Charter of the United Nations, in which all Members pledged themselves to take joint and separate action in co-operation with the Organization for the achievement of universal respect for, and observance of, human rights and fundamental freedoms for all without distinction as to race, sex, language or religion,

Considering the Universal Declaration of Human Rights, which states that all human beings are born free and equal in dignity and rights and that everyone is entitled to all the rights and freedoms set forth in the Declaration, without distinction of any kind, such as race, colour or national origin, Considering the Declaration on the Granting of Independence to Colonial Countries and Peoples, in which the General Assembly stated that the process of liberation is irresistible and irreversible and that, in the interests of human dignity, progress and justice, an end must be put to colonialism and all practices of segregation and discrimination associated therewith,

Observing that, in accordance with the International Convention on the Elimination of All Forms of Racial Discrimination, States particularly condemn racial segregation and apartheid and undertake to prevent, prohibit and eradicate all practices of this nature in territories under their jurisdiction,

Observing that, in the Convention on the Prevention and Punishment of the Crime of Genocide, certain acts which may also be qualified as acts of apartheid constitute a crime under international law,

Observing that, in the Convention on the Non-Applicability of Statutory Limitations to War Crimes and Crimes against Humanity, "inhuman acts resulting from the policy of apartheid" are qualified as crimes against humanity, Observing that the General Assembly of the United Nations has adopted a number of resolutions in which the policies and practices of apartheid are condemned as a crime against humanity,

Observing that the Security Council has emphasized that apartheid and its continued intensification and expansion seriously disturb and threaten international peace and security, Convinced that an International Convention on the Suppression and Punishment of the Crime of Apartheid would make it possible to take more effective measures at the international and national levels with a view to the suppression and punishment of the crime of apartheid, Have agreed as follows:

Article I

1. The States Parties to the present Convention declare that apartheid is a crime against humanity and that inhuman acts resulting from the policies and practices of apartheid and similar policies and practices of racial segregation and discrimination, as defined in Article II of the Convention, are crimes violating the principles of international law, in particular the purposes and principles of the Charter of the United Nations, and constituting a serious threat to international peace and security.

2. The States Parties to the present Convention declare criminal those organizations, institutions and individuals committing the crime of apartheid.

Article II

For the purpose of the present Convention, the term "the crime of apartheid", which shall include similar policies and practices of racial segregation and discrimination as practised in southern Africa, shall apply to the following inhuman acts committed for the purpose of establishing and maintaining domination by one racial group of persons over any other racial group of persons and systematically oppressing them:
a. Denial to a member or members of a racial group or groups of the right to life and liberty of person:
(i) By murder of members of a racial group or groups;
(ii) By the infliction upon the members of a racial group or groups of serious bodily or mental harm, by the infringement of their freedom or dignity, or by subjecting them to torture or to cruel, inhuman or degrading treatment or punishment;
(iii) By arbitrary arrest and illegal imprisonment of the members of a racial group or groups;
b. Deliberate imposition on a racial group or groups of living conditions calculated to cause its or their physical destruction in whole or in part;
c. Any legislative measures and other measures calculated to prevent a racial group or groups from participation in the political, social, economic and cultural life of the country and the deliberate creation of conditions preventing the full development of such a group or groups, in particular by denying to members of a racial group or groups basic human rights and freedoms, including the right to work, the right to form recognized trade unions, the right to education, the right to leave and to return to their country, the right to a nationality, the right to freedom of movement and residence, the right to freedom of opinion and expression, and the right to freedom of peaceful assembly and association;
d. Any measures including legislative measures, designed to divide the population along racial lines by the creation of separate reserves and ghettos for the members of a racial group or groups, the prohibition of mixed marriages among members of various racial groups, the expropriation of landed property belonging to a racial group or groups or to members thereof;
e. Exploitation of the labour of the members of a racial group or groups, in particular by submitting them to forced labour;
f. Persecution of organizations and persons, by depriving them of fundamental rights and freedoms, because they oppose apartheid.

Article III

International criminal responsibility shall apply, irrespective of the motive involved, to individuals, members of organizations and institutions and representatives of the State, whether residing in the territory of the State in which the acts are perpetrated or in some other State, whenever they:
a. Commit, participate in, directly incite or conspire in the commission of the acts mentioned in Article II of the present Convention;
b. Directly abet, encourage or co-operate in the commission of the crime of apartheid.

Article IV

The States Parties to the present Convention undertake:

a. To adopt any legislative or other measures necessary to suppress as well as to prevent any encouragement of the crime of apartheid and similar segregationist policies or their manifestations and to punish persons guilty of that crime;
b. To adopt legislative, judicial and administrative measures to prosecute, bring to trial and punish in accordance with their jurisdiction persons responsible for, or accused of, the acts defined in Article II of the present Convention, whether or not such persons reside in the territory of the State in which the acts are committed or are nationals of that State or of some other State or are stateless persons.

Article V

Persons charged with the acts enumerated in Article II of the present Convention may be tried by a competent tribunal of any State Party to the Convention which may acquire jurisdiction over the person of the accused or by an international penal tribunal having jurisdiction with respect to those States Parties which shall have accepted its jurisdiction.

Article VI

The States Parties to the present Convention undertake to accept and carry out in accordance with the Charter of the United Nations the decisions taken by the Security Council aimed at the prevention, suppression and punishment of the crime of apartheid, and to co-operate in the implementation of decisions adopted by other competent organs of the United Nations with a view to achieving the purposes of the Convention.

Article VII

1. The States Parties to the present Convention undertake to submit periodic reports to the group established under Article IX on the legislative, judicial, administrative or other measures that they have adopted and that give effect to the provisions of the Convention.
2. Copies of the reports shall be transmitted through the Secretary-General of the United Nations to the Special Committee on Apartheid.

Article VIII

Any State Party to the present Convention may call upon any competent organ of the United Nations to take such action under the Charter of the United Nations as it considers appropriate for the prevention and suppression of the crime of apartheid.

Article IX

1. The Chairman of the Commission on Human Rights shall appoint a group consisting of three members of the Commission on Human Rights, who are also representatives of States Parties to the present Convention, to consider reports submitted by States Parties in accordance with Article VII.
2. If, among the members of the Commission on Human Rights, there are no representatives of States Parties to the present Convention or if there are fewer than three such representatives, the Secretary-General of the United Nations shall, after consulting all States Parties to the Convention, designate a representative of the State Party or representatives of the States Parties which are not members of the Commission on Human Rights to take PART in the work of the group established in accordance with paragraph

1 of this Article, until such time as representatives of the States Parties to the Convention are elected to the Commission on Human Rights.
3. The group may meet for a period of not more than five days, either before the opening or after the closing of the session of the Commission on Human Rights, to consider the reports submitted in accordance with Article VII.

Article X

1. The States Parties to the present Convention empower the Commission on Human Rights:
(a) To request United Nations organs, when transmitting copies of petitions under Article 15 of the International Convention on the Elimination of All Forms of Racial Discrimination, to draw its attention to complaints concerning acts which are enumerated in Article II of the present Convention;
(b) To prepare, on the basis of reports from competent organs of the United Nations and periodic reports from States Parties to the present Convention, a list of individuals, organizations, institutions and representatives of States which are alleged to be responsible for the crimes enumerated in Article II of the Convention, as well as those against whom legal proceedings have been undertaken by States Parties to the Convention;
(c) To request information from the competent United Nations organs concerning measures taken by the authorities responsible for the administration of Trust and Non-Self-Governing Territories, and all other Territories to which General Assembly resolution 1514 (XV) of 14 December 1960 applies, with regard to such individuals alleged to be responsible for crimes under Article II of the Convention who are believed to be under their territorial and administrative jurisdiction.
2. Pending the achievement of the objectives of the Declaration on the Granting of Independence to Colonial Countries and Peoples, contained in General Assembly resolution 1514 (XV), the provisions of the present Convention shall in no way limit the right of petition granted to those peoples by other international instruments or by the United Nations and its specialized agencies.

Article XI

1. Acts enumerated in Article II of the present Convention shall not be considered political crimes for the purpose of extradition.
2. The States Parties to the present Convention undertake in such cases to grant extradition in accordance with their legislation and with the treaties in force.

Article XII

Disputes between States Parties arising out of the interpretation, application or implementation of the present Convention which have not been settled by negotiation shall, at the request of the States parties to the dispute, be brought before the International Court of Justice, save where the parties to the dispute have agreed on some other form of settlement.

Article XIII

The present Convention is open for signature by all States. Any State which does not sign the Convention before its entry into force may accede to it.

Article XIV

1. The present Convention is subject to ratification. Instruments of ratification shall be deposited with the Secretary-General of the United Nations.
2. Accession shall be effected by the deposit of an instrument of accession with the Secretary-General of the United Nations.

Article XV

1. The present Convention shall enter into force on the thirtieth day after the date of the deposit with the Secretary-General of the United Nations of the twentieth instrument of ratification or accession.
2. For each State ratifying the present Convention or acceding to it after the deposit of the twentieth instrument of ratification or instrument of accession, the Convention shall enter into force on the thirtieth day after the date of the deposit of its own instrument of ratification or instrument of accession.

Article XVI

A State Party may denounce the present Convention by written notification to the Secretary-General of the United Nations. Denunciation shall take effect one year after the date of receipt of the notification by the Secretary-General.

Article XVII

1. A request for the revision of the present Convention may be made at any time by any State Party by means of a notification in writing addressed to the Secretary-General of the United Nations.
2. The General Assembly of the United Nations shall decide upon the steps, if any, to be taken in respect of such request.

Article XVIII

The Secretary-General of the United Nations shall inform all States of the following particulars:
a. Signatures, ratifications and accessions under Articles XIII and XIV;
b. The date of entry into force of the present Convention under Article XV;
c. Denunciations under Article XVI;
d. Notifications under Article XVII.

Article XIX

1. The present Convention, of which the Chinese, English, French, Russian and Spanish texts are equally authentic, shall be deposited in the archives of the United Nations.
2. The Secretary-General of the United Nations shall transmit certified copies of the present Convention to all States.

Principles of international co-operation in the detection, arrest, extradition and punishment of persons guilty of war crimes and crimes against humanity

Adopted by General Assembly resolution 3074 (XXVIII) of 3 December 1973

The General Assembly,

Recalling its resolutions 2583 (XXIV) of 15 December 1969, 2712 (XXV) of 15 December 1970, 2840 (XXVI) of 18 December 1971 and 3020 (XXVII) of 18 December 1972,

Taking into account the special need for international action in order to ensure the prosecution and punishment of persons guilty of war crimes and crimes against humanity,

Having considered the draft principles of international co-operation in the detection, arrest, extradition and punishment of persons guilty of war crimes and crimes against humanity,

Declares that the United Nations, in pursuance of the principles and purposes set forth in the Charter concerning the promotion of co-operation between peoples and the maintenance of international peace and security, proclaims the following principles of international co-operation in the detection, arrest, extradition and punishment of persons guilty of war crimes and crimes against humanity:

1. War crimes and crimes against humanity, wherever they are committed, shall be subject to investigation and the persons against whom there is evidence that they have committed such crimes shall be subject to tracing, arrest, trial and, if found guilty, to punishment.
2. Every State has the right to try its own nationals for war crimes against humanity.
3. States shall co-operate with each other on a bilateral and multilateral basis with a view to halting and preventing war crimes and crimes against humanity, and shall take the domestic and international measures necessary for that purpose.
4. States shall assist each other in detecting, arresting and bringing to trial persons suspected of having committed such crimes and, if they are found guilty, in punishing them.
5. Persons against whom there is evidence that they have committed war crimes and crimes against humanity shall be subject to trial and, if found guilty, to punishment, as a general rule in the countries in which they committed those crimes. In that connection, States shall co-operate on questions of extraditing such persons.
6. States shall co-operate with each other in the collection of information and evidence which would help to bring to trial the persons indicated in para-graph 5 above and shall exchange such information.
7. In accordance with Article 1 of the Declaration on Territorial Asylum of 14 December 1967, States shall not grant asylum to any person with respect to whom there are serious reasons for considering that he has committed a crime against peace, a war crime or a crime against humanity.
8. States shall not take any legislative or other measures which may be prejudicial to the international obligations they have assumed in regard to the detection, arrest, extradition and punishment of persons guilty of war crimes and crimes against humanity.
9. In co-operating with a view to the detection, arrest and extradition of persons against whom there is evidence that they have committed war crimes and crimes against humanity and, if found guilty, their punishment, States shall act in conformity with the

provisions of the Charter of the United Nations and of the Declaration on Principles of International Law concerning Friendly Relations and Co-operation among States in accordance with the Charter of the United Nations.

Convention against Torture and Other Cruel, Inhuman or Degrading Treatment or Punishment

New York, 10 December 1984

PART I

Article 1

1. For the purposes of this Convention, the term "torture" means any act by which severe pain or suffering, whether physical or mental, is intentionally inflicted on a person for such purposes as obtaining from him or a third person information or a confession, punishing him for an act he or a third person has committed or is suspected of having committed, or intimidating or coercing him or a third person, or for any reason based on discrimination of any kind, when such pain or suffering is inflicted by or at the instigation of or with the consent or acquiescence of a public official or other person acting in an official capacity. It does not include pain or suffering arising only from, inherent in or incidental to lawful sanctions.
2. This Article is without prejudice to any international instrument or national legislation which does or may contain provisions of wider application.

Article 2

1. Each State Party shall take effective legislative, administrative, judicial or other measures to prevent acts of torture in any territory under its jurisdiction.
2. No exceptional circumstances whatsoever, whether a state of war or a threat of war, internal political in stability or any other public emergency, may be invoked as a justification of torture.
3. An order from a superior officer or a public authority may not be invoked as a justification of torture.

Article 3

1. No State Party shall expel, return ("refouler") or extradite a person to another State where there are substantial grounds for believing that he would be in danger of being subjected to torture.
2. For the purpose of determining whether there are such grounds, the competent authorities shall take into account all relevant considerations including, where applicable, the existence in the State concerned of a consistent pattern of gross, flagrant or mass violations of human rights.

Article 4

1. Each State Party shall ensure that all acts of torture are offences under its criminal law. The same shall apply to an attempt to commit torture and to an act by any person which constitutes complicity or participation in torture.
2. Each State Party shall make these offences punishable by appropriate penalties which take into account their grave nature.

Article 5

1. Each State Party shall take such measures as may be necessary to establish its jurisdiction over the offences referred to in Article 4 in the following cases:
(a) When the offences are committed in any territory under its jurisdiction or on board a ship or aircraft registered in that State;
(b)When the alleged offender is a national of that State;
(c) When the victim is a national of that State if that State considers it appropriate.
2. Each State Party shall likewise take such measures as may be necessary to establish its jurisdiction over such offences in cases where the alleged offender is present in any territory under its jurisdiction and it does not extradite him pursuant to Article 8 to any of the States mentioned in paragraph I of this Article.
3. This Convention does not exclude any criminal jurisdiction exercised in accordance with internal law.

Article 6

1. Upon being satisfied, after an examination of information available to it, that the circumstances so warrant, any State Party in whose territory a person alleged to have committed any offence referred to in Article 4 is present shall take him into custody or take other legal measures to ensure his presence. The custody and other legal measures shall be as provided in the law of that State but may be continued only for such time as is necessary to enable any criminal or extradition proceedings to be instituted. 2. Such State shall immediately make a preliminary inquiry into the facts.
3. Any person in custody pursuant to paragraph I of this Article shall be assisted in communicating immediately with the nearest appropriate representative of the State of which he is a national, or, if he is a stateless person, with the representative of the State where he usually resides.
4. When a State, pursuant to this Article, has taken a person into custody, it shall immediately notify the States referred to in Article 5, paragraph 1, of the fact that such person is in custody and of the circumstances which warrant his detention. The State which makes the preliminary inquiry contemplated in paragraph 2 of this Article shall promptly report its findings to the said States and shall indicate whether it intends to exercise jurisdiction.

Article 7

1. The State Party in the territory under whose jurisdiction a person alleged to have committed any offence referred to in Article 4 is found shall in the cases contemplated in Article 5, if it does not extradite him, submit the case to its competent authorities for the purpose of prosecution.
2. These authorities shall take their decision in the same manner as in the case of any ordinary offence of a serious nature under the law of that State. In the cases referred to in Article 5, paragraph 2, the standards of evidence required for prosecution and conviction shall in no way be less stringent than those which apply in the cases referred to in Article 5, paragraph 1.
3. Any person regarding whom proceedings are brought in connection with any of the offences referred to in Article 4 shall be guaranteed fair treatment at all stages of the proceedings.

Article 8

1. The offences referred to in Article 4 shall be deemed to be included as extraditable offences in any extradition treaty existing between States Parties. States Parties undertake to include such offences as extraditable offences in every extradition treaty to be concluded between them.
2. If a State Party which makes extradition conditional on the existence of a treaty receives a request for extradition from another State Party with which it has no extradition treaty, it may consider this Convention as the legal basis for extradition in respect of such offences. Extradition shall be subject to the other conditions provided by the law of the requested State.
3. States Parties which do not make extradition conditional on the existence of a treaty shall recognize such offences as extraditable offences between themselves subject to the conditions provided by the law of the requested State.
4. Such offences shall be treated, for the purpose of extradition between States Parties, as if they had been committed not only in the place in which they occurred but also in the territories of the States required to establish their jurisdiction in accordance with Article 5, paragraph 1.

Article 9

1. States Parties shall afford one another the greatest measure of assistance in connection with criminal proceedings brought in respect of any of the offences referred to in Article 4, including the supply of all evidence at their disposal necessary for the proceedings.
2. States Parties shall carry out their obligations under paragraph I of this Article in conformity with any treaties on mutual judicial assistance that may exist between them.

Article 10

1. Each State Party shall ensure that education and information regarding the prohibition against torture are fully included in the training of law enforcement personnel, civil or military, medical personnel, public officials and other persons who may be involved in the custody, interrogation or treatment of any individual subjected to any form of arrest, detention or imprisonment.
2. Each State Party shall include this prohibition in the rules or instructions issued in regard to the duties and functions of any such person.

Article 11

Each State Party shall keep under systematic review interrogation rules, instructions, methods and practices as well as arrangements for the custody and treatment of persons subjected to any form of arrest, detention or imprisonment in any territory under its jurisdiction, with a view to preventing any cases of torture.

Article 12

Each State Party shall ensure that its competent authorities proceed to a prompt and impartial investigation, wherever there is reasonable ground to believe that an act of torture has been committed in any territory under its jurisdiction.

Article 13

Each State Party shall ensure that any individual who alleges he has been subjected to torture in any territory under its jurisdiction has the right to complain to, and to have his case promptly and impartially examined by, its competent authorities. Steps shall be taken to ensure that the complainant and witnesses are protected against all ill-treatment or intimidation as a consequence of his complaint or any evidence given.

Article 14

1. Each State Party shall ensure in its legal system that the victim of an act of torture obtains redress and has an enforceable right to fair and adequate compensation, including the means for as full rehabilitation as possible. In the event of the death of the victim as a result of an act of torture, his dependants shall be entitled to compensation.
2. Nothing in this Article shall affect any right of the victim or other persons to compensation which may exist under national law.

Article 15

Each State Party shall ensure that any statement which is established to have been made as a result of torture shall not be invoked as evidence in any proceedings, except against a person accused of torture as evidence that the statement was made.

Article 16

1. Each State Party shall undertake to prevent in any territory under its jurisdiction other acts of cruel, inhuman or degrading treatment or punishment which do not amount to torture as defined in Article I, when such acts are committed by or at the instigation of or with the consent or acquiescence of a public official or other person acting in an official capacity. In particular, the obligations contained in Articles 10, 11, 12 and 13 shall apply with the substitution for references to torture of references to other forms of cruel, inhuman or degrading treatment or punishment.
2. The provisions of this Convention are without prejudice to the provisions of any other international instrument or national law which prohibits cruel, inhuman or degrading treatment or punishment or which relates to extradition or expulsion.

PART II

Article 17

1. There shall be established a Committee against Torture (hereinafter referred to as the Committee) which shall carry out the functions hereinafter provided. The Committee shall consist of ten experts of high moral standing and recognized competence in the field of human rights, who shall serve in their personal capacity. The experts shall be elected by the States Parties, consideration being given to equitable geographical distribution and to the usefulness of the participation of some persons having legal experience.
2. The members of the Committee shall be elected by secret ballot from a list of persons nominated by States Parties. Each State Party may nominate one person from among its own nationals. States Parties shall bear in mind the usefulness of nominating persons who are also members of the Human Rights Committee established under the International Covenant on Civil and Political Rights and who are willing to serve on the Committee against Torture.

3. Elections of the members of the Committee shall be held at biennial meetings of States Parties convened by the Secretary-General of the United Nations. At those meetings, for which two thirds of the States Parties shall constitute a quorum, the persons elected to the Committee shall be those who obtain the largest number of votes and an absolute majority of the votes of the representatives of States Parties present and voting.
4. The initial election shall be held no later than six months after the date of the entry into force of this Convention. At. Ieast four months before the date of each election, the Secretary-General of the United Nations shall address a letter to the States Parties inviting them to submit their nominations within three months. The Secretary-General shall prepare a list in alphabetical order of all persons thus nominated, indicating the States Parties which have nominated them, and shall submit it to the States Parties.
5. The members of the Committee shall be elected for a term of four years. They shall be eligible for re-election if renominated. However, the term of five of the members elected at the first election shall expire at the end of two years; immediately after the first election the names of these five members shall be chosen by lot by the chairman of the meeting referred to in paragraph 3 of this Article.
6. If a member of the Committee dies or resigns or for any other cause can no longer perform his Committee duties, the State Party which nominated him shall appoint another expert from among its nationals to serve for the remainder of his term, subject to the approval of the majority of the States Parties. The approval shall be considered given unless half or more of the States Parties respond negatively within six weeks after having been informed by the Secretary-General of the United Nations of the proposed appointment.
7. States Parties shall be responsible for the expenses of the members of the Committee while they are in performance of Committee duties.

Article 18

1. The Committee shall elect its officers for a term of two years. They may be re-elected.
2. The Committee shall establish its own rules of procedure, but these rules shall provide, inter alia, that:
(a) Six members shall constitute a quorum;
(b)Decisions of the Committee shall be made by a majority vote of the members present.
3. The Secretary-General of the United Nations shall provide the necessary staff and facilities for the effective performance of the functions of the Committee under this Convention.
4. The Secretary-General of the United Nations shall convene the initial meeting of the Committee. After its initial meeting, the Committee shall meet at such times as shall be provided in its rules of procedure.
5. The States Parties shall be responsible for expenses incurred in connection with the holding of meetings of the States Parties and of the Committee, including reimbursement to the United Nations for any expenses, such as the cost of staff and facilities, incurred by the United Nations pursuant to paragraph 3 of this Article.

Article 19

1. The States Parties shall submit to the Committee, through the Secretary-General of the United Nations, reports on the measures they have taken to give effect to their undertakings under this Convention, within one year after the entry into force of the Convention for the State Party concerned. Thereafter the States Parties shall submit supplementary reports every four years on any new measures taken and such other reports as the Committee may request.

2. The Secretary-General of the United Nations shall transmit the reports to all States Parties.
3. Each report shall be considered by the Committee which may make such general comments on the report as it may consider appropriate and shall forward these to the State Party concerned. That State Party may respond with any observations it chooses to the Committee.
4. The Committee may, at its discretion, decide to include any comments made by it in accordance with paragraph 3 of this Article, together with the observations thereon received from the State Party concerned, in its annual report made in accordance with Article 24. If so requested by the State Party concerned, the Committee may also include a copy of the report submitted under paragraph I of this Article.

Article 20

1. If the Committee receives reliable information which appears to it to contain well-founded indications that torture is being systematically practised in the territory of a State Party, the Committee shall invite that State Party to co-operate in the examination of the information and to this end to submit observations with regard to the information concerned.
2. Taking into account any observations which may have been submitted by the State Party concerned, as well as any other relevant information available to it, the Committee may, if it decides that this is warranted, designate one or more of its members to make a confidential inquiry and to report to the Committee urgently.
3. If an inquiry is made in accordance with paragraph 2 of this Article, the Committee shall seek the co-operation of the State Party concerned. In agreement with that State Party, such an inquiry may include a visit to its territory.
4. After examining the findings of its member or members submitted in accordance with paragraph 2 of this Article, the Commission shall transmit these findings to the State Party concerned together with any comments or suggestions which seem appropriate in view of the situation.
5. All the proceedings of the Committee referred to in paragraphs I to 4 of th is Article s hall be con fidential , and at all stages of the proceedings the co-operation of the State Party shall be sought. After such proceedings have been completed with regard to an inquiry made in accordance with paragraph 2, the Committee may, after consultations with the State Party concerned, decide to include a summary account of the results of the proceedings in its annual report made in accordance with Article 24.

Article 21

1. A State Party to this Convention may at any time declare under this Article that it recognizes the competence of the Committee to receive and consider communications to the effect that a State Party claims that another State Party is not fulfilling its obligations under this Convention. Such communications may be received and considered according to the procedures laid down in this Article only if submitted by a State Party which has made a declaration recognizing in regard to itself the competence of the Committee. No communication shall be dealt with by the Committee under this Article if it concerns a State Party which has not made such a declaration. Communications received under this Article shall be dealt with in accordance with the following procedure;
(a) If a State Party considers that another State Party is not giving effect to the provisions ofthis Convention, it may, by written communication, bring the matter to the attention of that State Party. Within three months afler the receipt of the communication the receiving State shall afford the State which sent the communication an explanation or any other

statement in writing clarifying the matter, which should include, to the extent possible and pertinent, reference to domestic procedures and remedies taken, pending or available in the matter;
(b)If the matter is not adjusted to the satisfaction of both States Parties concerned within six months after the receipt by the receiving State of the initial communication, either State shall have the right to refer the matter to the Committee, by notice given to the Committee and to the other State;
(c) The Committee shall deal with a matter referred to it under this Article only after it has ascertained that all domestic remedies have been invoked and exhausted in the matter, in conformity with the generally recognized principles of international law. This shall not be the rule where the application of the remedies is unreasonably prolonged or is unlikely to bring effective relief to the person who is the victim of the violation of this Convention;
(d)The Committee shall hold closed meetings when examining communications under this Article;
(e)Subject to the provisions of subparagraph (c), the Committee shall make available its good offices to the States Parties concerned with a view to a friendly solution of the matter on the basis of respect for the obligations provided for in this Convention. For this purpose, the Committee may, when appropriate, set up an ad hoc conciliation commission;
(f) In any matter referred to it under this Article, the Committee may call upon the States Parties concerned, referred to in subparagraph (b), to supply any relevant information;
(g)The States Parties concerned, referred to in subparagraph (b), shall have the right to be represented when the matter is being considered by the Committee and to make submissions orally and/or in writing;
(h)The Committee shall, within twelve months after the date of receipt of notice under subparagraph (b), submit a report:
(i) If a solution within the terms of subparagraph (e) is reached, the Committee shall confine its report to a brief statement of the facts and of the solution reached;
(ii)If a solution within the terms of subparagraph (e) is not reached, the Committee shall confine its report to a brief statement of the facts; the written submissions and record of the oral submissions made by the States Parties concerned shall be attached to the report. In every matter, the report shall be communicated to the States Parties concerned.
2. The provisions of this Article shall come into force when five States Parties to this Convention have made declarations under paragraph 1 of this Article. Such declarations shall be deposited by the States Parties with the Secretary-General of the United Nations, who shall transmit copies thereof to the other States Parties. A declaration may be withdrawn at any time by notification to the Secretary-General. Such a withdrawal shall not prejudice the consideration of any matter which is the subject of a communication already transmitted under this Article; no further communication by any State Party shall be received under this Article after the notification of withdrawal of the declaration has been received by the Secretary-General, unless the State Party concerned has made a new declaration.

Article 22

1. A State Party to this Convention may at any time declare under this Article that it recognizes the competence of the Committee to receive and consider communications from or on behalf of individuals subject to its jurisdiction who claim to be victims of a violation by a State Party of the provisions of the Convention. No communication shall be received by the Committee if it concerns a State Party which has not made such a declaration.

2. The Committee shall consider inadmissible any communication under this Article which is anonymous or which it considers to be an abuse of the right of submission of such communications or to be incompatible with the provisions of this Convention.
3. Subject to the provisions of paragraph 2, the Committee shall bring any communications submitted to it under this Article to the attention of the State Party to this Convention which has made a declaration under paragraph I and is alleged to be violating any provisions of the Convention. Within six months, the receiving State shall submit to the Committee written explanations or statements clarifying the matter and the remedy, if any, that may have been taken by that State.
4. The Committee shall consider communications received under this Article in the light of all information made available to it by or on behalf of the individual and by the State Party concerned.
5. The Committee shall not consider any communications from an individual under this Article unless it has ascertained that:
(a) The same matter has not been, and is not being, examined under another procedure of international investigation or settlement;
(b)The individual has exhausted all available domestic remedies; this shall not be the rule where the application of the remedies is unreasonably prolonged or is unlikely to bring effective reliefto the person who is the victim of the violation of this Convention.
6. The Committee shall hold closed meetings when examining communications under this Article.
7. The Committee shall forward its views to the State Party concerned and to the individual.
8. The provisions of this Article shall come into force when five States Parties to this Convention have made declarations under paragraph 1 of this Article. Such declarations shall be deposited by the States Parties with the Secretary-General of the United Nations, who shall transmit copies thereof to the other States Parties. A declaration may be withdrawn at any time by notification to the Secretary-General. Such a withdrawal shall not prejudice the consideration of any matter which is the subject of a communication already transmitted under this Article; no further communication by or on behalf of an individual shall be received under this Article after the notification of withdrawal of the declaration has been received by the SecretaryGeneral, unless the State Party has made a new declaration.

Article 23

The members of the Committee and of the ad hoc conciliation commissions which may be appointed under Article 21, paragraph I (e), shall be entitled to the facilities, privileges and immunities of experts on mission for the United Nations as laid down in the relevant sections of the Convention on the Privileges and Immunities of the United Nations.

Article 24

The Committee shall submit an annual report on its activities under this Convention to the States Parties and to the General Assembly of the United Nations.

PART III

Article 25

1. This Convention is open for signature by all States.

2. This Convention is subject to ratification. Instruments of ratification shall be deposited with the Secretary-General of the United Nations.

Article 26

This Convention is open to accession by all States. Accession shall be effected by the deposit of an instrument of accession with the Secretary General of the United Nations.

Article 27

1. This Convention shall enter into force on the thirtieth day after the date of the deposit with the Secretary-General of the United Nations of the twentieth instrument of ratification or accession.
2. For each State ratifying this Convention or acceding to it after the deposit of the twentieth instrument of ratification or accession, the Convention shall enter into force onthe thirtieth day after the date of the deposit of its own instrument of ratification or accession.

Article 28

1. Each State may, at the time of signature or ratification of this Convention or accession thereto, declare that it does not recognize the competence of the Committee provided for in Article 20.
2. Any State Party having made a reservation in accordance with paragraph I of this Article may, at any time, withdraw this reservation by notification to the Secretary-General of the United Nations.

Article 29

1. Any State Party to this Convention may propose an amendment and file it with the Secretary-General of the United Nations. The Secretary General shall thereupon communicate the proposed amendment to the States Parties with a request that they notify him whether they favour a conference of States Parties for the purpose of considering an d voting upon the proposal. In the event that within four months from the date of such communication at least one third of the States Parties favours such a conference, the SecretaryGeneral shall convene the conference under the auspices of the United Nations. Any amendment adopted by a majority of the States Parties present and voting at the conference shall be submitted by the Secretary-General to all the States Parties for acceptance.
2. An amendment adopted in accordance with paragraph I of this Article shall enter into force when two thirds of the States Parties to this Convention have notified the Secretary-General of the United Nations that they have accepted it in accordance with their respective constitutional processes.
3. When amendments enter into force, they shall be binding on those States Parties which have accepted them, other States Parties still being bound by the provisions of this Convention and any earlier amendments which they have accepted.

Article 30

1. Any dispute between two or more States Parties concerning the interpretation or application of this Convention which cannot be settled through negotiation shall, at the request of one of them, be submitted to arbitration. If within six months from thc date

of the request for arbitration the Parties are unable to agree on the organization of the arbitration, any one of those Parties may refer the dispute to the International Court of Justice by request in conformity with the Statute of the Court.
2. Each State may, at the time of signature or ratification of this Convention or accession thereto, declare that it does not consider itself bound by paragraph I of this Article. The other States Parties shall not be bound by paragraph I of this Article with respect to any State Party having made such a reservation.
3. Any State Party having made a reservation in accordance with paragraph 2 of this Article may at any time withdraw this reservation by notification to the Secretary-General of the United Nations.

Article 31

1. A State Party may denounce this Convention by written notification to the Secretary-General of the United Nations. Denunciation becomes effective one year after the date of receipt of- the notification by the Secretary-General.
2. Such a denunciation shall not have the effect of releasing the State Party from its obligations under this Convention in regard to any act or omission which occurs prior to the date at which the denunciation becomes effective, nor shall denunciation prejudice in any way the continued consideration of any matter which is already under consideration by the Committee prior to the date at which the denunciation becomes effective.
3. Following the date at which the denunciation of a State Party becomes effective, the Committee shall not commence consideration of any new matter regarding that State.

Article 32

The Secretary-General of the United Nations shall inform all States Members of the United Nations and all States which have signed this Convention or acceded to it of the following:
(a) Signatures, ratifications and accessions under Articles 25 and 26;
(b)The date of entry into force of this Convention under Article 27 and the date of the entry into force of any amendments under Article 29;
(c) Denunciations under Article 31.

Article 33

1. This Convention, of which the Arabic, Chinese, English, French, Russian and Spanish texts are equally authentic, shall be deposited with the Secretary-General of the United Nations.
2. The Secretary-General of the United Nations shall transmit certified copies of this Convention to all States.

Statute Of The International Tribunal For Rwanda

As amended by the Security Council acting under Chapter VII of the Charter of the United Nations, the International Criminal Tribunal for the Prosecution of Persons Responsible for Genocide and Other Serious Violations of International Humanitarian Law Committed in the Territory of Rwanda and Rwandan Citizens responsible for genocide and other such violations committed in the territory of neighbouring States, between 1 January 1994 and 31 December 1994 (hereinafter referred to as "The International Tribunal for Rwanda") shall function in accordance with the provisions of the present Statute.

Article 1Competence of the International Tribunal for Rwanda

The International Tribunal for Rwanda shall have the power to prosecute persons responsible for serious violations of international humanitarian law committed in the territory of Rwanda and Rwandan citizens responsible for such violations committed in the territory of neighbouring States between 1 January 1994 and 31 December 1994, in accordance with the provisions of the present Statute.

Article 2 Genocide

1. The International Tribunal for Rwanda shall have the power to prosecute persons committing genocide as defined in paragraph 2 of this Article or of committing any of the other acts enumerated in paragraph 3 of this Article.
2. Genocide means any of the following acts committed with intent to destroy, in whole or in part, a national, ethnical, racial or religious group, as such:
(a) Killing members of the group;
(b) Causing serious bodily or mental harm to members of the group;
(c) Deliberately inflicting on the group conditions of life calculated to bring about its physical destruction in whole or in part;
(d) Imposing measures intended to prevent births within the group;
(e) Forcibly transferring children of the group to another group.
3. The following acts shall be punishable:
(a) Genocide;
(b) Conspiracy to commit genocide;
(c) Direct and public incitement to commit genocide;
(d) Attempt to commit genocide;
(e) Complicity in genocide.

Article 3 Crimes against Humanity

The International Tribunal for Rwanda shall have the power to prosecute persons responsible for the following crimes when committed as part of a widespread or systematic attack against any civilian population on national, political, ethnic, racial or religious grounds:
(a) Murder;
(b) Extermination;
(c) Enslavement;
(d) Deportation;
(e) Imprisonment;
(f) Torture;
(g) Rape;

(h) Persecutions on political, racial and religious grounds;
(i) Other inhumane acts.

Article 4 Violations of Article 3 Common to the Geneva Conventions and of Additional Protocol II

The International Tribunal for Rwanda shall have the power to prosecute persons committing or ordering to be committed serious violations of Article 3 common to the Geneva Conventions of 12 August 1949 for the Protection of War Victims, and of Additional Protocol II thereto of 8 June 1977. These violations shall include, but shall not be limited to:
(a) Violence to life, health and physical or mental well-being of persons, in particular murder as well as cruel treatment such as torture, mutilation or any form of corporal punishment;
(b) Collective punishments;
(c) Taking of hostages;
(d) Acts of terrorism;
(e) Outrages upon personal dignity, in particular humiliating and degrading treatment, rape, enforced prostitution and any form of indecent assault;
(f) Pillage;
(g) The passing of sentences and the carrying out of executions without previous judgement pronounced by a regularly constituted court, affording all the judicial guarantees which are recognized as indispensable by civilised peoples;
(h) Threats to commit any of the foregoing acts.

Article 5 Personal Jurisdiction

The International Tribunal for Rwanda shall have jurisdiction over natural persons pursuant to the provisions of the present Statute.

Article 6 Individual Criminal Responsibility

1. A person who planned, instigated, ordered, committed or otherwise aided and abetted in the planning, preparation or execution of a crime referred to in Articles 2 to 4 of the present Statute, shall be individually responsible for the crime.
2. The official position of any accused person, whether as Head of state or government or as a responsible government official, shall not relieve such person of criminal responsibility nor mitigate punishment.
3. The fact that any of the acts referred to in Articles 2 to 4 of the present Statute was committed by a subordinate does not relieve his or her superior of criminal responsibility if he or she knew or had reason to know that the subordinate was about to commit such acts or had done so and the superior failed to take the necessary and reasonable measures to prevent such acts or to punish the perpetrators thereof.
4. The fact that an accused person acted pursuant to an order of a government or of a superior shall not relieve him or her of criminal responsibility, but may be considered in mitigation of punishment if the International Tribunal for Rwanda determines that justice so requires.

Article 7 Territorial and Temporal Jurisdiction

The territorial jurisdiction of the International Tribunal for Rwanda shall extend to the territory of Rwanda including its land surface and airspace as well as to the territory of neighbouring States in respect of serious violations of international humanitarian law committed by Rwandan citizens. The temporal jurisdiction of the International Tribunal for Rwanda shall extend to a period beginning on 1 January 1994 and ending on 31 December 1994.

Article 8 Concurrent Jurisdiction

1. The International Tribunal for Rwanda and national courts shall have concurrent jurisdiction to prosecute persons for serious violations of international humanitarian law committed in the territory of Rwanda and Rwandan citizens for such violations committed in the territory of the neighbouring States, between 1 January 1994 and 31 December 1994.
2. The International Tribunal for Rwanda shall have the primacy over the national courts of all States. At any stage of the procedure, the International Tribunal for Rwanda may formally request national courts to defer to its competence in accordance with the present Statute and the Rules of Procedure and Evidence of the International Tribunal for Rwanda.

Article 9 Non Bis in Idem

1. No person shall be tried before a national court for acts constituting serious violations of international humanitarian law under the present Statute, for which he or she has already been tried by the International Tribunal for Rwanda.
2. A person who has been tried before a national court for acts constituting serious violations of international humanitarian law may be subsequently tried by the International Tribunal for Rwanda only if:
(a) The act for which he or she was tried was characterised as an ordinary crime; or
(b) The national court proceedings were not impartial or independent, were designed to shield the accused from international criminal responsibility, or the case was not diligently prosecuted.
3. In considering the penalty to be imposed on a person convicted of a crime under the present Statute, the International Tribunal for Rwanda shall take into account the extent to which any penalty imposed by a national court on the same person for the same act has already been served.

Article 10 Organisation of the International Tribunal for Rwanda

The International Tribunal for Rwanda shall consist of the following organs:
(a) The Chambers, comprising three Trial Chambers and an Appeals Chamber;
(b) The Prosecutor;
(c) A Registry.

Article 11 Composition of the Chambers

1. The Chambers shall be composed of 16 permanent independent judges, no two of whom may be nationals of the same State, and a maximum at any one time of four *ad litem* independent judges appointed in accordance with article 12 *ter*, paragraph 2, of the present Statute, no two of whom may be nationals of the same State.
2. Three permanent judges and a maximum at any one time of four *ad litem* judges shall be members of each Trial Chamber. Each Trial Chamber to which *ad litem* judges are assigned may be divided into sections of three judges each, composed of both permanent and *ad litem* judges. A section of a Trial Chamber shall have the same powers and

responsibilities as a Trial Chamber under the present Statute and shall render judgement in accordance with the same rules.
3. Seven of the permanent judges shall be members of the Appeals Chamber. The Appeals Chamber shall, for each appeal, be composed of five of its members.
4. A person who for the purposes of membership of the Chambers of the International Tribunal for Rwanda could be regarded as a national of more than one State shall be deemed to be a national of the State in which that person ordinarily exercises civil and political rights.

Article 12 Qualification and Election of Judges

The permanent and *ad litem* judges shall be persons of high moral character, impartiality and integrity who possess the qualifications required in their respective countries for appointment to the highest judicial offices. In the overall composition of the Chambers and sections of the Trial Chambers, due account shall be taken of the experience of the judges in criminal law, international law, including international humanitarian law and human rights law.

Article 12 bis Election of Permanent Judges

1. Eleven of the permanent judges of the International Tribunal for Rwanda shall be elected by the General Assembly from a list submitted by the Security Council, in the following manner:
(a) The Secretary-General shall invite nominations for permanent judges of the International Tribunal for Rwanda from States Members of the United Nations and non-member States maintaining permanent observer missions at United Nations Headquarters;
(b) Within sixty days of the date of the invitation of the Secretary-General, each State may nominate up to two candidates meeting the qualifications set out in article 12 of the present Statute, no two of whom shall be of the same nationality and neither of whom shall be of the same nationality as any judge who is a member of the Appeals Chamber and who was elected or appointed a permanent judge of the International Tribunal for the Prosecution of Persons Responsible for Serious Violations of International Humanitarian Law Committed in the Territory of the Former Yugoslavia since 1991 (hereinafter referred to as 'the International Tribunal for the Former Yugoslavia') in accordance with article 13 *bis* of the Statute of that Tribunal;
(c) The Secretary-General shall forward the nominations received to the Security Council. From the nominations received the Security Council shall establish a list of not less than twenty-two and not more than thirty-three candidates, taking due account of the adequate representation on the International Tribunal for Rwanda of the principal legal systems of the world;
(d) The President of the Security Council shall transmit the list of candidates to the President of the General Assembly. From that list the General Assembly shall elect eleven permanent judges of the International Tribunal for Rwanda. The candidates who receive an absolute majority of the votes of the States Members of the United Nations and of the non-member States maintaining permanent observer missions at United Nations Headquarters, shall be declared elected. Should two candidates of the same nationality obtain the required majority vote, the one who received the higher number of votes shall be considered elected.
2. In the event of a vacancy in the Chambers amongst the permanent judges elected or appointed in accordance with this article, after consultation with the Presidents of the Security Council and of the General Assembly, the Secretary-General shall appoint a

person meeting the qualifications of article 12 of the present Statute, for the remainder of the term of office concerned.
3. The permanent judges elected in accordance with this article shall be elected for a term of four years. The terms and conditions of service shall be those of the permanent judges of the International Tribunal for the Former Yugoslavia. They shall be eligible for re-election.

Article 12 ter Election and Appointment of Ad Litem Judges

1. The *ad litem* judges of the International Tribunal for Rwanda shall be elected by the General Assembly from a list submitted by the Security Council, in the following manner:
(a) The Secretary-General shall invite nominations for *ad litem* judges of the International Tribunal for Rwanda from States Members of the United Nations and non-member States maintaining permanent observer missions at United Nations Headquarters;
(b) Within sixty days of the date of the invitation of the Secretary-General, each State may nominate up to four candidates meeting the qualifications set out in article 12 of the present Statute, taking into account the importance of a fair representation of female and male candidates;
(c) The Secretary-General shall forward the nominations received to the Security Council. From the nominations received the Security Council shall establish a list of not less than thirty-six candidates, taking due account of the adequate representation of the principal legal systems of the world and bearing in mind the importance of equitable geographical distribution;
(d) The President of the Security Council shall transmit the list of candidates to the President of the General Assembly. From that list the General Assembly shall elect the eighteen *ad litem* judges of the International Tribunal for Rwanda. The candidates who receive an absolute majority of the votes of the States Members of the United Nations and of the non-member States maintaining permanent observer missions at United Nations Headquarters shall be declared elected;
(e) The *ad litem* judges shall be elected for a term of four years. They shall not be eligible for re-election.
2. During their term, *ad litem* judges will be appointed by the Secretary-General, upon request of the President of the International Tribunal for Rwanda, to serve in the Trial Chambers for one or more trials, for a cumulative period of up to, but not including, three years. When requesting the appointment of any particular *ad litem* judge, the President of the International Tribunal for Rwanda shall bear in mind the criteria set out in article 12 of the present Statute regarding the composition of the Chambers and sections of the Trial Chambers, the considerations set out in paragraphs 1 (b) and (c) above and the number of votes the *ad litem* judge received in the General Assembly.

Article 12 quarter Status of Ad Litem Judges

1. During the period in which they are appointed to serve in the International Tribunal for Rwanda, *ad litem* judges shall:
(a) Benefit from the same terms and conditions of service *mutatis mutandis* as the permanent judges of the International Tribunal for Rwanda;
(b) Enjoy, subject to paragraph 2 below, the same powers as the permanent judges of the International Tribunal for Rwanda;
(c) Enjoy the privileges and immunities, exemptions and facilities of a judge of the International Tribunal for Rwanda.
2. During the period in which they are appointed to serve in the International Tribunal for Rwanda, *ad litem* judges shall not:

(a) Be eligible for election as, or to vote in the election of, the President of the International Tribunal for Rwanda or the Presiding Judge of a Trial Chamber pursuant to article 13 of the present Statute;
(b) Have power:
(i) To adopt rules of procedure and evidence pursuant to article 14 of the present Statute. They shall, however, be consulted before the adoption of those rules;
(ii) To review an indictment pursuant to article 18 of the present Statute;
(iii) To consult with the President of the International Tribunal for Rwanda in relation to the assignment of judges pursuant to article 13 of the present Statute or in relation to a pardon or commutation of sentence pursuant to article 27 of the present Statute;
(iv) To adjudicate in pre-trial proceedings.

Article 13 Officers and Members of the Chambers

1. The permanent judges of the International Tribunal for Rwanda shall elect a President from amongst their number.
2. The President of the International Tribunal for Rwanda shall be a member of one of its Trial Chambers.
3. After consultation with the permanent judges of the International Tribunal for Rwanda, the President shall assign two of the permanent judges elected or appointed in accordance with article 12 *bis* of the present Statute to be members of the Appeals Chamber of the International Tribunal for the Former Yugoslavia and eight to the Trial Chambers of the International Tribunal for Rwanda.
4. The members of the Appeals Chamber of the International Tribunal for the Former Yugoslavia shall also serve as the members of the Appeals Chamber of the International Tribunal for Rwanda.
5. After consultation with the permanent judges of the International Tribunal for Rwanda, the President shall assign such *ad litem* judges as may from time to time be appointed to serve in the International Tribunal for Rwanda to the Trial Chambers.
6. A judge shall serve only in the Chamber to which he or she was assigned.
7. The permanent judges of each Trial Chamber shall elect a Presiding Judge from amongst their number, who shall oversee the work of that Trial Chamber as a whole.

Article 14 Rules of Procedure and Evidence

The Judges of the International Tribunal for Rwanda shall adopt, for the purpose of proceedings before the International Tribunal for Rwanda, the Rules of Procedure and Evidence for the conduct of the pre-trial phase of the proceedings, trials and appeals, the admission of evidence, the protection of victims and witnesses and other appropriate matters of the International Tribunal for the former Yugoslavia with such changes as they deem necessary.

Article 15 The Prosecutor

1. The Prosecutor shall be responsible for the investigation and prosecution of persons responsible for serious violations of international humanitarian law committed in the territory of Rwanda and Rwandan citizens responsible for such violations committed in the territory of neighbouring States, between 1 January 1994 and 31 December 1994.
2. The Prosecutor shall act independently as a separate organ of the International Tribunal for Rwanda. He or she shall not seek or receive instructions from any government or from any other source.

3. The Prosecutor of the International Tribunal for the Former Yugoslavia shall also serve as the Prosecutor of the International Tribunal for Rwanda. He or she shall have additional staff, including an additional Deputy Prosecutor, to assist with prosecutions before the International Tribunal for Rwanda. Such staff shall be appointed by the Secretary-General on the recommendation of the Prosecutor.

Article 16 The Registry

1. The Registry shall be responsible for the administration and servicing of the International Tribunal for Rwanda.
2. The Registry shall consist of a Registrar and such other staff as may be required.
3. The Registrar shall be appointed by the Secretary-General after consultation with the President of the International Tribunal for Rwanda. He or she shall serve for a four-year term and be eligible for re-appointment. The terms and conditions of service of the Registrar shall be those of an Assistant Secretary-General of the United Nations.
4. The Staff of the Registry shall be appointed by the Secretary-General on the recommendation of the Registrar.

Article 17 Investigation and Preparation of Indictment

1. The Prosecutor shall initiate investigations ex-officio or on the basis of information obtained from any source, particularly from governments, United Nations organs, intergovernmental and non-governmental organizations. The Prosecutor shall assess the information received or obtained and decide whether there is sufficient basis to proceed.
2. The Prosecutor shall have the power to question suspects, victims and witnesses, to collect evidence and to conduct on-site investigations. In carrying out these tasks, the Prosecutor may, as appropriate, seek the assistance of the State authorities concerned.
3. If questioned, the suspect shall be entitled to be assisted by Counsel of his or her own choice, including the right to have legal assistance assigned to the suspect without payment by him or her in any such case if he or she does not have sufficient means to pay for it, as well as necessary translation into and from a language he or she speaks and understands.
4. Upon a determination that a *prima facie* case exists, the Prosecutor shall prepare an indictment containing a concise statement of the facts and the crime or crimes with which the accused is charged under the Statute. The indictment shall be transmitted to a judge of the Trial Chamber.

Article 18 Review of the Indictment

1. The judge of the Trial Chamber to whom the indictment has been transmitted shall review it. If satisfied that a *prima facie* case has been established by the Prosecutor, he or she shall confirm the indictment. If not so satisfied, the indictment shall be dismissed.
2. Upon confirmation of an indictment, the judge may, at the request of the Prosecutor, issue such orders and warrants for the arrest, detention, surrender or transfer of persons, and any other orders as may be required for the conduct of the trial.

Article 19 Commencement and Conduct of Trial Proceedings

1. The Trial Chambers shall ensure that a trial is fair and expeditious and that proceedings are conducted in accordance with the Rules of Procedure and Evidence, with full respect for the rights of the accused and due regard for the protection of victims and witnesses.

2. A person against whom an indictment has been confirmed shall, pursuant to an order or an arrest warrant of the International Tribunal for Rwanda, be taken into custody, immediately informed of the charges against him or her and transferred to the International Tribunal for Rwanda.
3. The Trial Chamber shall read the indictment, satisfy itself that the rights of the accused are respected, confirm that the accused understands the indictment, and instruct the accused to enter a plea. The Trial Chamber shall then set the date for trial.
4. The hearings shall be public unless the Trial Chamber decides to close the proceedings in accordance with its Rules of Procedure and Evidence.

Article 20 Rights of the Accused

1. All persons shall be equal before the International Tribunal for Rwanda.
2. In the determination of charges against him or her, the accused shall be entitled to a fair and public hearing, subject to Article 21 of the Statute.
3. The accused shall be presumed innocent until proven guilty according to the provisions of the present Statute.
4. In the determination of any charge against the accused pursuant to the present Statute, the accused shall be entitled to the following minimum guarantees, in full equality:
(a) To be informed promptly and in detail in a language which he or she understands of the nature and cause of the charge against him or her;
(b) To have adequate time and facilities for the preparation of his or her defence and to communicate with counsel of his or her own choosing;
(c) To be tried without undue delay;
(d) To be tried in his or her presence, and to defend himself or herself in person or through legal assistance of his or her own choosing; to be informed, if he or she does not have legal assistance, of this right; and to have legal assistance assigned to him or her, in any case where the interest of justice so require, and without payment by him or her in any such case if he or she does not have sufficient means to pay for it;
(e) To examine, or have examined, the witnesses against him or her and to obtain the attendance and examination of witnesses on his or her behalf under the same conditions as witnesses against him or her;
(f) To have the free assistance of an interpreter if he or she cannot understand or speak the language used in the International Tribunal for Rwanda;
(g) Not to be compelled to testify against himself or herself or to confess guilt.

Article 21 Protection of Victims and Witnesses

The International Tribunal for Rwanda shall provide in its Rules of Procedure and Evidence for the protection of victims and witnesses. Such protection measures shall include, but shall not be limited to, the conduct of in camera proceedings and the protection of the victim's identity.

Article 22 Judgement

1. The Trial Chambers shall pronounce judgements and impose sentences and penalties on persons convicted of serious violations of international humanitarian law.
2. The judgement shall be rendered by a majority of the judges of the Trial Chamber, and shall be delivered by the Trial Chamber in public. It shall be accompanied by a reasoned opinion in writing, to which separate or dissenting opinions may be appended.

Article 23 Penalties

1. The penalty imposed by the Trial Chamber shall be limited to imprisonment. In determining the terms of imprisonment, the Trial Chambers shall have recourse to the general practice regarding prison sentences in the courts of Rwanda.
2. In imposing the sentences, the Trial Chambers should take into account such factors as the gravity of the offence and the individual circumstances of the convicted person.
3. In addition to imprisonment, the Trial Chambers may order the return of any property and proceeds acquired by criminal conduct, including by means of duress, to their rightful owners.

Article 24 Appellate Proceedings

1. The Appeals Chamber shall hear appeals from persons convicted by the Trial Chambers or from the Prosecutor on the following grounds:
(a) An error on a question of law invalidating the decision; or
(b) An error of fact which has occasioned a miscarriage of justice.
2. The Appeals Chamber may affirm, reverse or revise the decisions taken by the Trial Chambers.

Article 25 Review Proceedings

Where a new fact has been discovered which was not known at the time of the proceedings before the Trial Chambers or the Appeals Chamber and which could have been a decisive factor in reaching the decision, the convicted person or the Prosecutor may submit to the International Tribunal for Rwanda an application for review of the judgement.

Article 26 Enforcement of Sentences

Imprisonment shall be served in Rwanda or any of the States on a list of States which have indicated to the Security Council their willingness to accept convicted persons, as designated by the International Tribunal for Rwanda. Such imprisonment shall be in accordance with the applicable law of the State concerned, subject to the supervision of the International Tribunal for Rwanda.

Article 27 Pardon or Commutation of Sentences

If, pursuant to the applicable law of the State in which the convicted person is imprisoned, he or she is eligible for pardon or commutation of sentence, the State concerned shall notify the International Tribunal for Rwanda accordingly. There shall only be pardon or commutation of sentence if the President of the International Tribunal for Rwanda, in consultation with the judges, so decides on the basis of the interests of justice and the general principles of law.

Article 28 Cooperation and Judicial Assistance

1. States shall cooperate with the International Tribunal for Rwanda in the investigation and prosecution of persons accused of committing serious violations of international humanitarian law.
2. States shall comply without undue delay with any request for assistance or an order issued by a Trial Chamber, including but not limited to:
(a) The identification and location of persons;

(b) The taking of testimony and the production of evidence;
(c) The service of documents;
(d) The arrest or detention of persons;
(e) The surrender or the transfer of the accused to the International Tribunal for Rwanda.

Article 29 The Status, Privileges and Immunities of the International Tribunal for Rwanda

The Convention on the Privileges and Immunities of the United Nations of 13 February 1946 shall apply to the International Tribunal for Rwanda, the judges, the Prosecutor and his or her staff, and the Registrar and his or her staff.
The judges, the Prosecutor and the Registrar shall enjoy the privileges and immunities, exemptions and facilities accorded to diplomatic envoys, in accordance with international law.
The staff of the Prosecutor and of the Registrar shall enjoy the privileges and immunities accorded to officials of the United Nations under Articles V and VII of the Convention referred to in paragraph 1 of this article.
Other persons, including the accused, required at the seat or meeting place of the International Tribunal for Rwanda shall be accorded such treatment as is necessary for the proper functioning of the International Tribunal for Rwanda.

Article 30 Expenses of the International Tribunal for Rwanda

The expenses of the International Tribunal for Rwanda shall be expenses of the Organisation in accordance with Article 17 of the Charter of the United Nations.

Article 31 Working Languages

The working languages of the International Tribunal for Rwanda shall be English and French.

Article 32 Annual Report

The President of the International Tribunal for Rwanda shall submit an annual report of the International Tribunal for Rwanda to the Security Council and to the General Assembly.

Statute Of The Special Court For Sierra Leone

Having been established by an Agreement between the United Nations and the Government of Sierra Leone pursuant to Security Council resolution 1315 (2000) of 14 August 2000, the Special Court for Sierra Leone (hereinafter "the Special Court") shall function in accordance with the provisions of the present Statute.

Article 1Competence of the Special Court

1. The Special Court shall, except as provided in subparagraph (2), have the power to prosecute persons who bear the greatest responsibility for serious violations of international humanitarian law and Sierra Leonean law committed in the territory of Sierra Leone since 30 November 1996, including those leaders who, in committing such crimes, have threatened the establishment of and implementation of the peace process in Sierra Leone.
2. Any transgressions by peacekeepers and related personnel present in Sierra Leone pursuant to the Status of Mission Agreement in force between the United Nations and the Government of Sierra Leone or agreements between Sierra Leone and other Governments or regional organizations, or, in the absence of such agreement, provided that the peacekeeping operations were undertaken with the consent of the Government of Sierra Leone, shall be within the primary jurisdiction of the sending State.
3. In the event the sending State is unwilling or unable genuinely to carry out an investigation or prosecution, the Court may, if authorized by the Security Council on the proposal of any State, exercise jurisdiction over such persons.

Article 2 Crimes against humanity

The Special Court shall have the power to prosecute persons who committed the following crimes as part of a widespread or systematic attack against any civilian population:
Murder;
Extermination;
Enslavement;
Deportation;
Imprisonment;
Torture;
Rape, sexual slavery, enforced prostitution, forced pregnancy and any other form of sexual violence;
Persecution on political, racial, ethnic or religious grounds;
Other inhumane acts.

Article 3 Violations of Article 3 common to the Geneva Conventions and of Additional Protocol II

The Special Court shall have the power to prosecute persons who committed or ordered the commission of serious violations of article 3 common to the Geneva Conventions of 12 August 1949 for the Protection of War Victims, and of Additional Protocol II thereto of 8 June 1977. These violations shall include:
- Violence to life, health and physical or mental well-being of persons, in particular murder as well as cruel treatment such as torture, mutilation or any form of corporal punishment;
- Collective punishments;
- Taking of hostages;

- Acts of terrorism;
- Outrages upon personal dignity, in particular humiliating and degrading treatment, rape, enforced prostitution and any form of indecent assault;
- Pillage;
- The passing of sentences and the carrying out of executions without previous judgement pronounced by a regularly constituted court, affording all the judicial guarantees which are recognized as indispensable by civilized peoples;
- Threats to commit any of the foregoing acts.

Article 4 Other serious violations of international humanitarian law

The Special Court shall have the power to prosecute persons who committed the following serious violations of international humanitarian law:
- Intentionally directing attacks against the civilian population as such or against individual civilians not taking direct part in hostilities;
- Intentionally directing attacks against personnel, installations, material, units or vehicles involved in a humanitarian assistance or peacekeeping mission in accordance with the Charter of the United Nations, as long as they are entitled to the protection given to civilians or civilian objects under the international law of armed conflict;
- Conscripting or enlisting children under the age of 15 years into armed forces or groups or using them to participate actively in hostilities.

Article 5 Crimes under Sierra Leonean law

The Special Court shall have the power to prosecute persons who have committed the following crimes under Sierra Leonean law:
- Offences relating to the abuse of girls under the Prevention of Cruelty to Children Act, 1926 (Cap. 31):
i. Abusing a girl under 13 years of age, contrary to section 6;
ii. Abusing a girl between 13 and 14 years of age, contrary to section 7;
iii. Abduction of a girl for immoral purposes, contrary to section 12.
- Offences relating to the wanton destruction of property under the Malicious Damage Act, 1861:
i. Setting fire to dwelling - houses, any person being therein, contrary to section 2;
ii. Setting fire to public buildings, contrary to sections 5 and 6;
iii. Setting fire to other buildings, contrary to section 6.

Article 6 Individual criminal responsibility

1. A person who planned, instigated, ordered, committed or otherwise aided and abetted in the planning, preparation or execution of a crime referred to in articles 2 to 4 of the present Statute shall be individually responsible for the crime.
2. The official position of any accused persons, whether as Head of State or Government or as a responsible government official, shall not relieve such person of criminal responsibility nor mitigate punishment.
3. The fact that any of the acts referred to in articles 2 to 4 of the present Statute was committed by a subordinate does not relieve his or her superior of criminal responsibility if he or she knew or had reason to know that the subordinate was about to commit such acts or had done so and the superior had failed to take the necessary and reasonable measures to prevent such acts or to punish the perpetrators thereof.

4. The fact that an accused person acted pursuant to an order of a Government or of a superior shall not relieve him or her of criminal responsibility, but may be considered in mitigation of punishment if the Special Court determines that justice so requires.
5. Individual criminal responsibility for the crimes referred to in article 5 shall be determined in accordance with the respective laws of Sierra Leone.

Article 7 Jurisdiction over persons of 15 years of age

1. The Special Court shall have no jurisdiction over any person who was under the age of 15 at the time of the alleged commission of the crime. Should any person who was at the time of the alleged commission of the crime between 15 and 18 years of age come before the Court, he or she shall be treated with dignity and a sense of worth, taking into account his or her young age and the desirability of promoting his or her rehabilitation, reintegration into and assumption of a constructive role in society, and in accordance with international human rights standards, in particular the rights of the child.
2. In the disposition of a case against a juvenile offender, the Special Court shall order any of the following: care guidance and supervision orders, community service orders, counselling, foster care, correctional, educational and vocational training programmes, approved schools and, as appropriate, any programmes of disarmament, demobilization and reintegration or programmes of child protection agencies.

Article 8 Concurrent jurisdiction

1. The Special Court and the national courts of Sierra Leone shall have concurrent jurisdiction.
2. The Special Court shall have primacy over the national courts of Sierra Leone. At any stage of the procedure, the Special Court may formally request a national court to defer to its competence in accordance with the present Statute and the Rules of Procedure and Evidence.

Article 9 Non bis in idem

1. No person shall be tried before a national court of Sierra Leone for acts for which he or she has already been tried by the Special Court.
2. A person who has been tried by a national court for the acts referred to in articles 2 to 4 of the present Statute may be subsequently tried by the Special Court if:
- The act for which he or she was tried was characterized as an ordinary crime; or
- The national court proceedings were not impartial or independent, were designed to shield the accused from international criminal responsibility or the case was not diligently prosecuted.

3. In considering the penalty to be imposed on a person convicted of a crime under the present Statute, the Special Court shall take into account the extent to which any penalty imposed by a national court on the same person for the same act has already been served.

Article 10 Amnesty

An amnesty granted to any person falling within the jurisdiction of the Special Court in respect of the crimes referred to in articles 2 to 4 of the present Statute shall not be a bar to prosecution.

Article 11 Organization of the Special Court

The Special Court shall consist of the following organs:
- The Chambers, comprising one or more Trial Chambers and an Appeals Chamber;
- The Prosecutor; and
- The Registry.

Article 12 Composition of the Chambers

1. The Chambers shall be composed of not less than eight (8) or more than eleven (11) independent judges, who shall serve as follows:
- Three judges shall serve in the Trial Chamber, of whom one shall be a judge appointed by the Government of Sierra Leone, and two judges appointed by the Secretary-General of the United Nations (hereinafter "the Secretary-General").
- Five judges shall serve in the Appeals Chamber, of whom two shall be judges appointed by the Government of Sierra Leone, and three judges appointed by the Secretary-General.
2. Each judge shall serve only in the Chamber to which he or she has been appointed.
3. The judges of the Appeals Chamber and the judges of the Trial Chamber, respectively, shall elect a presiding judge who shall conduct the proceedings in the Chamber to which he or she was elected. The presiding judge of the Appeals Chamber shall be the President of the Special Court.
4. If, at the request of the President of the Special Court, an alternate judge or judges have been appointed by the Government of Sierra Leone or the Secretary-General, the presiding judge of a Trial Chamber or the Appeals Chamber shall designate such an alternate judge to be present at each stage of the trial and to replace a judge if that judge is unable to continue sitting.

Article 13 Qualification and appointment of judges

1. The judges shall be persons of high moral character, impartiality and integrity who possess the qualifications required in their respective countries for appointment to the highest judicial offices. They shall be independent in the performance of their functions, and shall not accept or seek instructions from any Government or any other source.
2. In the overall composition of the Chambers, due account shall be taken of the experience of the judges in international law, including international humanitarian law and human rights law, criminal law and juvenile justice.
3. The judges shall be appointed for a three-year period and shall be eligible for reappointment.

Article 14 Rules of Procedure and Evidence

1. The Rules of Procedure and Evidence of the International Criminal Tribunal for Rwanda obtaining at the time of the establishment of the Special Court shall be applicable *mutatis mutandis* to the conduct of the legal proceedings before the Special Court.
2. The judges of the Special Court as a whole may amend the Rules of Procedure and Evidence or adopt additional rules where the applicable Rules do not, or do not adequately, provide for a specific situation. In so doing, they may be guided, as appropriate, by the Criminal Procedure Act, 1965, of Sierra Leone.

Article 15 The Prosecutor

1. The Prosecutor shall be responsible for the investigation and prosecution of persons who bear the greatest responsibility for serious violations of international humanitarian law and crimes under Sierra Leonean law committed in the territory of Sierra Leone since 30 November 1996. The Prosecutor shall act independently as a separate organ of the Special Court. He or she shall not seek or receive instructions from any Government or from any other source.
2. The Office of the Prosecutor shall have the power to question suspects, victims and witnesses, to collect evidence and to conduct on-site investigations. In carrying out these tasks, the Prosecutor shall, as appropriate, be assisted by the Sierra Leonean authorities concerned.
3. The Prosecutor shall be appointed by the Secretary-General for a three-year term and shall be eligible for re-appointment. He or she shall be of high moral character and possess the highest level of professional competence, and have extensive experience in the conduct of investigations and prosecutions of criminal cases.
4. The Prosecutor shall be assisted by a Sierra Leonean Deputy Prosecutor, and by such other Sierra Leonean and international staff as may be required to perform the functions assigned to him or her effectively and efficiently. Given the nature of the crimes committed and the particular sensitivities of girls, young women and children victims of rape, sexual assault, abduction and slavery of all kinds, due consideration should be given in the appointment of staff to the employment of prosecutors and investigators experienced in gender-related crimes and juvenile justice.
5. In the prosecution of juvenile offenders, the Prosecutor shall ensure that the child-rehabilitation programme is not placed at risk and that, where appropriate, resort should be had to alternative truth and reconciliation mechanisms, to the extent of their availability.

Article 16 The Registry

1. The Registry shall be responsible for the administration and servicing of the Special Court.
2. The Registry shall consist of a Registrar and such other staff as may be required.
3. The Registrar shall be appointed by the Secretary-General after consultation with the President of the Special Court and shall be a staff member of the United Nations. He or she shall serve for a three-year term and be eligible for re-appointment.
4. The Registrar shall set up a Victims and Witnesses Unit within the Registry. This Unit shall provide, in consultation with the Office of the Prosecutor, protective measures and security arrangements, counselling and other appropriate assistance for witnesses, victims who appear before the Court and others who are at risk on account of testimony given by such witnesses. The Unit personnel shall include experts in trauma, including trauma related to crimes of sexual violence and violence against children.

Article 17 Rights of the accused

1. All accused shall be equal before the Special Court.
2. The accused shall be entitled to a fair and public hearing, subject to measures ordered by the Special Court for the protection of victims and witnesses.
3. The accused shall be presumed innocent until proved guilty according to the provisions of the present Statute.
4. In the determination of any charge against the accused pursuant to the present Statute, he or she shall be entitled to the following minimum guarantees, in full equality:

- To be informed promptly and in detail in a language which he or she understands of the nature and cause of the charge against him or her;
- To have adequate time and facilities for the preparation of his or her defence and to communicate with counsel of his or her own choosing;
- To be tried without undue delay;
- To be tried in his or her presence, and to defend himself or herself in person or through legal assistance of his or her own choosing; to be informed, if he or she does not have legal assistance, of this right; and to have legal assistance assigned to him or her, in any case where the interests of justice so require, and without payment by him or her in any such case if he or she does not have sufficient means to pay for it;
- To examine, or have examined, the witnesses against him or her and to obtain the attendance and examination of witnesses on his or her behalf under the same conditions as witnesses against him or her;
- To have the free assistance of an interpreter if he or she cannot understand or speak the language used in the Special Court;
- Not to be compelled to testify against himself or herself or to confess guilt.

Article 18 Judgement

The judgement shall be rendered by a majority of the judges of the Trial Chamber or of the Appeals Chamber, and shall be delivered in public. It shall be accompanied by a reasoned opinion in writing, to which separate or dissenting opinions may be appended.

Article 19 Penalties

1. The Trial Chamber shall impose upon a convicted person, other than a juvenile offender, imprisonment for a specified number of years. In determining the terms of imprisonment, the Trial Chamber shall, as appropriate, have recourse to the practice regarding prison sentences in the International Criminal Tribunal for Rwanda and the national courts of Sierra Leone.
2. In imposing the sentences, the Trial Chamber should take into account such factors as the gravity of the offence and the individual circumstances of the convicted person.
3. In addition to imprisonment, the Trial Chamber may order the forfeiture of the property, proceeds and any assets acquired unlawfully or by criminal conduct, and their return to their rightful owner or to the State of Sierra Leone.

Article 20 Appellate proceedings

1. The Appeals Chamber shall hear appeals from persons convicted by the Trial Chamber or from the Prosecutor on the following grounds:
- A procedural error;
- An error on a question of law invalidating the decision;
- An error of fact which has occasioned a miscarriage of justice.
2. The Appeals Chamber may affirm, reverse or revise the decisions taken by the Trial Chamber.
3. The judges of the Appeals Chamber of the Special Court shall be guided by the decisions of the Appeals Chamber of the International Tribunals for the former Yugoslavia and for Rwanda. In the interpretation and application of the laws of Sierra Leone, they shall be guided by the decisions of the Supreme Court of Sierra Leone.

Article 21 Review proceedings

1. Where a new fact has been discovered which was not known at the time of the proceedings before the Trial Chamber or the Appeals Chamber and which could have been a decisive factor in reaching the decision, the convicted person or the Prosecutor may submit an application for review of the judgement.
2. An application for review shall be submitted to the Appeals Chamber. The Appeals Chamber may reject the application if it considers it to be unfounded. If it determines that the application is meritorious, it may, as appropriate:
- Reconvene the Trial Chamber;
- Retain jurisdiction over the matter.

Article 22 Enforcement of sentences

1. Imprisonment shall be served in Sierra Leone. If circumstances so require, imprisonment may also be served in any of the States which have concluded with the International Criminal Tribunal for Rwanda or the International Criminal Tribunal for the former Yugoslavia an agreement for the enforcement of sentences, and which have indicated to the Registrar of the Special Court their willingness to accept convicted persons. The Special Court may conclude similar agreements for the enforcement of sentences with other States.
2. Conditions of imprisonment, whether in Sierra Leone or in a third State, shall be governed by the law of the State of enforcement subject to the supervision of the Special Court. The State of enforcement shall be bound by the duration of the sentence, subject to article 23 of the present Statute.

Article 23 Pardon or commutation of sentences

If, pursuant to the applicable law of the State in which the convicted person is imprisoned, he or she is eligible for pardon or commutation of sentence, the State concerned shall notify the Special Court accordingly. There shall only be pardon or commutation of sentence if the President of the Special Court, in consultation with the judges, so decides on the basis of the interests of justice and the general principles of law.

Article 24 Working language

The working language of the Special Court shall be English.

Article 25 Annual Report

The President of the Special Court shall submit an annual report on the operation and activities of the Court to the Secretary-General and to the Government of Sierra Leone.

Statute of the International Criminal Tribunal for the former Yugoslavia[1]

Having been established by the Security Council acting under Chapter VII of the Charter of the United Nations, the International Tribunal for the Prosecution of Persons Responsible for Serious Violations of International Humanitarian Law Committed in the Territory of the Former Yugoslavia since 1991 (hereinafter referred to as "the International Tribunal") shall function in accordance with the provisions of the present Statute.

Article 1 Competence of the International Tribunal

The International Tribunal shall have the power to prosecute persons responsible for serious violations of international humanitarian law committed in the territory of the former Yugoslavia since 1991 in accordance with the provisions of the present Statute.

Article 2 Grave breaches of the Geneva Conventions of 1949

The International Tribunal shall have the power to prosecute persons committing or ordering to be committed grave breaches of the Geneva Conventions of 12 August 1949, namely the following acts against persons or property protected under the provisions of the relevant Geneva Convention:
(a) willful killing;
(b) torture or inhuman treatment, including biological experiments;
(c) willfully causing great suffering or serious injury to body or health;
(d) extensive destruction and appropriation of property, not justified by military necessity and carried out unlawfully and wantonly;
(e) compelling a prisoner of war or a civilian to serve in the forces of a hostile power;
(f) willfully depriving a prisoner of war or a civilian of the rights of fair and regular trial;
(g) unlawful deportation or transfer or unlawful confinement of a civilian;
(h) taking civilians as hostages.

Article 3 Violations of the laws or customs of war

The International Tribunal shall have the power to prosecute persons violating the laws or customs of war. Such violations shall include, but not be limited to:
(a) employment of poisonous weapons or other weapons calculated to cause unnecessary suffering;
(b) wanton destruction of cities, towns or villages, or devastation not justified by military necessity;
(c) attack, or bombardment, by whatever means, of undefended towns, villages, dwellings, or buildings;
(d) seizure of, destruction or willful damage done to institutions dedicated to religion, charity and education, the arts and sciences, historic monuments and works of art and science;
(e) plunder of public or private property.

1 As amended 29 September 2008 by Resolution 1837.

Article 4 Genocide

1. The International Tribunal shall have the power to prosecute persons committing genocide as defined in paragraph 2 of this article or of committing any of the other acts enumerated in paragraph 3 of this article.
2. Genocide means any of the following acts committed with intent to destroy, in whole or in part, a national, ethnical, racial or religious group, as such:
(a) killing members of the group;
(b) causing serious bodily or mental harm to members of the group; 6
(c) deliberately inflicting on the group conditions of life calculated to bring about its physical destruction in whole or in part;
(d) imposing measures intended to prevent births within the group;
(e) forcibly transferring children of the group to another group.
3. The following acts shall be punishable:
(a) genocide;
(b) conspiracy to commit genocide;
(c) direct and public incitement to commit genocide;
(d) attempt to commit genocide;
(e) complicity in genocide.

Article 5 Crimes against humanity

The International Tribunal shall have the power to prosecute persons responsible for the following crimes when committed in armed conflict, whether international or internal in character, and directed against any civilian population:
(a) murder;
(b) extermination;
(c) enslavement;
(d) deportation;
(e) imprisonment;
(f) torture;
(g) rape;
(h) persecutions on political, racial and religious grounds;
(i) other inhumane acts.

Article 6 Personal jurisdiction

The International Tribunal shall have jurisdiction over natural persons pursuant to the provisions of the present Statute.

Article 7 Individual criminal responsibility

1. A person who planned, instigated, ordered, committed or otherwise aided and abetted in the planning, preparation or execution of a crime referred to in articles 2 to 5 of the present Statute, shall be individually responsible for the crime.
2. The official position of any accused person, whether as Head of State or Government or as a responsible Government official, shall not relieve such person of criminal responsibility nor mitigate punishment.
3. The fact that any of the acts referred to in articles 2 to 5 of the present Statute was committed by a subordinate does not relieve his superior of criminal responsibility if he knew or had reason to know that the subordinate was about to commit such acts or had

done so and the superior failed to take the necessary and reasonable measures to prevent such acts or to punish the perpetrators thereof.
4. The fact that an accused person acted pursuant to an order of a Government or of a superior shall not relieve him of criminal responsibility, but may be considered in mitigation of punishment if the International Tribunal determines that justice so requires.

Article 8 Territorial and temporal jurisdiction

The territorial jurisdiction of the International Tribunal shall extend to the territory of the former Socialist Federal Republic of Yugoslavia, including its land surface, airspace and territorial waters. The temporal jurisdiction of the International Tribunal shall extend to a period beginning on 1 January 1991.

Article 9 Concurrent jurisdiction

1. The International Tribunal and national courts shall have concurrent jurisdiction to prosecute persons for serious violations of international humanitarian law committed in the territory of the former Yugoslavia since 1 January 1991.
2. The International Tribunal shall have primacy over national courts. At any stage of the procedure, the International Tribunal may formally request national courts to defer to the competence of the International Tribunal in accordance with the present Statute and the Rules of Procedure and Evidence of the International Tribunal.

Article 10 Non-bis-in-idem

1. No person shall be tried before a national court for acts constituting serious violations of international humanitarian law under the present Statute, for which he or she has already been tried by the International Tribunal.
2. A person who has been tried by a national court for acts constituting serious violations of international humanitarian law may be subsequently tried by the International Tribunal only if:
(a) the act for which he or she was tried was characterized as an ordinary crime; or
(b) the national court proceedings were not impartial or independent, were designed to shield the accused from international criminal responsibility, or the case was not diligently prosecuted.
3. In considering the penalty to be imposed on a person convicted of a crime under the present Statute, the International Tribunal shall take into account the extent to which any penalty imposed by a national court on the same person for the same act has already been served.

Article 11 Organization of the International Tribunal

The International Tribunal shall consist of the following organs:
(a) the Chambers, comprising three Trial Chambers and an Appeals Chamber;
(b) the Prosecutor; and
(c) a Registry, servicing both the Chambers and the Prosecutor.

Article 12 Composition of the Chambers

1. The Chambers shall be composed of a maximum of sixteen permanent independent judges, no two of whom may be nationals of the same State, and a maximum at any one

time of twelve *ad litem* independent judges appointed in accordance with article 13 *ter*, paragraph 2, of the Statute, no two of whom may be nationals of the same State.
2. A maximum at any one time of three permanent judges and six *ad litem* judges shall be members of each Trial Chamber. Each Trial Chamber to which *ad litem* judges are assigned may be divided into sections of three judges each, composed of both permanent and *ad litem* judges, except in the circumstances specified in paragraph 5 below. A section of a Trial Chamber shall have the same powers and responsibilities as a Trial Chamber under the Statute and shall render judgement in accordance with the same rules.
3. Seven of the permanent judges shall be members of the Appeals Chamber. The Appeals Chamber shall, for each appeal, be composed of five of its members.
4. A person who for the purposes of membership of the Chambers of the International Tribunal could be regarded as a national of more than one State shall be deemed to be a national of the State in which that person ordinarily exercises civil and political rights.
5. The Secretary-General may, at the request of the President of the International Tribunal appoint, from among the *ad litem* judges elected in accordance with Article 13 *ter*, reserve judges to be present at each stage of a trial to which they have been appointed and to replace a judge if that judge is unable to continue sitting.
6. Without prejudice to paragraph 2 above, in the event that exceptional circumstances require for a permanent judge in a section of a Trial Chamber to be replaced resulting in a section solely comprised of *ad litem* judges, that section may continue to hear the case, notwithstanding that its composition no longer includes a permanent judge.

Article 13 Qualifications of judges

The permanent and *ad litem* judges shall be persons of high moral character, impartiality and integrity who possess the qualifications required in their respective countries for appointment to the highest judicial offices. In the overall composition of the Chambers and sections of the Trial Chambers, due account shall be taken of the experience of the judges in criminal law, international law, including international humanitarian law and human rights law.

Article 13 bis **Election of permanent judges**

1. Fourteen of the permanent judges of the International Tribunal shall be elected by the General Assembly from a list submitted by the Security Council, in the following manner:
(a) The Secretary-General shall invite nominations for judges of the International Tribunal from States Members of the United Nations and non-member States maintaining permanent observer missions at United Nations Headquarters;
(b) Within sixty days of the date of the invitation of the Secretary-General, each State may nominate up to two candidates meeting the qualifications set out in article 13 of the Statute, no two of whom shall be of the same nationality and neither of whom shall be of the same nationality as any judge who is a member of the Appeals Chamber and who was elected or appointed a permanent judge of the International Criminal Tribunal for the Prosecution of Persons Responsible for Genocide and Other Serious Violations of International Humanitarian Law Committed in the Territory of Rwanda and Rwandan Citizens Responsible for Genocide and Other Such Violations Committed in the Territory of Neighbouring States, between 1 January 1994 and 31 December 1994 (hereinafter referred to as "The International Tribunal for Rwanda") in accordance with article 12 *bis* of the Statute of that Tribunal;
(c) The Secretary-General shall forward the nominations received to the Security Council. From the nominations received the Security Council shall establish a list of not

less than twenty-eight and not more than forty-two candidates, taking due account of the adequate representation of the principal legal systems of the world;
(d) The President of the Security Council shall transmit the list of candidates to the President of the General Assembly. From that list the General Assembly shall elect fourteen permanent judges of the International Tribunal. The candidates who receive an absolute majority of the votes of the States Members of the United Nations and of the non-member States maintaining permanent observer missions at United Nations Headquarters, shall be declared elected. Should two candidates of the same nationality obtain the required majority vote, the one who received the higher number of votes shall be considered elected.
2. In the event of a vacancy in the Chambers amongst the permanent judges elected or appointed in accordance with this article, after consultation with the Presidents of the Security Council and of the General Assembly, the Secretary-General shall appoint a person meeting the qualifications of article 13 of the Statute, for the remainder of the term of office concerned.
3. The permanent judges elected in accordance with this article shall be elected for a term of four years. The terms and conditions of service shall be those of the judges of the International Court of Justice. They shall be eligible for re-election.

Article 13 ter **Election and appointment of** ad litem **judges**

1. The *ad litem* judges of the International Tribunal shall be elected by the General Assembly from a list submitted by the Security Council, in the following manner:
(a) The Secretary-General shall invite nominations for *ad litem* judges of the International Tribunal from States Members of the United Nations and non-member States maintaining permanent observer missions at United Nations Headquarters.
(b) Within sixty days of the date of the invitation of the Secretary-General, each State may nominate up to four candidates meeting the qualifications set out in article 13 of the Statute, taking into account the importance of a fair representation of female and male candidates.
(c) The Secretary-General shall forward the nominations received to the Security Council. From the nominations received the Security Council shall establish a list of not less than fifty-four candidates, taking due account of the adequate representation of the principal legal systems of the world and bearing in mind the importance of equitable geographical distribution.
(d) The President of the Security Council shall transmit the list of candidates to the President of the General Assembly. From that list the General Assembly shall elect the twenty-seven *ad litem* judges of the International Tribunal. The candidates who receive an absolute majority of the votes of the States Members of the United Nations and of the non-member States maintaining permanent observer missions at United Nations Headquarters shall be declared elected.
(e) The *ad litem* judges shall be elected for a term of four years. They shall be eligible for re-election.
2. During any term, *ad litem* judges will be appointed by the Secretary-General, upon request of the President of the International Tribunal, to serve in the Trial Chambers for one or more trials, for a cumulative period of up to, but not including, three years. When requesting the appointment of any particular *ad litem* judge, the President of the International Tribunal shall bear in mind the criteria set out in article 13 of the Statute regarding the composition of the Chambers and sections of the Trial Chambers, the considerations set out in paragraphs 1 (b) and (c) above and the number of votes the *ad litem* judge received in the General Assembly.

Article 13 quater **Status of** ad litem **judges**

1. During the period in which they are appointed to serve in the International Tribunal, *ad litem* judges shall:
(a) Benefit from the same terms and conditions of service mutatis mutandis as the permanent judges of the International Tribunal;
(b) Enjoy, subject to paragraph 2 below, the same powers as the permanent judges of the International Tribunal;
(c) Enjoy the privileges and immunities, exemptions and facilities of a judge of the International Tribunal;
(d) Enjoy the power to adjudicate in pre-trial proceedings in cases other than those that they have been appointed to try.
2. During the period in which they are appointed to serve in the International Tribunal, *ad litem* judges shall not:
(a) Be eligible for election as, or to vote in the election of, the President of the Tribunal or the Presiding Judge of a Trial Chamber pursuant to article 14 of the Statute;
(b) Have power:
(i) To adopt rules of procedure and evidence pursuant to article 15 of the Statute. They shall, however, be consulted before the adoption of those rules;
(ii) To review an indictment pursuant to article 19 of the Statute;
(iii) To consult with the President in relation to the assignment of judges pursuant to article 14 of the Statute or in relation to a pardon or commutation of sentence pursuant to article 28 of the Statute.
3. Notwithstanding, paragraphs 1 and 2 above, an *ad litem* judge who is serving as a reserve judge shall, during such time as he or she so serves:
(a) Benefit from the same terms and conditions of service mutatis mutandis as the permanent judges of the International Tribunal;
(b) Enjoy the privileges and immunities, exemptions and facilities of a judge of the International Tribunal;
(c) Enjoy the power to adjudicate in pre-trial proceedings in cases other than those that they have been appointed to and for that purpose to enjoy subject to paragraph 2 above, the same powers as permanent judges.
4. In the event that a reserve judge replaces a judge who is unable to continue sitting, he or she will, as of that time, benefit from the provisions of paragraph 1 above.

Article 14 Officers and members of the Chambers

1. The permanent judges of the International Tribunal shall elect a President from amongst their number.
2. The President of the International Tribunal shall be a member of the Appeals Chamber and shall preside over its proceedings.
3. After consultation with the permanent judges of the International Tribunal, the President shall assign four of the permanent judges elected or appointed in accordance with Article 13 *bis* of the Statute to the Appeals Chamber and nine to the Trial Chambers.
4. Two of the permanent judges of the International Tribunal for Rwanda elected or appointed in accordance with article 12 *bis* of the Statute of that Tribunal shall be assigned by the President of that Tribunal, in consultation with the President of the International Tribunal, to be members of the Appeals Chamber and permanent judges of the International Tribunal.
5. After consultation with the permanent judges of the International Tribunal, the President shall assign such *ad litem* judges as may from time to time be appointed to serve in the International Tribunal to the Trial Chambers.

6. A judge shall serve only in the Chamber to which he or she was assigned.
7. The permanent judges of each Trial Chamber shall elect a Presiding Judge from amongst their number, who shall oversee the work of the Trial Chamber as a whole.

Article 15 Rules of procedure and evidence

The judges of the International Tribunal shall adopt rules of procedure and evidence for the conduct of the pre-trial phase of the proceedings, trials and appeals, the admission of evidence, the protection of victims and witnesses and other appropriate matters.

Article 16 The Prosecutor

1. The Prosecutor shall be responsible for the investigation and prosecution of persons responsible for serious violations of international humanitarian law committed in the territory of the former Yugoslavia since 1 January 1991.
2. The Prosecutor shall act independently as a separate organ of the International Tribunal. He or she shall not seek or receive instructions from any Government or from any other source.
3. The Office of the Prosecutor shall be composed of a Prosecutor and such other qualified staff as may be required.
4. The Prosecutor shall be appointed by the Security Council on nomination by the Secretary-General. He or she shall be of high moral character and possess the highest level of competence and experience in the conduct of investigations and prosecutions of criminal cases. The Prosecutor shall serve for a four-year term and be eligible for reappointment. The terms and conditions of service of the Prosecutor shall be those of an Under-Secretary-General of the United Nations.
5. The staff of the Office of the Prosecutor shall be appointed by the Secretary-General on the recommendation of the Prosecutor.

Article 17 The Registry

1. The Registry shall be responsible for the administration and servicing of the International Tribunal.
2. The Registry shall consist of a Registrar and such other staff as may be required.
3. The Registrar shall be appointed by the Secretary-General after consultation with the President of the International Tribunal. He or she shall serve for a four-year term and be eligible for reappointment. The terms and conditions of service of the Registrar shall be those of an Assistant Secretary-General of the United Nations.
4. The staff of the Registry shall be appointed by the Secretary-General on the recommendation of the Registrar.

Article 18 Investigation and preparation of indictment

1. The Prosecutor shall initiate investigations *ex-officio* or on the basis of information obtained from any source, particularly from Governments, United Nations organs, intergovernmental and nongovernmental organisations. The Prosecutor shall assess the information received or obtained and decide whether there is sufficient basis to proceed.
2. The Prosecutor shall have the power to question suspects, victims and witnesses, to collect evidence and to conduct on-site investigations. In carrying out these tasks, the Prosecutor may, as appropriate, seek the assistance of the State authorities concerned.
3. If questioned, the suspect shall be entitled to be assisted by counsel of his own choice, including the right to have legal assistance assigned to him without payment by him in

any such case if he does not have sufficient means to pay for it, as well as to necessary translation into and from a language he speaks and understands.
4. Upon a determination that a *prima facie* case exists, the Prosecutor shall prepare an indictment containing a concise statement of the facts and the crime or crimes with which the accused is charged under the Statute. The indictment shall be transmitted to a judge of the Trial Chamber.

Article 19 Review of the indictment

1. The judge of the Trial Chamber to whom the indictment has been transmitted shall review it. If satisfied that a *prima facie* case has been established by the Prosecutor, he shall confirm the indictment. If not so satisfied, the indictment shall be dismissed.
2. Upon confirmation of an indictment, the judge may, at the request of the Prosecutor, issue such orders and warrants for the arrest, detention, surrender or transfer of persons, and any other orders as may be required for the conduct of the trial.

Article 20 Commencement and conduct of trial proceedings

1. The Trial Chambers shall ensure that a trial is fair and expeditious and that proceedings are conducted in accordance with the rules of procedure and evidence, with full respect for the rights of the accused and due regard for the protection of victims and witnesses.
2. A person against whom an indictment has been confirmed shall, pursuant to an order or an arrest warrant of the International Tribunal, be taken into custody, immediately informed of the charges against him and transferred to the International Tribunal.
3. The Trial Chamber shall read the indictment, satisfy itself that the rights of the accused are respected, confirm that the accused understands the indictment, and instruct the accused to enter a plea. The Trial Chamber shall then set the date for trial.
4. The hearings shall be public unless the Trial Chamber decides to close the proceedings in accordance with its rules of procedure and evidence.

Article 21 Rights of the accused

1. All persons shall be equal before the International Tribunal.
2. In the determination of charges against him, the accused shall be entitled to a fair and public hearing, subject to article 22 of the Statute.
3. The accused shall be presumed innocent until proved guilty according to the provisions of the present Statute.
4. In the determination of any charge against the accused pursuant to the present Statute, the accused shall be entitled to the following minimum guarantees, in full equality:
(a) to be informed promptly and in detail in a language which he understands of the nature and cause of the charge against him;
(b) to have adequate time and facilities for the preparation of his defence and to communicate with counsel of his own choosing;
(c) to be tried without undue delay;
(d) to be tried in his presence, and to defend himself in person or through legal assistance of his own choosing; to be informed, if he does not have legal assistance, of this right; and to have legal assistance assigned to him, in any case where the interests of justice so require, and without payment by him in any such case if he does not have sufficient means to pay for it;
(e) to examine, or have examined, the witnesses against him and to obtain the attendance and examination of witnesses on his behalf under the same conditions as witnesses against him;

(f) to have the free assistance of an interpreter if he cannot understand or speak the language used in the International Tribunal;
(g) not to be compelled to testify against himself or to confess guilt.

Article 22 Protection of victims and witnesses

The International Tribunal shall provide in its rules of procedure and evidence for the protection of victims and witnesses. Such protection measures shall include, but shall not be limited to, the conduct of in camera proceedings and the protection of the victim's identity.

Article 23 Judgement

1. The Trial Chambers shall pronounce judgements and impose sentences and penalties on persons convicted of serious violations of international humanitarian law.
2. The judgement shall be rendered by a majority of the judges of the Trial Chamber, and shall be delivered by the Trial Chamber in public. It shall be accompanied by a reasoned opinion in writing, to which separate or dissenting opinions may be appended.

Article 24 Penalties

1. The penalty imposed by the Trial Chamber shall be limited to imprisonment. In determining the terms of imprisonment, the Trial Chambers shall have recourse to the general practice regarding prison sentences in the courts of the former Yugoslavia.
2. In imposing the sentences, the Trial Chambers should take into account such factors as the gravity of the offence and the individual circumstances of the convicted person.
3. In addition to imprisonment, the Trial Chambers may order the return of any property and proceeds acquired by criminal conduct, including by means of duress, to their rightful owners.

Article 25 Appellate proceedings

1. The Appeals Chamber shall hear appeals from persons convicted by the Trial Chambers or from the Prosecutor on the following grounds:
(a) an error on a question of law invalidating the decision; or
(b) an error of fact which has occasioned a miscarriage of justice.
2. The Appeals Chamber may affirm, reverse or revise the decisions taken by the Trial Chambers.

Article 26 Review proceedings

Where a new fact has been discovered which was not known at the time of the proceedings before the Trial Chambers or the Appeals Chamber and which could have been a decisive factor in reaching the decision, the convicted person or the Prosecutor may submit to the International Tribunal an application for review of the judgement.

Article 27 Enforcement of sentences

Imprisonment shall be served in a State designated by the International Tribunal from a list of States which have indicated to the Security Council their willingness to accept convicted persons. Such imprisonment shall be in accordance with the applicable law of the State concerned, subject to the supervision of the International Tribunal.

Article 28 Pardon or commutation of sentences

If, pursuant to the applicable law of the State in which the convicted person is imprisoned, he or she is eligible for pardon or commutation of sentence, the State concerned shall notify the International Tribunal accordingly. The President of the International Tribunal, in consultation with the judges, shall decide the matter on the basis of the interests of justice and the general principles of law.

Article 29 Co-operation and judicial assistance

1. States shall co-operate with the International Tribunal in the investigation and prosecution of persons accused of committing serious violations of international humanitarian law.
2. States shall comply without undue delay with any request for assistance or an order issued by a Trial Chamber, including, but not limited to:
(a) the identification and location of persons;
(b) the taking of testimony and the production of evidence;
(c) the service of documents;
(d) the arrest or detention of persons;
(e) the surrender or the transfer of the accused to the International Tribunal.

Article 30 The status, privileges and immunities of the International Tribunal

1. The Convention on the Privileges and Immunities of the United Nations of 13 February 1946 shall apply to the International Tribunal, the judges, the Prosecutor and his staff, and the Registrar and his staff.
2. The judges, the Prosecutor and the Registrar shall enjoy the privileges and immunities, exemptions and facilities accorded to diplomatic envoys, in accordance with international law.
3. The staff of the Prosecutor and of the Registrar shall enjoy the privileges and immunities accorded to officials of the United Nations under articles V and VII of the Convention referred to in paragraph 1 of this article.
4. Other persons, including the accused, required at the seat of the International Tribunal shall be accorded such treatment as is necessary for the proper functioning of the International Tribunal.

Article 31 Seat of the International Tribunal

The International Tribunal shall have its seat at The Hague.

Article 32 Expenses of the International Tribunal

The expenses of the International Tribunal shall be borne by the regular budget of the United Nations in accordance with Article 17 of the Charter of the United Nations.

Article 33 Working languages

The working languages of the International Tribunal shall be English and French.

Article 34 Annual report

The President of the International Tribunal shall submit an annual report of the International Tribunal to the Security Council and to the General Assembly.

Rome Statute of the International Criminal Court

Preamble

The States Parties to this Statute,

Conscious that all peoples are united by common bonds, their cultures pieced together in a shared heritage, and concerned that this delicate mosaic may be shattered at any time,
Mindful that during this century millions of children, women and men have been victims of unimaginable atrocities that deeply shock the conscience of humanity,
Recognizing that such grave crimes threaten the peace, security and well-being of the world,
Affirming that the most serious crimes of concern to the international community as a whole must not go unpunished and that their effective prosecution must be ensured by taking measures at the national level and by enhancing international cooperation,
Determined to put an end to impunity for the perpetrators of these crimes and thus to contribute to the prevention of such crimes,
Recalling that it is the duty of every State to exercise its criminal jurisdiction over those responsible for international crimes,
Reaffirming the Purposes and Principles of the Charter of the United Nations, and in particular that all States shall refrain from the threat or use of force against the territorial integrity or political independence of any State, or in any other manner inconsistent with the Purposes of the United Nations,
Emphasizing in this connection that nothing in this Statute shall be taken as authorizing any State Party to intervene in an armed conflict or in the internal affairs of any State,
Determined to these ends and for the sake of present and future generations, to establish an independent permanent International Criminal Court in relationship with the United Nations system, with jurisdiction over the most serious crimes of concern to the international community as a whole,
Emphasizing that the International Criminal Court established under this Statute shall be complementary to national criminal jurisdictions,
Resolved to guarantee lasting respect for and the enforcement of international justice,
Have agreed as follows

Part 1. Establishment of the Court

Article 1 The Court

An International Criminal Court ("the Court") is hereby established. It shall be a permanent institution and shall have the power to exercise its jurisdiction over persons for the most serious crimes of international concern, as referred to in this Statute, and shall be complementary to national criminal jurisdictions. The jurisdiction and functioning of the Court shall be governed by the provisions of this Statute.

Article 2 Relationship of the Court with the United Nations

The Court shall be brought into relationship with the United Nations through an agreement to be approved by the Assembly of States Parties to this Statute and thereafter concluded by the President of the Court on its behalf.

Article 3 Seat of the Court

1. The seat of the Court shall be established at The Hague in the Netherlands ("the host State").
2. The Court shall enter into a headquarters agreement with the host State, to be approved by the Assembly of States Parties and thereafter concluded by the President of the Court on its behalf.
3. The Court may sit elsewhere, whenever it considers it desirable, as provided in this Statute.

Article 4 Legal status and powers of the Court

1. The Court shall have international legal personality. It shall also have such legal capacity as may be necessary for the exercise of its functions and the fulfillment of its purposes.
2. The Court may exercise its functions and powers, as provided in this Statute, on the territory of any State Party and, by special agreement, on the territory of any other State.

Part 2. Jurisdiction, Admissibility and Applicable Law

Article 5 Crimes within the jurisdiction of the Court

1. The jurisdiction of the Court shall be limited to the most serious crimes of concern to the international community as a whole. The Court has jurisdiction in accordance with this Statute with respect to the following crimes:
(a) The crime of genocide;
(b) Crimes against humanity;
(c) War crimes;
(d) The crime of aggression.
2. The Court shall exercise jurisdiction over the crime of aggression once a provision is adopted in accordance with articles 121 and 123 defining the crime and setting out the conditions under which the Court shall exercise jurisdiction with respect to this crime. Such a provision shall be consistent with the relevant provisions of the Charter of the United Nations.

Article 6 Genocide

For the purpose of this Statute, "genocide" means any of the following acts committed with intent to destroy, in whole or in part, a national, ethnical, racial or religious group, as such:
Killing members of the group;
Causing serious bodily or mental harm to members of the group;
Deliberately inflicting on the group conditions of life calculated to bring about its physical destruction in whole or in part;
Imposing measures intended to prevent births within the group;
Forcibly transferring children of the group to another group.

Article 7 Crimes against humanity

1. For the purpose of this Statute, "crime against humanity" means any of the following acts when committed as part of a widespread or systematic attack directed against any civilian population, with knowledge of the attack:

Murder;
Extermination;
Enslavement;
Deportation or forcible transfer of population;
Imprisonment or other severe deprivation of physical liberty in violation of fundamental rules of international law;
Torture;
Rape, sexual slavery, enforced prostitution, forced pregnancy, enforced sterilization, or any other form of sexual violence of comparable gravity;
Persecution against any identifiable group or collectivity on political, racial, national, ethnic, cultural, religious, gender as defined in paragraph 3, or other grounds that are universally recognized as impermissible under international law, in connection with any act referred to in this paragraph or any crime within the jurisdiction of the Court;
Enforced disappearance of persons;
The crime of apartheid;
Other inhumane acts of a similar character intentionally causing great suffering, or serious injury to body or to mental or physical health.

2. For the purpose of paragraph 1:
"Attack directed against any civilian population" means a course of conduct involving the multiple commission of acts referred to in paragraph 1 against any civilian population, pursuant to or in furtherance of a State or organizational policy to commit such attack;
"Extermination" includes the intentional infliction of conditions of life, inter alia the deprivation of access to food and medicine, calculated to bring about the destruction of part of a population;
"Enslavement" means the exercise of any or all of the powers attaching to the right of ownership over a person and includes the exercise of such power in the course of trafficking in persons, in particular women and children;
"Deportation or forcible transfer of population" means forced displacement of the persons concerned by expulsion or other coercive acts from the area in which they are lawfully present, without grounds permitted under international law;
"Torture" means the intentional infliction of severe pain or suffering, whether physical or mental, upon a person in the custody or under the control of the accused; except that torture shall not include pain or suffering arising only from, inherent in or incidental to, lawful sanctions;
"Forced pregnancy" means the unlawful confinement of a woman forcibly made pregnant, with the intent of affecting the ethnic composition of any population or carrying out other grave violations of international law. This definition shall not in any way be interpreted as affecting national laws relating to pregnancy;
"Persecution" means the intentional and severe deprivation of fundamental rights contrary to international law by reason of the identity of the group or collectivity;
"The crime of apartheid" means inhumane acts of a character similar to those referred to in paragraph 1, committed in the context of an institutionalized regime of systematic oppression and domination by one racial group over any other racial group or groups and committed with the intention of maintaining that regime;
"Enforced disappearance of persons" means the arrest, detention or abduction of persons by, or with the authorization, support or acquiescence of, a State or a political organization, followed by a refusal to acknowledge that deprivation of freedom or to give information on the fate or whereabouts of those persons, with the intention of removing them from the protection of the law for a prolonged period of time.

3. For the purpose of this Statute, it is understood that the term "gender" refers to the two sexes, male and female, within the context of society. The term "gender" does not indicate any meaning different from the above.

Article 8 War crimes

1. The Court shall have jurisdiction in respect of war crimes in particular when committed as part of a plan or policy or as part of a large-scale commission of such crimes.
2. For the purpose of this Statute, "war crimes" means:
(a) Grave breaches of the Geneva Conventions of 12 August 1949, namely, any of the following acts against persons or property protected under the provisions of the relevant Geneva Convention:
(i) Willful killing;
(ii) Torture or inhuman treatment, including biological experiments;
(iii) Willfully causing great suffering, or serious injury to body or health;
(iv) Extensive destruction and appropriation of property, not justified by military necessity and carried out unlawfully and wantonly;
(v) Compelling a prisoner of war or other protected person to serve in the forces of a hostile Power;
(vi) Willfully depriving a prisoner of war or other protected person of the rights of fair and regular trial;
(vii) Unlawful deportation or transfer or unlawful confinement;
(viii) Taking of hostages.
(b) Other serious violations of the laws and customs applicable in international armed conflict, within the established framework of international law, namely, any of the following acts:
(i) Intentionally directing attacks against the civilian population as such or against individual civilians not taking direct part in hostilities;
(ii) Intentionally directing attacks against civilian objects, that is, objects which are not military objectives;
(iii) Intentionally directing attacks against personnel, installations, material, units or vehicles involved in a humanitarian assistance or peacekeeping mission in accordance with the Charter of the United Nations, as long as they are entitled to the protection given to civilians or civilian objects under the international law of armed conflict;
(iv) Intentionally launching an attack in the knowledge that such attack will cause incidental loss of life or injury to civilians or damage to civilian objects or widespread, long-term and severe damage to the natural environment which would be clearly excessive in relation to the concrete and direct overall military advantage ant(v) Attacking or bombarding, by whatever means, towns, villages, dwellings or buildings which are undefended and which are not military objectives;
(vi) Killing or wounding a combatant who, having laid down his arms or having no longer means of defence, has surrendered at discretion;
(vii) Making improper use of a flag of truce, of the flag or of the military insignia and uniform of the enemy or of the United Nations, as well as of the distinctive emblems of the Geneva Conventions, resulting in death or serious personal injury;
(viii) The transfer, directly or indirectly, by the Occupying Power of parts of its own civilian population into the territory it occupies, or the deportation or transfer of all or parts of the population of the occupied territory within or outside this territory;
(ix) Intentionally directing attacks against buildings dedicated to religion, education, art, science or charitable purposes, historic monuments, hospitals and places where the sick and wounded are collected, provided they are not military objectives;
(x) Subjecting persons who are in the power of an adverse party to physical mutilation or to medical or scientific experiments of any kind which are neither justified by the medical, dental or hospital treatment of the person concerned nor carried out in his or her interest, and which cause death to or seriously endanger the health of such person or persons;

(xi) Killing or wounding treacherously individuals belonging to the hostile nation or army;
(xii) Declaring that no quarter will be given;
(xiii) Destroying or seizing the enemy's property unless such destruction or seizure be imperatively demanded by the necessities of war;
(xiv) Declaring abolished, suspended or inadmissible in a court of law the rights and actions of the nationals of the hostile party;
(xv) Compelling the nationals of the hostile party to take part in the operations of war directed against their own country, even if they were in the belligerent's service before the commencement of the war;
(xvi) Pillaging a town or place, even when taken by assault;
(xvii) Employing poison or poisoned weapons;
(xviii) Employing asphyxiating, poisonous or other gases, and all analogous liquids, materials or devices;
(xix) Employing bullets which expand or flatten easily in the human body, such as bullets with a hard envelope which does not entirely cover the core or is pierced with incisions;
(xx) Employing weapons, projectiles and material and methods of warfare which are of a nature to cause superfluous injury or unnecessary suffering or which are inherently indiscriminate in violation of the international law of armed conflict, provided that such weapons, projectiles and material and methods of warfare are the subject of a comprehensive prohibition and are included in an annex to this Statute, by an amendment in accordance with the relevant provisions set forth in articles 121 and 123;
(xxi) Committing outrages upon personal dignity, in particular humiliating and degrading treatment;
(xxii) Committing rape, sexual slavery, enforced prostitution, forced pregnancy, as defined in article 7, paragraph 2 (f), enforced sterilization, or any other form of sexual violence also constituting a grave breach of the Geneva Conventions;
(xxiii) Utilizing the presence of a civilian or other protected person to render certain points, areas or military forces immune from military operations;
(xxiv) Intentionally directing attacks against buildings, material, medical units and transport, and personnel using the distinctive emblems of the Geneva Conventions in conformity with international law;
(xxv) Intentionally using starvation of civilians as a method of warfare by depriving them of objects indispensable to their survival, including wilfully impeding relief supplies as provided for under the Geneva Conventions;
(xxvi) Conscripting or enlisting children under the age of fifteen years into the national armed forces or using them to participate actively in hostilities.
(c) In the case of an armed conflict not of an international character, serious violations of article 3 common to the four Geneva Conventions of 12 August 1949, namely, any of the following acts committed against persons taking no active part in the hostilities, including members of armed forces who have laid down their arms and those placed hors de combat by sickness, wounds, detention or any other cause:
(i) Violence to life and person, in particular murder of all kinds, mutilation, cruel treatment and torture;
(ii) Committing outrages upon personal dignity, in particular humiliating and degrading treatment;
(iii) Taking of hostages;
(iv) The passing of sentences and the carrying out of executions without previous judgement pronounced by a regularly constituted court, affording all judicial guarantees which are generally recognized as indispensable.

(d) Paragraph 2 (c) applies to armed conflicts not of an international character and thus does not apply to situations of internal disturbances and tensions, such as riots, isolated and sporadic acts of violence or other acts of a similar nature.
(e) Other serious violations of the laws and customs applicable in armed conflicts not of an international character, within the established framework of international law, namely, any of the following acts:
(i) Intentionally directing attacks against the civilian population as such or against individual civilians not taking direct part in hostilities;
(ii) Intentionally directing attacks against buildings, material, medical units and transport, and personnel using the distinctive emblems of the Geneva Conventions in conformity with international law;
(iii) Intentionally directing attacks against personnel, installations, material, units or vehicles involved in a humanitarian assistance or peacekeeping mission in accordance with the Charter of the United Nations, as long as they are entitled to the protection given to civilians or civilian objects under the international law of armed conflict;
(iv) Intentionally directing attacks against buildings dedicated to religion, education, art, science or charitable purposes, historic monuments, hospitals and places where the sick and wounded are collected, provided they are not military objectives;
(v) Pillaging a town or place, even when taken by assault;
(vi) Committing rape, sexual slavery, enforced prostitution, forced pregnancy, as defined in article 7, paragraph 2 (f), enforced sterilization, and any other form of sexual violence also constituting a serious violation of article 3 common to the four Geneva Conventions;
(vii) Conscripting or enlisting children under the age of fifteen years into armed forces or groups or using them to participate actively in hostilities;
(viii) Ordering the displacement of the civilian population for reasons related to the conflict, unless the security of the civilians involved or imperative military reasons so demand;
(ix) Killing or wounding treacherously a combatant adversary;
(x) Declaring that no quarter will be given;
(xi) Subjecting persons who are in the power of another party to the conflict to physical mutilation or to medical or scientific experiments of any kind which are neither justified by the medical, dental or hospital treatment of the person concerned nor carried out in his or her interest, and which cause death to or seriously endanger the health of such person or persons;
(xii) Destroying or seizing the property of an adversary unless such destruction or seizure be imperatively demanded by the necessities of the conflict;
(f) Paragraph 2 (e) applies to armed conflicts not of an international character and thus does not apply to situations of internal disturbances and tensions, such as riots, isolated and sporadic acts of violence or other acts of a similar nature. It applies to armed conflicts that take place in the territory of a State when there is protracted armed conflict between governmental authorities and organized armed groups or between such groups.
3. Nothing in paragraph 2 (c) and (e) shall affect the responsibility of a Government to maintain or re-establish law and order in the State or to defend the unity and territorial integrity of the State, by all legitimate means.

Article 9 Elements of Crimes

1. Elements of Crimes shall assist the Court in the interpretation and application of articles 6, 7 and 8. They shall be adopted by a two-thirds majority of the members of the Assembly of States Parties.
2. Amendments to the Elements of Crimes may be proposed by:
- Any State Party;

- The judges acting by an absolute majority;
- The Prosecutor.

Such amendments shall be adopted by a two-thirds majority of the members of the Assembly of States Parties.

3. The Elements of Crimes and amendments thereto shall be consistent with this Statute.

Article 10

Nothing in this Part shall be interpreted as limiting or prejudicing in any way existing or developing rules of international law for purposes other than this Statute.

Article 11 Jurisdiction ratione temporis

1. The Court has jurisdiction only with respect to crimes committed after the entry into force of this Statute.
2. If a State becomes a Party to this Statute after its entry into force, the Court may exercise its jurisdiction only with respect to crimes committed after the entry into force of this Statute for that State, unless that State has made a declaration under article 12, paragraph 3.

Article 12 Preconditions to the exercise of jurisdiction

1. A State which becomes a Party to this Statute thereby accepts the jurisdiction of the Court with respect to the crimes referred to in article 5.
2. In the case of article 13, paragraph (a) or (c), the Court may exercise its jurisdiction if one or more of the following States are Parties to this Statute or have accepted the jurisdiction of the Court in accordance with paragraph 3:
(a) The State on the territory of which the conduct in question occurred or, if the crime was committed on board a vessel or aircraft, the State of registration of that vessel or aircraft;
(b) The State of which the person accused of the crime is a national.
3. If the acceptance of a State which is not a Party to this Statute is required under paragraph 2, that State may, by declaration lodged with the Registrar, accept the exercise of jurisdiction by the Court with respect to the crime in question. The accepting State shall cooperate with the Court without any delay or exception in accordance with Part 9.

Article 13 Exercise of jurisdiction

The Court may exercise its jurisdiction with respect to a crime referred to in article 5 in accordance with the provisions of this Statute if:
(a) A situation in which one or more of such crimes appears to have been committed is referred to the Prosecutor by a State Party in accordance with article 14;
(b) A situation in which one or more of such crimes appears to have been committed is referred to the Prosecutor by the Security Council acting under Chapter VII of the Charter of the United Nations; or
(c) The Prosecutor has initiated an investigation in respect of such a crime in accordance with article 15.

Article 14 Referral of a situation by a State Party

A State Party may refer to the Prosecutor a situation in which one or more crimes within the jurisdiction of the Court appear to have been committed requesting the Prosecutor

to investigate the situation for the purpose of determining whether one or more specific persons should be charged with the commission of such crimes.
As far as possible, a referral shall specify the relevant circumstances and be accompanied by such supporting documentation as is available to the State referring the situation.

Article 15 Prosecutor

The Prosecutor may initiate investigations proprio motu on the basis of information on crimes within the jurisdiction of the Court.
The Prosecutor shall analyse the seriousness of the information received. For this purpose, he or she may seek additional information from States, organs of the United Nations, intergovernmental or non-governmental organizations, or other reliable sources that he or she deems appropriate, and may receive written or oral testimony at the seat of the Court.
If the Prosecutor concludes that there is a reasonable basis to proceed with an investigation, he or she shall submit to the Pre-Trial Chamber a request for authorization of an investigation, together with any supporting material collected. Victims may make representations to the Pre-Trial Chamber, in accordance with the Rules of Procedure and Evidence.
If the Pre-Trial Chamber, upon examination of the request and the supporting material, considers that there is a reasonable basis to proceed with an investigation, and that the case appears to fall within the jurisdiction of the Court, it shall authorize the commencement of the investigation, without prejudice to subsequent determinations by the Court with regard to the jurisdiction and admissibility of a case.
The refusal of the Pre-Trial Chamber to authorize the investigation shall not preclude the presentation of a subsequent request by the Prosecutor based on new facts or evidence regarding the same situation.
If, after the preliminary examination referred to in paragraphs 1 and 2, the Prosecutor concludes that the information provided does not constitute a reasonable basis for an investigation, he or she shall inform those who provided the information. This shall not preclude the Prosecutor from considering further information submitted to him or her regarding the same situation in the light of new facts or evidence.

Article 16 Deferral of investigation or prosecution

No investigation or prosecution may be commenced or proceeded with under this Statute for a period of 12 months after the Security Council, in a resolution adopted under Chapter VII of the Charter of the United Nations, has requested the Court to that effect; that request may be renewed by the Council under the same conditions.

Article 17 Issues of admissibility

1. Having regard to paragraph 10 of the Preamble and article 1, the Court shall determine that a case is inadmissible where:
(a) The case is being investigated or prosecuted by a State which has jurisdiction over it, unless the State is unwilling or unable genuinely to carry out the investigation or prosecution;
(b) The case has been investigated by a State which has jurisdiction over it and the State has decided not to prosecute the person concerned, unless the decision resulted from the unwillingness or inability of the State genuinely to prosecute;
(c) The person concerned has already been tried for conduct which is the subject of the complaint, and a trial by the Court is not permitted under article 20, paragraph 3;

(d) The case is not of sufficient gravity to justify further action by the Court.
2. In order to determine unwillingness in a particular case, the Court shall consider, having regard to the principles of due process recognized by international law, whether one or more of the following exist, as applicable:
(a) The proceedings were or are being undertaken or the national decision was made for the purpose of shielding the person concerned from criminal responsibility for crimes within the jurisdiction of the Court referred to in article 5;
(b) There has been an unjustified delay in the proceedings which in the circumstances is inconsistent with an intent to bring the person concerned to justice;
(c) The proceedings were not or are not being conducted independently or impartially, and they were or are being conducted in a manner which, in the circumstances, is inconsistent with an intent to bring the person concerned to justice.
3. In order to determine inability in a particular case, the Court shall consider whether, due to a total or substantial collapse or unavailability of its national judicial system, the State is unable to obtain the accused or the necessary evidence and testimony or otherwise unable to carry out its proceedings.

Article 18 Preliminary rulings regarding admissibility

When a situation has been referred to the Court pursuant to article 13 (a) and the Prosecutor has determined that there would be a reasonable basis to commence an investigation, or the Prosecutor initiates an investigation pursuant to articles 13 (c) and 15, the Prosecutor shall notify all States Parties and those States which, taking into account the information available, would normally exercise jurisdiction over the crimes concerned. The Prosecutor may notify such States on a confidential basis and, where the Prosecutor believes it necessary to protect persons, prevent destruction of evidence or prevent the absconding of persons, may limit the scope of the information provided to States.
Within one month of receipt of that notification, a State may inform the Court that it is investigating or has investigated its nationals or others within its jurisdiction with respect to criminal acts which may constitute crimes referred to in article 5 and which relate to the information provided in the notification to States. At the request of that State, the Prosecutor shall defer to the State's investigation of those persons unless the Pre-Trial Chamber, on the application of the Prosecutor, decides to authorize the investigation.
The Prosecutor's deferral to a State's investigation shall be open to review by the Prosecutor six months after the date of deferral or at any time when there has been a significant change of circumstances based on the State's unwillingness or inability genuinely to carry out the investigation.
The State concerned or the Prosecutor may appeal to the Appeals Chamber against a ruling of the Pre-Trial Chamber, in accordance with article 82. The appeal may be heard on an expedited basis.
When the Prosecutor has deferred an investigation in accordance with paragraph 2, the Prosecutor may request that the State concerned periodically inform the Prosecutor of the progress of its investigations and any subsequent prosecutions. States Parties shall respond to such requests without undue delay.
Pending a ruling by the Pre-Trial Chamber, or at any time when the Prosecutor has deferred an investigation under this article, the Prosecutor may, on an exceptional basis, seek authority from the Pre-Trial Chamber to pursue necessary investigative steps for the purpose of preserving evidence where there is a unique opportunity to obtain important evidence or there is a significant risk that such evidence may not be subsequently available.

A State which has challenged a ruling of the Pre-Trial Chamber under this article may challenge the admissibility of a case under article 19 on the grounds of additional significant facts or significant change of circumstances.

Article 19 Challenges to the jurisdiction of the Court or the admissibility of a case

1. The Court shall satisfy itself that it has jurisdiction in any case brought before it. The Court may, on its own motion, determine the admissibility of a case in accordance with article 17.
2. Challenges to the admissibility of a case on the grounds referred to in article 17 or challenges to the jurisdiction of the Court may be made by:
(a) An accused or a person for whom a warrant of arrest or a summons to appear has been issued under article 58;
(b) A State which has jurisdiction over a case, on the ground that it is investigating or prosecuting the case or has investigated or prosecuted; or
(c) A State from which acceptance of jurisdiction is required under article 12.
3. The Prosecutor may seek a ruling from the Court regarding a question of jurisdiction or admissibility. In proceedings with respect to jurisdiction or admissibility, those who have referred the situation under article 13, as well as victims, may also submit observations to t4. The admissibility of a case or the jurisdiction of the Court may be challenged only once by any person or State referred to in paragraph 2. The challenge shall take place prior to or at the commencement of the trial. In exceptional circumstances, the Court may grant leave for a challenge to be brought more than once or at a time later than the commencement of the trial. Challenges to the admissibility of a case, at the commencement of a trial, or subsequently with the leave of the Court, may be based only on article 17, paragraph 1 (c).
5. A State referred to in paragraph 2 (b) and (c) shall make a challenge at the earliest opportunity.
6. Prior to the confirmation of the charges, challenges to the admissibility of a case or challenges to the jurisdiction of the Court shall be referred to the Pre-Trial Chamber. After confirmation of the charges, they shall be referred to the Trial Chamber. Decisions with respect to jurisdiction or admissibility may be appealed to the Appeals Chamber in accordance with article 82.
7. If a challenge is made by a State referred to in paragraph 2 (b) or (c), the Prosecutor shall suspend the investigation until such time as the Court makes a determination in accordance with article 17.
8. Pending a ruling by the Court, the Prosecutor may seek authority from the Court:
(a) To pursue necessary investigative steps of the kind referred to in article 18, paragraph 6;
(b) To take a statement or testimony from a witness or complete the collection and examination of evidence which had begun prior to the making of the challenge; and
(c) In cooperation with the relevant States, to prevent the absconding of persons in respect of whom the Prosecutor has already requested a warrant of arrest under article 58.
9. The making of a challenge shall not affect the validity of any act performed by the Prosecutor or any order or warrant issued by the Court prior to the making of the challenge.
10. If the Court has decided that a case is inadmissible under article 17, the Prosecutor may submit a request for a review of the decision when he or she is fully satisfied that new facts have arisen which negate the basis on which the case had previously been found inadmissible under article 17.
11. If the Prosecutor, having regard to the matters referred to in article 17, defers an investigation, the Prosecutor may request that the relevant State make available to the

Prosecutor information on the proceedings. That information shall, at the request of the State concerned, be confidential. If the Prosecutor thereafter decides to proceed with an investigation, he or she shall notify the State to which deferral of the proceedings has taken place.

Article 20 Ne bis in idem

Except as provided in this Statute, no person shall be tried before the Court with respect to conduct which formed the basis of crimes for which the person has been convicted or acquitted by the Court.
No person shall be tried by another court for a crime referred to in article 5 for which that person has already been convicted or acquitted by the Court.
No person who has been tried by another court for conduct also proscribed under article 6, 7 or 8 shall be tried by the Court with respect to the same conduct unless the proceedings in the other court:
- Were for the purpose of shielding the person concerned from criminal responsibility for crimes within the jurisdiction of the Court; or
- Otherwise were not conducted independently or impartially in accordance with the norms of due process recognized by international law and were conducted in a manner which, in the circumstances, was inconsistent with an intent to bring the person concerned to justice.

Article 21 Applicable law

1. The Court shall apply:
(a) In the first place, this Statute, Elements of Crimes and its Rules of Procedure and Evidence;
(b) In the second place, where appropriate, applicable treaties and the principles and rules of international law, including the established principles of the international law of armed conflict;
(c) Failing that, general principles of law derived by the Court from national laws of legal systems of the world including, as appropriate, the national laws of States that would normally exercise jurisdiction over the crime, provided that those principles are not inconsistent with this Statute and with international law and internationally recognized norms and standards.
2. The Court may apply principles and rules of law as interpreted in its previous decisions.
3. The application and interpretation of law pursuant to this article must be consistent with internationally recognized human rights, and be without any adverse distinction founded on grounds such as gender as defined in article 7, paragraph 3, age, race, colour, language, religion or belief, political or other opinion, national, ethnic or social origin, wealth, birth or other status.

Part 3. General Principles of Criminal Law

Article 22 Nullum crimen sine lege

A person shall not be criminally responsible under this Statute unless the conduct in question constitutes, at the time it takes place, a crime within the jurisdiction of the Court.
The definition of a crime shall be strictly construed and shall not be extended by analogy. In case of ambiguity, the definition shall be interpreted in favour of the person being investigated, prosecuted or convicted.

This article shall not affect the characterization of any conduct as criminal under international law independently of this Statute.

Article 23 Nulla poena sine lege

A person convicted by the Court may be punished only in accordance with this Statute.

Article 24 Non-retroactivity ratione personae

No person shall be criminally responsible under this Statute for conduct prior to the entry into force of the Statute.
In the event of a change in the law applicable to a given case prior to a final judgement, the law more favourable to the person being investigated, prosecuted or convicted shall apply.

Article 25 Individual criminal responsibility

The Court shall have jurisdiction over natural persons pursuant to this Statute.
A person who commits a crime within the jurisdiction of the Court shall be individually responsible and liable for punishment in accordance with this Statute.
In accordance with this Statute, a person shall be criminally responsible and liable for punishment for a crime within the jurisdiction of the Court if that person:
(a) Commits such a crime, whether as an individual, jointly with another or through another person, regardless of whether that other person is criminally responsible;
(b) Orders, solicits or induces the commission of such a crime which in fact occurs or is attempted;
(c) For the purpose of facilitating the commission of such a crime, aids, abets or otherwise assists in its commission or its attempted commission, including providing the means for its commission;
(d) In any other way contributes to the commission or attempted commission of such a crime by a group of persons acting with a common purpose. Such contribution shall be intentional and shall either:
(i) Be made with the aim of furthering the criminal activity or criminal purpose of the group, where such activity or purpose involves the commission of a crime within the jurisdiction of the Court; or
(ii) Be made in the knowledge of the intention of the group to commit the crime;
(e) In respect of the crime of genocide, directly and publicly incites others to commit genocide;
(f) Attempts to commit such a crime by taking action that commences its execution by means of a substantial step, but the crime does not occur because of circumstances independent of the person's intentions. However, a person who abandons the effort to commit the crime or otherwise prevents the completion of the crime shall not be liable for punishment under this Statute for the attempt to commit that crime if that person completely and voluntarily gave up the criminal purpose.
No provision in this Statute relating to individual criminal responsibility shall affect the responsibility of States under international law.

Article 26 Exclusion of jurisdiction over persons under eighteen

The Court shall have no jurisdiction over any person who was under the age of 18 at the time of the alleged commission of a crime.

Article 27 Irrelevance of official capacity

1. This Statute shall apply equally to all persons without any distinction based on official capacity. In particular, official capacity as a Head of State or Government, a member of a Government or parliament, an elected representative or a government official shall in no case exempt a person from criminal responsibility under this Statute, nor shall it, in and of itself, constitute a ground for reduction of sentence.
2. Immunities or special procedural rules which may attach to the official capacity of a person, whether under national or international law, shall not bar the Court from exercising its jurisdiction over such a person.

Article 28 Responsibility of commanders and other superiors

In addition to other grounds of criminal responsibility under this Statute for crimes within the jurisdiction of the Court:
(a) A military commander or person effectively acting as a military commander shall be criminally responsible for crimes within the jurisdiction of the Court committed by forces under his or her effective command and control, or effective authority and control as the case may be, as a result of his or her failure to exercise control properly over such forces, where:
(i) That military commander or person either knew or, owing to the circumstances at the time, should have known that the forces were committing or about to commit such crimes; and
(ii) That military commander or person failed to take all necessary and reasonable measures within his or her power to prevent or repress their commission or to submit the matter to the competent authorities for investigation and prosecution.
(b) With respect to superior and subordinate relationships not described in paragraph (a), a superior shall be criminally responsible for crimes within the jurisdiction of the Court committed by subordinates under his or her effective authority and control, as a result of his or her failure to exercise control properly over such subordinates, where:
(i) The superior either knew, or consciously disregarded information which clearly indicated, that the subordinates were committing or about to commit such crimes;
(ii) The crimes concerned activities that were within the effective responsibility and control of the superior; and
(iii) The superior failed to take all necessary and reasonable measures within his or her power to prevent or repress their commission or to submit the matter to the competent authorities for investigation and prosecution.

Article 29 Non-applicability of statute of limitations

The crimes within the jurisdiction of the Court shall not be subject to any statute of limitations.

Article 30 Mental element

Unless otherwise provided, a person shall be criminally responsible and liable for punishment for a crime within the jurisdiction of the Court only if the material elements are committed with intent and knowledge.
For the purposes of this article, a person has intent where:
(a) In relation to conduct, that person means to engage in the conduct;
(b) In relation to a consequence, that person means to cause that consequence or is aware that it will occur in the ordinary course of events.

For the purposes of this article, "knowledge" means awareness that a circumstance exists or a consequence will occur in the ordinary course of events. "Know" and "knowingly" shall be construed accordingly.

Article 31 Grounds for excluding criminal responsibility

In addition to other grounds for excluding criminal responsibility provided for in this Statute, a person shall not be criminally responsible if, at the time of that person's conduct:
- The person suffers from a mental disease or defect that destroys that person's capacity to appreciate the unlawfulness or nature of his or her conduct, or capacity to control his or her conduct to conform to the requirements of law;
- The person is in a state of intoxication that destroys that person's capacity to appreciate the unlawfulness or nature of his or her conduct, or capacity to control his or her conduct to conform to the requirements of law, unless the person has become voluntarily intoxicated under such circumstances that the person knew, or disregarded the risk, that, as a result of the intoxication, he or she was likely to engage in conduct constituting a crime within the jurisdiction of the Court;
- The person acts reasonably to defend himself or herself or another person or, in the case of war crimes, property which is essential for the survival of the person or another person or property which is essential for accomplishing a military mission, against an imminent and unlawful use of force in a manner proportionate to the degree of danger to the person or the other person or property protected. The fact that the person was involved in a defensive operation conducted by forces shall not in itself constitute a ground for excluding criminal responsibility under this subparagraph;
- The conduct which is alleged to constitute a crime within the jurisdiction of the Court has been caused by duress resulting from a threat of imminent death or of continuing or imminent serious bodily harm against that person or another person, and the person acts necessarily and reasonably to avoid this threat, provided that the person does not intend to cause a greater harm than the one sought to be avoided. Such a threat may either be:

(i) Made by other persons; or
(ii) Constituted by other circumstances beyond that person's control.

The Court shall determine the applicability of the grounds for excluding criminal responsibility provided for in this Statute to the case before it.

At trial, the Court may consider a ground for excluding criminal responsibility other than those referred to in paragraph 1 where such a ground is derived from applicable law as set forth in article 21. The procedures relating to the consideration of such a ground shall be provided for in the Rules of Procedure and Evidence.

Article 32 Mistake of fact or mistake of law

A mistake of fact shall be a ground for excluding criminal responsibility only if it negates the mental element required by the crime.

A mistake of law as to whether a particular type of conduct is a crime within the jurisdiction of the Court shall not be a ground for excluding criminal responsibility. A mistake of law may, however, be a ground for excluding criminal responsibility if it negates the mental element required by such a crime, or as provided for in article 33.

Article 33 Superior orders and prescription of law

The fact that a crime within the jurisdiction of the Court has been committed by a person pursuant to an order of a Government or of a superior, whether military or civilian, shall not relieve that person of criminal responsibility unless:

(a) The person was under a legal obligation to obey orders of the Government or the superior in question;
(b) The person did not know that the order was unlawful; and
(c) The order was not manifestly unlawful.
For the purposes of this article, orders to commit genocide or crimes against humanity are manifestly unlawful.

Part 4. Composition and Administration of the Court

Article 34 Organs of the Court

The Court shall be composed of the following organs:
- The Presidency;
- An Appeals Division, a Trial Division and a Pre-Trial Division;
- The Office of the Prosecutor;
- The Registry.

Article 35 Service of judges

All judges shall be elected as full-time members of the Court and shall be available to serve on that basis from the commencement of their terms of office.
The judges composing the Presidency shall serve on a full-time basis as soon as they are elected.
The Presidency may, on the basis of the workload of the Court and in consultation with its members, decide from time to time to what extent the remaining judges shall be required to serve on a full-time basis. Any such arrangement shall be without prejudice to the provisions of article 40.
The financial arrangements for judges not required to serve on a full-time basis shall be made in accordance with article 49.

Article 36 Qualifications, nomination and election of judges

Subject to the provisions of paragraph 2, there shall be 18 judges of the Court.
(a) The Presidency, acting on behalf of the Court, may propose an increase in the number of judges specified in paragraph 1, indicating the reasons why this is considered necessary and appropriate. The Registrar shall promptly circulate any such proposal to all States Parties.
(b) Any such proposal shall then be considered at a meeting of the Assembly of States Parties to be convened in accordance with article 112. The proposal shall be considered adopted if approved at the meeting by a vote of two thirds of the members of the Assembly of States Parties and shall enter into force at such time as decided by the Assembly of States Parties.
(c)
(i) Once a proposal for an increase in the number of judges has been adopted under subparagraph (b), the election of the additional judges shall take place at the next session of the Assembly of States Parties in accordance with paragraphs 3 to 8, and article 37, paragraph 2;
(ii) Once a proposal for an increase in the number of judges has been adopted and brought into effect under subparagraphs (b) and (c) (i), it shall be open to the Presidency at any time thereafter, if the workload of the Court justifies it, to propose a reduction in the number of judges, provided that the number of judges shall not be reduced below that specified in paragraph 1. The proposal shall be dealt with in accordance with the

procedure laid down in subparagraphs (a) and (b). In the event that the proposal is adopted, the number of judges shall be progressively decreased as the terms of office of serving judges expire, until the necessary number has been reached.
(d) The judges shall be chosen from among persons of high moral character, impartiality and integrity who possess the qualifications required in their respective States for appointment to the highest judicial offices.
(e) Every candidate for election to the Court shall:
(i) Have established competence in criminal law and procedure, and the necessary relevant experience, whether as judge, prosecutor, advocate or in other similar capacity, in criminal proceedings; or
(ii) Have established competence in relevant areas of international law such as international humanitarian law and the law of human rights, and extensive experience in a professional legal capacity which is of relevance to the judicial work of the Court;
(f) Every candidate for election to the Court shall have an excellent knowledge of and be fluent in at least one of the working languages of the Court.
For the purposes of the election, there shall be two lists of candidates:
List A containing the names of candidates with the qualifications specified in paragraph 3 (b) (i); and
List B containing the names of candidates with the qualifications specified in paragraph 3 (b) (ii).
A candidate with sufficient qualifications for both lists may choose on which list to appear. At the first election to the Court, at least nine judges shall be elected from list A and at least five judges from list B. Subsequent elections shall be so organized as to maintain the equivalent proportion on the Court of judges qualified on the two lists.
(a) The judges shall be elected by secret ballot at a meeting of the Assembly of States Parties convened for that purpose under article 112. Subject to paragraph 7, the persons elected to the Court shall be the 18 candidates who obtain the highest number of votes and a two-thirds majority of the States Parties pr(b) In the event that a sufficient number of judges is not elected on the first ballot, successive ballots shall be held in accordance with the procedures laid down in subparagraph (a) until the remaining places have been filled.
No two judges may be nationals of the same State. A person who, for the purposes of membership of the Court, could be regarded as a national of more than one State shall be deemed to be a national of the State in which that person ordinarily exercises civil and political rights.
(a) The States Parties shall, in the selection of judges, take into account the need, within the membership of the Court, for:
The representation of the principal legal systems of the world;
Equitable geographical representation; and
A fair representation of female and male judges.
(b) States Parties shall also take into account the need to include judges with legal expertise on specific issues, including, but not limited to, violence against women or children.
(c) Subject to subparagraph (b), judges shall hold office for a term of nine years and, subject to subparagraph (c) and to article 37, paragraph 2, shall not be eligible for re-election.
(d) At the first election, one third of the judges elected shall be selected by lot to serve for a term of three years; one third of the judges elected shall be selected by lot to serve for a term of six years; and the remainder shall serve for a term of nine years.
(e) A judge who is selected to serve for a term of three years under subparagraph (b) shall be eligible for re-election for a full term.

10. Notwithstanding paragraph 9, a judge assigned to a Trial or Appeals Chamber in accordance with article 39 shall continue in office to complete any trial or appeal the hearing of which has already commenced before that Chamber.

Article 37 Judicial vacancies

1. In the event of a vacancy, an election shall be held in accordance with article 36 to fill the vacancy.
2. A judge elected to fill a vacancy shall serve for the remainder of the predecessor's term and, if that period is three years or less, shall be eligible for re-election for a full term under article 36.

Article 38 The Presidency

1. The President and the First and Second Vice-Presidents shall be elected by an absolute majority of the judges. They shall each serve for a term of three years or until the end of their respective terms of office as judges, whichever expires earlier. They shall be eligible for re-election once.
2. The First Vice-President shall act in place of the President in the event that the President is unavailable or disqualified. The Second Vice-President shall act in place of the President in the event that both the President and the First Vice-President are unavailable or disqualified.
3. The President, together with the First and Second Vice-Presidents, shall constitute the Presidency, which shall be responsible for:

(a) The proper administration of the Court, with the exception of the Office of the Prosecutor; and
(b) The other functions conferred upon it in accordance with this Statute.

4. In discharging its responsibility under paragraph 3 (a), the Presidency shall coordinate with and seek the concurrence of the Prosecutor on all matters of mutual concern.

Article 39 Chambers

1. As soon as possible after the election of the judges, the Court shall organize itself into the divisions specified in article 34, paragraph (b). The Appeals Division shall be composed of the President and four other judges, the Trial Division of not less than six judges and the Pre-Trial Division of not less than six judges. The assignment of judges to divisions shall be based on the nature of the functions to be performed by each division and the qualifications and experience of the judges elected to the Court, in such a way that each division shall contain an appropriate combination of expertise in criminal law and procedure and in international law. The Trial and Pre-Trial Divisions shall be composed predominantly of judges with criminal trial experience.
2. (a) The judicial functions of the Court shall be carried out in each division by Chambers.
(b)(i) The Appeals Chamber shall be composed of all the judges of the Appeals Division;
(ii) The functions of the Trial Chamber shall be carried out by three judges of the Trial Division;
(iii) The functions of the Pre-Trial Chamber shall be carried out either by three judges of the Pre-Trial Division or by a single judge of that division in accordance with this Statute and the Rules of Procedure and Evidence;

(c) Nothing in this paragraph shall preclude the simultaneous constitution of more than one Trial Chamber or Pre-Trial Chamber when the efficient management of the Court's workload so requires.
3. (a) Judges assigned to the Trial and Pre-Trial Divisions shall serve in those divisions for a period of three years, and thereafter until the completion of any case the hearing of which has already commenced in the division concerned.
(b) Judges assigned to the Appeals Division shall serve in that division for their entire term of office.
4. Judges assigned to the Appeals Division shall serve only in that division. Nothing in this article shall, however, preclude the temporary attachment of judges from the Trial Division to the Pre-Trial Division or vice versa, if the Presidency considers that the efficient management of the Court's workload so requires, provided that under no circumstances shall a judge who has participated in the pre-trial phase of a case be eligible to sit on the Trial Chamber hearing that case.

Article 40 Independence of the judges

1. The judges shall be independent in the performance of their functions.
2. Judges shall not engage in any activity which is likely to interfere with their judicial functions or to affect confidence in their independence.
3. Judges required to serve on a full-time basis at the seat of the Court shall not engage in any other occupation of a professional nature.
4. Any question regarding the application of paragraphs 2 and 3 shall be decided by an absolute majority of the judges. Where any such question concerns an individual judge, that judge shall not take part in the decision.

Article 41 Excusing and disqualification of judges

1. The Presidency may, at the request of a judge, excuse that judge from the exercise of a function under this Statute, in accordance with the Rules of Procedure and Evidence.
2.(a) A judge shall not participate in any case in which his or her impartiality might reasonably be doubted on any ground. A judge shall be disqualified from a case in accordance with this paragraph if, inter alia, that judge has previously been involved in any capacity in that case before the Court or in a related criminal case at the national level involving the person being investigated or prosecuted. A judge shall also be disqualified on such other grounds as may be provided for in the Rules of Procedure and Evidence.
(b) The Prosecutor or the person being investigated or prosecuted may request the disqualification of a judge under this paragraph.
(c) Any question as to the disqualification of a judge shall be decided by an absolute majority of the judges. The challenged judge shall be entitled to present his or her comments on the matter, but shall not take part in the decision.

Article 42The Office of the Prosecutor

1. The Office of the Prosecutor shall act independently as a separate organ of the Court. It shall be responsible for receiving referrals and any substantiated information on crimes within the jurisdiction of the Court, for examining them and for conducting investigations and prosecutions before the Court. A member of the Office shall not seek or act on instructions from any external source.
2. The Office shall be headed by the Prosecutor. The Prosecutor shall have full authority over the management and administration of the Office, including the staff, facilities and other resources thereof. The Prosecutor shall be assisted by one or more Deputy

Prosecutors, who shall be entitled to carry out any of the acts required of the Prosecutor under this Statute. The Prosecutor and the Deputy Prosecutors shall be of different nationalities. They shall serve on a full-time basis.
3. The Prosecutor and the Deputy Prosecutors shall be persons of high moral character, be highly competent in and have extensive practical experience in the prosecution or trial of criminal cases. They shall have an excellent knowledge of and be fluent in at least one of the working languages of the Court.
4. The Prosecutor shall be elected by secret ballot by an absolute majority of the members of the Assembly of States Parties. The Deputy Prosecutors shall be elected in the same way from a list of candidates provided by the Prosecutor. The Prosecutor shall nominate three candidates for each position of Deputy Prosecutor to be filled. Unless a shorter term is decided upon at the time of their election, the Prosecutor and the Deputy Prosecutors shall hold office for a term of nine years and shall not be eligible for re-election.
5. Neither the Prosecutor nor a Deputy Prosecutor shall engage in any activity which is likely to interfere with his or her prosecutorial functions or to affect confidence in his or her independence. They shall not engage in any other occupation of a professional nature.
6. The Presidency may excuse the Prosecutor or a Deputy Prosecutor, at his or her request, from acting in a particular case.
7. Neither the Prosecutor nor a Deputy Prosecutor shall participate in any matter in which their impartiality might reasonably be doubted on any ground. They shall be disqualified from a case in accordance with this paragraph if, inter alia, they have previously been involved in any capacity in that case before the Court or in a related criminal case at the national level involving the person being investigated or prosecuted.
8. Any question as to the disqualification of the Prosecutor or a Deputy Prosecutor shall be decided by the Appeals Chamber.
- The person being investigated or prosecuted may at any time request the disqualification of the Prosecutor or a Deputy Prosecutor on the grounds set out in this article;
- The Prosecutor or the Deputy Prosecutor, as appropriate, shall be entitled to present his or her comments on the matter;
9. The Prosecutor shall appoint advisers with legal expertise on specific issues, including, but not limited to, sexual and gender violence and violence against children.

Article 43 The Registry

The Registry shall be responsible for the non-judicial aspects of the administration and servicing of the Court, without prejudice to the functions and powers of the Prosecutor in accordance with article 42.
The Registry shall be headed by the Registrar, who shall be the principal administrative officer of the Court. The Registrar shall exercise his or her functions under the authority of the President of the Court.
The Registrar and the Deputy Registrar shall be persons of high moral character, be highly competent and have an excellent knowledge of and be fluent in at least one of the working languages of the Court.
The judges shall elect the Registrar by an absolute majority by secret ballot, taking into account any recommendation by the Assembly of States Parties. If the need arises and upon the recommendation of the Registrar, the judges shall elect, in the same manner, a Deputy Registrar.
The Registrar shall hold office for a term of five years, shall be eligible for re-election once and shall serve on a full-time basis. The Deputy Registrar shall hold office for a term of five years or such shorter term as may be decided upon by an absolute majority of the

judges, and may be elected on the basis that the Deputy Registrar shall be called upon to serve as required.
The Registrar shall set up a Victims and Witnesses Unit within the Registry. This Unit shall provide, in consultation with the Office of the Prosecutor, protective measures and security arrangements, counselling and other appropriate assistance for witnesses, victims who appear before the Court, and others who are at risk on account of testimony given by such witnesses. The Unit shall include staff with expertise in trauma, including trauma related to crimes of sexual violence.

Article 44 Staff

The Prosecutor and the Registrar shall appoint such qualified staff as may be required to their respective offices. In the case of the Prosecutor, this shall include the appointment of investigators.
In the employment of staff, the Prosecutor and the Registrar shall ensure the highest standards of efficiency, competency and integrity, and shall have regard, mutatis mutandis, to the criteria set forth in article 36, paragraph 8.
The Registrar, with the agreement of the Presidency and the Prosecutor, shall propose Staff Regulations which include the terms and conditions upon which the staff of the Court shall be appointed, remunerated and dismissed. The Staff Regulations shall be approved by the Assembly of States Parties.
The Court may, in exceptional circumstances, employ the expertise of gratis personnel offered by States Parties, intergovernmental organizations or non-governmental organizations to assist with the work of any of the organs of the Court. The Prosecutor may accept any such offer on behalf of the Office of the Prosecutor. Such gratis personnel shall be employed in accordance with guidelines to be established by the Assembly of States Parties.

Article 45 Solemn undertaking

Before taking up their respective duties under this Statute, the judges, the Prosecutor, the Deputy Prosecutors, the Registrar and the Deputy Registrar shall each make a solemn undertaking in open court to exercise his or her respective functions impartially and conscientiously.

Article 46 Removal from office

1. A judge, the Prosecutor, a Deputy Prosecutor, the Registrar or the Deputy Registrar shall be removed from office if a decision to this effect is made in accordance with paragraph 2, in cases where that person:
(a) Is found to have committed serious misconduct or a serious breach of his or her duties under this Statute, as provided for in the Rules of Procedure and Evidence; or
(b) Is unable to exercise the functions required by this Statute.
2. A decision as to the removal from office of a judge, the Prosecutor or a Deputy Prosecutor under paragraph 1 shall be made by the Assembly of States Parties, by secret ballot:
(a) In the case of a judge, by a two-thirds majority of the States Parties upon a recommendation adopted by a two-thirds majority of the other judges;
(b) In the case of the Prosecutor, by an absolute majority of the States Parties;
(c) In the case of a Deputy Prosecutor, by an absolute majority of the States Parties upon the recommendation of the Prosecutor.

3. A decision as to the removal from office of the Registrar or Deputy Registrar shall be made by an absolute majority of the judges.
5. A judge, Prosecutor, Deputy Prosecutor, Registrar or Deputy Registrar whose conduct or ability to exercise the functions of the office as required by this Statute is challenged under this article shall have full opportunity to present and receive evidence and to make submissions in accordance with the Rules of Procedure and Evidence. The person in question shall not otherwise participate in the consideration of the matter.

Article 47 Disciplinary measures

A judge, Prosecutor, Deputy Prosecutor, Registrar or Deputy Registrar who has committed misconduct of a less serious nature than that set out in article 46, paragraph 1, shall be subject to disciplinary measures, in accordance with the Rules of Procedure and Evidence.

Article 48 Privileges and immunities

The Court shall enjoy in the territory of each State Party such privileges and immunities as are necessary for the fulfillment of its purposes.
The judges, the Prosecutor, the Deputy Prosecutors and the Registrar shall, when engaged on or with respect to the business of the Court, enjoy the same privileges and immunities as are accorded to heads of diplomatic missions and shall, after the expiry of their terms of office, continue to be accorded immunity from legal process of every kind in respect of words spoken or written and acts performed by them in their official capacity.
The Deputy Registrar, the staff of the Office of the Prosecutor and the staff of the Registry shall enjoy the privileges and immunities and facilities necessary for the performance of their functions, in accordance with the agreement on the privileges and immunities of the Court.
Counsel, experts, witnesses or any other person required to be present at the seat of the Court shall be accorded such treatment as is necessary for the proper functioning of the Court, in accordance with the agreement on the privileges and immunities of the Court.
The privileges and immunities of:
(a) A judge or the Prosecutor may be waived by an absolute majority of the judges;
(b) The Registrar may be waived by the Presidency;
(c) The Deputy Prosecutors and staff of the Office of the Prosecutor may be waived by the Prosecutor;
(d) The Deputy Registrar and staff of the Registry may be waived by the Registrar.

Article 49 Salaries, allowances and expenses

The judges, the Prosecutor, the Deputy Prosecutors, the Registrar and the Deputy Registrar shall receive such salaries, allowances and expenses as may be decided upon by the Assembly of States Parties. These salaries and allowances shall not be reduced during their terms of office.

Article 50 Official and working languages

The official languages of the Court shall be Arabic, Chinese, English, French, Russian and Spanish. The judgements of the Court, as well as other decisions resolving fundamental issues before the Court, shall be published in the official languages. The Presidency shall, in accordance with the criteria established by the Rules of Procedure and Evidence,

determine which decisions may be considered as resolving fundamental issues for the purposes of this paragraph.
The working languages of the Court shall be English and French. The Rules of Procedure and Evidence shall determine the cases in which other official languages may be used as working languages.
At the request of any party to a proceeding or a State allowed to intervene in a proceeding, the Court shall authorize a language other than English or French to be used by such a party or State, provided that the Court considers such authorization to be adequately justified.
Article 51 Rules of Procedure and Evidence

The Rules of Procedure and Evidence shall enter into force upon adoption by a two-thirds majority of the members of the Assembly of States Parties.
Amendments to the Rules of Procedure and Evidence may be proposed by:
(a) Any State Party;
(b) The judges acting by an absolute majority; or
(c) The Prosecutor.
Such amendments shall enter into force upon adoption by a two-thirds majority of the members of the Assembly of States Parties.
After the adoption of the Rules of Procedure and Evidence, in urgent cases where the Rules do not provide for a specific situation before the Court, the judges may, by a two-thirds majority, draw up provisional Rules to be applied until adopted, amended or rejected at the next ordinary or special session of the Assembly of States Parties.
The Rules of Procedure and Evidence, amendments thereto and any provisional Rule shall be consistent with this Statute. Amendments to the Rules of Procedure and Evidence as well as provisional Rules shall not be applied retroactively to the detriment of the person who is being investigated or prosecuted or who has been convicted.
In the event of conflict between the Statute and the Rules of Procedure and Evidence, the Statute s

Article 52 Regulations of the Court

The judges shall, in accordance with this Statute and the Rules of Procedure and Evidence, adopt, by an absolute majority, the Regulations of the Court necessary for its routine functioning.
The Prosecutor and the Registrar shall be consulted in the elaboration of the Regulations and any amendments thereto.
The Regulations and any amendments thereto shall take effect upon adoption unless otherwise decided by the judges. Immediately upon adoption, they shall be circulated to States Parties for comments. If within six months there are no objections from a majority of States Parties, they shall remain in force.

Part 5. Investigation and Prosecution

Article 53 Initiation of an investigation

1. The Prosecutor shall, having evaluated the information made available to him or her, initiate an investigation unless he or she determines that there is no reasonable basis to proceed under this Statute. In deciding whether to initiate an investigation, the Prosecutor shall consider whether:
(a) The information available to the Prosecutor provides a reasonable basis to believe that a crime within the jurisdiction of the Court has been or is being committed;

(b) The case is or would be admissible under article 17; and
(c) Taking into account the gravity of the crime and the interests of victims, there are nonetheless substantial reasons to believe that an investigation would not serve the interests of justice.
If the Prosecutor determines that there is no reasonable basis to proceed and his or her determination is based solely on subparagraph (c) above, he or she shall inform the Pre-Trial Chamber.
2. If, upon investigation, the Prosecutor concludes that there is not a sufficient basis for a prosecution because:
(a) There is not a sufficient legal or factual basis to seek a warrant or summons under article 58;
(b) The case is inadmissible under article 17; or
(c) A prosecution is not in the interests of justice, taking into account all the circumstances, including the gravity of the crime, the interests of victims and the age or infirmity of the alleged perpetrator, and his or her role in the alleged crime;
the Prosecutor shall inform the Pre-Trial Chamber and the State making a referral under article 14 or the Security Council in a case under article 13, paragraph (b), of his or her conclusion and the reasons for the conclusion.
3. (a) At the request of the State making a referral under article 14 or the Security Council under article 13, paragraph (b), the Pre-Trial Chamber may review a decision of the Prosecutor under paragraph 1 or 2 not to proceed and may request the Prosecutor to reconsider that decision.
(b) In addition, the Pre-Trial Chamber may, on its own initiative, review a decision of the Prosecutor not to proceed if it is based solely on paragraph 1 (c) or 2 (c). In such a case, the decision of the Prosecutor shall be effective only if confirmed by the Pre-Trial Chamber.
4. The Prosecutor may, at any time, reconsider a decision whether to initiate an investigation or prosecution based on new facts or information.

Article 54 Duties and powers of the Prosecutor with respect to investigations

1. The Prosecutor shall:
(a) In order to establish the truth, extend the investigation to cover all facts and evidence relevant to an assessment of whether there is criminal responsibility under this Statute, and, in doing so, investigate incriminating and exonerating circumstances equally;
(b) Take appropriate measures to ensure the effective investigation and prosecution of crimes within the jurisdiction of the Court, and in doing so, respect the interests and personal circumstances of victims and witnesses, including age, gender as defined in article 7, paragraph 3, and health, and take into account the nature of the crime, in particular where it involves sexual violence, gender violence or violence against children; and
(c) Fully respect the rights of persons arising under this Statute.
2. The Prosecutor may conduct investigations on the territory of a State:
(a) In accordance with the provisions of Part 9; or
(b) As authorized by the Pre-Trial Chamber under article 57, paragraph 3 (d).
3. The Prosecutor may:
(a) Collect and examine evidence;
(b) Request the presence of and question persons being investigated, victims and witnesses;
(c) Seek the cooperation of any State or intergovernmental organization or arrangement in accordance with its respective competence and/or mandate;

(d) Enter into such arrangements or agreements, not inconsistent with this Statute, as may be necessary to facilitate the cooperation of a State, intergovernmental organization or person;
(e) Agree not to disclose, at any stage of the proceedings, documents or information that the Prosecutor obtains on the condition of confidentiality and solely for the purpose of generating new evidence, unless the provider of the information consents; and
(f) Take necessary measures, or request that necessary measures be taken, to ensure the confidentiality of information, the protection of any person or the preservation of evidence.

Article 55 Rights of persons during an investigation

1. In respect of an investigation under this Statute, a person:
(a) Shall not be compelled to incriminate himself or herself or to confess guilt;
(b) Shall not be subjected to any form of coercion, duress or threat, to torture or to any other form of cruel, inhuman or degrading treatment or punishment;
(c) Shall, if questioned in a language other than a language the person fully understands and speaks, have, free of any cost, the assistance of a competent interpreter and such translations as are necessary to meet the requirements of fairness; and
(d) Shall not be subjected to arbitrary arrest or detention, and shall not be deprived of his or her liberty except on such grounds and in accordance with such procedures as are established in this Statute.
2. Where there are grounds to believe that a person has committed a crime within the jurisdiction of the Court and that person is about to be questioned either by the Prosecutor, or by national authorities pursuant to a request made under Part 9, that person shall also have the following rights of which he or she shall be informed prior to being questioned:
(a) To be informed, prior to being questioned, that there are grounds to believe that he or she has committed a crime within the jurisdiction of the Court;
(b) To remain silent, without such silence being a consideration in the determination of guilt or innocence;
(c) To have legal assistance of the person's choosing, or, if the person does not have legal assistance, to have legal assistance assigned to him or her, in any case where the interests of justice so require, and without payment by the person in any such case if the person does not have sufficient means to pay for it; and
(d) To be questioned in the presence of counsel unless the person has voluntarily waived his or her right to counsel.

Article 56Role of the Pre-Trial Chamber in relation to a unique investigative opportunity

1. (a) Where the Prosecutor considers an investigation to present a unique opportunity to take testimony or a statement from a witness or to examine, collect or test evidence, which may not be available subsequently for the purposes of a trial, the Prosecutor shall so inform the Pre-Trial Chamber.
(b) In that case, the Pre-Trial Chamber may, upon request of the Prosecutor, take such measures as may be necessary to ensure the efficiency and integrity of the proceedings and, in particular, to protect the rights of the defence.
(c) Unless the Pre-Trial Chamber orders otherwise, the Prosecutor shall provide the relevant information to the person who has been arrested or appeared in response to a summons in connection with the investigation referred to in subparagraph (a), in order that he or she may be heard on the matter.

2. The measures referred to in paragraph 1 (b) may include:
Making recommendations or orders regarding procedures to be followed;
Directing that a record be made of the proceedings;
Appointing an expert to assist;
Authorizing counsel for a person who has been arrested, or appeared before the Court in response to a summons, to participate, or where there has not yet been such an arrest or appearance or counsel has not been designated, appointing another counsel to attend and represent the interests of the defence;
Naming one of its members or, if necessary, another available judge of the Pre-Trial or Trial Division to observe and make recommendations or orders regarding the collection and preservation of evidence and the questioning of persons;
Taking such other action as may be necessary to collect or preserve evidence.
3. (a) Where the Prosecutor has not sought measures pursuant to this article but the Pre-Trial Chamber considers that such measures are required to preserve evidence that it deems would be essential for the defence at trial, it shall consult with the Prosecutor as to whether there is good reason for the Prosecutor's failure to request the measures. If upon consultation, the Pre-Trial Chamber concludes that the Prosecutor's failure to request such measures is unjustified, the Pre-Trial Chamber may take such measures on its own initiative.
(b) A decision of the Pre-Trial Chamber to act on its own initiative under this paragraph may be appealed by the Prosecutor. The appeal shall be heard on an expedited basis.
4. The admissibility of evidence preserved or collected for trial pursuant to this article, or the record thereof, shall be governed at trial by article 69, and given such weight as determined by the Trial Chamber.

Article 57 Functions and powers of the Pre-Trial Chamber

1. Unless otherwise provided in this Statute, the Pre-Trial Chamber shall exercise its functions in accordance with the provisions of this article.
2. (a) Orders or rulings of the Pre-Trial Chamber issued under articles 15, 18, 19, 54, paragraph 2, 61, paragraph 7, and 72 must be concurred in by a majority of its judges.
(b) In all other cases, a single judge of the Pre-Trial Chamber may exercise the functions provided for in this Statute, unless otherwise provided for in the Rules of Procedure and Evidence or by a majority of the Pre-Trial Chamber.
3. In addition to its other functions under this Statute, the Pre-Trial Chamber may:
(a) At the request of the Prosecutor, issue such orders and warrants as may be required for the purposes of an investigation;
(b) Upon the request of a person who has been arrested or has appeared pursuant to a summons under article 58, issue such orders, including measures such as those described in article 56, or seek such cooperation pursuant to Part 9 as may be necessary to assist the person in the preparation of his or her defence;
(c) Where necessary, provide for the protection and privacy of victims and witnesses, the preservation of evidence, the protection of persons who have been arrested or appeared in response to a summons, and the protection of national security information;
(d) Authorize the Prosecutor to take specific investigative steps within the territory of a State Party without having secured the cooperation of that State under Part 9 if, whenever possible having regard to the views of the State concerned, the Pre-Trial Chamber has determined in that case that the State is clearly unable to execute a request for cooperation due to the unavailability of any authority or any component of its judicial system competent to execute the request for cooperation under Part 9.
(e) Where a warrant of arrest or a summons has been issued under article 58, and having due regard to the strength of the evidence and the rights of the parties concerned,

as provided for in this Statute and the Rules of Procedure and Evidence, seek the cooperation of States pursuant to article 93, paragraph 1 (k), to take protective measures for the purpose of forfeiture, in particular for the ultimate benefit of victims.

Article 58 Issuance by the Pre-Trial Chamber of a warrant of arrest or a summons to appear

1. At any time after the initiation of an investigation, the Pre-Trial Chamber shall, on the application of the Prosecutor, issue a warrant of arrest of a person if, having examined the application and the evidence or other information submitted by the Prosecutor, it is satisfied that:
(a) There are reasonable grounds to believe that the person has committed a crime within the jurisdiction of the Court; and
(b) The arrest of the person appears necessary:
(i) To ensure the person's appearance at trial,
(ii) To ensure that the person does not obstruct or endanger the investigation or the court proceedings, or
(iii) Where applicable, to prevent the person from continuing with the commission of that crime or a related crime which is within the jurisdiction of the Court and which arises out of the same circumstances.
2. The application of the Prosecutor shall contain:
(a) The name of the person and any other relevant identifying information;
(b) A specific reference to the crimes within the jurisdiction of the Court which the person is alleged to have committed;
(c) A concise statement of the facts which are alleged to constitute those crimes;
(d) A summary of the evidence and any other information which establish reasonable grounds to believe that the person committed those crimes; and
(e) The reason why the Prosecutor believes that the arrest of the person is necessary.
3. The warrant of arrest shall contain:
(a) The name of the person and any other relevant identifying information;
(b) A specific reference to the crimes within the jurisdiction of the Court for which the person's arrest is sought; and
(c) A concise statement of the facts which are alleged to constitute those crimes.
4. The warrant of arrest shall remain in effect until otherwise ordered by the Court.
5. On the basis of the warrant of arrest, the Court may request the provisional arrest or the arrest and surrender of the person under Part 9.
6. The Prosecutor may request the Pre-Trial Chamber to amend the warrant of arrest by modifying or adding to the crimes specified therein. The Pre-Trial Chamber shall so amend the warrant if it is satisfied that there are reasonable grounds to believe that the person committed the modified or additional crimes.
7. As an alternative to seeking a warrant of arrest, the Prosecutor may submit an application requesting that the Pre-Trial Chamber issue a summons for the person to appear. If the Pre-Trial Chamber is satisfied that there are reasonable grounds to believe that the person committed the crime alleged and that a summons is sufficient to ensure the person's appearance, it shall issue the summons, with or without conditions restricting liberty (other than detention) if provided for by national law, for the person to appear. The summons shall contain:
(a) The name of the person and any other relevant identifying information;
(b) The specified date on which the person is to appear;
(c) A specific reference to the crimes within the jurisdiction of the Court which the person is alleged to have committed; and
(d) A concise statement of the facts which are alleged to constitute the crime.

The summons shall be served on the person.

Article 59 Arrest proceedings in the custodial State

1. A State Party which has received a request for provisional arrest or for arrest and surrender shall immediately take steps to arrest the person in question in accordance with its laws and the provisions of Part 9.
2. A person arrested shall be brought promptly before the competent judicial authority in the custodial State which shall determine, in accordance with the law of that State, that:

(a) The warrant applies to that person;
(b) The person has been arrested in accordance with the proper process; and
(c) The person's rights have been respected.
3. The person arrested shall have the right to apply to the competent authority in the custodial State for interim release pending surrender.
4. In reaching a decision on any such application, the competent authority in the custodial State shall consider whether, given the gravity of the alleged crimes, there are urgent and exceptional circumstances to justify interim release and whether necessary safeguards exist to ensure that the custodial State can fulfil its duty to surrender the person to the Court. It shall not be open to the competent authority of the custodial State to consider whether the warrant of arrest was properly issued in accordance with article 58, paragraph 1 (a) and (b).
5. The Pre-Trial Chamber shall be notified of any request for interim release and shall make recommendations to the competent authority in the custodial State. The competent authority in the custodial State shall give full consideration to such recommendations, including any recommendations on measures to prevent the escape of the person, before rendering its decision.
6. If the person is granted interim release, the Pre-Trial Chamber may request periodic reports on the status of the interim release.
7. Once ordered to be surrendered by the custodial State, the person shall be delivered to the Court as soon as possible.

Article 60 Initial proceedings before the Court

Upon the surrender of the person to the Court, or the person's appearance before the Court voluntarily or pursuant to a summons, the Pre-Trial Chamber shall satisfy itself that the person has been informed of the crimes which he or she is alleged to have committed, and of his or her rights under this Statute, including the right to apply for interim release pending trial.
A person subject to a warrant of arrest may apply for interim release pending trial. If the Pre-Trial Chamber is satisfied that the conditions set forth in article 58, paragraph 1, are met, the person shall continue to be detained. If it is not so satisfied, the Pre-Trial Chamber shall release the person, with or without conditions.
The Pre-Trial Chamber shall periodically review its ruling on the release or detention of the person, and may do so at any time on the request of the Prosecutor or the person. Upon such review, it may modify its ruling as to detention, release or conditions of release, if it is satisfied that changed circumstances so require.
The Pre-Trial Chamber shall ensure that a person is not detained for an unreasonable period prior to trial due to inexcusable delay by the Prosecutor. If such delay occurs, the Court shall consider releasing the person, with or without conditions.
If necessary, the Pre-Trial Chamber may issue a warrant of arrest to secure the presence of a person who has been released.

Article 61 Confirmation of the charges before trial

1. Subject to the provisions of paragraph 2, within a reasonable time after the person's surrender or voluntary appearance before the Court, the Pre-Trial Chamber shall hold a hearing to confirm the charges on which the Prosecutor intends to seek trial. The hearing shall be held in the presence of the Prosecutor and the person charged, as well as his or her counsel.
2. The Pre-Trial Chamber may, upon request of the Prosecutor or on its own motion, hold a hearing in the absence of the person charged to confirm the charges on which the Prosecutor intends to seek trial when the person has:
(a) Waived his or her right to be present; or
(b) Fled or cannot be found and all reasonable steps have been taken to secure his or her appearance before the Court and to inform the person of the charges and that a hearing to confirm those charges will be held.
In that case, the person shall be represented by counsel where the Pre-Trial Chamber determines that it is in the interests of justice.
3. Within a reasonable time before the hearing, the perso(a) Be provided with a copy of the document containing the charges on which the Prosecutor intends to bring the person to trial; and
(b) Be informed of the evidence on which the Prosecutor intends to rely at the hearing.
The Pre-Trial Chamber may issue orders regarding the disclosure of information for the purposes of the hearing.
4. Before the hearing, the Prosecutor may continue the investigation and may amend or withdraw any charges. The person shall be given reasonable notice before the hearing of any amendment to or withdrawal of charges. In case of a withdrawal of charges, the Prosecutor shall notify the Pre-Trial Chamber of the reasons for the withdrawal.
5. At the hearing, the Prosecutor shall support each charge with sufficient evidence to establish substantial grounds to believe that the person committed the crime charged. The Prosecutor may rely on documentary or summary evidence and need not call the witnesses expected to testify at the trial.
6. At the hearing, the person may:
(a) Object to the charges;
(b) Challenge the evidence presented by the Prosecutor; and
(c) Present evidence.
7. The Pre-Trial Chamber shall, on the basis of the hearing, determine whether there is sufficient evidence to establish substantial grounds to believe that the person committed each of the crimes charged. Based on its determination, the Pre-Trial Chamber shall:
(a) Confirm those charges in relation to which it has determined that there is sufficient evidence, and commit the person to a Trial Chamber for trial on the charges as confirmed;
(b) Decline to confirm those charges in relation to which it has determined that there is insufficient evidence;
(c) Adjourn the hearing and request the Prosecutor to consider:
(i) Providing further evidence or conducting further investigation with respect to a particular charge; or
(ii) Amending a charge because the evidence submitted appears to establish a different crime within the jurisdiction of the Court.
8. Where the Pre-Trial Chamber declines to confirm a charge, the Prosecutor shall not be precluded from subsequently requesting its confirmation if the request is supported by additional evidence.
9. After the charges are confirmed and before the trial has begun, the Prosecutor may, with the permission of the Pre-Trial Chamber and after notice to the accused, amend

the charges. If the Prosecutor seeks to add additional charges or to substitute more serious charges, a hearing under this article to confirm those charges must be held. After commencement of the trial, the Prosecutor may, with the permission of the Trial Chamber, withdraw the charges.
10. Any warrant previously issued shall cease to have effect with respect to any charges which have not been confirmed by the Pre-Trial Chamber or which have been withdrawn by the Prosecutor.
11. Once the charges have been confirmed in accordance with this article, the Presidency shall constitute a Trial Chamber which, subject to paragraph 9 and to article 64, paragraph 4, shall be responsible for the conduct of subsequent proceedings and may exercise any function of the Pre-Trial Chamber that is relevant and capable of application in those proceedings.

Part 6. The Trial

Article 62 Place of trial

Unless otherwise decided, the place of the trial shall be the seat of the Court.

Article 63 Trial in the presence of the accused

1. The accused shall be present during the trial.
2. If the accused, being present before the Court, continues to disrupt the trial, the Trial Chamber may remove the accused and shall make provision for him or her to observe the trial and instruct counsel from outside the courtroom, through the use of communications technology, if required. Such measures shall be taken only in exceptional circumstances after other reasonable alternatives have proved inadequate, and only for such duration as is strictly required.

Article 64 Functions and powers of the Trial Chamber

1. The functions and powers of the Trial Chamber set out in this article shall be exercised in accordance with this Statute and the Rules of Procedure and Evidence.
2. The Trial Chamber shall ensure that a trial is fair and expeditious and is conducted with full respect for the rights of the accused and due regard for the protection of victims and witnesses.
3. Upon assignment of a case for trial in accordance with this Statute, the Trial Chamber assigned to deal with the case shall:
(a) Confer with the parties and adopt such procedures as are necessary to facilitate the fair and expeditious conduct of the proceedings;
(b) Determine the language or languages to be used at trial; and
(c) Subject to any other relevant provisions of this Statute, provide for disclosure of documents or information not previously disclosed, sufficiently in advance of the commencement of the trial to enable adequate preparation for trial.
4. The Trial Chamber may, if necessary for its effective and fair functioning, refer preliminary issues to the Pre-Trial Chamber or, if necessary, to another available judge of the Pre-Trial Division.
5. Upon notice to the parties, the Trial Chamber may, as appropriate, direct that there be joinder or severance in respect of charges against more than one accused.
6. In performing its functions prior to trial or during the course of a trial, the Trial Chamber may, as necessary:

(a) Exercise any functions of the Pre-Trial Chamber referred to in article 61, paragraph 11;
(b) Require the attendance and testimony of witnesses and production of documents and other evidence by obtaining, if necessary, the assistance of States as provided in this Statute;
(c) Provide for the protection of confidential information;
(d) Order the production of evidence in addition to that already collected prior to the trial or presented during the trial by the parties;
(e) Provide for the protection of the accused, witnesses and victims; and
(f) Rule on any other relevant matters.
7. The trial shall be held in public. The Trial Chamber may, however, determine that special circumstances require that certain proceedings be in closed session for the purposes set forth in article 68, or to protect confidential or sensitive information to be given in evidence.
8.
(a) At the commencement of the trial, the Trial Chamber shall have read to the accused the charges previously confirmed by the Pre-Trial Chamber. The Trial Chamber shall satisfy itself that the accused understands the nature of the charges. It shall afford him or her the opportunity to make an admission of guilt in accordance with article 65 or to plead not guilty.
(b) At the trial, the presiding judge may give directions for the conduct of proceedings, including to ensure that they are conducted in a fair and impartial manner. Subject to any directions of the presiding judge, the parties may submit evidence in accordance with the provisions of this Statute.
9. The Trial Chamber shall have, inter alia, the power on application of a party or on its own motion to:
(a) Rule on the admissibility or relevance of evidence; and
(b) Take all necessary steps to maintain order in the course of a hearing.
10. The Trial Chamber shall ensure that a complete record of the trial, which accurately reflects the proceedings, is made and that it is maintained and preserved by the Registrar.

Article 65 Proceedings on an admission of guilt

1. Where the accused makes an admission of guilt pursuant to article 64, paragraph 8 (a), the Trial Chamber shall determine whether:
(a) The accused understands the nature and consequences of the admission of guilt;
(b) The admission is voluntarily made by the accused after sufficient consultation with defence counsel; and
(c) The admission of guilt is supported by the facts of the case that are contained in:
(i) The charges brought by the Prosecutor and admitted by the accused;
(ii) Any materials presented by the Prosecutor which supplement the charges and which the accused accepts; and
(iii) Any other evidence, such as the testimony of witnesses, presented by the Prosecutor or the accused.
2. Where the Trial Chamber is satisfied that the matters referred to in paragraph 1 are established, it shall consider the admission of guilt, together with any additional evidence presented, as establishing all the essential facts that are required to prove the crime to which the admission of guilt relates, and may convict the accused of that crime.
3. Where the Trial Chamber is not satisfied that the matters referred to in paragraph 1 are established, it shall consider the admission of guilt as not having been made, in which case it shall order that the trial be continued under the ordinary trial procedures provided by this Statute and may remit the case to another Trial Chamber.

4. Where the Trial Chamber is of the opinion that a more complete presentation of the facts of the case is required in the interests of justice, in particular the interests of the victims, the Trial Chamber may:
(a) Request the Prosecutor to present additional evidence, including the testimony of witnesses; or
(b) Order that the trial be continued under the ordinary trial procedures provided by this Statute, in which case it shall consider the admission of guilt as not having been made and may remit the case to another Trial Chamber.
Any discussions between the Prosecutor and the defence regarding modification of the charges, the admission of guilt or the penalty to be imposed shall not be binding on the Court.

Article 66 Presumption of innocence

1. Everyone shall be presumed innocent until proved guilty before the Court in accordance with the applicable law.
2. The onus is on the Prosecutor to prove the guilt of the accused.
3. In order to convict the accused, the Court must be convinced of the guilt of the accused beyond reasonable doubt.

Article 67 Rights of the accused

1. In the determination of any charge, the accused shall be entitled to a public hearing, having regard to the provisions of this Statute, to a fair hearing conducted impartially, and to the following minimum guarantees, in full equality:
(a) To be informed promptly and in detail of the nature, cause and content of the charge, in a language which the accused fully understands and speaks;
(b) To have adequate time and facilities for the preparation of the defence and to communicate freely with counsel of the accused's choosing in confidence;
(c) To be tried without undue delay;
(d) Subject to article 63, paragraph 2, to be present at the trial, to conduct the defence in person or through legal assistance of the accused's choosing, to be informed, if the accused does not have legal assistance, of this right and to have legal assistance assigned by the Court in any case where the interests of justice so require, and without payment if the accused lacks sufficient means to pay for it;
(e) To examine, or have examined, the witnesses against him or her and to obtain the attendance and examination of witnesses on his or her behalf under the same conditions as witnesses against him or her. The accused shall also be entitled to raise defences and to present other evidence admissible under this Statute;
(f) To have, free of any cost, the assistance of a competent interpreter and such translations as are necessary to meet the requirements of fairness, if any of the proceedings of or documents presented to the Court are not in a language which the accused fully understands and speaks;
(g) Not to be compelled to testify or to confess guilt and to remain silent, without such silence being a consideration in the determination of guilt or innocence;
(h) To make an unsworn oral or written statement in his or her defence; and
(i) Not to have imposed on him or her any reversal of the burden of proof or any onus of rebuttal.
2. In addition to any other disclosure provided for in this Statute, the Prosecutor shall, as soon as practicable, disclose to the defence evidence in the Prosecutor's possession or control which he or she believes shows or tends to show the innocence of the accused, or to mitigate the guilt of the accused, or which may affect the credibility of prosecution evidence. In case of doubt as to the application of this paragraph, the Court shall decide.

Article 68 Protection of the victims and witnesses and their participation in the proceedings

The Court shall take appropriate measures to protect the safety, physical and psychological well-being, dignity and privacy of victims and witnesses. In so doing, the Court shall have regard to all relevant factors, including age, gender as defined in article 7, paragraph 3, and health, and the nature of the crime, in particular, but not limited to, where the crime involves sexual or gender violence or violence against children. The Prosecutor shall take such measures particularly during the investigation and prosecution of such crimes. These measures shall not be prejudicial to or inconsistent with the rights of the accused and a fair and impartial trial.

As an exception to the principle of public hearings provided for in article 67, the Chambers of the Court may, to protect victims and witnesses or an accused, conduct any part of the proceedings in camera or allow the presentation of evidence by electronic or other special means. In particular, such measures shall be implemented in the case of a victim of sexual violence or a child who is a victim or a witness, unless otherwise ordered by the Court, having regard to all the circumstances, particularly the views of the victim or witness.

Where the personal interests of the victims are affected, the Court shall permit their views and concerns to be presented and considered at stages of the proceedings determined to be appropriate by the Court and in a manner which is not prejudicial to or inconsistent with the rights of the accused and a fair and impartial trial. Such views and concerns may be presented by the legal representatives of the victims where the Court considers it appropriate, in accordance with the Rules of Procedure and Evidence.

The Victims and Witnesses Unit may advise the Prosecutor and the Court on appropriate protective measures, security arrangements, counseling and assistance as referred to in article 43, paragraph 6.

Where the disclosure of evidence or information pursuant to this Statute may lead to the grave endangerment of the security of a witness or his or her family, the Prosecutor may, for the purposes of any proceedings conducted prior to the commencement of the trial, withhold such evidence or information and instead submit a summary thereof. Such measures shall be exercised in a manner which is not prejudicial to or inconsistent with the rights of the accused and a fair and impartial trial.

A State may make an application for necessary measures to be taken in respect of the protection of its servants or agents and the protection of confidential or sensitive information.

Article 69 Evidence

Before testifying, each witness shall, in accordance with the Rules of Procedure and Evidence, give an undertaking as to the truthfulness of the evidence to be given by that witness.

The testimony of a witness at trial shall be given in person, except to the extent provided by the measures set forth in article 68 or in the Rules of Procedure and Evidence. The Court may also permit the giving of viva voce (oral) or recorded testimony of a witness by means of video or audio technology, as well as the introduction of documents or written transcripts, subject to this Statute and in accordance with the Rules of Procedure and Evidence. These measures shall not be prejudicial to or inconsistent with the rights of the accused.

The parties may submit evidence relevant to the case, in accordance with article 64. The Court shall have the authority to request the submission of all evidence that it considers necessary for the determination of the truth.

The Court may rule on the relevance or admissibility of any evidence, taking into account, inter alia, the probative value of the evidence and any prejudice that such evidence may cause to a fair trial or to a fair evaluation of the testimony of a witness, in accordance with the Rules of Procedure and Evidence.

The Court shall respect and observe privileges on confidentiality as provided for in the Rules of Procedure and Evidence.

The Court shall not require proof of facts of common knowledge but may take judicial notice of them.
Evidence obtained by means of a violation of this Statute or internationally recognized human rights shall not be admissible if:
(a) The violation casts substantial doubt on the reliability of the evidence; or
(b) The admission of the evidence would be antithetical to and would seriously damage the integrity of the proceedings.
When deciding on the relevance or admissibility of evidence collected by a State, the Court shall not rule on the application of the State's national law.

Article 70 Offences against the administration of justice

The Court shall have jurisdiction over the following offences against its administration of justice when committed intentionally:
(a) Giving false testimony when under an obligation pursuant to article 69, paragraph 1, to tell the truth;
(b) Presenting evidence that the party knows is false or forged;
(c) Corruptly influencing a witness, obstructing or interfering with the attendance or testimony of a witness, retaliating against a witness for giving testimony or destroying, tampering with or interfering with the collection of evidence;
(d) Impeding, intimidating or corruptly influencing an official of the Court for the purpose of forcing or persuading the official not to perform, or to perform improperly, his or her duties;
(e) Retaliating against an official of the Court on account of duties performed by that or another official;
(f) Soliciting or accepting a bribe as an official of the Court in connection with his or her official duties.
The principles and procedures governing the Court's exercise of jurisdiction over offences under this article shall be those provided for in the Rules of Procedure and Evidence. The conditions for providing international cooperation to the Court with respect to its proceedings under this article shall be governed by the domestic laws of the requested State.
In the event of conviction, the Court may impose a term of imprisonment not exceeding five years, or a fine in accordance with the Rules of Procedure and Evidence, or both.
(a) Each State Party shall extend its criminal laws penalizing offences against the integrity of its own investigative or judicial process to offences against the administration of justice referred to in this article, committed on its territory, or by one of its nationals;
(b) Upon request by the Court, whenever it deems it proper, the State Party shall submit the case to its competent authorities for the purpose of prosecution. Those authorities

shall treat such cases with diligence and devote sufficient resources to enable them to be conducted effectively.

Article 71 Sanctions for misconduct before the Court

1. The Court may sanction persons present before it who commit misconduct, including disruption of its proceedings or deliberate refusal to comply with its directions, by administrative measures other than imprisonment, such as temporary or permanent removal from the courtroom, a fine or other similar measures provided for in the Rules of Procedure and Evidence.
2. The procedures governing the imposition of the measures set forth in paragraph 1 shall be those provided for in the Rules of Procedure and Evidence.

Article 72 Protection of national security information

1. This article applies in any case where the disclosure of the information or documents of a State would, in the opinion of that State, prejudice its national security interests. Such cases include those falling within the scope of article 56, paragraphs 2 and 3, article 61, paragraph 3, article 64, paragraph 3, article 67, paragraph 2, article 68, paragraph 6, article 87, paragraph 6 and article 93, as well as cases arising at any other stage of the proceedings where such disclosure may be 2. This article shall also apply when a person who has been requested to give information or evidence has refused to do so or has referred the matter to the State on the ground that disclosure would prejudice the national security interests of a State and the State concerned confirms that it is of the opinion that disclosure would prejudice its national security interests.
3. Nothing in this article shall prejudice the requirements of confidentiality applicable under article 54, paragraph 3 (e) and (f), or the application of article 73.
4. If a State learns that information or documents of the State are being, or are likely to be, disclosed at any stage of the proceedings, and it is of the opinion that disclosure would prejudice its national security interests, that State shall have the right to intervene in order to obtain resolution of the issue in accordance with this article.
5. If, in the opinion of a State, disclosure of information would prejudice its national security interests, all reasonable steps will be taken by the State, acting in conjunction with the Prosecutor, the defence or the Pre-Trial Chamber or Trial Chamber, as the case may be, to seek to resolve the matter by cooperative means. Such steps may include:
(a) Modification or clarification of the request;
(b) A determination by the Court regarding the relevance of the information or evidence sought, or a determination as to whether the evidence, though relevant, could be or has been obtained from a source other than the requested State;
(c) Obtaining the information or evidence from a different source or in a different form; or
(d) Agreement on conditions under which the assistance could be provided including, among other things, providing summaries or redactions, limitations on disclosure, use of in camera or ex parte proceedings, or other protective measures permissible under the Statute and the Rules of Procedure and Evidence.
6. Once all reasonable steps have been taken to resolve the matter through cooperative means, and if the State considers that there are no means or conditions under which the information or documents could be provided or disclosed without prejudice to its national security interests, it shall so notify the Prosecutor or the Court of the specific reasons for its decision, unless a specific description of the reasons would itself necessarily result in such prejudice to the State's national security interests.

7. Thereafter, if the Court determines that the evidence is relevant and necessary for the establishment of the guilt or innocence of the accused, the Court may undertake the following actions:
(a) Where disclosure of the information or document is sought pursuant to a request for cooperation under Part 9 or the circumstances described in paragraph 2, and the State has invoked the ground for refusal referred to in article 93, paragraph 4:
(i) The Court may, before making any conclusion referred to in subparagraph 7 (a) (ii), request further consultations for the purpose of considering the State's representations, which may include, as appropriate, hearings in camera and ex parte;
(ii) If the Court concludes that, by invoking the ground for refusal under article 93, paragraph 4, in the circumstances of the case, the requested State is not acting in accordance with its obligations under this Statute, the Court may refer the matter in accordance with article 87, paragraph 7, specifying the reasons for its conclusion; and
(iii) The Court may make such inference in the trial of the accused as to the existence or non-existence of a fact, as may be appropriate in the circumstances; or
(b) In all other circumstances:
(i) Order disclosure; or
(ii) To the extent it does not order disclosure, make such inference in the trial of the accused as to the existence or non-existence of a fact, as may be appropriate in the circumstances.

Article 73 Third-party information or documents

If a State Party is requested by the Court to provide a document or information in its custody, possession or control, which was disclosed to it in confidence by a State, intergovernmental organization or international organization, it shall seek the consent of the originator to disclose that document or information. If the originator is a State Party, it shall either consent to disclosure of the information or document or undertake to resolve the issue of disclosure with the Court, subject to the provisions of article 72. If the originator is not a State Party and refuses to consent to disclosure, the requested State shall inform the Court that it is unable to provide the document or information because of a pre-existing obligation of confidentiality to the originator.

Article 74 Requirements for the decision

All the judges of the Trial Chamber shall be present at each stage of the trial and throughout their deliberations. The Presidency may, on a case-by-case basis, designate, as available, one or more alternate judges to be present at each stage of the trial and to replace a member of the Trial Chamber if that member is unable to continue attending.
The Trial Chamber's decision shall be based on its evaluation of the evidence and the entire proceedings. The decision shall not exceed the facts and circumstances described in the charges and any amendments to the charges. The Court may base its decision only on evidence submitted and discussed before it at the trial.
The judges shall attempt to achieve unanimity in their decision, failing which the decision shall be taken by a majority of the judges.
The deliberations of the Trial Chamber shall remain secret.
The decision shall be in writing and shall contain a full and reasoned statement of the Trial Chamber's findings on the evidence and conclusions.
The Trial Chamber shall issue one decision. When there is no unanimity, the Trial Chamber's decision shall contain the views of the majority and the minority. The decision or a summary thereof shall be delivered in open court.

Article 75 Reparations to victims

The Court shall establish principles relating to reparations to, or in respect of, victims, including restitution, compensation and rehabilitation. On this basis, in its decision the Court may, either upon request or on its own motion in exceptional circumstances, determine the scope and extent of any damage, loss and injury to, or in respect of, victims and will state the principles on which it is acting.
The Court may make an order directly against a convicted person specifying appropriate reparations to, or in respect of, victims, including restitution, compensation and rehabilitation. Where appropriate, the Court may order that the award for reparations be made through the Trust Fund provided for in article 79.
Before making an order under this article, the Court may invite and shall take account of representations from or on behalf of the convicted person, victims, other interested persons or interested States.
In exercising its power under this article, the Court may, after a person is convicted of a crime within the jurisdiction of the Court, determine whether, in order to give effect to an order which it may make under this article, it is necessary to seek measures under article 93, paragraph 1.
A State Party shall give effect to a decision under this article as if the provisions of article 109 were applicable to this article.
Nothing in this article shall be interpreted as prejudicing the rights of victims under national or international law.

Article 76 Sentencing

In the event of a conviction, the Trial Chamber shall consider the appropriate sentence to be imposed and shall take into account the evidence presented and submissions made during the trial that are relevant to the sentence.
Except where article 65 applies and before the completion of the trial, the Trial Chamber may on its own motion and shall, at the request of the Prosecutor or the accused, hold a further hearing to hear any additional evidence or submissions relevant to the sentence, in accordance with the Rules of Procedure and Evidence.
Where paragraph 2 applies, any representations under article 75 shall be heard during the further hearing referred to in paragraph 2 and, if necessary, during any additional hearing.
The sentence shall be pronounced in public and, wherever possible, in the presence of the accused.

Part 7. Penalties

Article 77 Applicable penalties

1. Subject to article 110, the Court may impose one of the following penalties on a person convicted of a crime referred to in article 5 of this Statute:
(a) Imprisonment for a specified number of years, which may not exceed a maximum of 30 years; or
(b) A term of life imprisonment when justified by the extreme gravity of the crime and the individual circumstances of the convicted person.
2. In addition to imprisonment, the Court may order:
(a) A fine under the criteria provided for in the Rules of Procedure and Evidence;
(b) A forfeiture of proceeds, property and assets derived directly or indirectly from that crime, without prejudice to the rights of bona fide third parties.

Article 78 Determination of the sentence

In determining the sentence, the Court shall, in accordance with the Rules of Procedure and Evidence, take into account such factors as the gravity of the crime and the individual circumstances of the convicted person.
In imposing a sentence of imprisonment, the Court shall deduct the time, if any, previously spent in detention in accordance with an order of the Court. The Court may deduct any time otherwise spent in detention in connection with conduct underlying the crime.
When a person has been convicted of more than one crime, the Court shall pronounce a sentence for each crime and a joint sentence specifying the total period of imprisonment. This period shall be no less than the highest individual sentence pronounced and shall not exceed 30 years imprisonment or a sentence of life imprisonment in conformity with article 77, paragraph 1 (b).

Article 79 Trust Fund

A Trust Fund shall be established by decision of the Assembly of States Parties for the benefit of victims of crimes within the jurisdiction of the Court, and of the families of such victims.
The Court may order money and other property collected through fines or forfeiture to be transferred, by order of the Court, to the Trust Fund.
The Trust Fund shall be managed according to criteria to be determined by the Assembly of States Parties.

Article 80 Non-prejudice to national application of penalties and national laws

Nothing in this Part affects the application by States of penalties prescribed by their national law, nor the law of States which do not provide for penalties prescribed in this Part.

Part 8. Appeal and Revision

Article 81 Appeal against decision of acquittal or conviction or against sentence

1. A decision under article 74 may be appealed in accordance with the Rules of Procedure and Evidence as follows:
(a) The Prosecutor may make an appeal on any of the following grounds:
(i) Procedural error,
(ii) Error of fact, or
(iii) Error of law;
(b) The convicted person, or the Prosecutor on that person's behalf, may make an appeal on any of the following grounds:
(i) Procedural error,
(ii) Error of fact,
(iii) Error of law, or
(iv) Any other ground that affects the fairness or reliability of the proceedings or decision.
2. (a) A sentence may be appealed, in accordance with the Rules of Procedure and Evidence, by the Prosecutor or the convicted person on the ground of disproportion between the crime and the sentence;
(b) If on an appeal against sentence the Court considers that there are grounds on which the conviction might be set aside, wholly or in part, it may invite the Prosecutor and the

convicted person to submit grounds under article 81, paragraph 1 (a) or (b), and may render a decision on conviction in accordance with article 83;
(c) The same procedure applies when the Court, on an appeal against conviction only, considers that there are grounds to reduce the sentence under paragraph 2 (a).
3. (a) Unless the Trial Chamber orders otherwise, a convicted person shall remain in custody pending an appeal;
(b) When a convicted person's time in custody exceeds the sentence of imprisonment imposed, that person shall be released, except that if the Prosecutor is also appealing, the release may be subject to the conditions under subparagraph (c) below;
(c) In case of an acquittal, the accused shall be released immediately, subject to the following:
(i) Under exceptional circumstances, and having regard, inter alia, to the concrete risk of flight, the seriousness of the offence charged and the probability of success on appeal, the Trial Chamber, at the request of the Prosecutor, may maintain the detention of the person pending appeal;
(ii) A decision by the Trial Chamber under subparagraph (c) (i) may be appealed in accordance with the Rules of Procedure and Evidence.
4. Subject to the provisions of paragraph 3 (a) and (b), execution of the decision or sentence shall be suspended during the period allowed for appeal and for the duration of the appeal proceedings.

Article 82Appeal against other decisions

1. Either party may appeal any of the following decisions in accordance with the Rules of Procedure and Evidence:
(a) A decision with respect to jurisdiction or admissibility;
(b) A decision granting or denying release of the person being investigated or prosecuted;
(c) A decision of the Pre-Trial Chamber to act on its own initiative under article 56, paragraph 3;
(d) A decision that involves an issue that would significantly affect the fair and expeditious conduct of the proceedings or the outcome of the trial, and for which, in the opinion of the Pre-Trial or Trial Chamber, an immediate resolution by the Appeals Chamber may materially advance the proceedings.
2. A decision of the Pre-Trial Chamber under article 57, paragraph 3 (d), may be appealed against by the State concerned or by the Prosecutor, with the leave of the Pre-Trial Chamber. The appeal shall be heard on an expedited basis.
3. An appeal shall not of itself have suspensive effect unless the Appeals Chamber so orders, upon request, in accordance with the Rules of Procedure and Evidence.
4. A legal representative of the victims, the convicted person or a bona fide owner of property adversely affected by an order under article 75 may appeal against the order for reparations, as provided in the Rules of Procedure and Evidence.

Article 83 Proceedings on appeal

For the purposes of proceedings under article 81 and this article, the Appeals Chamber shall have all the powers of the Trial Chamber.
If the Appeals Chamber finds that the proceedings appealed from were unfair in a way that affected the reliability of the decision or sentence, or that the decision or sentence appealed from was materially affected by error of fact or law or procedural error, it may:
- Reverse or amend the decision or sentence; or
- Order a new trial before a different Trial Chamber.

For these purposes, the Appeals Chamber may remand a factual issue to the original Trial Chamber for it to determine the issue and to report back accordingly, or may itself call evidence to determine the issue. When the decision or sentence has been appealed only by the person convicted, or the Prosecutor on that person's behalf, it cannot be amended to his or her detriment.
If in an appeal against sentence the Appeals Chamber finds that the sentence is disproportionate to the crime, it may vary the sentence in accordance with Part 7.
The judgement of the Appeals Chamber shall be taken by a majority of the judges and shall be delivered in open court. The judgement shall state the reasons on which it is based. When there is no unanimity, the judgement of the Appeals Chamber shall contain the views of the majority and the minority, but a judge may deliver a separate or dissenting opinion on a question of law.

The Appeals Chamber may deliver its judgement in the absence of the person acquitted or convicted.

Article 84 Revision of conviction or sentence

1. The convicted person or, after death, spouses, children, parents or one person alive at the time of the accused's death who has been given express written instructions from the accused to bring such a claim, or the Prosecutor on the person's behalf, may apply to the Appeals Chamber to revise the final judgement of conviction or sentence on the grounds that:
(a) New evidence has been discovered that:
(i) Was not available at the time of trial, and such unavailability was not wholly or partially attributable to the party making application; and
(ii) Is sufficiently important that had it been proved at trial it would have been likely to have resulted in a different verdict;
(b) It has been newly discovered that decisive evidence, taken into account at trial and upon which the conviction depends, was false, forged or falsified;
(c) One or more of the judges who participated in conviction or confirmation of the charges has committed, in that case, an act of serious misconduct or serious breach of duty of sufficient gravity to justify the removal of that judge or those judges from office under article 46.
2. The Appeals Chamber shall reject the application if it considers it to be unfounded. If it determines that the application is meritorious, it may, as appropriate:
(a) Reconvene the original Trial Chamber;
(b) Constitute a new Trial Chamber; or
(c) Retain jurisdiction over the matter, with a view to, after hearing the parties in the manner set forth in the Rules of Procedure and Evidence, arriving at a determination on whether the judgement should be revised.

Article 85 Compensation to an arrested or convicted person

Anyone who has been the victim of unlawful arrest or detention shall have an enforceable right to compensation.
When a person has by a final decision been convicted of a criminal offence, and when subsequently his or her conviction has been reversed on the ground that a new or newly discovered fact shows conclusively that there has been a miscarriage of justice, the person who has suffered punishment as a result of such conviction shall be compensated according to law, unless it is proved that the non-disclosure of the unknown fact in time is wholly or partly attributable to him or her.

In exceptional circumstances, where the Court finds conclusive facts showing that there has been a grave and manifest miscarriage of justice, it may in its discretion award compensation, according to the criteria provided in the Rules of Procedure and Evidence, to a person who has been released from detention following a final decision of acquittal or a termination of the proceedings for that reason.

Part 9. International Cooperation and Judicial Assistance

Article 86 General obligation to cooperate

States Parties shall, in accordance with the provisions of this Statute, cooperate fully with the Court in its investigation and prosecution of crimes within the jurisdiction of the Court.

Article 87
Requests for cooperation: general provisions

1.
(a) The Court shall have the authority to make requests to States Parties for cooperation. The requests shall be transmitted through the diplomatic channel or any other appropriate channel as may be designated by each State Party upon ratification, acceptance, approval or accession. Subsequent changes to the designation shall be made by each State Party in accordance with the Rules of Procedure and Evidence.
(b) When appropriate, without prejudice to the provisions of subparagraph (a), requests may also be transmitted through the International Criminal Police Organization or any appropriate regional organization.
2. Requests for cooperation and any documents supporting the request shall either be in or be accompanied by a translation into an official language of the requested State or one of the working languages of the Court, in accordance with the choice made by that State upon ratification, acceptance, approval or accession. Subsequent changes to this choice shall be made in accordance with the Rules of Procedu
3. The requested State shall keep confidential a request for cooperation and any documents supporting the request, except to the extent that the disclosure is necessary for execution of the request.
4. In relation to any request for assistance presented under this Part, the Court may take such measures, including measures related to the protection of information, as may be necessary to ensure the safety or physical or psychological well-being of any victims, potential witnesses and their families. The Court may request that any information that is made available under this Part shall be provided and handled in a manner that protects the safety and physical or psychological well-being of any victims, potential witnesses and their families.
5.
(a) The Court may invite any State not party to this Statute to provide assistance under this Part on the basis of an ad hoc arrangement, an agreement with such State or any other appropriate basis.
(b) Where a State not party to this Statute, which has entered into an ad hoc arrangement or an agreement with the Court, fails to cooperate with requests pursuant to any such arrangement or agreement, the Court may so inform the Assembly of States Parties or, where the Security Council referred the matter to the Court, the Security Council.
6. The Court may ask any intergovernmental organization to provide information or documents. The Court may also ask for other forms of cooperation and assistance which

may be agreed upon with such an organization and which are in accordance with its competence or mandate.
7. Where a State Party fails to comply with a request to cooperate by the Court contrary to the provisions of this Statute, thereby preventing the Court from exercising its functions and powers under this Statute, the Court may make a finding to that effect and refer the matter to the Assembly of States Parties or, where the Security Council referred the matter to the Court, to the Security Council.

Article 88 Availability of procedures under national law

States Parties shall ensure that there are procedures available under their national law for all of the forms of cooperation which are specified under this Part.

Article 89 Surrender of persons to the Court

1. The Court may transmit a request for the arrest and surrender of a person, together with the material supporting the request outlined in article 91, to any State on the territory of which that person may be found and shall request the cooperation of that State in the arrest and surrender of such a person. States Parties shall, in accordance with the provisions of this Part and the procedure under their national law, comply with requests for arrest and surrender.
2. Where the person sought for surrender brings a challenge before a national court on the basis of the principle of ne bis in idem as provided in article 20, the requested State shall immediately consult with the Court to determine if there has been a relevant ruling on admissibility. If the case is admissible, the requested State shall proceed with the execution of the request. If an admissibility ruling is pending, the requested State may postpone the execution of the request for surrender of the person until the Court makes a determination on admissibility.
3. a) A State Party shall authorize, in accordance with its national procedural law, transportation through its territory of a person being surrendered to the Court by another State, except where transit through that State would impede or delay the surrender.
(b) A request by the Court for transit shall be transmitted in accordance with article 87. The request for transit shall contain:
(i) A description of the person being transported;
(ii) A brief statement of the facts of the case and their legal characterization; and
(iii) The warrant for arrest and surrender;
(c) A person being transported shall be detained in custody during the period of transit;
(d) No authorization is required if the person is transported by air and no landing is scheduled on the territory of the transit State;
(e) If an unscheduled landing occurs on the territory of the transit State, that State may require a request for transit from the Court as provided for in subparagraph (b). The transit State shall detain the person being transported until the request for transit is received and the transit is effected, provided that detention for purposes of this subparagraph may not be extended beyond 96 hours from the unscheduled landing unless the request is received within that time.
4. If the person sought is being proceeded against or is serving a sentence in the requested State for a crime different from that for which surrender to the Court is sought, the requested State, after making its decision to grant the request, shall consult with the Court.

Article 90 Competing requests

1. A State Party which receives a request from the Court for the surrender of a person under article 89 shall, if it also receives a request from any other State for the extradition of the same person for the same conduct which forms the basis of the crime for which the Court seeks the person's surrender, notify the Court and the requesting State of that fact.
2. Where the requesting State is a State Party, the requested State shall give priority to the request from the Court if:
- The Court has, pursuant to article 18 or 19, made a determination that the case in respect of which surrender is sought is admissible and that determination takes into account the investigation or prosecution conducted by the requesting State in respect of its request for extradition; or
- The Court makes the determination described in subparagraph (a) pursuant to the requested State's notification under paragraph 1.
3. Where a determination under paragraph 2 (a) has not been made, the requested State may, at its discretion, pending the determination of the Court under paragraph 2 (b), proceed to deal with the request for extradition from the requesting State but shall not extradite the person until the Court has determined that the case is inadmissible. The Court's determination shall be made on an expedited basis.
4. If the requesting State is a State not Party to this Statute the requested State, if it is not under an international obligation to extradite the person to the requesting State, shall give priority to the request for surrender from the Court, if the Court has determined that the case is admissible.
5. Where a case under paragraph 4 has not been determined to be admissible by the Court, the requested State may, at its discretion, proceed to deal with the request for extradition from the requesting State.
6. In cases where paragraph 4 applies except that the requested State is under an existing international obligation to extradite the person to the requesting State not Party to this Statute, the requested State shall determine whether to surrender the person to the Court or extradite the person to the requesting State. In making its decision, the requested State shall consider all the relevant factors, including but not limited to:
- The respective dates of the requests;
- The interests of the requesting State including, where relevant, whether the crime was committed in its territory and the nationality of the victims and of the person sought; and
- The possibility of subsequent surrender between the Court and the requesting State.
7. Where a State Party which receives a request from the Court for the surrender of a person also receives a request from any State for the extradition of the same person for conduct other than that which constitutes the crime for which the Court seeks the person's surrender:
- The requested State shall, if it is not under an existing international obligation to extradite the person to the requesting State, give priority to the request from the Court;
- The requested State shall, if it is under an existing international obligation to extradite the person to the requesting State, determine whether to surrender the person to the Court or to extradite the person to the requesting State. In making its decision, the requested State shall consider all the relevant factors, including but not limited to those set out in paragraph 6, but shall give special consideration to the relative nature and gravity of the conduct in question.
8. Where pursuant to a notification under this article, the Court has determined a case to be inadmissible, and subsequently extradition to the requesting State is refused, the requested State shall notify the Court of this decision.

Article 91 Contents of request for arrest and surrender

1. A request for arrest and surrender shall be made in writing. In urgent cases, a request may be made by any medium capable of delivering a written record, provided that the request shall be confirmed through the channel provided for in article 87, paragraph 1 (a).
2. In the case of a request for the arrest and surrender of a person for whom a warrant of arrest has been issued by the Pre-Trial Chamber under article 58, the request shall contain or be supported by:
- Information describing the person sought, sufficient to identify the person, and information as to that person's probable location;
- A copy of the warrant of arrest; and
- Such documents, statements or information as may be necessary to meet the requirements for the surrender process in the requested State, except that those requirements should not be more burdensome than those applicable to requests for extradition pursuant to treaties or arrangements between the requested State and other States and should, if possible, be less burdensome, taking into account the distinct nature of the Court.
3. In the case of a request for the arrest and surrender of a person already convicted, the request shall contain or be supported by:
- A copy of any warrant of arrest for that person;
- A copy of the judgement of conviction;
- Information to demonstrate that the person sought is the one referred to in the judgement of conviction; and
- If the person sought has been sentenced, a copy of the sentence imposed and, in the case of a sentence for imprisonment, a statement of any time already served and the time remaining to be served.
4. Upon the request of the Court, a State Party shall consult with the Court, either generally or with respect to a specific matter, regarding any requirements under its national law that may apply under paragraph 2 (c). During the consultations, the State Party shall advise the Court of the specific requirements of its national law.

Article 92 Provisional arrest

1. In urgent cases, the Court may request the provisional arrest of the person sought, pending presentation of the request for surrender and the documents supporting the request as specified in article 91.
2. The request for provisional arrest shall be made by any medium capable of delivering a written record and shall contain:
- Information describing the person sought, sufficient to identify the person, and information as to that person's probable location;
- A concise statement of the crimes for which the person's arrest is sought and of the facts which are alleged to constitute those crimes, including, where possible, the date and location of the crime;
- A statement of the existence of a warrant of arrest or a judgement of conviction against the person sought; and
- A statement that a request for surrender of the person sought will follow.
3. A person who is provisionally arrested may be released from custody if the requested State has not received the request for surrender and the documents supporting the request as specified in article 91 within the time limits specified in the Rules of Procedure and Evidence. However, the person may consent to surrender before the expiration of this period if permitted by the law of the requested State. In such a case, the requested State shall proceed to surrender the person to the Court as soon as possible.

4. The fact that the person sought has been released from custody pursuant to paragraph 3 shall not prejudice the subsequent arrest and surrender of that person if the request for surrender and the documents supporting the request are delivered at a later date.

Article 93 Other forms of cooperation

1. States Parties shall, in accordance with the provisions of this Part and under procedures of national law, comply with requests by the Court to provide the following assistance in relation to investigations or prosecutions:
- The identification and whereabouts of persons or the location of items;
- The taking of evidence, including testimony under oath, and the production of evidence, including expert opinions and reports necessary to the Court;
- The questioning of any person being investigated or prosecuted;
- The service of documents, including judicial documents;
- Facilitating the voluntary appearance of persons as witnesses or experts before the Court;
- The temporary transfer of persons as provided in paragraph 7;
- The examination of places or sites, including the exhumation and examination of grave sites;
- The execution of searches and seizures;
- The provision of records and documents, including official records and documents;
- The protection of victims and witnesses and the preservation of evidence;
- The identification, tracing and freezing or seizure of proceeds, property and assets and instrumentalities of crimes for the purpose of eventual forfeiture, without prejudice to the rights of bona fide third parties; and
- Any other type of assistance which is not prohibited by the law of the requested State, with a view to facilitating the investigation and prosecution of crimes within the jurisdiction of the Court.

2. The Court shall have the authority to provide an assurance to a witness or an expert appearing before the Court that he or she will not be prosecuted, detained or subjected to any restriction of personal freedom by the Court in respect of any act or omission that preceded the departure of that person from the requested State.
3. Where execution of a particular measure of assistance detailed in a request presented under paragraph 1, is prohibited in the requested State on the basis of an existing fundamental legal principle of general application, the requested State shall promptly consult with the Court to try to resolve the matter. In the consultations, consideration should be given to whether the assistance can be rendered in another manner or subject to conditions. If after consultations the matter cannot be resolved, the Court shall modify the request as necessary.
4. In accordance with article 72, a State Party may deny a request for assistance, in whole or in part, only if the request concerns the production of any documents or disclosure of evidence which relates to its national security.
5. Before denying a request for assistance under paragraph 1 (l), the requested State shall consider whether the assistance can be provided subject to specified conditions, or whether the assistance can be provided at a later date or in an alternative manner, provided that if the Court or the Prosecutor accepts the assistance subject to conditions, the Court or the Prosecutor shall abide by them.
6. If a request for assistance is denied, the requested State Party shall promptly inform the Court or the Prosecutor of the reasons for such denial.
7.

- The Court may request the temporary transfer of a person in custody for purposes of identification or for obtaining testimony or other assistance. The person may be transferred if the following conditions are fulfilled:
- The person freely gives his or her informed consent to the transfer; and
- The requested State agrees to the transfer, subject to such conditions as that State and the Court may agree.

- The person being transferred shall remain in custody. When the purposes of the transfer have been fulfilled, the Court shall return the person without delay to the requested State.
8.
- The Court shall ensure the confidentiality of documents and information, except as required for the investigation and proceedings described in the request.
- The requested State may, when necessary, transmit documents or information to the Prosecutor on a confidential basis. The Prosecutor may then use them solely for the purpose of generating new evidence.
- The requested State may, on its own motion or at the request of the Prosecutor, subsequently consent to the disclosure of such documents or information. They may then be used as evidence pursuant to the provisions of Parts 5 and 6 and in accordance with the Rules of Procedure and Evidence.
9.
(a)
(i) In the event that a State Party receives competing requests, other than for surrender or extradition, from the Court and from another State pursuant to an international obligation, the State Party shall endeavour, in consultation with the Court and the other State, to meet both requests, if necessary by postponing or attaching conditions to one or the other request.
(ii) Failing that, competing requests shall be resolved in accordance with the principles established in article 90.
(b) Where, however, the request from the Court concerns information, property or persons which are subject to the control of a third State or an international organization by virtue of an international agreement, the requested States shall so inform the Court and the Court shall direct its request to the third State or international organization.
10. (a) The Court may, upon request, cooperate with and provide assistance to a State Party conducting an investigation into or trial in respect of conduct which constitutes a crime within the jurisdiction of the Court or which constitutes a serious crime under the national law of the requesting State.
(b)(i) The assistance provided under subparagraph (a) shall include, inter alia:
- The transmission of statements, documents or other types of evidence obtained in the course of an investigation or a trial conducted by the Court; and
- The questioning of any person detained by order of the Court;
(ii) In the case of assistance under subparagraph (b) (i) a:
- If the documents or other types of evidence have been obtained with the assistance of a State, such transmission shall require the consent of that State;
- If the statements, documents or other types of evidence have been provided by a witness or expert, such transmission shall be subject to the provisions of article 68.
(c) The Court may, under the conditions set out in this paragraph, grant a request for assistance under this paragraph from a State which is not a Party to this Statute.

Article 94 Postponement of execution of a request in respect of ongoing investigation or prosecution

1. If the immediate execution of a request would interfere with an ongoing investigation or prosecution of a case different from that to which the request relates, the requested

State may postpone the execution of the request for a period of time agreed upon with the Court. However, the postponement shall be no longer than is necessary to complete the relevant investigation or prosecution in the requested State. Before making a decision to postpone, the requested State should consider whether the assistance may be immediately provided subject to certain conditions.
2. If a decision to postpone is taken pursuant to paragraph 1, the Prosecutor may, however, seek measures to preserve evidence, pursuant to article 93, paragraph 1 (j).

Article 95 Postponement of execution of a request in respect of an admissibility challenge

Where there is an admissibility challenge under consideration by the Court pursuant to article 18 or 19, the requested State may postpone the execution of a request under this Part pending a determination by the Court, unless the Court has specifically ordered that the Prosecutor may pursue the collection of such evidence pursuant to article 18

Article 96 Contents of request for other forms of assistance under article 93

1. A request for other forms of assistance referred to in article 93 shall be made in writing. In urgent cases, a request may be made by any medium capable of delivering a written record, provided that the request shall be confirmed through the channel provided for in article 87, paragraph 1 (a).
2. The request shall, as applicable, contain or be supported by the following:
- A concise statement of the purpose of the request and the assistance sought, including the legal basis and the grounds for the request;
- As much detailed information as possible about the location or identification of any person or place that must be found or identified in order for the assistance sought to be provided;
- A concise statement of the essential facts underlying the request;
- The reasons for and details of any procedure or requirement to be followed;
- Such information as may be required under the law of the requested State in order to execute the request; and
- Any other information relevant in order for the assistance sought to be provided.

3. Upon the request of the Court, a State Party shall consult with the Court, either generally or with respect to a specific matter, regarding any requirements under its national law that may apply under paragraph 2 (e). During the consultations, the State Party shall advise the Court of the specific requirements of its national law.
4. The provisions of this article shall, where applicable, also apply in respect of a request for assistance made to the Court.

Article 97 Consultations

Where a State Party receives a request under this Part in relation to which it identifies problems which may impede or prevent the execution of the request, that State shall consult with the Court without delay in order to resolve the matter. Such problems may include, inter alia:
- Insufficient information to execute the request;
- In the case of a request for surrender, the fact that despite best efforts, the person sought cannot be located or that the investigation conducted has determined that the person in the requested State is clearly not the person named in the warrant; or
- The fact that execution of the request in its current form would require the requested State to breach a pre-existing treaty obligation undertaken with respect to another State.

Article 98 Cooperation with respect to waiver of immunity and consent to surrender

1. The Court may not proceed with a request for surrender or assistance which would require the requested State to act inconsistently with its obligations under international law with respect to the State or diplomatic immunity of a person or property of a third State, unless the Court can first obtain the cooperation of that third State for the waiver of the immunity.
2. The Court may not proceed with a request for surrender which would require the requested State to act inconsistently with its obligations under international agreements pursuant to which the consent of a sending State is required to surrender a person of that State to the Court, unless the Court can first obtain the cooperation of the sending State for the giving of consent for the surrender.

Article 99 Execution of requests under articles 93 and 96

1. Requests for assistance shall be executed in accordance with the relevant procedure under the law of the requested State and, unless prohibited by such law, in the manner specified in the request, including following any procedure outlined therein or permitting persons specified in the request to be present at and assist in the execution process.
2. In the case of an urgent request, the documents or evidence produced in response shall, at the request of the Court, be sent urgently.
3. Replies from the requested State shall be transmitted in their original language and form.
4. Without prejudice to other articles in this Part, where it is necessary for the successful execution of a request which can be executed without any compulsory measures, including specifically the interview of or taking evidence from a person on a voluntary basis, including doing so without the presence of the authorities of the requested State Party if it is essential for the request to be executed, and the examination without modification of a public site or other public place, the Prosecutor may execute such request directly on the territory of a State as follows:
(a) When the State Party requested is a State on the territory of which the crime is alleged to have been committed, and there has been a determination of admissibility pursuant to article 18 or 19, the Prosecutor may directly execute such request following all possible consultations with the requested State Party;
(b) In other cases, the Prosecutor may execute such request following consultations with the requested State Party and subject to any reasonable conditions or concerns raised by that State Party. Where the requested State Party identifies problems with the execution of a request pursuant to this subparagraph it shall, without delay, consult with the Court to resolve the matter.
5. Provisions allowing a person heard or examined by the Court under article 72 to invoke restrictions designed to prevent disclosure of confidential information connected with national security shall also apply to the execution of requests for assistance under this article.

Article 100 Costs

1. The ordinary costs for execution of requests in the territory of the requested State shall be borne by that State, except for the following, which shall be borne by the Court:
- Costs associated with the travel and security of witnesses and experts or the transfer under article 93 of persons in custody;
- Costs of translation, interpretation and transcription;

- Travel and subsistence costs of the judges, the Prosecutor, the Deputy Prosecutors, the Registrar, the Deputy Registrar and staff of any organ of the Court;
- Costs of any expert opinion or report requested by the Court;
- Costs associated with the transport of a person being surrendered to the Court by a custodial State; and
- Following consultations, any extraordinary costs that may result from the execution of a request.

2. The provisions of paragraph 1 shall, as appropriate, apply to requests from States Parties to the Court. In that case, the Court shall bear the ordinary costs of execution.

Article 101 Rule of speciality

1. A person surrendered to the Court under this Statute shall not be proceeded against, punished or detained for any conduct committed prior to surrender, other than the conduct or course of conduct which forms the basis of the crimes for which that person has been surrendered.

2. The Court may request a waiver of the requirements of paragraph 1 from the State which surrendered the person to the Court and, if necessary, the Court shall provide additional information in accordance with article 91. States Parties shall have the authority to provide a waiver to the Court and should endeavour to do so.

Article 102 Use of terms

For the purposes of this Statute:
"surrender" means the delivering up of a person by a State to the Court, pursuant to this Statute.
"extradition" means the delivering up of a person by one State to another as provided by treaty, convention or national legislation.

Part 10. Enforcement

Article 103 Role of States in enforcement of sentences of imprisonment

1.
(a) A sentence of imprisonment shall be served in a State designated by the Court from a list of States which have indicated to the Court their willingness to accept sentenced persons.
(b) At the time of declaring its willingness to accept sentenced persons, a State may attach conditions to its acceptance as agreed by the Court and in accordance with this Part.
(c) A State designated in a particular case shall promptly inform the Court whether it accepts the Court's designation.
2.
(a) The State of enforcement shall notify the Court of any circumstances, including the exercise of any conditions agreed under paragraph 1, which could materially affect the terms or extent of the imprisonment. The Court shall be given at least 45 days' notice of any such known or foreseeable circumstances. During this period, the State of enforcement shall take no action that might prejudice its obligations under article 110.
(b) Where the Court cannot agree to the circumstances referred to in subparagraph (a), it shall notify the State of enforcement and proceed in accordance with article 104, paragraph 1.

3. In exercising its discretion to make a designation under paragraph 1, the Court shall take into account the following:
- The principle that States Parties should share the responsibility for enforcing sentences of imprisonment, in accordance with principles of equitable distribution, as provided in the Rules of Procedure and Evidence;
- The application of widely accepted international treaty standards governing the treatment of prisoners;
- The views of the sentenced person;
- The nationality of the sentenced person;
- Such other factors regarding the circumstances of the crime or the person sentenced, or the effective enforcement of the sentence, as may be appropriate in designating the State of enforcement.

4. If no State is designated under paragraph 1, the sentence of imprisonment shall be served in a prison facility made available by the host State, in accordance with the conditions set out in the headquarters agreement referred to in article 3, paragraph 2. In such a case, the costs arising out of the enforcement of a sentence of imprisonment shall be borne by the Court.

Article 104 Change in designation of State of enforcement

1. The Court may, at any time, decide to transfer a sentenced person to a prison of another State.
2. A sentenced person may, at any time, apply to the Court to be transferred from the State of enforcement.

Article 105 Enforcement of the sentence

1. Subject to conditions which a State may have specified in accordance with article 103, paragraph 1 (b), the sentence of imprisonment shall be binding on the States Parties, which shall in no case modify it.
2. The Court alone shall have the right to decide any application for appeal and revision. The State of enforcement shall not impede the making of any such application by a sentenced person.

Article 106 Supervision of enforcement of sentences and conditions of imprisonment

1. The enforcement of a sentence of imprisonment shall be subject to the supervision of the Court and shall be consistent with widely accepted international treaty standards governing treatment of prisoners.
2. The conditions of imprisonment shall be governed by the law of the State of enforcement and shall be consistent with widely accepted international treaty standards governing treatment of prisoners; in no case shall such conditions be more or less favourable than those available to prisoners convicted of similar offences in the State of enforcement.
3. Communications between a sentenced person and the Court shall be unimpeded and confidential.

Article 107 Transfer of the person upon completion of sentence

1. Following completion of the sentence, a person who is not a national of the State of enforcement may, in accordance with the law of the State of enforcement, be transferred to a State which is obliged to receive him or her, or to another State which agrees to receive him or her, taking into account any wishes of the person to be transferred to that State, unless the State of enforcement authorizes the person to remain in its territory.

2. If no State bears the costs arising out of transferring the person to another State pursuant to paragraph 1, such costs shall be borne by the Court.
3. Subject to the provisions of article 108, the State of enforcement may also, in accordance with its national law, extradite or otherwise surrender the person to a State which has requested the extradition or surrender of the person for purposes of trial or enforcement of a sentence.

Article 108 Limitation on the prosecution or punishment of other offences

1. A sentenced person in the custody of the State of enforcement shall not be subject to prosecution or punishment or to extradition to a third State for any conduct engaged in prior to that person's delivery to the State of enforcement, unless such prosecution, punishment or extradition has been approved by the Court at the request of the State of enforcement.
2. The Court shall decide the matter after having heard the views of the sentenced person.
3. Paragraph 1 shall cease to apply if the sentenced person remains voluntarily for more than 30 days in the territory of the State of enforcement after having served the full sentence imposed by the Court, or returns to the territory of that State after having left it.

Article 109 Enforcement of fines and forfeiture measures

1. States Parties shall give effect to fines or forfeitures ordered by the Court under Part 7, without prejudice to the rights of bona fide third parties, and in accordance with the procedure of their national law.
2. If a State Party is unable to give effect to an order for forfeiture, it shall take measures to recover the value of the proceeds, property or assets ordered by the Court to be forfeited, without prejudice to the rights of bona fide third parties.
3. Property, or the proceeds of the sale of real property or, where appropriate, the sale of other property, which is obtained by a State Party as a result of its enforcement of a judgement of the Court shall be transferred to the Court.

Article 110 Review by the Court concerning reduction of sentence

1. The State of enforcement shall not release the person before expiry of the sentence pronounced by the Court.
2. The Court alone shall have the right to decide any reduction of sentence, and shall rule on the matter after having heard the person.
3. When the person has served two thirds of the sentence, or 25 years in the case of life imprisonment, the Court shall review the sentence to determine whether it should be reduced. Such a review shall not be conducted before that time.
4. In its review under paragraph 3, the Court may reduce the sentence if it finds that one or more of the following factors are present:
- The early and continuing willingness of the person to cooperate with the Court in its investigations and prosecutions;
- The voluntary assistance of the person in enabling the enforcement of the judgements and orders of the Court in other cases, and in particular providing assistance in locating assets subject to orders of fine, forfeiture or reparation which may be used for the benefit of victims; or
- Other factors establishing a clear and significant change of circumstances sufficient to justify the reduction of sentence, as provided in the Rules of Procedure and Evidence.
5. If the Court determines in its initial review under paragraph 3 that it is not appropriate to reduce the sentence, it shall thereafter review the question of reduction of sentence at

such intervals and applying such criteria as provided for in the Rules of Procedure and Evidence.

Article 111 Escape

If a convicted person escapes from custody and flees the State of enforcement, that State may, after consultation with the Court, request the person's surrender from the State in which the person is located pursuant to existing bilateral or multilateral arrangements, or may request that the Court seek the person's surrender, in accordance with Part 9. It may direct that the person be delivered to the State in which he or she was serving the sentence or to another State designated by the Court.

Part 11. Assembly of States Parties

Article 112 Assembly of States Parties

1. An Assembly of States Parties to this Statute is hereby established. Each State Party shall have one representative in the Assembly who may be accompanied by alternates and advisers. Other States which have signed this Statute or the Final Act may be observers in the Assembly.
2. The Assembly shall:
- Consider and adopt, as appropriate, recommendations of the Preparatory Commission;
- Provide management oversight to the Presidency, the Prosecutor and the Registrar regarding the administration of the Court;
- Consider the reports and activities of the Bureau established under paragraph 3 and take appropriate action in regard thereto;
- Consider and decide the budget for the Court;
- Decide whether to alter, in accordance with article 36, the number of judges;
- Consider pursuant to article 87, paragraphs 5 and 7, any question relating to non-cooperation;
- Perform any other function consistent with this Statute or the Rules of Procedure and Evidence.
3.
(a) The Assembly shall have a Bureau consisting of a President, two Vice-Presidents and 18 members elected by the Assembly for three-year terms.
(b) The Bureau shall have a representative character, taking into account, in particular, equitable geographical distribution and the adequate representation of the principal legal systems of the world.
(c) The Bureau shall meet as often as necessary, but at least once a year. It shall assist the Assembly in the discharge of its responsibilities.
4. The Assembly may establish such subsidiary bodies as may be necessary, including an independent oversight mechanism for inspection, evaluation and investigation of the Court, in order to enhance its efficiency and economy.
5. The President of the Court, the Prosecutor and the Registrar or their representatives may participate, as appropriate, in meetings of the Assembly and of the Bureau.
6. The Assembly shall meet at the seat of the Court or at the Headquarters of the United Nations once a year and, when circumstances so require, hold special sessions. Except as otherwise specified in this Statute, special sessions shall be convened by the Bureau on its own initiative or at the request of one third of the States Parties.
7. Each State Party shall have one vote. Every effort shall be made to reach decisions by consensus in the Assembly and in the Bureau. If consensus cannot be reached, except as otherwise provided in the Statute:

- Decisions on matters of substance must be approved by a two-thirds majority of those present and voting provided that an absolute majority of States Parties constitutes the quorum for voting;
- Decisions on matters of procedure shall be taken by a simple majority of States Parties present and voting.

8. A State Party which is in arrears in the payment of its financial contributions towards the costs of the Court shall have no vote in the Assembly and in the Bureau if the amount of its arrears equals or exceeds the amount of the contributions due from it for the preceding two full years. The Assembly may, nevertheless, permit such a State Party to vote in the Assembly and in the Bureau if it is satisfied that the failure to pay is due to conditions beyond the control of the State Party.
9. The Assembly shall adopt its own rules of procedure.
10. The official and working languages of the Assembly shall be those of the General Assembly of the United Nations.

(...)

Article 121 Amendments

After the expiry of seven years from the entry into force of this Statute, any State Party may propose amendments thereto. The text of any proposed amendment shall be submitted to the Secretary-General of the United Nations, who shall promptly circulate it to all States Parties.
No sooner than three months from the date of notification, the Assembly of States Parties, at its next meeting, shall, by a majority of those present and voting, decide whether to take up the proposal. The Assembly may deal with the proposal directly or convene a Review Conference if the issue involved so warrants.
The adoption of an amendment at a meeting of the Assembly of States Parties or at a Review Conference on which consensus cannot be reached shall require a two-thirds majority of States Parties.
Except as provided in paragraph 5, an amendment shall enter into force for all States Parties one year after instruments of ratification or acceptance have been deposited with the Secretary-General of the United Nations by seven-eighths of them.
Any amendment to articles 5, 6, 7 and 8 of this Statute shall enter into force for those States Parties which have accepted the amendment one year after the deposit of their instruments of ratification or acceptance. In respect of a State Party which has not accepted the amendment, the Court shall not exercise its jurisdiction regarding a crime covered by the amendment when committed by that State Party's nationals or on its territory.
If an amendment has been accepted by seven-eighths of States Parties in accordance with paragraph 4, any State Party which has not accepted the amendment may withdraw from this Statute with immediate effect, notwithstanding article 127, paragraph 1, but subject to article 127, paragraph 2, by giving notice no later than one year after the entry into force of such amendment.
The Secretary-General of the United Nations shall circulate to all States Parties any amendment adopted at a meeting of the Assembly of States Parties or at a Review Conference.

Article 122 Amendments to provisions of an institutional nature

1. Amendments to provisions of this Statute which are of an exclusively institutional nature, namely, article 35, article 36, paragraphs 8 and 9, article 37, article 38, article

39, paragraphs 1 (first two sentences), 2 and 4, article 42, paragraphs 4 to 9, article 43, paragraphs 2 and 3, and articles 44, 46, 47 and 49, may be proposed at any time, notwithstanding article 121, paragraph 1, by any State Party. The text of any proposed amendment shall be submitted to the Secretary-General of the United Nations or such other person designated by the Assembly of States Parties who shall promptly circulate it to all States Parties and to others participating in the Assembly.
2. Amendments under this article on which consensus cannot be reached shall be adopted by the Assembly of States Parties or by a Review Conference, by a two-thirds majority of States Parties. Such amendments shall enter into force for all States Parties six months after their adoption by the Assembly or, as the case may be, by the Conference.

Article 123 Review of the Statute

1. Seven years after the entry into force of this Statute the Secretary-General of the United Nations shall convene a Review Conference to consider any amendments to this Statute. Such review may include, but is not limited to, the list of crimes contained in article 5. The Conference shall be open to those participating in the Assembly of States Parties and on the same conditions.
2. At any time thereafter, at the request of a State Party and for the purposes set out in paragraph 1, the Secretary-General of the United Nations shall, upon approval by a majority of States Parties, convene a Review Conference.
3. The provisions of article 121, paragraphs 3 to 7, shall apply to the adoption and entry into force of any amendment to the Statute considered at a Review Conference.

Article 124 Transitional Provision

Notwithstanding article 12, paragraphs 1 and 2, a State, on becoming a party to this Statute, may declare that, for a period of seven years after the entry into force of this Statute for the State concerned, it does not accept the jurisdiction of the Court with respect to the category of crimes referred to in article 8 when a crime is alleged to have been committed by its nationals or on its territory. A declaration under this article may be withdrawn at any time. The provisions of this article shall be reviewed at the Review Conference convened in accordance with article 123, paragraph 1.

Article 125 Signature, ratification, acceptance, approval or accession

1. This Statute shall be open for signature by all States in Rome, at the headquarters of the Food and Agriculture Organization of the United Nations, on 17 July 1998. Thereafter, it shall remain open for signature in Rome at the Ministry of Foreign Affairs of Italy until 17 October 1998. After that date, the Statute shall remain open for signature in New York, at United Nations Headquarters, until 31 December 2000.
2. This Statute is subject to ratification, acceptance or approval by signatory States. Instruments of ratification, acceptance or approval shall be deposited with the Secretary-General of the United Nations.
3. This Statute shall be open to accession by all States. Instruments of accession shall be deposited with the Secretary-General of the United Nations.

Article 126 Entry into force

This Statute shall enter into force on the first day of the month after the 60th day following the date of the deposit of the 60th instrument of ratification, acceptance, approval or accession with the Secretary-General of the United Nations.

For each State ratifying, accepting, approving or acceding to this Statute after the deposit of the 60th instrument of ratification, acceptance, approval or accession, the Statute shall enter into force on the first day of the month after the 60th day following the deposit by such State of its instrument of ratification, acceptance, approval or accession.

Article 127 Withdrawal

A State Party may, by written notification addressed to the Secretary-General of the United Nations, withdraw from this Statute. The withdrawal shall take effect one year after the date of receipt of the notification, unless the notification specifies a later date.

A State shall not be discharged, by reason of its withdrawal, from the obligations arising from this Statute while it was a Party to the Statute, including any financial obligations which may have accrued. Its withdrawal shall not affect any cooperation with the Court in connection with criminal investigations and proceedings in relation to which the withdrawing State had a duty to cooperate and which were commenced prior to the date on which the withdrawal became effective, nor shall it prejudice in any way the continued consideration of any matter which was already under consideration by the Court prior to the date on which the withdrawal became effective.

Article 128 Authentic texts

The original of this Statute, of which the Arabic, Chinese, English, French, Russian and Spanish texts are equally authentic, shall be deposited with the Secretary-General of the United Nations, who shall send certified copies thereof to all States.
In Witness Whereof, the undersigned, being duly authorized thereto by their respective Governments, have signed this Statute.

Done at Rome, this 17th day of July 1998.

Elements of Crime

General introduction

1. Pursuant to article 9, the following Elements of Crimes shall assist the Court in the interpretation and application of articles 6, 7 and 8, consistent with the Statute. The provisions of the Statute, including article 21 and the general principles set out in Part 3, are applicable to the Elements of Crimes.
2. As stated in article 30, unless otherwise provided, a person shall be criminally responsible and liable for punishment for a crime within the jurisdiction of the Court only if the material elements are committed with intent and knowledge. Where no reference is made in the Elements of Crimes to a mental element for any particular conduct, consequence or circumstance listed, it is understood that the relevant mental element, i.e., intent, knowledge or both, set out in article 30 applies. Exceptions to the article 30 standard, based on the Statute, including applicable law under its relevant provisions, are indicated below.
3. Existence of intent and knowledge can be inferred from relevant facts and circumstances.
4. With respect to mental elements associated with elements involving valuejudgement, such as those using the terms 'inhumane' or 'severe', it is notnecessary that the perpetrator personally completed a particular valuejudgement, unless otherwise indicated.
5. Grounds for excluding criminal responsibility or the absence thereof are generally not specified in the elements of crimes listed under each crime.[2]
6. The requirement of 'unlawfulness' found in the Statute or in other parts of international law, in particular international humanitarian law, is generally not specified in the elements of crimes.
7. The elements of crimes are generally structured in accordance with the following principles:
- As the elements of crimes focus on the conduct, consequences and circumstances associated with each crime, they are generally listed in that order;
- When required, a particular mental element is listed after the affected conduct, consequence or circumstance;
- Contextual circumstances are listed last.
8. As used in the Elements of Crimes, the term 'perpetrator' is neutral as to guilt or innocence. The elements, including the appropriate mental elements, apply, *mutatis mutandis*, to all those whose criminal responsibility may fall under articles 25 and 28 of the Statute.
9. A particular conduct may constitute one or more crimes.
10. The use of short titles for the crimes has no legal effect.

Article 6
Genocide - Introduction

With respect to the last element listed for each crime:
- The term 'in the context of' would include the initial acts in an emerging pattern;
- The term 'manifest' is an objective qualification;
- Notwithstanding the normal requirement for a mental element provided for in article 30, and recognizing that knowledge of the circumstances will usually be addressed in

2 This paragraph is without prejudice to the obligation of the Prosecutor under article 54, paragraph 1, of the Statute.

proving genocidal intent, the appropriate requirement, if any, for a mental element regarding this circumstance will need to be decided by the Court on a case-by-case basis.

Article 6 (a)
Genocide by killing - Elements

1. The perpetrator killed[3] one or more persons.
2. Such person or persons belonged to a particular national, ethnical, racial or religious group.
3. The perpetrator intended to destroy, in whole or in part, that national, ethnical, racial or religious group, as such.
4. The conduct took place in the context of a manifest pattern of similar conduct directed against that group or was conduct that could itself effect such destruction.

Article 6 (b)
Genocide by causing serious bodily or mental harm - Elements

1. The perpetrator caused serious bodily or mental harm to one or more persons.[4]
2. Such person or persons belonged to a particular national, ethnical, racial or religious group.
3. The perpetrator intended to destroy, in whole or in part, that national, ethnical, racial or religious group, as such.
4. The conduct took place in the context of a manifest pattern of similar conduct directed against that group or was conduct that could itself effect such destruction.

Article 6 (c)
Genocide by deliberately inflicting conditions of life calculated to bring about physical destruction - Elements

1. The perpetrator inflicted certain conditions of life upon one or more persons.
2. Such person or persons belonged to a particular national, ethnical, racial or religious group.
3. The perpetrator intended to destroy, in whole or in part, that national, ethnical, racial or religious group, as such.
4. The conditions of life were calculated to bring about the physical destruction of that group, in whole or in part.[5]
5. The conduct took place in the context of a manifest pattern of similar conduct directed against that group or was conduct that could itself effect such destruction.

Article 6 (d)
Genocide by imposing measures intended to prevent births - Elements

1. The perpetrator imposed certain measures upon one or more persons.

3 The term 'killed' is interchangeable with the term 'caused death'.
4 This conduct may include, but is not necessarily restricted to, acts of torture, rape, sexual violence or inhuman or degrading treatment.
5 The term 'conditions of life' may include, but is not necessarily restricted to, deliberate deprivation of resources indispensable for survival, such as food or medical services, or systematic expulsion from home

2. Such person or persons belonged to a particular national, ethnical, racial or religious group.
3. The perpetrator intended to destroy, in whole or in part, that national, ethnical, racial or religious group, as such.
4. The measures imposed were intended to prevent births within that group.
5. The conduct took place in the context of a manifest pattern of similar conduct directed against that group or was conduct that could itself effect such destruction.

Article 6 (e)
Genocide by forcibly transferring children
Elements

1. The perpetrator forcibly transferred one or more persons.[6]
2. Such person or persons belonged to a particular national, ethnical, racial or religious group.
3. The perpetrator intended to destroy, in whole or in part, that national, ethnical, racial or religious group, as such.
4. The transfer was from that group to another group.
5. The person or persons were under the age of 18 years.
6. The perpetrator knew, or should have known, that the person or persons were under the age of 18 years.
7. The conduct took place in the context of a manifest pattern of similar conduct directed against that group or was conduct that could itself effect such destruction.

Article 7
Crimes against humanity
Introduction

1. Since article 7 pertains to international criminal law, its provisions, consistent with article 22, must be strictly construed, taking into account that crimes against humanity as defined in article 7 are among the most serious crimes of concern to the international community as a whole, warrant and entail individual criminal responsibility, and require conduct which is impermissible under generally applicable international law, as recognized by the principal legal systems of the world.
2. The last two elements for each crime against humanity describe the context in which the conduct must take place. These elements clarify the requisite participation in and knowledge of a widespread or systematic attack against a civilian population. However, the last element should not be interpreted as requiring proof that the perpetrator had knowledge of all characteristics of the attack or the precise details of the plan or policy of the State or organization. In the case of an emerging widespread or systematic attack against a civilian population, the intent clause of the last element indicates that this mental element is satisfied if the perpetrator intended to further such an attack.
3. 'Attack directed against a civilian population' in these context elements is understood to mean a course of conduct involving the multiple commission of acts referred to in article 7, paragraph 1, of the Statute against any civilian population, pursuant to or in furtherance of a State or organizational policy to commit such attack. The acts need not constitute a military attack. It is understood that 'policy to commit such attack' requires

6 The term 'forcibly' is not restricted to physical force, but may include threat of force or coercion, such as that caused by fear of violence, duress, detention, psychological oppression or abuse of power, against such person or persons or another person, or by taking advantage of a coercive environment.

that the State or organization actively promote or encourage such an attack against a civilian population.[7]

Article 7 (1) (a)
Crime against humanity of murder
Elements

1. The perpetrator killed [8]one or more persons.
2. The conduct was committed as part of a widespread or systematic attack directed against a civilian population.
3. The perpetrator knew that the conduct was part of or intended the conduct to be part of a widespread or systematic attack against a civilian population.

Article 7 (1) (b)
Crime against humanity of extermination
Elements

1. The perpetrator killed[9] one or more persons, including by inflicting conditions of life calculated to bring about the destruction of part of a population.[10]
2. The conduct constituted, or took place as part of,[11]a mass killing of members of a civilian population.
3. The conduct was committed as part of a widespread or systematic attack directed against a civilian population.
4. The perpetrator knew that the conduct was part of or intended the conduct to be part of a widespread or systematic attack directed against a civilian population.

Article 7 (1) (c)
Crime against humanity of enslavement
Elements

1. The perpetrator exercised any or all of the powers attaching to the right of ownership over one or more persons, such as by purchasing, selling, lending or bartering such a person or persons, or by imposing on them a similar deprivation of liberty.[12]
2. The conduct was committed as part of a widespread or systematic attack directed against a civilian population.
3. The perpetrator knew that the conduct was part of or intended the conduct to be part of a widespread or systematic attack directed against a civilian population.

7 A policy which has a civilian population as the object of the attack would be implemented by State or organizational action. Such a policy may, in exceptional circumstances, be implemented by a deliberate failure to take action, which is consciously aimed at encouraging such attack. The existence of such a policy cannot be inferred solely from the absence of governmental or organizational action.
8 The term 'killed' is interchangeable with the term 'caused death'. This footnote applies to all elements which use either of these concepts.
9 The conduct could be committed by different methods of killing, either directly or indirectly.
10 The infliction of such conditions could include the deprivation of access to food and medicine.
11 The term 'as part of' would include the initial conduct in a mass killing.
12 It is understood that such deprivation of liberty may, in some circumstances, include exacting forced labour or otherwise reducing a person to a servile status as defined in the Supplementary Convention on the Abolition of Slavery, the Slave Trade, and Institutions and Practices Similar to Slavery of 1956. It is also understood that the conduct described in this element includes trafficking in persons, in particular women and children.

Article 7 (1) (d)
Crime against humanity of deportation or forcible transfer of population - Elements

1. The perpetrator deported or forcibly [13]transferred,[14] without grounds permitted under international law, one or more persons to another State or location, by expulsion or other coercive acts.
2. Such person or persons were lawfully present in the area from which they were so deported or transferred.
3. The perpetrator was aware of the factual circumstances that established the lawfulness of such presence.
4. The conduct was committed as part of a widespread or systematic attack directed against a civilian population.
5. The perpetrator knew that the conduct was part of or intended the conduct to be part of a widespread or systematic attack directed against a civilian population.

Article 7 (1) (e)
Crime against humanity of imprisonment or other severe deprivation of physical liberty
Elements

1. The perpetrator imprisoned one or more persons or otherwise severely deprived one or more persons of physical liberty.
2. The gravity of the conduct was such that it was in violation of fundamental rules of inter
3. The perpetrator was aware of the factual circumstances that established the gravity of the conduct.
4. The conduct was committed as part of a widespread or systematic attack directed against a civilian population.
5. The perpetrator knew that the conduct was part of or intended the conduct to be part of a widespread or systematic attack directed against a civilian population.

Article 7 (1) (f)
Crime against humanity of torture[15]
Elements

1. The perpetrator inflicted severe physical or mental pain or suffering upon one or more persons.
2. Such person or persons were in the custody or under the control of the perpetrator.
3. Such pain or suffering did not arise only from, and was not inherent in or incidental to, lawful sanctions.
4. The conduct was committed as part of a widespread or systematic attack directed against a civilian population.
5. The perpetrator knew that the conduct was part of or intended the conduct to be part of a widespread or systematic attack directed against a civilian population.

13 The term 'forcibly' is not restricted to physical force, but may include threat of force or coercion, such as that caused by fear of violence, duress, detention, psychological oppression or abuse of power against such person or persons or another person, or by taking advantage of a coercive environment.
14 'Deported or forcibly transferred' is interchangeable with 'forcibly displaced'.
15 It is understood that no specific purpose need be proved for this crime.

Article 7 (1) (g)-1
Crime against humanity of rape
Elements

1. The perpetrator invaded[16] the body of a person by conduct resulting in penetration, however slight, of any part of the body of the victim or of the perpetrator with a sexual organ, or of the anal or genital opening of the victim with any object or any other part of the body.
2. The invasion was committed by force, or by threat of force or coercion, such as that caused by fear of violence, duress, detention, psychological oppression or abuse of power, against such person or another person, or by taking advantage of a coercive environment, or the invasion was committed against a person incapable of giving genuine consent.[17]
3. The conduct was committed as part of a widespread or systematic attack directed against a civilian population.
4. The perpetrator knew that the conduct was part of or intended the conduct to be part of a widespread or systematic attack directed against a civilian population.

Article 7 (1) (g)-2
Crime against humanity of sexual slavery[18]
Elements

1. The perpetrator exercised any or all of the powers attaching to the right of ownership over one or more persons, such as by purchasing, selling, lending or bartering such a person or persons, or by imposing on them a similar deprivation of liberty.[19]
2. The perpetrator caused such person or persons to engage in one or more acts of a sexual nature.
3. The conduct was committed as part of a widespread or systematic attack directed against a civilian population.
4. The perpetrator knew that the conduct was part of or intended the conduct to be part of a widespread or systematic attack directed against a civilian population.

Article 7 (1) (g)-3
Crime against humanity of enforced prostitution
Elements

1. The perpetrator caused one or more persons to engage in one or more acts of a sexual nature by force, or by threat of force or coercion, such as that caused by fear of violence, duress, detention, psychological oppression or abuse of power, against such person or persons or another person, or by taking advantage of a coercive environment or such person's or persons' incapacity to give genuine consent.

16 The concept of 'invasion' is intended to be broad enough to be gender-neutral.

17 It is understood that a person may be incapable of giving genuine consent if affected by natural, induced or age-related incapacity. This footnote also applies to the corresponding elements of article 7 (1) (g)-3, 5 and 6.

18 Given the complex nature of this crime, it is recognized that its commission could involve more than one perpetrator as a part of a common criminal purpose.

19 It is understood that such deprivation of liberty may, in some circumstances, include exacting forced labour or otherwise reducing a person to a servile status as defined in the Supplementary Convention on the Abolition of Slavery, the Slave Trade, and Institutions and Practices Similar to Slavery of 1956. It is also understood that the conduct described in this element includes trafficking in persons, in particular women and children.

2. The perpetrator or another person obtained or expected to obtain pecuniary or other advantage in exchange for or in connection with the acts of a sexual nature.
3. The conduct was committed as part of a widespread or systematic attack directed against a civilian population.
4. The perpetrator knew that the conduct was part of or intended the conduct to be part of a widespread or systematic attack directed against a civilian population.

Article 7 (1) (g)-4
Crime against humanity of forced pregnancy
Elements

1. The perpetrator confined one or more women forcibly made pregnant, with the intent of affecting the ethnic composition of any population or carrying out other grave violations of international law.
2. The conduct was committed as part of a widespread or systematic attack directed against a civilian population.
3. The perpetrator knew that the conduct was part of or intended the conduct to be part of a widespread or systematic attack directed against a civilian population.

Article 7 (1) (g)-5
Crime against humanity of enforced sterilization
Elements

1. The perpetrator deprived one or more persons of biological reproductive capacity.[20]
2. The conduct was neither justified by the medical or hospital treatment of the person or persons concerned nor carried out with their genuine consent.[21]
3. The conduct was committed as part of a widespread or systematic attack directed against a civilian population.
4. The perpetrator knew that the conduct was part of or intended the conduct to be part of a widespread or systematic attack directed against a civilian population.

Article 7 (1) (g)-6
Crime against humanity of sexual violence
Elements

1. The perpetrator committed an act of a sexual nature against one or more persons or caused such person or persons to engage in an act of a sexual nature by force, or by threat of force or coercion, such as that caused by fear of violence, duress, detention, psychological oppression or abuse of power, against such person orpersons or another person, or by taking advantage of a coercive environment or such person's or persons' incapacity to give genuine consent.
2. Such conduct was of a gravity comparable to the other offences in article 7, paragraph 1 (g), of the Statute.
3. The perpetrator was aware of the factual circumstances that established the gravity of the conduct.
4. The conduct was committed as part of a widespread or systematic attack directed against a civilian population.

20 The deprivation is not intended to include birth-control measures which have a non-permanent effect in practice.
21 It is understood that 'genuine consent' does not include consent obtained through deception.

5. The perpetrator knew that the conduct was part of or intended the conduct to be part of a widespread or systematic attack directed against a civilian population.

Article 7 (1) (h)
Crime against humanity of persecution
Elements

1. The perpetrator severely deprived, contrary to international law,[22] one or more persons of fundamental rights.
2. The perpetrator targeted such person or persons by reason of the identity of a group or collectivity or targeted the group or collectivity as such.
3. Such targeting was based on political, racial, national, ethnic, cultural, religious, gender as defined in article 7, paragraph 3, of the Statute, or other grounds that are universally recognized as impermissible under international law.
4. The conduct was committed in connection with any act referred to in article 7, paragraph 1, of the Statute or any crime within the jurisdiction of the Court.[23]
5. The conduct was committed as part of a widespread or systematic attack directed against a civilian population.
6. The perpetrator knew that the conduct was part of or intended the conduct to be part of a widespread or systematic attack directed against a civilian population.

Article 7 (1) (i)
Crime against humanity of enforced disappearance of persons[24],[25]
Elements

1. The perpetrator:
(a) Arrested, detained[26], [27] or abducted one or more persons; or
(b) Refused to acknowledge the arrest, detention or abduction, or to give information on the fate or whereabouts of such person or persons.
2.
(a) Such arrest, detention or abduction was followed or accompanied by a refusal to acknowledge that deprivation of freedom or to give information on the fate or whereabouts of such person or persons; or
(b) Such refusal was preceded or accompanied by that deprivation of freedom.
3. The perpetrator was aware that:[28]
(a) Such arrest, detention or abduction would be followed in the ordinary course of events by a refusal to acknowledge that deprivation of freedom or to give information on the fate or whereabouts of such person or persons;[29] or

22 This requirement is without prejudice to paragraph 6 of the General Introduction to the Elements of Crimes.
23 It is understood that no additional mental element is necessary for this element other than that inherent inelement 6.
24 Given the complex nature of this crime, it is recognized that its commission will normally involve more than one perpetrator as a part of a common criminal purpose.
25 This crime falls under the jurisdiction of the Court only if the attack referred to in elements 7 and 8 occurs after the entry into force of the Statute.
26 The word 'detained' would include a perpetrator who maintained an existing detention.
27 It is understood that under certain circumstances an arrest or detention may have been lawful.
28 This element, inserted because of the complexity of this crime, is without prejudice to the General Introduction to the Elements of Crimes.
29 It is understood that, in the case of a perpetrator who maintained an existing detention, this element would be satisfied if the perpetrator was aware that such a refusal had already taken

(b) Such refusal was preceded or accompanied by that deprivation of freedom.
4. Such arrest, detention or abduction was carried out by, or with the authorization, support or acquiescence of, a State or a political organization.
5. Such refusal to acknowledge that deprivation of freedom or to give information on the fate or whereabouts of such person or persons was carried out by, or with the authorization or support of, such State or political organization.
6. The perpetrator intended to remove such person or persons from the protection of the law for a prolonged period of time.
7. The conduct was committed as part of a widespread or systematic attack directed against a civilian population.
8. The perpetrator knew that the conduct was part of or intended the conduct to be part of a widespread or systematic attack directed against a civilian population.

Article 7 (1) (j)
Crime against humanity of apartheid
Elements

1. The perpetrator committed an inhumane act against one or more persons.
2. Such act was an act referred to in article 7, paragraph 1, of the Statute, or was an act of a character similar to any of those acts.[30]
3. The perpetrator was aware of the factual circumstances that established the character of the act.
4. The conduct was committed in the context of an institutionalized regime of systematic oppression and domination by one racial group over any other racial group or groups.
5. The perpetrator intended to maintain such regime by that conduct.
6. The conduct was committed as part of a widespread or systematic attack directed against a civilian population.
7. The perpetrator knew that the conduct was part of or intended the conduct to be part of a widespread or systematic attack directed against a civilian population.

Article 7 (1) (k)
Crime against humanity of other inhumane acts
Elements

1. The perpetrator inflicted great suffering, or serious injury to body or to mental or physical health, by means of an inhumane act.
2. Such act was of a character similar to any other act referred to in article 7, paragraph 1, of the Statute.[31]
3. The perpetrator was aware of the factual circumstances that established the character of the act.
4. The conduct was committed as part of a widespread or systematic attack directed against a civilian population.
5. The perpetrator knew that the conduct was part of or intended the conduct to be part of a widespread or systematic attack directed against a civilian population.

place.
30 It is understood that 'character' refers to the nature and gravity of the act.
31 It is understood that 'character' refers to the nature and gravity of the act.

Article 8
War crimes
Introduction

The elements for war crimes under article 8, paragraph 2 (c) and (e), are subject to the limitations addressed in article 8, paragraph 2 (d) and (f), which are not elements of crimes.
The elements for war crimes under article 8, paragraph 2, of the Statute shall be interpreted within the established framework of the international law of armed conflict including, as appropriate, the international law of armed conflict applicable to armed conflict at sea.
With respect to the last two elements listed for each crime:
– There is no requirement for a legal evaluation by the perpetrator as to the existence of an armed conflict or its character as international or non-international;
– In that context there is no requirement for awareness by the perpetrator of the facts that established the character of the conflict as international or non-international;
– There is only a requirement for the awareness of the factual circumstances that established the existence of an armed conflict that is implicit in the terms 'took place in the context of and was associated with'.

Article 8 (2) (a)
Article 8 (2) (a) (i)
War crime of wilful killing
Elements

1. The perpetrator killed one or more persons.[32]
2. Such person or persons were protected under one or more of the Geneva Conventions of 1949.
3. The perpetrator was aware of the factual circumstances that established that protected status.[33], [34]
4. The conduct took place in the context of and was associated with an international armed conflict.[35]
5. The perpetrator was aware of factual circumstances that established the existence of an armed conflict.

32 The term 'killed' is interchangeable with the term 'caused death'. This footnote applies to all elements which use either of these concepts.
33 This mental element recognizes the interplay between articles 30 and 32. This footnote also applies to the corresponding element in each crime under article 8 (2) (a), and to the element in other crimes in article 8 (2) concerning the awareness of factual circumstances that establish the status of persons or property protected under the relevant international law of armed conflict.
34 With respect to nationality, it is understood that the perpetrator needs only to know that the victim belonged to an adverse party to the conflict. This footnote also applies to the corresponding element in each crime under article 8 (2) (a).
35 The term 'international armed conflict' includes military occupation. This footnote also applies to the corresponding element in each crime under article 8 (2) (a).

Article 8 (2) (a) (ii)-1
War crime of torture
Elements[36]

1. The perpetrator inflicted severe physical or mental pain or suffering upon one or more persons.
2. The perpetrator inflicted the pain or suffering for such purposes as: obtaining information or a confession, punishment, intimidation or coercion or for any reason based on discrimination of any kind.
3. Such person or persons were protected under one or more of the Geneva Conventions of 1949.
4. The perpetrator was aware of the factual circumstances that established that protected status.
5. The conduct took place in the context of and was associated with an international armed conflict.
6. The perpetrator was aware of factual circumstances that established the existence of an armed conflict.

Article 8 (2) (a) (ii)-2
War crime of inhuman treatment
Elements

1. The perpetrator inflicted severe physical or mental pain or suffering upon one or more persons.
2. Such person or persons were protected under one or more of the Geneva Conventions of 1949.
3. The perpetrator was aware of the factual circumstances that established that protected status.
4. The conduct took place in the context of and was associated with an international armed conflict.
5. The perpetrator was aware of factual circumstances that established the existence of an armed conflict.

Article 8 (2) (a) (ii)-3
War crime of biological experiments
Elements

1. The perpetrator subjected one or more persons to a particular biological experiment.
2. The experiment seriously endangered the physical or mental health or integrity of such person or persons.
3. The intent of the experiment was non-therapeutic and it was neither justified by medical reasons nor carried out in such person's or persons' interest.
4. Such person or persons were protected under one or more of the Geneva Conventions of 1949.
5. The perpetrator was aware of the factual circumstances that established that protected status.

36 As element 3 requires that all victims must be 'protected persons' under one or more of the Geneva Conventions of 1949, these elements do not include the custody or control requirement found in the elements of article 7 (1) (e).

6. The conduct took place in the context of and was associated with an international armed conflict.
7. The perpetrator was aware of factual circumstances that established the existence of an armed conflict.

Article 8 (2) (a) (iii)
War crime of wilfully causing great suffering
Elements

1. The perpetrator caused great physical or mental pain or suffering to, or serious injury to body or health of, one or more persons.
2. Such person or persons were protected under one or more of the Geneva Conventions of 1949.
3. The perpetrator was aware of the factual circumstances that established that protected status.
4. The conduct took place in the context of and was associated with an international armed conflict.
5. The perpetrator was aware of factual circumstances that established the existence of an armed conflict.

Article 8 (2) (a) (iv)
War crime of destruction and appropriation of property
Elements

1. The perpetrator destroyed or appropriated certain property.
2. The destruction or appropriation was not justified by military necessity.
3. The destruction or appropriation was extensive and carried out wantonly.
4. Such property was protected under one or more of the Geneva Conventions of 1949.
5. The perpetrator was aware of the factual circumstances that established that protected status.
6. The conduct took place in the context of and was associated with an international armed conflict.
7. The perpetrator was aware of factual circumstances that established the existence of an armed conflict.

Article 8 (2) (a) (v)
War crime of compelling service in hostile forces
Elements

1. The perpetrator coerced one or more persons, by act or threat, to take part in military operations against that person's own country or forces or otherwise serve in the forces of a hostile power.
2. Such person or persons were protected under one or more of the Geneva Conventions of 1949.
3. The perpetrator was aware of the factual circumstances that established that protected status.
4. The conduct took place in the context of and was associated with an international armed conflict.
5. The perpetrator was aware of factual circumstances that established the existence of an armed conflict.

Article 8 (2) (a) (vi)
War crime of denying a fair trial
Elements

1. The perpetrator deprived one or more persons of a fair and regular trial by denying judicial guarantees as defined, in particular, in the third and the fourth Geneva Conventions of 1949.
2. Such person or persons were protected under one or more of the Geneva Conventions of 1949.
3. The perpetrator was aware of the factual circumstances that established that protected status.
4. The conduct took place in the context of and was associated with an international armed conflict.
5. The perpetrator was aware of factual circumstances that established the existence of an armed conflict.

Article 8 (2) (a) (vii)-1
War crime of unlawful deportation and transfer
Elements

1. The perpetrator deported or transferred one or more persons to another State or to another location.
2. Such person or persons were protected under one or more of the Geneva Conventions of 1949.
3. The perpetrator was aware of the factual circumstances that established that protected status.
4. The conduct took place in the context of and was associated with an international armed conflict.
5. The perpetrator was aware of factual circumstances that established theexistence of an armed conflict.

Article 8 (2) (a) (vii)-2
War crime of unlawful confinement
Elements

1. The perpetrator confined or continued to confine one or more persons to a certain location.
2. Such person or persons were protected under one or more of the Geneva Conventions of 1949.
3. The perpetrator was aware of the factual circumstances that established that protected status.
4. The conduct took place in the context of and was associated with an international armed conflict.
5. The perpetrator was aware of factual circumstances that established the existence of an armed conflict.

Article 8 (2) (a) (viii)
War crime of taking hostages
Elements

1. The perpetrator seized, detained or otherwise held hostage one or more persons.
2. The perpetrator threatened to kill, injure or continue to detain such person or persons.
3. The perpetrator intended to compel a State, an international organization, a natural or legal person or a group of persons to act or refrain from acting as an explicit or implicit condition for the safety or the release of such person or persons.
4. Such person or persons were protected under one or more of the Geneva Conventions of 1949.
5. The perpetrator was aware of the factual circumstances that established that protected status.
6. The conduct took place in the context of and was associated with an international armed conflict.
7. The perpetrator was aware of factual circumstances that established the existence of an armed conflict.

Article 8 (2) (b)
Article 8 (2) (b) (i)
War crime of attacking civilians
Elements

1. The perpetrator directed an attack.
2. The object of the attack was a civilian population as such or individual civilians not taking direct part in hostilities.
3. The perpetrator intended the civilian population as such or individual civilians not taking direct part in hostilities to be the object of the attack.
4. The conduct took place in the context of and was associated with an international armed conflict.
5. The perpetrator was aware of factual circumstances that established the existence of an armed conflict.

Article 8 (2) (b) (ii)
War crime of attacking civilian objects
Elements

1. The perpetrator directed an attack.
2. The object of the attack was civilian objects, that is, objects which are not military objectives.
3. The perpetrator intended such civilian objects to be the object of the attack.
4. The conduct took place in the context of and was associated with an international armed conflict.
5. The perpetrator was aware of factual circumstances that established the existence of an armed conflict.

Article 8 (2) (b) (iii)
War crime of attacking personnel or objects involved in a humanitarian assistance or peacekeeping mission
Elements

1. The perpetrator directed an attack.

2. The object of the attack was personnel, installations, material, units or vehicles involved in a humanitarian assistance or peacekeeping mission in accordance with the Charter of the United Nations.
3. The perpetrator intended such personnel, installations, material, units or vehicles so involved to be the object of the attack.
4. Such personnel, installations, material, units or vehicles were entitled to thatprotection given to civilians or civilian objects under the international law of armed conflict.

5. The perpetrator was aware of the factual circumstances that established that protection.
6. The conduct took place in the context of and was associated with an international armed conflict.
7. The perpetrator was aware of factual circumstances that established the existence of an armed conflict.

Article 8 (2) (b) (iv)
War crime of excessive incidental death, injury, or damage
Elements

1. The perpetrator launched an attack.
2. The attack was such that it would cause incidental death or injury to civilians or damage to civilian objects or widespread, long-term and severe damage to the natural environment and that such death, injury or damage would be of such an extent as to be clearly excessive in relation to the concrete and direct overall military advantage anticipated..[37]
3. The perpetrator knew that the attack would cause incidental death or injury to civilians or damage to civilian objects or widespread, long-term and severe damage to the natural environment and that such death, injury or damage would be of such an extent as to be clearly excessive in relation to the concrete and direct overall military advantage anticipated.[38]
4. The conduct took place in the context of and was associated with an international armed conflict.
5. The perpetrator was aware of factual circumstances that established the existence of an armed conflict.

37 The expression 'concrete and direct overall military advantage' refers to a military advantage that is foreseeable by the perpetrator at the relevant time. Such advantage may or may not be temporally or geographically related to the object of the attack. The fact that this crime admits the possibility of lawful incidental injury and collateral damage does not in any way justify any violation of the law applicable in armed conflict. It does not address justifications for war or other rules related to jus ad bellum. It reflects the proportionality requirement inherent in determining the legality of any military activity undertaken in the context of an armed conflict.

38 As opposed to the general rule set forth in paragraph 4 of the General Introduction, this knowledge element requires that the perpetrator make the value judgement as described therein. An evaluation of that value judgement must be based on the requisite information available to the perpetrator at the time.

Article 8 (2) (b) (v)
War crime of attacking undefended places[39]
Elements

1. The perpetrator attacked one or more towns, villages, dwellings or buildings.
2. Such towns, villages, dwellings or buildings were open for unresisted occupation.
3. Such towns, villages, dwellings or buildings did not constitute military objectives.
4. The conduct took place in the context of and was associated with an international armed conflict.
5. The perpetrator was aware of factual circumstances that established the existence of an armed conflict.

Article 8 (2) (b) (vi)
War crime of killing or wounding a person hors de combat
Elements

1. The perpetrator killed or injured one or more persons.
2. Such person or persons were *hors de combat.*
3. The perpetrator was aware of the factual circumstances that established this status.
4. The conduct took place in the context of and was associated with an international armed conflict.
5. The perpetrator was aware of factual circumstances that established the existence of an armed conflict.

Article 8 (2) (b) (vii)-1
War crime of improper use of a flag of truce
Elements

1. The perpetrator used a flag of truce.
2. The perpetrator made such use in order to feign an intention to negotiate when there was no such intention on the part of the perpetrator.
3. The perpetrator knew or should have known of the prohibited nature of such use.[40]
4. The conduct resulted in death or serious personal injury.
5. The perpetrator knew that the conduct could result in death or serious personal injury.
6. The conduct took place in the context of and was associated with an international armed conflict.
7. The perpetrator was aware of factual circumstances that established the existence of an armed conflict.

Article 8 (2) (b) (vii)-2
War crime of improper use of a flag, insignia or uniform of the hostile party
Elements

1. The perpetrator used a flag, insignia or uniform of the hostile party.

39 The presence in the locality of persons specially protected under the Geneva Conventions of 1949 or of police forces retained for the sole purpose of maintaining law and order does not by itself render the locality a military objective.

40 This mental element recognizes the interplay between article 30 and article 32. The term 'prohibited nature' denotes illegality.

2. The perpetrator made such use in a manner prohibited under the international law of armed conflict while engaged in an attack.
3. The perpetrator knew or should have known of the prohibited nature of such use.[41]

4. The conduct resulted in death or serious personal injury.
5. The perpetrator knew that the conduct could result in death or serious personal injury.
6. The conduct took place in the context of and was associated with an international armed conflict.
7. The perpetrator was aware of factual circumstances that established the existence of an armed conflict.

Article 8 (2) (b) (vii)-3
War crime of improper use of a flag, insignia or uniform of the United Nations - Elements

1. The perpetrator used a flag, insignia or uniform of the United Nations.
2. The perpetrator made such use in a manner prohibited under the international law of armed conflict.
3. The perpetrator knew of the prohibited nature of such use.[42]
4. The conduct resulted in death or serious personal injury.
5. The perpetrator knew that the conduct could result in death or serious personal injury.
6. The conduct took place in the context of and was associated with an international armed conflict.
7. The perpetrator was aware of factual circumstances that established the existence of an armed conflict.

Article 8 (2) (b) (vii)-4
War crime of improper use of the distinctive emblems of the Geneva Conventions- Elements

1. The perpetrator used the distinctive emblems of the Geneva Conventions.
2. The perpetrator made such use for combatant purposes[43] in a manner prohibited under the international law of armed conflict.
3. The perpetrator knew or should have known of the prohibited nature of such use.[44]
4. The conduct resulted in death or serious personal injury.
5. The perpetrator knew that the conduct could result in death or serious personal injury.
6. The conduct took place in the context of and was associated with an international armed conflict.
7. The perpetrator was aware of factual circumstances that established the existence of an armed conflict.

41 This mental element recognizes the interplay between article 30 and article 32. The term 'prohibited nature' denotes illegality.

42 This mental element recognizes the interplay between article 30 and article 32. The 'should have known' test required in the other offences found in article 8 (2) (b) (vii) is not applicable here because of the variable and regulatory nature of the relevant prohibitions.

43 'Combatant purposes' in these circumstances means purposes directly related to hostilities and not including medical, religious or similar activities.

44 This mental element recognizes the interplay between article 30 and article 32. The term 'prohibited nature' denotes illegality.

Article 8 (2) (b) (viii)
The transfer, directly or indirectly, by the Occupying Power of parts of its own civilian population into the territory it occupies, or the deportation or transfer of all or parts of the population of the occupied territory within or outside this territory
Elements

1. The perpetrator:
(a) Transferred,[45] directly or indirectly, parts of its own population into the territory it occupies; or
(b) Deported or transferred all or parts of the population of the occupied territory within or outside this territory.
2. The conduct took place in the context of and was associated with an international armed conflict.
3. The perpetrator was aware of factual circumstances that established the existence of an armed conflict.

Article 8 (2) (b) (ix)
War crime of attacking protected objects[46]
Elements

1. The perpetrator directed an attack.
2. The object of the attack was one or more buildings dedicated to religion, education, art, science or charitable purposes, historic monuments, hospitals or places where the sick and wounded are collected, which were not military objectives.
3. The perpetrator intended such building or buildings dedicated to religion, education, art, science or charitable purposes, historic monuments, hospitals or places where the sick and wounded are collected, which were not military objectives, to be the object of the attack.
4. The conduct took place in the context of and was associated with an international armed conflict.
5. The perpetrator was aware of factual circumstances that established the existence of an armed conflict.

Article 8 (2) (b) (x)-1
War crime of mutilation
Elements

1. The perpetrator subjected one or more persons to mutilation, in particular by permanently disfiguring the person or persons, or by permanently disabling or removing an organ or appendage.
2. The conduct caused death or seriously endangered the physical or mental health of such person or persons.
3. The conduct was neither justified by the medical, dental or hospital treatment of the person or persons concerned nor carried out in such person's or persons' interest.[47]

45 The term 'transfer' needs to be interpreted in accordance with the relevant provisions of international humanitarian law.
46 The presence in the locality of persons specially protected under the Geneva Conventions of 1949 or of police forces retained for the sole purpose of maintaining law and order does not by itself render the locality a military objective.
47 Consent is not a defence to this crime. The crime prohibits any medical procedure which is not indicated by the state of health of the person concerned and which is not consistent with gener-

4. Such person or persons were in the power of an adverse party.
5. The conduct took place in the context of and was associated with an international armed conflict.
6. The perpetrator was aware of factual circumstances that established the existence of an armed conflict.

Article 8 (2) (b) (x)-2
War crime of medical or scientific experiments
Elements

1. The perpetrator subjected one or more persons to a medical or scientific experiment.
2. The experiment caused death or seriously endangered the physical or mental health or integrity of such person or persons.
3. The conduct was neither justified by the medical, dental or hospital treatment of such person or persons concerned nor carried out in such person's or persons' interest.
4. Such person or persons were in the power of an adverse party.
5. The conduct took place in the context of and was associated with an international armed conflict.
6. The perpetrator was aware of factual circumstances that established the existence of an armed conflict.

Article 8 (2) (b) (xi)
War crime of treacherously killing or wounding
Elements

1. The perpetrator invited the confidence or belief of one or more persons that they were entitled to, or were obliged to accord, protection under rules of international law applicable in armed conflict.
2. The perpetrator intended to betray that confidence or belief.
3. The perpetrator killed or injured such person or persons.
4. The perpetrator made use of that confidence or belief in killing or injuring such person or persons.
5. Such person or persons belonged to an adverse party.
6. The conduct took place in the context of and was associated with an international armed conflict.
7. The perpetrator was aware of factual circumstances that established the existence of an armed conflict.

Article 8 (2) (b) (xii)
War crime of denying quarter
Elements

1. The perpetrator declared or ordered that there shall be no survivors.
2. Such declaration or order was given in order to threaten an adversary or to conduct hostilities on the basis that there shall be no survivors.
3. The perpetrator was in a position of effective command or control over the subordinate forces to which the declaration or order was directed.

---

ally accepted medical standards which would be applied under similar medical circumstances to persons who are nationals of the party conducting the procedure and who are in no way deprived of liberty. This footnote also applies to the same element for article 8 (2) (b) (x)-2.

4. The conduct took place in the context of and was associated with an international armed conflict.
5. The perpetrator was aware of factual circumstances that established the existence of an armed conflict.

Article 8 (2) (b) (xiii)
War crime of destroying or seizing the enemy's property
Elements

1. The perpetrator destroyed or seized certain property.
2. Such property was property of a hostile party.
3. Such property was protected from that destruction or seizure under the international law of armed conflict.
4. The perpetrator was aware of the factual circumstances that established the status of the property.
5. The destruction or seizure was not justified by military necessity.
6. The conduct took place in the context of and was associated with an international armed conflict.
7. The perpetrator was aware of factual circumstances that established the existence of an armed conflict.

Article 8 (2) (b) (xiv)
War crime of depriving the nationals of the hostile power of rights or actions – Elements

1. The perpetrator effected the abolition, suspension or termination of admissibility in a court of law of certain rights or actions.
2. The abolition, suspension or termination was directed at the nationals of a hostile party.
3. The perpetrator intended the abolition, suspension or termination to be directed at the nationals of a hostile party.
4. The conduct took place in the context of and was associated with an international armed conflict.
5. The perpetrator was aware of factual circumstances that established the existence of an armed conflict.

Article 8 (2) (b) (xv)
War crime of compelling participation in military operations
Elements

1. The perpetrator coerced one or more persons by act or threat to take part in military operations against that person's own country or forces.
2. Such person or persons were nationals of a hostile party.
3. The conduct took place in the context of and was associated with an international armed conflict.
4. The perpetrator was aware of factual circumstances that established the existence of an armed conflict.

Article 8 (2) (b) (xvi)
War crime of pillaging
Elements

1. The perpetrator appropriated certain property.
2. The perpetrator intended to deprive the owner of the property and to appropriate it for private or personal use.[48]
3. The appropriation was without the consent of the owner.
4. The conduct took place in the context of and was associated with an international armed conflict.
5. The perpetrator was aware of factual circumstances that established the existence of an armed conflict.

Article 8 (2) (b) (xvii)
War crime of employing poison or poisoned weapons
Elements

1. The perpetrator employed a substance or a weapon that releases a substance as a result of its employment.
2. The substance was such that it causes death or serious damage to health in the ordinary course of events, through its toxic properties.
3. The conduct took place in the context of and was associated with an international armed conflict.
4. The perpetrator was aware of factual circumstances that established the existence of an armed conflict.

Article 8 (2) (b) (xviii)
War crime of employing prohibited gases, liquids, materials or devices - Elements

1. The perpetrator employed a gas or other analogous substance or device.
2. The gas, substance or device was such that it causes death or serious damage to health in the ordinary course of events, through its asphyxiating or toxic properties.[49]
3. The conduct took place in the context of and was associated with an international armed conflict.
4. The perpetrator was aware of factual circumstances that established the existence of an armed conflict.

Article 8 (2) (b) (xix)
War crime of employing prohibited bullets
Elements

1. The perpetrator employed certain bullets.
2. The bullets were such that their use violates the international law of armed conflict because they expand or flatten easily in the human body.
3. The perpetrator was aware that the nature of the bullets was such that their employment would uselessly aggravate suffering or the wounding effect.
4. The conduct took place in the context of and was associated with an international armed conflict.

48 As indicated by the use of the term 'private or personal use', appropriations justified by military necessity cannot constitute the crime of pillaging.

49 Nothing in this element shall be interpreted as limiting or prejudicing in any way existing or developing rules of international law with respect to the development, production, stockpiling and use of chemical weapons.

5. The perpetrator was aware of factual circumstances that established the existence of an armed conflict.

Article 8 (2) (b) (xx)
War crime of employing weapons, projectiles or materials or methods of warfare listed in the Annex to the Statute - Elements
[Elements will have to be drafted once weapons, projectiles or material or methods of warfare have been included in an annex to the Statute]

Article 8 (2) (b) (xxi)
War crime of outrages upon personal dignity
Elements

1. The perpetrator humiliated, degraded or otherwise violated the dignity of one or more persons.[50]
2. The severity of the humiliation, degradation or other violation was of such degree as to be generally recognized as an outrage upon personal dignity.
3. The conduct took place in the context of and was associated with an international armed conflict.
4. The perpetrator was aware of factual circumstances that established the existence of an armed conflict.

Article 8 (2) (b) (xxii)-1
War crime of rape
Elements

1. The perpetrator invaded[51] the body of a person by conduct resulting in penetration, however slight, of any part of the body of the victim or of the perpetrator with a sexual organ, or of the anal or genital opening of the victim with any object or any other part of the body.
2. The invasion was committed by force, or by threat of force or coercion, such as that caused by fear of violence, duress, detention, psychological oppression or abuse of power, against such person or another person, or by taking advantage of a coercive environment, or the invasion was committed against a person incapable of giving genuine consent.[52]
3. The conduct took place in the context of and was associated with an international armed conflict.
4. The perpetrator was aware of factual circumstances that established the existence of an armed conflict.

Article 8 (2) (b) (xxii)-2
War crime of sexual slavery[53]
Elements

50 For this crime, 'persons' can include dead persons. It is understood that the victim need not personally be aware of the existence of the humiliation or degradation or other violation. This element takes into account relevant aspects of the cultural background of the victim.
51 The concept of 'invasion' is intended to be broad enough to be gender-neutral.
52 It is understood that a person may be incapable of giving genuine consent if affected by natural, induced or age-related incapacity. This footnote also applies to the corresponding elements of article 8 (2) (b) (xxii)-3, 5 and 6.
53 Given the complex nature of this crime, it is recognized that its commission could involve more than one perpetrator as a part of a common criminal purpose.

1. The perpetrator exercised any or all of the powers attaching to the right of ownership over one or more persons, such as by purchasing, selling, lending or bartering such a person or persons, or by imposing on them a similar deprivation of liberty.[54]
2. The perpetrator caused such person or persons to engage in one or more acts of a sexual nature.
3. The conduct took place in the context of and was associated with an international armed conflict.
4. The perpetrator was aware of factual circumstances that established the existence of an armed conflict.

Article 8 (2) (b) (xxii)-3
War crime of enforced prostitution
Elements

1. The perpetrator caused one or more persons to engage in one or more acts of a sexual nature by force, or by threat of force or coercion, such as that caused by fear of violence, duress, detention, psychological oppression or abuse of power, against such person or persons or another person, or by taking advantage of a coercive environment or such person's or persons' incapacity to give genuine consent.
2. The perpetrator or another person obtained or expected to obtain pecuniary or other advantage in exchange for or in connection with the acts of a sexual nature.
3. The conduct took place in the context of and was associated with an international armed conflict.
4. The perpetrator was aware of factual circumstances that established the existence of an armed conflict.

Article 8 (2) (b) (xxii)-4
War crime of forced pregnancy
Elements

1. The perpetrator confined one or more women forcibly made pregnant, with the intent of affecting the ethnic composition of any population or carrying out other grave violations of international law.
2. The conduct took place in the context of and was associated with an international armed conflict.
3. The perpetrator was aware of factual circumstances that established the existence of an armed conflict.

Article 8 (2) (b) (xxii)-5
War crime of enforced sterilization
Elements

1. The perpetrator deprived one or more persons of biological reproductive capacity.[55]

54 It is understood that such deprivation of liberty may, in some circumstances, include exacting forced labour or otherwise reducing a person to servile status as defined in the Supplementary Convention on the Abolition of Slavery, the Slave Trade, and Institutions and Practices Similar to Slavery of 1956. It is also understood that the conduct described in this element includes trafficking in persons, in particular women and children.

55 The deprivation is not intended to include birth-control measures which have a non-permanent effect in practice.

2. The conduct was neither justified by the medical or hospital treatment of the person or persons concerned nor carried out with their genuine consent.[56]
3. The conduct took place in the context of and was associated with an international armed conflict.
4. The perpetrator was aware of factual circumstances that established the existence of an armed conflict.

Article 8 (2) (b) (xxii)-6
War crime of sexual violence
Elements

1. The perpetrator committed an act of a sexual nature against one or more persons or caused such person or persons to engage in an act of a sexual nature by force, or by threat of force or coercion, such as that caused by fear of violence, duress,detention, psychological oppression or abuse of power, against such person or persons or another person, or by taking advantage of a coercive environment or such person's or persons' incapacity to give genuine consent.
2. The conduct was of a gravity comparable to that of a grave breach of the Geneva Conventions.
3. The perpetrator was aware of the factual circumstances that established the gravity of the conduct.
4. The conduct took place in the context of and was associated with an international armed conflict.
5. The perpetrator was aware of factual circumstances that established the existence of an armed conflict.

Article 8 (2) (b) (xxiii)
War crime of using protected persons as shields
Elements

1. The perpetrator moved or otherwise took advantage of the location of one or more civilians or other persons protected under the international law of armed conflict.
2. The perpetrator intended to shield a military objective from attack or shield, favour or impede military operations.
3. The conduct took place in the context of and was associated with an international armed conflict.
4. The perpetrator was aware of factual circumstances that established the existence of an armed conflict.

Article 8 (2) (b) (xxiv)
War crime of attacking objects or persons using the distinctive emblems of the Geneva Conventions - Elements

1. The perpetrator attacked one or more persons, buildings, medical units or transports or other objects using, in conformity with international law, a distinctive emblem or other method of identification indicating protection under the Geneva Conventions.
2. The perpetrator intended such persons, buildings, units or transports or other objects so using such identification to be the object of the attack.
3. The conduct took place in the context of and was associated with an international armed conflict.

56 It is understood that 'genuine consent' does not include consent obtained through deception.

4. The perpetrator was aware of factual circumstances that established the existence of an armed conflict.

Article 8 (2) (b) (xxv)
War crime of starvation as a method of warfare
Elements

1. The perpetrator deprived civilians of objects indispensable to their survival.
2. The perpetrator intended to starve civilians as a method of warfare.
3. The conduct took place in the context of and was associated with an international armed conflict.
4. The perpetrator was aware of factual circumstances that established the existence of an armed conflict.

Article 8 (2) (b) (xxvi)
War crime of using, conscripting or enlisting children
Elements

1. The perpetrator conscripted or enlisted one or more persons into the national armed forces or used one or more persons to participate actively in hostilities.
2. Such person or persons were under the age of 15 years.
3. The perpetrator knew or should have known that such person or persons were under the age of 15 years.
4. The conduct took place in the context of and was associated with an international armed conflict.
5. The perpetrator was aware of factual circumstances that established the existence of an armed conflict.

Article 8 (2) (c)
Article 8 (2) (c) (i)-1
War crime of murder - Elements

1. The perpetrator killed one or more persons.
2. Such person or persons were either *hors de combat*, or were civilians, medical personnel, or religious personnel[57] taking no active part in the hostilities.
3. The perpetrator was aware of the factual circumstances that established this status.
4. The conduct took place in the context of and was associated with an armed conflict not of an international character.
5. The perpetrator was aware of factual circumstances that established the existence of an armed conflict.

Article 8 (2) (c) (i)-2
War crime of mutilation
Elements

1. The perpetrator subjected one or more persons to mutilation, in particular by permanently disfiguring the person or persons, or by permanently disabling or removing an organ or appendage.

57 The term 'religious personnel' includes those non-confessional non-combatant military personnel carrying out a similar function.

2. The conduct was neither justified by the medical, dental or hospital treatment of the person or persons concerned nor carried out in such person's or persons' interests.
3. Such person or persons were either *hors de combat*, or were civilians, medical personnel or religious personnel taking no active part in the hostilities.
4. The perpetrator was aware of the factual circumstances that established this status.
5. The conduct took place in the context of and was associated with an armed conflict not of an international character.
6. The perpetrator was aware of factual circumstances that established the existence of an armed conflict.

Article 8 (2) (c) (i)-3
War crime of cruel treatment
Elements

1. The perpetrator inflicted severe physical or mental pain or suffering upon one o more persons.
2. Such person or persons were either *hors de combat*, or were civilians, medical personnel, or religious personnel taking no active part in the hostilities.
3. The perpetrator was aware of the factual circumstances that established this status.
4. The conduct took place in the context of and was associated with an armed conflict not of an international character.
5. The perpetrator was aware of factual circumstances that established the existence of an armed conflict.

Article 8 (2) (c) (i)-4
War crime of torture
Elements

1. The perpetrator inflicted severe physical or mental pain or suffering upon one or more persons.
2. The perpetrator inflicted the pain or suffering for such purposes as: obtaining information or a confession, punishment, intimidation or coercion or for any reason based on discrimination of any kind.
3. Such person or persons were either *hors de combat*, or were civilians, medical personnel or religious personnel taking no active part in the hostilities.
4. The perpetrator was aware of the factual circumstances that established this status.
5. The conduct took place in the context of and was associated with an armed conflict not of an international character.
6. The perpetrator was aware of factual circumstances that established the existence of an armed conflict.

Article 8 (2) (c) (ii)
War crime of outrages upon personal dignity
Elements

1. The perpetrator humiliated, degraded or otherwise violated the dignity of one or more persons.[58]

58 For this crime, 'persons' can include dead persons. It is understood that the victim need not personally be aware of the existence of the humiliation or degradation or other violation. This element takes into account relevant aspects of the cultural background of the victim.

2. The severity of the humiliation, degradation or other violation was of such degree as to be generally recognized as an outrage upon personal dignity.
3. Such person or persons were either *hors de combat*, or were civilians, medical personnel or religious personnel taking no active part in the hostilities.
4. The perpetrator was aware of the factual circumstances that established this status.
5. The conduct took place in the context of and was associated with an armed conflict not of an international character.
6. The perpetrator was aware of factual circumstances that established the existence of an armed conflict.

Article 8 (2) (c) (iii)
War crime of taking hostages
Elements

1. The perpetrator seized, detained or otherwise held hostage one or more persons.
2. The perpetrator threatened to kill, injure or continue to detain such person or persons.
3. The perpetrator intended to compel a State, an international organization, a natural or legal person or a group of persons to act or refrain from acting as an explicit or implicit condition for the safety or the release of such person or persons.
4. Such person or persons were either *hors de combat*, or were civilians, medical personnel or religious personnel taking no active part in the hostilities.
5. The perpetrator was aware of the factual circumstances that established this status.
6. The conduct took place in the context of and was associated with an armed conflict not of an international character.
7. The perpetrator was aware of factual circumstances that established the existence of an armed conflict.

Article 8 (2) (c) (iv)
War crime of sentencing or execution without due process
Elements

1. The perpetrator passed sentence or executed one or more persons.[59]
2. Such person or persons were either *hors de combat*, or were civilians, medical personnel or religious personnel taking no active part in the hostilities.
3. The perpetrator was aware of the factual circumstances that established this status.
4. There was no previous judgement pronounced by a court, or the court that rendered judgement was not 'regularly constituted', that is, it did not afford the essential guarantees of independence and impartiality, or the court that rendered judgement did not afford all other judicial guarantees generally recognized as indispensable under international law.[60]
5. The perpetrator was aware of the absence of a previous judgement or of the denial of relevant guarantees and the fact that they are essential or indispensable to a fair trial.
6. The conduct took place in the context of and was associated with an armed conflict not of an international character.
7. The perpetrator was aware of factual circumstances that established the existence of an armed conflict.

59 The elements laid down in these documents do not address the different forms of individual criminal responsibility, as enunciated in articles 25 and 28 of the Statute.

60 With respect to elements 4 and 5, the Court should consider whether, in the light of all relevant circumstances, the cumulative effect of factors with respect to guarantees deprived the person or persons of a fair trial.

Article 8 (2) (e)
Article 8 (2) (e) (i)
War crime of attacking civilians
Elements

1. The perpetrator directed an attack.
2. The object of the attack was a civilian population as such or individual civilians not taking direct part in hostilities.
3. The perpetrator intended the civilian population as such or individual civilians not taking direct part in hostilities to be the object of the attack.
4. The conduct took place in the context of and was associated with an armed conflict not of an international character.
5. The perpetrator was aware of factual circumstances that established the existence of an armed conflict.

Article 8 (2) (e) (ii)
War crime of attacking objects or persons using the distinctive emblems of the Geneva Conventions
Elements

1. The perpetrator attacked one or more persons, buildings, medical units or transports or other objects using, in conformity with international law, a distinctive emblem or other method of identification indicating protection under the Geneva Conventions.
2. The perpetrator intended such persons, buildings, units or transports or other objects so using such identification to be the object of the attack.
3. The conduct took place in the context of and was associated with an armed conflict not of an international character.
4. The perpetrator was aware of factual circumstances that established the existence of an armed conflict.

Article 8 (2) (e) (iii)
War crime of attacking personnel or objects involved in a humanitarian assistance or peacekeeping mission
Elements

1. The perpetrator directed an attack.
2. The object of the attack was personnel, installations, material, units or vehicles involved in a humanitarian assistance or peacekeeping mission in accordance with the Charter of the United Nations.
3. The perpetrator intended such personnel, installations, material, units or vehicles so involved to be the object of the attack.
4. Such personnel, installations, material, units or vehicles were entitled to that protection given to civilians or civilian objects under the international law of armed conflict.
5. The perpetrator was aware of the factual circumstances that established that protection.
6. The conduct took place in the context of and was associated with an armed conflict not of an international character.
7. The perpetrator was aware of factual circumstances that established the existence of an armed conflict.

Article 8 (2) (e) (iv)
War crime of attacking protected objects[61]
Elements

1. The perpetrator directed an attack.
2. The object of the attack was one or more buildings dedicated to religion, education, art, science or charitable purposes, historic monuments, hospitals or places where the sick and wounded are collected, which were not military objectives.
3. The perpetrator intended such building or buildings dedicated to religion, education, art, science or charitable purposes, historic monuments, hospitals or places where the sick and wounded are collected, which were not military objectives, to be the object of the attack.
4. The conduct took place in the context of and was associated with an armed conflict not of an international character.
5. The perpetrator was aware of factual circumstances that established the existence of an armed conflict.

Article 8 (2) (e) (v)
War crime of pillaging
Elements

1. The perpetrator appropriated certain property.
2. The perpetrator intended to deprive the owner of the property and to appropriate it for private or personal use.[62]
3. The appropriation was without the consent of the owner.
4. The conduct took place in the context of and was associated with an armed conflict not of an international character.
5. The perpetrator was aware of factual circumstances that established the existence of an armed conflict.

Article 8 (2) (e) (vi)-1
War crime of rape
Elements

1. The perpetrator invaded[63] the body of a person by conduct resulting in penetration, however slight, of any part of the body of the victim or of the perpetrator with a sexual organ, or of the anal or genital opening of the victim with any object or any other part of the body.
2. The invasion was committed by force, or by threat of force or coercion, such as that caused by fear of violence, duress, detention, psychological oppression or abuse of power, against such person or another person, or by taking advantage of a coercive environment, or the invasion was committed against a person incapable of giving genuine consent.[64]

61 The presence in the locality of persons specially protected under the Geneva Conventions of 1949 or of police forces retained for the sole purpose of maintaining law and order does not by itself render the locality a military objective.
62 As indicated by the use of the term 'private or personal use', appropriations justified by military necessity cannot constitute the crime of pillaging.
63 The concept of 'invasion' is intended to be broad enough to be gender-neutral.
64 It is understood that a person may be incapable of giving genuine consent if affected by natural, induced or age-related incapacity. This footnote also applies to the corresponding elements in article 8 (2) (e) (vi)-3, 5 and 6.

3. The conduct took place in the context of and was associated with an armed conflict not of an international character.
4. The perpetrator was aware of factual circumstances that established the existence of an armed conflict.

Article 8 (2) (e) (vi)-2
War crime of sexual slavery[65]
Elements

1. The perpetrator exercised any or all of the powers attaching to the right of ownership over one or more persons, such as by purchasing, selling, lending or bartering such a person or persons, or by imposing on them a similar deprivation of liberty.[66]
2. The perpetrator caused such person or persons to engage in one or more acts of sexual nature.
3. The conduct took place in the context of and was associated with an armed conflict not of an international character.
4. The perpetrator was aware of factual circumstances that established the existence of an armed conflict.

Article 8 (2) (e) (vi)-3
War crime of enforced prostitution
Elements

1. The perpetrator caused one or more persons to engage in one or more acts of a sexual nature by force, or by threat of force or coercion, such as that caused by fear of violence, duress, detention, psychological oppression or abuse of power, against such person or persons or another person, or by taking advantage of a coercive environment or such person's or persons' incapacity to give genuine consent.
2. The perpetrator or another person obtained or expected to obtain pecuniary or other advantage in exchange for or in connection with the acts of a sexual nature.
3. The conduct took place in the context of and was associated with an armed conflict not of an international character.
4. The perpetrator was aware of factual circumstances that established the existence of an armed conflict.

Article 8 (2) (e) (vi)-4
War crime of forced pregnancy
Elements

1. The perpetrator confined one or more women forcibly made pregnant, with the intent of affecting the ethnic composition of any population or carrying out other grave violations of international law.
2. The conduct took place in the context of and was associated with an armed conflict not of an international character.

65 Given the complex nature of this crime, it is recognized that its commission could involve more than one perpetrator as a part of a common criminal purpose.
66 It is understood that such deprivation of liberty may, in some circumstances, include exacting forced labour or otherwise reducing a person to servile status as defined in the Supplementary Convention on the Abolition of Slavery, the Slave Trade, and Institutions and Practices Similar to Slavery of 1956. It is also understood that the conduct described in this element includes trafficking in persons, in particular women and children.

3. The perpetrator was aware of factual circumstances that established the existence of an armed conflict.

Article 8 (2) (e) (vi)-5
War crime of enforced sterilization
Elements

1. The perpetrator deprived one or more persons of biological reproductive capacity.[67]
2. The conduct was neither justified by the medical or hospital treatment of the person or persons concerned nor carried out with their genuine consent.[68]
3. The conduct took place in the context of and was associated with an armed conflict not of an international character.
4. The perpetrator was aware of factual circumstances that established the existence of an armed conflict.

Article 8 (2) (e) (vi)-6
War crime of sexual violence
Elements

1. The perpetrator committed an act of a sexual nature against one or more persons or caused such person or persons to engage in an act of a sexual nature by force, or by threat of force or coercion, such as that caused by fear of violence, duress, detention, psychological oppression or abuse of power, against such person or persons or another person, or by taking advantage of a coercive environment or such person's or persons' incapacity to give genuine consent.
2. The conduct was of a gravity comparable to that of a serious violation of article 3 common to the four Geneva Conventions.
3. The perpetrator was aware of the factual circumstances that established the gravity of the conduct.
4. The conduct took place in the context of and was associated with an armed conflict not of an international character.
5. The perpetrator was aware of factual circumstances that established the existence of an armed conflict.

Article 8 (2) (e) (vii)
War crime of using, conscripting and enlisting children
Elements

1. The perpetrator conscripted or enlisted one or more persons into an armed force or group or used one or more persons to participate actively in hostilities.
2. Such person or persons were under the age of 15 years.
3. The perpetrator knew or should have known that such person or persons were under the age of 15 years.
4. The conduct took place in the context of and was associated with an armed conflict not of an international character.
5. The perpetrator was aware of factual circumstances that established the existence of an armed conflict.

67 The deprivation is not intended to include birth-control measures which have a non-permanent effect in practice.
68 It is understood that 'genuine consent' does not include consent obtained through deception.

Article 8 (2) (e) (viii)
War crime of displacing civilians
Elements

1. The perpetrator ordered a displacement of a civilian population.
2. Such order was not justified by the security of the civilians involved or by military necessity.
3. The perpetrator was in a position to effect such displacement by giving such order.
4. The conduct took place in the context of and was associated with an armed conflict not of an international character.
5. The perpetrator was aware of factual circumstances that established the existence of an armed conflict.

Article 8 (2) (e) (ix)
War crime of treacherously killing or wounding
Elements

1. The perpetrator invited the confidence or belief of one or more combatant adversaries that they were entitled to, or were obliged to accord, protection under rules of international law applicable in armed conflict.
2. The perpetrator intended to betray that confidence or belief.
3. The perpetrator killed or injured such person or persons.
4. The perpetrator made use of that confidence or belief in killing or injuring such person or persons.
5. Such person or persons belonged to an adverse party.
6. The conduct took place in the context of and was associated with an armed conflict not of an international character.
7. The perpetrator was aware of factual circumstances that established the existence of an armed conflict.

Article 8 (2) (e) (x)
War crime of denying quarter
Elements

1. The perpetrator declared or ordered that there shall be no survivors.
2. Such declaration or order was given in order to threaten an adversary or to conduct hostilities on the basis that there shall be no survivors.
3. The perpetrator was in a position of effective command or control over the subordinate forces to which the declaration or order was directed.
4. The conduct took place in the context of and was associated with an armed conflict not of an international character.
5. The perpetrator was aware of factual circumstances that established the existence of an armed conflict.

Article 8 (2) (e) (xi)-1
War crime of mutilation
Elements

1. The perpetrator subjected one or more persons to mutilation, in particular by permanently disfiguring the person or persons, or by permanently disabling or removing an organ or appendage.

2. The conduct caused death or seriously endangered the physical or mental health of such person or persons.
3. The conduct was neither justified by the medical, dental or hospital treatment of the person or persons concerned nor carried out in such person's or persons' interest.[69]
4. Such person or persons were in the power of another party to the conflict.
5. The conduct took place in the context of and was associated with an armed conflict not of an international character.
6. The perpetrator was aware of factual circumstances that established the existence of an armed conflict.

Article 8 (2) (e) (xi)-2
War crime of medical or scientific experiments
Elements

1. The perpetrator subjected one or more persons to a medical or scientific experiment.
2. The experiment caused the death or seriously endangered the physical or mental health or integrity of such person or persons.
3. The conduct was neither justified by the medical, dental or hospital treatment of such person or persons concerned nor carried out in such person's or persons' interest.
4. Such person or persons were in the power of another party to the conflict.
5. The conduct took place in the context of and was associated with an armed conflict not of an international character.
6. The perpetrator was aware of factual circumstances that established the existence of an armed conflict.

Article 8 (2) (e) (xii)
War crime of destroying or seizing the enemy's property
Elements

1. The perpetrator destroyed or seized certain property.
2. Such property was property of an adversary.
3. Such property was protected from that destruction or seizure under the international law of armed conflict.
4. The perpetrator was aware of the factual circumstances that established the status of the property.
5. The destruction or seizure was not required by military necessity.
6. The conduct took place in the context of and was associated with an armed conflict not of an international character.
7. The perpetrator was aware of factual circumstances that established the existence of an armed conflict.

69 Consent is not a defence to this crime. The crime prohibits any medical procedure which is not indicated by the state of health of the person concerned and which is not consistent with generally accepted medical standards which would be applied under similar medical circumstances to persons who are nationals of the party conducting the procedure and who are in no way deprived of liberty. This footnote also applies to the similar element in article 8 (2) (e) (xi)-2.